Contents

IF YOU ARE NOT SURE WHICH UNITS YOU NEED TO STUDY, USE THE **STUDY GUIDE** ON PAGE 326.

IF YOU ARE NOT SURE WHICH UNITS YOU NEED TO STUDY, USE THE **STUDY GUIDE** ON PAGE 326.

IF YOU ARE NOT SURE WHICH UNITS YOU NEED TO STUDY, USE THE **STUDY GUIDE** ON PAGE 326.

IF YOU ARE NOT SURE WHICH UNITS YOU NEED TO STUDY, USE THE **STUDY GUIDE** ON PAGE 326.

Thanks

This is the fifth edition of *English Grammar in Use*. I wrote the original edition when I was a teacher at the Swan School of English, Oxford. I would like to repeat my thanks to my former colleagues and students at the school for their help, encouragement and interest at that time.

Regarding the production of this fifth edition, I would like to thank Rebecca Winthrop and Chris Capper.

Design & Illustrations
Q2A Media Services Pvt. Ltd.

To the student

This book is for students who want help with English grammar. It is written for you to use without a teacher.

The book will be useful for you if you are not sure of the answers to questions like these:

- ○ What is the difference between *I did* and *I have done*?
- ○ When do we use *will* for the future?
- ○ What is the structure after *I wish*?
- ○ When do we say *used to do* and when do we say *used to doing*?
- ○ When do we use *the*?
- ○ What is the difference between *like* and *as*?

These and many other points of English grammar are explained in the book, and there are exercises on each point.

Level

The book is intended mainly for *intermediate* students (students who have already studied the basic grammar of English). It concentrates on those structures that intermediate students want to use, but that often cause difficulty. Some advanced students who have problems with grammar will also find the book useful.

The book is *not* suitable for elementary learners.

How the book is organised

There are 145 units in the book. Each unit concentrates on a particular point of grammar. Some problems (for example, the present perfect or the use of *the*) are covered in more than one unit. For a list of units, see the *Contents* at the beginning of the book.

Each unit consists of two facing pages. On the left there are explanations and examples; on the right there are exercises. At the back of the book there is an Answer Key for you to check your answers to the exercises (page 336).

There are also seven *Appendices* at the back of the book (pages 292–301). These include irregular verbs, summaries of verb forms, spelling, and American English.

Finally, there is a detailed *Index* at the back of the book (page 373).

How to use the book

The units are not in order of difficulty, so it is not intended that you work through the book from beginning to end. Every learner has different problems, and you should use this book to help you with the grammar that *you* find difficult.

It is suggested that you work in this way:

- ○ Use the *Contents* and/or *Index* to find which unit deals with the point you are interested in.
- ○ If you are not sure which units you need to study, use the *Study guide* on page 326.
- ○ Study the explanations and examples on the left-hand page of the unit you have chosen.
- ○ Do the exercises on the right-hand page.
- ○ Check your answers with the *Key*.
- ○ If your answers are not correct, study the left-hand page again to see what went wrong.

You can, of course, use the book simply as a reference book without doing the exercises.

Additional exercises

At the back of the book there are *Additional exercises* (pages 302–325). These exercises bring together some of the grammar points from a number of different units. For example, Exercise 16 brings together grammar points from Units 26–36. You can use these exercises for extra practice after you have studied and practised the grammar in the units concerned.

ebook

An ebook version of *English Grammar in Use* is also available to buy.

To the teacher

English Grammar in Use was written as a self-study grammar book, but teachers may also find it useful as additional course material in cases where further work on grammar is necessary.

The book will probably be most useful at middle- and upper-intermediate levels (where all or nearly all of the material will be relevant), and can serve both as a basis for revision and as a means for practising new structures. It will also be useful for some more advanced students who have problems with grammar and need a book for reference and practice. The book is not intended to be used by elementary learners.

The units are organised in grammatical categories (*Present and past*, *Articles and nouns*, *Prepositions* etc.). They are not ordered according to level of difficulty, so the book should not be worked through from beginning to end. It should be used selectively and flexibly in accordance with the grammar syllabus being used and the difficulties students are having.

The book can be used for immediate consolidation or for later revision or remedial work. It might be used by the whole class or by individual students needing extra help. The left-hand pages (explanations and examples) are written for the student to use individually, but they may of course be used by the teacher as a source of ideas and information on which to base a lesson. The student then has the left-hand page as a record of what has been taught and can refer to it in the future. The exercises can be done individually, in class or as homework. Alternatively (and additionally), individual students can be directed to study certain units of the book by themselves if they have particular difficulties not shared by other students in their class. Don't forget the *Additional exercises* at the back of the book (see **To the student**).

English Grammar in Use Fifth Edition
This is a new edition of English Grammar in Use. The differences between this edition and the fourth edition are:

- ☐   Much of the material has been revised or reorganised, and in most units there are changes in the examples, explanations and exercises.
- ☐   The book has been redesigned with new, updated illustrations.
- ☐   There is a new ebook available with all the contents of the book as well as audio, access to a dictionary and more.

An edition of English Grammar in Use without the Key is also available. Some teachers may prefer to use this with their students.

ENGLISH GRAMMAR IN USE

CAMBRIDGE
UNIVERSITY PRESS

Present continuous (**I am doing**)

A Study this example situation:

Sarah is in her car. She is on her way to work.
She**'s driving** to work. (= She **is driving** …)

This means: she is driving *now*, at the time of speaking.
The action is not finished.

am/is/are + -ing is the *present continuous*:

I	**am**	(= I**'m**)	**driving**
he/she/it	**is**	(= he**'s** etc.)	**working**
we/you/they	**are**	(= we**'re** etc.)	**doing** etc.

B **I am doing** something = I started doing it and I haven't finished; I'm in the middle of doing it.

- ○ Please don't make so much noise. I**'m trying** to work. (*not* I try)
- ○ 'Where's Mark?' 'He**'s having** a shower.' (*not* He has a shower)
- ○ Let's go out now. It **isn't raining** any more. (*not* It doesn't rain)
- ○ How's your new job? **Are** you **enjoying** it?
- ○ What's all that noise? What**'s going** on? *or* What**'s happening**?

Sometimes the action is not happening at the time of speaking. For example:

Steve is talking to a friend on the phone. He says:

I**'m reading** a really good book at the moment.
It's about a man who …

Steve says 'I**'m reading** …' but he is *not* reading the book at
the time of speaking.
He means that he has started reading the book, but has not
finished it yet. He is in the middle of reading it.

Some more examples:

- ○ Kate wants to work in Italy, so she**'s learning** Italian.
  (but perhaps she isn't learning Italian at the time of speaking)
- ○ Some friends of mine **are building** their own house. They hope to finish it next summer.

C You can use the present continuous with **today** / **this week** / **this year** etc. (periods around now):

- ○ A: You**'re working** hard **today**. (*not* You work hard today)
  B: Yes, I have a lot to do.
- ○ The company I work for **isn't doing** so well **this year**.

D We use the present continuous when we talk about a change that has started to happen. We often use
these verbs in this way:

getting, becoming   **changing, improving**
starting, beginning   **increasing, rising, falling, growing**

- ○ Is your English **getting** better? (*not* Does your English get better)
- ○ The population of the world **is increasing** very fast. (*not* increases)
- ○ At first I didn't like my job, but I**'m starting** to enjoy it now. (*not* I start)

>> Present continuous and present simple → **Units 3–4**   Present tenses for the future → **Unit 19**

Exercises

1.1 What's happening in the pictures? Choose from these verbs:

cross   hide   scratch   ~~take~~   tie   wave

1   _She's taking_ a picture.
2   He .... a shoelace.
3   .... the road.

4   .... his head.
5   .... behind a tree.
6   .... to somebody.

1.2 The sentences on the right follow those on the left. Which sentence goes with which?

1 Please don't make so much noise.	a I'm getting hungry.	1 _f_
2 We need to leave soon.	b They're lying.	2 ....
3 I don't have anywhere to live right now.	c It's starting to rain.	3 ....
4 I need to eat something soon.	d They're trying to sell it.	4 ....
5 They don't need their car any more.	e It's getting late.	5 ....
6 Things are not so good at work.	f ~~I'm trying to work.~~	6 ....
7 It isn't true what they say.	g I'm staying with friends.	7 ....
8 We're going to get wet.	h The company is losing money.	8 ....

1.3 Write questions. Use the present continuous.

1   What's all that noise? _What's happening?_ .... (what / happen?)
2   What's the matter? .... (why / you / cry?)
3   Where's your mother? .... (she / work / today?)
4   I haven't seen you for ages. .... (what / you / do / these days?)
5   Amy is a student. .... (what / she / study?)
6   Who are those people? .... (what / they / do?)
7   I heard you started a new job. .... (you / enjoy / it?)
8   We're not in a hurry. .... (why / you / walk / so fast?)

1.4 Put the verb into the correct form, positive (**I'm doing** etc.) or negative (**I'm not doing** etc.).

1   Please don't make so much noise. _I'm trying_ (I / try) to work.
2   Let's go out now. _It isn't raining_ (it / rain) any more.
3   You can turn off the radio. .... (I / listen) to it.
4   Kate phoned last night. She's on holiday with friends. .... (She / have) a great time and doesn't want to come back.
5   Andrew started evening classes recently. .... (He / learn) Japanese.
6   Paul and Sarah have had an argument and now .... (they / speak) to one another.
7   The situation is already very bad and now .... (it / get) worse.
8   Tim .... (work) today. He's taken the day off.
9   .... (I / look) for Sophie. Do you know where she is?
10 The washing machine has been repaired. .... (It / work) now.
11 .... (They / build) a new hospital. It will be finished next year.
12 Ben is a student, but he's not very happy. .... (He / enjoy) his course.
13 .... (The weather / change). Look at those clouds. I think it's going to rain.
14 Dan has been in the same job for a long time. .... (He / start) to get bored with it.

3

Present simple (**I do**)

A Study this example situation:

Alex is a bus driver, but now he is in bed asleep.
He is not driving a bus. (He is asleep.)

but He **drives** a bus. He is a bus driver.

drive(**s**), **work**(**s**), **do**(**es**) etc. is the *present simple*:

I/we/you/they	**drive/work/do** etc.
he/she/it	**drives/works/does** etc.

B We use the present simple to talk about things in general. We use it to say that something happens all the time or repeatedly, or that something is true in general:
- ☐ Nurses **look** after patients in hospitals.
- ☐ I usually **go** away at weekends.
- ☐ The earth **goes** round the sun.
- ☐ The cafe **opens** at 7.30 in the morning.

We say:

I **work**	*but*	he **works**		you **go**	*but*	it **goes**
they **teach**	*but*	my sister **teaches**		I **have**	*but*	he **has**

For spelling (-**s** or -**es**), see Appendix 6.

C We use **do**/**does** to make questions and negative sentences:

do **does**	I/we/you/they he/she/it	**work**? **drive**? **do**?		I/we/you/they he/she/it	**don't** **doesn't**	**work** **drive** **do**

- ☐ I come from Canada. Where **do** you **come** from?
- ☐ I **don't go** away very often.
- ☐ What **does** this word **mean**? (*not* What means this word?)
- ☐ Rice **doesn't grow** in cold climates.

In the following examples, **do** is also the main verb (do you **do** / doesn't **do** etc.):
- ☐ 'What **do** you **do**?' 'I work in a shop.'
- ☐ He's always so lazy. He **doesn't do** anything to help.

D We use the present simple to say how often we do things:
- ☐ **I get** up at 8 o'clock **every morning**.
- ☐ **How often do** you **go** to the dentist?
- ☐ Julie **doesn't drink** tea **very often**.
- ☐ Robert usually **goes** away **two or three times a year**.

E **I promise / I apologise** etc.

Sometimes we do things by saying something. For example, when you promise to do something, you can say '**I promise** …'; when you suggest something, you can say '**I suggest** …':
- ☐ **I promise** I won't be late. (*not* I'm promising)
- ☐ 'What do **you suggest** I do?' '**I suggest** that you …'

In the same way we say: **I apologise** … / **I advise** … / **I insist** … / **I agree** … / **I refuse** … etc.

>> Present simple and present continuous ➜ **Units 3–4**   Present tenses for the future ➜ **Unit 19**

Exercises

2.1 Complete the sentences using the following verbs:

> cause(s)   close(s)   connect(s)   go(es)   live(s)   ~~speak(s)~~   take(s)

1 Tanya __speaks__ German very well.
2 Ben and Jack .... to the same school.
3 Bad driving .... many accidents.
4 The museum .... at 4 o'clock on Sundays.
5 My parents .... in a very small flat.
6 The Olympic Games .... place every four years.
7 The Panama Canal .... the Atlantic and Pacific oceans.

2.2 Put the verb into the correct form.

1 Julia __doesn't drink__ (not / drink) tea very often.
2 What time .... (the banks / close) here?
3 I have a car, but I .... (not / use) it much.
4 Where .... (Maria / come) from? Is she Spanish?
5 'What .... (you / do)?' 'I'm an electrician.'
6 Look at this sentence. What .... (this word / mean)?
7 David isn't very fit. He .... (not / do) any sport.
8 It .... (take) me an hour to get to work in the morning. How long .... (it / take) you?

2.3 Complete the sentences using these verbs. Sometimes you need the negative.

> believe   eat   flow   ~~go~~   ~~grow~~   make   rise   tell   translate

1 The earth __goes__ round the sun.
2 Rice __doesn't grow__ in cold climates.
3 The sun .... in the east.
4 Bees .... honey.
5 Vegetarians .... meat.
6 An atheist .... in God.
7 An interpreter .... from one language into another.
8 Liars are people who .... the truth.
9 The River Amazon .... into the Atlantic Ocean.

2.4 You ask Lisa questions about herself and her family. Write the questions.

1 You know that Lisa plays tennis. You want to know how often. Ask her.
  How often __do you play tennis__ ?
2 Perhaps Lisa's sister plays tennis too. You want to know. Ask Lisa.
  .... your sister .... ?
3 You know that Lisa goes to the cinema a lot. You want to know how often. Ask her.
  .... ?
4 You know that Lisa's brother works. You want to know what he does. Ask Lisa.
  .... ?
5 You're not sure whether Lisa speaks Spanish. You want to know. Ask her.
  .... ?
6 You don't know where Lisa's grandparents live. You want to know. Ask Lisa.
  .... ?

2.5 Complete using the following:

> I agree   I apologise   I insist   I promise   I recommend   ~~I suggest~~

1 Mr Evans is not in the office today. __I suggest__ you try calling him tomorrow.
2 I won't tell anybody what you said. ....
3 (in a restaurant) You must let me pay for the meal. ....
4 .... for what I said. I shouldn't have said it.
5 The new restaurant in Baker Street is very good. .... it.
6 I think you're absolutely right. .... with you.

Present continuous and present simple 1 (**I am doing** and **I do**)

Compare:

present continuous (**I am doing**)	*present simple* (**I do**)

present continuous (**I am doing**)

We use the continuous for things happening at or around the time of speaking. The action is not complete.

```
            I am doing
───────────────────────────────────
past          now          future
```

- ☐ The water **is boiling**. Be careful.
- ☐ Listen to those people. What language **are** they **speaking**?
- ☐ Let's go out. It **isn't raining** now.
- ☐ 'I'm busy.' 'What **are you doing**?'
- ☐ I**'m getting** hungry. Let's go and eat.
- ☐ Kate wants to work in Italy, so she**'s learning** Italian.
- ☐ The population of the world **is increasing** very fast.

We use the continuous for *temporary* situations (things that continue for a short time):

- ☐ I**'m living** with some friends until I find a place of my own.
- ☐ A: You**'re working** hard today.
    B: Yes, I have a lot to do.

See Unit 1 for more information.

present simple (**I do**)

We use the simple for things in general or things that happen repeatedly.

```
←──────────── I do ────────────→
past          now          future
```

- ☐ Water **boils** at 100 degrees Celsius.
- ☐ Excuse me, **do** you **speak** English?

- ☐ It **doesn't rain** very much in summer.
- ☐ What **do** you usually **do** at weekends?
- ☐ I always **get** hungry in the afternoon.
- ☐ Most people **learn** to swim when they are children.
- ☐ Every day the population of the world **increases** by about 200,000 people.

We use the simple for *permanent* situations (things that continue for a long time):

- ☐ My parents **live** in London. They have lived there all their lives.
- ☐ Joe isn't lazy. He **works** hard most of the time.

See Unit 2 for more information.

I always do and **I'm always doing**

I always do something = I do it every time:
- ☐ I **always go** to work by car. (*not* I'm always going)

I'm always doing something = I do it too often or more often than normal.
For example:

I've lost my keys again. **I'm always losing** them.

I**'m always losing** them = I lose them too often, or more often than normal.

- ☐ Paul is never satisfied. He**'s always complaining**. (= he complains too much)
- ☐ You**'re always looking** at your phone. Don't you have anything else to do?

» Present continuous and simple 2 → **Unit 4**   Present tenses for the future → **Unit 19**

Exercises

3.1 Are the <u>underlined</u> verbs OK? Correct them where necessary.

1 Water <u>boils</u> at 100 degrees Celsius.   *OK*
2 How often <u>are you going</u> to the cinema?   *do you go*
3 Ben <u>tries</u> to find a job, but he hasn't had any luck yet.
4 Martina <u>is phoning</u> her mother every day.
5 The moon <u>goes</u> round the earth in about 27 days.
6 Can you hear those people? What <u>do they talk</u> about?
7 What <u>do you do</u> in your spare time?
8 Sarah is a vegetarian. She <u>doesn't eat</u> meat.
9 I must go now. It <u>gets</u> late.
10 'Come on! It's time to leave.' 'OK, I <u>come</u>.'
11 Paul is never late. He<u>'s always starting</u> work on time.
12 They don't get on well. They<u>'re always arguing</u>.

3.2 Put the verb into the correct form, present continuous or present simple.

1 a   *I usually get* (I / usually / get) hungry in the afternoon.
   b   *I'm getting* (I / get) hungry. Let's go and eat something.
2 a '... (you / listen) to the radio?' 'No, you can turn it off.'
   b '... (you / listen) to the radio a lot?' 'No, not very often.'
3 a The River Nile .... (flow) into the Mediterranean.
   b The river .... (flow) very fast today – much faster than usual.
4 a I'm not very active. .... (I / not / do) any sport.
   b What .... (you / usually / do) at weekends?
5 a Rachel is in New York right now. .... (She / stay) at the Park Hotel.
   b .... (She / always / stay) there when she's in New York.

3.3 Put the verb into the correct form, present continuous or present simple.

1 Why are all these people here? *What's happening* (What / happen)?
2 Julia is good at languages. .... (She / speak) four languages very well.
3 Are you ready yet? .... (Everybody / wait) for you.
4 I've never heard this word. How .... (you / pronounce) it?
5 Kate .... (not / work) this week. She's on holiday.
6 I think my English .... (improve) slowly. It's better than it was.
7 Nicola .... (live) in Manchester. She has never lived anywhere else.
8 Can we stop walking soon? .... (I / start) to get tired.
9 Sam and Tina are in Madrid right now. .... (They / visit) a friend of theirs.
10 'What .... (your father / do)?' 'He's an architect.'
11 It took me an hour to get to work this morning. Most days ....
(it / not / take) so long.
12 I .... (I / learn) to drive. My driving test is next month. My father
.... (teach) me.

3.4 Finish B's sentences. Use always -ing.

1 A: I've lost my keys again.
   B: Not again! *You're always losing your keys* .
2 A: The car has broken down again.
   B: That car is useless. It ....
3 A: Look! You've made the same mistake again.
   B: Oh no, not again! I ....
4 A: Oh, I've left my phone at home again.
   B: Typical! ....

Present continuous and present simple 2 (**I am doing** and **I do**)

A

We use continuous forms (I**'m waiting**, it**'s raining** etc.) for actions and happenings that have started but not finished.

Some verbs (for example, **know** and **like**) are not normally used in this way. We don't say 'I am knowing', 'they are liking'. We say 'I **know**', 'they **like**'.

The following verbs are not normally used in the present continuous:

like	want	need	prefer	
know	realise	understand		recognise
believe	suppose	remember		mean
belong	fit	contain	consist	seem

- ○ I'm hungry. I **want** something to eat. (*not* I'm wanting)
- ○ **Do** you **understand** what I **mean**?
- ○ Anna **doesn't seem** very happy right now.

B **think**

When **think** means 'believe' or 'have an opinion', we do not use the continuous:
- ○ I **think** Mary is Canadian, but I'm not sure. (*not* I'm thinking)
- ○ What **do** you **think** of my idea? (= what is your opinion?)

When **think** means 'consider', the continuous is possible:
- ○ I**'m thinking** about what happened. I often **think** about it.
- ○ Nicky **is thinking** of giving up her job. (= she is considering it)

C see   hear   smell   taste   look   feel

We normally use the present simple (not continuous) with **see/hear/smell/taste**:
- ○ **Do** you **see** that man over there? (*not* are you seeing)
- ○ The room **smells**. Let's open a window.
- ○ This soup **doesn't taste** very good.

You can use the present simple or continuous to say how somebody **looks** or **feels** now:
- ○ You **look** well today.   *or*   You**'re looking** well today.
- ○ How **do** you **feel** now?   *or*   How **are** you **feeling** now?

but
- ○ I usually **feel** tired in the morning. (*not* I'm usually feeling)

D **am/is/are being**

You can say **he's being** …, **you're being** … etc. to say how somebody is behaving *now*:
- ○ I can't understand why he**'s being** so selfish. He isn't usually like that.
  (**being** selfish = behaving selfishly now)
- ○ 'The path is icy. Don't slip.' 'Don't worry. I**'m being** very careful.'

Compare:
- ○ He never thinks about other people. He**'s** very selfish.
  (= he is selfish generally, not only now)
- ○ I don't like to take risks. I**'m** a very careful person.

We use **am/is/are being** to say how a person is *behaving* (= doing something they can control) now. It is not usually possible in other situations:
- ○ Sam **is** ill. (*not* is being ill)
- ○ **Are** you tired? (*not* are you being tired)

Present continuous and simple 1 → **Unit 3**   have → **Unit 17**   Present tenses for the future → **Unit 19**

Exercises

4.1 Put the verb into the correct form, present continuous or present simple.

1 Are you hungry? __Do you want__ (you / want) something to eat?
2 Alan says he's 90 years old, but nobody __doesn't__ (believe) him.
3 She told me her name, but __I don't__ (I / not / remember) it now.
4 Don't put the dictionary away. _____ (I / use) it.
5 Don't put the dictionary away. _____ (I / need) it.
6 Air _____ (consist) mainly of nitrogen and oxygen.
7 Who is that man? What _____ (he / want)?
8 Who is that man? Why _____ (he / look) at us?
9 Who is that man? _____ (you / recognise) him?
10 _____ (I / think) of selling my car. Would you be interested in buying it?
11 I can't make up my mind. What _____ (you / think) I should do?
12 Gary wasn't well earlier, but _____ (he / seem) OK now.

4.2 Use the words in brackets to make sentences.

1 (you / not / seem / very happy today)
You don't seem very
happy today.

2 Are you OK?
You look worried.
(I / think)

3 (who / this umbrella / belong to?)
I've no idea.

4 (this / smell / good)

5 Excuse me. (anybody / sit / there?)
No, it's free.

6 GLOVES
(these gloves / not / fit / me)
They're too small.

4.3 Are the underlined verbs OK? Correct them where necessary.

1 Nicky is thinking of giving up her job.   OK
2 It's not true. I'm not believing it.   I don't believe it.
3 I'm feeling hungry. Is there anything to eat?   _____
4 I've never eaten that fruit. What is it tasting like? _____
5 I'm not sure what she does. I think she works in a shop. _____
6 Look over there. What are you seeing?   _____
7 You're very quiet. What are you thinking about? _____

4.4 Complete the sentences. Use is/are being (continuous) or is/are (simple).

1 I can't understand why __he's being__ so selfish. He isn't usually like that.
2 You'll like Sophie when you meet her. She _____ very nice.
3 Sarah _____ very nice to me at the moment. I wonder why.
4 They _____ very happy. They've just got married.
5 You're normally very patient, so why _____ so unreasonable about waiting ten more minutes?
6 Would you like something to eat? _____ hungry?

Past simple (**I did**)

Study this example:

> Wolfgang Amadeus Mozart **was** an Austrian musician and composer. He **lived** from 1756 to 1791. He **started** composing at the age of five and **wrote** more than 600 pieces of music. He **was** only 35 years old when he **died**.
>
> **lived**/**started**/**wrote**/**was**/**died** are all *past simple*.

W.A. Mozart

1756-1791

Very often the past simple ends in -**ed** (*regular* verbs):
- ○ I work in a travel agency now. Before that I **worked** in a department store.
- ○ They **invited** us to their party, but we **decided** not to go.
- ○ The police **stopped** me on my way home last night.
- ○ Laura **passed** her exam because she **studied** very hard.

For spelling (sto**pp**ed, stud**ied** etc.), see Appendix 6.

But many verbs are *irregular*. The past simple does *not* end in -**ed**. For example:

write	→ **wrote**	○ Mozart **wrote** more than 600 pieces of music.
see	→ **saw**	○ We **saw** Alice in town a few days ago.
go	→ **went**	○ I **went** to the cinema three times last week.
shut	→ **shut**	○ It was cold, so I **shut** the window.

For a list of irregular verbs, see Appendix 1.

In questions and negative sentences we use **did**/**didn't** + infinitive (**enjoy**/**see**/**go** etc.):

I	enjoy**ed**
she	**saw**
they	**went**

	you	**enjoy**?
did	she	**see**?
	they	**go**?

I		**enjoy**
she	**didn't**	**see**
they		**go**

- ○ I enjoyed the party a lot. **Did** you **enjoy** it?
- ○ How many people **did** they **invite** to the wedding?
- ○ I **didn't buy** anything because I **didn't have** any money.
- ○ '**Did** you **go** out?' 'No, I **didn't**.'

Sometimes **do** is the main verb in the sentence (did you **do**?, I didn't **do**):
- ○ What **did** you **do** at the weekend? (*not* What did you at the weekend?)
- ○ I **didn't do** anything. (*not* I didn't anything)

The past of **be** (**am**/**is**/**are**) is **was**/**were**:

I/he/she/it	**was**/**wasn't**
we/you/they	**were**/**weren't**

was	I/he/she/it?
were	we/you/they?

- ○ **I was** annoyed because **they were** late.
- ○ **Was the weather** good when **you were** on holiday?
- ○ **They weren't** able to come because **they were** so busy.
- ○ **I wasn't** hungry, so I **didn't eat** anything.
- ○ Did you go out last night or **were you** too tired?

Exercises

5.1 Read what Laura says about a typical working day:

I usually get up at 7 o'clock and have a big breakfast. I walk to work, which takes me about half an hour. I start work at 8.45. I never have lunch. I finish work at 5 o'clock. I'm always tired when I get home. I usually cook a meal in the evening. I don't usually go out. I go to bed at about 11 o'clock, and I always sleep well.

LAURA

Yesterday was a typical working day for Laura. Write what she did or didn't do yesterday.

1 *She got up* .... at 7 o'clock.
2 She .... a big breakfast.
3 She ....
4 It .... to get to work.
5 .... at 8.45.
6 .... lunch.
7 .... at 5 o'clock.
8 .... tired when .... home.
9 .... a meal yesterday evening.
10 .... out yesterday evening.
11 .... at 11 o'clock.
12 .... well last night.

5.2 Complete the sentences using the following verbs in the correct form:

| buy | catch | cost | fall | hurt | sell | spend | teach | throw | ~~write~~ |

1 Mozart ....**wrote**.... more than 600 pieces of music.
2 'How did you learn to drive?' 'My father .... me.'
3 We couldn't afford to keep our car, so we .... it.
4 Dave .... down the stairs this morning and .... his leg.
5 Joe .... the ball to Sue, who .... it.
6 Kate .... a lot of money yesterday. She .... a dress which .... £100.

5.3 You ask James about his holiday in the US. Write your questions.

1 YOU: Where ....*did you go*.... ?
   JAMES: To the US. We went on a trip from San Francisco to Denver.
2 YOU: How .... ? By car?
   JAMES: Yes, we hired a car in San Francisco.
3 YOU: It's a long way to drive. How long .... ?
   JAMES: Two weeks. We stopped at a lot of places along the way.
4 YOU: Where .... ? In hotels?
   JAMES: Yes, small hotels or motels.
5 YOU: .... good?
   JAMES: Yes, but it was very hot – sometimes too hot.
6 YOU: .... the Grand Canyon?
   JAMES: Of course. It was wonderful.

5.4 Complete the sentences. Put the verb into the correct form, positive or negative.

1 It was warm, so I ....**took**.... off my coat. (take)
2 The film wasn't very good. I ....**didn't enjoy**.... it much. (enjoy)
3 I knew Sarah was busy, so I .... her. (disturb)
4 We were very tired, so we .... the party early. (leave)
5 It was hard carrying the bags. They .... really heavy. (be)
6 The bed was very uncomfortable. I .... well. (sleep)
7 This watch wasn't expensive. It .... much. (cost)
8 The window was open and a bird .... into the room. (fly)
9 I was in a hurry, so I .... time to call you. (have)
10 I didn't like the hotel. The room .... very clean. (be)

Past continuous (I was doing)

A Study this example situation:

Yesterday Karen and Joe played tennis. They started at 10 o'clock and finished at 11.30.
So, at 10.30 they **were playing** tennis.

they **were playing** =
they were in the middle of playing, they had not finished

was/were + -ing is the past continuous:

he/she/it	**was**	playing
we/you/they	**were**	doing working etc.

B I **was doing** something = I was in the middle of doing it at a certain time. The action or situation started before this time, but had not finished:

I started doing   **I was doing**   **I finished doing**

past   *past*   *now*

- ○ This time last year I **was living** in Hong Kong.
- ○ What **were** you **doing** at 10 o'clock last night?
- ○ I waved to Helen, but she **wasn't looking**.

C Compare I **was doing** (*past continuous*) and I **did** (*past simple*):

I **was doing** (= in the middle of an action)	I **did** (= complete action)
○ We were **walking** home when I met Dan. (in the middle of walking home)	○ We **walked** home after the party last night. (= all the way, completely)
○ Kate **was watching** TV when we arrived.	○ Kate **watched** TV a lot when she was ill last year.

D You can say that something **happened** (past simple) in the middle of something else (past continuous):
- ○ Matt **phoned** while we **were having** dinner.
- ○ It **was raining** when I **got** up.
- ○ I **saw** you in the park yesterday. You **were sitting** on the grass and **reading** a book.
- ○ I **hurt** my back while I **was working** in the garden.

But we use the past simple to say that one thing happened *after* another:
- ○ I **was walking** along the road when I **saw** Dan. So I **stopped**, and we **talked** for a while.

Compare:

○ When Karen arrived, we **were having** dinner. (= we had already started before she arrived)	○ When Karen arrived, we **had** dinner. (= Karen arrived, and then we had dinner)

E Some verbs (for example, **know** and **want**) are not normally used in continuous forms (**is** + **-ing**, **was** + **-ing** etc.). See Unit 4A for a list of these verbs.
- ○ We were good friends. We **knew** each other well. (*not* we were knowing)
- ○ I was enjoying the party, but Chris **wanted** to go home. (*not* was wanting)

≫ Past simple (**I did**) → Unit 5

Exercises

6.1 Complete the sentences. Choose from:

was looking	~~was wearing~~	wasn't listening	weren't looking
was snowing	was working	were sitting	were you going

1 Today Helen is wearing a skirt. Yesterday she ....**was wearing**.... trousers.
2 'What did he say?' 'I don't know. I ....'
3 We .... at the back of the theatre. We couldn't hear very well.
4 This time last year Steve .... on a farm.
5 They didn't see me. They .... in my direction.
6 The weather was bad. It was very cold and it ....
7 I saw you in your car. Where .... ?
8 I saw Kate a few minutes ago. She .... for you.

6.2 Which goes with which?

1 When I got to the cafe	a when she was living in Rome.
2 We fell asleep	b she was working in a clothes shop.
3 Amy learnt Italian	c when I was driving home.
4 Tom didn't come out with us	e while we were watching a film.
5 The car began to make a strange noise	f ~~my friends were waiting for me.~~
6 The TV was on	d but nobody was watching it.
7 When I first met Jessica	g because he wasn't feeling well.

1 _f_
2 _e_
3 _a_
4 _g_
5 ....
6 _d_
7 _b_

6.3 Put the verb into the correct form, past continuous or past simple.

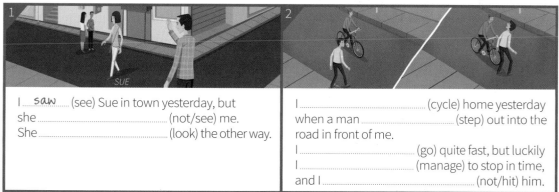

1 I ....**saw**.... (see) Sue in town yesterday, but she .... (not-see) me. She .... (look) the other way.

2 I .... (cycle) home yesterday when a man .... (step) out into the road in front of me. I .... (go) quite fast, but luckily I .... (manage) to stop in time, and I .... (not/hit) him.

6.4 Put the verb into the correct form, past continuous or past simple.

1 Jenny ....**was waiting**.... (wait) for me when I ....**arrived**.... (arrive).
2 'What .... (you / do) at this time yesterday?' 'I was asleep.'
3 '... (you / go) out last night?' 'No, I was too tired.'
4 How fast .... (you / drive) when the accident .... (happen)?
5 Sam .... (take) a picture of me while I .... (not / look).
6 We were in a very difficult position. We .... (not / know) what to do, so we .... (do) nothing.
7 I haven't seen Alan for ages. When I last .... (see) him, he .... (try) to find a job.
8 I .... (walk) along the street when suddenly I .... (hear) something behind me. Somebody .... (follow) me. I was scared and I .... (start) to run.
9 When I was young, I .... (want) to be a pilot. Later I .... (change) my mind.
10 Last night I .... (drop) a plate when I .... (do) the washing up. Fortunately it .... (not / break).

➔ **Additional exercise 1** (page 302)

Present perfect 1 (**I have done**)

A Study this example situation:

I've lost my key.

Tom can't find his key.
He**'s lost** his key. (= He **has lost** …)

he **has lost** his key =
he lost it and he doesn't have it now

have lost / **has lost** is the *present perfect simple*:

| I/we/they/you **have** (= I**'ve** etc.) | **finished** **lost** |
| he/she/it **has** (= he**'s** etc.) | **done** **been** etc. |

The present perfect simple is **have**/**has** + *past participle*. The past participle often ends in -**ed** (finish**ed**/decid**ed** etc.), but many verbs are *irregular* (**lost**/**done**/**written** etc.).

For a list of irregular verbs, see Appendix 1.

B When we say 'something **has happened**', this is usually new information:
- ○ Ow! I**'ve cut** my finger.
- ○ The road is closed. There**'s been** an accident. (= There **has been** …)
- ○ Police **have arrested** two men in connection with the robbery.

When we use the present perfect, there is a connection with *now*. The action in the past has a result *now*:
- ○ Tom **has lost** his key. (= he doesn't have it *now*)
- ○ He told me his name, but I**'ve forgotten** it. (= I can't remember it *now*)
- ○ Sally is still here. She **hasn't gone** out. (= she is here *now*)
- ○ I can't find my bag. **Have** you **seen** it? (= do you know where it is *now*?)

Compare **gone** (**to**) and **been** (**to**):
- ○ James is on holiday. He **has gone to** Italy. (= he is there now or on his way there)
- ○ Amy is back home now. She **has been** to Italy. (= she has now come back)

C You can use the present perfect with **just**, **already** and **yet**.

Just = a short time ago:
- ○ 'Are you hungry?' 'No, I**'ve just had** lunch.'
- ○ Hello. **Have** you **just arrived**?

Already = sooner than expected:
- ○ 'Don't forget to pay the bill.' 'I**'ve already paid** it.'
- ○ 'What time is Mark leaving?' 'He**'s already left**.'

Yet = until now. We use **yet** to show that we are expecting something to happen.
We use **yet** in questions and negative sentences:
- ○ **Has** it **stopped** raining **yet**?
- ○ I've written the email, but I **haven't sent** it **yet**.

D You can also use the past simple (**did**, **went**, **had** etc.) in the examples on this page. So you can say:
- ○ Ben isn't here. He**'s gone** out. *or* He **went** out.
- ○ 'Are you hungry?' 'No, I**'ve** just **had** lunch.' *or* 'No, I just **had** lunch.'

Present perfect → **Units 8**, **11**   been to → **Units 8A**, **126A**   Present perfect continuous → **Units 9–10**
Present perfect and past → **Units 12–14**   yet and already → **Unit 111**   American English → **Appendix 7**

Exercises

7.1 Read the situations and complete the sentences using the present perfect. Choose from these verbs:

> break   disappear   go up   grow   improve   ~~lose~~   shrink   stop

1 Tom is looking for his key. He can't find it.   Tom *has lost his key.*
2 Maria's English wasn't very good. Now it is better.   Her English ....
3 My bag was here, but it isn't here any more.   My bag ....
4 Lisa can't walk and her leg is in plaster.   Lisa ....
5 Last week the bus fare was £1.80. Now it is £2.   The bus fare ....
6 Dan didn't have a beard before. Now he has a beard.   Dan ....
7 It was raining ten minutes ago. It isn't raining now.   It ....
8 I washed my sweater, and now it's too small for me.   My sweater ....

7.2 Put in **been** or **gone**.

1 My parents are on holiday. They've ......*gone*...... to Italy.
2 Hello! I've just .... to the shops. I've bought lots of things.
3 Tom has just .... out. He'll be back in about an hour.
4 Alice isn't here at the moment. I don't know where she's ....
5 You're very late. Where have you ....?

7.3 Complete the sentences using the present perfect.

1 Sally is still here. ......*She hasn't gone*...... (she / not / go) out.
2 I can't find my bag. .... (you / see / it) anywhere?
3 I can't log on to the website. .... (I / forget) my password.
4 I sent Joe an email this morning, but .... (he / not / reply).
5 Is the meeting still going on, or .... (it / finish)?
6 .... (the weather / change). It's colder now.
7 .... (you / not / sign) the form. Could you sign it now, please?
8 Are your friends still here, or .... (they / go) home?
9 Paul doesn't know what he's going to do. ....
   (he / not / decide / yet).
10 'Do you know where Julia is?' 'Yes, ... (I / just / see / her).'
11 'When is David going away?' '...................... (he / already / go).'
12 A: .... (your course / start / yet)?
   B: Not yet. It starts next week.

7.4 Read the situations and write sentences with **just**, **already** or **yet**.

1 After lunch you go to see a friend at her house. She says, 'Would you like something to eat?'
   You say: No thank you. ......*I've just had lunch*...... . (have lunch)
2 Joe goes out. Five minutes later, the phone rings and the caller says, 'Can I speak to Joe?'
   You say: I'm afraid .... (go out)
3 You are eating in a restaurant. The waiter thinks you have finished and starts to take your plate away.
   You say: Wait a minute! .... (not / finish)
4 You plan to eat at a restaurant tonight. You phone to reserve a table. Later your friend says,
   'Shall I phone to reserve a table?' You say: No, ... (do it)
5 You know that Lisa is looking for a place to live. Perhaps she has been successful.
   You ask her: .... ? (find)
6 You are still thinking about where to go for your holiday. A friend asks, 'Where are you going
   for your holiday?' You say: .... (not / decide)
7 Laura went out, but a few minutes ago she returned. Somebody asks, 'Is Laura still out?'
   You say: No, ... (come back)

Present perfect 2 (**I have done**)

A Study this example conversation:

DAVE: **Have** you **travelled** a lot, Jane?
JANE: Yes, I**'ve been** to lots of places.
DAVE: Really? **Have** you ever **been** to China?
JANE: Yes, I**'ve been** to China twice.
DAVE: What about India?
JANE: No, I **haven't been** to India.

Jane's life
(a period until now)

past   now

When we talk about a period of time that continues from the past until now, we use the *present perfect* (**have been / have travelled** etc.). Here, Dave and Jane are talking about the places Jane **has visited** in her life, which is a period that continues until now.

In the same way we say:
- [ ] **Have** you **ever eaten** caviar?
- [ ] We**'ve** never **had** a car.
- [ ] I don't know what the film is about. I **haven't seen** it.
- [ ] Susan really loves that book. She**'s read** it three times. (She**'s** = She **has**)
- [ ] It's a really boring movie. It's the most boring movie I**'ve ever seen**.

been (**to**) = visited:
- [ ] I**'ve** never **been to** Canada. Have you **been** there?

B In the following examples too, the speakers are talking about a period that continues until now (**recently**, **in the last few days**, **so far**, **since I arrived** etc.):

- [ ] **Have** you **heard** anything from Ben **recently**?
- [ ] I**'ve met** a lot of people **in the last few days**.
- [ ] Everything is going well. There **haven't been** any problems **so far**.
- [ ] The weather is bad here. It**'s** (= It **has**) **rained** every day **since I arrived**. (= from when I arrived until now)
- [ ] It's good to see you again. We **haven't seen** each other **for a long time**.

recently
in the last few days
since I arrived

past   now

In the same way we use the present perfect with **today**, **this evening**, **this year** etc. when these periods are not finished at the time of speaking:
- [ ] I**'ve drunk** four cups of coffee **today**.
- [ ] **Have** you **had** a holiday **this year**?
- [ ] I **haven't seen** Tom **this morning**. **Have** you?

today

past   now

C We say 'It's the (first) time something **has happened**'. For example:
Don is having a driving lesson. It's his first lesson.
We can say:

- [ ] It's the first time he **has driven** a car. (*not* drives)
- *or* He **hasn't driven** a car **before**.
- *or* He **has never driven** a car **before**.

In the same way we say:
- [ ] Sarah has lost her passport again. This is the second time this **has happened**. (*not* happens)
- [ ] Andy is phoning his girlfriend again. It's the third time he**'s phoned** her **this evening**.

This is the first time I**'ve driven** a car.

DRIVING SCHOOL

Present perfect 1 → **Unit 7**   Present perfect + **for/since** → **Units 11–12**   Present perfect and past → **Units 12–14**

Exercises

8.1 You ask people about things they have done. Write questions with ever.

1 (ride / horse?) <u>Have you ever ridden a horse?</u>
2 (be / California?) Have ....
3 (run / marathon?) ....
4 (speak / famous person?) ....
5 (most beautiful place / visit?) What's ....

8.2 Complete B's answers. Some sentences are positive and some negative. Use these verbs:

be   be   eat   happen   ~~have~~   have   ~~meet~~   play   read   see   try

	A	B
1	What's Mark's sister like?	I've no idea. <u>I've never met</u> her.
2	Is everything going well?	Yes, we <u>haven't had</u> any problems so far.
3	Are you hungry?	Yes. I .... much today.
4	Can you play chess?	Yes, but .... for ages.
5	Are you enjoying your holiday?	Yes, it's the best holiday .... for a long time.
6	What's that book about?	I don't know. .... it.
7	Is Brussels an interesting place?	I've no idea. .... there.
8	I hear your car broke down again yesterday.	Yes, it's the second time .... this month.
9	Do you like caviar?	I don't know. .... it.
10	Mike was late for work again today.	Again? He .... late every day this week.
11	Who's that woman by the door?	I don't know. .... her before.

8.3 Write four sentences about yourself. Use I haven't and choose from the boxes.

| used a computer | travelled by bus | eaten any fruit |
| been to the cinema | read a book | lost anything |

today
this week
recently
for ages
since …
this year

1 <u>I haven't used a computer today.</u>
2 ....
3 ....
4 ....
5 ....

8.4 Read the situations and complete the sentences.

1 Jack is driving a car for the first time. He's very nervous and not sure what to do.
   <u>It's the first time he's driven</u> a car.
2 Some children at the zoo are looking at a giraffe. They've never seen one before.
   It's the first time .... a giraffe.
3 Sue is riding a horse. She doesn't look very confident or comfortable.
   She .... before.
4 Joe and Lisa are on holiday in Japan. They've been to Japan once before.
   This is the second time ....
5 Emily is staying at the Prince Hotel. She stayed there a few years ago.
   It's not the first .... this hotel.
6 Ben is playing tennis for the first time. He's a complete beginner.
   .... before.

Present perfect continuous (**I have been doing**)

A   **It's been raining.**

Study this example situation:

Is it raining?
No, but the ground is wet.
It's been raining. (= It **has** been ...)

have/has been + **-ing** is the *present perfect continuous*:

I/we/they/you he/she/it	**have** **has**	(= I**'ve** etc.) (= he**'s** etc.)	**been**	**doing** **working** **learning** etc.

We use the present perfect continuous for an activity that has recently stopped or just stopped:
- ○ Why are you out of breath? **Have** you **been running**?
- ○ Paul is very tired. He**'s been working** hard.
- ○ Why are you so tired? What **have** you **been doing**?
- ○ I**'ve been talking** to Amanda and she agrees with me.
- ○ Where have you been? I**'ve been looking** for you.

have/has been + -ing
present perfect continuous

now

B   **It's been raining for two hours.**

Study this example situation:

It began raining two hours ago and it is still raining.

How long **has** it **been raining**?
It**'s been raining** for two hours. (= It **has** been ...)

We use the present perfect continuous in this way, especially with **how long**, **for** ... and **since** ... . The activity is still happening (as in this example) or has just stopped.

- ○ **How long have** you **been learning** English? (= you're still learning English)
- ○ Ben is watching TV. He**'s been watching** TV **all day**.
- ○ Where have you been? I**'ve been looking** for you **for the last half hour**.
- ○ Chris **hasn't been feeling** well **recently**.

You can use the present perfect continuous for repeated actions:
- ○ Silvia is a very good tennis player. She**'s been playing since she was eight**.
- ○ Every morning they meet in the same cafe. They**'ve been going** there **for years**.

C   Compare **I am doing** and **I have been doing**:

I am doing
present continuous

now

I have been doing
present perfect continuous

now

- ○ Don't disturb me now. I**'m working**.

- ○ We need an umbrella. It**'s raining**.
- ○ Hurry up! We**'re waiting**.

- ○ I**'ve been working** hard. Now I'm going to have a break.
- ○ The ground is wet. It**'s been raining**.
- ○ We**'ve been waiting** for an hour.

Exercises

9.1 **What have these people been doing or what has been happening?**

1 It's been raining.

2 She _____

3 They _____

4 He _____

9.2 **Write a question for each situation.**

1 You meet Kate as she is leaving the swimming pool. You say:
Hi, Kate. (you / swim?) __Have you been swimming?__

2 You have arrived a little late to meet Ben who is waiting for you. You say:
I'm sorry I'm late, Ben. (you / wait / long?) _____

3 Jane's little boy comes into the house with a very dirty face and dirty hands. His mother says:
Why are you so dirty? (what / you / do?) _____

4 You are in a shop and see Anna. You didn't know she worked there. You say:
Hi, Anna. (how long / you / work / here?) _____

5 A friend tells you about his job – he sells phones. You say:
You sell phones? (how long / you / do / that?) _____

9.3 **Read the situations and complete the sentences.**

1 It's raining. The rain started two hours ago.
It __'s been raining__ for two hours.

2 We are waiting for the bus. We started waiting 20 minutes ago.
We _____ for 20 minutes.

3 I'm learning Japanese. I started classes in December.
I _____ since December.

4 Jessica is working in a hotel. She started working there on 18 January.
_____ since 18 January.

5 Our friends always go to Italy for their holidays. The first time was years ago.
_____ for years.

9.4 **Put the verb into the present continuous (am/is/are + -ing) or present perfect continuous (have/has been + -ing).**

1 __Maria has been learning__ (Maria / learn) English for two years.

2 Hi, Tom. _____ (I / look) for you. I need to ask you something.

3 Why _____ (you / look) at me like that? Stop it!

4 Rachel is a teacher. _____ (she / teach) for ten years.

5 _____ (I / think) about what you said and I've decided to take your advice.

6 'Is Paul on holiday this week?' 'No, _____ (he / work).'

7 Sarah is very tired. _____ (she / work) very hard recently.

8 It's dangerous to use your phone when _____ (you / drive).

9 Laura _____ (travel) in South America for the last three months.

19

Present perfect continuous and simple (I have been doing and I have done)

A Compare these two situations:

> I've been painting my bedroom.

> I've painted my bedroom.

There is paint on Kate's clothes.
She **has been painting** her bedroom.

has been painting is the *present perfect continuous*.

We are thinking of the activity. It does not matter whether it has been finished or not. In this example, the activity (painting the bedroom) has not been finished.

The bedroom was green. Now it is yellow.
She **has painted** her bedroom.

has painted is the *present perfect simple*.

Here, the important thing is that something has been finished. 'She **has painted**' is a completed action. We are thinking about the *result* of the activity (the painted bedroom), not the activity itself.

B Compare these examples:

- ○ My hands are very dirty. **I've been repairing** my bike.
- ○ Joe **has been eating** too much recently. He should eat less.
- ○ It's nice to see you again. What **have** you **been doing** since we last met?
- ○ Where have you been? **Have** you **been playing** tennis?

- ○ My bike is OK again now. **I've repaired it**. (= I've finished repairing it)
- ○ Somebody **has eaten** all the chocolates. The box is empty.
- ○ Where's the book I gave you? What **have** you **done** with it?
- ○ **Have** you ever **played** tennis?

C

We use the continuous to say *how long* (for something that is still happening):
- ○ How long **have** you **been reading** that book?
- ○ Amy is writing emails. She**'s been writing** emails all morning.
- ○ They**'ve been playing** tennis since 2 o'clock.
- ○ I'm learning Arabic, but I **haven't been learning** it very long.

We use the simple to say *how much, how many* or *how many times* (for completed actions):
- ○ How many pages of that book **have** you **read**?
- ○ Amy **has sent** lots of emails this morning.
- ○ They**'ve played** tennis three times this week.
- ○ I'm learning Arabic, but I **haven't learnt** very much yet.

D Some verbs (for example, **know**) are not normally used in continuous forms (**be** + **-ing**):
- ○ I**'ve known** about the problem for a long time. (*not* I've been knowing)
- ○ How long **have** you **had** that camera? (*not* have you been having)

For a list of these verbs, see Unit 4A. For **have**, see Unit 17.
But note that you *can* use **want** and **mean** in the present perfect continuous (**have/has been** + **-ing**):
- ○ I**'ve been meaning** to phone Anna, but I keep forgetting.

>> Present perfect simple → Units 7–8   Present perfect continuous → Unit 9
Present perfect + for/since → Units 11–12

Exercises

10.1 **Read the situation and complete the sentences. Use the verbs in brackets.**

1 Tom started reading a book two hours ago. He is still reading it and now he is on page 53.
   He has been reading for two hours. (read)
   He has read 53 pages so far. (read)

2 Rachel is from Australia. She is travelling round Europe. She began her trip three months ago.
   She .... for three months. (travel)
   .... six countries so far. (visit)

3 Patrick is a tennis player. He began playing tennis when he was 10 years old. This year he won the national championship again – for the fourth time.
   .... the national championship four times. (win)
   .... since he was ten. (play)

4 When they left college, Lisa and Sue started making films together. They still make films.
   They .... films since they left college. (make)
   .... five films since they left college. (make)

10.2 **Ask questions using the words in brackets. Use the present perfect simple (have/has done) or continuous (have/has been doing).**

1 You have a friend who is learning Arabic. You ask:
   (how long / learn / Arabic?) _How long have you been learning Arabic?_

2 You have just arrived to meet a friend. She is waiting for you. You ask:
   (wait / long?) Have ....

3 You see somebody fishing by the river. You ask:
   (catch / any fish?) ....

4 Some friends of yours are having a party next week. You ask:
   (how many people / invite?) ....

5 A friend of yours is a teacher. You ask:
   (how long / teach?) ....

6 You meet somebody who is a writer. You ask:
   (how many books / write?) ....
   (how long / write / books?) ....

7 A friend of yours is saving money to go on a world trip. You ask:
   (how long / save?) ....
   (how much money / save?) ....

10.3 **Put the verb into the present perfect simple or continuous.**

1 Where have you been? _Have you been playing_ (you / play) tennis?
2 Look! .... (somebody / break) that window.
3 You look tired. .... (you / work) hard?
4 '.. (you / ever / work) in a factory?' 'No, never.'
5 Where's Lisa? Where .... (she / go)?
6 This is a very old book. .... (I / have) it since I was a child.
7 'Have you been busy?' 'No, ... (I / watch) TV.'
8 My brother is an actor. .... (he / appear) in several films.
9 'Sorry I'm late.' 'That's all right. .... (I / not / wait) long.'
10 Are you OK? You look as if .... (you / cry).
11 'Is it still raining?' 'No, ... (it / stop).'
12 The children are tired now. .... (they / play) in the garden.
13 .... (I / lose) my phone. .... (you / see) it?
14 .... (I / read) the book you lent me, but ....
   .... (I / not / finish) it yet. It's really interesting.
15 .... (I / read) the book you lent me, so you can have it back now.

21

how long have you (been) ... ?

A Study this example situation:

Dan and Kate are married. They got married exactly 20 years ago, so today is their 20th wedding anniversary.

They **have been** married **for 20 years**.

We say: They **are** married. *(present)*

but   How long have they **been** married?
(*not* How long are they married?)
They **have been** married **for 20 years**.
(*not* They are married for 20 years) } *(present perfect)*

We use the *present perfect* to talk about something that began in the past and still continues now.
Compare the *present* and *present perfect*:

	○ Paul is in hospital.
but	He**'s been** in hospital **since Monday**. (= He **has** been ...)
	(*not* Paul is in hospital since Monday)

	○ We **know** each other very well.
but	We**'ve known** each other **for a long time**.
	(*not* We know)

| | ○ **Do** they **have** a car? |
| *but* | **How long have** they **had** their car? |

| | ○ She**'s waiting** for somebody. |
| *but* | She **hasn't been waiting** very long. |

present
he is
we know
do they have
she is waiting

present perfect
he has been
we have known
have they had
she has been waiting

past   *now*

B **I've known / I've had / I've lived** etc. is the *present perfect simple*.
I've been learning / I've been waiting etc. is the *present perfect continuous*.

When we ask or say 'how long', the continuous is more usual (see Unit 10):
○ **I've been learning** English **since January**.
○ It**'s been raining all morning**.
○ Richard **has been doing** the same job **for 20 years**.
○ '**How long have** you **been driving**?' 'Since I was 17.'

Some verbs (for example, **know** and **like**) are not normally used in the continuous:
○ How long **have** you **known** Jane? (*not* have you been knowing)
○ **I've had** these shoes for ages. (*not* I've been having)
See also Units 4A and 10C. For **have**, see Unit 17.

C You can use either the continuous or simple with **live** and **work**:
○ Julia **has been living** in this house for a long time. *or* Julia **has lived** ...
○ How long **have** you **been working** here? *or* How long **have** you **worked** here?

But we use the simple (**have lived** etc.) with **always**:
○ **I've always lived** in the country. (*not* always been living)

D We say 'I haven't (done something) **since/for** ...' *(present perfect simple)*:
○ I **haven't seen** Tom since Monday. (= Monday was the last time I saw him)
○ Sarah **hasn't phoned** for ages. (= the last time she phoned was ages ago)

Exercises

Which is right?

1 Ben is a friend of mine. <u>I know</u> / ~~I've known~~ him very well. (<u>I know</u> *is correct*)
2 I like your house. How long <u>do you live / have you lived</u> here?
3 You'll need an umbrella if you go out now. <u>It's raining / It's been raining</u>.
4 The weather <u>is / has been</u> awful since I arrived here.
5 I'm sorry I'm late. <u>Are you waiting / Have you been waiting</u> long?
6 We've moved. <u>We're living / We've been living</u> in New Street now.
7 I met Maria only recently. <u>I don't know / I haven't known</u> her very long.
8 Lisa is in Germany. <u>She's / She's been</u> there on a business trip.
9 That's a very old bike. How long <u>do you have / have you had</u> it?
10 I'm not feeling good. <u>I'm feeling / I've been feeling</u> ill all day.

Read the situations and write questions using the words in brackets.

1 A friend tells you that Paul is in hospital. You ask him:
(how long / Paul / hospital?) <u>How long has Paul been in hospital?</u>
2 You know that Jane is a good friend of Katherine's. You ask Jane:
(how long / you / know / Katherine?) ....
3 Your friend's sister went to Australia some time ago and she's still there. You ask your friend:
(how long / sister / in Australia?) ....
4 You meet a woman who tells you that she teaches English. You ask her:
(how long / you / teach / English?) ....

5 Tom always wears the same jacket. It's very old. You ask him:
(how long / you / have / that jacket?) ....
6 You are talking to a friend about Joe, who now works at the airport. You ask your friend:
(how long / Joe / work / airport?) ....

7 You meet somebody on a plane. She says that she lives in Chicago. You ask her:
(you / always / live / in Chicago?) ....

Complete B's answers to A's questions.

	A	B
1	Paul is in hospital, isn't he?	Yes, he <u>has been</u> in hospital since Monday.
2	Do you see Lisa very often?	No, I <u>haven't seen</u> her for three months.
3	Is Paul married?	Yes, he .... married for ten years.
4	Is Amy married?	Yes, she .... married to a German guy.
5	Do you still play tennis?	No, I .... tennis for years.
6	Are you waiting for the bus?	Yes, I .... for about 20 minutes.
7	You know Mel, don't you?	Yes, we .... each other a long time.
8	Jack is never ill, is he?	No, he .... ill since I've known him.
9	Martin lives in Italy, doesn't he?	Yes, he .... in Milan.
10	Sue lives in Berlin, doesn't she?	Yes, she .... in Berlin for many years.
11	Is Joe watching TV?	Yes, he .... TV all evening.
12	Do you watch TV a lot?	No, I .... TV since last weekend.
13	Do you have a headache?	Yes, I .... a headache all morning.
14	Do you go to the cinema a lot?	No, I .... to the cinema for ages.
15	Would you like to go to New York one day?	Yes, I .... to go to New York. (*use* **always / want**)

A   We use **for** and **since** to say how long something has been happening.

We use **for** + a period of time:
- ○   We've been waiting **for two hours**.

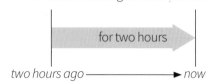

two hours ago ──────▶ *now*

for		
two hours	a long time	a week
20 minutes	six months	ages
five days	50 years	years

- ○   Sally has been working here **for six months**. (*not* since six months)
- ○   I haven't seen Tom **for three days**.

We use **since** + the start of a period:
- ○   We've been waiting **since 8 o'clock**.

8 o'clock ──────▶ *now*

since		
8 o'clock	April	lunchtime
Monday	2001	we arrived
12 May	Christmas	I got up

- ○   Sally has been working here **since April**. (= from April until now)
- ○   I haven't seen Tom **since Monday**.

B   We often leave out **for** (but not usually in negative sentences):
- ○   They've been married **for ten years**. *or*   They've been married **ten years**.
- ○   They **haven't had** a holiday **for** ten years. (you need **for**)

You can use **in** instead of **for** in negative sentences (**I haven't** … etc.):
- ○   They **haven't had** a holiday **in ten years**. (= **for** ten years)

We do *not* use **for** + **all** … (**all day / all my life** etc.):
- ○   I've lived here **all my life**. (*not* for all my life)

C   Compare **when** … ? (+ *past simple*) and **how long** … ? (+ *present perfect*):

A: **When** did it start raining?
B: It started raining **an hour ago / at 1 o'clock**.

A: **How long** has it been raining?
B: It's been raining **for an hour / since 1 o'clock**.

A: **When** did Joe and Kate first meet?
B: They first met { **a long time ago.**
                  { **when they were at school.**
A: **How long** have they known each other?
B: They've known each other { **for a long time.**
                       { **since they were at school.**

D   We say:

it's (= it **is**) *or* **it's been** (= it **has been**)	a long time six months (*etc.*)	since something happened

- ○   **It's two years since** I last saw Joe.   *or*   **It's been two years since** … (= I **haven't seen** Joe for two years)
- ○   **It's ages since** we went to the cinema.   *or*   **It's been ages since** … (= We **haven't been** to the cinema for ages)
- ○   **How long is it since** Mrs Hill died?   *or*   **How long has it been since** … (= when did she die?)

>>   How long have you (been) … ? → Unit 11

Exercises

12.1 Write **for** or **since**.

1 It's been raining ....._since_..... lunchtime.
2 Paul has lived in Brazil .... ten years.
3 I'm tired of waiting. We've been sitting here .... an hour.
4 Kevin has been looking for a job .... he left school.
5 I haven't been to a party .... ages.
6 I wonder where Joe is. I haven't seen him .... last week.
7 Jane is away on holiday. She's been away .... Friday.
8 The weather is dry. It hasn't rained .... a few weeks.

12.2 Look at each answer and choose the right question.

1   ~~How long have they been married ?~~
    When did they get married?   Ten years ago.

   (When did they get married? *is correct*)

2   How long have you had this car?
    When did you buy this car?   About five years.

3   How long have you been waiting?
    When did you get here?   Only a few minutes.

4   How long have you been doing your course?
    When did your course start?   September.

5   How long has Anna been in London?
    When did Anna arrive in London?   Last week.

6   How long have you known each other?
    When did you first meet each other?   A long time.

12.3 Read the situations and complete the sentences.

1 It's raining. It's been raining since lunchtime. It ...._started raining_.... at lunchtime.
2 Ann and Jess are friends. They first met years ago. They've ...._known each other for_.... years.
3 Mark is unwell. He became ill on Sunday. He has .... Sunday.
4 Sarah is married. She's been married for a year. She got ....
5 You have a headache. It started when you woke up.
   I've .... I woke up.
6 Sue is in a meeting at work. It's been going on since 9 o'clock.
   The meeting .... at 9 o'clock.
7 You're working in a hotel. You started working there six months ago.
   I've been ....
8 Kate is learning Japanese. She's been doing this for a long time.
   Kate started ....

12.4 Complete B's sentences.

    A   B
1   Do you often go on holiday?   No, I ...._haven't had a holiday for_.... five years.
2   Have you seen Lisa recently?   No, I .... about a month.
3   Do you still go swimming regularly?   No, I .... a long time.
4   Do you still ride a bike these days? No, I .... ages.

Now write B's answers again. This time use **It's . . . since . . . .**

5 (1) No, ..._it's five years since I last had a holiday._....
6 (2) No, it's ....
7 (3) No, ...
8 (4) ....

25

Present perfect and past 1 (**I have done** and **I did**)

A Study this example situation:

Tom is looking for his key. He can't find it.

He **has lost** his key. (*present perfect*)

This means that he doesn't have his key *now*.

Ten minutes later:

Now Tom **has found** his key. He has it now.

Has he **lost** his key? No, he **has found** it.
Did he **lose** his key? Yes, he **did**.

He **lost** his key (*past simple*)
but now he **has found** it. (*present perfect*)

The *present perfect* (something **has happened**) is a *present* tense. It tells us about the situation *now*.
'Tom **has lost** his key' = he doesn't have his key *now* (see Unit 7).

The *past simple* (something **happened**) tells us only about the *past*. If somebody says 'Tom **lost** his key',
we don't know whether he has the key now or not. We know only that he lost it at some time in the past.

Compare *present perfect* and *past simple*:
- ○ They**'ve gone** away. They'll be back on Friday. (they are away *now*)
- ○ They **went** away, but I think they're back at home now. (*not* They've gone away)
- ○ It **has stopped** raining now, so we don't need the umbrella. (it isn't raining *now*)
- ○ It **stopped** raining for a while, but now it's raining again. (*not* It has stopped)

B You can use the present perfect for new or recent happenings:
- ○ I**'ve repaired** the washing machine. It's working OK now.
- ○ 'Hannah **has had** a baby! It's a boy.' 'That's great news.'

Usually, you can also use the past simple:
- ○ I **repaired** the washing machine. It's working OK now.

Use the past simple (*not* the present perfect) for things that are not recent or new:
- ○ Mozart **was** a composer. He **wrote** more than 600 pieces of music.
  (*not* has been … has written)
- ○ My mother **grew** up in Italy. (*not* has grown)

Compare:
Somebody **has invented** a new type of washing machine.
Who **invented** the telephone? (*not* has invented)

C We use the present perfect to give new information (see Unit 7). But if we continue to talk about it,
we normally use the past simple:
- ○ A: Ow! I**'ve burnt** myself.
  B: How **did** you **do** that? (*not* have you done)
  A: I **picked** up a hot dish. (*not* have picked)

- ○ A: Look! Somebody **has spilt** something on the sofa.
  B: Well, it **wasn't** me. I **didn't do** it. (*not* hasn't been … haven't done)

>> Past simple → **Unit 5**   Present perfect → **Units 7–8**   Present perfect and past 2 → **Unit 14**
American English → **Appendix 7**

Exercises

13.1 Complete the sentences. Use the present perfect where possible. Otherwise use the past simple.

1. I can't get in. I __'ve lost__ (lose) my key.
2. The office is empty now. Everybody .... (go) home.
3. I meant to call you last night, but I .... (forget).
4. Helen .... (go) to New York for a holiday, but she's back home in London now.
5. Are you OK? — Yes, I .... (have) a headache, but it's OK now. *before*
6. Can you help us? Our car .... (break) down.

13.2 Are the underlined parts of these sentences OK? Correct them where necessary.

1. Did you hear about Sophie? <u>She's given up</u> her job.   *OK*
2. <u>My mother has grown up</u> in Italy.   *My mother grew up*
3. How many plays <u>has William Shakespeare written</u>?   ....
4. <u>I've forgotten</u> his name. Is it Joe or Jack?   ....
5. Who <u>has invented</u> paper?   ....
6. <u>Drugs have become</u> a big problem everywhere.   ....
7. <u>We've washed</u> the car, but now it's dirty again.   ....
8. Where <u>have you been born</u>?   ....
9. <u>Ellie has gone</u> shopping. She'll be back in about an hour.   ....
10. <u>Albert Einstein has been</u> the scientist who <u>has developed</u> the theory of relativity.   ....

13.3 Put the verb into the correct form, present perfect or past simple.

1. __It stopped__ raining for a while, but now it's raining again. (it / stop)
2. The town where I live is very different now. __It has changed__ a lot. (it / change)
3. I studied German at school, but .... most of it now. (I / forget)
4. The police .... three people, but later they let them go. (arrest)
5. What do you think of my English? Do you think ....? (it / improve)
6. Are you ready to go? .... your coffee? (you / finish)
7. .... for a job as a tour guide, but I wasn't successful. (I / apply)
8. Where's my bike? .... outside the house, but it's not there now. (it / be)
9. Quick! We need to call an ambulance. .... an accident. (there / be)
10. A: I've found my phone.
    B: Oh, good. Where .... it? (you / find)
    A: .... at the bottom of my bag. (It / be)
11. A: Ben won't be able to play tennis for a while. .... his arm. (He / break)
    B: Oh. How ....? (that / happen)
    A: .... off a ladder. (He / fall)

27

A

We do not use the present perfect (**I have done**) when we talk about a *finished* time (for example, **yesterday** / **last year** / **ten minutes ago** etc.). We use a past tense:

○ It **was** very cold **yesterday**. (*not* has been)
○ Paul and Lucy **arrived ten minutes ago**. (*not* have arrived)
○ **Did** you **eat** a lot of sweets **when you were a child**? (*not* have you eaten)
○ I **got** home late **last night**. I **was** very tired and **went** straight to bed.

Use the past to ask **When** …? *or* **What time** …?:

○ **When did** your friends **arrive**? (*not* have … arrived)
○ **What time did** you **finish** work?

Compare:

Present perfect	*Past simple*
○ Tom **has lost** his key. He can't get into the house.	○ Tom **lost** his key **yesterday**. He couldn't get into the house.
○ Is Carla here or **has** she **left**?	○ **When did** Carla **leave**?

B

Compare:

Present perfect (**have done**)	*Past simple* (**did**)
○ I**'ve done** a lot of work **today**.	○ I **did** a lot of work **yesterday**.

We use the present perfect for a period of time that continues *until now*. For example: **today** / **this week** / **since 2010**.

We use the past simple for a *finished* time in the past. For example: **yesterday** / **last week** / **from 2010 to 2014**.

○ It **hasn't rained this week**.	○ It **didn't rain last week**.
○ **Have** you **seen** Anna **this morning**? (it is still morning now)	○ **Did** you **see** Anna **this morning**? (it is now afternoon or evening)
○ **Have** you **seen** Ben **recently**? (in the last few days or weeks)	○ **Did** you **see** Ben **on Sunday**?
○ I**'ve been working** here **since 2010**. (I still work here now)	○ I **worked** here **from 2010 to 2014**. (I don't work here now)
○ I don't know where Lisa is. I **haven't seen** her. (= I haven't seen her recently)	○ A: **Was** Lisa at the party **on Sunday**? B: I don't think so. I **didn't see** her.
○ We**'ve been waiting** for an hour. (we are still waiting now)	○ We **waited** (*or* **were waiting**) for an hour. (we are no longer waiting)
○ Jack lives in Los Angeles. He **has lived** there for seven years.	○ Jack **lived** in New York for ten years. Now he lives in Los Angeles.
○ I**'ve never ridden** a horse. (in my life)	○ I **never rode** a bike **when I was a child**.
○ *It's the last day of your holiday. You say*: It**'s been** a really good holiday. I**'ve** really **enjoyed** it.	○ *After you come back from holiday you say*: It **was** a really good holiday. I really **enjoyed** it.

Exercises

14.1 Are the <u>underlined</u> parts of these sentences OK? Correct them where necessary.

1 <u>I've lost</u> my key. I can't find it anywhere.   *OK*
2 <u>Have you eaten</u> a lot of sweets when you were a child?   *Did you eat*
3 <u>I've bought</u> a new car. You must come and see it.
4 <u>I've bought</u> a new car last week.
5 Where <u>have you been</u> yesterday evening?
6 Maria <u>has left</u> school in 1999.
7 I'm looking for Mike. <u>Have you seen</u> him?
8 '<u>Have you been</u> to Paris?' 'Yes, many times.'
9 I'm very hungry. <u>I haven't eaten</u> much today.
10 When <u>has this bridge been</u> built?

14.2 Make sentences from the words in brackets. Use the present perfect or past simple.

1 (it / not / rain / this week)   *It hasn't rained this week.*
2 (the weather / be / cold / recently)   The weather
3 (it / cold / last week)   It
4 (I / not / eat / any fruit yesterday)   I
5 (I / not / eat / any fruit today)
6 (Emily / earn / a lot of money / this year)
7 (she / not / earn / so much / last year)
8 (you / have / a holiday recently?)

14.3 Put the verb into the correct form, present perfect or past simple.

1 *I haven't been* (I / not / be) to Canada, but I'd like to go there.
2 Paul and Lucy *arrived* (arrive) about ten minutes ago.
3 I'm tired. .... (I / not / sleep) well last night.
4 .... (There / be) a bus drivers' strike last week, so .... (there / be) no buses.
5 Edward .... (work) in a bank for 15 years. Then .... (he / give) it up. Now he works as a gardener.
6 Mary lives in Dublin. .... (She / live) there all her life.
7 My grandfather .... (die) before I was born. .... (I / never / meet) him.
8 I don't know Karen's husband. .... (I / never / meet) him.
9 It's nearly lunchtime, and .... (I / not / see) Martin all morning. I wonder where he is.
10 A: .... (you / go) to the cinema last night?
    B: Yes, but the movie .... (be) awful.
11 A: .... (It / be) very warm here since we arrived.
    B: Yes, ... (it / be) 35 degrees yesterday.
12 A: Where do you live?   B: In Boston.
    A: How long .... (you / live) there?   B: Five years.
    A: Where .... (you / live) before that?   B: In Chicago.
    A: And how long .... (you / live) in Chicago?   B: Two years.

14.4 Write sentences about yourself using the ideas in brackets.

1 (something you haven't done today)   *I haven't eaten any fruit today.*
2 (something you haven't done today)
3 (something you didn't do yesterday)
4 (something you did yesterday evening)
5 (something you haven't done recently)
6 (something you've done a lot recently)

Past perfect (**I had done**)

A   Study this example situation:

Sarah and Paul went to the same party last week, but they didn't see each other. Paul left the party at 10.30 and Sarah arrived at 11 o'clock.

So when Sarah arrived at the party, Paul wasn't there.

He **had gone** home.

had gone is the *past perfect*:

I/we/they/you he/she/it	had	(= I**'d** etc.) (= he**'d** etc.)	gone seen finished etc.

The past perfect (simple) is **had** + *past participle* (**gone**/**seen**/**finished** etc.).

Sometimes we talk about something that happened in the past:
- ○ Sarah **arrived** at the party.

This is the starting point of the story. Then, if we want to talk about things that happened *before* this time, we use the past perfect (**had** …):
- ○ **When Sarah arrived** at the party, Paul **had** already **gone** home.

Some more examples:
- ○ When we got home last night, we found that somebody **had broken** into the flat.
- ○ Karen didn't come to the cinema with us. She**'d** already **seen** the movie.
- ○ At first I thought I**'d done** the right thing, but I soon realised that I**'d made** a big mistake.
- ○ The people sitting next to me on the plane were nervous. They **hadn't flown** before.
  or They**'d** never **flown** before.

B   Compare *present perfect* (**have seen** etc.) and *past perfect* (**had seen** etc.):

Present perfect

have seen →

_____|_____
past   *now*

- ○ Who is that woman? I**'ve seen** her before, but I can't remember where.
- ○ We aren't hungry. We**'ve** just **had** lunch.
- ○ The house is dirty. They **haven't cleaned** it for weeks.

Past perfect

had seen →

_____|_____|____
           past   *now*

- ○ I wasn't sure who she was. I**'d seen** her before, but I couldn't remember where.
- ○ We weren't hungry. We**'d** just **had** lunch.
- ○ The house was dirty. They **hadn't cleaned** it for weeks.

C   Compare *past simple* (**left**, **was** etc.) and *past perfect* (**had left**, **had been** etc.):

Past simple

- ○ A: Was Tom there when you arrived?
  B: Yes, but he **left** soon afterwards.

- ○ Kate **wasn't** at home when I phoned.
  She **was** at her mother's house.

Past perfect

- ○ A: Was Tom there when you arrived?
  B: No, he**'d** already **left**.

- ○ Kate **had** just **got** home when I phoned.
  She**'d been** at her mother's house.

Exercises

15.1 Read the situations and write sentences using the words in brackets.

1 There was a picture lying on the floor.
(It / fall / off the wall) _It had fallen off the wall._

2 The people sitting next to you on the plane were nervous. It was their first flight.
(They / not / fly / before) _They hadn't flown before._

3 You went back to your home town recently after many years. It wasn't the same as before.
(It / change / a lot) It ....

4 Somebody sang a song. You didn't know it.
(I / not / hear / it / before) I ....

5 I invited Rachel to the party, but she couldn't come.
(She / arrange / to do something else) ....

6 You went to the cinema last night. You got to the cinema late.
(The film / already / start) ....

7 Last year we went to Mexico. It was our first time there.
(We / not / be / there / before) We ....

8 I met Daniel last week. It was good to see him again after such a long time.
(I / not / see / him for five years) ....

9 I offered my friends something to eat, but they weren't hungry.
(They / just / have / lunch) ....

10 Sam played tennis yesterday. He wasn't very good at it because it was his first game ever.
(He / never / play / before) ....

15.2 Use the sentences on the left to complete the paragraphs on the right. These sentences are in the order in which they happened – so (a) happened before (b), (b) before (c) etc. But your paragraph begins with the <u>underlined</u> sentence, so sometimes you need the past perfect.

1 (a) Somebody broke into the office during the night.
(b) <u>We arrived at work in the morning</u>.
(c) We called the police.

We arrived at work in the morning and found that ...._somebody had broken_.... into the office during the night. So ...._we called_.... the police.

2 (a) Laura went out this morning.
(b) <u>I rang her doorbell</u>.
(c) There was no answer.

I went to Laura's house this morning and rang her doorbell, but .... no answer. .... out.

3 (a) Joe came back from holiday a few days ago.
(b) <u>I met him the same day</u>.
(c) He looked very well.

I met Joe a few days ago. .... just .... holiday. .... very well.

4 (a) James sent Amy lots of emails.
(b) She never replied to them.
(c) <u>Yesterday he got a phone call from her.</u>
(d) He was surprised.

Yesterday James .... from Amy. .... surprised. .... lots of emails, but ....

15.3 Put the verb into the correct form, past perfect (**I had done**) or past simple (**I did**).

1 Paul wasn't at the party when I arrived. ...._He'd gone_.... (He / go) home.

2 I felt very tired when I got home, so .... (I / go) straight to bed.

3 The house was very quiet when I got home. Everybody .... (go) to bed.

4 Mark travels a lot. When I first met him, ... (he / already / travel) round the world.

5 Sorry I'm late. The car .... (break) down on my way here.

6 We were driving along the road when .... (we / see) a car which .... (break) down, so .... (we / stop) to help.

→ **Additional exercises 5–8** (pages 304–07)

Past perfect continuous (**I had been doing**)

Study this example situation:

yesterday morning

Yesterday morning I got up and looked out of the window. The sun was shining, but the ground was very wet.

It **had been raining**.

It was *not* raining when I looked out of the window. The sun was shining. But it **had been raining** before.

had been -ing is the *past perfect continuous*:

I/we/you/they he/she/it	**had**	(= I**'d** etc.) (= he**'d** etc.)	**been**	do**ing** work**ing** play**ing** etc.

Some more examples:
- ○ My hands were dirty because I**'d been repairing** my bike.
- ○ Tom was tired when he got home. He**'d been working** hard all day.
- ○ I went to Madrid a few years ago and stayed with a friend of mine. **She hadn't been living** there very long, but she knew the city very well.

You can say that something **had been happening** before something else happened:
- ○ We**'d been playing** tennis for about half an hour when it **started** to rain heavily.

Compare **have been -ing** (*present perfect continuous*) and **had been -ing** (*past perfect continuous*):

Present perfect continuous

I have been -ing

past   *now*

- ○ I hope the bus comes soon. I**'ve been waiting** for 20 minutes. (*before now*)
- ○ James **is** out of breath. He**'s been running**. (= he **has** been …)

Past perfect continuous

I had been -ing

past   *now*

- ○ At last the bus came. I**'d been waiting** for 20 minutes. (*before the bus came*)
- ○ James **was** out of breath. He**'d been running**. (= he **had** been …)

Compare **was -ing** (*past continuous*) and **had been -ing**:
- ○ It **wasn't raining** when we went out. The sun **was shining**. But it **had been raining**, so the ground was wet.
- ○ Katherine **was lying** on the sofa. She was tired because she**'d been working** hard.

Some verbs (for example, **know**) are not normally used in *continuous* forms (**be** + **-ing**):
- ○ We were good friends. We **had known** each other for years. (*not* had been knowing)
- ○ A few years ago Lisa cut her hair really short. I was surprised because she**'d** always **had** long hair. (*not* she'd been having)

For a list of these verbs, see **Unit 4A**. For **have**, see **Unit 17**

Present perfect continuous → **Units 9–10**   Past perfect simple → **Unit 15**

Exercises

16.1 **Read the situations and make sentences using the words in brackets.**

1 Tom was very tired when he got home.
(He / work / hard all day)   He'd been working hard all day.

2 The children came into the house. They had a football and they were both very tired.
(They / play / football) ....

3 I was disappointed when I had to cancel my holiday.
(I / look / forward to it) ....

4 Anna woke up in the middle of the night. She was frightened and didn't know where she was.
(She / have / a bad dream) ....

5 When I got home, Mark was sitting in front of the TV. He had just turned it off.
(He / watch / a film) ....

6 The people waiting at the bus stop were getting impatient. The bus was very late.
(They / wait / a long time) ....

16.2 **Read the situations and complete the sentences.**

1 We played tennis yesterday. We didn't finish our game.
    We'd been playing (We / play) for half an hour when   it started (it / start) to rain.

2 I had arranged to meet Tom in a restaurant. I arrived and waited for him to come.
.... (I / wait) for 20 minutes when ....
(I / realise) that .... (I / be) in the wrong restaurant.

3 Sarah worked in a company for a long time. The company no longer exists.
At the time the company .... (go) out of business, Sarah
.... (work) there for twelve years.

4 I went to a concert. Soon after the orchestra began playing, something strange happened.
The orchestra .... (play) for about ten minutes when a man in
the audience suddenly .... (start) shouting.

Now make your own sentence:

5 I began walking along the road. I ....
when ....

16.3 **Which is right?**

1 It was noisy next door last night. Our neighbours <u>were having</u> / <del>had been having</del> a party.
(were having *is correct*)

2 At the end of our journey we were extremely tired. <u>We were travelling</u> / <u>We'd been travelling</u> for more than 24 hours.

3 James was on his hands and knees on the floor. <u>He was looking</u> / <u>He'd been looking</u> for his contact lens.

4 Sue was sitting on the ground. She was out of breath. <u>She was running</u> / <u>She'd been running</u>.

5 John and I went for a walk. <u>He was walking</u> / <u>He'd been walking</u> very fast and I had difficulty keeping up with him.

6 I was sad when I sold my car. <u>I've had it</u> / <u>I'd had it</u> for a very long time.

7 I was sad when my local cafe closed. <u>I was going</u> / <u>I'd been going</u> there for many years.

8 I'm running a marathon next month. <u>I've been training</u> / <u>I'd been training</u> for it every day.

9 I had arranged to meet Kate, but I was late. When I finally arrived, <u>she was waiting</u> / <u>she'd been waiting</u> for me. She was annoyed because <u>she was waiting</u> / <u>she'd been waiting</u> such a long time.

10a Joe and I work for the same company. He joined the company before me. When I started a few years ago, <u>he was already working</u> / <u>he'd already been working</u> there.

10b I started working at the company a few years ago. At the time I started, Joe <u>was already working</u> / <u>had already been working</u> there for two years.

10c Joe still works for the company. <u>He's been working</u> / <u>He'd been working</u> there a long time now.

➜ **Additional exercises 5–8** (pages 304–07)

have and have got

A

have and **have got** (= for possession, relationships, illnesses, appointments etc.)

You can use **have** or **have got**. There is no difference in meaning. You can say:
- They **have** a new car.   *or*   They**'ve got** a new car.
- Lisa **has** two brothers.   *or*   Lisa **has got** two brothers.
- I **have** a headache.   *or*   I**'ve got** a headache.
- Our house **has** a small garden.   *or*   Our house **has got** a small garden.
- He **has** a few problems.   *or*   He**'s got** a few problems.
- I **have** a driving lesson tomorrow.   *or*   I**'ve got** a driving lesson tomorrow.

With these meanings (possession etc.), we do not use continuous forms (**I'm having** etc.):
- We're enjoying our holiday. We **have** / We**'ve got** a nice room in the hotel.
  (*not* We're having a nice room)

For the past we use **had** (usually without **got**):
- Lisa **had** long hair when she was a child. (*not* Lisa had got)

B

In questions and negative sentences there are three possible forms:

	Do you have any questions?		I **don't have** any questions.	
or	**Have you got** any questions?	*or*	I **haven't got** any questions.	
or	**Have you** any questions? *(less usual)*	*or*	I **haven't** any questions. *(less usual)*	
	Does she have a car?		She **doesn't have** a car.	
or	**Has she got** a car?	*or*	She **hasn't got** a car.	
or	**Has she** a car? *(less usual)*	*or*	She **hasn't** a car. *(less usual)*	

In past questions and negative sentences, we use **did/didn't**:
- **Did** you **have** a car when you were living in Paris?
- I **didn't have** my phone, so I couldn't call you.
- Lisa **had** long hair, **didn't** she?

C

have breakfast / **have a shower** / **have a good time** etc.

We also use **have** (*but not* have got) for things we do or experience. For example:

have	**breakfast** / **dinner** / **a cup of coffee** / **something to eat** etc. **a bath** / **a shower** / **a swim** / **a break** / **a rest** / **a party** / **a holiday** **an accident** / **an experience** / **a dream** **a look** (at something) **a chat** / **a discussion** / **a conversation** (with somebody) **trouble** / **difficulty** / **fun** / **a good time** etc. **a baby** (= give birth to a baby)

Have got is *not* possible in these expressions. Compare:
- Sometimes I **have** (= eat) a sandwich for my lunch. (*not* I've got)
- *but*   I**'ve got** / I **have** some sandwiches. Would you like one?

You can use continuous forms (I**'m having** etc.) with these expressions:
- We're enjoying our holiday. We**'re having** a great time.
- 'Where's Mark?' 'He**'s having** a shower.'

In questions and negative sentences we use **do/does/did**:
- I **don't** usually **have** a big breakfast. (*not* I usually haven't)
- Where **does** Chris usually **have** lunch?
- **Did** you **have** trouble finding somewhere to stay? (*not* Had you)

    have (got) to ... → Unit 31   American English **→ Appendix 7**

Exercises

17.1 Which goes with which?

1 I'm not free tomorrow morning.	a She's got a degree in physics.
2 Rachel is an only child.	b I've got a sore throat.
3 We've got plenty of time.	c There's no need to hurry.
4 You've got a really good voice.	d I've got a driving lesson.
5 I don't feel very well this morning.	e Maybe you can answer it.
6 Laura studied at university.	f I think he should get the job.
7 I've got a question.	g I wish I could sing as well as you.
8 James has got a lot of experience.	h She's got no brothers or sisters.

1 _d_
2 _____
3 _____
4 _____
5 _____
6 _____
7 _____
8 _____

17.2 Complete the sentences using **have**.

1 She couldn't get into the house. __She didn't have__ a key.
2 Is there anything you'd like to ask? __Do you have__ any questions?
3 They can't pay their bills. They _____ any money.
4 We got wet in the rain yesterday. We _____ an umbrella.
5 Jack _____ a car. He can't afford one and he can't drive anyway.
6 'Excuse me, _____ a pen I could borrow?' 'Yes, sure. Here you are.'
7 I was very busy yesterday. I _____ time to go shopping.
8 'Tell me about Jack. _____ a job?' 'Yes, he works at the hospital.'
9 When you worked in your last job, _____ your own office?
10 'Where's the remote control?' 'I don't know. I _____ it.'
11 'Tom _____ a motorbike, _____ he?' 'Yes, that's right. A long time ago.'

17.3 Are the underlined words OK? Change them where necessary.

1 I'm not free tomorrow morning. <u>I've got a driving lesson.</u>
2 <u>Lisa had got long hair</u> when she was a child.
3 I couldn't contact you because <u>I hadn't my phone</u>.
4 'Are you feeling OK?' 'No, <u>I'm having a cold.</u>'
5 I'm not working right now. <u>I'm having a break.</u>
6 I felt really tired. <u>I hadn't any energy</u>.
7 It's a small town. <u>It doesn't have many shops.</u>
8 Was your trip OK? <u>Had you any problems</u>?
9 My friend called me when <u>I was having breakfast</u>.
10 The last time I saw Steve, <u>he was having a beard</u>.
11 We don't need to hurry. <u>We have plenty of time</u>.
12 How often <u>have you a shower</u>?

_OK_
Lisa had long hair
_____
_____
_____
_____
_____
_____
_____
_____
_____
_____

17.4 Complete the sentences. Use an expression with **have** in the correct form. Choose from:

have a baby	have a break	have a chat	have trouble	have a shower
have a look	~~have lunch~~	have a party	have a nice time	have a holiday

1 I don't eat much during the day. I never __have lunch__ .
2 David starts work at 8 o'clock and _____ at 10.30.
3 We _____ last week. We invited lots of people.
4 There's something wrong with my bike. Can you _____ at it for me?
5 Joe is away on holiday at the moment. I hope he _____ .
6 I met some friends in the supermarket yesterday. We stopped and _____ .
7 '_____ finding the book you wanted?' 'No, I found it OK.'
8 Suzanne _____ a few weeks ago. It's her second child.
9 I _____ when the light went out suddenly.
10 I'd like to go away somewhere. I _____ for a long time.

A Study this example situation:

a few years ago

these days

Nicola doesn't travel much these days.
She prefers to stay at home.

But she **used to travel** a lot.
She **used to go** away two or three times a year.

She **used to travel** a lot = she travelled often in the past, but she doesn't do this any more.

she used to travel

she doesn't travel

past   now

B I **used to** do something = I did it often in the past, but not any more:
  ○ I **used to play** tennis a lot, but I don't play very much now.
  ○ David **used to spend** a lot of money on clothes. These days he can't afford it.
  ○ 'Do you go to the cinema much?' 'Not now, but I **used to**.' (= I used to go)

We also use **used to** … for things that were true, but are not true any more:
  ○ This building is now a furniture shop. It **used to be** a cinema.
  ○ I **used to think** Mark was unfriendly, but now I realise he's a very nice person.
  ○ I've started drinking coffee recently. I never **used to like** it before.
  ○ Lisa **used to have** very long hair when she was a child.

C '**I used to** do something' is past. There is no present. You cannot say 'I use to do'.
To talk about the present, we use the present simple (**I do**).

Compare:

past	he **used to play**	we **used to live**	there **used to be**
present	he **plays**	we **live**	there **is**

  ○ We **used to live** in a small village, but now we **live** in a city.
  ○ There **used to be** four cinemas in the town. Now there **is** only one.

D The normal question form is **did** (you) **use to** …? :
  ○ **Did** you **use to eat** a lot of sweets when you were a child? (= did you do this often?)

The negative form is **didn't use to** … (**used not to** … is also possible):
  ○ I **didn't use to like** him. (*or* I **used not to like** him.)

E Compare **I used to do** and **I was doing**:
  ○ I **used to watch** TV a lot. (= I watched TV often in the past, but I don't do this any more)
  ○ I **was watching** TV when Rob called. (= I was in the middle of watching TV)

F Do not confuse **I used to do** and **I am used to doing** (see Unit 61). The structures and meanings are different:
  ○ I **used to live** alone. (= I lived alone in the past, but I no longer live alone.)
  ○ I **am** used to **living** alone. (= I live alone, and it's not a problem for me because I've lived alone for some time.)

>> Past continuous (**I was doing**) ➜ Unit 6   would (= used to) ➜ Unit 36
be/get used to (**doing** something) ➜ Unit 61

Exercises

18.1 **Complete the sentences with used to + a suitable verb.**

1 Nicola _used to travel_ a lot, but she doesn't go away much these days.
2 Sophie _____ a motorbike, but last year she sold it and bought a car.
3 Our friends moved to Spain a few years ago. They _____ in Paris.
4 Jackie _____ my best friend, but we aren't friends any more.
5 I rarely eat ice cream now, but I _____ it when I was a child.
6 It only takes me about 40 minutes to get to work now that the new road is open.
   It _____ more than an hour.
7 There _____ a hotel near the airport, but it closed a long time ago.
8 I _____ in a factory. It wasn't my favourite job.

18.2 **Complete the sentences. Choose from the box.**

1 Lisa _used to have_ very long hair when she was a child.
2 We _____ to watch TV a lot, but we don't have a TV any more.
3 Lisa works in a shop now. She _____ a receptionist in a hotel.
4 What games _____ you use to play when you were a child?
5 I _____ like big cities, but now I prefer the countryside.
6 In your last job, how many hours a day did you _____ to work?
7 I don't travel very much these days, but I used _____ .
8 I used to _____ to run ten kilometres, but I can't run that far now.
9 These days I eat more than before. I _____ use to eat as much.

did
didn't
to
use
used
used to
used to be
~~used to have~~
be able

18.3 **Compare what Karen said ten years ago and what she says today:**

TEN YEARS AGO

~~I travel a lot.~~

I'm very lazy.

I don't like cheese.

I play the piano.

I never drink tea.

I have a dog.

TODAY

I eat lots of cheese now.

My dog died two years ago.

I work very hard these days.

I haven't played the piano for a long time.

~~I don't go away much these days.~~

Tea's great! I like it now.

Now write about how Karen has changed. Use used to / didn't use to / never used to in the first part of your sentence.

1 _She used to travel a lot,_ but _she doesn't go away much these days._
2 She used _____ but _____
3 _____ but _____
4 _____ but _____
5 _____ but _____
6 _____ but _____

18.4 **Write sentences about yourself. Begin I used to … (I used to be/work/like/play etc.)**

1 _I used to live in a small village, but now I live in a city._
2 _I used to play tennis a lot, but I don't play any more._
3 I used _____ , but _____
4 I _____
5 _____

Now begin with I didn't use to … .

6 _I didn't use to read a lot, but I do now._
7 I didn't _____
8 _____

A *Present continuous* (**I am doing**) with a future meaning

This is Ben's diary for next week.

He **is playing** tennis on Monday afternoon.
He **is going** to the dentist on Tuesday morning.
He **is meeting** Kate on Friday.

In all these examples, Ben has already decided and arranged to do these things.

I'm doing something (tomorrow etc.) = I have already decided and arranged to do it:
- ○ A: What **are** you **doing** on Saturday evening? (*not* What do you do)
  B: I**'m going** to the cinema. (*not* I go)
- ○ A: What time **is** Katherine **arriving** tomorrow?
  B: Half past ten. We**'re meeting** her at the station.
- ○ I**'m not working** tomorrow, so we can go out somewhere.
- ○ Steve **isn't playing** football next Saturday. He's hurt his leg.

We do not normally use **will** to talk about what we have arranged to do:
- ○ What **are** you **doing** tonight? (*not* What will you do)
- ○ Alex **is getting** married next month. (*not* will get)

We also use the present continuous for an action *just before you start to do it*. This happens especially with verbs of movement (**go**/**come**/**leave** etc.):
- ○ I'm tired. I**'m going** to bed now. Goodnight. (*not* I go to bed now)
- ○ 'Tina, are you ready yet?' 'Yes, I**'m coming**.' (*not* I come)

B *Present simple* (**I do**) with a future meaning

We use the present simple when we talk about timetables and programmes (for example, transport or cinema times):
- ○ I have to go. My train **leaves** at 11.30.
- ○ What time **does** the film **start** tonight?
- ○ The meeting **is** at nine o'clock tomorrow.

You can use the present simple to talk about people if their plans are fixed like a timetable:
- ○ I **start** my new job on Monday.
- ○ What time **do** you **finish** work tomorrow?

But the continuous is more usual for other personal arrangements:
- ○ What time **are** you **meeting** Kate tomorrow? (*not* do you meet)

Compare:

Present continuous	Present simple
○ What time **are** you **arriving**?	○ What time **does** the train **arrive**?
○ I**'m going** to the cinema this evening.	○ The film **starts** at 8.15.

When you talk about appointments, lessons, exams etc., you can use **I have** or **I've got**:
- ○ **I have** an exam next week. *or* **I've got** an exam next week.

▶▶ I'm going to → Units 20, 23   will → Units 21–22   Present simple after **when** and **if** → Unit 25

Exercises

19.1 Ask Anna about her holiday plans.

1 (where / go?) _Where are you going?_
2 (how long / go for?) _____
3 (when / leave?) _____
4 (go / alone?) _____
5 (travel / by car?) _____
6 (where / stay?) _____

ANNA

Scotland.
Ten days.
Next Friday.
No, with a friend.
No, by train.
In a hotel.

19.2 Complete the sentences.

1 Steve __isn't playing__ (not / play) football on Saturday. He's hurt his leg.
2 _____ (We / have) a party next week. We've invited all our friends.
3 _____ (I / not / work) tomorrow. It's a public holiday.
4 _____ (I / leave) now. I've come to say goodbye.
5 'What time _____ (you / go) out this evening?' 'Seven o'clock.'
6 _____ (Laura / not / come) to the party tomorrow. She isn't well.
7 I love New York. _____ (I / go) there soon.
8 Ben can't meet us on Monday. _____ (He / work) late.

19.3 Have you arranged to do anything at these times? Write sentences about yourself.

1 (this evening) _I'm not doing anything this evening._
2 (tomorrow morning) I _____
3 (tomorrow evening) I _____
4 (next Sunday) I _____
5 (*another day or time*) _____

19.4 Complete the sentences. Use the present continuous or present simple.

1 A: Tina, are you ready yet?
   B: Yes, __I'm coming__ (I / come).
2 A: _____ (you / go) to Sam's party on Saturday?
   B: No, I haven't been invited.
3 A: Has Jack moved into his new apartment yet?
   B: Not yet, but _____ (he / move) soon – probably at the end of the month.
4 A: _____ (I / go) to a concert tonight.
   B: That's nice. What time _____ (it / start)?
5 A: Have you seen Chris recently?
   B: No, but _____ (we / meet) for lunch next week.
6 A: _____ (you / do) anything tomorrow morning?
   B: No, I'm free. Why?
7 A: When _____ (this term / end)?
   B: Next Friday. And next term _____ (start) four weeks after that.
8 A: _____ (We / go) to a wedding at the weekend.
   B: Really? _____ (Who / get) married?
9 A: There's football on TV later tonight. _____ (you / watch) it?
   B: No, I'm not interested.
10 A: What time is your train tomorrow?
    B: It _____ (leave) at 9.35 and _____ (arrive) at 12.47.
11 A: I'd like to go and see the exhibition at the museum. How long is it on for?
    B: _____ (It / finish) next week.
12 A: Do you need the car this evening?
    B: No, you can have it. _____ (I / not / use) it.

I'm going to (do)

I **am going to do** something = I have already decided to do it, I intend to do it:
- ○ '**Are** you **going to eat** anything?' 'No, I'm not hungry.'
- ○ A: I hear Sarah won the lottery. What **is** she **going to do** with the money?
  B: She**'s going to buy** a new car.
- ○ I**'m** just **going to make** a quick phone call. Can you wait for me?
- ○ This cheese smells horrible. I**'m not going to eat** it.

B **I am doing** and **I am going to do**

I am doing = it is *already fixed or arranged*. For example, you have arranged to go somewhere or meet somebody:
- ○ I**'m leaving** next week. I've booked my flight.
- ○ What time **are** you **meeting** Emily this evening?

I am going to do something = I've decided to do it. Maybe I've arranged to do it, maybe not.
- ○ A: Your shoes are dirty.
  B: Yes, I know. I**'m going to clean** them.
      (= I've *decided* to clean them, but I haven't arranged this with anybody)
- ○ I don't want to stay here. Tomorrow I**'m going to look** for somewhere else to stay.

Compare:
- ○ I don't know what I**'m doing** tomorrow. (= I don't know my schedule or plans)
- ○ I don't know what I**'m going to do** about the problem. (= I haven't decided what to do)

Often the difference is small and either form is possible.

C You can also say that 'something **is going to happen**' in the future. For example:

The man isn't looking where he is going.

He **is going to walk** into the wall.

When we say that 'something **is going to happen**', the situation *now* makes this clear.
The man is walking towards the wall now, so we can see that he **is going to walk** into it.

now going to *future*

Some more examples:
- ○ Look at those black clouds! It**'s going to rain**. (we can see the clouds *now*)
- ○ I feel terrible. I think I**'m going to be** sick. (I feel terrible *now*)
- ○ The economic situation is bad now and things **are going to get** worse.

D I **was going to** do something = I intended to do it, but didn't do it:
- ○ We **were going to travel** by train, but then we decided to drive instead.
- ○ I **was** just **going to cross** the road when somebody shouted 'Stop!'

You can say that 'something **was going to happen**' (but didn't happen):
- ○ I thought it **was going to rain**, but it didn't.

Exercises

20.1 **Write questions with going to.**

1 Your friend has won some money. You ask:
(what / do?)   _What are you going to do with it?_
2 Your friend is going to a wedding next week. You ask:
(what / wear?) ....
3 Your friend has just bought a new table. You ask:
(where / put?) ....
4 Your friend has decided to have a party. You ask:
(who / invite?) ....
5 Your friend has bought some fish for dinner. You ask:
(how / cook?) ....

20.2 **Complete the sentences using I'm going to … / I'm not going to … . Choose from:**

| complain | learn | run | say | try | wash | not/accept | ~~not/eat~~ | not/tell |

1 This cheese smells horrible.   _I'm not going to eat_   it.
2 I haven't been trying hard enough. From now on .... harder.
3 I have to make a speech tomorrow, but I don't know what ....
4 'The car is very dirty.' 'I know. .... it.'
5 I've been offered a job, but .... it. The pay is too low.
6 .... a language, but I haven't decided yet which one.
7 One day .... in a marathon. It's my ambition.
8 The food in this restaurant is awful. ....
9 Ben doesn't need to know what happened, so .... him.

20.3 **What is going to happen in these situations? Use the words in brackets.**

1 There are a lot of black clouds in the sky.
(rain)   _It's going to rain._
2 It is 8.30. Tom is leaving home. He has to be at work at 8.45, but the journey takes 30 minutes.
(late)   He ....
3 There is a hole in the bottom of the boat. A lot of water is coming in through the hole.
(sink)   The boat ....
4 Amy and Ben are driving. The tank is nearly empty. It's a long way to the nearest petrol station.
(run out)   They ....
5 Sarah's car was badly damaged in an accident. Now it has to be repaired.
(cost a lot)   It .... to repair the car.

20.4 **Complete the sentences with was/were going to. Choose from:**

| be | buy | give up | phone | play | say | ~~travel~~ |

1 We _were going to travel_ by train, but then we decided to go by car instead.
2 I .... some new clothes yesterday, but I didn't have time to
go to the shops.
3 Tom and I .... tennis last week, but he'd hurt his knee and had
to cancel.
4 I .... Jane, but I sent her an email instead.
5 I thought the exam .... hard, but it was easier than I expected.
6 Peter .... his job, but in the end he decided to stay where
he was.
7 I'm sorry I interrupted you. What .... you .... ?

will and shall 1

A

We use **I'll** ... (= **I will**) when we've just decided to do something. When we say '**I'll** do something', we announce our decision:

- ○ Oh, I left the door open. **I'll go** and shut it.
- ○ 'What would you like to drink?'   '**I'll have** orange juice, please.'
- ○ 'Did you call Max?'   'Oh no, I forgot. **I'll call** him now.'

We do not use the *present simple* (**I do** / **I go** etc.) in these sentences:

- ○ **I'll phone** him now. (*not* I phone him now)

We often use **I think I'll** ... / **I don't think I'll** ...:

- ○ I'm a little hungry. **I think I'll have** something to eat.
- ○ **I don't think I'll go** out tonight. I'm too tired.

In spoken English **will not** is usually **won't**:

- ○ I can see you're busy, so **I won't stay** long. (= I will not stay long)

B

We often use **I'll** in these situations:

Offering to do something
- ○ That bag looks heavy. **I'll help** you with it. (*not* I help)

Agreeing to do something
- ○ A: Can you give Tom this book?
     B: Sure, **I'll give** it to him when I see him this afternoon.

Promising to do something
- ○ Thanks for lending me the money. **I'll pay** you back on Friday.
- ○ I **won't tell** anyone what happened. I promise.

> I'll help you.

We use **won't** to say that somebody refuses to do something:

- ○ I've tried to give her advice, but she **won't listen**.
- ○ The car **won't start**. (= the car 'refuses' to start)

> The car won't start.

Will you (do something)? = please do it:

- ○ **Will you** please turn the music down? It's too loud.

C

We do *not* use **will** to talk about what has been decided or arranged before:

- ○ **I'm going** on holiday next Saturday. (*not* I'll go)

Compare:

- ○ **I'm meeting** Kate tomorrow morning. (decided before)
- ○ A: **I'll meet** you at half past ten, OK?
     B: Fine. See you then.   (decided now)

D

We use **shall** mostly in the questions **shall I** ... ? / **shall we** ... ?

We use **shall I** ... ? / **shall we** ... ? to ask if it's OK to do something or to ask for a suggestion:

- ○ **Shall I** open the window? (= do you want me to open it?)
- ○ I've got no money. What **shall I** do? (= what do you suggest?)
- ○ '**Shall we** go?' 'Just a minute. I'm not ready yet.'
- ○ 'Where **shall we** have lunch?' 'Let's go to Marino's.'

Compare **shall I** ... ? and **will you** ... ?:

- ○ **Shall I** shut the door? (= do you want me to shut it?)
- ○ **Will you** shut the door? (= I want you to shut it)

>> **I am doing** (future) ➔ **Unit 19**   **will and shall 2** ➔ **Unit 22**   **I will** and **I'm going to** ➔ **Unit 23**
American English ➔ **Appendix 7**

Exercises

21.1 **Complete the sentences with I'll + a suitable verb.**

1 'How are you going to get home?'   'I think _____I'll take_____ a taxi.'
2 'It's cold in this room.'   'Is it? _____ on the heating then.'
3 'Are you free next Friday?'   'Let me see. _____ my diary.'
4 'Shall I do the washing-up?'   'No, it's all right. _____ it later.'
5 'I don't know how to use this phone.'   'OK, _____ you.'
6 'Would you like tea or coffee?'   '_____ coffee, please.'
7 'Are you coming with us?'   'No, I think _____ here.'
8 'Can you finish this report today?'   'Well, _____ , but I can't promise.'

21.2 **Read the situations and write sentences with I think I'll … or I don't think I'll … .**

1 It's a bit cold. The window is open and you decide to close it. You say:
   It's cold with the window open. _____I think I'll close it._____
2 You are feeling tired and it's getting late. You decide to go to bed. You say:
   I'm tired, so _____ . Goodnight!
3 The weather is nice and you need some exercise. You decide to go for a walk. You say:
   It's a lovely morning. _____ . Do you want to come too?
4 You were going to have lunch. Now you decide you don't want to eat anything. You say:
   I don't feel hungry any more. _____ lunch.
5 You planned to go swimming today. Now you decide not to go. You say:
   I've got a lot to do, so _____ today.

21.3 **Which is correct?**

1 'Did you call Max?'   'Oh no, I forgot. I call / I'll call him now.'   (I'll call *is correct*)
2 I can't meet you tomorrow morning. I'm playing / I'll play tennis.   (I'm playing *is correct*)
3 'I meet / I'll meet you outside the hotel at 10.30, OK?'   'Yes, that's fine.'
4 'Please don't go yet.'   'OK, I'm staying / I'll stay a little longer, but I have to go soon.'
5 I'm having / I'll have a party next Saturday. I hope you can come.
6 'Remember to lock the door when you go out.'   'OK. I don't forget / I won't forget.'
7 'Do you have any plans for the weekend?'   'Yes, we're going / we'll go to a wedding.'
8 'Are you doing / Will you do anything tomorrow evening?'   'No, I'm free. Why?'
9 'Do you do / Will you do something for me?'   'It depends. What do you want me to do?'
10 'Do you go / Will you go to work by car?'   'Not usually. I prefer to walk.'
11 I asked Sue what happened, but she doesn't tell / won't tell me.
12 I don't know if I can win the race tomorrow, but I'm doing / I'll do my best.

21.4 **What do you say in these situations? Write sentences with shall I … ? or shall we … ?**

1 You and a friend want to do something this evening, but you don't know what.
   You say: _____What shall we do this evening?_____   Do you want to go somewhere?
2 You and a friend are going on holiday together, but you have to decide where.
   You ask your friend: _____ ?
3 You try on a jacket in a shop. You are not sure whether to buy it or not.
   You ask a friend for advice: _____ ? What do you think?
4 You and a friend are going out. You have to decide whether to get a taxi or to walk.
   You ask your friend: _____ or _____ ?
5 It's Helen's birthday soon. You want to give her a present, but what?
   You ask a friend: What _____ ? Any ideas?
6 You're meeting a friend tomorrow, but you have to decide what time.
   You say: _____ ? Is 10.30 OK for you?

➜ Additional exercises 10–13 (pages 308–10)   43

will and shall 2

A We do *not* use **will** to say what somebody has *already arranged* or *decided* to do:
- ○ Lisa **is working** next week. (*not* Lisa will work)
- ○ **Are** you **going to watch** TV this evening? (*not* will you watch)

See Units 19–20.

We use **will** to say what we know or believe about the future (not what someone has already decided).
For example:

Kate has her driving test next week.
Chris and Joe are talking about it.

Do you think
Kate will pass?

CHRIS

Yes, she's a good driver.
She'll pass easily.

JOE

Joe believes that Kate **will pass**
the driving test.
He is *predicting* the future.

When we predict a future
happening or situation, we use
will/won't.

Some more examples:
- ○ They've been away a long time. When they return, they**'ll find** a lot of changes here.
- ○ 'Where **will** you **be** this time next year?' 'I**'ll be** in Japan.'
- ○ That plate is hot. If you touch it, you**'ll burn** yourself.
- ○ Anna looks completely different now. You **won't recognise** her.
- ○ When **will** you **get** your exam results?

Compare:
- ○ I think James **is going** to the party on Friday. (= I think he has already decided to go)
- ○ I think James **will go** to the party on Friday. (= I think he will decide to go)

B We often use **will** (**'ll**) with:

probably	○ I**'ll probably** be home late tonight.
I'm sure	○ Don't worry about the exam. **I'm sure** you**'ll** pass.
I think	○ Do you **think** Sarah **will** like the present we bought her?
I don't think	○ I **don't think** the exam **will** be very difficult.
I wonder	○ I **wonder** what **will** happen.

After **I hope**, we generally use the present:
- ○ I hope Kate **passes** the driving test.
- ○ I hope it **doesn't rain** tomorrow.

C Generally we use **will** to talk about *the future*, but sometimes we use **will** to talk about *now*:
- ○ Don't phone Amy now. She**'ll be** busy. (= she'll be busy *now*)

D Normally we use **shall** only with **I** and **we**. You can say:
I shall *or* **I will** (**I'll**)   **we shall** *or* **we will** (**we'll**)

- ○ **I shall** be late this evening. (*or* **I will** be)
- ○ **We shall** probably go to France in June. (*or* **We will** probably go)

In spoken English we normally use **I'll** and **we'll**:
- ○ **We'll** probably go to France.

The negative of **shall** is **shall not** or **shan't**:
- ○ I **shan't** be here tomorrow. (*or* I **won't** be)

We do not normally use **shall** with **he/she/it/you/they**:
- ○ She **will** be very angry. (*not* She shall be)

>> will and shall 1 ➜ Unit 21   I will and I'm going to ➜ Unit 23   will be doing and will have done ➜ Unit 24
will have to ➜ Unit 31A   The future ➜ Appendix 3   American English ➜ Appendix 7

Exercises

22.1 **Put in will ('ll) or won't.**

1 Can you wait for me? I ___won't___ be long.
2 There's no point in asking Amanda for advice. She _____ know what to do.
3 I'm glad I'm meeting Emma tomorrow. It _____ be good to see her again.
4 I'm sorry about what happened yesterday. It _____ happen again.
5 You don't need to take an umbrella with you. I don't think it _____ rain.
6 I've got some incredible news! You _____ believe it.

22.2 **Complete the sentences using will ('ll). Choose from the following:**

it/be	she/come	you/get	you/like	you/enjoy
people/live	it/look	we/meet	~~you/pass~~	she/mind

1 Don't worry about your exam. I'm sure ___you'll pass___ .
2 Why don't you try on this jacket? _____ nice on you.
3 You must meet Max sometime. I think _____ him.
4 It's a very nice hotel. _____ your stay there.
5 It's raining hard. Don't go out. _____ very wet.
6 Do you think _____ longer in the future?
7 Goodbye! I'm sure _____ again before long.
8 I've invited Anna to the party, but I don't think _____ .
9 You can borrow Amy's umbrella. I don't think _____ .
10 It takes me an hour to get to work at the moment. When the new road is finished,
   _____ much quicker.

22.3 **Write questions using do you think ... will ... ? + the following:**

be back	cost	end	get married	happen	~~like~~	rain

1 I've bought this picture for Karen. ___Do you think she'll like it___ ?
2 The weather doesn't look very good. Do you _____ ?
3 The meeting is still going on. When do you _____ ?
4 My car needs to be repaired. How much _____ ?
5 Sally and David are in love. Do _____ ?
6 'I'm going out now.' 'OK. What time _____ ?'
7 The future situation is uncertain. What _____ ?

22.4 **Where do you think you will be at these times? Write sentences about yourself. Use:**

I'll be ... *or* **I'll probably be ...** *or* **I don't know where ...**

1 (next Monday evening at 7.45)   ___I'll probably be at home.___
2 (at 3 am tomorrow) _____
3 (at 10.30 tomorrow morning) _____
4 (next Friday afternoon at 4.15) _____
5 (this time next year) _____

22.5 **Which is better in these sentences?**

1 Lisa isn't free on Saturday. ~~She'll work~~ / She's working. (She's working *is correct*)
2 It was an amazing experience. I never forget it. / I'll never forget it.
3 Something very funny happened. You're laughing / You'll laugh when I tell you about it.
4 I'll go / I'm going to a party tomorrow night. Would you like to come too?
5 Who do you think will win / is winning the game tomorrow?
6 I can't meet you this evening. A friend of mine will come / is coming to see me.
7 Don't be afraid of the dog. It won't hurt / It isn't hurting you.
8 What's happening / What will happen if I press this button?
9 A: Have you decided where to go for your holidays?
   B: Yes, we'll go / we're going to Italy.

→ **Additional exercises 10–13** (pages 308–10)

I will and I'm going to

Future actions

Compare **will** and **(be) going to**:

Sarah is talking to Helen:

SARAH

HELEN

Let's have a party.

That's a great idea.
We'**ll invite** lots of people.

will (We'**ll invite** ...)

We use **will** (We'**ll** invite ...) to announce a new decision. The party is a new idea.

Later that day, Helen meets Max:

HELEN

MAX

Sarah and I have decided to have a party.
We'**re going to invite** lots of people.

(be) going to (We'**re going to** invite ...)

We use **(be) going to** when we have *already decided* to do something.
Helen had already decided to invite lots of people *before* she spoke to Max.

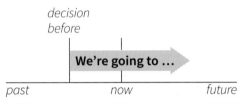

Compare:

- 'Gary has been trying to contact you.' 'Has he? OK, I'**ll call** him.'
  'Gary has been trying to contact you.' 'Yes, I know. I'**m going to call** him.'

- 'Anna is in hospital.' 'Really? I didn't know. I'**ll go** and visit her.'
  'Anna is in hospital.' 'Yes, I know. I'**m going to visit** her this evening.'

Future happenings and situations (predicting the future)

We use both **will** and **going to** for future happenings and situations. So you can say:

- I think the weather **will be** nice later. *or*
  I think the weather **is going to be** nice later.
- Those shoes are well-made. They'**ll last** a long time. *or*
  Those shoes are well-made. They'**re going to last** a long time.

When we say something **is going to** happen, we believe this because of the situation *now*. What is happening *now* shows that something **is going to** happen in the future. For example:

- Look at those black clouds. It'**s going to rain**. (*not* it will rain)
  (we can see that it **is going to rain** – the black clouds are in the sky *now*)

Compare:

- We'**re going to be** late. The meeting starts in five minutes and it takes 15 minutes to get there.
  (it is clear *now* that we don't have enough time to get there)
- Jane **will be** late for the meeting. She's always late.
  (I believe this because I know what Jane is like)

>> I'm going to → Unit 20   will → Units 21–22   The future → Appendix 3

Exercises

23.1 **Complete the sentences using will ('ll) or (be) going to.**

1 A: Why are you turning on the TV?
   B: ......*I'm going to watch*...... the news. (I / watch)

2 A: I forgot my wallet. I don't have any money.
   B: Not to worry. .... you some. (I / lend)

3 A: Why are you filling that bucket with water?
   B: .... the car. (I / wash)

4 A: I don't know how to use the washing machine.
   B: It's easy. .... you. (I / show)

5 A: I've decided to paint this room.
   B: That's nice. What colour .... it? (you / paint)

6 A: Where are you going? Are you going shopping?
   B: Yes, ... some things for dinner tonight. (I / buy)

7 A: What would you like to eat?
   B: .... a pizza, please. (I / have)

8 A: This food doesn't taste very good, does it?
   B: No, it's horrible. .... it. (I / not / finish)

9 A: Tom is starting an evening class next month.
   B: Is he? What .... ? (he / study)

10 A: Did you call Lisa?
    B: Oh, no. I completely forgot. .... her now. (I / call)

11 A: Has Dan decided what to do when he leaves school?
    B: Yes. Everything is planned.
      First .... a holiday for a few weeks. (he / have)
      Then .... a management training course. (he / do)

23.2 **Read the situations and complete the sentences using will ('ll) or (be) going to.**

1 You want some coffee. You go to the kitchen to make some.
   You say (to your friend): ......*I'm going to make*...... some coffee. Would you like some?

2 You're speaking to a friend and arranging to meet. You suggest a time and place.
   You say: .... you at 10.30 in the hotel lobby, OK? (I/see)

3 You have decided to sell your car. You tell a friend of yours.
   You say: I don't need my car any more. .... it. (I/sell)

4 Your friend is worried because she has lost her driving licence.
   You say: Don't worry. I'm sure .... it. (you/find)

5a You have an old camera that is broken. You have decided to throw it away. You tell your friend.
   You say: This camera is broken. .... it away. (I/throw)

5b Your friend loves and collects old cameras. He doesn't want you to throw it away.
   He says: Don't throw it away! .... it. (I/have)

6a Joe has to go to the airport tomorrow. He doesn't know how to get there. Amy offers to take him.
   Amy says: Don't worry about getting to the airport, Joe. .... you. (I/take)

6b Later that day, Paul offers to take Joe to the airport. Joe tells him that it's not necessary.
   Joe says: Thanks, Paul, but .... me. (Amy/take)

23.3 **Which goes with which?**

1	Why don't you come to the party with us?	a	He'll get what he wants.	1	*f*
2	That ceiling looks dangerous.	b	He probably won't remember me.	2	
3	He's looking very tired.	c	It's going to be a nice day.	3	
4	This table is too big.	d	It looks as if it's going to fall down.	4	
5	The weather forecast is good.	e	It's going to be 200 metres high.	5	
6	Jack is very determined.	f	~~You'll enjoy it.~~	6	
7	They are building a new skyscraper here.	g	I don't think it will fit in the room.	7	
8	I haven't seen Ben for ages.	h	I think he's going to fall asleep.	8	

→ **Additional exercises 10–13** (pages 308–10)

will be doing and **will have done**

A Study this example situation:

These people are standing in a queue to get into the cinema.

now

Half an hour from now, the cinema will be full. Everyone **will be watching** the film.

half an hour from now

Three hours from now, the cinema will be empty. The film **will have finished**. Everyone **will have gone** home.

three hours from now

B I **will be doing** something (*future continuous*) = I will be in the middle of doing it:
- ○ This time next week I'll be on holiday. **I'll be lying** on the beach or **swimming** in the sea.
- ○ You have no chance of getting the job. You**'ll be wasting** your time if you apply.

Compare **will be** (do)**ing** and **will** (do):
- ○ Don't phone between 7 and 8. We**'ll be eating**.
- ○ Let's wait for Liz to arrive and then we**'ll eat**.

Compare:
- ○ At 10 o'clock yesterday, Tina **was** in her office. She **was working**. (*past continuous*)
  It's 10 o'clock now. She **is** in her office. She **is working**. (*present continuous*)
  At 10 o'clock tomorrow, she **will be** in her office. She **will be working**. (*future continuous*)

C We also use **will be -ing** to talk about complete actions in the future. For example:
- ○ The government **will be making** a statement about the crisis later today.
- ○ Later in the programme, I**'ll be talking** to the Minister of Education.
- ○ The team's star player is injured and **won't be playing** in the game on Saturday.

When we use it in this way, **will be** (**doing**) is similar to **will** (**do**) and **going to** (**do**).

Later in the programme, I'll be talking to …

D I **will have done** something (*future perfect*) = it will be complete before a time in the future. For example:
- ○ Sally always leaves for work at 8.30 in the morning. She won't be at home at 9 o'clock – she**'ll have gone** to work.
- ○ We're late. The film **will** already **have started** by the time we get to the cinema.

Compare:
- ○ Ted and Amy **have been** married for 24 years. (*present perfect*)
  Next year they **will have been** married for 25 years. (*future perfect*)
  When their son was born, they **had been** married for three years. (*past perfect*)

>> will → Units 21–22   by then / by the time → Unit 120   The future → Appendix 3

Exercises

24.1 Read about Andy. Then tick (✓) the sentences which are true. In each group of sentences at least one is true.

Andy goes to work every day. He leaves home at 8 o'clock and arrives at work at about 8.45. He starts work immediately and continues until 12.30 when he has lunch (which takes about half an hour). He starts work again at 1.15 and goes home at exactly 4.30. Every day he follows the same routine and tomorrow will be no exception.

1 **At 7.45**
    a he'll be leaving the house
    b he'll have left the house
    c he'll be at home ✓
    d he'll be having breakfast ✓

4 **At 12.45**
    a he'll have lunch
    b he'll be having lunch
    c he'll have finished his lunch
    d he'll have started his lunch

2 **At 8.15**
    a he'll be leaving the house
    b he'll have left the house
    c he'll have arrived at work
    d he'll be arriving at work

5 **At 4 o'clock**
    a he'll have finished work
    b he'll finish work
    c he'll be working
    d he won't have finished work

3 **At 9.15**
    a he'll be working
    b he'll start work
    c he'll have started work
    d he'll be arriving at work

6 **At 4.45**
    a he'll leave work
    b he'll be leaving work
    c he'll have left work
    d he'll have arrived home

24.2 Complete the sentences. Choose from the box.

1 There's an election next week. Who ___will you be voting___ for?
2 I'll .... shopping later. Can I get you anything?
3 Emily is not well, so she .... volleyball tomorrow.
4 Little Emma .... school soon. She's growing up fast.
5 The match is on TV tonight. Will you .... it?
6 What .... in your new job? The same as before?
7 I .... to the wedding. I'll be away on holiday.
8 Please fasten your seat belts. The plane .... in ten minutes.

> be watching
> will be landing
> won't be playing
> will be starting
> ~~will you be voting~~
> won't be going
> be going
> will you be doing

24.3 Put the verb into the correct form, **will be (do)ing** or **will have (done)**.

1 Don't phone between 7 and 8. ___We'll be eating___ then. (we / eat)
2 Tomorrow afternoon we're going to play tennis from 3 o'clock until 4.30. So at 4 o'clock,
  .... tennis. (we / play)
3 Sarah will meet you at the station. .... for you when you arrive.
  (she / wait)
4 The meeting starts at 9.30 and won't last longer than an hour. You can be sure that
  .... by 11 o'clock. (it / finish)
5 Do you think .... in the same place in ten years' time? (you / still / live)
6 Lisa is travelling in Europe and so far she has travelled about 1,000 miles. By the end of the trip,
  .... more than 3,000 miles. (she / travel)
7 If you need to contact me, ... at the Lion Hotel until Friday. (I / stay)
8 Ben is on holiday and is spending his money very quickly. If he continues like this,
  .... all his money before the end of his holiday. (he / spend)
9 I'm fed up with my job. I hope .... it much longer. (I / not / do)

when I do and when I've done   if and when

A

Study this example:

Amy is on a train. She's calling a friend.

I'll call you again later **when I arrive.**

'I'll call you again later when I arrive' is a sentence with two parts:

| the main part: | I'll call you again later |
| and **when** …: | when I arrive |

The time is *future* ('later'), but Amy says:

… **when I arrive** (*not* when I will arrive)

We say

when I **do** something (*not* will do)

when something **happens** (*not* will happen)

Some more examples:

- ○ We'll go out **when** it **stops** raining. (*not* when it will stop)
- ○ **When** you **are** here again, you must come and see us. (*not* When you will be)
- ○ Don't forget to lock the door **when** you **go** out. (*not* will go)

The same thing happens after **while / before / after / as soon as / until**:

- ○ What are you going to do **while** I'**m** away? (*not* while I will be)
- ○ **Before** you **go**, there's something I want to ask you.
- ○ Wait here **until** I **come** back. *or* … **till** I **come** back.

B

You can also use the *present perfect* (**have done**) after **when / after / until / as soon as**:

- ○ Can I have the newspaper **when** you'**ve finished** with it?
- ○ Don't say anything while Ian is here. Wait **until** he **has gone**.

We use the present perfect to show that one thing is complete *before* the other. The two things do *not* happen together:

- ○ **When** I'**ve phoned** Kate, we can go out.
  (= first I'll phone Kate and *after that* we can go out)

Do not use the present perfect if the two things happen together:

- ○ **When** I **phone** Kate, I'll ask her about the party. (*not* when I've phoned)

It is often possible to use either the present simple or the present perfect:

- ○ I'll come **as soon as I finish**. *or* I'll come **as soon as I've finished**.
- ○ You'll feel better **after** you **have** something to eat. *or* You'll feel better **after** you'**ve had** something to eat.

C   if and when

After **if**, we normally use the present (**if** I **do** / **if** I **see** etc.) for the future:

- ○ I'll be angry **if** it **happens** again. (*not* if it will happen)
- ○ Hurry up! **If** we **don't** hurry, we'll be late.

We use **if** (*not* when) for things that will *possibly* happen (or not happen):

- ○ **If** it is raining this evening, I won't go out. (*not* when it is raining)
- ○ Don't worry **if** I'm late tonight. (*not* when I'm late)
- ○ **If** they don't come soon, I'm not going to wait for them.

We use **when** for things which are *sure* to happen. Compare:

- ○ I might go out later. *(it's possible)* **If** I go out, I'll get some bread.
- ○ I'm going out later. *(for sure)* **When** I go out, I'll get some bread.

>> if → Units 38–40   even if / even when → Unit 112D   unless → Unit 115

Exercises

25.1 **Which is correct?**

1 Don't forget to lock the door when <u>you go out</u> / ~~you'll go out~~. (you go out *is correct*)
2 As soon as we get any more information, <u>we let</u> / <u>we'll let</u> you know.
3 I want to get to the cinema before the film <u>starts</u> / <u>will start</u>.
4 Don't drive through a red light. Wait until <u>it changes</u> / <u>it will change</u> to green.
5 Sarah will be here soon. <u>I make</u> / <u>I'll make</u> some coffee when she comes.
6 I'm 20 now. I wonder where I'll be when <u>I'm 40</u> / <u>I'll be 40</u>.
7 <u>I wait</u> / <u>I'll wait</u> for you until you're ready, but don't be long.
8 Oliver is five years old. He wants to be a TV presenter when <u>he grows up</u> / <u>he'll grow up</u>.
9 We could meet for coffee tomorrow morning if <u>you're</u> / <u>you will be</u> free.
10 If the weather <u>is</u> / <u>will be</u> nice tomorrow, we're going to the beach.
11 Vicky <u>is</u> / <u>will be</u> very disappointed if she doesn't get a place at university.
12 You'll feel better after <u>you've had</u> / <u>you'll have</u> something to eat.

25.2 **Complete the sentences using the verbs in brackets. Use will/won't or the present
(see/plays/are etc.).**

1 When ....*you are*.... (you / be) here again, you must come and see us.
2 I want to see Sophie before .... (she / go) away next week.
3 Call me when .... (you / know) what time you're going to get here.
4 There's no need to hurry. .... (I / wait) for you until
.... (you / be) ready.
5 I'm going out for about an hour. .... (you / still / be) here when
.... (I / get) back?
6 I think everything will be fine, but if .... (there / be) any problems,
.... (I / let) you know, OK?
7 Kate looks completely different now. .... (you / not / recognise)
her when .... (you / see) her again.
8 I'm going to be away for a few days. If .... (you / need) to contact me
while .... (I / be) away, you can call me.

25.3 **Read the situations and complete the sentences.**

1 You and a friend want to go out, but it's raining hard. You don't want to get wet.
You say: Let's wait until ....*it stops raining*... .
2 You're visiting a friend. It's going to get dark soon, and you want to leave before that.
You ask: I'd better go now before ....
3 You want to sell your car. Mark is interested in buying it, but he hasn't decided yet.
You ask: Let me know as soon as ....
4 Your friends are going to Hong Kong soon. You want to know where they're going to stay.
You ask: Where are you going to stay when .... ?
5 The traffic is bad in your town, but they are going to build a new road.
You say: I think things will be better when they ....
6 Someone you know has been very rude to you. You want her to apologise.
You say (to someone else): I won't speak to her until ....

25.4 **Put in when or if.**

1 Don't worry ....*if*.... I'm late tonight.
2 Be careful. You'll hurt yourself .... you fall.
3 I'm going shopping. .... you want anything, I can get it for you.
4 I'm going away for a few days. I'll call you .... I get back.
5 .... I don't see you tomorrow, when will I see you again?
6 I'm watching a programme on TV right now. .... it finishes, I'm going to bed.
7 We can eat at home or, ... you prefer, we can go to a restaurant.
8 I hope Sarah can come to the party. It will be a shame .... she can't come.

→ **Additional exercises 12–15** (pages 309–11), **32** (page 321)

Unit 26   can, could and (be) able to

A

We use **can** to say that something is possible or allowed, or that somebody has the ability to do something. We use **can** + *infinitive* (**can do** / **can see** etc.):

- ○ We **can see** the lake from our hotel.
- ○ 'I don't have a pen.' 'You **can use** mine.'
- ○ **Can** you **speak** any foreign languages?
- ○ I **can come** and see you tomorrow if you like.
- ○ The word 'dream' **can be** a noun or a verb.

The negative is **can't** (= **cannot**):

- ○ I'm afraid I **can't come** to the party on Friday.

B

You can say that somebody **is able to** do something, but **can** is more usual:

- ○ We **are able to see** the lake from our hotel.

But **can** has only two forms: **can** *(present)* and **could** *(past)*. So sometimes it is necessary to use **(be) able to**. Compare:

○ I **can't** sleep.	○ I **haven't been able to** sleep recently.
○ Tom **can** come tomorrow.	○ Tom **might be able to** come tomorrow.
○ Maria **can** speak French, Spanish and English.	○ Applicants for the job **must be able to** speak two foreign languages.

C

Sometimes **could** is the past of **can**. We use **could** especially with:

see   hear   smell   taste   feel   remember   understand

- ○ We had a lovely room in the hotel. We **could see** the lake.
- ○ As soon as I walked into the room, I **could smell** gas.
- ○ I was sitting at the back of the theatre and **couldn't hear** very well.

We also use **could** to say that somebody had the ability to do something, or was allowed to do something:

- ○ My grandfather **could speak** five languages.
- ○ We were totally free. We **could do** what we wanted. (= we were allowed to do)

D

could and **was able to**

We use **could** for *general* ability and with **see**, **hear** etc. :

- ○ My grandfather **could speak** five languages.
- ○ I **could see** them, but not very clearly.

But to say that somebody succeeded in doing something in a specific situation, we normally use **was/were able to** or **managed to** (*not* **could**):

- ○ The fire spread quickly, but everybody **was able to escape**. (*not* could escape)
- ○ I didn't know where Max was, but I **managed to find** him in the end. (*not* could find)

Compare:

- ○ Jack was an excellent tennis player when he was younger. He **could beat** anybody.
  (= he was good enough to beat anybody, he had the ability)
- *but* Jack and Andy played a match yesterday. Andy played well, but Jack **managed to beat** him.
  (= he succeeded in beating him this time)

The negative **couldn't** (**could not**) is possible in all situations:

- ○ My grandfather **couldn't swim**.
- ○ I looked for Max everywhere, but I **couldn't find** him.
- ○ Andy played well, but he **couldn't beat** Jack.

»   could (do) and could have (done) → Unit 27   must and can't → Unit 28   can/could you … ? → Unit 37

Exercises

26.1 Complete the sentences using **can** or **(be) able to**. If **can** is not possible, use **(be) able to**.

1 Gary has travelled a lot. He ___*can*___ speak five languages.
2 I haven't ___*been able to*___ sleep very well recently.
3 Nicole _____ drive, but she doesn't have a car.
4 I used to _____ stand on my head, but I can't do it any more.
5 I can't understand Mark. I've never _____ understand him.
6 I can't see you on Friday, but I _____ meet you on Saturday morning.
7 Ask Katherine about your problem. She might _____ help you.
8 You have to be careful in this part of the city. It _____ be dangerous.
9 Michael has lived in Italy a long time, so he should _____ speak Italian.

26.2 Write sentences about yourself using the ideas in brackets.

1 (something you used to be able to do)
   ___*I used to be able to sing well.*___
2 (something you used to be able to do)
   I used _____
3 (something you would like to be able to do)
   I'd _____
4 (something you have never been able to do)
   I've _____

26.3 Complete the sentences with **can/can't/could/couldn't** + the following:

believe	~~come~~	hear	run	sleep	wait

1 I'm afraid I ___*can't come*___ to your party next week.
2 When Dan was 16, he _____ 100 metres in 11 seconds.
3 'Are you in a hurry?'   'No, I've got plenty of time. I _____.'
4 I don't feel good this morning. I _____ last night.
5 Can you speak a little louder? I _____ you very well.
6 I was amazed when I heard the news. I _____ it.

26.4 Complete the answers to the questions with **was/were able to** ... .

1 A: Did everybody escape from the fire?
   B: Yes. The fire spread quickly, but everybody ___*was able to escape*___ .
2 A: Did you finish your work this afternoon?
   B: Yes, there was nobody to disturb me, so I _____ .
3 A: Did you solve the problem?
   B: Yes, we did. It wasn't easy, but we _____ .
4 A: Did the thief get away?
   B: Yes. No-one realised what was happening and the thief _____ .

26.5 Complete the sentences using **could**, **couldn't** or **managed to**.

1 My grandfather travelled a lot. He ___*could*___ speak five languages.
2 I looked everywhere for the book, but I ___*couldn't*___ find it.
3 They didn't want to come with us at first, but we ___*managed to*___ persuade them.
4 Jessica had hurt her foot and _____ walk very well.
5 There was a small fire in the kitchen, but fortunately I _____ put it out.
6 The walls were thin and I _____ hear people talking in the next room.
7 I ran my first marathon recently. It was very hard, but I _____ finish.
8 My grandmother loved music. She _____ play the piano very well.
9 We wanted to go to the concert, but we _____ get tickets.
10 A girl fell into the river, but some people _____ pull her out. She's all right now.

could (do) and could have (done)

A Sometimes **could** is the past of **can** (see Unit 26):
- ○ Listen. I **can hear** something. *(now)*
- ○ I listened. I **could hear** something. *(past)*

But **could** is not always past. We also use **could** for possible actions now or in the future, especially to make suggestions. For example:

- ○ A: What shall we do tonight?
     B: We **could go** to the cinema.

- ○ A: When you go to Paris next month,
         you **could stay** with Sarah.
     B: Yes, I suppose I **could**.

Can is also possible in these sentences ('We can go to the cinema.' etc.). **Could** is less sure than **can**.

What shall we
do tonight?

We **could go** to the cinema.

B We also use **could** (*not* **can**) for actions that are not realistic. For example:
- ○ I'm so tired, I **could sleep** for a week. (*not* I can sleep for a week)

Compare **can** and **could**:
- ○ I **can stay** with Sarah when I go to Paris. (realistic)
- ○ Maybe I **could stay** with Sarah when I go to Paris. (possible, but less sure)
- ○ This is a wonderful place. I **could stay** here for ever. (unrealistic)

C We also use **could** (*not* **can**) to say that something is possible now or in the future:
- ○ The story **could be** true, but I don't think it is. (*not* can be true)
- ○ I don't know what time Lisa is coming. She **could get** here at any time.

Compare **can** and **could**:
- ○ The weather **can** change very quickly in the mountains. (in general)
- ○ The weather is nice now, but it **could** change later. (the weather now, not in general)

D We use **could have** (done) to talk about the past. Compare:
- ○ I'm so tired, I **could sleep** for a week. *(now)*
     I was so tired, I **could have slept** for a week. *(past)*
- ○ The situation is bad, but it **could be** worse. *(now)*
     The situation was bad, but it **could have been** worse. *(past)*

Something **could have** happened = it was possible, but did *not* happen:
- ○ Why did you stay at a hotel? You **could have stayed** with me.
- ○ David was lucky. He **could have hurt** himself when he fell, but he's all right.

E **I couldn't do** something = it would not be possible:
- ○ I **couldn't live** in a big city. I'd hate it. (= it wouldn't be possible for me)
- ○ Everything is fine right now. Things **couldn't be** better.

For the past we use **couldn't have** … (= would not have been possible):
- ○ We had a really good holiday. It **couldn't have been** better.

Note that 'I **couldn't do** something' has two meanings:
(1) I **couldn't** = it would not be possible now, I would not be able:
- ○ I **couldn't run** ten kilometres now. I'm not fit enough. (= I would not be able)
(2) I **couldn't** = I was not able (past)
- ○ I **couldn't run** yesterday because I'd hurt my leg. (= I was not able)

>> **can** and **could** → **Unit 26**   **couldn't have** (done) → **Unit 28B**   **could** and **might** → **Unit 29C**
    could I/you … ? → **Unit 37**   **could** with **if** → **Units 38C, 39E, 40D**   Modal verbs (**can/will** etc.) → **Appendix 4**

Exercises

27.1 Which goes with which?

1	What shall we eat tonight?	a	We could go away somewhere.	1	c
2	I need to phone Vicky sometime.	b	You could give her a book.	2	
3	What shall I get Ann for her birthday?	c	~~We could have fish.~~	3	
4	Where shall we put this picture?	d	You could wear your brown suit.	4	
5	What would you like to do at the weekend?	e	You could do it now.	5	
6	I don't know what to wear to the wedding.	f	We could hang it in the kitchen.	6	

27.2 Put in can or could.

1 This is a wonderful place. I __could__ stay here forever.
2 I'm so angry with him. I _____ kill him!
3 I _____ hear a strange noise. What is it?
4 It's so nice here. I _____ sit here all day but unfortunately I have to go.
5 I _____ understand your point of view, but I don't agree with you.
6 Peter is a keen musician. He plays the flute and he _____ also play the piano.
7 The company Amy works for isn't doing well. She _____ lose her job.
8 Some people are unlucky. Life _____ be very unfair.
9 I've been really stupid. I _____ kick myself.
10 Be careful climbing that tree. You _____ fall.

27.3 Complete the sentences. Choose from:

gone	could be	could come	~~could sleep~~
have moved	could have	could have come	could have been

1 A: Are you tired?
  B: Yes, very tired. I feel as if I __could sleep__ for a week.
2 A: I spent a very boring evening at home yesterday.
  B: Why did you stay at home? You _____ out with us.
3 A: Shall I open this letter?
  B: Yes. It _____ important.
4 A: How was your exam? Was it difficult?
  B: It wasn't so bad. It _____ worse.
5 A: I got very wet walking home in the rain.
  B: Why did you walk? You _____ taken a taxi.
6 A: Where shall we meet tomorrow?
  B: Well, I _____ to your office if you like.
7 A: Does Tom still live in the same place?
  B: I'm not sure. He could _____ .
8 A: Did you go to university?
  B: No. I could have _____ , but I didn't want to.

27.4 Complete the sentences. Use couldn't or couldn't have + these verbs (in the correct form):

afford	be	~~be~~	~~live~~	manage	stand	study	wear

1 I __couldn't live__ in a big city. I'd hate it.
2 We had a really good holiday. It __couldn't have been__ better.
3 I _____ that hat. People would laugh at me.
4 You helped me a lot. I _____ without you.
5 The staff at the hotel were really good. They _____ more helpful.
6 There's no way we could buy a car now. We _____ it.
7 Jack prepared for the exam as well as he could. He _____ harder.
8 I wouldn't like to live near the motorway. I _____ the noise of the traffic.

→ Additional exercises 16–18 (pages 311–13)

must and can't

Study this example:

My house is very near the motorway.

It **must be** very noisy.

We use **must** to say that we believe something is certain:
- ○ You've been travelling all day. You **must be** tired.
  (travelling is tiring and you've been travelling all day, so you **must** be tired)
- ○ 'Joe is a hard worker.' 'Joe? You **must be joking**. He doesn't do anything.'
- ○ Louise **must get** very bored in her job. She does the same thing every day.

We use **can't** to say that we believe something is not possible:
- ○ You've just had lunch. You **can't be** hungry already.
  (we don't expect people to be hungry immediately after a meal)
- ○ They haven't lived here for very long. They **can't know** many people.

The structure is:

you/she/they (etc.)	must can't	**be** (tired / hungry / at work etc.) **be -ing** (doing / going / joking etc.) **get** / **know** / **have** etc.

Study this example:

There's nobody at home. They **must have gone** out.

Martin and Lucy expected their friends to be at home.
They rang the doorbell twice, but nobody has answered. Lucy says:

They **must have gone** out.
(= there is no other possibility)

For the past we use **must have** ... and **can't have** ...:
- ○ I lost one of my gloves. I **must have dropped** it somewhere.
  (that's the only explanation I can think of)
- ○ 'We used to live very near the motorway.' 'Did you? It **must have been** noisy.'
- ○ Sarah hasn't contacted me. She **can't have got** my message.
- ○ Max walked into a wall. He **can't have been looking** where he was going.

The structure is:

I/you/he (etc.)	must can't	have	**been** (asleep / at work etc.) **been -ing** (doing / looking etc.) **gone** / **got** / **known** etc.

You can use **couldn't have** instead of **can't have**:
- ○ Sarah **couldn't have got** my message.
- ○ Max **couldn't have been looking** where he was going.

---

can't ('I can't swim' etc.) → Unit 26   must ('I must go' etc.) → Units 31–32
Modal verbs (can/will etc.) → Appendix 4   American English → Appendix 7

Exercises

28.1 **Put in must or can't.**

1 You've been travelling all day. You ___must___ be tired.
2 That restaurant .... be very good. It's always full of people.
3 That restaurant .... be very good. It's always empty.
4 I'm sure Kate gave me her address. I .... have it somewhere.
5 I often see that man in this street. He .... live near here.
6 It rained every day during their holiday. It .... have been very nice for them.
7 Congratulations on passing your exam. You .... be very pleased.
8 This bill .... be correct. It's much too high.
9 You got here very quickly. You .... have driven very fast.
10 Bill and Sue always stay at five-star hotels. They .... be short of money.
11 Karen hasn't left the office yet. She .... be working late tonight.

28.2 **Complete each sentence with a verb (one or two words).**

1 I've lost one of my gloves. I must ___have dropped___ it somewhere.
2 Their house is very near the motorway. It must ___be___ very noisy.
3 You've lived in this village a long time. You must .... everybody who lives here.
4 I don't seem to have my wallet with me. I must .... it at home.
5 'How old is Ed?' 'He's older than me. He must .... at least 40.'
6 I didn't hear my phone. I must .... asleep.
7 'You're going on holiday soon. You must .... forward to it.' 'Yes, I am.'
8 I'm sure you know this song. You must .... it before.
9 The road is closed, so we have to go another way. There must .... an accident.
10 'Do you have a car?' 'You must .... ! How could I afford to have a car?'
11 David is the managing director of a large company, so he must .... quite a high salary.

28.3 **Use the words in brackets to write sentences with must have and can't have.**

1 We went to our friends' house and rang the doorbell, but nobody answered. (they / go out)
   ___They must have gone out.___
2 Sarah hasn't contacted me. (she / get / my message)
   ___She can't have got my message.___
3 The jacket you bought is very good quality. (it / be / very expensive)
   ....
4 I haven't seen our neighbours for the last few days. (they / go away)
   ....
5 I can't find my umbrella. (I / leave / it in the restaurant last night)
   ....
6 Amy was in a very difficult situation when she lost her job. (it / be / easy for her)
   ....
7 There was a man standing outside the cafe. He was there a long time. (he / wait / for somebody)
   ....
8 Rachel did the opposite of what I asked her to do. (she / understand / what I said)
   ....
9 When I got back to my car, it was unlocked. (I / forget / to lock it)
   ....
10 My neighbours were making a lot of noise in the night. It woke me up. (they / have / a party)
   ....
11 The light was red, but the car didn't stop. (the driver / see / the red light)
   ....
12 Paul has had these shoes for years, but they still look new. (he / wear / them much)
   ....

may and might 1

A

Study this example situation:

You are looking for Ben. Nobody is sure where he is, but you get some suggestions.

Where's Ben?

He **may be** in his office. (= perhaps he is in his office)

He **might be** having lunch. (= perhaps he is having lunch)

Ask Kate. She **might know**. (= perhaps she knows)

We use **may** or **might** to say that something is possible. You can use **may** or **might**:

- It **may** be true. *or* It **might** be true. (= perhaps it is true)
- She **might** know. *or* She **may** know.

The negative forms are **may not** and **might not**:

- It **may not** be true. (= perhaps it isn't true)
- She **might not** know. (= perhaps she doesn't know)

I/you/he (etc.)	may might	(not)	**be** (true / in his office etc.) **be -ing** (doing / working / having etc.) **know** / **work** / **want** etc.

Note the difference between **may be** (2 words) and **maybe** (1 word):

- It **may be** true. (**may** + verb)
- 'Is it true?' '**Maybe**. I'm not sure.' (**maybe** = it's possible, perhaps)

B

For the past we use **may have** … or **might have** …:

- A: I wonder why Kate didn't answer her phone.
B: She **may have been** asleep. (= perhaps she was asleep)
- A: I can't find my phone anywhere.
B: You **might have left** it at work. (= perhaps you left it at work)
- A: Why wasn't Amy at the meeting yesterday?
B: She **might not have known** about it. (= perhaps she didn't know)
- A: I wonder why David was in such a bad mood yesterday.
B: He **may not have been feeling** well. (= perhaps he wasn't feeling well)

I/you/he (etc.)	may might	(not) have	**been** (asleep / at home etc.) **been -ing** (doing / working / feeling etc.) **known** / **had** / **wanted** / **left** etc.

C

could is similar to **may** and **might**:

- It's a strange story, but it **could be** true. (= it is possible that it's true)
- You **could have left** your phone at work. (= it's possible that you left it there)

But **couldn't** (*negative*) is different from **may not** and **might not**. Compare:

- Sarah **couldn't have received** my message. Otherwise she would have replied.
(= it is not possible that she got my message)
- Why hasn't Sarah replied to my message? I suppose she **might not have received** it.
(= it's possible that she didn't receive it – perhaps she did, perhaps she didn't)

>> could → Unit 27   may/might 2 → Unit 30   may I …? → Unit 37C
might with if → Units 30B, 38C, 40D   Modal verbs (can/will etc.) → Appendix 4

Exercises

29.1 **Complete the sentences. Choose from the box.**

1 A: Do you know where Helen is?
   B: I'm not sure. She __might be in her room__ .
2 A: Is there a bookshop near here?
   B: I'm not sure, but ask Anna. She _____ .
3 A: Where are those people from?
   B: I don't know. They _____ .
4 A: I hope you can help me.
   B: I'll try, but it _____ .
5 A: Whose phone is this?
   B: It's not mine. It _____ .
6 A: Why doesn't George answer his phone?
   B: He _____ .
7 A: Do you know anyone who has a key to this cupboard?
   B: Rachel _____ , but I'm not sure.
8 A: Gary is in a strange mood today.
   B: Yes, he is. He _____ .

> may be Tom's
> may not be feeling well
> may not be possible
> ~~might be in her room~~
> might be Brazilian
> might be driving
> might have one
> might know

29.2 **Complete each sentence using the verb in brackets.**

1 A: Where's Ben?
   B: I'm not sure. He might __be having__ lunch. (have)
2 A: Who was the guy we saw with Anna yesterday?
   B: I'm not sure. It may _____ her brother. (be)
3 A: Is Ellie here?
   B: I can't see her. She may not _____ yet. (arrive)
4 A: Gary said he would meet us in the cafe, but he isn't here.
   B: He might _____ outside. I'll go and look. (wait)
5 A: How did John know that I'd lost my job?
   B: I don't know. I suppose Sam may _____ him. (tell)
6 A: Do you know where Jeff is? Is he still in the office?
   B: He was here earlier, but he might _____ home. (go)
7 A: Where's Emma? What's she doing?
   B: I'm not sure. She might _____ TV. (watch)
8 A: Does Max have any brothers or sisters?
   B: I'm not sure. I think he may _____ a younger sister. (have)
9 A: I can't find my umbrella. Have you seen it?
   B: You may _____ it in the restaurant last night. (leave)
10 A: I rang Dan's doorbell, but he didn't answer. I'm sure he was there.
    B: He might not _____ the doorbell. (hear)
11 A: Hannah is supposed to meet us here, and she's already 20 minutes late.
    B: She may _____ . She's always forgetting things. (forget)

29.3 **Complete the sentences using might not have … or couldn't have … .**

1 A: I was surprised Amy wasn't at the meeting. Perhaps she didn't know about it.
   B: Maybe. __She might not have known__ about it.
2 A: I wonder why Tom didn't come to the party. Perhaps he didn't want to come.
   B: It's possible. He _____ to come.
3 A: I wonder how the fire started. Was it an accident?
   B: No, the police say it _____ an accident. It was deliberate.
4 A: Mike says he needs to see you. He tried to find you yesterday.
   B: Well, he _____ very hard. I was in my office all day.
5 A: The man you spoke to – are you sure he was American?
   B: No, I'm not sure. He _____ .

may and **might** 2

A

We use **may** and **might** to talk about possible actions or happenings in the future:

- ☐ I haven't decided where to go on holiday. I **may go** to Ireland. (= perhaps I will go there)
- ☐ Take an umbrella with you. It **might rain** later. (= perhaps it will rain)
- ☐ The bus isn't always on time. We **might have** to wait a few minutes.
  (= perhaps we will have to wait)

The negative forms are **may not** and **might not** (**mightn't**):

- ☐ Amy **may not go** out tonight. She isn't feeling well. (= perhaps she will not go out)
- ☐ There **might not be** enough time to discuss everything at the meeting.
  (= perhaps there will not be enough time)

Compare:

- ☐ **I'm going** to buy a car. (for sure)
- ☐ I **may buy** a car. *or* I **might buy** a car. (possible)

B

Usually you can use **may** or **might**. So you can say:

- ☐ I **may go** to Ireland. *or* I **might go** to Ireland.
- ☐ Jane **might be** able to help you. *or* Jane **may be** able to help you.

But we use **might** (*not* **may**) when the situation is *not real*:

- ☐ If they paid me better, I **might** work harder. (*not* I may work)

This situation (**If they paid** me better) is not real. They do *not* pay me well, so I'm not going to work harder.

C

Compare **may/might be -ing** and **will be -ing**:

- ☐ Don't phone at 8.30. I'**ll be watching** the football on TV.
- ☐ Don't phone at 8.30. I **might be watching** the football on TV. (= perhaps I'll be watching it)

We also use **may/might be -ing** for possible plans. Compare:

- ☐ **I'm going** to Ireland soon. (for sure)
- ☐ I **might be going** (*or* I **may be going**) to Ireland soon. (possible)

D

might as well

Helen and Clare have just missed the bus.
The buses run every hour.

> What shall we do? Shall we walk?

> We **might as well**. It's a nice day and I don't want to wait here for an hour.

We **might as well** do something = we should do it because there is no better alternative. There is no reason not to do it.

You can also use **may as well**.

- ☐ A: What time are you going out?
  B: Well, I'm ready, so I **might as well go** now. *or* … I **may as well go** now.
- ☐ Buses are so expensive these days, you **might as well get** a taxi.
  (= taxis are as good, no more expensive than buses)

---

will be -ing ➔ Unit 24   **may/might 1** ➔ Unit 29   **may I … ?** ➔ Unit 37
might with **if** ➔ Units 38C, 40D

Exercises

30.1 **Which alternative makes sense?**

1 A: Where are you going for your holidays?
 B: I haven't decided yet. <u>I might go</u> / <s>I'm going</s> to Ireland. (<u>I might go</u> *makes sense*)
2 A: Have you decided what sort of car you want to buy?
 B: Yes, <u>I might get / I'm going to get</u> a sports car.
3 A: When is Tom coming to see us?
 B: He hasn't said yet. <u>He might come / He's coming</u> on Sunday.
4 A: Where are you going to put that picture?
 B: I don't know yet. <u>I might hang / I'm going to hang</u> it in the bedroom.
5 A: What's Tanya going to do when she leaves school? Does she know yet?
 B: Yes, she's decided. <u>She might go / She's going</u> to university.
6 A: Do you have plans for the weekend?
 B: Nothing fixed. <u>I might go away / I'm going away</u>.

30.2 **Complete the sentences using might + a verb from the box:**

1 Take an umbrella with you when you go out. It __might rain__ later.
2 Don't make too much noise. You .... the baby.
3 Be careful with your coffee. You .... it.
4 Don't forget your phone. You .... it.
5 It's better if we don't talk so loud. Somebody .... us.
6 Be careful. This footpath is icy. You ....

hear
need
~~**rain**~~
slip
spill
wake

30.3 **Complete the sentences. Use might be able to or might have to + one of these verbs:**

> fix   ~~help~~   leave   meet   pay   wait

1 Tell me about your problem. I __might be able to help__ you.
2 I can come to the meeting, but I .... before the end.
3 I'm not free this evening, but I .... you tomorrow evening.
4 I'm not sure whether this car park is free or not. We ....
5 There's a long queue. We .... a long time.
6 'I've got a problem with my bike.'   'Let me have a look. I .... it.'

30.4 **Write sentences with might not.**

1 Lisa's not feeling very well. I'm not sure that she will go to the party.
 Lisa might not come to the party.
2 I haven't seen him for a long time. I don't know if I will recognise him or not.
 I might .... him.
3 We want to go to the game, but I don't know whether we'll be able to get tickets.
 We .... for the game.
4 I said I'd do the shopping, but it's possible I won't have time.
 I .... to do the shopping.
5 I've been invited to the wedding, but I'm not sure that I'll be able to go.
 I ....

30.5 **Read the situations and write sentences with might as well.**

1 You and a friend have just missed the bus. The buses run every hour.
 You say: We'll have to wait an hour for the next bus. __We might as well walk__ .
2 Your computer doesn't work any more. It will cost a lot to repair.
 You say: It's not worth repairing. I .... a new one.
3 You've painted the kitchen. You still have a lot of paint, so why not paint the bathroom too?
 You say: I .... too. There's plenty of paint left.
4 You and a friend are at home. You're bored. There's a film on TV starting in a few minutes.
 You say: We .... it. There's nothing else to do.

have to and **must**

A I **have to** do something = it is necessary to do it, I am obliged to do it:
- ○ You can't turn right here. You **have to turn** left.
- ○ I **have to wear** glasses for reading.
- ○ Robert can't come out with us this evening.
  He **has to work** late.
- ○ Last week Tina broke her arm and **had to go** to hospital.
- ○ I haven't **had to go** to the doctor for ages.

> You **have to turn** left here.

We use **do/does/did** in questions and negative sentences
(for the present and past simple):
- ○ What **do** I **have to do** to get a new driving licence? (*not* What have I to do?)
- ○ Karen **doesn't have to work** Saturdays. (*not* Karen hasn't to)
- ○ '**Did** you **have to wait** a long time for a bus?' 'No, only ten minutes.'

You can say **I'll have to** … , **I'm going to have to** … , **I might have to** … , **I may have to** … :
- ○ They can't repair my computer, so **I'll have to buy** a new one. *or*
  … **I'm going to have to buy** a new one.
- ○ We **might have to change** our plans. *or* We **may have to change** …
  (= it's possible that we will have to change them)

B **Must** is similar to **have to**. You can say:
- ○ It's later than I thought. I **must go**. *or* I **have to go**.

You can use **must** or **have to** when you give your own opinion (for example, to say what *you* think is
necessary, or to recommend someone to do something):
- ○ I haven't spoken to Sue for ages. I **must phone** her. / I **have to phone** her.
  (= I say this is necessary)
- ○ Mark is a really nice person. You **must meet** him. / You **have to meet** him.
  (= I recommend this)

We use **have to** (*not usually* **must**) to say what someone is *obliged* to do. This is a *fact*, not the speaker's
own opinion:
- ○ I **have to work** from 8.30 to 5.30 every day. (a fact, not an opinion)
- ○ Jane **has to travel** a lot for her work.

But we use **must** in written rules and instructions:
- ○ Applications for the job **must be received** by 18 May.
- ○ Seat belts **must be worn**.

> Seat belts
> must be
> worn

We use **had to** (*not* **must**) to talk about the past:
- ○ I went to the meeting yesterday, but I **had** to leave early. (*not* I must)

C **Mustn't** and **don't have to** are completely different:

> You **mustn't** do something = *don't* do it:
> - ○ You **must keep** this a secret. You **mustn't tell** anyone. (= don't tell anyone)
> - ○ I promised I would be on time. I **mustn't be** late. (= I must be on time)
>
> You **don't have to** do something = you don't need to do it (but you can if you want):
> - ○ You **don't have to come** with me. I can go alone.
> - ○ I **don't have to be** at the meeting, but I'm going anyway.

D You can use **have got to** instead of **have to**. You can say:
- ○ I**'ve got to** work tomorrow. *or* I **have to** work tomorrow.
- ○ When **has** Helen **got to** go? *or* When **does** Helen **have to** go?

>> **must** ('You must be tired') → Unit 28   **must/mustn't/needn't** → Unit 32

Exercises

31.1 Complete the sentences using have/has/had to … . Use the verbs in brackets.

1 Robert can't come out with us this evening. _He has to work_ late. (he / work)
2 'The bus was late this morning.' 'How long _did you have to wait_ ?' (you / wait)
3 I don't have much time. .... in ten minutes. (I / go)
4 'I'm afraid I can't stay long.' 'What time .... ?' (you / go)
5 Joe starts work at 5 am every day, which means .... at four. (he / get up)
6 We nearly missed the bus this morning. .... to catch it. (we / run)
7 Is Lisa usually free on Saturdays or .... ? (she / work)
8 There was nobody to help me. .... everything by myself. (I / do)
9 How old .... to have a driving licence? (you / be)
10 There was a lot of noise from the street. .... the window. (we / close)
11 Was the exhibition free, or .... to go in? (you / pay)

31.2 Complete the sentences using have/has/had to + the verbs in the list. Some sentences are negative
(I don't have to … etc.):

| ask | decide | drive | ~~get up~~ | go | make | make | pay | ~~show~~ | stand |

1 I'm not working tomorrow, so _I don't have to get up_ early.
2 Steve didn't know how to change the settings on his phone. I _had to show_ him.
3 Excuse me a moment – I .... a phone call. I won't be long.
4 You can let me know later what you want to do. You .... now.
5 I couldn't find the street I wanted. I .... somebody for directions.
6 This car park is free. You ....
7 A man was slightly injured in the accident, but he .... to hospital.
8 Jane has a senior position in the company. She .... important decisions.
9 The train was very full and there were no seats free. We .... all the way.
10 When Patrick starts his new job next month, he .... 50 miles to work
every day.

31.3 In some of these sentences, must is wrong or unnatural. Correct the sentences where necessary.

1 It's later than I thought. I must go.   _OK (I have to go_ is also correct)
2 I must start work every day at 8.30.   _I have to start work_
3 I must remember to call Sarah tomorrow.   ....
4 I couldn't get a taxi last night. I must walk home. ....
5 You must come and see us again soon.   ....
6 Tom isn't going out this evening. He must study   ....
for his exam.   ....
7 We can't go the usual way because the road   ....
is closed. We must go another way.   ....
8 Julia wears glasses. She must wear glasses   ....
since she was very young.

31.4 Complete the sentences with mustn't, don't have to or doesn't have to.

1 I don't want anyone to know about our plan. You _mustn't_ tell anyone.
2 Richard _doesn't have to_ wear a suit to work, but he usually does.
3 There's a lift in the building, so we .... climb the stairs.
4 I promised Kate I'd call her tomorrow. I .... forget.
5 I'm not very busy. I have a few things to do, but I .... do them now.
6 Sophie likes weekends because she .... get up early.
7 You .... be a good player to enjoy a game of tennis.
8 You should keep trying to find a job. You .... give up.
9 I .... eat too much. I'm supposed to be on a diet.
10 We have plenty of time before our flight. We .... check in yet.

→ Additional exercise 16 (page 311)

Unit 32 must   mustn't   needn't

A   must and mustn't

You **must** do something = it is necessary that you do it:
- ○ Don't tell anybody what I said. You **must keep** it a secret.
- ○ We don't have much time. We **must hurry**.

You **mustn't** do something = don't do it:
- ○ You **must** keep it a secret. You **mustn't** tell anyone. (= don't tell anyone)
- ○ We **must** be very quiet. We **mustn't** make any noise.

B   needn't and don't need to

You **needn't** do something = it's not necessary to do it (but you can if you want):
- ○ We have plenty of time. We **needn't hurry**. (= it is not necessary to hurry)
- ○ Joe can stay here. He **needn't come** with us. (= it is not necessary for him to come)

You can also use **don't/doesn't need to**:
- ○ We **don't need to** hurry.

Note that we say '**don't need to** do', but '**needn't do**' (*without* **to**).

Compare **needn't** and **mustn't**:
- ○ You **needn't** tell Steve. I can tell him myself. (= it is not necessary)
- ○ You **mustn't** tell Steve. I don't want him to know. (= don't tell him)

C   needn't have (done)

Study this example situation:

Can I reserve a table for two?

We **needn't have reserved** a table.

Paul and Sarah reserved a table at a restaurant.

But when they went to the restaurant, it was almost empty.

They **needn't have reserved** a table.

This means: they reserved a table, but now they know this was not necessary.

Compare **needn't** (do) and **needn't have** (done):
- ○ Everything will be OK. You **needn't worry**. (it is not necessary)
- ○ Everything was OK. You **needn't have worried**. (you worried, but it was not necessary)

D   needn't have (done) and didn't need to (do)

He **needn't have done** something = he did it, but now we know that it was not necessary:
- ○ Why did he get up at 5 o'clock? He **needn't have got** up so early. He could have stayed in bed longer.

He **didn't need to do** something = it was not necessary to do it. It doesn't matter whether he did it or not:
- ○ He **didn't need to get** up early, so he didn't.
- ○ He **didn't need to get** up early, but it was a beautiful morning, so he did.

You can also say 'He **didn't have to** get up' in these examples.

>> **must** ('You must be tired') → Unit 28   **have to** and **must** → Unit 31
Modal verbs (**can/could/will/would** etc.) → Appendix 4   American English → Appendix 7

Exercises

32.1 **Which goes with which? Find the sentences with a similar meaning.**

1 You must be very quiet.	a You mustn't stay here.	1	_f_
2 You must remember your password.	b You mustn't be afraid.	2	
3 You must be brave.	c You mustn't think about it.	3	
4 You must be on time.	d You mustn't forget it.	4	
5 You must leave the furniture as it is.	e You mustn't be late.	5	
6 You must go away.	f ~~You mustn't make any noise.~~	6	
7 You must forget what happened.	g You mustn't move anything.	7	

32.2 **Which is correct?**

1 We have plenty of time. We ~~mustn't~~ / needn't hurry. (needn't *is correct*)
2 I have to talk to Gary. I must / mustn't remember to call him.
3 I have to talk to Gary. I mustn't / needn't forget to call him.
4 There's plenty of time for you to decide. You mustn't / don't need to decide now.
5 These are important documents. We mustn't / needn't lose them.
6 You mustn't / needn't wait for me. You go on and I'll join you later.
7 This is a dangerous situation and we need to be careful. We mustn't / needn't do anything stupid.
8 I understand the situation perfectly. You mustn't / don't need to explain further.
9 A: What sort of house do you want to buy? Something big?
   B: It mustn't / needn't be big – that's not so important. But it must / mustn't have a nice garden.

32.3 **Complete the sentences. Use needn't + verb. Choose from:**

come	keep	~~leave~~	walk	worry

1 We have plenty of time. We ___needn't leave___ yet.
2 I can manage the shopping alone. You _____ with me.
3 We _____ all the way home. We can get a taxi.
4 You can delete these emails. You _____ them.
5 I'll be all right. You _____ about me.

32.4 **Write two sentences for each situation. Use needn't have in the first sentence and could have in the second (as in the example). For could have, see Unit 27.**

1 Why did you rush? Why didn't you take your time?
  You needn't have rushed. You could have taken your time.
2 Why did you walk home? Why didn't you take a taxi?
  _____
3 Why did they stay at a hotel? Why didn't they stay with us?
  _____
4 Why did she phone me at 3 am? Why didn't she wait until the morning?
  _____
5 Why did you shout at me? Why weren't you more patient?
  _____

32.5 **Are these sentences OK? Change them where necessary.**

1 We have plenty of time. We don't need hurry.   _We don't need to hurry_
2 Keep it a secret. You mustn't tell anybody.   _Ok_
3 You needn't to shout. I can hear you perfectly.   _____
4 I needn't have gone out, so I stayed at home.   _____
5 This train is direct. You don't need to change.   _____
6 You mustn't lock the door. It's OK to leave it unlocked. _____
7 I needn't have said anything, so I kept quiet.   _____
8 I needn't have said anything. I should have kept quiet. _____

→ **Additional exercises 16–17** (pages 311–12)   65

should 1

A You **should do** something = it is a good thing to do or the right thing to do.
You can use **should** to give advice or to give an opinion:

- ◯ You look tired. You **should go** to bed.
- ◯ The government **should do** more to improve schools.
- ◯ A: **Should** we **invite** Stephanie to the party?
  B: Yes, I think we **should**.
- ◯ The man on the motorbike **should be wearing** a helmet.

You **shouldn't** do something = it isn't a good thing to do:
- ◯ You **shouldn't believe** everything you read in newspapers.

We often use **should** with **I think** / **I don't think** / **Do you think** … ? :
- ◯ **I think** the government **should do** more to improve schools.
- ◯ **I don't think** you **should work** so hard.
- ◯ A: **Do you think** I **should apply** for this job?
  B: Yes, **I think** you **should**.

Should is not as strong as **must** or **have to**:
- ◯ You **should** apologise. (= it would be a good thing to do)
- ◯ You **must** apologise. / You **have to** apologise. (= you have no alternative)

B We use **should** when something is not right or what we expect:
- ◯ Where's Tina? She **should be** here by now.
  (= she isn't here yet, and this is not normal)
- ◯ The price on this packet is wrong. It **should be** £2.50, not £3.50.

We also use **should** to say that we expect something to happen:
- ◯ Helen has been studying hard for the exam, so she **should pass**.
  (= I expect her to pass)
- ◯ There are plenty of hotels in the town. It **shouldn't be** hard to find a place to stay.
  (= I don't expect it to be hard)

C You **should have done** something = you didn't do it, but it would have been a good thing to do:
- ◯ You missed a great party last night. You **should have come**. Why didn't you?
  (= you didn't come, but it would have been good to come)
- ◯ I wonder why they're so late. They **should have been** here long ago.

You **shouldn't have done** something = you did it, but it wasn't a good thing to do:
- ◯ I'm feeling sick. I **shouldn't have eaten** so much. (= I ate too much)
- ◯ She **shouldn't have been listening** to our conversation. It was private.
  (= she was listening)

Compare **should** (do) and **should have** (done):
- ◯ You look tired. You **should go** to bed now.
- ◯ You went to bed very late last night. You **should have gone** to bed earlier.

D **ought to** …

You can use **ought to** instead of **should** in the sentences on this page.
We say 'ought **to** do' (with **to**):
- ◯ Do you think I **ought to apply** for this job? (= Do you think I **should apply** … ?)
- ◯ Jack **ought not to go** to bed so late. (= Jack **shouldn't go** …)
- ◯ It was a great party last night. You **ought to have come**. (= You **should have come**)

➤➤ should 2 → Unit 34   should and had better → Unit 35B
Modal verbs (**can/could/will/would** etc.) → Appendix 4

Exercises

33.1 For each situation, write a sentence with **should** or **shouldn't** + one of the following:

~~go away for a few days~~	stay up so late	look for another job
put some pictures on the walls	take a picture	worry so much

1 Anna needs a change.   *She should go away for a few days.*
2 Your salary is very low.   You ....
3 Jack always finds it hard to get up.   He ....
4 What a beautiful view!   You ....
5 Laura is always anxious.   She ....
6 Dan's room isn't very nice.

33.2 Complete the sentences. Choose from:

should solve	should be working OK	shouldn't cost more	shouldn't take long
should receive	~~should pass the exam~~	should be much warmer	should be here soon

1 Helen has been studying hard, so she ...*should pass the exam*... .
2 Joe hasn't arrived yet, but he ....
3 The TV has been repaired. It .... now.
4 It .... to get to the hotel. About 20 minutes.
5 I sent the documents to you today, so you .... them tomorrow.
6 The weather is unusually cold. It .... at this time of year.
7 The best way to get to the airport is by taxi. It .... than ten pounds.
8 If you have a problem with the computer, try restarting it. That .... the problem.

33.3 Complete the sentences. Use **should ...** or **should have ...** + the verb in brackets.

1 You look tired. You ...*should go*............................. to bed. (go)
2 You missed a great party last night. ...*You should have come*.... . (come)
3 I'm in a difficult position. What do you think I .... now? (do)
4 I'm sorry that I didn't take your advice. I .... what you said. (do)
5 We lost the game, but we were the better team. We .... (win)
6 We don't see you enough. You .... and see us more often. (come)
7 We went the wrong way and got lost. We .... right, not left. (turn)
8 My exam results weren't good. I .... better. (do)

33.4 Read the situations and write sentences with **should** / **should have** / **shouldn't** / **shouldn't have**.

1 I'm feeling sick. I ate too much.
   I shouldn't have eaten so much.
2 When we got to the restaurant, there were no free tables. We hadn't reserved one.
   We ....
3 Laura told me her address, but I didn't write it down. Now I can't remember the house number.
   I ....
4 The shop is open every day from 8.30. It is 9 o'clock now, but the shop isn't open yet.
   ....
5 I was looking at my phone. I wasn't looking where I was going. I walked into a wall.
   ....
6 Kate is driving. The speed limit is 30 miles an hour, but Kate is doing 50.
   She ....
7 I wasn't feeling well yesterday, but I went to work. That was a mistake. Now I feel worse.
   ....
8 Tomorrow there is a football match between Team A and Team B. Team A are much better.
   ....
9 I was driving. The car in front stopped suddenly and I drove into it. It wasn't my fault.
   The driver in front ....

A You can use **should** after:

> insist   demand   recommend   suggest   propose

- ○ I **insisted** that he **should apologise**.
- ○ Doctors **recommend** that everyone **should eat** plenty of fruit.
- ○ What do you **suggest** we **should do**?
- ○ Many people are **demanding** that something **should be done** about the problem.

also

It's important/vital/necessary/essential that … **should** … :

- ○ **It's essential** that everyone **should be** here on time.

B You can also leave out **should** in the sentences in section A. So you can say:

- ○ **It's essential** that everyone **be** here on time. (= … that everyone **should be** here …)
- ○ I **insisted** that he **apologise**. (= … that he **should apologise**)
- ○ What do you **suggest** we **do**?
- ○ Many people are **demanding** that something **be done** about the problem.

This form (**be/do/apologise** etc.) is called the *subjunctive*. It is the same as the *infinitive* (without **to**). You can also use normal present and past forms:

- ○ It's **essential** that everyone **is** here on time.
- ○ I **insisted** that he **apologised**.

C We do not use **to** … with **suggest**. You can say:

- ○ What do you **suggest we should do**?
- *or*   What do you **suggest we do**? (*but not* What do you suggest us to do?)

- ○ Jane won the lottery.
  I **suggested** that she **should buy** a car with the money she won.
- *or*   I **suggested** that she **buy** a car.
- *or*   I **suggested** that she **bought** a car. (*but not* I suggested her to buy)

You can also use -**ing** after **suggest** (What do you **suggest doing**?). See Unit 53.

D You can use **should** after some adjectives, especially:

> strange   odd   funny   typical   natural   interesting   surprised   surprising

- ○ It's **strange** that he **should be** late. He's usually on time.
- ○ I was **surprised** that he **should say** such a thing.

E You can say '**if** something **should** happen …'. For example:

- ○ We have no jobs at present, but **if** the situation **should change**, we will contact you.

You can also begin with **should** (**Should** something happen …):

- ○ **Should** the situation **change**, we will contact you.

This means the same as '**If** the situation **changes**, …'. With **should**, the speaker feels that the possibility is smaller.

F You can use **I should** … / **I shouldn't** … to give advice. For example:

- ○ 'Shall I leave now?'   'No, **I should wait** a bit.' (= I advise you to wait)

Here, **I should** … = 'I would … if I were you', 'I advise you to …'. Two more examples:

- ○ 'I'm going out now. Is it cold outside?'   'Yes, **I should wear** a coat.'
- ○ **I shouldn't stay** up too late. You have to be up early tomorrow.

Exercises

34.1 Complete the second sentence so that it means the same as the first.

1 'It would be a good idea to eat more fruit,' the doctor said to me.
   The doctor recommended that ___I should eat more fruit___ .
2 'You really must stay a little longer,' she said to me.
   She insisted that I ....
3 'Why don't you visit the museum after lunch?' I said to them.
   I suggested that ....
4 'You must pay the rent by Friday,' the landlord said to us.
   The landlord demanded that ....
5 'Let's go to the cinema,' Chris said to me.
   Chris suggested that ....

34.2 Two of these sentences are not correct. Change the two that are not correct.

1 Tom suggested that I look for another job.   ___OK___
2 I called Tina and suggested that we meet for coffee. ....
3 What do you suggest me to do? ....
4 What sort of car do you suggest I should buy? ....
5 I suggest you to read this book. ....
6 I suggested that Anna learn to drive. ....

34.3 Complete the sentences using should + verb. Choose from:

| ask | ~~be~~ | be done | leave | say | vote | worry |

1 It's strange that he ___should be___ late. He's usually on time.
2 It's funny that you .... that. I was thinking the same thing.
3 It's only natural that parents .... about their children.
4 Isn't it typical of Joe that he .... without saying goodbye to anybody?
5 I was surprised that they .... me for advice. What advice could I give them?
6 This is a democratic election, and it's important that you ....
7 The bridge needs to be repaired. It's essential that the work .... as soon
   as possible.

34.4 Complete the sentences using If ... should ... . Choose from:

| anyone / ask | ~~the situation / change~~ | it / rain | there / any problems |

1 We have no jobs at present. ___If the situation should change___ , we'll let you know.
2 I've hung out the washing to dry on the balcony. If .... , can you bring it inside?
3 I think everything will be OK. .... , I'm sure we'll be
   able to solve them.
4 I don't want anyone to know where I'm going. .... , say you don't know.

Now complete the same sentences beginning with Should ... .

5 ___Should the situation change___ , we'll let you know.
6 .... , can you bring the washing inside?
7 .... , I'm sure we'll be able to solve them.
8 .... where I'm going, say you don't know.

34.5 Complete the sentences using I should. Choose from:

| call | get | keep | ~~wait~~ |

1 'Shall I leave now?'   'No, ___I should wait___ a bit.'
2 'Shall I throw these things away?'   'No, ... them. You may need them.'
3 'Shall I go and see Paul?'   'Yes, but .... him first.'
4 'Is it worth getting this computer repaired?'   'No, ... a new one.'

I'd better ...   it's time ...

A   had better (I'd better / you'd better etc.)

I'd better do something = it is advisable to do it. If I don't do it, there will be a problem or a danger:
- ○   I have to meet Amy in ten minutes. **I'd better go** now or I'll be late.
- ○   'Shall I take an umbrella?'   'Yes, **you'd better**. It might rain.'
- ○   **We'd better stop** for petrol soon. The tank is almost empty.

The negative is **I'd better not** (= I **had** better not):
- ○   A: That jacket looks good on you. Are you going to buy it?
       B: **I'd better not**. It's very expensive.
- ○   You don't look very well. **You'd better not go** out tonight.

Remember that:

> **I'd** better = **I had** better, **you'd** better = you **had** better etc.
> - ○   **I'd better** phone Chris, **hadn't** I?
> - ○   We **had better** go now.
>
> **Had** is normally past, but we use **had better** for the present or future, *not* past.
> - ○   I'd better go **now** / **tomorrow**.
>
> We say 'I'd better **do**' (*not* to do).
> - ○   It might rain. We'd better **take** an umbrella. (*not* We'd better to take)

B   had better and should

Had better is similar to **should** but not exactly the same. We use **had better** only for a specific situation, not for things in general. You can use **should** in all types of situations to give an opinion or give advice:
- ○   It's late. You**'d better go**. *or* You **should go**. (a specific situation)
- ○   You're always at home. You **should go** out more often. (in general – *not* 'had better go')

Also, with **had better**, there is always a danger or a problem if you don't follow the advice.
Should means only 'it is a good thing to do'. Compare:
- ○   It's a great film. You **should** go and see it. (but no problem if you don't)
- ○   The film starts at 8.30. You**'d better** go now or you'll miss the beginning.

C   it's time ...

You can say **It's time** (for somebody) **to** ... :
- ○   It's time **to go** home. / It's time for us **to go** home.

But you can also say:
- ○   It's late. It's time **we went** home.
When we use **it's time** + past ('it's time we **went**' etc.), the meaning is present, *not* past:
- ○   **It's time** they **were** here. Why are they so late? (*not* It's time they are here)

It's time somebody **did** something = they should have already done it or started it.
We often use this structure to criticise or to complain:
- ○   This situation can't continue. **It's time** you **did** something about it.
- ○   He's very selfish. **It's time he realised** that he isn't the most important person in the world.

You can also say **It's about time** ... :
- ○   Jack is a great talker, but **it's about time** he **did** something instead of just talking.

≫ should 1 **→ Unit 33**

Exercises

35.1 Read the situations and write sentences with **'d better** or **'d better not**. Choose a verb from:

check   disturb   go   put   reserve   ~~take~~

1 You're going out for a walk with a friend. It looks as if it might rain.
You say: ___We'd better take___ an umbrella.
2 You and Kate plan to go to a restaurant tonight. It will be busy.
You say to Kate: We .... a table.
3 Oliver has just cut himself. It's bleeding and he'll need a plaster on it.
You say to him: You .... on it.
4 Rebecca doesn't look well this morning – not well enough to go to work.
You say to her: .... this morning.
5 You're going to the cinema, but you're not sure what time the film starts.
You say: .... the film starts.
6 You need to talk to your boss, but she's very busy right now.
You say to a colleague: .... right now.

35.2 Is **had better** OK in these sentences? Change to **should** where necessary.

1 I have an appointment in ten minutes. <u>I'd better go now</u> or I'll be late.   ___OK___
2 <u>You'd better set your alarm</u>. You have to get up early tomorrow.
3 I'm glad you came to see us. <u>You'd better come more often</u>.
4 She'll be sad if we don't invite her to the party, so <u>we'd better invite her</u>.
5 It's nearly time to go out. <u>I'd better get ready</u>.
6 I think <u>everybody had better learn</u> a foreign language.
7 We've just missed the last bus. <u>We'd better get a taxi</u>.

35.3 Complete the sentences. Choose from the box.

1 It might rain. We'd better ___take___ an umbrella.
2 Ben needs to know what happened. Somebody .... better tell him.
3 We'd better .... park the car here. The road is too narrow.
4 You .... brush your teeth at least twice a day.
5 What are we going to do? It's time .... decide.
6 .... better not be late. It's an important meeting.
7 It's time they .... here. They promised they wouldn't be late.
8 The window is open. You'd .... close it before you go out.
9 We'd better leave as soon as possible, ... we?
10 The government should .... something about the problem.
11 It's time the government .... something about the problem.
12 It's time something .... done about the problem.

better
do
did
had
hadn't
I'd
not
to
~~**take**~~
should
was
were

35.4 Read the situations and write sentences with **It's time** (somebody **did** something).

1 You're at a friend's house. You planned to go home at 11 o'clock. It's already 11 o'clock now.
(I / go) ___It's time I went home.___
2 You haven't had a holiday for a very long time. You need one now.
(I / holiday) It's time ....
3 It's 10 o'clock. It's after the children's bedtime. You think they should be in bed.
(children / bed) ....
4 You didn't realise it was so late. You need to start cooking dinner.
(start / cook) .... dinner.
5 Kate is always complaining about everything. You think she complains too much.
(stop / complaining) .... about everything.
6 The company you work for has been badly managed for a long time. You think some changes should
be made.
(changes / make) .... in the way the company is run.

would

A We use **would** (**'d**) / **wouldn't** when we *imagine* a situation or action (= we think of something that is not real):

- ○ It **would be** nice to buy a new car, but we can't afford it.
- ○ I**'d love** to live by the sea.
- ○ A: Shall I tell Chris what happened?
  B: No, I **wouldn't say** anything.
    (= I wouldn't say anything in your situation)

We use **would have** (**done**) when we imagine something that didn't happen in the past:

- ○ They helped us a lot. I don't know what we**'d have done** without their help.
  (we**'d** have done = we **would** have done)
- ○ It's a shame you didn't see the film. You **would have liked** it.
- ○ I didn't tell Sam what happened. He **wouldn't have been** pleased.

Compare **would** (**do**) and **would have** (**done**):

- ○ I **would call** Lisa, but I don't have her number. *(now)*
  I **would have called** Lisa, but I didn't have her number. *(past)*
- ○ I'm not going to invite them to the party. They **wouldn't come** anyway.
  I didn't invite them to the party. They **wouldn't have come** anyway.

We often use **would** in sentences with **if** (see Units 38–40):

- ○ I **would call** Lisa **if** I had her number.
- ○ I **would have called** Lisa **if** I'd had her number.

B Compare **will** (**'ll**) and **would** (**'d**):

- ○ I**'ll stay** a little longer. I've got plenty of time.
  I**'d stay** a little longer, but I really have to go now. (so I can't stay longer)
- ○ I**'ll call** Lisa. I have her number.
  I**'d call** Lisa, but I don't have her number. (so I can't call her)

Sometimes **would/wouldn't** is the past of **will/won't**.
Compare:

present		*past*
○ TOM: I**'ll call** you on Sunday.	→	Tom said he**'d call** me on Sunday.
○ AMY: I promise I **won't be** late.	→	Amy promised that she **wouldn't be** late.
○ LISA: Oh, no! The car **won't start**.	→	Lisa was annoyed because her car **wouldn't start**.

Somebody **wouldn't do** something = he/she refused to do it:

- ○ I tried to warn him, but he **wouldn't listen** to me. (= he refused to listen)
- ○ The car **wouldn't start**. (= it 'refused' to start)

C You can also use **would** to talk about things that happened regularly in the past:

- ○ When we were children, we lived by the sea. In summer, if the weather was fine, we **would** all get up early and go for a swim. (= we did this regularly)
- ○ Whenever Richard was angry, he **would** walk out of the room.

With this meaning, **would** is similar to **used to** (see Unit 18):

- ○ Whenever Richard was angry, he **used to walk** out of the room.

---

will → Units 21–22   **would … if** → Units 38–40   **wish … would** → Unit 41   **would like** → Units 37D, 58
would prefer / would rather → Unit 59   Modal verbs → Appendix 4

Exercises

36.1 Write sentences about yourself. Imagine things you would like or wouldn't like.

1 (a place you'd love to live)   I'd love to live by the sea.
2 (a job you wouldn't like to do) ....
3 (something you would love to do) ....
4 (something that would be nice to have) ....
5 (a place you'd like to go to) ....

36.2 Complete the sentences using **would** + the following verbs (in the correct form):

| be | be | ~~do~~ | do | enjoy | enjoy | have | stop |

1 They helped us a lot. I don't know what we __would have done__ without their help.
2 You should go and see the film. I think you .... it.
3 It's a pity you couldn't come to the party last night. You .... it.
4 Shall I apply for the job or not? What .... you .... in my position?
5 I was in a hurry when I saw you. Otherwise I .... to talk.
6 We took a taxi home last night, but got stuck in the traffic. It ....
   quicker to walk.
7 Why don't you go and see Clare? She .... very pleased to see you.
8 In an ideal world, everybody .... enough to eat.

36.3 Each sentence on the right follows a sentence on the left. Which follows which?

1 I'd like to go to Australia one day.	a It wouldn't have been very nice.	1 __c__
2 I wouldn't like to live on a busy road.	b It would have been fun.	2 ....
3 I'm sorry your trip was cancelled.	c ~~It would be nice.~~	3 ....
4 I'm looking forward to going out tonight.	d It won't be much fun.	4 ....
5 I'm glad we didn't go out in the rain.	e It wouldn't be very nice.	5 ....
6 I'm not looking forward to the trip.	f It will be fun.	6 ....

36.4 Write sentences using **promised** + **would/wouldn't**.

1 I wonder why Laura is late.   She promised she wouldn't be late.
2 I wonder why Steve hasn't called me. He promised ....
3 Why did you tell Amy what I said? You ....
4 I'm surprised they didn't wait for us. They ....

36.5 Complete the sentences. Use **wouldn't** + a suitable verb.

1 I tried to warn him, but he __wouldn't listen__ to me.
2 I asked Amanda what had happened, but she .... me.
3 Paul was angry about what I'd said and he .... to me for two weeks.
4 Martina insisted on carrying all her luggage. She .... me help her.

36.6 Complete the sentences using **would** (section C). Choose from these verbs:

| forget | shake | share | smile | stay | ~~walk~~ |

1 Whenever Richard was angry, he __would walk__ out of the room.
2 We used to live next to a railway line. Every time a train went past, the house ....
3 Katherine was always very generous. She didn't have much, but she .... what
   she had with everyone else.
4 You could never rely on Joe. It didn't matter how many times you reminded him to do something,
   he .... always ....
5 When we were children, we used to go to the beach a lot. We .... there all day
   playing in the sand and swimming in the sea.
6 Lucy was always friendly. Whenever I saw her, she .... always .... and say hello.

can/could/would you … ? etc.
(Requests, offers, permission and invitations)

A Asking people to do things (requests)

We use **can** or **could** to ask people to do things:

○ **Can you** wait a moment, please?
or **Could you** wait a moment, please?
○ Helen, **can you** do me a favour?
○ Excuse me, **could you** tell me how to get to the bus station?

> Could you open the door, please?

You can say **Do you think** you **could** … ? :
○ **Do you think you could** take me to the airport?
(*not* Do you think you can)

B Asking for things

To ask for something, we use **Can** (I) **have** … ? / **Could** (I) **have** … ? or **Can** (I) **get** …?:
○ *(in a shop)*
Can I have these postcards, please? *or* **Can I get** these postcards, please?
○ *(in a restaurant)*
Could we have the menu, please? *or* **Can we have** the menu, please?

May I have … ? is also possible:
○ **May I have** these postcards, please?

C Asking to do things

We use **can I** or **could I** to ask to do something:
○ *(on the phone)* Hello, **can I** speak to Steve, please?
○ '**Could I** use your phone charger?' 'Sure.'
○ **Do you think I could** borrow your bike?

> Could I use your phone charger?

May is also possible:
○ **May I ask** you a question?
May is more formal than **can** or **could**.

You can also say:
Do you mind if I … ?
Is it all right if I … ? / **Is it OK if I** … ?
○ **Do you mind if I** use your phone charger?
○ '**Is it all right if I** sit here?' 'Yes, of course.'

D Offering and inviting

You can use **Can I** … ? to offer to do something:
○ '**Can I** help you?' 'No, it's OK. I can manage, thanks.'
○ '**Can I** get you some coffee?' 'That would be nice.'

To offer or to invite, we use **Would you like** … ? (*not* Do you like):
○ '**Would you like** some coffee?' 'No, thanks.'
○ '**Would you like** to eat with us tonight?' 'That would be great.'

I'd like … (= I **would** like) is a polite way to say what you want:
○ *(at a tourist information office)* **I'd like** some information about hotels, please.
○ *(in a shop)* **I'd like** to try on this jacket, please.

>> **can** and **could** → Units 26–27   mind -ing → Unit 53   would like → Units 55A, 58B
Modal verbs (**can/could/will/would** etc.) → Appendix 4

Exercises

37.1 **Which goes with which?**

1 Could you pass the sugar?	a It depends what you want me to do.	1 __e__
2 Would you like to go to the cinema?	b No, that's fine.	2 ....
3 Can I use your toilet?	c Me too. Let's go out for a walk.	3 ....
4 Do you mind if I leave work early?	d Sure. It's the door on the left.	4 ....
5 Can you do me a favour?	e Yes, here you are.	5 ....
6 Would you like something to eat?	f No, it's all right. I can manage, thanks.	6 ....
7 Can I give you a hand?	g Maybe. What's on?	7 ....
8 I'd like some fresh air.	h No, thanks. I'm not hungry.	8 ....

37.2 **Complete the sentences. Choose from:**

I'd like	Would you like to try	Do you mind	Can I take
Can I give	Would you like to come	Would you like	I'd like to

1 You're driving and you see a friend walking along the road. You stop and say:
   Hi Joe. ___Can I give___ you a lift?
2 You're making a cold drink for your friend. Perhaps he wants ice. You ask:
   .... ice in your drink?
3 You're ordering something to eat in a cafe. You say:
   .... a chicken salad, please.
4 You have an extra ticket for a concert. Maybe your friend will come. You ask:
   .... to a concert tomorrow night?
5 You answer the phone. The caller wants to speak to Lisa. You say:
   Lisa's not here. .... a message?
6 You need to see a dentist. You phone for an appointment. You say:
   Hello. .... make an appointment, please.
7 You work in a shoe shop. A customer asks you about some shoes. You ask:
   .... them on?
8 You go into a cafe and see some people you know. You ask:
   .... if I join you?

37.3 **What would you say in these situations?**

1 You're carrying a lot of things. You can't open the door yourself. There's a man near the door.
   You say to him: ___Could you open the door, please?___
2 You've finished your meal in a restaurant and now you want the bill.
   You ask the waiter: ....
3 You've filled in some forms in English. You want your friend to check them for you.
   You ask your friend: ....
4 The woman in the next room is playing music. It's very loud. You want her to turn it down.
   You say to her: ....
5 You're on a train. The window is open and you're cold. You'd like to close it.
   You ask the man next to you: ....
6 You're on a bus. You have a seat, but an elderly man is standing. You offer him your seat.
   You say to him: ....
7 You're a tourist. You want to go to the station, but you don't know how to get there.
   You ask at your hotel: ....
8 You are in a clothes shop. You see some trousers you like and you want to try them on.
   You say to the shop assistant: ....
9 You meet a very famous person. You want to get his/her autograph.
   You ask: ....

if I do … and if I did …

Compare these examples:

(1)   LISA: Shall we take the bus or the train?
JESS: **If we take** the bus, it **will** be cheaper.

For Jess, it is possible that they will take the bus,
so she says:
If we **take** the bus, it **will** be …

If we take the bus,
it will be cheaper.

(2)   Lisa and Jess decide to take the train.
Later, Jess talks to Joe.

JOE: How are you going to travel?
JESS: We're going to take the train. **If we took** the bus,
it **would** be cheaper, but the train is quicker.

Now Jess knows they are *not* going to take the bus,
so she says:
If we **took** the bus, it **would** be …

If we took the bus, it would be cheaper.

JOE   JESS

When we talk about something that will not happen,
or we don't expect that it will happen, we use
if + *past* (**if** we **went** / **if** there **was** etc.).
But the meaning is *not* past:
○   What would you do **if** you **won** a lot of money?
(I don't really expect this to happen)
○   **If** there **was** an election tomorrow, who would
you vote for?
(there will not be an election tomorrow)
○   I'd be surprised **if** they **didn't come** to the party.
(I expect them to come)

If I won a lot of money …

Compare **if I find** and **if I found**:
○   I think I left my watch at your house. **If you find** it, can you call me?
but
○   **If you found** a wallet in the street, what would you do with it?

We do not normally use **would** in the **if**-part of the sentence:
○   I'd be very scared **if** somebody **pointed** a gun at me. (*not* if somebody would point)
○   **If** we **went** by bus, it would be cheaper. (*not* If we would go)

In the other part of the sentence (not the **if**-part) we use **would** (**'d**) / **wouldn't**:
○   **I'd be** (= I **would** be) scared if somebody pointed a gun at me.
○   I'm not going to bed yet. I'm not tired. If I went to bed now, I **wouldn't sleep**.
○   What **would** you **do** if you were bitten by a snake?

Could and **might** are also possible:
○   If I won a lot of money, I **might** buy a house.
(= it is possible that I would buy a house)
○   If it stopped raining, we **could go** out.
(= we would be able to go out)

⟫   will → Units 21–22   if and when → Unit 25D   would → Unit 36   if I knew → Unit 39
if … was/were → Unit 39C   if I had known → Unit 40

Exercises

38.1 Complete the sentences. Choose from:

did	dropped	~~found~~	happened	lost	was	went

1 If you ....**found**.... a wallet in the street, what would you do with it?
2 Be careful with that vase. If you .... it, it would break into small pieces.
3 This notebook is very important to me. I'd be very upset if I .... it.
4 I don't expect to lose my job but if that .... , I'd have to find another one.
5 We're thinking about our holiday for next year. If we .... to Italy, would you come with us?
6 I don't think he'll fail the exam. I'd be very surprised if he ....
7 If there .... a fire in the building, would you know how to put the fire out?

38.2 What do you say in these situations?

1 Of course you don't expect to win the lottery. Which do you say?
  a If I win the lottery, I'll buy a big house. ☐
  b If I won the lottery, I'd buy a big house. ☑ (b *is correct*)
2 You're not going to sell your car because it's old and not worth much. Which do you say?
  a If I sell my car, I won't get much money for it. ☐
  b If I sold my car, I wouldn't get much money for it. ☐
3 You often see Sarah. A friend of yours wants to contact her. Which do you say?
  a If I see Sarah, I'll tell her to call you. ☐
  b If I saw Sarah, I'd tell her to call you. ☐
4 You don't expect that there will be a fire in the building. Which do you say?
  a What will you do if there is a fire in the building? ☐
  b What would you do if there was a fire in the building? ☐
5 You've never lost your passport. You can only imagine it.
  a I don't know what I'll do if I lose my passport. ☐
  b I don't know what I'd do if I lost my passport. ☐
6 Somebody stops you and asks the way to a bank. Which do you say?
  a If you go right at the end of this street, you'll see a bank on your left. ☐
  b If you went right at the end of this street, you'd see a bank on your left. ☐
7 You're in a lift. There is an emergency button. Nobody is going to press it. Which do you say?
  a What will happen if somebody presses that button? ☐
  b What would happen if somebody pressed that button? ☐

38.3 Complete the sentences.

1 I'd be very scared if ....**somebody pointed**.... (somebody / point) a gun at me.
2 I can't afford to buy a car. If .... (I / buy) a car, I'd have to borrow the money.
3 If you had a party, who .... (you / invite)?
4 Don't lend James your car. If .... (he / ask) me, I wouldn't lend him mine.
5 I don't think Gary and Emma will get married. .... (I / be) amazed if they did.
6 If .... (somebody / give) me $20,000, ... (I / have) a long holiday.
7 .... (you / be) nervous if .... (you / meet) a famous person?
8 What .... (you / do) if .... (you / be) in a lift
and .... (it / stop) between floors?

38.4 Write sentences beginning **If ...** .

1 We're not going to take the 10.30 train. (we / arrive too early)
  ....If we took the 10.30 train, we'd arrive too early.....
2 We're not going to stay at a hotel. (it / cost too much)
  If we .... , it ....
3 There's no point in telling you what happened. (you / not / believe)
  If I ....
4 Sally has no plans to leave her job. (it / hard to find another one)
  If she ....
5 Kevin is not going to apply for the job. (he / not / get it).

if I knew ... I wish I knew ...

A Study this example situation:

Sarah wants to phone Paul, but she can't do this because she doesn't know his number. She says:

I'd phone him **if** I **knew** his number.
(I'd phone = I **would** phone)

Sarah *doesn't* know Paul's number, so she says 'if I **knew**'.
She *imagines* what she **would** do **if** she **knew** his number.

... **if I knew** his number ...

When we imagine a situation like this, we use **if** + *past* (**if** I **knew** / **if** you **were** / **if** we **didn't** etc.).
But the meaning is present, *not* past:
- ○ There are many things I'd like to do **if** I **had** more time. (but I don't have time)
- ○ **If** I **didn't** want to go to the party, I wouldn't go. (but I want to go)
- ○ **If** you **were** in my position, what would you do?
- ○ It's a pity he can't drive. It would be useful **if** he **could**.

B We use the past in the same way after **wish** (I **wish** I **knew** / I **wish** you **were** etc.).
We use **wish** to say that we regret something, that something is not as we would like it to be:
- ○ I **wish** I **knew** Paul's phone number.
  (= I don't know it and I regret this)
- ○ Do you ever **wish** you **could** fly?
  (you can't fly)
- ○ It's very crowded here. I **wish** there **weren't** so many people. (there are a lot of people)
- ○ I **wish** I **didn't** have to work tomorrow, but unfortunately I do.

I wish I had an umbrella.

Compare:
- ○ **I'm glad** I **live** here. (I live here and that's good)
- ○ I **wish** I **lived** here. (I don't live here unfortunately)

C After **if** and **wish**, you can use **were** instead of **was** (**if** I **were** / I **wish** it **were** etc.).
You can also use **was**. So you can say:
- ○ **If** I **were** you, I wouldn't buy that coat.　　*or*　　**If** I **was** you, ...
- ○ I'd go for a walk **if it weren't** so cold.　　*or*　　... **if it wasn't** so cold.
- ○ I **wish** Anna **were** here.　　*or*　　I **wish** Anna **was** here.

D We do not usually say 'if ... would'. We use **would** (**'d**) in the other part of the sentence:
- ○ **If** I **were** rich, I **would** travel a lot. (*not* If I would be rich)
- ○ Who **would** you ask **if** you **needed** help? (*not* if you would need)
In the same way we say:
- ○ I **wish** I **had** something to read. (*not* I wish I would have)
- ○ I **wish** she **were** here now. (*not* I wish she would be)

For '**I wish ... would ...**' see Unit 41.

E **Could** sometimes means 'would be able to' and sometimes 'was/were able to':
- ○ She **could get** a better job
  if she **could speak** another language.
- ○ I wish I **could** help you.

(she **could get** = she **would be able** to get)
(if she **could speak** = if she **was able** to speak)
(I wish I **could** = I wish I **was able**)

>> could → Units 26–27　　if I do / if I did → Unit 38
if I had known / I wish I had known → Unit 40　　wish → Unit 41

Exercises

39.1 Put the verb into the correct form.

1 If ___I knew___ (I / know) his number, I would phone him.
2 ___I wouldn't buy___ (I / not / buy) that coat if I were you.
3 _____ (I / help) you if I could, but I'm afraid I can't.
4 This soup isn't very nice. _____ (it / taste) better if it wasn't so salty.
5 We live in a city and don't need a car, but we would need one if _____ (we / live) in the country.
6 If we had the choice, _____ (we / live) in the country.
7 I'd make a lot of changes if _____ (I / be) the manager of the company.
8 I wouldn't call someone in the middle of the night if _____ (it / not / be) important.
9 If I were you, _____ (I / not / wait). _____ (I / go) now.
10 You're always tired because you go to bed so late. If _____ (you / not / go) to bed so late every night, _____ (you / not / be) tired all the time.
11 I think there are too many cars. If _____ (there / not / be) so many cars, _____ (there / not / be) so much pollution.
12 We all need jobs and money, but what _____ (you / do) if _____ (you / not / have) to work?

39.2 Write a sentence with if … for each situation.

1 We don't see you very often because you live so far away.
   ___If you didn't live so far away, we'd see you more often.___
2 I like these shoes but they're too expensive, so I'm not going to buy them.
   I _____ them if _____ so
3 We'd like to go on holiday, but we can't afford it.
   We _____ if _____
4 It would be nice to have lunch outside but it's raining, so we can't.
   We _____
5 I don't want his advice, and that's why I'm not going to ask for it.
   If _____

39.3 Write sentences beginning I wish … .

1 I don't know many people (and I'm lonely). ___I wish I knew more people.___
2 I don't have much free time (and I need more). I wish _____
3 Helen isn't here (and I need to see her). _____
4 It's cold (and I hate cold weather). _____
5 I live in a big city (and I don't like it). _____
6 I can't find my phone (which is a problem). _____
7 I'm not feeling well (which isn't good). _____
8 I have to get up early tomorrow (but I'd prefer to sleep late).
   _____
9 I don't know much about science (and I should know more). _____

39.4 Write your own sentences beginning I wish … .

1 (somewhere you'd like to be now – on the beach, in New York, in bed etc.)
   I wish I _____
2 (something you'd like to have – a motorbike, more friends, lots of money etc.)
   _____
3 (something you'd like to be able to do – sing, travel more, cook etc.)
   _____
4 (something you'd like to be – famous, more intelligent, good at sport etc.)
   _____

if I had known ...   I wish I had known ...

A

Study this example situation:

> Last month Gary was in hospital for a few days. Rachel didn't know this.
> A few days ago they met by chance. Rachel said:
>
> **If I'd known** you were in hospital, **I would have gone** to visit you.
> (= I didn't know, so I didn't go to visit you)
>
> **If I'd known** = If I **had** known. This tells us that she *didn't* know before.

We use **if** + **had** (**'d**) ... to talk about the past (**if I'd known** / **if you'd done** etc.):
- ○ I didn't see you when you passed me in the street. **If I'd seen** you, I would have said hello.
- ○ They didn't go out last night. They would have gone out **if** they **hadn't been** so tired.
  (but they were tired)
- ○ **If you'd been looking** where you were going, you wouldn't have walked into the wall.
  (but you weren't looking)
- ○ The view was wonderful. I would have taken some pictures **if** I'd had (= if I **had had**)
  a camera with me. (but I didn't have a camera)

Compare:
- ○ I'm not hungry. **If** I **was** hungry, I would eat something. *(now)*
- ○ I wasn't hungry. **If** I **had been** hungry, I would have eaten something. *(past)*

B

We do *not* say 'if something would have happened'. We use **would** in the other part of the sentence:
- ○ **If** I **had seen** you, I **would have said** hello. (*not* If I would have seen you)

The short form **'d** can be **would** or **had**:
- ○ If I**'d seen** you,   (I**'d** seen = I **had** seen)
  I**'d have said** hello.   (I**'d** have said = I **would** have said)

C

We use **had done/known/been** etc. in the same way after **wish**.

I **wish** something **had happened** = I am sorry that it didn't happen
I **wish** something **hadn't happened** = I am sorry that it happened
- ○ I **wish** I**'d known** that Gary was ill. I would have gone to see him. (but I didn't know)
- ○ I feel sick. I **wish** I **hadn't eaten** so much. (I ate too much)
- ○ Do you **wish** you**'d studied** science instead of languages? (you didn't study science)

Compare:
- ○ **I'm glad I saw** him. (= I **saw** him)
- ○ **I wish I'd seen** him. (= I **didn't see** him)

We do *not* say 'wish ... would have ...'.
- ○ The weather was cold. I wish it **had been** warmer. (*not* I wish it would have been)

D

Compare **would** (**do**) and **would have** (**done**):
- ○ If I'd gone to the party last night, I **would be** tired now. (I am not tired now – *present*)
- ○ If I'd gone to the party last night, I **would have met** lots of people. (I didn't meet lots
  of people – *past*)

Compare **would have**, **could have** and **might have**:
- ○ If the weather hadn't been so bad, { we **would have gone** out.
    we **could have gone** out.
    (= we would have been able to go out)
    we **might have gone** out.
    (= maybe we would have gone out)

---

had done → Unit 15   **if I do / if I did →** Unit 38   **if I knew / I wish I knew →** Unit 39   **wish →** Unit 41

Exercises

40.1 **Put the verb into the correct form.**

1 I didn't see you. If __I'd seen__ (I / see) you, __I would have said__ (I / say) hello.
2 Sarah got to the station just in time to catch her train to the airport. If ....
.... (she / miss) the train, ... (she / miss) her flight too.
3 Thanks for reminding me about Lisa's birthday. .... (I / forget)
if .... (you / not / remind) me.
4 I didn't have your email address, so I couldn't contact you. If .... (I / have)
your email address, ... (I / send) you an email.
5 Their trip was OK, but .... (they / enjoy) it more if
the weather .... (be) better.
6 Sorry we're late. Our taxi got stuck in the traffic. .... (it / be)
quicker if .... (we / walk).
7 Why didn't you tell me about your problem? If .... (you / tell) me,
.... (I / try) to help you.
8 I'm not tired. If .... (I / be) tired, I'd go home now.
9 I wasn't tired last night. If .... (I / be) tired, I would have
gone home earlier.

40.2 **For each situation, write a sentence beginning with If.**

1 I wasn't hungry, so I didn't eat anything.
__If I'd been hungry, I would have eaten something.__
2 The accident happened because the road was icy.
If the road ....
3 I didn't know that you had to get up early, so I didn't wake you up.
If I ....
4 Unfortunately I lost my phone, so I couldn't call you.
....
5 Karen wasn't injured in the crash, because fortunately she was wearing a seat belt.
....
6 You didn't have any breakfast – that's why you're hungry now.
....
7 I didn't get a taxi because I didn't have enough money.
....
8 Dan didn't do well at school, so he couldn't go to university.
....

40.3 **Imagine that you are in these situations. For each situation, write a sentence with I wish.**

1 You've eaten too much and now you feel sick.
You say: __I wish I hadn't eaten so much.__
2 When you were younger, you never learned to play a musical instrument. Now you regret this.
You say: ....
3 You've painted the gate red. Now you think it doesn't look good. Red was the wrong colour.
You say: ....
4 You decided to travel by car, but the journey was long and tiring. Going by train would have been better.
You say: I wish we ....
5 Last year you went to New York with a friend. You didn't have time to do all the things you wanted to do.
You say: ....
6 You moved to a new flat a few months ago. Now you don't like your new flat. You think that moving
was a bad idea.
You say: ....

➔ Additional exercises 19–21 (pages 313–14)

A

We say 'wish somebody **luck / all the best / success**' etc. :
- ◯ **I wish you all the best** in the future.
- ◯ I saw Mark before the exam and **he wished me luck**.

We say 'wish somebody *something*' (**luck**, **happiness** etc.), but we do not say 'I wish something *happens*'. We use **hope** in this situation:
- ◯ I'm sorry you're not well. I **hope** you **feel** better soon. (*not* I wish you feel)

Compare **I wish** and **I hope**:
- ◯ **I wish** you **a pleasant stay** at this hotel.
- ◯ **I hope** you **enjoy** your stay at this hotel. (*not* I wish you enjoy)

B

We also use **wish** to say that we regret something, that something is not as we would like it. When we use **wish** in this way, we use the *past* (**knew/lived** etc.), but the meaning is *present*:
- ◯ I **wish** I **knew** what to do about the problem. (but I don't know)
- ◯ I **wish** you **didn't** have to go so soon. (but you have to go)
- ◯ Do you **wish** you **lived** near the sea? (you don't live near the sea)
- ◯ Jack's going on a trip to Mexico soon. I **wish** I **was** going too. (but I'm not going)

To say that we regret something that happened before, we use **wish** + **had** known / **had** said etc. :
- ◯ I **wish** I'd **known** about the party. I'd have gone if I'd known. (but I didn't know)
- ◯ It was a stupid thing to say. I **wish** I **hadn't said** it. (but I said it)

See also Units 39 and 40.

C

I wish I could (**do** something) = I regret that I cannot do it:
- ◯ I'm sorry you have to go. I **wish** you **could stay** longer. (but you can't)
- ◯ I've met that man before. I **wish** I **could remember** his name. (but I can't)

I wish I could have (**done** something) = I regret that I could not do it:
- ◯ I hear the party was great. I **wish** I **could have gone**. (but I couldn't go)

D

You can say '**I wish** something **would** happen'. For example:

I wish it **would** stop raining.

It's been raining all day. Tanya doesn't like it. She says:
I wish it **would stop** raining.

Tanya would like the rain to stop, but this will probably not happen.

We use **I wish** … **would** when we would like something to happen or change.

We often use **I wish** … **would** to complain about a situation:
- ◯ The phone has been ringing for five minutes. **I wish** somebody **would answer** it.
- ◯ **I wish** you'**d do** (= you **would** do) something instead of just sitting and doing nothing.

You can use **I wish** … **wouldn't** … to complain about things that people do repeatedly:
- ◯ **I wish** you **wouldn't keep** interrupting me. (= please stop interrupting me)

E

We use **I wish** … **would** … to say that we want something *to happen*. We do not use **I wish** … **would** … to say how we would like things *to be*. Compare:
- ◯ **I wish** Sarah **would** come. (= I want her to come)
- *but*   **I wish** Sarah **was** (*or* **were**) here now. (*not* I wish Sarah would be)

- ◯ **I wish** somebody **would buy** me a car.
- *but*   **I wish** I **had** a car. (*not* I wish I would have)

▸▸ would ➜ Unit 36   I wish I knew ➜ Unit 39   I wish I was / I wish I were ➜ Unit 39C
     I wish I had known ➜ Unit 40

Exercises

41.1 **Put in wish(ed) or hope(d).**

1 I ....*wish*.... you a pleasant stay at this hotel.
2 Enjoy your holiday. I .... you have a great time.
3 Goodbye. I .... you all the best for the future.
4 We said goodbye to each other and .... each other luck.
5 We're going to have a picnic tomorrow, so I .... the weather is nice.
6 Congratulations on your new job. I .... you every success.
7 Good luck in your new job. I .... it works out well for you.

41.2 **Complete the sentences.**

1 Jack is going on a trip to Mexico soon. I wish I ....*was going*.... too.
2 I'm very tired and I have so much to do. I wish I .... so tired.
3 You didn't tell me you were ill. Why not? I wish you .... me.
4 I don't have enough free time. I wish I .... more free time.
5 I can't make up my mind what to do. I wish I .... decide.
6 I bought these shoes, but now I don't like them. I wish I .... them.
7 We have to go out now and I don't want to go. I wish we .... to go out now.
8 Unfortunately I couldn't go to the wedding last month. I wish I could ....

41.3 **What do you say in these situations? Write sentences with I wish … would … .**

1 It's raining. You want to go out, but not in the rain.
   You say: ..*I wish it would stop raining.*..
2 You're waiting for Jane. She's late and you're getting impatient.
   You say to yourself: I wish she ....
3 You're looking for a job – so far without success. Nobody will give you a job.
   You say: I wish somebody ....
4 You can hear a dog barking. It's been barking a long time and you're trying to study.
   You say: ....

For the following situations, write sentences with I wish … wouldn't … .

5 Your friend is driving very fast. She always drives fast and you don't like this.
   You say to her: I wish you ....
6 Joe leaves the door open all the time. This annoys you.
   You say to Joe: ....
7 A lot of people drop litter in the street. You don't like this.
   You say: I wish people ....

41.4 **Put the verb into the correct form.**

1 It was a stupid thing to say. I wish ...*I hadn't said*... it. (I / not / say)
2 I'm fed up with this rain. I wish ...*it would stop*... . (it / stop)
3 It's a difficult question. I wish .... the answer. (I / know)
4 I really didn't enjoy the party. I wish .... (we / not / go)
5 I wish .... We've been waiting for 20 minutes. (the bus / come)
6 You're lucky to be going away. I wish .... with you. (I / can / come)
7 Our flat is rather small. I wish .... a bit bigger. (it / be)
8 I should have listened to you. I wish .... your advice. (I / take)
9 You keep interrupting me! I wish .... (you / listen)
10 You're always complaining. I wish .... all the time.
   (you / not / complain)
11 It's freezing today. I wish .... so cold. I hate cold weather. (it / not / be)
12 I wish .... It's horrible! (the weather / change)
13 I wish .... a piano. I'd love to have one. (I / have)
14 When we were in London last year, we didn't have time to see all the things we wanted to see.
   I wish .... there longer. (we / can / stay)

Passive 1 (**is done / was done**)

A   Study this example:

This house **was built** in 1981.

'This house **was built**' is *passive*.

Compare active and passive:

Somebody **built** | this house | in 1981. *(active)*
        subject   *object*

This house | **was built** in 1981. *(passive)*
  subject

When we use an *active* verb, we say *what the subject does*:
- ○   My grandfather was a builder. **He built** this house in 1981.
- ○   It's a big company. **It employs** two hundred people.

When we use a *passive* verb, we say *what happens to the subject*:
- ○   'How old is this house?'   '**It was built** in 1981.'
- ○   **Two hundred people are employed** by the company.

B   When we use the passive, who or what causes the action is often unknown or unimportant:
- ○   A lot of money **was stolen** in the robbery. (somebody stole it, but we don't know who)
- ○   **Is** this room **cleaned** every day? (does somebody clean it? – it's not important who)

If we want to say who does or what causes the action, we use **by**:
- ○   This house was built **by my grandfather**.
- ○   Two hundred people are employed **by the company**.

C   The passive is **be** (**is/was** etc.) + *past participle* (**done/cleaned/seen** etc.):
    (**be**) **done**   (**be**) **cleaned**   (**be**) **damaged**   (**be**) **built**   (**be**) **seen** etc.

The *past participle* often ends in -**ed** (clean**ed**/damag**ed** etc.), but many important verbs are
irregular (**built/done/stolen** etc.). See Appendix 1.

Compare active and passive, *present simple* and *past simple*:

Present simple

active: **clean**(**s**) / **see**(**s**) etc.

passive: **am/is/are** + **cleaned/seen** etc.

Somebody **cleans** this room every day.

This room **is cleaned** every day.

- ○   Many accidents **are caused** by careless driving.
- ○   I**'m not invited** to parties very often.
- ○   How **is** this word **pronounced**?

Past simple

active: **cleaned/saw** etc.

passive: **was/were** + **cleaned/seen** etc.

Somebody **cleaned** this room yesterday.

This room **was cleaned** yesterday.

- ○   We **were woken** up by a loud noise during the night.
- ○   'Did you go to the party?'   'No, I **wasn't invited**.'
- ○   How much money **was stolen** in the robbery?

>>   Passive 2–3 ➜ Units 43–44   by ➜ Unit 128

Exercises

42.1 Complete the sentences. Use these verbs in the correct form, present or past:

cause	damage	find	hold	injure	invite
make	overtake	own	send	show	surround

1 Many accidents ....are caused.... by careless driving.
2 Cheese .... from milk.
3 The roof of the building .... in a storm a few days ago.
4 A cinema is a place where films ....
5 You .... to the party. Why didn't you go?
6 This plant is very rare. It .... in very few places.
7 Although we were driving fast, we .... by a lot of other cars.
8 In the US, elections for president .... every four years.
9 There was an accident last night, but fortunately nobody ....
10 You can't see the house from the road. It .... by trees.
11 I never received the letter. It .... to the wrong address.
12 The company I work for .... by a much larger company.

42.2 Write questions using the passive. Some are present and some are past.

1 Ask about glass. (how / make?)   How is glass made?
2 Ask about television. (when / invent?) When ....
3 Ask about mountains. (how / form?) ....
4 Ask about DNA. (when / discover?) ....
5 Ask about silver. (what / use for?) ....

42.3 Put the verb into the correct form, present or past, active or passive.

1 a Two hundred people ...are employed... (employ) by the company.
   b The company ...employs... (employ) 200 people.
2 a Water .... (cover) most of the earth's surface.
   b How much of the earth's surface .... (cover) by water?
3 a While I was on holiday, my camera .... (steal) from my hotel room.
   b While I was on holiday, my camera .... (disappear) from my hotel room.
4 a Robert's parents .... (die) when he was very young.
   b Robert and his sister .... (bring up) by their grandparents.
5 a The boat hit a rock and .... (sink) quickly.
   b Fortunately everybody .... (rescue).
6 a Bill .... (fire) from his job. He wasn't very good at it.
   b Sue .... (resign) from her job because she didn't enjoy it any more.
7 a It can be noisy living here, but it .... (not / bother) me.
   b It can be noisy living here, but I .... (not / bother) by it.
8 a Maria had an accident. She .... (knock) off her bike.
   b Maria had an accident. She .... (fall) off her bike.
9 a I haven't seen these flowers before. What .... (they / call)?
   b I haven't seen these flowers before. What .... (you / call) them?

42.4 Instead of using somebody, they, people etc., write a passive sentence.

1 Somebody cleans the room every day.   The room is cleaned every day .
2 They cancelled all flights because of fog.   All ....
3 Somebody accused me of stealing money.   .... money.
4 How do you use this word?   How .... used?
5 The price includes all taxes.   All .... in the price.
6 People warned us not to go out alone.   We ....
7 We don't use this office any more.   This ....
8 They invited five hundred people to the   Five hundred ....
   wedding.

Passive 2 (**be done** / **been done** / **being done**)

Infinitive

active: (to) **do/clean/see** etc.

Somebody **will clean** this room later.

passive: (to) **be** + **done/cleaned/seen** etc.

This room **will be cleaned** later.

- ○ The situation is serious. Something must **be done** before it's too late.
- ○ A mystery is something that can't **be explained**.
- ○ The music was very loud and could **be heard** from a long way away.
- ○ A new supermarket is going **to be built** next year.
- ○ Please go away. I want **to be left** alone.

Perfect infinitive

active: (to) **have** + **done/cleaned/seen** etc.

Somebody **should have cleaned** the room .

passive: (to) **have been** + **done/cleaned/seen** etc.

The room **should have been cleaned**.

- ○ I haven't received the letter yet. It might **have been sent** to the wrong address.
- ○ If you had locked the car, it wouldn't **have been stolen**.
- ○ There were some problems at first, but they seem **to have been solved**.

Present perfect

active: **have/has** + **done** etc.

The room looks nice. Somebody **has cleaned** it .

passive: **have/has been** + **done** etc.

The room looks nice. It **has been cleaned**.

- ○ Have you heard? The trip **has been cancelled**.
- ○ **Have** you ever **been bitten** by a dog?
- ○ 'Are you going to the party?' 'No, I **haven't been invited**.'

Past perfect

active: **had** + **done** etc.

The room looked nice. Somebody **had cleaned** it .

passive: **had been** + **done** etc.

The room looked nice. It **had been cleaned**.

- ○ The vegetables didn't taste good. They **had been cooked** too long.
- ○ The car was three years old, but **hadn't been used** very much.

Present continuous

active: **am/is/are** + **(do)ing**

Somebody **is cleaning** the room at the moment.

passive: **am/is/are** + **being (done)**

The room **is being cleaned** at the moment.

- ○ There's somebody walking behind us. I think we **are being followed**.
- ○ A new bridge **is being built** across the river. It will be finished next year.

Past continuous

active: **was/were** + **(do)ing**

Somebody **was cleaning** the room when I arrived.

passive: **was/were** + **being (done)**

The room **was being cleaned** when I arrived.

- ○ There was somebody walking behind us. I think we **were being followed**.

Passive 1, 3 → Units 42, 44

43.1 Complete these sentences. Use the following verbs in the passive:

> arrest   carry   cause   delay   ~~do~~   forget   keep   knock   know   make   repair   ~~send~~

Sometimes you need have (might have, would have etc.).

1 The situation is serious. Something must ....be done.... before it's too late.
2 I haven't received the letter yet. It might ....have been sent.... to the wrong address.
3 A decision will not .... until the next meeting.
4 These documents are important. They should always .... in a safe place.
5 This road is in bad condition. It should .... a long time ago.
6 The injured man couldn't walk and had to ....
7 If you hadn't shouted at the policeman, you wouldn't ....
8 I'm not sure what time I'll arrive tomorrow. I may ....
9 It's not certain how the fire started. It might .... by an electrical fault.
10 A new school is being built. The old one is going to .... down.
11 The election is next Sunday. The full results will .... on Tuesday.
12 Last week they weren't speaking to one another. Now they're happy again. The problem seems to
   ....

43.2 Make sentences from the words in brackets. Sometimes the verb is active, sometimes passive.

1 There's somebody behind us. (We / follow) ...We're being followed.
2 This door is a different colour, isn't it? (you / paint?) ...Have you painted it?
3 My bike has disappeared. (It / steal!) It ....
4 My umbrella has disappeared. (Somebody / take) Somebody ....
5 A neighbour of mine disappeared six months ago.
   (He / not / see / since then) He ....
6 I wonder how Jessica is these days.
   (I / not / see / for ages) I ....
7 A friend of mine was stung by a bee recently.
   (you / ever / sting / bee?) .... you
8 The bridge was damaged recently.
   (It / repair / at the moment) It ....
9 Tom's car was stolen recently.
   (It / not / find / yet) ....
10 I went into the room and saw that the table and chairs were not in the same place.
   (The furniture / move) The ....

43.3 Instead of using 'somebody', 'they' etc., write a passive sentence.

1 Somebody has cleaned the room. The ...room has been cleaned.... .
2 They are building a new road around the city.
   A .... around the city.
3 They have built two new hotels near the airport.
   Two .... near the airport.
4 When I last visited, they were building some new houses here.
   When I last visited, some ....
5 The meeting is now on 15 April. They have changed the date.
   The date of ....
6 I didn't know that somebody was recording our conversation.
   I didn't know that our ....
7 Is anyone doing anything about the problem?
   .... anything .... the problem?
8 The windows were very dirty. Nobody had cleaned them for ages.
   The windows were very dirty. They ....

Passive 3

A   I was offered … / we were given … etc.

Some verbs can have two objects. For example, **give**:

- My grandfather gave **me this watch**.
  - object 1   object 2

It is possible to make two passive sentences:

- **I was given** this watch (by my grandfather). *or*
  This watch was given to me (by my grandfather).

Other verbs which can have two objects are:

ask   offer   pay   show   tell

When we use these verbs in the passive, most often we begin with the *person*:

- **I've been offered** the job, but I don't think I want it. (= somebody has offered me the job)
- **You will be given** plenty of time to decide. (= we will give you plenty of time)
- I didn't see the original document, but **I was shown** a copy. (= somebody showed me a copy)
- Tim has an easy job – **he's paid a lot of money** to do very little. (= somebody pays him a lot)

B   I don't like being …

The passive of **doing/seeing** etc. is **being done / being seen** etc. Compare:

active: I don't like **people telling me** what to do.
passive: I don't like **being told** what to do.

- I remember **being taken** to the zoo when I was a child.
  (= I remember **somebody taking** me to the zoo)
- Steve hates **being kept** waiting. (= he hates **people keeping** him waiting)
- We climbed over the wall without **being seen**. (= without **anybody seeing** us)

C   I was born …

We say '**I was** born …' (*not* I am born):

- I **was born** in Chicago.
- Where **were** you **born**? (*not* Where are you born?) } *past*

but

- How many babies **are born** every day?   *present*

D   get

You can use **get** for the passive:

- There was a fight, but nobody **got hurt**. (= nobody **was** hurt)
- I don't **get invited** to many parties. (= **I'm** not invited)
- I'm surprised Liz **didn't get offered** the job. (= Liz **wasn't offered** the job)

We use **get** only when things *happen*. For example, you cannot use **get** in these sentences:

- Jessica **is liked** by everybody. (*not* gets liked – this is not a 'happening')
- Peter was a mystery man. Very little **was known** about him. (*not* got known)

We use **get** mainly in informal spoken English. You can use **be** in all situations.

We also use **get** in the following expressions (which are not passive in meaning):

get married, get divorced   **get dressed** (= put on your clothes)
get lost (= not know where you are)   **get changed** (= change your clothes)

Passive 1–2 ➔ **Units 42–43**

Exercises

44.1 **Complete the sentences using the correct form of the verb.**

1 I tried to contact Tom.
   I called his office but I ___was told___ (tell) that he was in a meeting.
2 Amy retired from her job recently.
   She _____ (give) a present by her colleagues.
3 I didn't know there was a meeting yesterday.
   I _____ (not / tell) about it.
4 Sarah's salary is very low.
   I don't understand why she _____ (pay) so little.
5 You will need to use this machine.
   Have you _____ (show) how it works?
6 I had an interview for a job recently. It wasn't easy.
   I _____ (ask) some questions that were very hard for me to answer.
7 They didn't tell us much about the project.
   We _____ (not / give) enough information.
8 I was surprised to get the job I applied for.
   I didn't expect _____ (offer) it.

44.2 **Complete the sentences using being + the following verbs (in the correct form):**

| bite | give | invite | ~~keep~~ | knock down | stick | treat |

1 Steve hates ___being kept___ waiting.
2 We went to the wedding without _____ .
3 I like giving presents and I also like _____ them.
4 It's a busy road and I don't like crossing it. I'm afraid of _____ .
5 How do you avoid _____ by mosquitoes?
6 I'm an adult. I don't like _____ like a child.
7 You can't do anything about _____ in a traffic jam.

44.3 **Complete the sentences using get or got + the following verbs (in the correct form):**

| ask | break | ~~hurt~~ | pay | steal | sting | stop | use |

1 There was a fight, but nobody ___got hurt___ .
2 Alex _____ by a bee while he was sitting in the garden.
3 These tennis courts don't _____ very often. Not many people want to play here.
4 I used to have a bike, but it _____ a few months ago.
5 Rachel works hard, but she doesn't _____ very much.
6 Please pack these things very carefully. I don't want anything to _____ .
7 People often want to know what my job is. I _____ that question a lot.
8 Last night I _____ by the police as I was driving home. One of the lights
   on my car wasn't working.

44.4 **Complete the sentences.**

1 I've been ___offered___ the job, but I don't think I'll accept it.
2 I ___don't___ get invited to many parties.
3 Which year _____ you born in?
4 I haven't been _____ any information yet.
5 I didn't know the way, so I got _____ .
6 He doesn't like _____ interrupted when he's speaking.
7 How did the window _____ broken? What happened?
8 She's a voluntary worker. She _____ get paid.
9 I _____ born in a small town in the north of the country.
10 We had to do what we did. We _____ given any choice.

→ **Additional exercises 22–24** (pages 314–15)   89

it is said that … he is said to …
he is supposed to …

Study this example situation:

GEORGE

George is very old. Nobody knows exactly how old he is, but:

It is said that he is 108 years old.

or He **is said to be** 108 years old.

Both these sentences mean: 'People say that he is 108 years old.'

You can use these structures with a number of other verbs, especially:

alleged   believed   considered   expected   known   reported   thought   understood

- Cathy loves running.
  It is said that she runs 10 miles a day. *or* **She is said to** run 10 miles a day.
- The police are looking for a missing boy.
  It is believed that the boy is wearing *or* **The boy is believed to** be wearing
  a white sweater and blue jeans. a white sweater and blue jeans.
- The strike started three weeks ago.
  It is expected that it will end soon. *or* **The strike is expected to** end soon.
- A friend of mine has been arrested.
  It is alleged that he stole a car. *or* **He is alleged to** have stolen a car.
- The two houses belong to the same family.
  It is said that there is a secret tunnel *or* **There is said to** be a secret tunnel
  between them. between them.

These structures are often used in news reports. For example, in a report about an accident:
- **It is reported that** two people were *or* **Two people are reported to** have
  injured in the explosion. been injured in the explosion.

supposed to …

You can use **supposed to** … in the same way as **said to** … :
- I want to see that film. It**'s supposed to be** good. (= people say it's good)
- There are many stories about Joe. He**'s supposed to have robbed** a bank many years ago.
- Fireworks **are supposed to have been invented** in China. Is it true?

Sometimes **supposed to** … has a different meaning. We use **supposed to** to say what is intended, arranged or expected. Often this is different from the real situation:
- The plan **is supposed to be** a secret, but everybody seems to know about it.
  (= the plan is intended to be a secret)
- What are you doing at work? You**'re supposed to be** on holiday.
  (= you arranged to be on holiday)
- Our guests **were supposed to come** at 7.30, but they were late.
- Jane **was supposed to phone** me last night, but she didn't.
- I'd better hurry. I**'m supposed to be meeting** Chris in ten minutes.

You're not supposed to do something = it is not allowed or advised:
- **You're not supposed to park** your car here. It's private parking only.
- Joe is much better after his illness, but **he's not supposed to exercise** too hard.

Exercises

45.1 Write these sentences in another way, beginning as shown. Use the <u>underlined</u> word each time.

1 It is <u>expected</u> that the strike will end soon.
  The strike _is expected to end soon._

2 It is <u>reported</u> that many people are homeless after the floods.
  Many people ....

3 It is <u>thought</u> that the thieves got in through a window in the roof.
  The thieves ....

4 It is <u>alleged</u> that the driver of the car was driving at 110 miles an hour.
  The driver ....

5 It is <u>reported</u> that the building has been badly damaged by the fire.
  The building ....

6 It is <u>said</u> that the company is losing a lot of money.
  The company ....

7 It is <u>believed</u> that the company lost a lot of money last year.
  The company ....

8 It is <u>expected</u> that the company will make a loss this year.
  The company ....

45.2 Complete the sentences. Use the words in brackets and any other necessary words.

1 A: What's the City Hotel like? Can you recommend it?
  B: I've never stayed there, but _it's supposed to be_ (it / supposed) very good.

2 A: How much are these paintings worth?
  B: I'm not sure, but .... (they / supposed) very valuable.

3 A: This looks an interesting building.
  B: Yes, ... (it / supposed) a prison a long time ago.

4 A: Is it true that your neighbours were lucky in the lottery?
  B: Yes, ... (they / supposed / win) a lot of money.

5 A: Is it possible to climb to the top of the tower?
  B: Yes, ... (the view / supposed) very nice.

6 A: I heard that Laura has gone away.
  B: Yes, ... (she / supposed / living) in London now.

45.3 Write sentences using **supposed to be** + the following:

on a diet	a flower	my friend	a joke	open every day	~~a secret~~	working

1 How is it that everybody knows about the plan? _It's supposed to be a secret._
2 You shouldn't criticise me all the time. You ....
3 I shouldn't be eating this cake really. I ....
4 I'm sorry for what I said. I was trying to be funny. It ....
5 What's this drawing? Is it a tree? Or maybe it ....
6 You shouldn't be playing a game now. ....
7 That's strange. The museum seems to be closed. ....

45.4 Write sentences with **supposed to ...** or **not supposed to ...** . Choose from the following verbs:

depart	lift	~~park~~	phone	put	start

1 You _'re not supposed to park_ your car here. It's private parking only.
2 We .... work at 8.15, but we rarely do anything before 8.30.
3 I .... Helen last night, but I completely forgot.
4 This door is a fire exit. We .... anything in front of it.
5 My flight .... at 10.15, but it didn't leave until 11.30.
6 Jonathan has a problem with his back. He .... anything heavy.

→ Additional exercises 22–24 (pages 314–15)   91

have something done

Study this example situation:

LISA

The roof of Lisa's house was damaged.
So she called a builder, and yesterday he came and repaired it.

Lisa **had** the roof **repaired** yesterday.

This means: Lisa arranged for somebody else to repair the roof. She didn't repair it herself.

If you **have something done**, you arrange for somebody to do it for you.
Compare:
- ○ Lisa **repaired** the roof. (= she repaired it herself)
- ○ Lisa **had** the roof **repaired**. (= she arranged for somebody else to repair it)

- ○ A: Did you **make** those curtains yourself?
     B: Yes, I like making things.
- ○ A: Did you **have** those curtains **made**?
     B: No, I made them myself.

Study the word order:

have	object	past participle
Lisa **had**	the roof	**repaired**.
Where did you **have**	your hair	**cut**?
We are **having**	the house	**painted**.
I think you should **have**	that coat	**cleaned**.
I don't like **having**	my picture	**taken**.

We say:
- ○ How often do you **have your car serviced**? (*not* have serviced your car)
- ○ Our neighbour is **having a garage built**. (*not* having built a garage)
- ○ Your hair looks nice. Did you **have it cut**?

get something done

You can say '**get** something done' instead of '**have** something done':
- ○ When are you going to **get the roof repaired**? (= have the roof repaired)
- ○ I think you should **get your hair cut** really short.

We also use **have something done** with a different meaning. For example:
- ○ Paul and Karen **had their bags stolen** while they were travelling.

This does not mean that they arranged for somebody to steal their bags. 'They **had their bags stolen**' means only: 'Their bags were stolen'.

With this meaning, we use **have something done** to say that something happens to somebody or their belongings:
- ○ Gary **had** his nose **broken** in a fight. (= his nose was broken)
- ○ Have you ever **had** your bike **stolen**?

Exercises

46.1 Tick (✓) the correct sentence, (a) or (b), for each picture.

SARAH

(a) Sarah is cutting her hair.
(b) Sarah is having her hair cut.

DAN

(a) Dan is cutting his hair.
(b) Dan is having his hair cut.

KATE

(a) Kate is painting the gate.
(b) Kate is having the gate painted.

SUE

(a) Sue is taking a picture.
(b) Sue is having her picture taken.

46.2 Put the words in the correct order.

1 (painted / had / a few weeks ago / the house)
We __had the house painted a few weeks ago.__

2 (serviced / car / once a year / her / has)
Sarah ....

3 (had / your / recently / tested / eyes / you?)
Have ....

4 (like / cut / my / having / don't / hair)
I ....

5 (fifteen pounds / have / cleaned / my suit / cost / to)
It ....

6 (as soon as possible / need / translated / to get / this document)
You ....

46.3 Write sentences in the way shown.

1 Lisa didn't repair the roof herself. She __had it repaired.__
2 I didn't cut my hair myself. I ....
3 We didn't clean the carpets ourselves. We ....
4 Ben didn't build that wall himself. He ....
5 I didn't deliver the flowers myself. I ....
6 Sarah didn't repair her shoes herself. She ....

46.4 Which goes with which?

1 My hair is getting long.	a I need to get it fixed.	1 __d__
2 I really like this picture.	b I'll have to get a new one made.	2 ....
3 The washing machine is broken.	c I need to get my teeth checked.	3 ....
4 I want to wear earrings.	d ~~I should get it cut.~~	4 ....
5 Can you recommend a dentist?	e I'm going to get my ears pierced.	5 ....
6 I've lost my key.	f I'm going to get it framed.	6 ....

46.5 Use the words in brackets to complete the sentences.

1 Did I tell you about Paul and Karen?
(They / their bags / steal) __They had their bags stolen.__

2 Security at the airport was strict.
(We / our bags / search) ....

3 I've had some good news!
(I / my salary / increase) I ....

4 Joe can't get a visa.
(He / his application / refuse) ....

93

Reported speech 1 (**he said that** …)

A Study this example situation:

I'm feeling ill.

PAUL

You saw Paul yesterday and you want to tell somebody
what he said.
There are two ways of doing this:

You can repeat Paul's words (direct speech):
Paul said, '**I'm feeling ill**.'

Or you can use reported speech:
Paul said **that he was feeling ill**.

Compare:

direct   Paul said, ' **I**   **am**   feeling ill.'   In writing we use these quotation
marks to show direct speech.

reported   Paul said that **he**   **was**   feeling ill.

B When we use reported speech, the main verb of the sentence is usually past (Paul **said** that … /
I **told** her that … etc.). The rest of the sentence is usually past too:
- ○ Paul **said** that he **was feeling** ill.
- ○ I **told** Lisa that I **didn't have** any money.

You can leave out **that**. So you can say:
- ○ Paul **said that** he was feeling ill. *or* Paul **said** he was feeling ill.

In general, the *present* in direct speech changes to the *past* in reported speech:
am/is → **was**	do/does → **did**	will → **would**
are → **were**	have/has → **had**	can → **could**
want/like/know/go etc. → **wanted/liked/knew/went** etc.		

See also Unit 48A.

Compare direct and reported speech:

You met Anna. Here are some of
the things she said in *direct* speech:

I**'ve** lost my phone.
I **want** to buy a car.
I **can't** come to the party on
Friday.
I **don't** have much free time.
My parents **are** fine.
I**'m** going away for a few days.
I**'ll** phone you when I **get** back.

ANNA

Later you tell somebody what Anna said.
You use *reported* speech:

- ○ Anna said that she **had** lost her phone.
- ○ She said that she **wanted** to buy a car.
- ○ She said that she **couldn't** come to
  the party on Friday.
- ○ She said that she **didn't** have much
  free time.
- ○ She said that her parents **were** fine.
- ○ She said that she **was** going away for a
  few days and **would** phone me when
  she **got** back.

C The *past simple* (**did/saw/knew** etc.) can stay the same in reported speech, or you can change it to the
past perfect (**had done / had seen / had known** etc.):
- ○ *direct*   Paul said: 'I **woke** up feeling ill, so I **didn't go** to work.'
-     *reported*   Paul said (that) he **woke** up feeling ill, so he **didn't go** to work. *or*
-             Paul said (that) he **had woken** up feeling ill, so he **hadn't gone** to work.

>>   Reported speech 2 → **Unit 48**   Reported questions → **Unit 50B**

Exercises

47.1 You talked to some friends of yours (Paul, Tom, Anna etc.). Read what they said on the left (direct speech). Later (the same day) you tell another friend what they said (reported speech). Complete the sentences.

		direct speech	*reported speech*
1	YOU:	Are you going to work today, Paul?	Paul didn't go to work today. He said
	PAUL:	No, I'm feeling ill.	<u>he was feeling</u> ill.
2	YOU:	Shall we walk to the station?	I wanted to walk to the station, but
	TOM:	No, it's too far. Let's get a taxi.	Tom said .... far.
3	YOU:	Have you been invited to the party?	Anna has been invited to the party but she
	ANNA:	Yes, but I don't want to go.	told me .... to go.
4	YOU:	When are you going away, Dan?	I asked Dan about his travel plans. He said
	DAN:	I'll let you know next week.	.... next week.
5	YOU:	Do you ever see Rachel these days?	I asked Ben about Rachel, but he told me
	BEN:	I haven't seen her for a while.	.... for a while.
6	YOU:	Where can I borrow a guitar?	I needed to borrow a guitar and Kate said
	KATE:	You can borrow mine.	....
7	YOU:	How's your job, Sue?	I asked Sue about her job. She said
	SUE:	I'm not enjoying it very much.	.... very much.
8	YOU:	Do you still have your car?	I asked James about his car. He told me
	JAMES:	No, I sold it a few months ago.	.... a few months ago.
9	YOU:	What's the name of the cafe we went to?	I asked Sarah the name of the cafe we went
	SARAH:	I don't know.	to but she said ....
10	YOU:	How many students are there in your class, Amy?	I asked Amy about her school and she told me ....
	AMY:	Twenty.	.... class.

47.2 Somebody says something to you which is not what you expected. Use your own ideas to complete your answers.

1 A: It's quite a long way from the hotel to the city centre.
  B: Is it? The man on the reception desk said <u>it was only five minutes' walk.</u>
2 A: Sue is coming to the party tonight.
  B: Is she? I saw her a few days ago and she said she ....
3 A: Sarah gets on fine with Paul.
  B: Does she? Last week you said .... each other.
4 A: Joe knows lots of people.
  B: That's not what he told me. He said .... anyone.
5 A: Jane will be here next week.
  B: Oh, really? When I spoke to her, she said .... away.
6 A: I'm going out tonight.
  B: Are you? I thought you said .... at home.
7 A: I speak French quite well.
  B: Do you? But earlier you said .... any other languages.
8 A: I haven't seen Ben recently.
  B: That's strange. He told me .... last weekend.

→ **Additional exercise 25** (page 316)

Reported speech 2

A

We do not always change the verb in reported speech. If the situation *is still the same*, it is not necessary to change the verb to the past. For example:

- ○ *direct*   Paul said, '**My** new job **is** boring.'
  reported Paul said that **his** new job **is** boring.
  (The situation is still the same. His job is still boring now.)
- ○ *direct*   Helen said, '**I want** to go to Canada next year.'
  reported Helen told me that **she wants** to go to Canada next year.
  (Helen still wants to go to Canada next year.)

You can also change the verb to the past:

- ○ Paul said that his new job **was** boring.
- ○ Helen told me that she **wanted** to go to Canada next year.

But if the situation has *changed* or *finished*, you need to use a past verb. Compare:

- ○ Paul left the room suddenly. He said '**I have to go**.' *(direct speech)*
  Paul left the room suddenly. He said (that) **he had to go**. *(not has to go)*

B

You need to use the past in reported speech when what was said is different from what is really true. For example:

You met Rachel a few days ago. She said:

- ○ Have you heard? **Joe is in hospital**.

Later that day you meet Joe in the street. You say:

- ○ Joe, this is a surprise. Rachel said you **were** in hospital. (*not* 'you are in hospital' – it's clear that he isn't)

Joe is in hospital.

RACHEL

Rachel said you **were** in hospital

JOE

C

say and **tell**

If you say *who* somebody is talking to, use **tell**:

- ○ Rachel **told me** that you were in hospital. (*not* Rachel said me)
- ○ What did you **tell the police**? (*not* say the police)

Otherwise use **say**:

- ○ Rachel **said** that you were in hospital.
  (*not* Rachel told that …)
- ○ What did you **say**?

TELL SOMEBODY

~~SAY SOMEBODY~~

You can '**say** something **to** somebody':

- ○ Anna **said** goodbye **to** me and left. (*not* Anna said me goodbye)
- ○ What did you **say to** the police?

D

We say '**tell** somebody **to** …' and '**ask** somebody **to** …'.

Compare direct and reported speech:

- ○ *direct*   '**Drink** plenty of water,' the doctor said to me.
  reported The doctor **told me to drink** plenty of water.
- ○ *direct*   '**Don't work** too hard,' I said to Joe.
  reported I **told Joe not to work** too hard.
- ○ *direct*   'Can you help me, please,' Jackie said to me.
  reported Jackie **asked me to help** her.

You can also say 'Somebody **said** (**not**) **to** do something':

- ○ Paul **said not to worry** about him. (*but not* Paul said me)

➤➤ Reported speech 1 ➔ **Unit 47**   Reported questions ➔ **Unit 50B**

Exercises

48.1 Here are some things that Sarah said to you earlier:

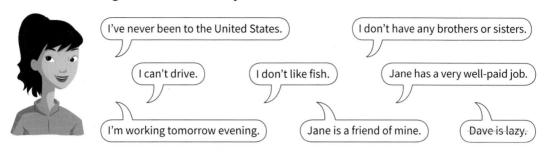

- I've never been to the United States.
- I don't have any brothers or sisters.
- I can't drive.
- I don't like fish.
- Jane has a very well-paid job.
- I'm working tomorrow evening.
- Jane is a friend of mine.
- Dave is lazy.

But later Sarah says something different to you. What do you say?

	Sarah	You
1	Dave works very hard.	*But you said he was lazy.*
2	Let's have fish for dinner.	But ....
3	I'm going to buy a car.	
4	Jane is always short of money.	
5	My sister lives in Paris.	
6	I think New York is a great place.	
7	Let's go out tomorrow evening.	
8	I've never spoken to Jane.	

48.2 Complete the sentences with **say** or **tell** (in the correct form). Use only one word each time.

1 Anna ___said___ goodbye to me and left.
2 .... us about your holiday. Did you have a nice time?
3 Don't just stand there! .... something!
4 I wonder where Sue is. She .... she would be here at 8 o'clock.
5 Dan .... me that he was bored with his job.
6 The doctor .... that I should rest for at least a week.
7 Gary couldn't help me. He .... me to ask Chris.
8 Gary couldn't help me. He .... to ask Chris.
9 Don't .... anybody what I .... It's a secret just between us.
10 'Did Kate .... you what happened?' 'No, she didn't .... anything to me.'

48.3 The following sentences are direct speech:

- Don't wait for me if I'm late.
- Mind your own business.
- Please slow down!
- Can you open your bag, please?
- Don't worry, Sue.
- Hurry up!
- Will you marry me?
- Do you think you could give me a hand, Tom?

Now choose one of these to complete each of the sentences below. Use <u>reported</u> speech.

1 Will was taking a long time to get ready, so I ___told him to hurry up___.
2 Sarah was driving too fast, so I asked ....
3 Sue was nervous about the situation. I told ....
4 I couldn't move the piano alone, so I ....
5 The security guard looked at me suspiciously and ....
6 The man started asking me personal questions, so I ....
7 Carl was in love with Maria, so he ....
8 I didn't want to delay Helen, so I ....

➜ Additional exercise 25 (page 316)

Questions 1

A

In questions the subject is usually after the first verb:

	subject + verb		verb + subject	
Tom	will	→	will	Tom?
you	have	→	have	you?
the house	was	→	was	the house?

- ☐ **Will Tom** be here tomorrow?
- ☐ **Have you** been working hard?
- ☐ When **was the house** built?

The subject is after the *first* verb:
- ☐ **Is Katherine** working today? (*not* Is working Katherine)

B

In *present simple* questions, we use **do/does**:

you	live	→	**do**	you **live**?
the film	starts	→	**does**	the film **start**?

- ☐ **Do** you **live** near here?
- ☐ What time **does** the film **start**?

In *past simple* questions, we use **did**:

you	sold	→	**did**	you **sell**?
the train	stopped	→	**did**	the train **stop**?

- ☐ **Did** you **sell** your car?
- ☐ Why **did** the train **stop**?

But do not use **do/does/did** if **who/what** etc. is the subject of the sentence. Compare:

who *object*

Emma phoned somebody .
  └── *object* ──┘

Who **did** Emma **phone**?

who *subject*

Somebody phoned Emma.
  └ *subject* ┘

Who **phoned** Emma?

In these examples, **who**/**what** etc. is the *subject*:
- ☐ **Who wants** something to eat? (*not* Who does want)
- ☐ **What happened** to you last night? (*not* What did happen)
- ☐ **How many people came** to the party? (*not* did come)
- ☐ **Which bus goes** to the centre? (*not* does go)

C

In questions beginning **who/what/which/where**, prepositions (**in, for** etc.) usually go at the end:
- ☐ **Where** are you **from**?
- ☐ **Who** do you want to speak **to**?
- ☐ **What** was the weather **like**?
- ☐ **Which** job has Tina applied **for**?

You can use *preposition* + **whom** in formal style:
- ☐ **To whom** do you wish to speak?

D

isn't it …? / **didn't you** …? etc. (negative questions)

We use negative questions especially to show surprise:
- ☐ **Didn't you** hear the doorbell? I rang it three times.
or when we expect the listener to agree with us:
- ☐ '**Haven't we** met before?'   'Yes, I think we have.'

Note the meaning of **yes** and **no** in answers to negative questions:
- ☐ '**Don't you** want to go?'   { '**Yes**.' (= Yes, I want to go)
                                    { '**No**.' (= No, I don't want to go)

We often use negative questions with **Why** …? :
- ☐ **Why don't we** eat out tonight? (*not* Why we don't eat)
- ☐ **Why wasn't Emma** at work yesterday? (*not* Why Emma wasn't)

>> Questions 2 → Unit 50   Question tags (do you? isn't it? etc.) → Unit 52

Exercises

49.1 **Ask Joe questions.**

JOE

1 (where / live)	Where do you live?
2 (born there?)	
3 (married?)	
4 (how long?)	
5 (what / do?)	
6 (what wife / do?)	
7 (children?)	
8 (how old?)	

In Manchester.
No, I was born in London.
Yes.
17 years.
I'm a journalist.
She's a doctor.
Yes, two boys.
12 and 15.

49.2 **Make questions with who or what.**

1	Somebody hit me.	Who hit you?
2	I hit somebody.	Who did you hit?
3	Somebody paid the bill.	Who
4	I'm worried about something.	What
5	Something happened.	
6	Diane said something.	
7	This book belongs to somebody.	
8	Somebody lives in that house.	
9	I fell over something.	
10	Something fell off the shelf.	
11	This word means something.	
12	Sarah was with somebody.	
13	I'm looking for something.	
14	Emma reminds me of somebody.	

49.3 **Put the words in brackets in the correct order.**

1 (when / was / built / this house?) When was this house built?
2 (how / cheese / is / made?)
3 (why / Sue / working / isn't / today?)
4 (what time / arriving / your friends / are?)
5 (why / was / cancelled / the meeting?)
6 (when / invented / paper / was?)
7 (where / your parents / were / born?)
8 (why / you / to the party / didn't / come?)
9 (how / the accident / did / happen?)
10 (why / happy / you / aren't?)
11 (how many / speak / can / languages / you?)

49.4 **Write negative questions from the words in brackets. In each situation you are surprised.**

1 A: We won't see Lisa this evening.
   B: Why not? (she / not / come / out with us?) Isn't she coming out with us?
2 A: I hope we don't meet Luke tonight.
   B: Why? (you / not / like / him?)
3 A: Don't go and see that film.
   B: Why not? (it / not / good?)
4 A: I'll have to borrow some money.
   B: Why? (you / not / have / any?)

99

Questions 2 (**do you know where** … **?** / **he asked me where** …)

Do you **know where** … ? / **I don't know why** … / **Could you tell me what** … ? etc.

We say: Where **has Tom** gone?

but **Do you know** where **Tom has** gone? (*not* has Tom gone)

When the question (**Where has Tom gone?**) is part of a longer sentence (**Do you know** … ? / **I don't know** … / **Can you tell me** … ? etc.), the word order changes. We say:

○ What time **is it**?	*but* **Do you know** what time **it is**?
○ Who **are those people**?	**I don't know** who **those people are**.
○ Where **can I** find Louise?	**Can you tell me** where **I can** find Louise?
○ How much **will it** cost?	**Do you have any idea** how much **it will** cost?

Be careful with **do/does/did** questions. We say:

○ What time **does the film start**?	*but* **Do you know** what time **the film starts**?
	(*not* does the film start)
○ What **do you mean**?	**Please explain** what **you mean**.
○ Why **did she leave** early?	**I wonder** why **she left** early.

Use **if** or **whether** where there is no other question word (**what**, **why** etc.):

○ Did anybody see you?	*but* I don't know **if** anybody saw me.
	or … **whether** anybody saw me.

He asked me where …

The same changes in word order happen in questions in reported speech. Compare:

○ *direct*	The police officer said to us 'Where **are you going** ?'
reported	The police officer asked us where **we were going** .
○ *direct*	Clare asked 'What time **do the shops close** ?'
reported	Clare wanted to know what time **the shops closed** .

In reported speech the verb usually changes to the past (**were**, **closed** etc.). See Unit 47.

Study these examples. You had a job interview and the interviewer asked you these questions:

> **Are you** willing to travel?

> **Why did you apply** for the job?

> What **do you do** in your spare time?

> **Can you speak** any other languages?

> How long **have you been working in** your present job?

> **Do you have** a driving licence?

Later you tell a friend what the interviewer asked you. You use *reported* speech:
- ○ She asked if (*or* whether) **I was** willing to travel.
- ○ She wanted to know what **I did** in my spare time.
- ○ She asked how long **I had been working** in my present job.
- ○ She asked why **I had applied** for the job. *or* … why I **applied** …
- ○ She wanted to know if (*or* whether) **I could** speak any other languages.
- ○ She asked if (*or* whether) **I had** a driving licence.

➤➤ Reported speech → Units 47–48

Exercises

50.1 **Which is right? Tick (✓) the correct alternative.**

1 a Do you know what time the film starts? ✓
    b Do you know what time does the film start?
    c Do you know what time starts the film?

2 a Why Amy does get up so early every day?
    b Why Amy gets up so early every day?
    c Why does Amy get up so early every day?

3 a I want to know what this word means.
    b I want to know what does this word mean.
    c I want to know what means this word.

4 a I can't remember where did I park the car.
    b I can't remember where I parked the car.
    c I can't remember where I did park the car.

5 a Why you didn't phone me yesterday?
    b Why didn't you phone me yesterday?
    c Why you not phoned me yesterday?

6 a Do you know where does Helen work?
    b Do you know where Helen does work?
    c Do you know where Helen works?

7 a How much it costs to park here?
    b How much does it cost to park here?
    c How much it does cost to park here?

8 a Tell me what you want.
    b Tell me what you do want.
    c Tell me what do you want.

50.2 **Put the words in the correct order.**

1 (it / you / what time / know / is) Do *you know what time it is* ?
2 (is / to the airport / far / it) How .... ?
3 (wonder / is / how / old / Tom) I ....
4 (they / married / been / have) How long .... ?
5 (they / married / how long / been / have / know)
   Do you .... ?
6 (tell / the station / you / me / is / where)
   Could .... ?
7 (in the accident / injured / anyone / don't / whether / know / was)
   I ....
8 (what / tomorrow / know / time / will / arrive / you / you)
   Do .... ?

50.3 **You were visiting London. You met a lot of people who asked you a lot of questions:**

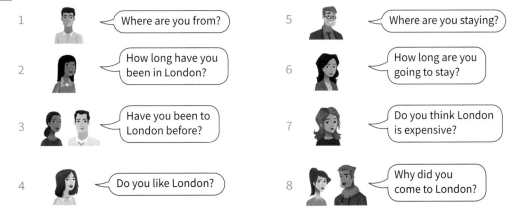

1 Where are you from?
2 How long have you been in London?
3 Have you been to London before?
4 Do you like London?
5 Where are you staying?
6 How long are you going to stay?
7 Do you think London is expensive?
8 Why did you come to London?

Now you tell a friend what people asked you. Use reported speech.

1 *He asked me where I was from.*
2 She asked me ....
3 They ....
4 ....
5 ....
6 ....
7 ....
8 ....

→ Additional exercise 25 (page 316)

Auxiliary verbs (**have/do/can** etc.)
I think so / I hope so etc.

A

In these sentences there is an *auxiliary* verb and a *main* verb:

	auxiliary	*main*	
I	**have**	**lost**	my keys.
She	**can't**	**come**	to the party.
The hotel	**was**	**built**	ten years ago.
Why	**do** you	**want**	to go home?

In these examples **have/can't/was/do** are *auxiliary* (= helping) verbs.

You can use an auxiliary verb when you don't want to repeat something:
- ○ 'Have you locked the door?' 'Yes, I **have**.' (= I have *locked the door*)
- ○ Gary wasn't working, but Laura **was**. (= Laura was *working*)
- ○ Jessica could lend me the money, but she **won't**. (= she won't *lend me the money*)

We use **do/does/did** for the present and past simple:
- ○ 'Do you like onions?' 'Yes, I **do**.' (= I *like onions*)
- ○ 'Does Simon live in London?' 'He **did**, but he **doesn't** any more.'

You can use auxiliary verbs to deny what somebody says (= say it is not true):
- ○ 'You're sitting in my place.' 'No, I**'m not**.' (= I'm not *sitting in your place*)
- ○ 'You didn't lock the door before you left.' 'Yes, I **did**.' (= I *locked the door*)

B

We use **have you**? / **isn't she**? / **are they**? etc. to show that we are interested in what somebody has said, or to show surprise:
- ○ 'I've just seen Steven.' 'Oh, **have you**? How is he?'
- ○ 'Lisa isn't very well today.' '**Isn't she**? What's wrong with her?'
- ○ 'It rained every day during our holiday.' '**Did it**? What a shame!'
- ○ 'James and Tanya are getting married.' '**Are they**? Really?'

C

We use auxiliary verbs with **so** and **neither**:
- ○ 'I'm tired.' '**So am I**.' (= I'm tired too)
- ○ 'I never read newspapers.' '**Neither do I**.' (= I never read newspapers either)
- ○ Sarah can't drive and **neither can Mark**.

Note the word order after **so** and **neither** (verb before subject):
- ○ I passed the exam and **so did Paul**. (*not* so Paul did)

Instead of **neither**, you can use **nor**. You can also use **not ... either**:
- ○ 'I don't know.' '**Neither** do I.' *or* '**Nor** do I.' *or* 'I do**n't either**.'

D

I think so / I suppose so etc.

You can say **I think so / I suppose so** etc. when we don't want to repeat something:
- ○ 'Are those people Korean?' '**I think so**.' (= I think *they are Korean*)
- ○ 'Is Kate working tomorrow?' '**I suppose so**.' (= I suppose *she is working tomorrow*)
- ○ 'Will you be at home this evening?' '**I expect so**.' (= I expect *I'll be at home ...*)

In the same way we say: **I hope so**, **I guess so** and **I'm afraid so**.

The usual negative forms are:

I think so / I expect so	→	I **don't think so** / I **don't expect so**
I hope so / I'm afraid so	→	I **hope not** / I**'m afraid not**
I guess so / I suppose so	→	I **guess not** / I **suppose not**

- ○ 'Is that woman American?' '**I think so**. / **I don't think so**.'
- ○ 'Do you think it will rain?' '**I hope so**. / **I hope not**.' (*not* I don't hope so)

>> American English → **Appendix 7**

Exercises

51.1 Complete each sentence with an auxiliary verb (do/was/could/might etc.). Sometimes the verb must be negative (don't/wasn't etc.).

1 I wasn't tired, but my friends ......were...... .
2 I like hot weather, but Ann ....
3 'Is Andy here?' 'He .... five minutes ago, but I think he's gone home now.'
4 I haven't travelled much, but Gary ....
5 Lisa said she might come and see us tomorrow, but I don't think she ....
6 I don't know whether to apply for the job or not. Do you think I ....?
7 'Please don't tell anybody what happened.' 'Don't worry. I ....'
8 'You never listen to me.' 'Yes, I ....!'
9 I usually work on Saturdays, but last Saturday I ....
10 'Do you think it's going to rain?' 'It .... Take an umbrella in case.'
11 'Are you and Chris going to the party?' 'I ...., but Chris ....'
12 'Please help me.' 'I'm sorry. I .... if I ...., but I ....'

51.2 You never agree with Amy. Answer in the way shown.

1	I'm hungry.	Are you? I'm not.
2	I don't like driving.	Don't you? I do.
3	I like football.	....
4	AMY I didn't enjoy the film.	....
5	I'm not tired.	....
6	I thought the exam was easy.	....

YOU

51.3 Tina tells you something. If the same is true for you, answer with So ... or Neither ... (as in the first example). Otherwise, ask Tina questions (as in the second example).

1	I'm not tired.	Neither am I.
2	I work hard.	Do you? What do you do?
3	I watched TV last night.	....
4	TINA I won't be at home tomorrow.	....
5	I like reading.	....
6	I'd like to live somewhere else.	....
7	I can't go out tonight.	....
8	I'm looking forward to the weekend.	....

YOU

51.4 What do you say to Sam? Use I think so, I hope not etc.

1 (You don't like rain.) SAM: Is it going to rain? YOU: ....I hope not.................... (hope)	5 (Jane has lived in Italy for many years.) SAM: Does Jane speak Italian? YOU: .... (suppose)
2 (You need more money.) SAM: Do you think you'll get a pay rise? YOU: .... (hope)	6 (You have to leave Sam's party early.) SAM: Do you have to leave already? YOU: .... (afraid)
3 (You're going to a party. You can't stand John.) SAM: Will John be at the party? YOU: .... (hope)	7 (You're not sure what time the film begins, but it's probably 7.30.) SAM: What time is the film? 7.30? YOU: .... (think)
4 (You're not sure whether Amy is married, but she probably isn't.) SAM: Is Amy married? YOU: .... (think)	8 (You are the receptionist at a hotel. The hotel is full.) SAM: Do you have a room for tonight? YOU: .... (afraid)

Question tags (**do you**? **isn't it**? etc.)

A Study these examples:

You haven't seen Lisa today, **have you**?

No, I haven't.

It was a good film, **wasn't it**?

Yes, it was great.

Have you? and **wasn't it**? are *question tags.* These are mini-questions that you can put on the end of a sentence.
In question tags, we use an auxiliary verb (**have**/**was**/**will** etc.).

We use **do**/**does**/**did** for the present and past simple (see Unit 51):
- ○ 'Karen plays the piano, **does**n't she?'   'Well, yes, but not very well.'
- ○ 'You didn't lock the door, **did** you?'   'No, I forgot.'

B Normally we use a *negative* question tag after a *positive* sentence:

... and a *positive* question tag after a *negative* sentence:

positive sentence + *negative tag*
Kate **will** be here soon,   **won't she**?
There **was** a lot of traffic,   **wasn't there**?
Joe **should** pass the exam,   **shouldn't he**?

negative sentence + *positive tag*
Kate **won't** be late,   **will she**?
They **don't** like us,   **do they**?
You **haven't** eaten yet,   **have you**?

Notice the meaning of **yes** and **no** in answer to a negative sentence:
- ○ 'You're **not** going out this morning, **are you**?'   { '**Yes.**'   (= Yes, I am going out)
                                                            '**No.**'   (= No, I am not going out)

C The meaning of a question tag depends on how you say it. If your voice goes *down*, you are not really asking a question. You expect the listener to agree with you:
- ○ 'It's a nice day, **isn't it**?'   'Yes, beautiful.'
- ○ 'Paul doesn't look well today, **does he**?'   'No, he looks very tired.'
- ○ 'Lisa's very funny. She's got a great sense of humour, **hasn't she**?'   'Yes, she has.'

But if the voice goes *up*, it is a real question:
- ○ 'You haven't seen Kate today, **have you**?'   'No, I haven't.'
   (= Have you seen Kate today?)

You can use a *negative sentence* + *positive tag* to ask for things or information, or to ask somebody to do something. The voice goes *up* at the end of the tag:
- ○ 'You couldn't do me a favour, **could you**?'   'It depends what it is.'
- ○ 'You don't know where Karen is, **do you**?'   'Sorry, I have no idea.'

D After **Let's** ... (= **Let us**) the question tag is **shall we**:
- ○ **Let's** go for a walk, **shall we**? (the voice goes *up*)

After **Don't** ..., the question tag is **will you**:
- ○ **Don't** be late, **will you**? (the voice goes *down*)

After **I'm** ..., the negative question tag is **aren't I**? (= am I not?):
- ○ 'I'm right, **aren't I**?'   'Yes, you are.'

>> Auxiliary verbs (**have**/**do**/**can** etc.) → Unit 51

Exercises

52.1 **Complete these sentences with a question tag.**

1	Kate won't be late,	_will she_ ?	No, she's never late.
2	You're tired,	_aren't you_ ?	Yes, a little.
3	You travel a lot,	?	Yes, I love travelling.
4	You weren't listening,	?	Yes, I was!
5	Sarah doesn't know Ann,	?	No, they've never met.
6	Jack's on holiday,	?	Yes, he's in Australia.
7	It didn't take long to get here,	?	No, just ten minutes.
8	You can speak German,	?	Yes, but not fluently.
9	They won't mind if I take a picture,	?	No, of course they won't.
10	There are a lot of people here,	?	Yes, more than I expected.
11	Let's go and have coffee,	?	Yes, let's do that.
12	This isn't very interesting	?	No, not really.
13	I'm too impatient	?	Yes, you are sometimes.
14	You wouldn't tell anyone,	?	No, of course not.
15	Helen has lived here a long time,	?	Yes, 20 years.
16	I shouldn't have lost my temper,	?	No, but that's all right.
17	He'd never met her before,	?	No, that was the first time.
18	Don't forget to call me,	?	No, I won't forget.

52.2 **In these situations you expect your friend to agree with you. Use a question tag in your sentences.**

1 You look out of the window. The sky is blue and the sun is shining. You say to your friend:
(beautiful day) _It's a beautiful day, isn't it?_

2 You're with a friend outside a restaurant. You're looking at the prices, which are very high.
You say: (expensive) It

3 You and a colleague have just finished a training course. You really enjoyed it. You say to your
colleague: (great) The course

4 Your friend's hair is much shorter than when you last met. You say to her/him:
(have / your hair / cut) You

5 You're listening to a woman singing. You like her voice very much. You say to your friend:
(a good voice) She

6 You're trying on a jacket in a shop. You look in the mirror and you don't like what you see.
You say to your friend:
(not / look / right) It

7 You and a friend are walking over a small wooden bridge. The bridge is old and some parts are
broken. You say:
(not / very safe) This bridge

52.3 **In these situations you are asking for information, asking people to do things etc.**

1 You need a pen. Perhaps Jane has one. Ask her.
Jane, you don't have a pen I could borrow, do you?

2 You have to move a heavy table. You want Joe to help you with it. Ask him.
Joe, you

3 You're looking for Sarah. Perhaps Lisa knows where she is. Ask her.
Lisa, you

4 You want to borrow a tennis racket. Perhaps Helen has one. Ask her.
Helen,

5 Anna has a car and you need a lift to the station. Perhaps she'll take you. Ask her.
Anna,

6 You're looking for your keys. Perhaps Robert has seen them. Ask him.
Robert,

A We say:
- ○ I **enjoy reading**. (*not* I enjoy to read)
- ○ Would you **mind closing** the door? (*not* mind to close)
- ○ Chris **suggested going** to the cinema. (*not* suggested to go)

Would you **mind closing** the door?

After **enjoy**, **mind** and **suggest**, we use -**ing** (*not* **to** …).

Some more verbs that are followed by -**ing**:

stop	recommend	admit	avoid	imagine
finish	consider	deny	risk	fancy

- ○ Suddenly everybody **stopped talking**. There was silence.
- ○ I'll do the shopping when I've **finished cleaning** the flat.
- ○ He tried to **avoid answering** my question.
- ○ I don't **fancy going** out this evening. (= I'm not enthusiastic about it)
- ○ Have you ever **considered going** to live in another country?
- ○ They said they were innocent. They **denied doing** anything wrong.

The negative form is **not** -**ing**:
- ○ When I'm on holiday, I enjoy **not having** to get up early.

B We also use -**ing** after:

> **give up** (= stop)
> **put off** (= delay until later)
> **go on** *or* **carry on** (= continue)
> **keep** *or* **keep on** (= do something continuously or repeatedly)

- ○ I've **given up buying** newspapers. I don't read them any more.
- ○ You shouldn't **put off telling** him what happened. You need to tell him now.
- ○ Katherine doesn't want to retire. She wants to **go on working**. *or* … to **carry on working**.
- ○ You **keep interrupting** when I'm talking. *or* You **keep on interrupting** …

C With some verbs you can use the structure *verb* + somebody + -**ing**:
- ○ You can't **stop people doing** what they want.
- ○ I can't **imagine George riding** a motorbike.
- ○ Did she really say that? I don't **remember her saying** that.
- ○ Sorry to **keep you waiting** so long.

D When you talk about finished actions, you can say **having done/stolen/said** etc. :
- ○ They admitted **having stolen** the money.

But it is not necessary to use **having** (done). You can say:
- ○ They admitted **stealing** the money.
- ○ I now regret **saying** that. *or* I now regret **having said** that.

E Other structures are possible with **admit**, **deny**, **suggest** and **recommend**. For example, you can say:
- ○ They **denied** (that) **they had done** anything wrong. (= They **denied doing** …)
- ○ Chris **suggested** (that) **we go** to the cinema. (= Chris **suggested going** …)
- ○ I **recommend** (that) **you travel** by train. (= I **recommend travelling** …)

>> **suggest** → Unit 34   **being done** (passive) → Unit 44B   Verb + **to** … → Unit 54
Verb + **to** … and -**ing** → Units 55C, 56–58   remember / regret / go on → Unit 56B
go on / carry on / keep on → Unit 141A

Exercises

53.1 Complete the sentences for each situation. Use -ing.

1 What shall we do? — We could go to the zoo.
She suggested ...going to the zoo.

2 Do you want to play tennis? — No, not really.
He didn't fancy ....

3 Let's go for a walk. — Good idea!
She suggested ....

4 You caused the accident. — No, I didn't.
He denied ....

5 Can you wait a few minutes? — Sure, no problem.
They didn't mind ....

6 You didn't tell the truth. — That's right. I didn't.
She admitted ....

53.2 Complete the sentences. Choose from these verbs (in the correct form):

answer	apply	forget	interrupt	listen	live
lose	make	pay	read	travel	try

1 He tried to avoid ....answering.... my question.
2 I'm trying to concentrate. Please stop .... so much noise!
3 I enjoy .... to music.
4 I considered .... for the job, but in the end I decided against it.
5 Have you finished .... the newspaper yet?
6 We need to change our routine. We can't go on .... like this.
7 It's better to avoid .... during the rush hour.
8 My memory is getting worse. I keep .... things.
9 I've put off .... this bill so many times. I really must do it today.
10 I've given up .... to learn Japanese. I was making no progress.
11 If you gamble, you risk .... your money.
12 Would you mind not .... me all the time? Let me speak!

53.3 Put the words in the right order.

1 Did she really say that? I (that / remember / her / saying / don't).
   I ..don't remember her saying that.
2 It's OK if you want to drive my car. I (driving / don't / it / you / mind).
   I ....
3 What a stupid thing to do! Can (imagine / so stupid / being / you / anybody)?
   Can ....
4 We can't control the weather. We (raining / stop / it / can't).
   We ....
5 I'll be as quick as I can. I (waiting / want / keep / you / don't / to).
   I ....

53.4 Use your own ideas to complete these sentences. Use -ing.

1 She's a very interesting person. I always enjoy ..talking to her.
2 I'm not feeling very well. I don't fancy ....
3 I'm afraid there aren't any chairs. I hope you don't mind ....
4 It was a beautiful day, so I suggested ....
5 The movie was very funny. I couldn't stop ....
6 My car is unreliable. It keeps ....

Verb + **to** … (**decide to** … / **forget to** … etc.)

A   After these verbs you can use **to** … *(infinitive)*:

offer	plan	manage	deserve
agree	arrange	fail	afford
refuse	hope	promise	learn
decide	forget	threaten	tend

- ○ It was a long way to walk, so we **decided to take** a taxi home.
- ○ Simon was in a difficult situation, so I **agreed to help** him.
- ○ I waved to Karen, but **failed to attract** her attention.
- ○ I like Dan, but I think he **tends to talk** too much.
- ○ How old were you when you **learnt to drive**?
  or … learnt **how** to drive?

Dan **tends to talk** too much.

The negative is **not to** … :
- ○ We **decided not to go** out because of the weather.
- ○ I **promised not to be** late.

After some verbs, we use **-ing** *(not* **to** …*)*. For example, **enjoy/think/suggest**:
- ○ I **enjoy reading**. *(not* enjoy to read*)*
- ○ Andy **suggested meeting** for coffee. *(not* suggested to meet*)*
- ○ Are you **thinking of buying** a car? *(not* thinking to buy*)*

For verb + **-ing**, see Units 53 and 62.

B   After **dare** you can use the infinitive with or without **to**:
- ○ I didn't **dare to tell** him. *or* I didn't **dare tell** him.

But after **dare not** *(or* **daren't**), we do not use **to**:
- ○ I **daren't tell** him what happened. *(not* I daren't to tell him*)*

C   We also use **to** … after **seem**, **appear**, **pretend** and **claim**. For example:
- ○ They **seem to have** plenty of money.
- ○ Ann **pretended not to see** me when she passed me in the street.

You can also use **to be -ing** *(continuous* infinitive) and **to have (done)** *(perfect* infinitive):
- ○ I **pretended to be reading** the newspaper. (= I pretended that I **was reading**)
- ○ Have you seen my keys? I **seem to have lost** them. (= it seems that I **have lost** them)
- ○ She **claimed not to have seen** me. (= she claimed that she **hadn't seen** me)

D   After these verbs you can use a question word (**what/how** etc.) + **to** … :

     ask   **know**   **decide**   **remember**   **forget**   **learn**   **explain**   **understand**   **wonder**

For example:

We **asked**	how	**to get**	to the station.
Have you **decided**	where	**to go**	on holiday?
I don't **know**	whether	**to apply**	for the job or not.
Do you **understand**	what	**to do?**	

also
show/tell/ask/advise/teach somebody **what/how/where** to do something:
- ○ Can somebody **show me how to use** this camera?
- ○ Ask Jack. He'll **tell you what to do**.

»   Verb + **-ing** ➜ **Unit 53**   Verb + object + **to** … (**want** etc.) ➜ **Unit 55**
     Verb + **to** … and **-ing** ➜ **Units 55C, 56–58**

Exercises

Unit
54

54.1 Complete the sentences for these situations.

1 Shall we get married? / Yes, let's.
They decided _to get married_ .

2 Please help me. / OK.
She agreed ....

3 Can I carry your bag for you? / No, thanks. I can manage.
He offered ....

4 Let's meet at 8 o'clock. / OK, fine.
They arranged ....

5 What's your name? / I'm not going to tell you.
She refused ....

6 Please don't tell anyone. / I won't. I promise.
She promised ....

54.2 Complete the sentences. Use a suitable verb.

1 Don't forget _to lock_ the door when you go out.
2 There was a lot of traffic, but we managed .... to the airport in time.
3 We couldn't afford .... in London. It's too expensive.
4 I can't play a musical instrument, but I'd like to learn .... the guitar.
5 I don't want Mark to know what happened. I decided not .... him.
6 We were all afraid to speak. Nobody dared .... anything.

54.3 Put the verb into the correct form, **to ...** or **-ing**. (See Unit 53 for verbs + -ing.)

1 When I'm tired, I enjoy _watching_ TV. It's relaxing. (watch)
2 I've decided .... for another job. I need a change. (look)
3 I'm not going anywhere! I refuse .... (move)
4 I'm not in a hurry. I don't mind .... (wait)
5 Tina ran in a marathon last week, but she failed .... (finish)
6 I wish that dog would stop .... It's driving me crazy. (bark)
7 They didn't know I was listening to them. I pretended .... asleep. (be)
8 We were hungry, so I suggested .... dinner early. (have)
9 Hurry up! I don't want to risk .... the train. (miss)
10 David is very quiet. He tends not .... much. (say)

54.4 Make a new sentence using the verb in brackets.

1 I've lost my keys. (seem) _I seem to have lost my keys._
2 Tom is worried about something. (appear) Tom appears ....
3 You know a lot of people. (seem) You ....
4 My English is getting better. (seem) ....
5 That car has broken down. (appear) ....
6 Rachel is enjoying her job. (seem) ....
7 They have solved the problem. (claim) ....

54.5 Complete each sentence using **what/how/where/whether** + these verbs:

do	~~get~~	go	put	ride	use

1 Do you know _how to get to_ the airport from here?
2 Would you know .... if there was a fire in the building?
3 You'll never forget .... a bike once you've learnt.
4 I've been invited to the party, but I haven't decided .... or not.
5 My room is very untidy. I've got so many things and I don't know .... them.
6 I have some clothes to wash. Can you show me .... the washing machine?

→ **Additional exercises 26–28** (pages 317–19)

109

Verb (+ object) + **to** … (**I want you to** …)

A We say:

verb	+	**to** …
want		
expect	**to go**	
ask	**to be**	
help	**to work**	
would like	etc.	
would prefer		

and

verb	+	object	+	**to** …
want				
expect				**to go**
ask		**somebody**		**to be**
help		**something**		**to work**
would like				etc.
would prefer				

- We **expected to be** late.
- Would you **like to go** now?
- He doesn't **want to know**.

- We expected **Dan to be** late.
- Would you like **me to go** now?
- He doesn't want **anybody to know**.

We do not usually say 'want that':
- Do you **want me to come** with you? (*not* want that I come)

You can use **help** with or without **to**. You can say:
- Can you help me **to move** this table? *or* Can you help me **move** this table?

B These verbs have the structure *verb* + *object* + **to** … :

verb	+	object	+	**to** …
tell				
advise				
remind				
warn				
invite				**to do**
encourage		**somebody**		**to be**
persuade				**to work**
get				etc.
force				
teach				
allow				
enable				

- It's not a nice hotel. I wouldn't **advise you to stay** there.
- Can you **remind me to call** Sam tomorrow?
- Joe said the switch was dangerous and **warned me not to touch** it.
- I didn't move the piano by myself. I **got somebody to help** me.
- Who **taught you to drive**?
- They don't **allow people to park** in front of the building.

In these examples, the verb is *passive* (**I was warned** / **we are allowed** etc.):
- **I was warned not to touch** the switch.
- **Are we allowed to park** here?

We do not use **suggest** with **to** … :
- Jane **suggested that I ask** you for advice. (*not* Jane suggested me to ask)

C We say '**make** somebody **do** something', '**let** somebody **do** something' (without **to**):
- I **made him promise** that he wouldn't tell anybody what happened.
  (*not* made him to promise)
- Hot weather **makes me feel** tired. (= causes me to feel tired)
- Her parents wouldn't **let her go** out alone. (= wouldn't allow her to go out)
- **Let me carry** your bag for you.

We say '**make** somebody **do**', but in the *passive* we say '(be) **made to do**' (with **to**):
- **We were made to wait** for two hours. (= They **made us wait** …)

| **suggest** → Units 34, 53 | **tell/ask** somebody **to** … → Unit 48D | Verb + **-ing** → Unit 53 |
| Verb + **to** … → Unit 54 | Verb + **to** … and **-ing** → Units 56–58 | **help** → Unit 57C |

Exercises

55.1 Complete the questions. Use *do you want me to ... ?* or *would you like me to ... ?* with these
verbs (and any other necessary words):

~~come~~   lend   repeat   show   shut   wait

1 Do you want to go alone, or _do you want me to come with you_ ?
2 Do you have enough money, or do you want .... ?
3 Shall I leave the window open, or would you .... ?
4 Do you know how to use the printer, or would .... ?
5 Did you hear what I said, or do .... ?
6 Can I go now, or do .... ?

55.2 Complete the sentences for these situations.

1 Meet me at the station. — OK.
She told _him to meet her at the station_ .

2 Why don't you come and stay with us? — That would be nice.
They invited him ....

3 Don't forget to call Joe. — No, I won't forget.
He reminded her ....

4 Be careful. — Don't worry. I will.
She warned ....

5 Can you give me a hand? — Sure.
He asked ....

55.3 Complete the second sentence so that the meaning is similar to the first sentence.

1 My father said I could use his car.
My father allowed _me to use his car._
2 I was surprised that it rained.
I didn't expect ....
3 Don't stop him doing what he wants.
Let ....
4 Tom looks older when he wears glasses.
Tom's glasses make ....
5 I think you should know the truth.
I want ....
6 At first I didn't want to apply for the
job, but Sarah persuaded me.
Sarah persuaded ....
7 My lawyer said I shouldn't say
anything to the police.
My lawyer advised ....
8 I was told that I shouldn't believe
everything he says.
I was warned ....
9 If you've got a car, you are able to get
around more easily.
Having a car enables ....

55.4 Which is right?

1 You aren't allowed ~~take~~ / to take pictures here. (to take *is correct*)
2 I'm in a difficult position. What do you advise me do / to do?
3 The film was very sad. It made me cry / to cry.
4 Lisa's parents always encouraged her study / to study hard at school.
5 Please don't interrupt me. Let me finish / to finish.
6 You can't make people do / to do things they don't want to do.
7 You can't force people do / to do things they don't want to do.
8 Sarah won't let me drive / to drive her car. She doesn't trust me.
9 Why did you change your decision? What made you change / to change your mind?
10 If you enter a country with a tourist visa, you are not allowed work / to work there.

Verb + -ing or to … 1 (remember, regret etc.)

A

Some verbs are followed by -ing and some are followed by to … .

Verbs that you can use with -ing (not to …):

admit	fancy	postpone
avoid	finish	risk
consider	imagine	stop
deny	keep (on)	suggest
enjoy	mind	

For examples, see Unit 53.

Verbs that you can use with to … :

afford	fail	offer
agree	forget	plan
arrange	hope	promise
decide	learn	refuse
deserve	manage	tend

For examples, see Unit 54.

B

Some verbs can be followed by -ing or to … with a difference of meaning:

remember

I **remember doing** something = I did it and now I remember this.
You **remember doing** something *after* you have done it.
- ○ I know I locked the door. I clearly **remember locking** it.
  (= I locked it, and now I remember this)
- ○ He could **remember driving** along the road just before the accident, but he couldn't remember the accident itself.

I **remembered to do** something = I remembered that I had to do it, so I did it.
You **remember to do** something *before* you do it.
- ○ I **remembered to lock** the door, but I forgot to shut the windows.
  (= I remembered that I had to lock it, and so I locked it)
- ○ **Remember to buy** some bananas.
  (= Don't forget to buy them)

regret

I **regret doing** something = I did it and now I am sorry about it:
- ○ I now **regret saying** what I said. I shouldn't have said it.
- ○ Do you **regret not** going to college?

I **regret to say** / **to tell** you / **to inform** you = I am sorry that I have to say:
- ○ (from a formal letter) I **regret to say** that we are unable to accept your offer.

go on

go on doing something = continue doing the same thing:
- ○ The president paused for a moment and then **went on talking**.
- ○ We need to change. We can't **go on living** like this.

go on to do something = do or say something new:
- ○ After discussing the economy, the president **went on to talk** about foreign policy.

C

We use the following verbs with -ing or to … with no difference of meaning:
    begin   **start**   **continue**   **intend**   **bother**

So you can say:
- ○ It **started raining**. *or* It **started to rain**.
- ○ Andy **intends buying** a house. *or* Andy **intends to buy** …
- ○ Don't **bother locking** the door. *or* Don't **bother to lock** …

Normally we do not use -ing after -ing:
- ○ It's **starting to rain**. (*not usually* It's starting raining)

Verb + -ing → Unit 53   Verb + to … → Units 54–55   Other verbs + -ing or to … → Units 57–58

Exercises

56.1 **Put the verb into the correct form, -ing or to … .**

1 They denied ......*stealing*...... the money. (steal)
2 I don't enjoy .... very much. (drive)
3 I can't afford .... away. I don't have enough money. (go)
4 Have you ever considered .... to live in another country? (go)
5 We were unlucky to lose the game. We played well and deserved .... (win)
6 Why do you keep .... me questions? Leave me alone! (ask)
7 Please stop .... me questions! (ask)
8 I refuse .... any more questions. (answer)
9 The driver of one of the cars admitted .... the accident. (cause)
10 Mark needed our help, and we promised .... what we could. (do)
11 I don't mind .... alone, but I'd rather be with other people. (be)
12 The wall was quite high, but I managed .... over it. (climb)
13 Sarah doesn't know about the meeting. I forgot .... her. (tell)
14 I've enjoyed .... to you. I hope .... you again soon. (talk, see)

56.2 **Tom can remember some things about his childhood, but he can't remember others. Write sentences with He remembers … or He doesn't remember … .**

1 He was in hospital when he was a small child. He can still remember this.
......*He remembers being in hospital*...... when he was a small child.
2 He cried on his first day at school. He doesn't remember this.
He doesn't .... on his first day at school.
3 Once he fell into the river. He remembers this.
He ....
4 He said he wanted to be a doctor. He doesn't remember this.
.... to be a doctor.
5 Once he was bitten by a dog. He doesn't remember this.
.... a dog.
6 His sister was born when he was four. He remembers this.
....

56.3 **Complete the sentences with a suitable verb in the correct form, -ing or to … .**

1 a Please remember ......*to lock*...... the door when you go out.
b He says we've met before, but I don't remember .... him.
c Someone must have taken my bag. I clearly remember .... it by the window and now it isn't there.
d When you see Steve, remember .... hello to him from me.
e A: You lent me some money a few months ago.
 B: Did I? Are you sure? I don't remember .... you any money.
f A: Did you remember .... your sister?
 B: No, I forgot. I'll phone her tomorrow.
2 a The course I did wasn't very good, but I don't regret .... it.
b I knew they were in trouble, but I regret .... I did nothing to help them.
c It started to get cold, and he regretted not .... his coat.
d I now regret .... my job. It was a big mistake.
3 a Ben joined the company nine years ago. He became assistant manager after two years, and a few years later he went on .... manager of the company.
b I can't go on .... here any more. I want a different job.
c When I came into the room, Lisa was reading a book. She looked up and said hello, and then went on .... her book.
d Food prices have gone up again. How are we going to manage if prices go on ....?

Verb + -ing or to ... 2 (try, need, help)

A try to ... and try -ing

try to do = attempt to do, make an effort to do:
- ○ I was very tired. I **tried to keep** my eyes open, but I couldn't.
- ○ Please **try to be** quiet when you come home. Everyone will be asleep.

try something or **try doing something** = do it as an experiment or test:
- ○ These cakes are delicious. You should **try one**. (= have one to see if you like it)
- ○ We couldn't find anywhere to stay. We **tried every hotel** in the town, but they were all full.
  (= we went to every hotel to see if they had a room)
- ○ A: The photocopier doesn't seem to be working.
  B: **Try pressing** the green button.
     (= press the green button – perhaps this will help to solve the problem)

Compare:
- ○ I **tried to move** the table, but it was too heavy. (so I couldn't move it)
- ○ I didn't like the way the furniture was arranged, so I **tried moving** the table to the other side of the room. But it didn't look right, so I moved it back again.
  (I **tried moving** it = I moved it to see if it looked better)

B need to ... and need -ing

I need to do something = it is necessary for me to do it:
- ○ He **needs to work** harder if he wants to make progress.
- ○ I don't **need to come** to the meeting, do I?

You can say that something **needs -ing**:
- ○ My phone **needs charging**. (= it **needs to be charged**)
- ○ Does your suit **need cleaning**? (= ... **need to be cleaned**)
- ○ It's a difficult problem. It **needs thinking about** carefully.
  (= it **needs to be thought about** carefully)

My phone **needs charging**.

Compare:
- ○ I need **to charge** my phone.
- *but* **My phone** needs **charging**.

C help and can't help

You can say **help to do** or **help do** (with or without **to**):
- ○ Everybody **helped to clean** up after the party. *or*
  Everybody **helped clean** up ...
- ○ Can you **help** me **move** this table? *or*
  Can you **help** me **to move** ...

I can't help doing something = I can't stop myself doing it:
- ○ I don't like him, but he has a lot of problems.
  I **can't help feeling** sorry for him.
- ○ She tried to be serious, but she **couldn't help laughing**.
  (= she couldn't stop herself laughing)
- ○ I'm sorry I'm so nervous. I **can't help it**.
  (= I can't help **being** nervous)

She **couldn't help laughing**.

Exercises

57.1 **Put the verb into the correct form.**

1 I was very tired. I tried ....*to keep*.... my eyes open, but I couldn't. (keep)
2 I tried .... the shelf, but I wasn't tall enough. (reach)
3 I rang the doorbell, but there was no answer. Then I tried .... on the window, but there was still no answer. (knock)
4 We tried .... the fire out, but without success. We had to call the fire brigade. (put)
5 Please leave me alone. I'm trying .... (concentrate)
6 Sue needed to borrow some money. She tried .... Carl, but he didn't have any. (ask)
7 Mr Bennett isn't here right now. Please try .... later. (call)
8 The woman's face was familiar. I tried .... where I'd seen her before. (remember)
9 If you have a problem with the computer, try .... it. (restart)

57.2 **For each picture, write a sentence with need(s) + one of the following verbs:**

> clean   cut   empty   ~~paint~~   tighten

1 This room isn't very nice. ...*It needs painting*............................. .
2 The grass is very long. It ....
3 The windows are dirty. They ....
4 The screws are loose. ....
5 The bin is full. ....

57.3 **Which is right?**

1 We spend too much time sitting down. We need ~~getting~~ / to get more exercise.
   (to get *is correct*)
2 These clothes are dirty. They all need washing / to wash.
3 My grandmother isn't able to look after herself any more. She needs looking / to look after.
4 I can't make a decision right now. I need thinking / to think about it.
5 Your hair is getting very long. It will need cutting / to cut soon.
6 I need a change. I need going / to go away for a while.
7 That shirt looks fine. You don't need ironing / to iron it.
8 That shirt looks fine. It doesn't need ironing / to iron.

57.4 **Put the verb into the correct form.**

1 I don't like him, but I can't help ....*feeling*.... sorry for him. (feel)
2 I've lost my phone. Can you help me .... for it? (look)
3 They were talking very loudly. We couldn't help .... what they said. (overhear)
4 He looks so funny. Whenever I see him, I can't help .... (smile)
5 The fine weather helped .... it a really nice holiday. (make)
6 Did you help .... the meeting? (organise)
7 I think about what happened all the time. I can't help .... about it. (think)
8 I can't help you .... a job. You have to find one yourself. (get)

Verb + -ing or to … 3 (like / would like etc.)

A like / love / hate

When you talk about repeated actions, you can use -ing or to … after these verbs.
So you can say:

- ◯ Do you **like getting** up early? *or* Do you **like to get** up early?
- ◯ Stephanie **hates flying**. *or* Stephanie **hates to fly**.
- ◯ I **love meeting** people. *or* I **love to meet** people.
- ◯ I don't **like being** kept waiting. *or* … **like to be** kept waiting.
- ◯ I don't **like** friends **calling** me at work. *or* … friends **to call** me at work.

but

(1) We use -ing (*not* to …) when we talk about a situation that already exists (or existed).
For example:

- ◯ Paul lives in Berlin now. He **likes living** there.
  (he lives there now and he likes it)
- ◯ Do you **like being** a student? (you are a student – do you like it?)
- ◯ The office I worked in was horrible. I **hated working** there. (I worked there and I hated it)

(2) There is sometimes a difference between **I like to do** and **I like doing**:

I like doing something = I do it and I enjoy it:
- ◯ I **like cleaning** the kitchen. (= I enjoy it.)

I like to do something = I choose to do it (but maybe I don't enjoy it):
- ◯ It's not my favourite job, but I **like to clean** the kitchen as often as possible.

Note that we use -ing (*not* to …) with **enjoy** and **mind**:
- ◯ I **enjoy cleaning** the kitchen. (*not* I enjoy to clean)
- ◯ I **don't mind cleaning** the kitchen. (*not* I don't mind to clean)

B would like / would love / would hate / would prefer

Would like / would love etc. are usually followed by **to** … :
- ◯ I**'d like** (= I **would** like) to go away for a few days.
- ◯ What **would** you **like to do** this evening?
- ◯ I **wouldn't like to go** on holiday alone.
- ◯ I**'d love to meet** your family.
- ◯ **Would** you **prefer to eat** now or later?

Compare **I like** and **I would like** (**I'd** like):
- ◯ I **like playing** tennis. / I **like to play** tennis. (= I like it in general)
- ◯ I**'d like to play** tennis today. (= I want to play today)

Would mind is followed by -ing:
- ◯ **Would** you **mind closing** the door, please? (*not* mind to close)

C I would like to have (done something)

I would like **to have done** something = I regret now that I didn't or couldn't do it:
- ◯ It's a shame we didn't see Anna. I **would like to have seen** her again.
- ◯ We**'d like to have gone** away, but we were too busy at home.

We use the same structure after **would love / would hate / would prefer**:
- ◯ Poor David! I **would hate to have been** in his position.
- ◯ I**'d love to have gone** to the party, but it was impossible.

>> enjoy/mind → Unit 53   would like → Units 37E, 55A   prefer → Unit 59

Exercises

58.1 Write sentences about yourself. Do you like these activities? Choose from these verbs:

like / don't like   love   hate   enjoy   don't mind

1 (flying) <u>I don't like flying.</u> or <u>I don't like to fly.</u>
2 (playing cards) ....
3 (being alone) ....
4 (going to museums) ....
5 (cooking) ....
6 (getting up early) ....

58.2 Make sentences using -ing or to … . Sometimes either form is possible.

1 Paul lives in Berlin now. It's nice. He likes it.
(He / like / live / there) <u>He likes living there.</u>
2 Jane is a biology teacher. She likes her job
(She / like / teach / biology) She ....
3 Joe always has his camera with him and takes a lot of pictures.
(He / like / take / pictures) ....
4 I used to work in a supermarket. I didn't like it much.
(I / not / like / work / there) ....
5 Rachel is studying medicine. She likes it.
(She / like / study / medicine) ....
6 Dan is famous, but he doesn't like it.
(He / not / like / be / famous) ....
7 Jennifer is a very careful person. She doesn't take many risks.
(She / not / like / take / risks) ....
8 I don't like surprises.
(I / like / know / things / in advance) ....

58.3 Complete the sentences with a verb in the correct form, -ing or to … . In two sentences either form is possible.

1 It's fun to go to new places – I enjoy <u>travelling</u> .
2 'Would you like .... down?' 'No, thanks. I'll stand.'
3 The music is very loud. Would you mind .... it down?
4 How do you relax? What do you like .... in your spare time?
5 When I have to take a train, I'm always worried that I'll miss it. So I like ....
to the station in plenty of time.
6 I enjoy .... busy. I don't like it when there's nothing to do.
7 I would love .... to your wedding, but I'm afraid I'll be away.
8 I don't like .... in this part of town. I want to move somewhere else.
9 Do you have a minute? I'd like .... to you about something.
10 If there's bad news and good news, I like .... the bad news first.
11 Shall we leave now, or would you prefer .... a little?
12 Steve wants to win every time. He hates ....

58.4 Write sentences using would … to have (done). Use the verbs in brackets.

1 It's a shame I couldn't go to the party. (like) <u>I would like to have gone to the party.</u>
2 It's a shame I didn't see the programme. (like) ....
3 I'm glad I didn't lose my watch. (hate) ....
4 It's too bad I didn't meet your parents. (love) ....
5 I'm glad I wasn't alone. (not / like) ....
6 We should have travelled by train. (prefer) ....

➜ Additional exercises 26–28 (pages 317–19)   117

prefer and would rather

A   prefer to … and prefer -ing

When you say what you prefer in general, you can use **prefer to** … or **prefer -ing**:

○   I don't like cities. I **prefer to live** in the country.   *or*   I **prefer living** in the country.

You can say:

prefer something	**to** something else
prefer doing something	**to doing** something else **rather than** (**doing**) something else
prefer to do something	**rather than** (**do**) something else

○   I **prefer** this coat **to** the other one.
○   I **prefer driving to travelling** by train.   *or*
    I **prefer driving rather than travelling** by train.
○   I **prefer to drive rather than travel** by train.
○   Sarah **prefers to live** in the country **rather than** in a city.

B   would prefer (I'd prefer …)

We use **would prefer** to say what somebody wants in a specific situation (not in general):

○   '**Would** you **prefer** tea or coffee?'   'Coffee, please.'

We say 'would prefer **to do** something' (*not usually* would prefer doing):

○   'Shall we go by train?'   '**I'd prefer to drive**.'   (= I **would** prefer …)
○   **I'd prefer to stay** at home tonight **rather than go** to the cinema.

C   would rather (I'd rather …)

I'd rather = I **would** rather. **I'd rather do** something = **I'd prefer to do** it.
We say **I'd rather** do (*not* to do). Compare:

○   'Shall we go by train?' { '**I'd rather drive**.'   (*not* to drive)
                          { '**I'd prefer to drive**.'
○   Which **would** you **rather do**,
    Which **would** you **prefer to do**, } go to the cinema or go shopping?

The negative is '**I'd rather not** …':

○   I'm tired. **I'd rather not go** out this evening, if you don't mind.
○   'Do you want to go out this evening?'   '**I'd rather not**.'

We say '**I'd rather do** one thing **than do** another':

○   **I'd rather stay** at home tonight **than go** to the cinema.

D   I'd rather somebody did something

We say '**I'd rather** you **did** something' (*not* I'd rather you do):

○   'Who's going to drive, you or me?'   '**I'd rather** you **drove**.'   (= I would prefer this)
○   'Jack says he'll repair your bike tomorrow, OK?'   '**I'd rather** he **did** it today.'
○   Are you going to tell Anna what happened, or **would** you **rather** I **told** her?

We use the *past* (**drove**, **did** etc.) here, but the meaning is present *not* past. Compare:

○   I'd rather **make** dinner now.
    I'd rather **you made** dinner now. (*not* I'd rather you make)

I'd rather **you didn't** (do something) = I'd prefer you not to do it:

○   **I'd rather you didn't tell** anyone what I said.
○   'Shall I tell Anna what happened?'   '**I'd rather you didn't**.'
○   'Are you going to tell Anna what happened?'   'No. **I'd rather** she **didn't** know.'

 >>   **would prefer** → Unit 58B   **prefer** (one thing) **to** (another) → Unit 136D

Exercises

59.1 **Which do you prefer? Write sentences using 'I prefer (something) to (something else)'.**

1 (driving / travelling by train)
   I prefer driving to travelling by train.

2 (basketball / football)
   I prefer ....

3 (going to the cinema / watching movies at home)
   I .... to ....

4 (being very busy / having nothing to do)
   I ....

Now rewrite sentences 3 and 4 using rather than:

5 (1) _I prefer to drive rather than travel by train._
   or _I prefer driving rather than travelling by train._

6 (3) I prefer ....

7 (4) ....

59.2 **Complete the sentences. Sometimes you need one word, sometimes more.**

A	B
1 Shall we walk home?	_I'd rather_ get a taxi.
2 Do you want to eat now?	I'd prefer _to wait_ till later.
3 Would you like to watch TV?	I'd .... to listen to some music.
4 Do you want to go to a restaurant?	I'd rather .... at home.
5 Let's go now.	.... wait a few minutes.
6 What about a game of tennis?	I'd prefer .... for a swim.
7 I think we should decide now.	I'd .... think about it for a while.
8 Would you like to sit down?	.... to stand.
9 Do you want me to come with you?	I'd rather .... alone.

Now use the same ideas to complete these sentences using than and rather than.

10 (1) I'd rather _get_ a taxi _than wait for a bus._

11 (3) I'd rather .... some music ....

12 (4) I'd prefer .... at home ....

13 (6) I'd rather .... for a swim ....

14 (7) I'd prefer .... about it for a while ....

59.3 **Complete the sentences using would you rather I ... .**

1 Are you going to make dinner or _would you rather I made it_ .... ?

2 Are you going to pay the bill or would you rather .... ?

3 Are you going to do the shopping or .... ?

4 Are you going to phone Tina or .... ?

59.4 **Use your own ideas (one or two words) to complete these sentences.**

1 'Shall I tell Anna what happened?' 'No, I'd rather she _didn't_ know.'

2 You can stay here if you want to, but I'd rather you .... with us.

3 I don't like this programme. I'd rather not .... it.

4 I'd rather work outdoors .... work in an office.

5 This is a private matter. I'd rather you .... tell anybody else.

6 The weather here isn't bad, but I'd rather it .... a little warmer.

7 I don't want to go to the match. I'd prefer .... it on TV.

8 'Do you mind if I open the window?' 'I'd rather you .... I'm feeling cold.'

9 I hate doing the shopping. I'd rather somebody else .... it.

10 I'd prefer to go to the beach .... go shopping.

A   If a preposition (**in/for/about** etc.) is followed by a verb, the verb ends in -**ing**:

	preposition	*verb* (-**ing**)	
Are you interested	**in**	**working**	for us?
I'm not good	**at**	**learning**	languages.
Kate must be fed up	**with**	**studying**.	
What are the advantages	**of**	**having**	a car?
Thanks very much	**for**	**inviting**	me to your party.
How	**about**	**meeting**	for lunch tomorrow?
Why don't you go out	**instead of**	**sitting**	at home all the time?
Amy went to work	**in spite of**	**feeling**	ill.

You can also say 'instead of **somebody** doing something', 'fed up with **people** doing something' etc. :
- ○ I'm fed up with **people** telling me what to do.

B   We say:

before -**ing**, **after** -**ing**:
- ○ **Before going** out, I phoned Sarah.   (*not* Before to go out)
- ○ What did you do **after leaving** school?

You can also say '**Before I went** out …' and '… **after you left** school'.

by -**ing** (to say *how* something happens):
- ○ You can improve your English **by reading** more.
- ○ She made herself ill **by** not **eating** properly.
- ○ Many accidents are caused **by** people **driving** too fast.
- ○ The burglars got into the house **by breaking** a window and **climbing** in.

without -**ing**:
- ○ We ran ten kilometres **without stopping**.
- ○ It was a stupid thing to say. I said it **without thinking**.
- ○ She needs to work **without** people **disturbing** her.   *or* … **without being** disturbed.
- ○ I have enough problems of my own **without having** to worry about yours.

C   **to** + -**ing** (look forward **to doing** something etc.)

We often use **to** + *infinitive* (**to do** / **to see** etc.):
- ○ We decided **to travel** by train.
- ○ Would you like **to meet** for lunch tomorrow?

But **to** is also a *preposition* (like **in/for/about/with** etc.). For example:
- ○ We went from Paris **to Geneva**.
- ○ I prefer tea **to coffee**.
- ○ Are you looking forward **to the weekend**?

If we use a *preposition* + *verb*, the verb ends in -**ing**:
- ○ I'm fed up **with travelling** by train.
- ○ How **about going** away this weekend?

So, when **to** is a preposition and it is followed by a verb, we use **to** -**ing**:
- ○ I prefer driving **to travelling** by train. (*not* to travel)
- ○ Are you looking forward **to going** on holiday? (*not* looking forward to go)

>> be/get used to -ing ➜ Unit 61   Verb + preposition + -ing ➜ Unit 62   while/when -ing ➜ Unit 68B
in spite of ➜ Unit 113   Prepositions ➜ Units 121–136

Exercises

60.1 **Complete the second sentence so that it means the same as the first.**

1 Why is it useful to have a car?
   What are the advantages of ..... *having a car* ..... ?

2 I don't intend to apply for the job.
   I have no intention of ..... .

3 Helen has a good memory for names.
   Helen is good at ..... .

4 You probably won't win the lottery. You have little chance.
   You have little chance of ..... .

5 Did you get into trouble because you were late?
   Did you get into trouble for ..... ?

6 We didn't eat at home. We went to a restaurant instead.
   We went to a restaurant instead of ..... .

7 We got into the exhibition. We didn't have to queue.
   We got into the exhibition without ..... .

8 Amy is 90 years old, but she's fit and healthy.
   Amy is fit and healthy despite ..... .

60.2 **Complete the sentences using by -ing. Choose from these verbs:**

borrow	break	drive	press	put	stand

1 The burglars got into the house ..... *by breaking* ..... a window.
2 I was able to reach the top shelf ..... on a chair.
3 You turn on the computer ..... the button at the back.
4 Kevin got himself into financial trouble ..... too much money.
5 You can put people's lives in danger ..... too fast.
6 We made the room look nicer ..... some pictures on the walls.

60.3 **Complete the sentences with a suitable word. Use only one word each time.**

1 We ran ten kilometres without ..... *stopping* ..... .
2 Dan left the hotel without ..... his bill.
3 It's a nice morning. How about ..... for a walk?
4 You need to think carefully before ..... an important decision.
5 It was a long trip. We were tired after ..... on a train for 36 hours.
6 I'm not looking forward to ..... away. I'd prefer to stay here.
7 I was annoyed because the decision was made without anybody ..... me.
8 After ..... the same job for ten years, Ellie felt she needed a change.
9 We got lost because we went straight on instead of ..... left.
10 I like these pictures you took. You're good at ..... pictures.
11 Can you touch your toes without ..... your knees?
12 We've decided to sell our car. Are you interested in ..... it?

60.4 **For each situation, write a sentence with I'm (not) looking forward to.**

1 You are going on holiday next week. How do you feel?
   I'm looking forward to going on holiday.

2 A good friend of yours is coming to visit you soon. It will be good to see her again. How do you feel?
   I'm .....

3 You're going to the dentist tomorrow. You don't enjoy visits to the dentist. How do you feel?
   I'm not .....

4 Rachel doesn't like school, but she's leaving next summer. How does she feel?
   .....

5 Joe and Helen are moving to a new apartment soon. It's much nicer than where they live now.
   How do they feel?
   .....

be/get used to … (I'm used to …)

A Study this example situation:

Lisa is American, but she lives in Britain.
When she first drove a car in Britain, driving on the left was a problem for her because:

She **wasn't used to it**.
She **wasn't used to driving** on the left.
(because Americans drive on the right)

But after some time, driving on the left became easier.
She **got used to driving** on the left.

Now it's no problem for Lisa:
She **is used to driving** on the left.

B **I'm used to** something = it is not new or strange for me

You can say:

be get	used to	something *or* **doing** something

- Paul lives alone. He has lived alone for a long time, so it is not strange for him. He**'s used to it**. He **is used to living** alone.
- I bought some new shoes. They felt a little strange at first because I **wasn't used to them**.
- Our new apartment is on a busy street. I expect we**'ll get used to the noise**, but at the moment it's very disturbing.
- Helen has a new job. She has to get up much earlier now than before – at 6.30. She finds this difficult because she **isn't used to getting** up so early.
- Katherine's husband is often away from home. She doesn't mind this. She**'s used to him being** away.

C We say 'be/get used **to doing** something' (*not* I'm used to do).
- Lisa is used **to driving** on the left. (*not* is used to drive)
- I'm used **to living** alone. (*not* I'm used to live)

When we say '**I am used to** …', **to** is a *preposition*:

- We're not used **to** { the noise.
it.
living here. (*not* live here) }

Compare **to** + *infinitive* (**to do**, **to live** etc.):
- We don't want **to live** here.

D Compare **I am used to doing** and **I used to do**:

I **am** used **to** (**doing**) something = it isn't strange or new for me:
- I'm used **to the weather** here.
- I'm used **to driving** on the left because I've lived in Britain a long time.

I **used to do** something = I did it regularly in the past but no longer do it. We use this only for the past (I **used** …), not for the present. See Unit 18.
- I **used to drive** to work every day, but these days I usually go by bike.
- We **used to live** just outside the town, but now we live near the centre.

>> used to (do) → Unit 18   to + -ing → Unit 60C

Exercises

61.1 Complete the sentences using **used to** + a suitable verb.

1 I'm not lonely. I don't need other people. I'm _used to being_ on my own.
2 I don't feel good. I stayed up until 3 am. I'm not _____ to bed so late.
3 Tomorrow I start a new job. I'll have to get _____ with new people.
4 My feet hurt. I can't go any further. I'm not _____ so far.
5 I like this part of town. I've been here a long time, so I'm _____ here.

61.2 Read about Sarah and Jack. Complete the sentences using **used to**.

1 Sarah is a nurse. A year ago she started working nights. At first it was hard for her.
   Sarah _wasn't used to working_ nights. It took her a few months to _____ it.
   Now, after a year, it's normal for her. She _____ nights.

2 Jack has to drive two hours to work every morning. Many years ago, when he first had to do this, it was hard for him and he didn't like it.
   When Jack started working in this job, he _____ driving two hours
   to work every morning, but after some time he _____ it. Now it's no
   problem for him. He _____ two hours every morning.

61.3 What do you say in these situations? Use **I'm (not) used to ...** .

1 You live alone. You don't mind this. You have always lived alone.
   FRIEND: Do you get lonely sometimes?
   YOU: No, _I'm used to living alone._
2 You sleep on the floor. It's OK for you. You have always slept on the floor.
   FRIEND: Wouldn't you prefer to sleep in a bed?
   YOU: No, I _____
3 You have to work long hours in your job. This is not a problem. You have always done this.
   FRIEND: You have to work long hours in your job, don't you?
   YOU: Yes, but I don't mind that. I _____
4 You've just moved from a village to a big city. It's busy and you don't like the crowds of people.
   FRIEND: How do you like living here now?
   YOU: It's different from living in a village. I _____

61.4 Read the situations and complete the sentences using **get/got used to**.

1 Some friends of yours have just moved into an apartment on a busy street. It is very noisy.
   They'll have to _get used to the noise_ .
2 The children got a new teacher. She was different from the teacher before her, but this wasn't
   a problem for the children. They soon _____ .
3 Kate moved from a big house to a much smaller one. She found it strange at first. She had to
   _____ in a much smaller house.
4 Anna has lived in Britain for ten years. She didn't like the weather when she first came, and she
   still doesn't like it. She can't _____ .
5 Lee got a new job, but his new salary was much less. So he had less money.
   He had to _____ .

61.5 Complete the sentences using only one word each time.

1 Lisa had to get used to _driving_ on the left.
2 Daniel used to _____ a lot of coffee. Now he prefers tea.
3 I feel very full after that meal. I'm not used to _____ so much.
4 I wouldn't like to share a room. I'm used to _____ my own room.
5 I used to _____ a car, but I sold it a few months ago.
6 When we were children, we used to _____ swimming very often.
7 There used to _____ a school here, but it was knocked down a few years ago.
8 I'm the boss here! I'm not used to _____ told what to do.

Verb + preposition + -ing
(succeed in -ing / insist on -ing etc.)

A

We use some verbs + *preposition* + *object*. For example:

	verb + preposition		+ object
We **talked**	about		the problem.
I **apologised**	for		what I said.

If the *object* is another verb, we use **-ing**:

	verb + preposition		+ **-ing**
We **talked**	about		**going** to South America.
You should **apologise**	for		not **telling** the truth.

You can use these verbs in the same way:

approve of	He doesn't **approve**	of		**swearing**.
decide against	We have **decided**	against		**moving** to London.
dream of	I wouldn't **dream**	of		**asking** them for money.
feel like	I don't **feel**	like		**going** out tonight.
insist on	They **insisted**	on		**paying** for the meal.
look forward to	Are you **looking forward**	to		**going** away?
succeed in	Has Paul **succeeded**	in		**finding** a job yet?
think of/about	I'm **thinking**	of/about		**buying** a house.

You can also say 'approve of **somebody** doing something', 'look forward to **somebody** doing something' etc. :

- ○ I don't approve **of people killing** animals as a sport.
- ○ We are all looking forward **to Andy coming** home next week.

B

Some verbs can have the structure *verb* + *object* + *preposition* + **-ing**.
For example:

	verb + object		+	preposition + **-ing**	
accuse ... of	He **accused**	me		of	**telling** lies.
congratulate ... on	We **congratulated**	Lisa		on	**winning** the first prize.
prevent ... from	What **prevented**	you		from	**coming** to see us?
stop ... from	The rain didn't **stop**	us		from	**enjoying** our holiday.
suspect ... of	Nobody **suspected**	the general		of	**being** a spy.
thank ... for	I **thanked**	everyone		for	**helping** me.

You can say '**stop** somebody **doing**' or '**stop** somebody **from doing**':
- ○ You can't **stop** me **doing** what I want.   *or*   You can't **stop** me **from doing** ...

Note this example with **not -ing**:
- ○ He accused me of **not telling** the truth.

Some of these verbs are often used in the *passive*. For example:
- ○ We **were accused of telling** lies. (*or* ... **accused of lying**.)
- ○ The general **was suspected of being** a spy.

Note that we say 'apologise **to somebody** for ...' :
- ○ I apologised **to them** for keeping them waiting. (*not* I apologised them)

>> **decide to ...** → Unit 54A   Preposition + **-ing** → Unit 60   Verb + preposition → **Units 132–136**

Exercises

62.1 Complete the sentences. Use only <u>one</u> word each time.

1 Our neighbours apologised for ......*making*.... so much noise.
2 I feel lazy. I don't feel like .... any work.
3 I wanted to go out alone, but Joe insisted on .... with me.
4 I'm fed up with my job. I'm thinking of .... something else.
5 We can't afford a car right now, so we've decided against .... one.
6 It took us a long time, but we finally succeeded in .... the problem.
7 I've always dreamed of .... a small house by the sea.
8 It's great that Amy and Sam are coming to visit us. I'm looking forward to .... them again.

62.2 Complete the sentences. Use a preposition + one of these verbs (in the correct form):

be	eat	get	~~go out~~	invite	steal
take off	tell	try	use	walk	

1 I don't feel ...*like going out*... this evening. I'm too tired.
2 The police stopped the car because they suspected the driver .... it.
3 Our flight was delayed. Bad weather prevented the plane ....
4 My phone is very old. I'm thinking .... a new one.
5 I didn't want to hear the story but Dan insisted .... me anyway.
6 I'm getting hungry. I'm really looking forward .... something.
7 I think you should apologise to Sarah .... so rude.
8 There's a fence around the lawn to stop people .... on the grass.
9 I'm sorry I can't come to your party, but thank you very much .... me.
10 The man who has been arrested is suspected .... a false passport.
11 I did my best. Nobody can accuse me .... not ....

62.3 Complete the sentences on the right.

1   YOU   KEVIN   *It was nice of you to help me. Thanks very much.*   Kevin thanked ...*me for helping him*... .

2   ANN   TOM   *I'll take you to the station. I insist.*   Tom insisted .... Ann ....

3   YOU   DAN   *I hear you got married. Congratulations!*   Dan congratulated me ....

4   SUE   JEN   *It was nice of you to come to see me. Thank you.*   Jen thanked ....

5   YOU   KATE   *Sorry I'm late.*   Kate apologised ....

6   YOU   JANE   *You don't care about other people.*   Jane accused ....

there's no point in -ing, it's worth -ing etc.

A We say:

there's no point in it's no use it's no good	**doing** something

- ○ **There's no point in having** a car if you never use it.
- ○ **There was no point in waiting** any longer, so we left.
- ○ **It's no use worrying** about what happened. There's nothing you can do about it.
- ○ **It's no good trying** to persuade me. You won't succeed.

We say '**no point in** …' but '**the point of** …':
- ○ There's **no point in** having a car.
- ○ What's **the point of** having a car if you never use it?

B We say:

it's worth it's not worth	**doing** something

- ○ It's a nice town. **It's worth spending** a few days there.
- ○ Our flight was very early in the morning, so **it wasn't worth going** to bed.

You can say that something is **worth it** or **not worth it**:
- ○ You should spend a couple of days here. **It's worth it**.
- ○ We didn't go to bed. **It wasn't worth it**.

You can also say that something is **worth doing**, a movie is **worth seeing** etc. :
- ○ It's a great movie. It's **worth seeing**.
- ○ Thieves broke into the house, but didn't take anything. There was nothing **worth stealing**.
- ○ It's an interesting idea. It's **worth thinking** about.

C We say:

have	trouble difficulty a problem	**doing** something

- ○ I had no **trouble finding** a place to stay. (*not* trouble to find)
- ○ Did you have **a problem getting** a visa?
- ○ People sometimes have **difficulty reading** my writing.

D We say:

spend waste	(time)	**doing** something

- ○ He **spent** hours **trying** to repair the clock.
- ○ I **waste** a lot of time **doing** nothing.

We also say '(be) **busy doing** something':
- ○ She said she couldn't meet me. She was too **busy doing** other things.

E We use **go -ing** for sports and other activities. For example:

| go sailing | go swimming | go fishing | go riding | go hiking |
| go surfing | go scuba diving | go skiing | go jogging | go camping |

- ○ How often do you **go swimming**?
- ○ We **went skiing** last year.
- ○ Tom isn't here. He's **gone shopping**.
- ○ I've never **been sailing**.

» gone and been … → Unit 7B

Exercises

63.1 **Which goes with which?**

1 It's a nice town.	a I don't believe you're sorry.
2 It's an interesting idea.	b We'll never find him.
3 It's no use standing here talking.	c It's not worth getting a taxi.
4 It's not important.	d We have to do something.
5 There's no point in looking for him.	e He won't change his opinion.
6 It's no good apologising to me.	f It's worth spending a few days here.
7 It's not worth arguing with him.	g It's not worth worrying about.
8 The hotel is a short walk from here.	h It's worth considering.

1 ___f___
2 _____
3 _____
4 _____
5 _____
6 _____
7 _____
8 _____

63.2 **Write sentences beginning There's no point … .**

1 Why have a car if you never use it?
   There's no point in having a car if you never use it.

2 Why work if you don't need money?
   ....

3 Don't try to study if you feel tired.
   ....

4 Why hurry if you have plenty of time?
   ....

63.3 **Complete the sentences.**

1 I managed to get a visa, but it was difficult.
   I had a problem ..._getting a visa_.. .
2 I find it hard to remember people's names.
   I have a problem ....
3 Lucy found a job easily. It wasn't a problem.
   She had no trouble ....
4 It will be easy to get a ticket for the game.
   You won't have any problems ....
5 It was easy for us to understand one another.
   We had no difficulty ....

63.4 **Complete the sentences. Use only one word each time.**

1 I waste a lot of time ...._doing_..... nothing.
2 How much time do you spend .... to and from work every day?
3 Karen is going on holiday tomorrow, so she's busy .... her things ready.
4 I waste too much time .... TV.
5 There was a beautiful view from the hill. It was worth .... to the top.
6 We need to stay calm. There's no point in .... angry.
7 Amy is learning to play the guitar. She spends a lot of time ....
8 Gary is enjoying his new job. He's busy .... on a new project.
9 I decided it wasn't worth .... for the job. I had no chance of getting it.
10 It's no good .... to escape. You won't be able to get out of here.

63.5 **Complete these sentences. Choose from the following and put the verb in the correct form.**

go riding	go sailing	go shopping	go skiing	go swimming

1 Ben lives by the sea and he's got a boat, so he often ...._goes sailing_.... .
2 It was a very hot day, so we .... in the lake.
3 There's plenty of snow in the mountains; so we'll be able to ....
4 Helen has two horses. She .... regularly.
5 Dan isn't here. He .... There were a few things he needed to buy.

to ... , for ... and so that ...

A

We say:
- ○ I called the restaurant **to reserve** a table.
- ○ What do you need **to make** bread?
- ○ We shouted **to warn** everybody of the danger.
- ○ This letter is **to confirm** the decisions we made at our meeting last week.
- ○ The president has a team of bodyguards **to protect** him.

In these examples **to** ... (**to reserve** ... / **to make** ... etc.) tells us the *purpose* of something: why somebody does something, has something, needs something etc., or why something exists.

B

We say 'a place **to park**', 'something **to eat**', 'work **to do**' etc. :
- ○ It's hard to find **a place to park** in the city centre. (= a place where you can park)
- ○ Would you like **something to eat**? (= something that you can eat)
- ○ Do you have **much work to do**? (= work that you must do)

Sometimes there is a preposition (**on**, **with** etc.) after the verb:
- ○ Is there **a chair to sit on**? (= a chair that I can sit on)
- ○ I get lonely if there's **nobody to talk to**.
- ○ I need **something to open** this bottle **with**.

We also say **money/time/chance/opportunity/energy/courage** (etc.) **to** do something:
- ○ They gave us **money to buy** food.
- ○ Do you have **much opportunity to practise** your English?
- ○ I need **a few days to think** about your proposal.

C

Compare **for** ... and **to** ...

for + *noun*	**to** + verb
○ We stopped **for petrol**. ○ I had to run **for the bus**.	○ We stopped **to get** petrol. ○ I had to run **to catch the bus**.

You can say '**for** somebody **to do** something':
- ○ There weren't any chairs **for us to sit on**, so we sat on the floor.

We use **for** (do)**ing** to say what something is used for:
- ○ This brush is **for washing** the dishes.

But we do not use **for** -ing to say why somebody does something:
- ○ I went into the kitchen **to wash** the dishes. (*not* for washing)

You can use **What** ... **for**? to ask about purpose:
- ○ **What** is this switch **for**? (= what is it used for?)
- ○ **What** did you do that **for**? (= why did you do that?)

D

so that

We use **so that** (*not* **to** ...) especially with **can/could** and **will/would**:
- ○ She's learning English **so that** she **can** study in Canada.
- ○ We moved to London **so that** we **could** see our friends more often.
- ○ I hurried **so that** I **wouldn't** be late.
  (= because I didn't want to be late)

You can leave out **that**. So you can say:
- ○ I hurried **so that** I wouldn't be late. *or* I hurried **so** I wouldn't be late.

Exercises

64.1 Choose from Box A and Box B to make sentences with **to** ... .

A
1	I shouted
2	I opened the box
3	I moved to a new apartment
4	I couldn't find a knife
5	I called the police
6	I called the hotel
7	I employed an assistant

B

I wanted to be nearer my friends
I wanted someone to help me with my work
I wanted to report the accident
~~I wanted to warn people of the danger~~
I wanted to see what was in it
I wanted to chop the onions
I wanted to find out if they had any rooms free

1   *I shouted to warn people of the danger.*
2   I opened the box ....
3   I ....
4   ....
5   ....
6   ....
7   ....

64.2 Complete these sentences using **to** + a suitable verb.

1   The president has a team of bodyguards ......*to protect*...... him.
2   I don't have enough time .... all the things I have to do.
3   I came home by taxi. I didn't have the energy ....
4   Would you like something .... ? Coffee? Tea?
5   Can you give me a bag .... these things in?
6   There will be a meeting next week .... the problem.
7   Do you need a visa .... to the United States?
8   I saw Helen at the party, but I didn't have a chance .... to her.
9   I need some new clothes. I don't have anything nice ....
10   They've passed their exams. They're going to have a party ....
11   I can't do all this work alone. I need somebody .... me.
12   Why are you so scared? There's nothing .... afraid of.

64.3 Put in **to** or **for**.

1   We stopped ....*for*.... petrol.
2   We'll need time .... make a decision.
3   I went to the dentist .... a check-up.
4   He's very old. He needs somebody .... take care of him.

5   Can you lend me money .... a taxi?
6   Do you wear glasses .... reading?
7   I put on my glasses .... read the letter.
8   I wish we had a garden .... the children .... play in.

64.4 Make one sentence from two, using **so that**.

1   I hurried. I didn't want to be late.
     I hurried ...*so that I wouldn't be late.*...
2   I wore warm clothes. I didn't want to get cold.
     I wore warm clothes ....
3   I gave Mark my phone number. I wanted him to be able to contact me.
     I gave Mark my phone number ....
4   We spoke very quietly. We didn't want anybody else to hear us.
     We spoke very quietly .... nobody else ....
5   Please arrive early. We want to be able to start the meeting on time.
     Please arrive early ....
6   We made a list of things to do. We didn't want to forget anything.
     We made a list of things to do ....
7   I slowed down. I wanted the car behind me to be able to overtake.
     I slowed down ....

Adjective + **to** …

hard to understand, interesting to talk to etc.

Compare sentences (a) and (b):

○ James doesn't speak clearly.
{ (a) **It** is hard to **understand** him .
{ (b) **He** is hard to **understand**.

Sentences (a) and (b) have the same meaning. Note that we say:
○ He is hard **to understand**. (*not* He is hard to understand him)

We use other adjectives in the same way. For example:

easy	nice	safe	cheap	exciting	impossible
difficult	good	dangerous	expensive	interesting	

○ Do you think it is **safe to drink this water**?
Do you think this water is **safe to drink**? (*not* to drink it)
○ The exam questions were very hard. It was **impossible to answer them**.
The exam questions were very hard. They were **impossible to answer**.
(*not* to answer them)
○ Nicola has lots of interesting ideas. It's **interesting to talk** to her.
Nicola is **interesting to talk to**. (*not* to talk to her)

We also use this structure with *adjective + noun*:
○ This is a **difficult question to answer**. (*not* to answer it)

nice of (you) to …

We say 'It's **nice of** somebody **to** …' :
○ It was **nice of** you **to take** me to the airport. Thank you very much.

We use other adjectives in the same way. For example:

kind	generous	careless	silly	stupid	inconsiderate	unfair	typical

○ It's **silly of Ruth to give** up her job when she needs the money.
○ I think it was **unfair of him to criticise** me.

sorry to … / surprised to … etc.

You can use *adjective +* **to** … to say how somebody reacts to something:
○ I'm **sorry to hear** that your mother isn't well.

We use other adjectives in the same way. For example:

glad	pleased	relieved	surprised	amazed	sad	disappointed

○ Was Julia **surprised to see** you?
○ It was a long and tiring journey. We were **glad to get** home.

You can use **to** … after **the next / the last / the only / the first / the second** (etc.):
○ **The next** train **to arrive** at platform 4 will be the 10.50 to Liverpool.
○ Everybody was late except me. I was **the only** one **to arrive** on time.
○ If I have any more news, you will be **the first to know**. (= the first person to know.)

You can say that something is **sure/likely/bound to** happen:
○ Carla is a very good student. She's **bound to pass** the exam. (= she is sure to pass)
○ It's possible I'll win the lottery one day, but it's not **likely to happen**. (= it's not probable)

>> afraid/interested/sorry ➜ Unit 66   it … ➜ Unit 84C   **enough** and **too** + adjective ➜ Unit 103

Exercises

65.1 **Write these sentences in another way, beginning as shown.**

1 It's hard to understand some things.   Some things *are hard to understand.*
2 It was difficult to open the window.   The window ....
3 It's impossible to translate some words.   Some words ....
4 It's expensive to maintain a car.   A ....
5 It's not safe to eat this meat.   This ....
6 It's easy to get to my house from here.   My ....

65.2 **Make sentences from the words in brackets.**

1 I couldn't answer the question.
   (difficult question / answer)   *It was a difficult question to answer* .
2 It's a very common mistake.
   (easy mistake / make)   It's ....
3 I like living in this town.
   (great place / live)   ....
4 I wonder why she said that.
   (strange thing / say)   ....

65.3 **Complete the sentences. Choose from the box.**

1 It's nice of Dan and Kate *to invite* me to their party.
2 I've been travelling a long time. Now I'm .... to be back home.
3 I heard about Tom's accident. I was relieved .... that he's OK.
4 It was nice .... to remember my birthday.
5 Let me know if you need any assistance. I'd be very pleased .... you.
6 I thought James was about 25. I was .... to discover he was 40.
7 It was inconsiderate of our neighbours .... so much noise.
8 My interview went well. I was disappointed .... to be offered the job.
9 It's .... of me to worry so much about things that are not important.

to hear
to help
~~to invite~~
to make
not
of you
silly
amazed
glad

65.4 **Complete the sentences. Use:** the first   the second   the last   the only

1 Nobody spoke before me. I was *the first person to speak.*
2 Everybody else arrived before Paul.
   Paul was ....
3 Emily passed the exam. All the other students failed.
   Emily ....
4 I complained to the manager. Another customer had already complained.
   I ....
5 Neil Armstrong walked on the moon in 1969. Nobody had done this before him.
   Neil Armstrong ....

65.5 **Complete the sentences using the words in brackets and a suitable verb.**

1 Carla is a very good student.
   (she / bound / pass) *She's bound to pass* the exam.
2 I'm not surprised you're tired after your trip.
   (you / bound / tired) .... after such a long journey.
3 Andy has a very bad memory.
   (he / sure / forget) .... anything you tell him.
4 I don't think you'll need an umbrella.
   (it / not / likely / rain) ....
5 The holidays begin this weekend.
   (there / sure / be) .... a lot of traffic on the roads.

to ... (afraid **to do**) and preposition + -ing (afraid **of** -ing)

A   **afraid to** (do) and **afraid of** (do)ing

I am **afraid to do** something =
I don't want to do it because it is dangerous or the result could be bad.
- ○   This part of town is dangerous. People are **afraid to walk** here at night.
  (= they don't walk here at night because it is dangerous)
- ○   James was **afraid to tell** his parents what had happened.
  (= he didn't tell them because he thought they would be angry)

I am **afraid of** something **happening** =
I am afraid that something bad will happen.
- ○   The path was icy, so we walked very carefully. We were **afraid of falling**.
  (= we were afraid that we would fall – *not* afraid to fall)
- ○   I don't like dogs. I'm always **afraid of being** bitten.
  (= I'm afraid that I will be bitten – *not* afraid to be bitten)

So, you are **afraid to do something** because you are **afraid of something happening** as a result:
- ○   I was **afraid to go** near the dog because I was **afraid of being** bitten.

B   **interested in** (do)ing and **interested to** (do)

I'm **interested in doing** something = I'm thinking of doing it, I would like to do it:
- ○   Let me know if you're **interested in joining** the club. (*not* to join)
- ○   I tried to sell my car, but nobody was **interested in buying** it. (*not* to buy)

I was **interested to hear/see/know** something = it was interesting for me. For example:
- ○   I was **interested to hear** that Tanya left her job.
  (= I heard this and it was interesting for me)
- ○   I'll ask Mike for his opinion. I would be **interested to know** what he thinks.
  (= it would be interesting for me to know what he thinks)
This structure is the same as **surprised to** ... / **glad to** ... etc. (see Unit 65C):
- ○   I was **surprised to hear** that Tanya left her job.

C   **sorry for** ... and **sorry to** ...

We use **sorry for** (doing) to apologise for something:
- ○   I'm **sorry for shouting** at you yesterday. (*not* sorry to shout)
You can also say:
- ○   I'm **sorry I shouted** at you yesterday.

We use **sorry to** ... to say that we regret something that happens:
- ○   I'm **sorry to hear** that Nicky lost her job. (*not* sorry for)
- ○   I've enjoyed my stay here. I'll be **sorry to leave**.

We also say '**I'm sorry to** ...' to apologise at the time we do something:
- ○   I'm **sorry to bother** you, but I need to ask you a question.

D

We say:

I **want to** (do), I'd **like to** (do) *but*	I'm **thinking of** (do)ing
I **hope to** (do)	I **dream of** (do)ing
I **failed to** (do)	I **succeeded in** (do)ing
I **allowed** them **to** (do)	I **prevented** them **from** (do)ing
I **plan to** (do)	I'm **looking forward to** (do)ing
I **promised to** (do)	I **insisted on** (do)ing

>>   Verb + **to** ... ➜ **Units 54–55**   Verb + preposition + **-ing** ➜ **Unit 62**   **sorry to** ... ➜ **Unit 65C**
Adjective + preposition ➜ **Units 130–131**   **sorry about/for** ➜ **Unit 130**

Exercises

66.1 **Write sentences using afraid to ... or afraid of -ing.**

1 The streets here are not safe at night.
(a lot of people / afraid / go / out) _A lot of people are afraid to go out._

2 We walked very carefully along the icy path.
(we / afraid / fall) _We were afraid of falling._

3 I don't usually carry my passport with me.
(I / afraid / lose / it) ....

4 I thought she would be angry if I told her what had happened.
(I / afraid / tell / her) ....

5 We ran to the station.
(we / afraid / miss / our train) ....

6 In the middle of the film there was a very horrifying scene.
(we / afraid / look) ....

7 The vase was very valuable, so I held it carefully.
(I / afraid / drop / it) ....

8 If there's anything you want to know, you can ask me.
(don't / afraid / ask) ....

9 I was worried because we didn't have much petrol.
(I / afraid / run out of petrol) ....

66.2 **Complete the sentences using interested in ... or interested to ... . Choose from these verbs:**

buy	hear	know	look	start	study

1 I'm trying to sell my car, but nobody is _interested in buying_ it.
2 Nicola is .... her own business.
3 I saw Joe recently. You'll be .... that he's getting married soon.
4 I didn't enjoy school. I wasn't ....
5 I went to a public meeting to discuss the plans for a new road. I was ....
how people felt about the project.
6 Paul doesn't enjoy sightseeing. He's not .... at old buildings.

66.3 **Complete the sentences using sorry for ... or sorry to ... . Use the verb in brackets.**

1 I'm _sorry to bother_ you, but I need to ask you something. (bother)
2 We were .... that you can't come to the wedding. (hear)
3 I'm .... bad things about you. I didn't mean what I said. (say)
4 It's a shame Alan is leaving the company. I'll be .... him go. (see)
5 I'm .... so much noise last night. (make)

66.4 **Complete the sentences in each group using the verb in brackets.**

1 a We wanted _to leave_ the building.
  b We weren't allowed .... the building.   } (leave)
  c We were prevented .... the building.

2 a Sam and Chris hoped .... the problem.
  b Sam failed .... the problem.   } (solve)
  c Chris succeeded .... the problem.

3 a I'm thinking .... away next week.
  b I'm planning .... away next week.
  c I'd like .... away next week.   } (go)
  d I'm looking forward .... away next week.

4 a Helen wanted .... me lunch.
  b Helen insisted .... me lunch.
  c Helen promised .... me lunch.   } (buy)
  d Helen wouldn't dream .... me lunch.

→ **Additional exercise 27** (page 318)   133

A Study this example situation:

Tom got into his car and drove off. You saw this.
You can say:

- ○ I saw Tom **get** into his car and **drive** off.

We say 'I saw him **do** something' (= he did it
and I saw this). In the same way, you can say:

hear listen to watch feel	somebody **do** something something **happen**

- ○ I didn't **hear** you **come** in. (you came in – I didn't hear this)
- ○ Lisa suddenly **felt** somebody **touch** her on the shoulder.

B Study this example situation:

Yesterday you saw Kate. She was waiting for a bus.
You can say:

- ○ I saw Kate **waiting** for a bus.

We say 'I saw her **doing** something' (= she was doing it and I saw this).
In the same way, you can say:

hear listen to watch feel smell find	somebody **doing** something something **happening**

- ○ I could **hear** it **raining**. (it was raining – I could hear it)
- ○ **Listen to** the birds **singing**!
- ○ Can you **smell** something **burning**?
- ○ We looked for Paul and finally we **found** him **sitting** under a tree **eating** an apple.

C Study the difference in meaning:

I **saw him do** something = he **did** something and I saw this.
I saw the complete action from start to finish:

- ○ He **jumped** over the wall and **ran** away. I saw this.
   → I **saw** him **jump** over the wall and **run** away.
- ○ They **went** out. I heard this. → I **heard** them **go** out.

I **saw him doing** something = he **was doing** something and I saw this.
I saw him *in the middle* of doing something (not from start to finish):

- ○ I saw Tom as I drove past in my car. He **was walking** along the street.
   → I **saw** Tom **walking** along the street.
- ○ I heard them. They **were talking**. → I **heard** them **talking**.

Sometimes the difference is not important and you can use either form:

- ○ I've never seen her **dance**. *or* I've never seen her **dancing**.

>> Past simple (**I did**) → Unit 5   Past continuous (**I was doing**) → Unit 6

Exercises

67.1 Complete the sentences with the verb in the correct form:

1   a   Tom doesn't have the keys. He ....*gave*.... them to Lisa. (give)
    b   Tom doesn't have the keys. I saw him .... them to Lisa. (give)
2   a   A car .... outside our house, and then it drove off again. (stop)
    b   We heard a car .... outside our house, and then it drove off again. (stop)
3   a   Ben gave me the envelope and watched me .... it. (open)
    b   Ben gave me the envelope and I .... it. (open)
4   a   Sarah is Canadian. I heard her .... she's from Toronto. (say)
    b   Sarah is Canadian. She .... she's from Toronto. (say)
5   a   A man .... over in the street, so we went to help him. (fall)
    b   We saw a man .... over in the street, so we went to help him. (fall)

67.2 You and a friend saw, heard or smelt something. Complete the sentences.

1   ....We saw Kate waiting for a bus...   .
2   We saw Clare .... in a restaurant.
3   We saw David and Helen ....
4   We could smell something ....
5   We could hear ....
6   ....

67.3 Complete the sentences. Use these verbs (in the correct form):

| crawl | cry | explode | ~~get~~ | happen | lie | put | ride | say | slam | ~~stand~~ | tell |

1   The bus stopped at the bus stop but I didn't see anybody ....*get*.... off.
2   I saw two people ....*standing*.... outside your house. I don't know who they were.
3   I thought I heard somebody .... 'Hi', so I turned round.
4   There was an accident outside my house, but I didn't see it ....
5   Listen. Can you hear a baby .... ?
6   I know you took the key. I saw you .... it in your pocket.
7   We listened to the old man .... his story from beginning to end.
8   Everybody heard the bomb .... It was a tremendous noise.
9   Oh! I can feel something .... up my leg. It must be an insect.
10 I looked out of the window and saw Dan .... his bike along the road.
11 I heard somebody .... a door in the middle of the night. It woke me up.
12 When I got home, I found a cat .... on the kitchen table.

-ing clauses (He hurt his knee **playing football**.)

A Study this example:

Kate is in the kitchen. She's making coffee.
You can say:
- ○ Kate is in the kitchen **making coffee**.
  └── *-ing clause* ──┘

You can use **-ing** in this way when two things happen at the same time:
- ○ A man ran out of the house **shouting**.
  (= he ran out of the house *and* he was shouting)
- ○ Do something! Don't just stand there **doing nothing**!
- ○ Be careful **crossing the road**.

We also use **-ing** when one action happens during another action:
- ○ Joe hurt his knee **playing football**. (= while he was playing)
- ○ Did you cut yourself **shaving**? (= while you were shaving)

You can also say '**while doing** something' and '**when doing** something':
- ○ Joe hurt his knee **while playing** football.
- ○ Be careful **when crossing** the road. (= when you are crossing)

B When one action happens before something else, we use **having (done)** for the first action:
- ○ **Having found** a hotel, we looked for somewhere to eat.
- ○ **Having finished** her work, she went home.

You can also say **after -ing**:
- ○ **After finishing** her work, she went home.

These structures are used more in written English than in spoken English.
When we begin a sentence with '**Having** (done something)' or '**After** (doing something)', we write a comma (**,**) after this part of the sentence:
- ○ **Having finished her work,** she went home.
                              ↑
                           comma

C You can also use **-ing** to explain something, or to say why somebody does something. The sentence usually begins with **-ing**:
- ○ **Feeling tired**, I went to bed early. (= because I felt tired)
  └── *-ing clause* ──┘

- ○ **Being** unemployed, he doesn't have much money. (= because he is unemployed)
- ○ **Not having** a car, she finds it difficult to get around.
  (= because she doesn't have a car)

We use **having (done)** for something that is complete before something else:
- ○ **Having seen** the film twice, I didn't want to see it again.
  (= because I had seen it twice)

These structures are used more in written English than in spoken English.
When we begin a sentence with **-ing** (**Feeling tired** … / **Not knowing** … / **Having seen** … etc.), we write a comma (**,**) after this part of the sentence.
- ○ **Not knowing what to do,** I called my friend to ask her advice.

Exercises

68.1 Choose from Box A and Box B to make sentences. Use -ing.

A
1 ~~Kate was in the kitchen.~~
2 Amy was sitting in an armchair.
3 Nicola opened the door carefully.
4 Sarah went out.
5 Lisa worked in Rome for two years.
6 Anna walked around the town.

B
She was trying not to make a noise.
She looked at the sights and took pictures.
She said she would be back in an hour.
She was reading a book.
~~She was making coffee.~~
She was teaching English.

1   Kate was in the kitchen making coffee.
2 Amy was sitting in an armchair ....
3 Nicola ....
4 ....
5 ....
6 ....

68.2 Put the words in the right order.

1 Joe (knee / football / his / hurt / playing) Joe   hurt his knee playing football.
2 I (in the rain / wet / got / very / walking)
   I ....
3 Laura (to work / had / driving / an accident)
   Laura ....
4 My friend (off / slipped / a bus / getting / and fell)
   My friend ....
5 Emily (trying / her back / a heavy box / to lift / hurt)
   Emily ....
6 Two people were (to put out / by smoke / the fire / overcome / trying)
   Two people were ....

68.3 Complete the sentences. Use Having + a suitable verb.

1   Having finished   her work, Katherine left the office and went home.
2 .... our tickets, we went into the theatre and took our seats.
3 .... the problem, I think we'll be able to find a solution.
4 .... he was hungry, Joe now says he doesn't want to eat anything.
5 .... his job recently, James is now unemployed.
6 .... most of his life in London, Sam has now gone to live in a small village
   in the country.

68.4 Make one sentence from two. Begin with -ing or Not -ing. Sometimes you need to begin with
Having ... . Don't forget the comma (,).

1 I felt tired. So I went to bed early.
   Feeling tired,   I went to bed early.
2 I thought they might be hungry. So I offered them something to eat.
   .... I offered them something to eat.
3 Robert is a vegetarian. So he doesn't eat any kind of meat.
   .... Robert doesn't eat any kind of meat.
4 I didn't have a phone. So I had no way of contacting anyone.
   .... I had no way of contacting anyone.
5 Sarah has travelled a lot. So she knows a lot about other countries.
   .... Sarah knows a lot about other countries.
6 I wasn't able to speak the local language. So I had trouble communicating.
   .... I had trouble communicating.
7 We had spent nearly all our money. So we couldn't afford to stay at a hotel.
   .... we couldn't afford to stay at a hotel.

Countable and uncountable 1

A

A noun can be *countable* or *uncountable*:

Countable
- ☐ I eat **a banana** every day.
- ☐ I like **bananas**.

Banana is a *countable* noun.

A countable noun can be singular (**banana**) or plural (**bananas**).

We can use numbers with countable nouns. So we can say **one banana**, **two bananas** etc.

Examples of nouns usually countable:
- ☐ Kate was singing **a song**.
- ☐ There's **a** nice **beach** near here.
- ☐ Do you have **a** ten-pound **note**?
- ☐ It wasn't your fault. It was **an accident**.
- ☐ There are no **batteries** in the radio.
- ☐ We don't have enough **cups**.

Uncountable
- ☐ I eat **rice** every day.
- ☐ I like **rice**.

Rice is an *uncountable* noun.

An uncountable noun has only one form (**rice**). There is no plural.

We cannot use numbers with uncountable nouns. We cannot say 'one rice', 'two rices' etc.

Examples of nouns usually uncountable:
- ☐ Kate was listening to **music**.
- ☐ There's **sand** in my shoes.
- ☐ Do you have any **money**?
- ☐ It wasn't your fault. It was bad **luck**.
- ☐ There is no **electricity** in this house.
- ☐ We don't have enough **water**.

B

You can use **a/an** with singular countable nouns:

    a beach   **a student**   **an umbrella**

You cannot use singular countable nouns alone (without **a/the/my** etc.):
- ☐ Do you want **a banana**?
  (*not* want banana)
- ☐ There's been **an accident**.
  (*not* There's been accident)

You can use *plural* countable nouns alone:
- ☐ I like **bananas**. (= bananas in general)
- ☐ **Accidents** can be prevented.

We do not use **a/an** with uncountable nouns. We do not say 'a sand', 'a music', 'a rice'.

But you can often use **a ... of**. For example:
    a bowl / a packet / a grain of rice

You can use uncountable nouns alone (without **the/my/some** etc.):
- ☐ I eat **rice** every day.
- ☐ There's **blood** on your shirt.
- ☐ Can you hear **music**?

C

You can use **some** and **any** with plural countable nouns:
- ☐ We sang **some songs**.
- ☐ Did you buy **any apples**?

We use **many** and **few** with plural countable nouns:
- ☐ We didn't take **many pictures**.
- ☐ I have a **few things** to do.

You can use **some** and **any** with uncountable nouns:
- ☐ We listened to **some music**.
- ☐ Did you buy **any** apple **juice**?

We use **much** and **little** with uncountable nouns:
- ☐ We didn't do **much shopping**.
- ☐ I have a **little work** to do.

➤➤ Countable and uncountable 2 ➜ **Unit 70**   **children / the children** ➜ **Unit 75**   **some and any** ➜ **Unit 85**
many/much/few/little ➜ **Unit 87**

Exercises

69.1 Some of these sentences need **a/an**. Correct the sentences where necessary.

1 Joe goes everywhere by bike. He doesn't have car.   He doesn't have **a** car.
2 Helen was listening to music when I arrived.   OK
3 We went to very nice restaurant last weekend.   ....
4 I brush my teeth with toothpaste.   ....
5 I use toothbrush to brush my teeth.   ....
6 Can you tell me if there's bank near here?   ....
7 My brother works for insurance company.   ....
8 I don't like violence.   ....
9 When we were in Rome, we stayed in big hotel.   ....
10 If you have problem, I'll try and help you.   ....
11 I like your suggestion. It's interesting idea.   ....
12 Can you smell paint?   ....
13 I like volleyball. It's good game.   ....
14 Lisa doesn't usually wear jewellery.   ....
15 Jane was wearing beautiful necklace.   ....
16 Does this city have airport?   ....

69.2 Complete the sentences using the following words. Use **a/an** where necessary.

~~accident~~	biscuit	blood	coat	decision	electricity
ice	interview	key	moment	~~music~~	question

1 The road is closed. There's been .... *an accident* ....
2 Listen! Can you hear .... *music* .... ?
3 I couldn't get into the house. I didn't have ....
4 It's very warm today. Why are you wearing ....?
5 Would you like .... in your drink?
6 Are you hungry? Have ....!
7 Our lives would be very difficult without ....
8 Excuse me, can I ask you .... ?
9 I'm not ready yet. Can you wait ...., please?
10 The heart pumps .... through the body.
11 We can't delay much longer. We have to make .... soon.
12 I had .... for a job yesterday. It went quite well.

69.3 Complete the sentences using the following words:

air	day	friend	joke	language	meat
patience	people	~~picture~~	queue	space	umbrella

Sometimes the word needs to be plural (-s), and sometimes you need to use a/an.

1 I had a camera with me, but I didn't take any .... *pictures* ....
2 There are seven .... in a week.
3 A vegetarian is a person who doesn't eat ....
4 Outside the cinema there was .... of people waiting to see the film.
5 I'm not good at telling ....
6 Last night I went out with some .... of mine.
7 There were very few .... in town today. The streets were almost empty.
8 I'm going out for a walk. I need some fresh ....
9 Paul always wants things quickly. He doesn't have much ....
10 I think it's going to rain. Do you have .... I could borrow?
11 How many .... can you speak?
12 Our flat is very small. We don't have much ....

Countable and uncountable 2

A Many nouns are sometimes countable, and sometimes uncountable. Usually there is a difference in meaning. Compare:

Countable	Uncountable
◯ Did you hear **a noise** just now? (= a specific noise)	◯ I can't work here. There's too much **noise**. (= noise in general)
◯ I bought **a paper** to read. (= a newspaper)	◯ I need **some paper** to write on. (= material for writing on)
◯ There's **a hair** in my soup! (= one single hair)	◯ You've got very long **hair**. (*not* hairs) (= all the hair on your head)
◯ This is **a** nice **room**. (= a room in a house)	◯ You can't sit here. There isn't **room**. (= space)
◯ I had some interesting **experiences** while I was travelling. (= things that happened to me)	◯ I was offered the job because I had a lot of **experience**. (*not* experiences) (= experience of that type of job)
◯ Enjoy your trip. Have **a** great **time**!	◯ I can't wait. I don't have **time**.

Coffee/tea/juice/beer etc. (drinks) are normally uncountable:
◯ I don't like **coffee** very much.
But you can say **a coffee** (= a cup of coffee), **two coffees** (= two cups) etc. :
◯ **Two coffees** and **an orange juice**, please.

B These nouns are usually uncountable:

accommodation	behaviour	damage	luck	permission	traffic
advice	bread	furniture	luggage	progress	weather
baggage	chaos	information	news	scenery	work

We do not normally use **a/an** with these nouns:
◯ I'm going to buy **some bread**. *or* … **a loaf of bread**. (*not* a bread)
◯ Enjoy your holiday! I hope you have good **weather**. (*not* a good weather)

These nouns are not usually plural (so we do not say 'breads', 'furnitures' etc.):
◯ Where are you going to put all your **furniture**? (*not* furnitures)
◯ Let me know if you need more **information**. (*not* informations)

News is uncountable, not plural:
◯ The **news was** unexpected. (*not* The news were)

Travel (*noun*) means 'travelling in general' (uncountable). We do not say 'a travel' to mean **a trip** or **a journey**:
◯ They spend a lot of money on **travel**.
◯ We had a very good **trip/journey**. (*not* a good travel)

Compare these countable and uncountable nouns:

Countable	Uncountable
◯ I'm looking for **a job**.	◯ I'm looking for **work**. (*not* a work)
◯ What **a** beautiful **view**!	◯ What beautiful **scenery**!
◯ It's **a** nice **day** today.	◯ It's nice **weather** today.
◯ We had a lot of **bags**.	◯ We had a lot of **baggage/luggage**.
◯ **These chairs** are mine.	◯ **This furniture** is mine.
◯ That's **a** good **suggestion**.	◯ That's good **advice**.
◯ There were a lot of **cars**.	◯ There **was** a lot of **traffic**.

▶▶ Countable and uncountable 1 → **Unit 69**   American English → **Appendix 7**

Exercises

70.1 **Which is correct?**

1 a The engine is making ~~strange noise~~ / a strange noise. What is it? (*a strange noise is correct*)
  b We live near a busy road so <u>there's a lot of noise / there are a lot of noises</u>.
2 a <u>Light / A light</u> comes from the sun.
  b I thought there was somebody in the house because there was <u>light / a light</u> on inside.
3 a I was in a hurry this morning. I didn't have <u>time / a time</u> for breakfast.
  b We really enjoyed our holiday. We had <u>great time / a great time</u>.
4 a Can I have <u>glass of water / a glass of water</u>, please?
  b Be careful. The window has been broken and there's <u>broken glass / a broken glass</u> on the floor.
5 a We stayed at a hotel. We had <u>very nice room / a very nice room</u>.
  b We have a big garage. There's <u>room / a room</u> for two cars.

70.2 **Which is correct?**

1 Did you have <u>nice weather</u> / ~~a nice weather~~ when you were away? (<u>nice weather</u> *is correct*)
2 We were very unfortunate. We had <u>bad luck / a bad luck</u>.
3 Our <u>travel / journey</u> from Paris to Moscow by train was very tiring.
4 When the fire alarm rang, there was <u>complete chaos / a complete chaos</u>.
5 Bad news <u>don't / doesn't</u> make people happy.
6 There's <u>some lovely scenery / a lovely scenery</u> in this part of the country.
7 I like my job, but it's <u>very hard work / a very hard work</u>.
8 I want to print some documents, but the printer is out of <u>paper / papers</u>.
9 The trip took a long time. There was <u>heavy traffic / a heavy traffic</u>.
10 <u>Your hair is / Your hairs are</u> too long. You should have <u>it / them</u> cut.

70.3 **Complete the sentences using the following words. Use the plural (-s) where necessary.**

advice	chair	damage	experience	experience
furniture	hair	~~luggage~~	permission	progress

1 We didn't have much ....**luggage**.... – just two small bags.
2 We have no .... , not even a bed or a table.
3 There is room for everybody to sit down. There are plenty of ....
4 Who is that woman with short .... ? Do you know her?
5 Carla's English is better than it was. She's made good ....
6 If you want to take pictures here, you need to ask for ....
7 I didn't know what I should do, so I asked Chris for ....
8 I don't think Dan should get the job. He doesn't have enough ....
9 Kate has done many interesting things. She could write a book about her ....
10 The .... caused by the storm will cost a lot to repair.

70.4 **What do you say in these situations? Use the word in brackets in your sentence.**

1 Your friends have just arrived at the station. You can't see any cases or bags. You ask:
  (luggage) Do ...**you have any luggage**............................ ?
2 You go to a tourist office. You want to know about places to visit in the town.
  (information) I'd like ....
3 You are a student. You want your teacher to advise you about which courses to do. You say:
  (advice) Can you give .... ?
4 You applied for a job and you've just heard that you were successful. You call Tom and say:
  (good news) Hi, Tom. I .... I got the job!
5 You are at the top of a mountain. You can see a very long way. It's beautiful. You say:
  (view) It .... , isn't it?
6 You look out of the window. The weather is horrible: cold, wet and windy. You say:
  (weather) What .... !

Countable nouns with **a/an** and **some**

A Countable nouns can be *singular* or *plural*:

a **dog**	a **child**	the **evening**	this **party**	an **umbrella**
dogs	some **children**	the **evenings**	these **parties**	two **umbrellas**

Before singular countable nouns you can use **a/an**:
- ○ Bye! Have **a** nice **evening**.
- ○ Do you need **an umbrella**?

You cannot use singular countable nouns alone (without **a/the/my** etc.):
- ○ She never wears **a hat**. (*not* wears hat)
- ○ Be careful of **the dog**.
- ○ What **a** beautiful **day**!
- ○ Did you hurt **your leg**?

B We use **a/an** … to say what kind of thing something is, or what kind of person somebody is:
- ○ That's a **nice table**.

In the plural we use the noun alone (*not* some …):
- ○ Those are **nice chairs**. (*not* some nice chairs)

Compare singular and plural:

- ○ A dog is **an animal**.
- ○ I'm **an optimist**.
- ○ My father is **a doctor**.
- ○ Jane is **a really nice person**.
- ○ What **a lovely dress**!

- ○ Dogs are **animals**.
- ○ We're **optimists**.
- ○ My parents are both **doctors**.
- ○ Jane and Ben are **really nice people**.
- ○ What **awful shoes**!

We say that somebody has **a long nose / a nice face / blue eyes / long fingers** etc. :

- ○ Jack has a long **nose**.
  (*not* the long nose)

- ○ Jack has **blue eyes**.
  (*not* the blue eyes)

We use **a/an** when we say what somebody's job is:
- ○ Sandra is **a nurse**. (*not* Sandra is nurse)
- ○ Would you like to be **an English teacher**?

C You can use **some** with plural countable nouns. We use **some** in two ways.

(1) **some** = a number (of) / a few (of) / a pair (of):
- ○ I've seen **some** good **movies** recently. (*not* I've seen good movies)
- ○ **Some friends** of mine are coming to stay at the weekend.
- ○ I need **some** new **sunglasses**. (= a new pair of sunglasses)

Often you can say the same thing with or without **some**. For example:
- ○ I need (**some**) **new clothes**.
- ○ The room was empty apart from a table and (**some**) **chairs**.

Do not use **some** when you are talking about things in general (see Unit 75):
- ○ I love **bananas**. (*not* some bananas)
- ○ My aunt is a writer. She writes **books**. (*not* some books)

(2) **some** = some but not all:
- ○ **Some children** learn very quickly. (but not all children)
- ○ Tomorrow there will be rain in **some places**, but most of the country will be dry.

>> Countable and uncountable → Units 69–70   a/an and the → Unit 72   some and any → Unit 85

Exercises

71.1 **What are these things? Choose from the box and write a sentence.**

1 an eagle   It's a bird.
2 a pigeon, a duck and a penguin   They're birds.
3 carrots and onions
4 a tulip
5 Earth, Mars and Jupiter
6 chess
7 a hammer, a saw and a screwdriver
8 the Nile, the Rhine and the Mekong
9 a mosquito
10 Hindi, Arabic and Swahili

bird(s)
flower(s)
game(s)
insect(s)
language(s)
planet(s)
river(s)
tool(s)
vegetable(s)

71.2 **Read about what these people do. What are their jobs? Choose from:**

| chef | interpreter | journalist | nurse | plumber | surgeon | tour guide | waiter |

1 Sarah looks after patients in hospital.   She's a nurse.
2 Gary works in a restaurant. He brings the food to the tables. He
3 Jane writes articles for a newspaper.
4 Kevin works in a hospital. He operates on people.
5 Jonathan cooks in a restaurant.
6 Dave installs and repairs water pipes.
7 Anna shows visitors round her city and tells them about it.
8 Lisa translates what people are saying from one language into another, so that they can understand each other.

71.3 **Which is right?**

1 Most of my friends are students / some students. (students is correct)
2 Are you careful driver / a careful driver?
3 I went to the library and borrowed books / some books.
4 Mark works in a bookshop. He sells books / some books.
5 I've been walking for hours. I've got sore feet / some sore feet.
6 I don't feel very well. I've got sore throat / a sore throat.
7 What lovely present / a lovely present! Thank you very much.
8 I met students / some students in a cafe yesterday. They were from China.
9 It might rain. Don't go out without umbrella / without an umbrella.
10 People / Some people learn languages more easily than others.

71.4 **Put in a/an or some where necessary. If no word is necessary, leave the space empty.**

1 I've seen ____some____ good movies recently.
2 Are you feeling all right? Do you have ____a____ headache?
3 I know lots of people. Most of them are ____−____ students.
4 When I was _____ child, I used to be very shy.
5 _____ birds, for example the penguin, cannot fly.
6 Would you like to be _____ actor?
7 Questions, questions, questions! You're always asking _____ questions!
8 I didn't expect to see you. What _____ surprise!
9 Do you like staying in _____ hotels?
10 Tomorrow is a holiday. _____ shops will be open, but most of them will be closed.
11 Those are _____ nice shoes. Where did you get them?
12 You need _____ visa to visit _____ countries, but not all of them.
13 Kate is _____ teacher. Her parents were _____ teachers too.
14 I don't believe him. He's _____ liar. He's always telling _____ lies.

Unit 72   a/an and the

A   Study this example:

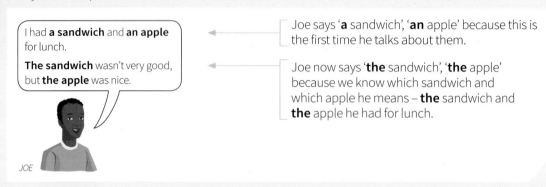

I had **a sandwich** and **an apple** for lunch.

The sandwich wasn't very good, but **the apple** was nice.

JOE

Joe says 'a sandwich', 'an apple' because this is the first time he talks about them.

Joe now says '**the** sandwich', '**the** apple' because we know which sandwich and which apple he means – **the** sandwich and **the** apple he had for lunch.

Compare **a** and **the** in these examples:

- ☐ **A man** and **a woman** were sitting opposite me. **The man** was American, but I think **the woman** was British.
- ☐ When we were on holiday, we stayed at **a hotel**. Sometimes we ate at **the hotel** and sometimes we went to **a restaurant**.

B   We use **the** when we are thinking of a specific thing. Compare **a/an** and **the**:

- ☐ Tim sat down on **a chair**. (maybe one of many chairs in the room)
  Tim sat down on **the chair nearest the door**. (a specific chair)
- ☐ Do you have **a car**? (not a specific car)
  I cleaned **the car** yesterday. (= my car)

We use **a/an** when we say what kind of thing or person we mean. Compare:

- ☐ We stayed at **a very cheap hotel**. (a type of hotel)
  The hotel where we stayed was very cheap. (a specific hotel)

C   We use **the** when it is clear which thing or person we mean. For example, in a room we talk about **the light / the floor / the ceiling / the door / the carpet** etc. :

- ☐ Can you turn off **the light**, please? (= the light in this room)
- ☐ I took a taxi to **the station**. (= the station in that town)
- ☐ *(in a shop)* I'd like to speak to **the manager**, please. (= the manager of this shop)

We also say '(go to) **the bank / the post office**':

- ☐ I have to go to **the bank** and then I'm going to **the post office**.
  (The speaker is usually thinking of a specific bank or post office.)

and '(go to) **the doctor / the dentist**':

- ☐ Clare isn't well. She's gone to **the doctor**.
- ☐ I don't like going to **the dentist**.

Compare **the** and **a**:

- ☐ I have to go to **the bank** today.
  Is there **a bank** near here?
- ☐ I don't like going to **the dentist**.
  My sister is **a dentist**.

D   We say 'once **a week** / three times **a day** / £1.50 **a kilo**' etc. :

- ☐ I go to the cinema about once **a month**.
- ☐ 'How much are those potatoes?' '£1.50 **a kilo**.'
- ☐ Helen works eight hours **a day**, six days **a week**.

>>   a/an → Unit 71   the → Units 73–78

Exercises

72.1 **Put in a/an or the.**

1 This morning I bought ....*a*.... book and .... magazine. .... book is in my bag, but I can't remember where I put .... magazine.
2 I saw .... accident this morning. .... car crashed into .... tree. .... driver of .... car wasn't hurt, but .... car was badly damaged.
3 There are two cars parked outside: .... blue one and .... grey one. .... blue one belongs to my neighbours. I don't know who .... owner of .... grey one is.
4 My friends live in .... old house in .... small village. There is .... beautiful garden behind .... house. I would like to have .... garden like that.

72.2 **Put in a/an or the.**

1 a This house is very nice. Does it have .... garden?
  b It's a beautiful day. Let's sit in .... garden.
  c I like living in this house, but it's a shame that .... garden is so small.
2 a Can you recommend .... good restaurant?
  b We had dinner in .... very nice restaurant.
  c We had dinner in .... best restaurant in town.
3 a What's .... name of that man we met yesterday?
  b We stayed at a very nice hotel – I can't remember .... name now.
  c My neighbour has .... French name, but in fact she's English, not French.
4 a Did Paula get .... job she applied for?
  b It's not easy to get .... job at the moment.
  c Do you enjoy your work? Is it .... interesting job?
5 a 'Are you going away next week?' 'No, ... week after next.'
  b I'm going away for .... week in September.
  c Gary has a part-time job. He works three mornings .... week.

72.3 **Put in a/an or the where necessary.**

1 Would you like apple?   *Would you like an apple?*
2 How often do you go to dentist?
3 Can you close door, please?
4 I have problem. I need your help.
5 How far is it from here to station?
6 I'm going to post office. I won't be long.
7 Paul plays tennis. He's very good player.
8 There isn't airport near where I live.
9 Nearest airport is 70 miles away.
10 There were no chairs, so we sat on floor.
11 Have you finished with book I lent you?
12 Chris has just got job in bank in Zurich.
13 We live in small apartment in city centre.
14 There's shop at end of street I live in.

72.4 **Answer these questions. Where possible, use once a week / three times a day etc.**

1 How often do you go to the cinema?   *Three or four times a year.*
2 How often do you go to the dentist?
3 How often do you go away on holiday?
4 How long do you usually sleep?
5 How often do you go out in the evening?
6 How many hours of TV do you watch (on average)?
7 What's the usual speed limit in towns in your country?

→ Additional exercise 29 (page 319)

Unit 73   the 1

A

We use **the** when there is only one of something:
- ○ Have you ever crossed **the equator**?
  (there is only one equator)
- ○ Our apartment is on **the tenth floor**.
- ○ Buenos Aires is **the capital of Argentina**.
- ○ I'm going away at **the end of this month**.

THE EQUATOR →

We use **the** + *superlative* (**best**, **oldest** etc.):
- ○ What's **the longest river in Europe**?

Compare **the** and **a/an** (see also Units 71–72):
- ○ **The sun** is **a star**. (= one of many stars)
- ○ **The hotel** where we stayed was **a very old hotel**.
- ○ We live in **an apartment** on **the tenth floor**.
- ○ What's **the best way** to learn **a language**?

B

We say '**the same**':
- ○ Your sweater is **the same** colour as mine. (*not* is same colour)
- ○ 'Are these keys **the same**?' 'No, they're different.'

C

We say: **the world**　**the universe**　**the sun**　**the moon**　**the earth**
the sky　**the sea**　**the ground**　**the country** (= not a town)

- ○ I love to look at the stars in **the sky**. (*not* in sky)
- ○ Do you live in a town or in **the country**?
- ○ **The earth** goes round **the sun**, and **the moon** goes round **the earth**.

We also use **Earth** (without **the**) when we think of it as a planet in space (like **Mars**, **Jupiter** etc.).
- ○ Which is the planet nearest **Earth**?

We say **space** (without **the**) when we mean 'space in the universe'. Compare:
- ○ There are millions of stars **in space**. (*not* in the space)
- ○ I tried to park my car, but **the space** was too small.

D

We say:
(go to) **the cinema**, **the theatre**
- ○ I go to **the cinema** a lot, but I haven't been to **the theatre** for ages.

TV / television (without **the**), but **the radio**
- ○ I watch **TV** a lot, but I don't listen to **the radio** much.
- *but* Can you turn off **the television**, please? (**the** television = the TV set)

the internet
- ○ **The internet** has changed the way we live.

E

We usually say **breakfast/lunch/dinner** (without **the**):
- ○ What did you have for **breakfast**?
- ○ We had **lunch** in a very nice restaurant.

But we say '**a big** lunch', '**a wonderful** dinner', '**an early** breakfast' etc.
- ○ We had **a very nice lunch**. (*not* We had very nice lunch)

F

We say: **size 43**, **platform 5** etc. (without **the**)
- ○ Our train leaves from **platform 5**. (*not* the platform 5)
- ○ Do you have these shoes in **size 43**? (*not* the size 43)

In the same way, we say: **room 126**, **page 29**, **vitamin A**, **section B** etc.

a/an → Unit 71　a/an and the → Unit 72　the 2–4 → Units 74–76
Names with and without **the** → Units 77–78

Exercises

73.1 Put in **the** or **a** where necessary. If no word is necessary, leave the space empty.

1 A: Our apartment is on ___the___ tenth floor.
  B: Is it? I hope there's _____ lift.
2 A: Did you have _____ nice holiday?
  B: Yes, it was _____ best holiday I've ever had.
3 A: Where's _____ nearest shop?
  B: There's one at _____ end of this street.
4 A: It's _____ lovely day, isn't it?
  B: Yes, there isn't _____ cloud in _____ sky.
5 A: We spent all our money because we stayed at _____ most expensive hotel in town.
  B: Why didn't you stay at _____ cheaper hotel?
6 A: Would you like to travel in _____ space?
  B: Yes, I'd love to go to _____ moon.
7 A: What did you think of _____ movie last night?
  B: It was OK, but I thought _____ ending was a bit strange.
8 A: What's Jupiter? Is it _____ star?
  B: No, it's _____ planet. It's _____ largest planet in _____ solar system.

73.2 Which is right? (For **the**, see also Unit 72.)

1 I haven't been to ~~cinema~~ / the cinema for ages. (_the cinema is correct_)
2 Sarah spends most of her free time watching TV / the TV.
3 Do you ever listen to radio / the radio?
4 Television / The television was on, but nobody was watching it.
5 Have you had dinner / the dinner yet?
6 It's confusing when two people have same name / the same name.
7 What do you want for breakfast / for the breakfast?
8 Fruit is an important source of vitamin C / the vitamin C.
9 This computer is not connected to internet / the internet.
10 I lay down on ground / the ground and looked up at sky / the sky.
11 Next train / The next train to London leaves from platform 3 / the platform 3.

73.3 Put in **the** or **a** where necessary. (For **a** and **the** see also Units 71–72.)

1 Sun is star. _The sun is a star._
2 I'm fed up with doing same thing every day. _____
3 Room 25 is on second floor. _____
4 It was very hot day. It was hottest day of year. _____
5 We had lunch in nice restaurant by sea. _____
6 What's on at cinema this week? _____
7 I had big breakfast this morning. _____
8 You'll find information you need at top of page 15. _____

73.4 Complete the sentences. Choose from the box and use **the** where necessary.

breakfast	cinema	gate	Gate 24	~~lunch~~	question	question 3	sea

1 I'm hungry. It's time for ___lunch___ .
2 There was no wind, so _____ was very calm.
3 Most of the questions in the test were OK, but I couldn't answer _____ .
4 'I'm going to _____ tonight.' 'Are you? What are you going to see?'
5 I'm sorry, but could you repeat _____ , please?
6 I didn't have _____ this morning because I was in a hurry.
7 _(airport announcement)_ Flight AB123 to Rome is now boarding at _____ .
8 I forgot to shut _____ . Can you shut it for me?

→ Additional exercise 29 (page 319)

the 2 (school / the school etc.)

A

Compare **school** and **the school**:

Ellie is ten years old. Every day she goes **to school**. She's **at school** now. **School** starts at 9 and finishes at 3.

We say a child goes **to school** or is **at school** (as a student). We are not thinking of a specific school. We are thinking of **school** as a *general* idea – children learning in a classroom.

Today Ellie's mother wants to speak to her daughter's teacher. So she has gone to **the school** to see her. She's at **the school** now.

Ellie's mother is not a student. She is not 'at school', she doesn't 'go to school'. If she wants to see Ellie's teacher, she goes to **the school** (= Ellie's school, a specific building).

B

We use **prison** (or **jail**), **hospital**, **university**, **college** and **church** in a similar way. We do not use **the** when we are thinking of the general idea of these places and what they are used for.
Compare:

- When I leave school, I plan to go **to university** / go **to college**. (as a student)

- Joe had an accident last week. He was taken **to hospital**. He's still **in hospital** now. (as a patient)

- Ken's brother is **in prison** for robbery. (He is a prisoner. We are not thinking of a specific prison.)

- Sarah's father goes **to church** every Sunday. (for a religious service)

- I went to **the university** to meet Professor Thomas. (as a visitor, not as a student)

- Jane has gone to **the hospital** to visit Joe. She's at **the hospital** now. (as a visitor, not as a patient)

- Ken went to **the prison** to visit his brother. (He went as a visitor, not as a prisoner.)

- Some workmen went to **the church** to repair the roof. (a specific building)

With most other places, you need **the**. For example, **the station**, **the cinema** (see Units 72C and 73D).

C

We say **go to bed** / **be in bed** etc. (*not* the bed):
- I'm going **to bed** now. Goodnight.
- Do you ever have breakfast **in bed**?

but
- I sat down on **the bed**. (a specific piece of furniture)

go to work / **be at work** / **start work** / **finish work** etc. (*not* the work):
- Chris didn't go to **work** yesterday.
- What time do you usually finish **work**?

go home / **come home** / **arrive home** / **get home** / **be (at) home** / do something **at home** etc. :
- It's late. Let's **go home**.
- I don't go out to work. I work **at home**.

>> the → Units 72–73, 75–78   Prepositions (**at school** / **in hospital** etc.) → **Units 123–125**
home → **Unit 126C**   American English → **Appendix 7**

Exercises

74.1 **Complete the sentences with school or the school.**

1 Why aren't your children at ....*school*.... today? Are they ill?
2 When he was younger, Ben hated ...., but he enjoys it now.
3 There were some parents waiting outside .... to meet their children.
4 What time does .... start in the morning?
5 How do your children get to and from ....? Do you take them?
6 What was the name of .... you attended?
7 What does Emily want to do when she leaves ....?
8 My children walk to .... isn't very far.

74.2 **Which is right?**

1 a Where is ~~university~~ / the university? Is it near here? (the university *is correct*)
  b Neil left school and got a job. He didn't want to go to university / the university.
  c In your country, what proportion of the population study at university / the university?
  d This is a small town, but university / the university is the biggest in the country.

2 a My brother has always been healthy. He's never been in hospital / the hospital.
  b When my friend was ill, I went to hospital / the hospital to see her.
  c When I was visiting my friend, I met Lisa, who is a nurse at hospital / the hospital.
  d I saw an accident. A woman was injured and was taken to hospital / the hospital.

3 a Why is she in prison / the prison? What crime did she commit?
  b There was a fire at prison / the prison. Firefighters were called to put it out.
  c Do you think too many people are sent to prison / the prison?

4 a John's mother is a regular churchgoer. She goes to church / the church every Sunday.
  b John himself doesn't go to church / the church.
  c The village is very nice. You should visit church / the church. It's interesting.

74.3 **Complete the sentences. Choose from the box.**

1 How did you get ....*home*.... after the party?
2 How do you usually go .... in the morning? By bus?
3 Sam likes to go to .... early and get up early.
4 I don't have my phone. I left it ....
5 'Have you seen my keys?' 'Yes, they're on ....'
6 Shall we meet .... tomorrow evening?
7 I like to read .... before going to sleep.
8 It was a long tiring journey. We arrived .... very late.
9 Tom usually finishes .... at five o'clock.
10 It's nice to travel around, but there's no place ....

bed
the bed
in bed
~~**home**~~
home
at home
like home
work
to work
after work

74.4 **Complete the sentences. Choose at/in/to + hospital, school etc.**

bed	home	~~hospital~~	hospital	prison	school	university	work

1 Kate's mother has to have an operation. She'll be ....*in hospital*.... for a few days.
2 In your country, from what age do children have to go ....?
3 Mark didn't go out last night. He stayed ....
4 There is a lot of traffic in the morning when people are going ....
5 When Sophie leaves school, she wants to study psychology ....
6 Ben never gets up before 9 o'clock. It's 8.30 now, so he is still ....
7 The accident wasn't serious. Nobody had to go ....
8 If people commit crimes, they may end up ....

the 3 (children / the children)

A When we are talking about things or people in general, we do *not* use **the**:
- ○ I'm afraid of **dogs**. (*not* the dogs)
  (**dogs** = dogs in general, not a specific group of dogs)
- ○ **Doctors** are usually paid more than **teachers**.
- ○ Do you know anybody who collects **stamps**?
- ○ **Life** has changed a lot in the last thirty years.
- ○ Do you like **classical music / Chinese food / fast cars**?
- ○ My favourite sport is **football/skiing/athletics**.
- ○ My favourite subject at school was **history/physics/English**.

We say '**most** people / **most** shops / **most** big cities' etc. (*not* the most …):
- ○ **Most shops** accept credit cards. (*not* The most shops)

B We use **the** when we mean specific things or people.
Compare:

In general (without **the**)	*Specific people or things* (with **the**)
○ **Children** learn from playing. (= children in general)	○ We took **the children** to the zoo. (= a specific group, perhaps the speaker's children)
○ I couldn't live without **music**.	○ The film wasn't very good, but I liked **the music**. (= the music in the film)
○ All **cars** have wheels.	○ All **the cars in this car park** belong to people who work here.
○ **Sugar** isn't very good for you.	○ Can you pass **the sugar**, please? (= the sugar on the table)
○ **English people** drink a lot of tea. (= English people in general)	○ **The English people I know** drink a lot of tea. (= only the English people I know, not English people in general)

C The difference between 'something in general' and 'something specific' is not always very clear.
Compare:

In general (without **the**)	*Specific people or things* (with **the**)
○ I like working with **people**. (= people in general)	
○ I like working with **people who say what they think**. (not all people, but 'people who say what they think' is still a general idea)	○ I like **the people I work with**. (= a specific group of people)
○ Do you like **coffee**? (= coffee in general)	
○ Do you like **strong black coffee**? (not all coffee, but 'strong black coffee' is still a general idea)	○ **The coffee we had after dinner** wasn't very good. (= specific coffee)

>> the 1–2 ➜ Units 73–74   the + adjective (**the young** / **the English** etc.) ➜ Unit 76

Exercises

75.1 Choose four of these things and write what you think about them:

bananas	boxing	cats	crowds	fast food	horror movies
~~hot weather~~	maths	opera	snow	supermarkets	zoos

Use: I like … / I don't like …   I think … is/are …   I don't mind …
I love … / I hate …   I'm (not) interested in …

1 I don't like hot weather very much.
2
3
4
5

75.2 Which is right?

1 a Apples / ~~The apples~~ are good for you. (Apples *is correct*)
   b Look at apples / the apples on that tree. They're very big.
2 a Who are people / the people in this picture?
   b It annoys me when people / the people throw rubbish on the ground.
3 a My memory isn't good. I'm not good at remembering names / the names.
   b What were names / the names of those people we met last night?
4 a First World War / The First World War began in 1914 and ended in 1918.
   b A pacifist is somebody who is against war / the war.
5 a He's lazy. He doesn't like hard work / the hard work.
   b Did you finish work / the work you were doing yesterday?

75.3 Complete the sentences using the following. Use **the** where necessary.

(the) ~~basketball~~	(the) **grass**	(the) **patience**	(the) **people**
(the) **questions**	(the) **meat**	~~(the) information~~	(the) **hotels**
(the) **biology**	(the) **water**	(the) **spiders**	(the) **lies**

1 My favourite sport is ....basketball.... .
2 ....The information.... we were given wasn't correct.
3 Some people are afraid of ....
4 A vegetarian is somebody who doesn't eat ....
5 The test wasn't hard. I answered .... without difficulty.
6 Do you know .... who live in the flat next to yours?
7 .... is the study of plants and animals.
8 It's better to tell the truth. Telling .... often causes problems.
9 We couldn't find anywhere to stay in the town. .... were all full.
10 Don't swim in this pool. .... doesn't look very clean.
11 Don't sit on .... It's wet after the rain.
12 You need .... to teach young children.

75.4 Which is right?

1 Steve is very good at telling stories / the stories.
2 I can't sing this song. I don't know words / the words.
3 Don't stay in that hotel. It's noisy and rooms / the rooms are very small.
4 I don't have a car, so I use public transport / the public transport most of the time.
5 All books / All the books on the top shelf belong to me.
6 Life / The life is strange sometimes. Some very strange things happen.
7 We enjoyed our holiday. Weather / The weather was good.
8 Everybody needs water / the water to live.
9 I don't like films / the films with unhappy endings.

A

Study these sentences:

- ○ **The giraffe** is the tallest of all animals.
- ○ **The bicycle** is an excellent means of transport.
- ○ When was **the camera** invented?
- ○ **The dollar** is the currency of the United States.

In these examples, **the** ... does not mean one specific thing.
The giraffe = a specific type of animal, not a specific giraffe.
We use **the** ... in this way to talk about a type of animal, machine etc.

In the same way we use **the** for musical instruments:

- ○ Can you play **the** guitar?
- ○ **The** piano is my favourite instrument.

Compare **a** and **the**:

- ○ I'd like to have **a piano**.   *but*   I can't play **the piano**.
- ○ We saw **a giraffe** at the zoo. *but*   **The giraffe** is my favourite animal.

Note that **man** (without **the**) = human beings in general, the human race:

- ○ What do you know about the origins of **man**? (*not* the man)

B

the old, the rich etc.

We use **the** + *adjective* (without a noun) to talk about groups of people. For example:

the old	the rich	the homeless	the sick
the elderly	the poor	the unemployed	the injured

the old = old people, **the rich** = rich people etc. :

- ○ Do you think **the rich** should pay higher taxes?
- ○ We need to do more to help **the homeless**.

Note that we say: the **old** (*not* the olds), the **poor** (*not* the poors) etc.

The rich, the homeless etc. are *plural*. For one person, we say:
   a rich **man** (*not* a rich)   **a** homeless **person** (*not* a homeless)

C

the French, the Chinese etc.

We use **the** + a few nationality adjectives that end in **-ch** or **-sh**. For example:
   the French   the Dutch   the British   the English   the Spanish

The meaning is *plural* – the people of that country.

- ○ **The French** are famous for their food. (*not* French are ...)

We do not say 'a French' or 'an English' (*singular*). For example, we say:

- ○ I met **a** French **woman** / **an** English **guy**.

We also use **the** + nationality words ending in **-ese** or **-ss**. For example:
   the Chinese   the Portuguese   the Swiss
These words can also be singular (**a Chinese, a Swiss** etc.).

With other nationality words, the plural ends in **-s** (usually without **the**). For example:
   an Italian → **Italians**   a Mexican → **Mexicans**   a Thai → **Thais**

- ○ **Italians / Mexicans / Thais** are very friendly.

In all cases you can use *adjective* + **people**. For example, you can say:

- ○ **French / Chinese / Mexican** people are very friendly.

>> **a/an** and **the** → Unit 72   **the** → Units 73–75   Names with and without **the** → Units 77–78

Exercises

76.1 **Answer the questions. Choose the right answer from the box. Don't forget the.**

1	2	3	4
animals	*birds*	*inventions*	*currencies*
tiger elephant rabbit cheetah giraffe kangaroo	eagle penguin swan owl parrot pigeon	telephone wheel telescope laser helicopter typewriter	dollar peso euro rupee rouble yen

1 a Which of the animals is the tallest?   *the giraffe*
  b Which animal can run the fastest?
  c Which of these animals is found in Australia?
2 a Which of these birds has a long neck?
  b Which of these birds cannot fly?
  c Which bird flies at night?
3 a Which of these inventions is the oldest?
  b Which one is the most recent?
  c Which one was especially important for astronomy?
4 a What is the currency of India?
  b What is the currency of Canada?
  c And the currency of your country?

76.2 **Put in the or a.**

1 When was ....*the*.... telephone invented?
2 Can you play .... musical instrument?
3 Jessica plays .... violin in an orchestra.
4 There was .... piano in the corner of the room.
5 I wish I could play .... piano.
6 Our society is based on .... family.
7 Martin comes from .... large family.
8 .... computer has changed the way we live.
9 When was .... bicycle invented?
10 Do you have .... car?

76.3 **Complete these sentences. Use the + adjective. Choose from:**

elderly   injured   rich   sick   unemployed   ~~young~~

1 ...*The young*.... have the future in their hands.
2 Helen is a nurse. She's spent her life caring for ....
3 Life is all right if you have a job, but things are hard for ....
4 Ambulances arrived at the scene of the accident and took ....
  to hospital.
5 More and more people are living longer. How are we going to care for .... ?
6 It's nice to have lots of money, but .... have their problems too.

76.4 **What do you call the people of these countries?**

	one person (a/an …)	*the people in general*
1 Canada	a Canadian	Canadians
2 Germany		
3 France		
4 Russia		
5 Japan		
6 Brazil		
7 England		
8 and your country		

Names with and without **the** 1

A

We do *not* use **the** with names of people ('Helen', 'Helen Taylor' etc.). In the same way, we do *not* use **the** with most names of places. For example:

continents	**Africa** (*not* the Africa), **South America**
countries, states etc.	**France** (*not* the France), **Japan**, **Texas**
islands	**Sicily**, **Tasmania**
cities, towns etc.	**Cairo**, **Bangkok**
mountains	**Everest**, **Kilimanjaro**

But we normally use **the** in names with **Republic**, **Kingdom**, **States** etc. :
> **the** Czech **Republic**   **the** United **Kingdom** (**the** UK)
> **the** Dominican **Republic**   **the** United **States** of America (**the** USA)

Compare:
- ⬭ Have you been to **Canada** or **the United States**?

B

When we use **Mr/Ms/Captain/Doctor** etc. + a name, we do not use **the**. So we say:
> **Mr** Johnson / **Doctor** Johnson / **Captain** Johnson / **President** Johnson etc. (*not* the …)
> **Uncle** Robert / **Saint** Catherine / **Queen** Catherine etc. (*not* the …)

Compare:
- ⬭ We called **the doctor**.
   We called **Doctor** Johnson. (*not* the Doctor Johnson)

We use **Mount** (= mountain) and **Lake** before a name in the same way (without **the**):
> **Mount** Everest (*not* the …)   **Mount** Etna   **Lake** Superior   **Lake** Victoria
- ⬭ They live near **the lake**.
   They live near **Lake Superior**. (*not* the Lake Superior)

C

We use **the** with the names of oceans, seas, rivers and canals:
> **the** Atlantic (Ocean)   **the** Red Sea   **the** Amazon
> **the** Indian Ocean   **the** Channel (between   **the** Nile
> **the** Mediterranean (Sea)   France and Britain)   **the** Suez Canal

We use **the** with the names of deserts:
> **the** Sahara (Desert)   **the** Gobi Desert

D

We use **the** with *plural* names of people and places:

people	**the** Taylor**s** (= the Taylor family), **the** Johnson**s**
countries	**the** Netherland**s**, **the** Philippine**s**, **the** United State**s**
groups of islands	**the** Canarie**s** (*or* **the** Canary Island**s**), **the** Bahama**s**
mountain ranges	**the** Ande**s**, **the** Alp**s**, **the** Ural**s**

- ⬭ The highest mountain in **the Andes** is (**Mount**) **Aconcagua**.

E

We say:
> **the north** (of Brazil)   *but*   **northern** Brazil (*without* the)
> **the southeast** (of Spain)   *but*   **southeastern** Spain

Compare:
- ⬭ Sweden is in **northern Europe**; Spain is in **the south**.

We also use **north/south** etc. (*without* **the**) in the names of some regions and countries:
> **North America**   **South Africa**   **southeast Asia**

Note that on maps, **the** is not usually included in the name.

≫ Names with and without **the** 2 ➜ Unit 78

Exercises

77.1 **Which is right?**

1 Who is <u>Doctor Johnson</u> / <s>the Doctor Johnson</s>? (<u>Doctor Johnson</u> *is correct*)
2 I was ill. <u>Doctor / The doctor</u> told me to rest for a few days.
3 <u>Doctor Thomas / The Doctor Thomas</u> is an expert on heart disease.
4 I'm looking for <u>Professor Brown / the Professor Brown</u>. Do you know where she is?
5 In the United States, <u>President / the President</u> is elected for four years.
6 <u>President Kennedy / The President Kennedy</u> was assassinated in 1963.
7 The officer I spoke to at the police station was <u>Inspector Roberts / the Inspector Roberts</u>.
8 Do you know <u>Wilsons / the Wilsons</u>? They're a very nice couple.
9 Julia spent three years as a student in <u>United States / the United States</u>.
10 <u>France / The France</u> has a population of about 66 million.

77.2 **Some of these sentences are OK, but some need the (sometimes more than once). Correct the sentences where necessary.**

1 Everest was first climbed in 1953.   OK
2 Milan and Turin are cities <u>in north</u> of Italy.   in the north of Italy
3 Africa is much larger than Europe.
4 Last year I visited Mexico and United States.
5 Southern England is warmer than north.
6 Thailand and Cambodia are in southeast Asia.
7 Chicago is on Lake Michigan.
8 Next year we're going skiing in Swiss Alps.
9 UK consists of Great Britain and Northern Ireland.
10 Seychelles are a group of islands in Indian Ocean.
11 I've never been to South Africa.
12 River Volga flows into Caspian Sea.

77.3 **Here are some geography questions. Choose the right answer from one of the boxes and use the if necessary. You do not need all the names in the boxes.**

continents	countries	oceans and seas	mountains	rivers and canals	
Africa	Canada	~~Atlantic~~	Alps	Amazon	Rhine
Asia	Denmark	Indian Ocean	Andes	Danube	Thames
Australia	Indonesia	Pacific	Himalayas	Nile	Volga
Europe	Sweden	Black Sea	Rockies	Suez Canal	
North America	Thailand	Mediterranean	Urals	Panama Canal	
South America	United States	Red Sea			

1 What do you have to cross to travel from Europe to America?   the Atlantic
2 Where is Argentina?
3 Which is the longest river in Africa?
4 Of which country is Stockholm the capital?
5 Of which country is Washington the capital?
6 What is the name of the mountain range in the west of North America?
7 What is the name of the sea between Africa and Europe?
8 Which is the smallest continent in the world?
9 What is the name of the ocean between North America and Asia?
10 What is the name of the ocean between Africa and Australia?
11 Which river flows through London?
12 Which river flows through Vienna, Budapest and Belgrade?
13 Of which country is Bangkok the capital?
14 What joins the Atlantic and Pacific Oceans?
15 Which is the longest river in South America?

Names with and without **the** 2

A Names without **the**

We do not use **the** with names of most city streets/roads/squares/parks etc. :

Union Street (*not* the …)	**Fifth Avenue**	**Hyde Park**
Abbey Road	**Broadway**	**Times Square**

Names of many public buildings and institutions (airports, stations, universities etc.), and also some geographical names, are two words:

Manchester Airport   **Harvard University**

The first word is the name of a place ('Manchester') or a person ('Harvard'). These names are usually without **the**. In the same way, we say:

Victoria Station (*not* the …)	**Canterbury Cathedral**	**Edinburgh Castle**
Buckingham Palace	**Cambridge University**	**Sydney Harbour**

Compare:

Buckingham Palace (*not* the …)   *but*   **the Royal Palace**
('Royal' is an adjective – it is not a name like 'Buckingham'.)

B Most other buildings have names with **the**. For example:

hotels	**the** Sheraton Hotel, **the** Holiday Inn
theatres/cinemas	**the** Palace Theatre, **the** Odeon (cinema)
museums	**the** Guggenheim Museum, **the** National Gallery
other buildings	**the** Empire State (Building), **the** White House, **the** Eiffel Tower

We often leave out the noun:

the Sheraton (Hotel)   **the Palace** (Theatre)   **the Guggenheim** (Museum)

Some names are only **the** + *noun*, for example:

the Acropolis   **the Kremlin**   **the Pentagon**

C Names with **of** usually have **the**. For example:

the Bank **of** England	**the** Museum **of** Modern Art
the Great Wall **of** China	**the** Tower **of** London

Note that we say:
the University **of** Cambridge   *but*   **Cambridge University** (*without* **the**)

D Many shops, restaurants, hotels etc. are named after people. These names end in -**'s** or -**s**. We do not use **the** with these names:

McDonald's (*not* the …)	**Barclays** (bank)
Joe's Diner (restaurant)	**Macy's** (department store)

Churches are often named after saints (St = Saint):

St John's Church (*not* the …)   **St Patrick's Cathedral**

E Most newspapers and many organisations have names with **the**:

the Washington Post	**the** Financial Times	**the** Sun (newspaper)
the European Union	**the** BBC	**the** Red Cross

Names of companies, airlines etc. are usually without **the**:

Fiat (*not* the Fiat)	**Sony**	**Singapore Airlines**
Kodak	**IBM**	**Yale University Press**

Names with and without **the** 1 ➔ Unit 77

Exercises

78.1 Use the map to answer the questions. Write the name of the place and the street it is in.
Use **the** if necessary. (Remember that on maps we do not normally use **the**.)

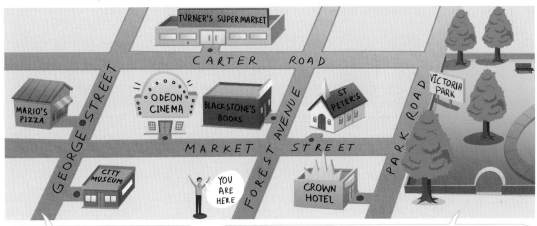

1	Is there a cinema near here?	Yes, __the Odeon__ in __Market Street__ .
2	Is there a supermarket near here?	Yes, ... in ....
3	Is there a hotel near here?	Yes, ... in ....
4	Is there a church near here?	Yes, ...
5	Is there a museum near here?	Yes, ...
6	Is there a bookshop near here?	Yes, ...
7	Is there a restaurant near here?	Yes, ...
8	Is there a park near here?	Yes, ... at the end of ....

78.2 Where are the following? Use **the** where necessary.

Acropolis	Broadway	Buckingham Palace	Eiffel Tower
Kremlin	White House	Gatwick Airport	~~Times Square~~

1 __Times Square__ is in New York.
2 .... is in Paris.
3 .... is in London.
4 .... is in Washington.
5 .... is in Moscow.
6 .... is in New York.
7 .... is in Athens.
8 .... is near London.

78.3 Which is right?

1 Have you ever been to ~~Science Museum~~ / the Science Museum? (<u>the Science Museum</u> *is correct*)
2 Many tourists in London visit <u>St Paul's Cathedral</u> / <u>the St Paul's Cathedral</u>.
3 The biggest park in New York is <u>Central Park</u> / <u>The Central Park</u>.
4 I'd like to go to China and see <u>Great Wall</u> / <u>the Great Wall</u>.
5 <u>Dublin Airport</u> / <u>The Dublin Airport</u> is situated about 12 kilometres from the city centre.
6 'Which cinema are we going to this evening?' '<u>Classic</u> / <u>The Classic</u>.'
7 Jack is a student at <u>Liverpool University</u> / <u>the Liverpool University</u>.
8 You should go to <u>National Museum</u> / <u>the National Museum</u>. It's very interesting.
9 If you're looking for a department store, I would recommend <u>Harrison's</u> / <u>the Harrison's</u>.
10 Andy is a flight attendant. He works for <u>Cathay Pacific</u> / <u>the Cathay Pacific</u>.
11 'Which newspaper do you want?' '<u>Morning News</u> / <u>The Morning News</u>.'
12 We went to Italy and saw <u>Leaning Tower</u> / <u>the Leaning Tower</u> of Pisa.
13 This book is published by <u>Cambridge University Press</u> / <u>the Cambridge University Press</u>.
14 The building across the street is <u>College of Art</u> / <u>the College of Art</u>.
15 <u>Imperial Hotel</u> / <u>The Imperial Hotel</u> is in <u>Baker Street</u> / <u>the Baker Street</u>.
16 <u>Statue of Liberty</u> / <u>The Statue of Liberty</u> is at the entrance to <u>New York Harbor</u> / <u>the New York Harbor</u>.

➜ Additional exercise 29 (page 319)

Singular and plural

Sometimes we use a *plural* noun for one thing that has two parts. For example:

trousers *(two legs)* also **jeans/tights/shorts/pants**	**pyjamas** *(top and bottom)*	**glasses**	**binoculars**	**scissors**

These words are plural, so they take a plural verb:
- My trousers **are** too long. (*not* My trousers is)

You can also use **a pair of** + these words:
- **Those are** nice **jeans**.   *or*   That**'s a** nice **pair of** jeans. (*not* a nice jeans)
- I need **some** new **glasses**.   *or*   I need **a** new **pair of** glasses.

Some nouns end in **-ics**, but are not usually plural. For example:

athletics	gymnastics	economics	politics
physics	electronics	maths (= mathematics)	

- **Gymnastics is** my favourite sport. (*not* Gymnastics are)

News is not plural (see Unit 70B):
- I have **some news** for you. **It's** good news!

Some words that end in **-s** can be singular or plural. For example:

means	**a means** of transport	**many means** of transport
series	**a** TV **series**	**two** TV **series**
species	**a species** of fish	**200 species** of fish

Some singular nouns are often used with a plural verb. For example:

audience	committee	company	family	firm	government	staff	team

These nouns are all groups of people. We often think of them as a number of people (= they), not as one thing (= it). So we often use a plural verb:
- **The government** (= they) **have decided** to increase taxes.
- **The staff** at the company (= they) **are** not happy with **their** working conditions.

In the same way, we often use a plural verb after the name of a company or a sports team:
- **Shell have** increased the price of petrol.
- **Italy are** playing Brazil next Sunday (in a football match).

You can also use a singular verb (The government **wants** ... / Shell **has** ... etc.).

We use a plural verb with **police**:
- **The police are** investigating the crime, but **haven't** arrested anyone yet.
  (*not* The police is ... hasn't)

Note that we say **a police officer / a policeman / a policewoman** (*not* a police).

We do not often use the plural of **person** ('persons'). We normally use **people** (a *plural* word):
- He's **a** nice **person**. *but* They are nice **people**. (*not* nice persons)
- **Many people don't** have enough to eat. (*not* Many people doesn't)

We think of a sum of money, a period of time, a distance etc. as *one* thing. So we use a singular verb:
- **Fifty thousand pounds** (= it) **was** stolen in the robbery. (*not* were stolen)
- **Three years** (= it) **is** a long time to be without a job. (*not* Three years are)
- **Two miles isn't** very far to walk.

>> American English → **Appendix 7**

Exercises

79.1 Complete the sentences. Choose from the box.

1 My eyesight is getting worse. I need ...._glasses_.... .
2 The trousers you bought for me .... fit me.
3 The jacket you bought for me .... fit me.
4 I need .... scissors to cut this piece of material.
5 I can't find my binoculars. Have you seen ....?
6 I went shopping and bought a .... of jeans.
7 Where .... my sunglasses?
8 I went shopping and bought .... pair of pyjamas.
9 I don't know much about politics. I'm not interested in ....

a
are
them
doesn't
pair
it
~~glasses~~
some
don't

79.2 Complete the sentences. Use a word from section B (**news**, **series** etc.).

1 'Have you heard the ...._news_....?' 'No. What's happened?'
2 The bicycle is a .... of transport.
3 A lot of American TV .... are shown in other countries.
4 The tiger is an endangered ....
5 There will be a .... of meetings to discuss the problem.
6 Fortunately the .... wasn't as bad as we expected.
7 How many .... of bird are there in the world?
8 I didn't have my phone, so I had no .... of contacting you.

79.3 Choose the correct form of the verb, singular or plural. In three sentences either the singular or plural verb is possible.

1 Gymnastics is / ~~are~~ my favourite sport. (_is is correct_)
2 My new glasses doesn't / don't fit very well.
3 The police want / wants to interview two men about the robbery.
4 Physics was / were my favourite subject at school.
5 It's a nice place to visit. The people is / are very friendly.
6 Germany is / are playing Spain tomorrow night. Are you going to watch it?
7 Does / Do the police know how the accident happened?
8 Where do / does your family live?
9 Most people enjoy / enjoys music.
10 I like this cafe. The staff here is / are really friendly and efficient.

79.4 Complete the sentences. Use **is** or **isn't**, and choose from the box.

1 Three years ...._is a long time_.... to be without a job.
2 Thirty degrees .... for Tom. He doesn't like hot weather.
3 Ten dollars .... We need more than that.
4 Four days .... for a holiday. You need at least a week.
5 Twenty kilos .... Are you sure you can manage?

a lot to carry
enough money
too hot
long enough
~~a long time~~

79.5 Are these sentences OK? Correct them where necessary.

1 <u>Three years are</u> a long time to be without a job.
2 The committee want to change the rules of the club.
3 Susan was wearing a black jeans.
4 I like Martin and Jane. They're very nice persons.
5 I'm going to buy some new pyjamas.
6 There was a police directing traffic in the street.
7 This scissors isn't very sharp.
8 The company have decided to open a new factory.
9 This plant is very rare species.
10 Twelve hours are a long time to be on a plane.

Three years is a long time
OK (wants is also correct)
....
....
....
....
....
....
....
....

Noun + noun (a **bus driver** / a **headache**)

A

You can use two nouns together (*noun + noun*) to mean *one* thing/person/idea etc. :

a **bus driver**   **income tax**   the **city centre**   an **apple tree**

The first noun is like an adjective. It tells us what kind of thing/person/idea etc. :

> a **bus driver** = the driver of a bus
> **income tax** = tax that you pay on your income
> the **city centre** = the centre of the city
> an **apple tree** = a tree that has apples
> a **Paris hotel** = a hotel in Paris
> my **life story** = the story of my life

So you can say:

a **television** camera   a **television** programme   a **television** studio   a **television** producer
(things or people to do with television)
language **problems**   marriage **problems**   health **problems**   work **problems**
(different kinds of problems)

Sometimes the first word ends in **-ing**:

a **frying** pan (= a pan for frying)
a **washing** machine
a **swimming** pool

B

Sometimes there are more than two nouns together:

- ○ I waited at the **hotel reception desk**.
- ○ We watched the **World Swimming Championships** on TV.
- ○ If you want to play table tennis (= a game), you need **a table tennis table** (= a table).

C

When two nouns are together like this, sometimes we write them as one word and sometimes as two separate words. For example:

a **headache**   **toothpaste**   a **weekend**   a **car park**   a **road sign**

There are no clear rules for this. If you are not sure, write two words.

D

Note the difference between:

a **coffee cup** (maybe empty) and a **cup of coffee** (= a cup with coffee in it)
a **shopping bag** (maybe empty) and a **bag of shopping** (= a bag full of shopping)

E

When we use *noun + noun*, the first noun is like an *adjective*. It is normally singular, but the meaning is often plural.
For example: a **car park** is a place to park **cars**, an **apple tree** is a tree that has **apples**.

In the same way we say:

a **three-hour** journey (= a journey that takes three **hours**)
a **ten-pound** note (= a note with the value of ten **pounds**)
a **four-week** course
a **six-mile** walk
two **14-year**-old girls

Compare:

- ○ It was **a four-week** course. (*not* a four weeks course)
- *but*   The course lasted four **weeks**.

>> -'s and of ... → Unit 81   a week's holiday / three weeks' holiday etc. → Unit 81E

Exercises

80.1 **What do we call these things and people?**

1 Someone who drives a bus is a _bus driver_.
2 Problems concerning health are _health problems_.
3 A ticket to travel by train is a _____.
4 A machine you use to get a ticket is a _____.
5 The staff at a hotel are the _____.
6 The results of your exams are your _____.
7 A horse that runs in races is a _____.
8 A race for horses is a _____.
9 Shoes for running are _____.
10 A shop that sells shoes is a _____.
11 The window of a shop is a _____.
12 A person who cleans windows is a _____.
13 A scandal involving a construction company is _____.
14 Workers at a car factory are _____.
15 A scheme for the improvement of a road is a _____.
16 A department store in New York is a _____.

80.2 **Answer the questions using two of the following words each time:**

~~accident~~	belt	birthday	card	credit	driver
forecast	machine	number	party	ring	~~road~~
room	seat	truck	washing	weather	wedding

1 This could be caused by bad driving.   a _road accident_
2 You should wear this when you're driving.   a _____
3 You can use this to pay for things.   a _____
4 This will tell you if it's going to rain or not. the _____
5 This is useful if you have a lot of dirty clothes. a _____
6 This is something you might wear if you're married. a _____
7 If you're staying at a hotel, you need to remember this. your _____
8 This is a way to celebrate getting older.   a _____
9 This person transports things by road.   a _____

80.3 **Put the words in the right order.**

1 I spilt coffee on the _living room carpet_. (room / carpet / living)
2 Jack likes sport. He plays for his _____. (team / school / football)
3 Anna works for a _____. (company / production / film)
4 Many people invest in a _____. (life / policy / insurance)
5 You can get a map at the _____. (information / office / tourist)

80.4 **Which is correct?**

1 It's quite a big book. There are more than ~~500 page~~ / 500 pages. (500 pages *is correct*)
2 It's only a two-hour / two hours flight from London to Madrid.
3 It took only two hour / two hours to fly to Madrid.
4 I don't have any change. I only have a twenty-pound / twenty pounds note.
5 I looked down and there were two ten-pound / ten pounds notes on the ground.
6 At work in the morning we usually have a 15-minute / 15 minutes break for coffee.
7 There are 60-minute / 60 minutes in an hour.
8 My office is on the tenth floor of a twelve-storey / twelve storeys building.
9 I work five-day / five days a week. Saturday and Sunday are free.
10 Five-star / Five stars hotels are the most expensive.
11 Sam's daughter is six-year-old / six years old.
12 Sam has a six-year-old / six-years-old daughter.

A

We use -'s (*apostrophe* + **s**) mostly for people or animals:
- ○ **Tom's** computer isn't working. (*not* the computer of Tom)
- ○ How old are **Chris's** children? (*not* the children of Chris)
- ○ What's (= What is) **your sister's** name?
- ○ What's **Tom's sister's** name?
- ○ Be careful. Don't step on **the cat's** tail.

You can use -'**s** without a noun after it:
- ○ This isn't my book. It's **my sister's**. (= my sister's book)

We do not use -'**s** after a long group of words. So we say:
    my friend's mother
but the mother **of the man we met yesterday** (*not* the man we met yesterday's mother)

Note that we say **a woman's hat** (= a hat for a woman), **a boy's name** (= a name for a boy), **a bird's egg** (= an egg laid by a bird) etc.

B

With a *singular* noun we use -'**s**:
    my **sister's** room (= **her** room – *one sister*)
    Mr Carter's house (= **his** house)

With a *plural* noun (sister**s**, friend**s** etc.) we put an apostrophe (**'**) after **s**:
    my **sisters'** room (= **their** room – *two or more* sisters)
    the Carters' house (= **their** house – *Mr and Mrs Carter*)

If a plural noun does not end in -**s** (for example **men/women/children/people**) we use -'**s**:
    the **men's** changing room   a **children's** book (= a book for children)

You can use -'**s** after more than one noun:
    Jack and Karen's children   **Mr and Mrs Carter's** house

C

For things, ideas etc., we normally use **of**:
    the temperature **of the water** (*not* the water's temperature)
    the name **of the book**   the owner **of the restaurant**

We say **the beginning/end/middle of** … / **the top/bottom of** … / **the front/back/side of** … :
    the beginning of the month (*not* the month's beginning)
    the top of the hill   **the back of** the car

D

You can usually use -'**s** or **of** … for an organisation (= a group of people). So you can say:
    the government's decision *or* the decision **of the government**
    the company's success *or* the success **of the company**

We also use -'**s** for places. So you can say:
    the city's streets   **the world's** population   **Italy's** prime minister

E

We use -'**s** with time words (**yesterday** / **next week** etc.):
- ○ Do you still have **yesterday's** newspaper?
- ○ **Next week's** meeting has been cancelled.

In the same way, you can say **today's** / **tomorrow's** / **this evening's** / **Monday's** etc.

We also use -'**s** (or -**s'** with plural words) with periods of time:
- ○ I've got **a week's holiday** starting on Monday.
- ○ Julia has got **three weeks' holiday**.
- ○ I live near the station – it's only **ten minutes' walk**.

⟫ Noun + noun (a **bus driver**) ➜ **Unit 80**   a **three-hour** journey, a **ten-pound** note ➜ **Unit 80E**
    -'**s** (= **is** or **has**) in short forms ➜ **Appendix 5.2**

Exercises

81.1 In some of these sentences, it is more natural to use -'s or -'. Change the underlined parts where necessary.

1 Who is the owner of this restaurant?   *OK*
2 How old are the children of Chris?   *Chris's children*
3 Is this the umbrella of your friend?
4 Write your name at the top of the page.
5 I've never met the daughter of James.
6 How old is the son of Helen and Andy?
7 We don't know the cause of the problem.
8 I don't know the words of this song.
9 The friends of your children are here.
10 What is the cost of a new washing machine?
11 The garden of our neighbours is very small.
12 The hair of David is very long.
13 I work on the ground floor of the building.
14 I couldn't go to the party of my best friend.
15 George is the brother of somebody I knew at college.
16 Have you seen the car of the parents of Ben?
17 What is the meaning of this expression?
18 Do you agree with the policy of the government?

81.2 Which is right?

1 Don't step on the ....*cat's*.... tail. (cat / cat's / cats')
2 It's my .... birthday tomorrow. (father / father's / fathers')
3 Those .... look nice. Shall we buy some? (apples / apple's / apples')
4 .... clothes are expensive. (Children / Children's / Childrens')
5 Zurich is .... largest city. (Switzerland / Switzerland's / Switzerlands')
6 Your .... parents are your grandparents. (parents / parent's / parents')
7 I took a lot of .... when I was on holiday. (photos / photo's / photos')
8 This isn't my coat. It's .... (someone else / someone else's / someone elses)
9 Have you read any of .... poems? (Shakespeare / Shakespeare's / Shakespeares')

81.3 Read each sentence and write a new sentence beginning with the underlined words.

1 The meeting tomorrow has been cancelled.
  Tomorrow's meeting has been cancelled.
2 The storm last week caused a lot of damage.
Last
3 The only cinema in the town has closed down.
The
4 The weather in Britain is very changeable.

5 Tourism is the main industry in the region.

81.4 Use the information given to complete the sentences.

1 If I leave my house at 9 o'clock and drive to the airport, I arrive at about 11.
So it's about ....*two hours' drive*.... from my house to the airport. (drive)
2 If I leave my house at 8.40 and walk to the centre, I get there at 9 o'clock.
So it's .... from my house to the centre. (walk)
3 I'm going on holiday on the 12th. I have to be back at work on the 26th.
So I've got .... (holiday)
4 I went to sleep at 3 o'clock this morning and woke up an hour later. After that I couldn't sleep.
So last night I only had .... (sleep)

A Study this example:

Hi, I'm Steve.

Steve **introduced himself** to the other guests.

We use **myself/yourself/himself** etc. (*reflexive pronouns*) when the *subject* and *object* are the same:

Steve introduced himself
subject   *object*

The reflexive pronouns are:

singular (-**self**)   my**self**   your**self** (*one person*)   him**self**/her**self**/it**self**
plural (-**selves**)   our**selves**   your**selves** (*more than one*)   them**selves**

- ○ I don't want you to pay for me. **I**'ll pay for **myself**. (*not* I'll pay for me)
- ○ Amy had a great holiday. **She** really enjoyed **herself**.
- ○ Do **you** talk to **yourself** sometimes? (*said to one person*)
- ○ If you want more to eat, help **yourselves**. (*said to more than one person*)

Compare:
- ○ **Lisa** introduced **me** to the other guests.
- ○ **I** introduced **myself** to the other guests.

B We do not use **myself** etc. after **feel/relax/concentrate/meet**:
- ○ I **feel** nervous. I can't **relax**.
- ○ You need to **concentrate**. (*not* concentrate yourself)
- ○ What time shall we **meet** tomorrow?

Normally we do not use **myself** etc. after **wash/shave/dress**:
- ○ He got up, **washed**, **shaved** and **dressed**. (*not* washed himself etc.)
You can also say **get dressed** (He **got dressed**).

C Compare -**selves** and **each other**:
- ○ Kate and Joe stood in front of the mirror and looked at **themselves**.
  (= *Kate and Joe together* looked at *Kate and Joe*)
- ○ Kate looked at Joe, and Joe looked at Kate. They looked at **each other**.

themselves

each other

You can use **one another** instead of **each other**:
- ○ How long have you and Ben known **each other**? *or* ... known **one another**?
- ○ Sue and Alice don't like **each other**. *or* ... don't like **one another**.
- ○ Do they live near **each other**? *or* ... near **one another**?

D We also use **myself/yourself** etc. in another way. For example:
- ○ 'Who repaired your bike?' '**I** repaired it **myself**.'

I repaired it myself = I repaired it, not another person. Here, **myself** is used to emphasise 'I' (= it makes it stronger). Some more examples:
- ○ I'm not going to do your work for you. **You** can do it **yourself**. (= you, not me)
- ○ **Let's** paint the house **ourselves**. It will be much cheaper.
- ○ **The film itself** wasn't very good, but I loved the music.
- ○ I don't think Lisa will get the job she applied for. **Lisa** doesn't think so **herself**. *or*
  Lisa herself doesn't think so.

>> get dressed / get married etc. → Unit 44D   by myself / by yourself etc. → Unit 83D

Exercises

82.1 Complete the sentences using myself/yourself etc. + these verbs (in the correct form):

> blame   burn   enjoy   express   hurt   ~~introduce~~   put

1 Steve ___introduced himself___ to the other guests at the party.
2 Ben fell down some steps, but fortunately he didn't _____ .
3 It isn't Sue's fault. She really shouldn't _____ .
4 Please try and understand how I feel. You have to _____ in my position.
5 The children had a great time at the beach. They really _____ .
6 Be careful! That pan is hot. Don't _____ .
7 Sometimes I can't say exactly what I mean. I wish I could _____ better.

82.2 Put in myself/yourself/ourselves etc. or me/you/us etc.

1 Amy had a great holiday. She enjoyed ___herself___ .
2 It's not my fault. You can't blame _____ .
3 What I did was really bad. I'm ashamed of _____ .
4 We have a problem. I hope you can help _____ .
5 'Can I take another biscuit?' 'Of course. Help _____ !'
6 I want you to meet Sarah. I'll introduce _____ to her.
7 Don't worry about us. We can take care of _____ .
8 Don't worry about the children. I'll take care of _____ .
9 I gave them a key to our house so that they could let _____ in.

82.3 Complete these sentences. Use myself/yourself etc. where necessary. Choose from:

> concentrate   defend   dry   ~~enjoy~~   feel   meet   relax   ~~shave~~

1 Neil grew a beard because he was fed up with ___shaving___ .
2 Amy had a great holiday. She ___enjoyed herself___ .
3 I wasn't very well yesterday, but I _____ much better today.
4 I climbed out of the swimming pool and _____ with a towel.
5 I tried to study, but I couldn't _____ .
6 If somebody attacks you, you have the right to _____ .
7 I'm going out with Chris this evening. We're _____ at 7.30.
8 You're always rushing. Why don't you sit down and _____ ?

82.4 Complete the sentences with ourselves/themselves or each other.

1 How long have you and Ben known ___each other___ ?
2 If people work too hard, they can make _____ ill.
3 I need you and you need me. We need _____ .
4 In Britain friends often give _____ presents at Christmas.
5 Some people are selfish. They only think of _____ .
6 Tracy and I don't see _____ very often these days.
7 We couldn't get back into the house. We had locked _____ out.
8 They've had an argument. Now they're not speaking to _____ .
9 We'd never met before, so we introduced _____ to _____ .

82.5 Complete the sentences using myself/yourself etc. Use the verb in brackets.

1 'Who repaired the bike for you?' 'Nobody. I ___repaired it myself___ .' (repair)
2 I didn't buy this cake from a shop. I _____ . (make)
3 'Who told you Laura was going away?' 'Laura _____ .' (tell)
4 I don't know what they're going to do. I don't think they _____ . (know)
5 'Who cuts Paul's hair for him?' 'Nobody. He _____ .' (cut)
6 'Can you phone Sam for me?' 'Why can't you _____ ?' (do)

→ Additional exercise 30 (page 320)

A   **a friend of mine / a friend of yours** etc.

We say '(a friend) **of mine/yours/his/hers/ours/theirs**'.
A friend of mine = one of my friends:

- ○ I'm going to a wedding on Saturday. **A friend of mine** is getting married. (*not* a friend of me)
- ○ We went on holiday with **some friends of ours**. (*not* some friends of us)
- ○ Harry had an argument with **a neighbour of his**.
- ○ It was **a good idea of yours** to go to the cinema.

In the same way we say '(a friend) **of my sister's** / (a friend) **of Tom's**' etc. :

- ○ That woman over there is **a friend of my sister's**. (= one of my sister's friends)
- ○ It was **a good idea of Tom's** to go to the cinema.

B   **my own** … / **your own** … etc.

We say **my own** / **your own** / **her own** … etc. :

     my own house   **your own** car   **her own** room
(*not* an own house, an own car etc.)

my own … / **your own** … etc. = something that is only mine/yours, not shared or borrowed:

- ○ I don't want to share a room with anybody. I want **my own room**.
- ○ Vicky and Gary would like to have **their own house**.
- ○ It's a shame that the apartment hasn't got **its own parking space**.
- ○ It's **my own fault** that I have no money. I buy too many things I don't need.
- ○ Why do you want to borrow my car? Why don't you use **your own**? (= your own car)

You can also say 'a room **of my own**', 'a house **of your own**', 'problems **of his own**' etc. :

- ○ I'd like to have a room **of my own**.
- ○ He won't be able to help you with your problems. He has too many problems **of his own**.

C   He cuts **his own** hair

We also use **own** to say that we do something ourselves instead of somebody else doing it
for us. For example:

- ○ Paul usually cuts **his own hair**.
  (= he cuts it himself)
- ○ I'd like to have a garden so that
  I could grow **my own vegetables**.
  (= grow them myself instead of
  buying them from shops)

PAUL

D   **on my own / by myself**

On my own and **by myself** both mean 'alone'. So you can say:

on { my / your his / her / its our / their } **own**	*or*	**by** { myself / yourself *(singular)* himself / herself / itself ourselves / yourselves *(plural)* / themselves }

- ○ I like living **on my own**. *or* I like living **by myself**.
- ○ Some people prefer to live **on their own**. *or* … live **by themselves**.
- ○ Jack was sitting **on his own** in a corner of the cafe. *or* Jack was sitting **by himself** …
- ○ Did you go on holiday **on your own**? *or* Did you go on holiday **by yourself**?

≫ myself/yourself/themselves etc. → Unit 82

Exercises

83.1 Change the <u>underlined</u> words and use the structure … of mine/yours etc.

1 I'm meeting <u>one of my friends</u> tonight.   <u>I'm meeting a friend of mine tonight.</u>
2 We met <u>one of your relatives</u>.   We met a ....
3 Jason borrowed <u>one of my books</u>.   Jason borrowed ....
4 I met Lisa and <u>some of her friends</u>.   I met Lisa and ....
5 We had dinner with <u>one of our neighbours</u>.   We had dinner with ....
6 I went on holiday with <u>two of my friends</u>.   I went on holiday with ....
7 I met <u>one of Amy's friends</u> at the party.   I met .... at the party.
8 It's always been <u>one of my ambitions</u> to   It's always been ....
   travel round the world.   to travel round the world.

83.2 Complete the sentences using my own / our own etc. + the following:

~~bathroom~~	business	opinions	private beach	words

1 I share a kitchen, but I have ... <u>my own bathroom</u> .
2 Gary doesn't think like me. He has ....
3 Julia doesn't want to work for other people. She wants to start ....
4 In the test we had to read a story, and then write it in ....
5 We stayed at a luxury hotel by the sea. The hotel had ....

83.3 Complete the sentences using my own / your own etc.

1 Why do you need to borrow my car? Why don't you ... <u>use your own car</u> ?
2 How can you blame me? It's not my fault. It's ....
3 She's always using my ideas. Why can't she use .... ?
4 Please don't worry about my problems. I'm sure you have ....
5 I can't make his decisions for him. He has to make ....

83.4 Complete the sentences using my own / your own etc. Use the verbs in brackets.

1 Paul never goes to a barber. He ... <u>cuts his own hair</u> . (cut)
2 Helen doesn't often buy clothes. She likes to .... (make)
3 I'm not going to clean your shoes. You can .... (clean)
4 We don't often buy bread. We usually .... (bake)
5 Jack and Joe are singers. They sing songs written by other people, but they also ....
   .... (write)

83.5 Complete the sentences using my own / your own etc. or myself/yourself etc.

1 Did you go on holiday on ... <u>your own</u> ?
2 The box was too heavy for me to lift by ....
3 We had no help decorating the apartment. We did it completely on ....
4 Very young children should not go swimming by ....
5 'Who was Tom with when you saw him?' 'Nobody. He was by .... '
6 I don't like strawberries with cream. I like them on ....
7 Do you like working with other people or do you prefer working by .... ?
8 I went out with Sally because she didn't want to go out on ....

83.6 Are these sentences OK? Correct them where necessary.

1 Katherine would like <u>to have the own house</u>.   ... <u>to have her own house.</u>
2 Sam and Chris are colleagues of me.   ....
3 I was scared. I didn't want to go out by my own.   ....
4 In my last job I had own office.   ....
5 He must be lonely. He's always with himself.   ....
6 My parents have gone away with some friends of them.   ....
7 Are there any countries that produce all own food?   ....

there … and it …

Study this example:

There's a new restaurant in Hill Street.

Yes, I know. I've heard it's very good.

We use **there** … when we talk about something for the first time, to say that it exists:

- ○ **There's** a new restaurant in Hill Street.
- ○ I'm sorry I'm late. **There was** a lot of traffic. (*not* It was a lot of traffic)
- ○ Things are very expensive now. **There has been** a big rise in the cost of living.

It = a specific thing, place, fact, situation etc. :

- ○ We went to the new restaurant. **It's** very good. (**It** = the restaurant)
- ○ I wasn't expecting her to call me. **It** was a complete surprise. (**It** = that she called)

Compare **there** and **it**:

- ○ I like this town. **There**'s a lot to do here. **It**'s an interesting place.

There also means 'to/at/in that place':

- ○ The house is unoccupied. There's nobody living **there**. (= in the house)

You can say:

there will be there must be there might be etc.	there must have been there should have been there would have been etc.	there is sure to be there is bound to be there is going to be	there is likely to be there is supposed to be there used to be

- ○ 'Is there a flight to Rome tonight?'   '**There might be**. I'll check online.'
- ○ If people drove more carefully, **there wouldn't be** so many accidents.
- ○ I could hear music coming from the house. **There must have been** somebody at home.
- ○ **There's bound to be** a cafe somewhere near here. (= There's **sure** to be …)

Compare **there** and **it**:

- ○ They live on a busy road. **There must be** a lot of noise from the traffic.
  They live on a busy road. **It must be** very noisy. (**It** = living on a busy road)
- ○ **There used to be** a cinema here, but it closed a few years ago.
  That building is now a supermarket. **It used to be** a cinema. (**It** = that building)
- ○ **There's sure to be** a flight to Rome tonight.
  There's a flight to Rome tonight, but **it's sure to be** full. (**it** = the flight)

We say:

- ○ **It**'s dangerous **to walk in the road**. (*not* To walk in the road is dangerous)

Normally we use **It** … at the beginning of sentences like this. Some more examples:

- ○ **It** didn't take us long **to get** here.
- ○ **It**'s a shame (**that**) **you can't come to the party**.
- ○ **It**'s not worth **waiting any longer**. Let's go.

We also use **it** to talk about distance, time and weather:

- ○ **How far is it** from here to the airport?
- ○ **It's a long time** since we last saw you.

Compare **it** and **there**:

- ○ **It** was **windy**. *but* **There** was **a cold wind**.

>> supposed to … → Unit 45B   it's worth / it's no use / there's no point → Unit 63A
sure to / bound to … etc. → Unit 65E   there is + -ing/-ed → Unit 97

Exercises

84.1 Put in **there is/was** or **it is/was**. Some sentences are questions (**is there … ? / was it … ?** etc.)
and some are negative (**there isn't / it wasn't** etc.).

1 The journey took a long time. ___There was___ a lot of traffic.
2 What's the new restaurant like? ___Is it___ good?
3 _____ something wrong with the washing machine. It's not working properly.
4 I wanted to visit the museum yesterday, but _____ enough time.
5 What's that new building over there? _____ a hotel?
6 How can we get across the river? _____ a bridge?
7 A few days ago _____ a big storm, which caused a lot of damage.
8 I can't find my phone. _____ in my bag – I just looked.
9 _____ anything interesting on TV, so I turned it off.
10 _____ often very cold here, but _____ much snow.
11 I couldn't see anything. _____ completely dark.
12 '_____ a bookshop near here?' 'Yes, _____ one in Hudson Street.'
13 _____ difficult to get a job right now. _____ a lot of unemployment.
14 When we got to the cinema, _____ a queue outside. _____ a very long
   queue, so we decided not to wait.

84.2 Read the first sentence and then write a sentence beginning **There …** .

1 The roads were busy yesterday.   ___There was a lot of traffic.___
2 This soup is very salty.   There _____ in the soup.
3 The box was empty.   _____ in the box.
4 About 50 people came to the meeting.   _____ at the meeting.
5 The film is very violent.   _____
6 I like this town – it's lively.   _____

84.3 Complete the sentences. Use **there would be**, **there used to be** etc. Choose from:

won't	may	~~would~~	wouldn't	should	used to	is going to

1 If people drove more carefully, ___there would be___ fewer accidents.
2 'Do we have any eggs?' 'I'm not sure. _____ some in the fridge.'
3 I think everything will be OK. _____ any problems.
4 Look at those clouds. _____ a storm. I'm sure of it.
5 There isn't a school in the village. _____ one, but it closed a few years ago.
6 People drive too fast on this road. I think _____ a speed limit.
7 If people weren't so aggressive, _____ any wars.

84.4 Are these sentences OK? Change **it** to **there** where necessary.

1 They live on a busy road. <u>It must be</u> a lot of noise.   ___There must be a lot of noise.___
2 It's a long way from my house to the nearest shop.   ___OK___
3 After the lecture it will be an opportunity to ask questions.   _____
4 Why was she so unfriendly? It must have been a reason.   _____
5 I like where I live, but it would be nicer to live by the sea. _____
6 How long is it since you last went to the theatre?   _____
7 It used to be a lot of tourists here, but not many come now.   _____
8 My phone won't work here. It's no signal.   _____
9 It was Ken's birthday yesterday. We had a party.   _____
10 We won't have any problem parking the car. It's sure to be
   a car park somewhere.   _____
11 I'm sorry about what happened. It was my fault.   _____
12 I was told that it would be somebody to meet me at the
   station, but it wasn't anybody.   _____

some and any

A

In general we use **some** (*also* **somebody/someone/something**) in positive sentences and **any** (*also* **anybody** etc.) in negative sentences:

some	any
○ We **bought some** flowers.	○ We **didn't** buy **any** flowers.
○ He's busy. He **has some** work to do.	○ He's lazy. He **never** does **any** work.
○ There**'s somebody** at the door.	○ There **isn't anybody** at the door.
○ I **want something** to eat.	○ I **don't** want **anything** to eat.

We use **any** in the following sentences because the meaning is negative:
- ○ She went out **without any** money. (she **didn't** take **any** money with her)
- ○ He **refused** to eat **anything**. (he **didn't** eat **anything**)
- ○ It's a very easy exam. **Hardly anybody** fails. (= almost **nobody** fails)

B

We use both **some** and **any** in questions. We use **some/somebody/something** to talk about a person or thing that we know exists, or we think exists:
- ○ Are you waiting for **somebody**? (I think you are waiting for somebody)

We use **some** in questions when we ask for or offer things:
- ○ Can I have **some** sugar, please? (there is probably some sugar that I can have)
- ○ Would you like **something** to eat? (there is something to eat)

But in most questions, we use **any**. We do not know if the thing or person exists:
- ○ Do you have **any** luggage? (maybe you do, maybe not)
- ○ Is there **anybody** in the house? (maybe there is, maybe not)

C

You can use **if** + **any**:
- ○ Let me know **if** you need **anything**.
- ○ **If anyone** has **any** questions, I'll be pleased to answer them.

The following sentences have the idea of **if**:
- ○ I'm sorry for **any** trouble I've caused. (= **if** I have caused **any** trouble)
- ○ The police want to speak to **anyone** who saw the accident. (= **if** there is **anyone**)

D

We also use **any** with the meaning 'it doesn't matter which':
- ○ You can take **any** bus. They all go to the centre. (= it doesn't matter which bus you take)
- ○ Come and see me **any** time you want.

We use **anybody/anyone/anything/anywhere** in the same way:
- ○ We forgot to lock the door. **Anybody** could have come in.

Compare **some**- and **any**-:
- ○ A: I'm hungry. I want **something** to eat.
  B: What would you like?
  A: I don't mind. **Anything**. (= it doesn't matter what)
- ○ B: Let's go out **somewhere**.
  A: Where shall we go?
  B: **Anywhere**. I just want to go out.

E

Somebody/someone/anybody/anyone are singular words:
- ○ **Someone** is here to see you.

But we use **they/them/their** after these words:
- ○ **Someone** has forgotten **their** umbrella. (= his or her umbrella)
- ○ If **anybody** wants to leave early, **they** can. (= he or she can)

>> not … any → Unit 86   some of / any of … → Unit 88   hardly any → Unit 101C

Exercises

85.1 Put in **some** or **any**.

1 We didn't buy ___any___ flowers.
2 Tonight I'm going out with _____ friends of mine.
3 Have you seen _____ good movies recently?
4 I'd like _____ information about what there is to see in this town.
5 I didn't have _____ money. I had to borrow _____ .
6 You can use your card to withdraw money at _____ cash machine.
7 Those apples look nice. Shall we get _____ ?
8 With the special tourist train ticket, you can travel on _____ train you like.
9 'Can I have _____ more coffee, please?' 'Sure. Help yourself.'
10 If there are _____ words you don't understand, look them up in a dictionary.
11 We wanted to buy _____ grapes, but they didn't have _____ in the shop.

85.2 Complete the sentences with **some-** or **any-** + **-body/-thing/-where**.

1 I was too surprised to say ___anything___ .
2 There's _____ at the door. Can you go and see who it is?
3 Does _____ mind if I open the window?
4 I can't drive and I don't know _____ about cars.
5 You must be hungry. Why don't I get you _____ to eat?
6 Emma is very tolerant. She never complains about _____ .
7 There was hardly _____ on the beach. It was almost deserted.
8 Let's go away. Let's go _____ warm and sunny.
9 I'm going out now. If _____ asks where I am, tell them you don't know.
10 Why are you looking under the bed? Have you lost _____ ?
11 This is a no-parking area. _____ who parks their car here will have to pay a fine.
12 Quick, let's go! There's _____ coming and I don't want _____ to see us.
13 They stay at home all the time. They never seem to go _____ .
14 Jonathan stood up and left the room without saying _____ .
15 'Can I ask you _____ ?' 'Sure. What do you want to ask?'
16 Sarah was upset about _____ and refused to talk to _____ .
17 I need _____ to translate. Is there _____ here who speaks English?
18 Sue is very secretive. She never tells _____ . (*2 words*)

85.3 Complete the sentences. Use **any** (+ noun) or **anybody/anything/anywhere**.

1	Which bus do I have to take?	___Any bus___ . They all go to the centre.
2	When shall we meet? Monday?	I don't mind. _____ next week will be OK for me.
3	What do you want to eat?	_____ . I don't mind. Whatever you have.
4	Who shall I invite to the party?	It's your party. You can invite _____ you want.
5	What sort of job are you looking for?	_____ . It doesn't matter what it is.
6	Where shall I sit?	It's up to you. You can sit _____ you like.
7	Is this machine difficult to use?	No, it's easy. _____ can learn to use it very quickly.

no/none/any   nothing/nobody etc.

A   no and none

We use **no** + *noun* (**no bus**, **no shops** etc.).
no = **not a** or **not any**:
- ○ We had to walk home. There was **no bus**. (= There **wasn't a** bus.)
- ○ Sarah will have **no trouble** finding a job. (= Sarah **won't** have **any** trouble …)
- ○ There were **no shops** open. (= There **weren't any** shops open.)

You can use **no** + *noun* at the beginning of a sentence:
- ○ **No reason** was given for the change of plan.

We use **none** *without* a noun:
- ○ 'How much money do you have?' '**None**.' (= no money)
- ○ All the tickets have been sold. There are **none** left. (= no tickets left)

Or we use **none of** … :
- ○ This money is all yours. **None of it** is mine.

Compare **no**, **none** and **any**:
- ○ I have **no luggage**.
- ○ 'How much luggage do you have?' '**None**.' *or* 'I **don't** have **any**.'

After **none of** + *plural* (none of **the students**, none of **them** etc.) the verb can be singular or plural:
- ○ None of the students **were** happy. *or* None of the students **was** happy.

B   nothing   nobody/no-one   nowhere

You can use these words at the beginning of a sentence or alone (as answers to questions):
- ○ 'What's going to happen?' '**Nobody** knows. / **No-one** knows.'
- ○ 'What happened?' '**Nothing**.'
- ○ 'Where are you going?' '**Nowhere**. I'm staying here.'

You can also use these words after a verb, especially after **be** and **have**:
- ○ The house is empty. There**'s nobody** living there.
- ○ . We **had nothing** to eat.

nothing/nobody etc. = **not** + **anything/anybody** etc. :
- ○ I said **nothing**. = I **didn't** say **anything**.
- ○ Jane told **nobody** about her plans. = Jane **didn't** tell **anybody** about her plans.
- ○ They have **nowhere** to live. = They **don't** have **anywhere** to live.

With **nothing/nobody** etc., we do *not* use a negative verb (**isn't**, **didn't** etc.):
- ○ I **said** nothing. (*not* I didn't say nothing)

C   After **nobody/no-one** you can use **they/them/their** (see also Unit 85E):
- ○ **Nobody** is perfect, are **they**? (= is he or she perfect?)
- ○ **No-one** did what I asked **them** to do. (= him or her)
- ○ **Nobody** in the class did **their** homework. (= his or her homework)

D   Sometimes **any/anything/anybody** etc. means 'it doesn't matter which/what/who' (see Unit 85D).
Compare **no-** and **any-**:
- ○ There was **no** bus, so we walked home.
  You can take **any** bus. They all go to the centre. (= it doesn't matter which bus)
- ○ 'What do you want to eat?' '**Nothing**. I'm not hungry.'
  I'm so hungry. I could eat **anything**. (= it doesn't matter what)
- ○ It's a difficult job. **Nobody** wants to do it.
  It's a very easy job. **Anybody** can do it. (= it doesn't matter who)

>>   **some** and **any** ➜ **Unit 85**   **none of** … ➜ **Unit 88**   **any bigger** / **no better** etc. ➜ **Unit 106B**

Exercises

86.1 **Complete these sentences with no, none or any.**

1 It was a public holiday, so there were ......*no*...... shops open.
2 I don't have ......*any*...... money. Can you lend me some?
3 We had to walk home. There were .... taxis.
4 We had to walk home. There weren't .... taxis.
5 'How many eggs do we have?'   '............................ . Shall I get some?'
6 There's nowhere to cross the river. There's .... bridge.
7 We took a few pictures, but .... of them were very good.
8 'Did you take lots of pictures?'   'No, I didn't take ....'
9 I had to do what I did. I had .... alternative.
10 I don't like .... of this furniture. It's horrible.
11 We cancelled the party because .... of the people we invited were able to come.
12 Everyone knows they are getting married. It's .... secret.
13 The two books are exactly the same. There isn't .... difference.
14 'Do you know where Chris is?'   'I'm sorry. I have .... idea.'

86.2 **Answer these questions using none/nobody/nothing/nowhere.**

1	What did you do at the weekend?	......*Nothing*...... . It was very boring.
2	Who are you waiting for?	.... I'm just standing here.
3	How much bread did you buy?	.... We already have enough.
4	Where are you going?	.... I'm staying here.
5	How many books have you read this year?	.... I don't read books.
6	How much does it cost to get into the museum?	.... It's free.

Now answer the same questions using any/anybody/anything/anywhere.

7 (1) ......*I didn't do anything.*......   10 (4) ....
8 (2) I'm ....   11 (5) ....
9 (3) I ....   12 (6) ....

86.3 **Complete these sentences with no- or any- + -body/-thing/-where.**

1 I don't want ......*anything*...... to drink. I'm not thirsty.
2 The bus was completely empty. There was .... on it.
3 'Where did you go for your holidays?'   '............................ . I didn't go away.'
4 'Can you smell gas?'   'No, I can't smell ....'
5 Everybody seemed satisfied. .... complained.
6 Let's go away. We can go .... you like.
7 The town is still the same as it was years ago. .... has changed.
8 'What did you buy?'   '............................ . I couldn't find .... I wanted.'
9 There was complete silence in the room. .... said ....

86.4 **Which is right?**

1 She didn't tell ~~nobody~~ / anybody about her plans. (anybody is correct)
2 The accident looked bad, but fortunately nobody / anybody was seriously injured.
3 I looked out of the window, but I couldn't see no-one / anyone.
4 The exam is very easy. Nobody / Anybody can pass it.
5 'What's in that box?'   'Nothing / Anything. It's empty.'
6 The future is uncertain. Nothing / Anything is possible.
7 I don't know nothing / anything about economics.
8 I'll try and answer no / any questions you ask me.
9 'Who were you talking to just now?'   'No-one / Anyone. I wasn't talking to no-one / anyone.'

➔ Additional exercise 30 (page 320)   173

much, many, little, few, a lot, plenty

A

We use **much** and **little** with *uncountable* nouns:

    much luck   much time   little energy   little money

We use **many** and **few** with *plural* nouns:

    many friends   many people   few cars   few children

We use **a lot of** / **lots of** / **plenty of** with both *uncountable* and *plural* nouns:

    a lot of luck   lots of time   plenty of money
    a lot of friends   lots of people   plenty of ideas

plenty = more than enough:
- There's no need to hurry. We've got **plenty of time**.
- There's **plenty to do** in this town.

B

Much is unusual in positive sentences (especially in spoken English). Compare:
- We **didn't** spend **much** money. *but* We **spent a lot of** money.
- **Do** you **see** David **much**?   *but* I **see** David **a lot**.

But we use **too much** / **so much** / **as much** in positive sentences:
- We **spent too much** money.

We use **many** and **a lot of** in all kinds of sentences:
- **Many** people drive too fast.   *or* **A lot of** people drive too fast.
- Do you know **many** people?   *or* Do you know **a lot of** people?
- There aren't **many** tourists here. *or* There aren't **a lot of** tourists here.

Note that we say **many years** / **many weeks** / **many days**:
- We've lived here for **many years**. (*not usually* a lot of years)

C

little = not much, **few** = not many:
- Gary is very busy with his job. He has **little time** for other things.
  (= not much time, less time than he would like)
- Vicky doesn't like living in London. She has **few friends** there.
  (= not many friends, not as many as she would like)

We often use **very little** and **very few**:
- Gary has **very little time** for other things.
- Vicky has **very few friends** in London.

D

a little = some, a small amount:
- Let's go and have coffee. We have **a little** time before the train leaves.
  (**a little time** = some time, enough time to have a coffee)
- 'Do you speak English?' '**A little**.' (so we can talk a bit)

a few = some, a small number:
- I enjoy my life here. I have **a few friends** and we meet quite often.
  (**a few friends** = not many, but enough to have a good time)
- 'When was the last time you saw Clare?' '**A few days** ago.' (= 3 or 4 days ago)

E

Compare **little** and **a little**, **few** and **a few**:
- He spoke **little English**, so it was difficult to communicate with him.
  He spoke **a little English**, so we were able to communicate with him.
- She's lucky. She has **few problems**. (= not many problems)
  Things are not going so well for her. She has **a few problems**. (= some problems)

We say **only a little** (*not* only little) and **only a few** (*not* only few):
- Hurry! We **only** have **a little** time. (= some, but not much time)
- The village was small. There were **only a few** houses. (= some but not many houses)

    >>   Countable and uncountable → Units 69–70

Exercises

87.1 In some of these sentences **much** is incorrect or unnatural. Change **much** to **many** or **a lot (of)** where necessary. Write '**OK**' if the sentence is correct.

1 We didn't eat much.   OK
2 My mother drinks <u>much tea</u>.   My mother drinks a lot of tea.
3 Be quick. We don't have much time.
4 It cost much to repair the car.
5 Did it cost much to repair the car?
6 You have much luggage. Let me help you.
7 There wasn't much traffic this morning.
8 I don't know much people in this town.
9 Do you eat much fruit?
10 Mike likes travelling. He travels much.

87.2 Complete the sentences using **plenty of ...** or **plenty to ...** . Choose from:

| hotels | learn | money | room | see | ~~time~~ |

1 There's no need to hurry. There's   plenty of time.
2 He has no financial problems. He has
3 Come and sit with us. There's
4 She knows a lot, but she still has
5 It's an interesting town to visit. There
6 I'm sure we'll find somewhere to stay.

87.3 Put in **much/many/little/few** (one word only).

1 She isn't popular. She has ..... **few** ..... friends.
2 Anna is very busy these days. She has .... free time.
3 Did you take .... pictures at the wedding?
4 This is a modern city. There are .... old buildings.
5 The weather has been very dry recently. We've had .... rain.
6 I don't know London well. I haven't been there for .... years.
7 The two cars are similar. There is .... difference between them.
8 I'm not very busy today. I don't have .... to do.
9 It's a wonderful place to live. There are .... better places to be.

87.4 Which is right?

1 She's lucky. She has <u>few problems / a few problems</u>. (few problems *is correct*)
2 Can you lend me <u>few dollars / a few dollars</u>?
3 It was the middle of the night, so there was <u>little traffic / a little traffic</u>.
4 They got married <u>few years ago / a few years ago</u>.
5 I can't give you a decision yet. I need <u>little time / a little time</u> to think.
6 I don't know much Russian – <u>only few words / only a few words</u>.
7 It was a surprise that he won the game. <u>Few people / A few people</u> expected him to win.

87.5 Put in **little / a little / few / a few**.

1 Gary is very busy with his job. He has ..... **little** ..... time for other things.
2 Listen carefully. I'm going to give you .... advice.
3 Do you mind if I ask you .... questions?
4 It's not a very interesting place, so .... tourists visit.
5 I don't think Amy would be a good teacher. She has .... patience.
6 'Would you like milk in your coffee?' 'Yes, ... , please.'
7 This is a boring place to live. There's .... to do.
8 I know Hong Kong quite well. I've been there .... times.
9 There were only .... people at the meeting.
10 'Did you do all this work on your own?' 'No, I had .... help from my friends.'

A

all	some	any	most	much	many	(a) little	(a) few	no

You can use these words with a noun (**some food** / **few books** etc.):
- ○ **All cars** have wheels.
- ○ **Some cars** can go faster than others.
- ○ **Many people** drive too fast.
- ○ I go away **most weekends**.
- ○ I feel really tired. I've got **no energy**.

We do not say 'all of cars', 'some of people' etc. (see Section B):
- ○ **Some people** learn more easily than others. (*not* Some of people)

B

all	half	some	any	most	much	many	(a) little	(a) few	none

You can use these words with **of** (**some of** / **most of** etc.):

some of		the …	my …
most of	+	this …	these …
none of etc.		that …	those … etc.

So you can say:
> some **of the people**, some **of those people** (*but not* some of people)
> most **of my time**, most **of the time** (*but not* most of time)

- ○ **Some of the people I work with** are very strange.
- ○ **None of this money** is mine.
- ○ Have you read **any of these books**?
- ○ I was ill yesterday. I spent **most of the day** in bed.

You don't need **of** after **all** or **half**. So you can say:
- ○ **All my friends** live near here. *or*   All **of** my friends …
- ○ **Half this money** is mine. *or*   Half **of** this money …

Compare:
- ○ **All flowers** are beautiful. (= all flowers in general)
  All (of) these flowers are beautiful. (= a specific group of flowers)
- ○ **Most problems** have a solution. (= most problems in general)
  We were able to solve **most of the problems we had**. (= a specific group of problems)

C

You can use **all of** / **some of** / **none of** etc. + **it/us/you/them**:

all of			
some of		it	
any of	+	us	
most of		you	
none of		them	
etc.			

- ○ A: Do you like this music?
  B: **Some of it**. Not **all of it**.
- ○ A: How many of these people do you know?
  B: **None of them**. / **A few of them**.
- ○ Do **any of you** want to come to a party tonight?
  (*said to more than 2 people*)

We say: **all of us** / **all of you** / **half of it** / **half of them** etc. You need **of** before **it/us/you/them**:
- ○ **All of us** were late. (*not* all us)
- ○ I haven't finished the book yet. I've only read **half of it**. (*not* half it)

D

We also use **some/most** etc. alone, *without* a noun:
- ○ Some cars have four doors and **some** have two.
- ○ A few of the shops were open, but **most** (of them) were closed.
- ○ Half this money is mine, and **half** (of it) is yours. (*not* the half)

» all ➜ Unit 75B, 90, 110D   some and any ➜ Unit 85   no and none ➜ Unit 86
much/many/little/few ➜ Unit 87   all of whom / most of which etc. ➜ Unit 96B

Exercises

88.1 Put in **of** where necessary. Leave the space empty if the sentence is already complete.

1   All ____–____ cars have wheels. *(the sentence is already complete)*
2   None __of__ this money is mine.
3   There were problems at the airport and some _____ flights were cancelled.
4   Some _____ the films I've seen recently have been very violent.
5   Joe never goes to museums. He says that all _____ museums are boring.
6   I think some _____ people watch too much TV.
7   Do you want any _____ these magazines or can I throw them away?
8   Kate has lived in London most _____ her life.
9   Joe has lived in Chicago all _____ his life.
10 Most _____ days I get up before 7 o'clock.
11 I usually have a little _____ sugar in my coffee.
12 They won the lottery a few years ago, but they've spent most _____ the money.

88.2 Choose from the list and complete the sentences. Use **of** (some of / most of etc.) where necessary.

accidents	European countries	my dinner	the players
birds	her friends	my spare time	the population
~~cars~~	her opinions	the buildings	~~these books~~

1   I haven't read many __of these books__ .
2   All __cars__ have wheels.
3   I spend much _____ gardening.
4   Many _____ are caused by bad driving.
5   It's a historic town. Many _____ are over 400 years old.
6   When Emily got married, she kept it a secret. She didn't tell any _____ .
7   Not many people live in the north of the country. Most _____ live
    in the south.
8   Not all _____ can fly. For example, the penguin can't fly.
9   Our team played badly and lost the game. None _____ played well.
10 Emma and I have different ideas. I don't agree with many _____ .
11 Sarah travels a lot in Europe. She has been to most _____ .
12 I had no appetite. I could only eat half _____ .

88.3 Use your own ideas to complete these sentences.

1   The building was damaged in the explosion. All __the windows__ were broken.
2   We argue sometimes, but get on well most of _____ .
3   I went to the cinema by myself. None of _____ wanted to come.
4   The test was hard. I could only answer half _____ .
5   Some of _____ you took at the wedding were really good.
6   'Did you spend all _____ I gave you?' 'No, there's some left.'

88.4 Complete the sentences. Use:

   all of / some of / none of + **it/them/us** (all of it / some of them etc.)

1   These books are all Sarah's. __None of them__ belong to me.
2   'How many of these books have you read?' '_____ . Every one.'
3   We all got wet in the rain because _____ had an umbrella.
4   Some of this money is yours and _____ is mine.
5   Many of my friends have travelled a lot, but _____ has ever been to Africa.
6   Not all the tourists in the group were Spanish. _____ were French.
7   I watched most of the film, but not _____ .
8   He told us his life story, but _____ was true. It was all invented.

both / both of   neither / neither of
either / either of

A

We use **both/neither/either** for *two* things.
You can use these words with a *noun* (**both books**, **neither book** etc.).

For example, you are going out to eat. There are two possible restaurants. You say:
- ○ **Both restaurants** are good. (*not* the both restaurants)
- ○ **Neither restaurant** is expensive.
- ○ We can go to **either restaurant**. I don't mind. (= one or the other, it doesn't matter which)
- ○ I haven't been to **either restaurant** before. (= not one or the other)

You can also use **both/neither/either** without a noun:
- ○ 'Which do you prefer, basketball or tennis?'   'It's hard to say. I like **both**.'
- ○ 'Is your friend British or American?'   '**Neither**. She's Australian.'
- ○ 'Do you want tea or coffee?'   '**Either**. I don't mind.'

B

both of … / neither of … / either of …

We use **both of / neither of / either of + the/these/my/Tom's** … etc. So we say 'both of **the** restaurants', 'both of **those** restaurants' etc. (*but not* both of restaurants):
- ○ **Both of these** restaurants are good.
- ○ **Neither of the** restaurants we went to was expensive.
- ○ I haven't been to **either of those** restaurants.

You don't need **of** after **both**. So you can say:
- ○ **Both of these** restaurants are good.   *or*   **Both these** restaurants are good.

We also use **both of / neither of / either of + us/you/them**:
- ○ *(talking to two people)* Can **either of you** speak Russian?
- ○ I asked two people how to get to the station, but **neither of them** knew.

We say 'both **of**' before **us/you/them** (you need to use **of**):
- ○ **Both of us** were tired. (*not* Both us were …)

After **neither of** … a verb can be singular or plural:
- ○ Neither of them **is** at home.   *or*   Neither of them **are** at home.

C

You can say:

both … and …	○ **Both** Chris **and** Paul were late.
	○ I was **both** tired **and** hungry when I arrived home.
neither … nor …	○ **Neither** Chris **nor** Paul came to the party.
	○ There was an accident outside our house, but we **neither** saw **nor** heard anything.
either … or …	○ I'm not sure where Maria's from. She's **either** Spanish **or** Italian.
	○ **Either** you apologise, **or** I'll never speak to you again.

D

Compare **either/neither/both** (two things) and **any/none/all** (more than two):

○ There are **two** good hotels here. You could stay at **either** of them.	○ There are **many** good hotels here. You could stay at **any** of them.

○ We tried **two** hotels.
   { **Neither** of them had a room.
     Both of them were full.
	○ We tried **a lot of** hotels.
	   { **None** of them had a room.
	     All of them were full.

≫   neither do I / I don't either → Unit 51C   any → Units 85–86   none → Units 86A, 88   all → Unit 88
     both of whom / neither of which → Unit 96B   both → Unit 110D

Exercises

89.1 Complete the sentences with **both**/**neither**/**either**.

1 'Do you want tea or coffee?' '___Either___. I really don't mind.'
2 'What day is it today – the 18th or the 19th?' '_____. It's the 20th.'
3 A: Where did you go on your trip – Korea or Japan?
   B: We went to _____. A week in Korea and a week in Japan.
4 'Shall we sit in the corner or by the window?' '_____. I don't mind.'
5 'Where's Lisa? Is she at work or at home?' '_____. She's away on holiday.'
6 'Is it true that Kate speaks Spanish and Arabic?' 'Yes, she speaks _____ fluently.'

89.2 Complete the sentences with **both**/**neither**/**either**. Use **of** where necessary.

1 ___Both___ my parents are from Egypt.
2 To get to the town centre, you can walk along the river or you can go along the road.
   You can go _____ way.
3 I went to Carl's house twice, but _____ times he wasn't at home.
4 _____ Tom's parents is English. His father is Polish and his mother is Italian.
5 I saw an accident this morning. One car drove into the back of another. Fortunately
   _____ driver was injured, but _____ cars were badly damaged.
6 I have two sisters and a brother. My brother is working, but _____ my sisters are still
   at school.

89.3 Complete the sentences with **both**/**neither**/**either** + **of us** / **of them**.

1 I asked two people how to get to the station, but ___neither of them___ knew.
2 I was invited to two parties last week, but I couldn't go to _____.
3 There were two windows in the room. It was very warm, so I opened _____.
4 Sam and I often play tennis, but we're not very good. _____ can play well.
5 I tried two bookshops for the book I wanted to buy, but _____ had it.

89.4 Write sentences with **both ... and ...** / **neither ... nor ...** / **either ... or ...** .

1 Chris was late. So was Pat. ___Both Chris and Pat were late.___
2 He didn't say hello, and he didn't smile. ___He neither said hello nor smiled.___
3 It was a boring movie. It was long too.
   The movie _____
4 Joe doesn't have a car. Sam doesn't have one either.
   _____
5 Emily speaks German and she speaks Russian too.
   _____
6 Ben doesn't watch TV and he doesn't read newspapers.
   Ben _____
7 Is that man's name Richard? Or is it Robert? It's one of the two.
   That man's name _____
8 I don't have time to go on holiday. And I don't have the money.
   I have _____
9 We can leave today or we can leave tomorrow – whichever you prefer.
   We _____

89.5 Complete the sentences with **neither**/**either**/**none**/**any**.

1 We tried a lot of hotels, but ___none___ of them had a room.
2 Sam has two sisters, but I haven't met _____ of them.
3 Emily has four brothers, but I haven't met _____ of them.
4 There were a few shops in the street, but _____ of them was open.
5 Spain, Italy, Greece, Turkey – have you been to _____ of these countries?
6 I could meet you next Monday or Thursday. Would _____ of those days suit you?
7 Mark and I couldn't get into the house because _____ of us had a key.

all every whole

A everybody/everyone/everything and all

We say:
- ○ **Everybody** was happy.   *or*   **Everyone** was happy.   (*not* all were happy)
- ○ He thinks he knows **everything**.   (*not* knows all)
- ○ Our holiday was a disaster. **Everything** went wrong.   (*not* all went wrong)

We do not often use **all** *alone* in this way. We do not say 'all were happy', 'he knows all' etc.

We use **all** in the following ways:

all + noun (**all cars, all my money** etc.)	○ **All my friends** were happy.
all of + us/you/them	○ **All of us** were happy.
we/you/they … **all** … (see also Unit 110D)	○ **We** were **all** happy.
all about …	○ He knows **all about computers**.
all … = the only thing(s)	○ **All I've eaten today** is a banana.
	(= the only thing I've eaten today)

B whole and all

Whole = complete, entire. We use **whole** mostly with *singular* nouns:
- ○ Did you read **the whole book**? (= all the book, not just a part of it)
- ○ Emily has lived **her whole life** in the same town.
- ○ I was so hungry, I ate **a whole packet** of biscuits. (= a complete packet)

We do not normally use **whole** with *uncountable* nouns (**water**, **food**, **money** etc.).
We say:
- ○ Did you spend **all the money** I gave you? (*not* the whole money)
- ○ I read **all the information** carefully. (*not* the whole information)

We use **the/my/a** etc. before **whole**. Compare **whole** and **all**:
- ○ I read **the whole** book. *but* I read **all the** information.

C every day / all day / the whole day

We use **every** to say how often something happens (**every day / every ten minutes** etc.):
- ○ When we were on holiday, we went to the beach **every day**. (*not* all days)
- ○ The bus service is excellent. There's a bus **every ten minutes**.
- ○ We don't see each other very often – about **every six months**.

All day *or* **the whole day** = the complete day from beginning to end:
- ○ We spent **all day** on the beach. *or* We spent **the whole day** …
- ○ Dan was very quiet. He didn't say a word **all evening**. *or* …**the whole evening**.

Note that we say **all day** (*not* all the day), **all week** (*not* all the week) etc.

Compare **all the time** and **every time**:
- ○ They never go out. They are at home **all the time**. (= always, continuously)
- ○ **Every time** I see you, you look different. (= each time, on every occasion)

D Every/everybody/everyone/everything are *singular* words, so we use a *singular* verb:
- ○ **Every seat** in the theatre **was** taken.
- ○ **Everybody has** arrived. (*not* have arrived)

But we use **they/them/their** after **everybody/everyone**:
- ○ **Everybody** said **they** enjoyed **themselves**. (= everybody enjoyed himself or herself)

>> Countable and uncountable → Units 69–70   all / all of → Unit 88   each and every → Unit 91
   every one → Unit 91D   all → Unit 110C

Exercises

90.1 Complete these sentences with **all**, **everything** or **everybody/everyone**.

1 It was a good party. ___Everybody___ had a great time.
2 ___All___ I've eaten today is a banana.
3 _____ has their faults. Nobody is perfect.
4 Nothing has changed. _____ is the same as it was.
5 Kate told me _____ about her new job. It sounds interesting.
6 Can _____ write their names on a piece of paper, please?
7 Why are you always thinking about money? Money isn't _____.
8 I'm really exhausted. _____ I want to do is sleep.
9 When the fire alarm rang, _____ left the building immediately.
10 Amy didn't say where she was going. _____ she said was that she was going away.
11 We have completely different opinions. I disagree with _____ she says.
12 We all did well in the exam. _____ in our class passed.
13 We all did well in the exam. _____ of us passed.
14 Why are you so lazy? Why do you expect me to do _____ for you?

90.2 Write sentences with **whole**.

1 I read the book from beginning to end. ___I read the whole book.___
2 Everyone in the team played well.
   The _____
3 Paul opened a box of chocolates. He started eating. When he finished, there were no chocolates left in the box. He ate _____
4 The police came to the house. They were looking for something. They searched everywhere, every room. They _____
5 Everyone in Ed and Jane's family plays tennis. Ed and Jane play, and so do all their children.
   The _____
6 Sarah worked from early in the morning until late in the evening.
   _____
7 Jack and Lisa had a week's holiday by the sea. It rained from the beginning of the week to the end of the week. It _____

Now write sentences 6 and 7 again using **all** instead of **whole**.

8 (6) Sarah _____
9 (7) _____

90.3 Complete these sentences using **every** with the following:

five minutes	~~ten minutes~~	four hours	six months	four years

1 The bus service is very good. There's a bus ___every ten minutes___ .
2 Tom is ill. He has some medicine. He has to take it _____ .
3 The Olympic Games take place _____ .
4 We live near a busy airport. A plane flies over our house _____ .
5 Martin goes to the dentist for a check-up _____ .

90.4 Which is right?

1 Did you spend ~~the whole money~~ / all the money I gave you? (all the money *is correct*)
2 Eve works every day / all days except Sunday.
3 I'm tired. I've been working hard all the day / all day.
4 It was a terrible fire. Whole building / The whole building was destroyed.
5 It's a very sad song. Every time / All the time I hear it, it makes me cry.
6 I don't like the weather here. It rains every time / all the time.
7 When I was on holiday, all my luggage / my whole luggage was stolen.

→ **Additional exercise 30** (page 320)   181

each and every

A

Each and **every** are similar. Often it is possible to use **each** or **every**:
- ◯ **Each** time I see you, you look different. *or* **Every** time I see you …

But **each** and **every** are not exactly the same.

We use **each** when we think of things separately, one by one. ◯ Study **each sentence** carefully. (= study the sentences one by one)	We use **every** when we think of things as a group. The meaning is similar to **all**. ◯ **Every window** in the house was open. (= all the windows in the house)

each = X + X + X + X

every = XXXXXXXXXXXX

Each is more usual for a small number: ◯ There were four books on the table. **Each book** was a different colour. ◯ *(in a card game)* At the beginning of the game, **each player** has three cards.	**Every** is more usual for a large number: ◯ Kate loves reading. She has read **every book** in the library. (= all the books) ◯ I'd like to visit **every country** in the world. (= all the countries)

Each (but not **every**) can be used for two things:
- ◯ In football, **each team** has eleven players. (*not* every team)

We use **every** (not **each**) to say how often something happens:
- ◯ 'How often do you use your car?' '**Every day**.' (*not* Each day)
- ◯ There's a bus **every ten minutes**. (*not* each ten minutes)

B

Compare the structures we use with **each** and **every**.

We use **each** with or without a noun: ◯ None of the rooms are the same. **Each room** is different. *or* **Each** is different. Or you can use **each one**: ◯ **Each one** is different. We say **each of** (**the/these/them** … etc.): ◯ **Each of the** books was a different colour. (*not* each of books) ◯ **Each of them** was a different colour. ◯ Read **each of these** sentences carefully.	We use **every** with a noun: ◯ She's read **every book** in the library. We don't use **every** alone, but you can say **every one**: ◯ A: Have you read all these books? B: Yes, **every one**. We say **every one of** … (*but not* every of): ◯ I've read **every one of those** books. (*not* every of those books) ◯ I've read **every one of them**.

C

We also use **each** in the middle of a sentence. For example:
- ◯ The students were **each** given a book. (= Each student was given a book.)

We say **a dollar each**, **ten pounds each** etc. :
- ◯ These oranges are **40 pence each**. (**each** = for one orange)

D

everyone and **every one**

Everyone (one word) is only for people (= everybody).
- ◯ **Everyone** enjoyed the party. (= **Everybody** …)

Every one (two words) is for things or people:
- ◯ Sarah is invited to lots of parties and she goes to **every one**. (= to **every party**)

》 **each other →** Unit 82C   **all** and **every →** Unit 90

Exercises

91.1 Look at the pictures and complete the sentences with **each** or **every**.

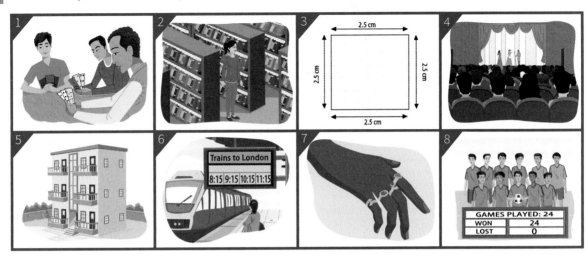

1. ...Each.... player has three cards.
2. Kate has read ....every.... book in the library.
3. .... side of a square is the same length.
4. .... seat in the theatre was taken.
5. There are six apartments in the building. .... one has a balcony.
6. There's a train to London .... hour.
7. She was wearing four rings – one on .... finger.
8. Our football team is playing well. We've won .... game this season.

91.2 Put in **each**, **each of** or **every**.

1. There were four books on the table. ...Each.... book was a different colour.
2. The Olympic Games are held ....every.... four years.
3. .... parent worries about their children.
4. In a game of tennis there are two or four players. .... player has a racket.
5. Nicola plays volleyball .... Thursday evening.
6. I understood most of what they said but not .... word.
7. The book is divided into five parts and .... these has three sections.
8. I get paid .... four weeks.
9. I called the office two or three times, but .... time it was closed.
10. Car seat belts save lives. .... driver should wear one.
11. A friend of mine has three children. I always give .... them a present at Christmas.
12. *(from an exam)* Answer all five questions. Write your answer to .... question on a separate sheet of paper.

91.3 Complete the sentences using **each**.

1. The price of one of those oranges is 40 pence. ..Those oranges are 40 pence each.. .
2. I had ten pounds and so did Sonia. Sonia and I ....
3. One of those postcards costs a pound. Those ....
4. The hotel was expensive. I paid 200 dollars and so did you. We ....

91.4 Put in **everyone** (1 word) or **every one** (2 words).

1. Sarah is invited to a lot of parties and she goes to ..every one.. .
2. I remember school very clearly. I remember .... in my class.
3. I asked her lots of questions and she answered .... correctly.
4. Amy is very popular. .... likes her.
5. I dropped a tray of glasses. Unfortunately .... broke.

183

Relative clauses 1: clauses with **who/that/which**

A Study this example situation:

Last week we had a party and a lot of people came. Everybody enjoyed it.

Everybody **who came to the party** enjoyed it.
———— *relative clause* ————

A *clause* is a part of a sentence. A *relative clause* tells us which person or thing (or what kind of person or thing) the speaker means:

the woman **who lives next door to me**
('who lives next door to me' tells us which woman)
people **who complain all the time**
('who complain all the time' tells us what kind of people)

We use **who** in a relative clause for people (not things):

- ○ **The woman who** lives next door to me is a doctor.
- ○ I don't like **people who** complain all the time.
- ○ An architect is **someone who** designs buildings.
- ○ What was the name of **the person who** called?
- ○ Do you know **anyone who** wants to buy a car?

We also use **that** for people, but not **which**:

- ○ The woman **that lives next door to me** is a doctor. (*not* the woman which)

Sometimes you must use **who** (*not* that) for people – see Unit 95.

B When we are talking about things, we use **that** or **which** (*not* who) in a relative clause:

- ○ I don't like **stories that** have unhappy endings.
  or … **stories which** have unhappy endings.
- ○ Grace works for **a company that** makes furniture.
  or … **a company which** makes furniture.
- ○ **The machine that** broke down is working again now.
  or **The machine which** broke down …

In these examples **that** is more usual than **which**, but sometimes you must use **which**. See Unit 95.

C In relative clauses we use **who/that/which**, not **he/she/they/it**.
Compare:

- ○ I met a Canadian woman at the party. **She** is an English teacher. *(2 sentences)*
  I met **a Canadian woman who** is an English teacher. *(1 sentence)*
- ○ I can't find the keys. **They** were on the table.
  Where are **the keys that** were on the table? *(not the keys they were)*

D **What** = the thing(s) that

Compare **what** and **that**:

- ○ **What happened** was my fault. (= the thing that happened)

but

- ○ Everything **that happened** was my fault.
  (*not* Everything what happened)
- ○ The machine **that broke down** is now working again.
  (*not* The machine what broke down)

>> Relative clauses 2–5 → Units 93–96

Exercises

92.1 What do these words mean? Choose from the box and write sentences with who.

steals from a shop	buys something from a shop
~~designs buildings~~	pays rent to live somewhere
doesn't tell the truth	breaks into a house to steal things
is not brave	expects the worst to happen

1 (an architect) _An architect is someone who designs buildings._
2 (a customer) ....
3 (a burglar) ....
4 (a coward) ....
5 (a tenant) ....
6 (a shoplifter) ....
7 (a liar) ....
8 (a pessimist) ....

92.2 Make one sentence from two. Use who/that/which.

1 A girl was injured in the accident. She is now in hospital.
   The girl who was injured in the accident is now in hospital.
2 A waiter served us. He was impolite and impatient.
   The ....
3 A building was destroyed in the fire. It has now been rebuilt.
   The ....
4 Some people were arrested. They have now been released.
   The ....
5 A bus goes to the airport. It runs every half hour.
   The ....

92.3 Complete the sentences. Choose from the box and use who/that/which.

happened in the past	~~makes furniture~~
runs away from home	can support life
cannot be explained	has stayed there
developed the theory of relativity	were hanging on the wall

1 Helen works for a company _that makes furniture_ .
2 The movie is about a girl ....
3 What happened to the pictures .... ?
4 A mystery is something ....
5 I've heard it's a good hotel, but I don't know anyone ....
6 History is the study of things ....
7 Albert Einstein was the scientist ....
8 It seems that Earth is the only planet ....

92.4 Are these sentences right or wrong? Correct them where necessary.

1 I don't like stories <u>who</u> have unhappy endings.   _stories that have_
2 What was the name of the person who phoned?   _OK_
3 Where's the nearest shop who sells bread?   ....
4 Dan said some things about me they were not true.   ....
5 The driver which caused the accident was fined £500.   ....
6 Do you know the person that took these pictures?   ....
7 We live in a world what is changing all the time.   ....
8 Gary apologised for what he said.   ....
9 What was the name of the horse what won the race?   ....

Relative clauses 2:
clauses with and without **who/that/which**

Look at these example sentences from Unit 92:

○ **The woman who lives** next door to me is a doctor. (*or* The woman **that** lives …)

The woman lives next door to me   **who** (= the woman) is the *subject*

○ Where are **the keys that were** on the table? (*or* … the keys **which** were …)

The keys were on the table   **that** (= the keys) is the *subject*

You must use **who/that/which** when it is the *subject* of the relative clause. You cannot leave out **who/that/which** in these examples.

Sometimes **who/that/which** is the *object* of the verb. For example:

○ **The woman who I wanted to see** was away on holiday.

I wanted to see the woman   **who** (= the woman) is the *object*
          I is the *subject*

○ Did you find **the keys that you lost**?

you lost the keys   **that** (= the keys) is the *object*
          you is the *subject*

When **who/that/which** is the object, you can leave it out. So you can say:
○ **The woman I wanted to see** was away. *or* The woman **who** I wanted to see …
○ Did you find **the keys you lost**? *or* … the keys **that** you lost?
○ **The dress Lisa bought** doesn't fit her very well. *or* The dress **that** Lisa bought …
○ Is there **anything I can do**? *or* … anything **that** I can do?
Note that we say:
the keys you lost (*not* the keys you lost them)
the dress Lisa bought (*not* the dress Lisa bought it)

Note the position of prepositions (**to/in/for** etc.) in relative clauses:

Tom is talking to a woman. Do you know her? (*2 sentences*)

→ Do you know the woman Tom is **talking to**? (*or* … the woman **who/that** Tom is talking to)

I slept in a bed. It wasn't comfortable. (*2 sentences*)

→ The bed I **slept in** wasn't comfortable. (*or* The bed **that/which** I slept in …)

○ Are these **the books you were looking for**? *or*
Are these the books **that/which** you were …
○ **The man I was sitting next to on the plane** talked all the time. *or*
The man **who/that** I was sitting next to …
Note that we say:
the books **you were looking for** (*not* the books you were looking for them)
the man **I was sitting next to** (*not* the man I was sitting next to him)

We say:
○ **Everything** (that) **they said** was true. (*not* Everything what they said)
○ I gave her **all the money** (that) **I had**. (*not* all the money what I had)

What = the thing(s) that:
○ **What they said** was true. (= The things that they said)

» Relative clauses 1 → Unit 92   Relative clauses 3–5 → Units 94–96   whom → Unit 94B

Exercises

93.1 In some of these sentences you need **who** or **that**. Correct the sentences where necessary.

1 The <u>woman lives next door</u> is a doctor.   The woman who lives next door
2 Did you find the keys you lost?   OK
3 The people we met last night were very friendly.
4 The people work in the office are very friendly.
5 I like the people I work with.
6 What have you done with the money I gave you?
7 What happened to the money was on the table?
8 What's the worst film you've ever seen?
9 What's the best thing it has ever happened to you?

93.2 What do you say in these situations? Complete each sentence with a relative clause.

1 Your friend lost some keys. You want to know if he found them. You say:
  Did you find _the keys you lost_ ?
2 A friend is wearing a dress. You like it. You tell her:
  I like the dress _____ .
3 A friend is going to the cinema. You want to know the name of the film. You say:
  What's the name of the film _____ ?
4 You wanted to visit a museum, but it was shut. You tell a friend:
  The museum _____ was shut.
5 You invited people to your party. Some of them couldn't come. You tell someone:
  Some of the people _____ couldn't come.
6 Your friend had to do some work. You want to know if she has finished. You say:
  Have you finished the work _____ ?
7 You rented a car. It broke down after a few miles. You tell a friend:
  Unfortunately the car _____ broke down after a few miles.

93.3 These sentences all have a relative clause with a preposition. Put the words in the correct order.

1 Did you find (looking / for / you / the books / were)?
  Did you find _the books you were looking for_ ?
2 We couldn't go to (we / invited / to / were / the wedding).
  We couldn't go to _____ .
3 What's the name of (the hotel / about / me / told / you)?
  What's the name of _____ ?
4 Unfortunately I didn't get (applied / I / the job / for).
  Unfortunately I didn't get _____ .
5 Did you enjoy (you / the concert / to / went)?
  Did you enjoy _____ ?
6 Gary is a good person to know. He's (on / rely / can / somebody / you).
  Gary is a good person to know. He's _____ .
7 Who were (the people / with / were / you) in the restaurant yesterday?
  Who were _____ in the restaurant yesterday?

93.4 Put in **that** or **what** where necessary. If the sentence is already complete, leave the space empty.

1 I gave her all the money __−__ I had. (all the money **that** I had *is also correct*)
2 Did you hear __what__ they said?
3 She gives her children everything _____ they want.
4 Tell me _____ you want and I'll try to get it for you.
5 Why do you blame me for everything _____ goes wrong?
6 I won't be able to do much, but I'll do _____ I can.
7 I won't be able to do much, but I'll do the best _____ I can.
8 I don't agree with _____ you said.
9 I don't trust him. I don't believe anything _____ he says.

Relative clauses 3: **whose/whom/where**

whose

Study this example situation:

> When we were driving home, we saw some people standing by the road. Their car had broken down, so we stopped to help them.
>
> We helped some people **whose** car had broken down.
> (= **their** car had broken down)

We use **whose** mostly for people:
- ○ A widow is a woman **whose husband is dead**.
  (**her** husband is dead)
- ○ I met someone **whose brother I went to school with**.
  (I went to school with **his**/**her** brother)

Compare **who** and **whose**:
- ○ I met a man **who** knows you. (**he** knows you)
- ○ I met a man **whose sister** knows you. (**his sister** knows you)

Do not confuse **whose** and **who's**. The pronunciation is the same, but **who's** = who **is** or who **has**:
- ○ I have a friend **who's learning** Arabic. (**who's** = who **is**)
- ○ I have a friend **who's** just **started** learning Arabic. (**who's** = who **has**)
- ○ I have a friend **whose** sister is learning Arabic.

whom

Whom is possible instead of **who** when it is the *object* of the verb (see Unit 93B):
- ○ George is a person **whom I admire** very much. (I admire **him**)

You can also use a preposition + **whom** (**to whom** / **from whom** / **with whom** etc.):
- ○ It's important to have friends **with whom** you can relax. (you can relax **with them**)

Whom is a formal word and we do not often use it in spoken English. We usually prefer to say:
- ○ **a person I admire** a lot   *or*   a person **who**/**that** I admire a lot
- ○ **friends you can relax with**   *or*   friends **who**/**that** you can relax with

where

We use **where** in a relative clause to talk about a place:
- ○ I recently went back to **the town where** I grew up. (I grew up **there**)
- ○ **The restaurant where** we had lunch was near the airport.
- ○ I would like to live in **a place where** there is plenty of sunshine.

the day, the time, the reason …

We say '**the day** we got married', '**the year** I was born', '**the last** time they met' etc. :
- ○ I can't meet you on Friday. That's **the day I'm going away**.
- ○ **The last time I saw her**, she looked great.

You can also use **that**:
- ○ The last time **that** I saw her, she looked great.

We say '**the reason** I'm calling you', '**the reason** she didn't get the job' etc.
- ○ **The reason I'm calling you** is to ask your advice.

You can also use **that**:
- ○ The reason **that** I'm calling you …   *or*   The reason **why** I'm calling you …

>> Relative clauses 1–2 → **Units 92–93**   Relative clauses 4–5 → **Units 95–96**   whom → **Unit 96**

Exercises

94.1 You met these people at a party:

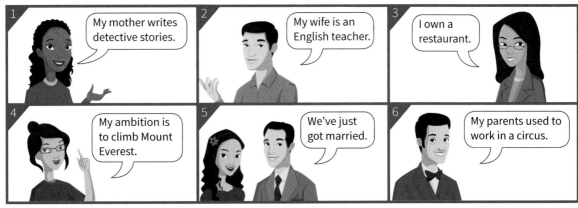

The next day you tell a friend about these people. Complete the sentences using **who** or **whose**.

1 I met somebody ___whose mother writes detective stories___ .
2 I met a man ....
3 I met a woman ....
4 I met somebody ....
5 I met a couple ....
6 I met somebody ....

94.2 For each situation write a sentence with **whom** (more formal) and without **whom** (less formal).

1 You met a friend. You hadn't seen him for years.
  more formal I met a friend ___whom I hadn't seen for years___ .
  less formal I met a friend ___I hadn't seen for years___ .
2 You needed a lawyer. A friend of yours recommended one.
  more formal I went to see a lawyer ....
  less formal I went to see a lawyer ....
3 You called your bank with a problem. You spoke to somebody, but he wasn't very helpful.
  more formal The person .... wasn't very helpful.
  less formal The person ....
4 Tom was in love with a woman, but she wasn't in love with Tom.
  more formal The woman .... wasn't in love with him.
  less formal The woman .... wasn't in love with him.

94.3 Complete the sentences using **who/whom/whose/where**.

1 We helped some people ___whose___ car had broken down.
2 A cemetery is a place .... people are buried.
3 A pacifist is a person .... believes that all wars are wrong.
4 An orphan is a child .... parents are dead.
5 What's the name of the hotel .... your parents are staying?
6 This school is only for children .... first language is not English.
7 The person from .... I bought my car is a friend of my father's.
8 I live in a friendly village .... everybody knows everybody else.

94.4 Use your own ideas to complete these sentences.

1 I can't meet you on Friday. That's the day ___I'm going away___ .
2 The reason .... was that the salary was too low.
3 I'll never forget the time ....
4 .... was the year ....
5 The reason .... is that neither of them can drive.
6 The last time I .... was ....
7 Do you remember the day .... ?

Relative clauses 4: extra information clauses (1)

A There are two types of relative clause. In these examples, the relative clauses are <u>underlined</u>. Compare:

Type 1
- ◯ The woman <u>who lives next door to me</u> is a doctor.
- ◯ Grace works for a company <u>that makes furniture</u>.
- ◯ We stayed at the hotel <u>(that) you recommended</u>.

In these examples, the relative clauses tell you which person or thing (or what kind of person or thing) the speaker means:

'The woman **who lives next door to me**' tells us *which* woman.
'A company **that makes furniture**' tells us *what kind* of company.
'The hotel **(that) you recommended**' tells us *which* hotel.

We do not use commas (,) with these clauses:
- ◯ We know a lot of people <u>who live in London</u>.

Type 2
- ◯ My brother Ben, <u>who lives in Hong Kong</u>, is an architect.
- ◯ Anna told me about her new job, <u>which she's enjoying a lot</u>.
- ◯ We stayed at the Park Hotel, <u>which a friend of ours recommended</u>.

In these examples, the relative clauses do not tell you which person or thing the speaker means. We already know which thing or person is meant: 'My brother Ben', 'Anna's new job' and 'the Park Hotel'.

The relative clauses in these sentences give us *extra information* about the person or thing.

We use commas (,) with these clauses:
- ◯ My brother Ben, <u>who lives in Hong Kong</u>, is an architect.

B In both types of relative clause we use **who** for people and **which** for things. But:

Type 1
You can use **that**:
- ◯ Do you know anyone **who/that** speaks French and Italian?
- ◯ Grace works for a company **which/that** makes furniture.

You can leave out **who/which/that** when it is the object (see Unit 93):
- ◯ We stayed at **the hotel** (that/which) **you recommended**.
- ◯ This morning I met **somebody** (who/that) **I hadn't seen for ages**.

We do not often use **whom** in this type of clause (see Unit 94B).

Type 2
You cannot use **that**:
- ◯ John, **who** speaks French and Italian, works as a tour guide. (*not* that speaks)
- ◯ Anna told me about her new job, **which** she's enjoying a lot.

You cannot leave out **who** or **which**:
- ◯ We stayed at the Park Hotel, **which** a friend of ours recommended.
- ◯ This morning I met Chris, **who** I hadn't seen for ages.

You can use **whom** for people (when it is the object):
- ◯ This morning I met Chris, **whom** I hadn't seen for ages.

C In both types of relative clause you can use **whose** and **where**:

- ◯ We helped some people **whose** car had broken down.
- ◯ What's the name of the place **where** you went on holiday?

- ◯ Lisa, **whose** car had broken down, was in a very bad mood.
- ◯ Kate has just been to Sweden, **where** her daughter lives.

>> Relative clauses (Type 1) → **Units 92–94**   Relative clauses (Type 2) → **Unit 96**

Exercises

95.1 Make one sentence from two. Use the information in brackets to make a relative clause (Type 2).
You will need to use who/whom/whose/which/where.

1 Catherine is very friendly. (She lives next door to us.)
  Catherine, who lives next door to us, is very friendly.

2 We stayed at the Park Hotel. (A friend of ours recommended this hotel.)
  We stayed at the Park Hotel, which a friend of ours recommended.

3 We drove to the airport. (The airport was not far from the city.)
  We drove to the airport,

4 Kate's husband is an airline pilot. (I have never met Kate's husband.)
  Kate's .... pilot.

5 Lisa is away from home a lot. (Lisa's job involves a lot of travelling.)
  Lisa

6 Paul and Emily have a daughter, Alice. (Alice has just started school.)
  Paul and Emily have

7 The new stadium will hold 90,000 spectators. (The stadium will be finished next month.)

8 My brother lives in Alaska. (Alaska is the largest state in the US.)

9 Our teacher was very kind. (I have forgotten her name.)

10 We enjoyed our visit to the museum. (We saw a lot of interesting things in the museum.)

95.2 Read the information and complete the sentences. Use a relative clause of Type 1 or Type 2.
Use commas where necessary.

1 My brother is an architect. (He lives in Hong Kong.)
  My _brother, who lives in Hong Kong, is an architect._

2 The strike at the factory has now ended. (The strike began ten days ago.)
  The strike at the factory

3 I was looking for a book this morning. (I've found it now.)
  I've found

4 I've had my car for 15 years. (This car has never broken down.)
  My car

5 A lot of people applied for the job. (Few of them had the necessary qualifications.)
  Few of

6 Amy showed me a picture of her son. (Her son is a police officer.)
  Amy showed me

95.3 Are these sentences OK? Correct them (and put in commas) where necessary. If the sentence is
correct, write 'OK'.

1 Anna told me about her new job that she's enjoying very much.
  Anna told me about her new job, which she's enjoying very much.

2 My office that is on the second floor is very small.

3 The office that I'm using at the moment is very small.

4 Sarah's father that used to be in the army now works for a TV company.

5 The doctor that examined me couldn't find anything wrong.

6 The sun that is one of millions of stars in the universe provides us with heat and light.

Relative clauses 5: extra information clauses (2)

A   preposition + whom/which

You can use a *preposition* + **whom** (for people) and **which** (for things).
So you can say:

| to whom | with whom | about whom | etc. |
| of which | without which | from which | etc. |

- ○ Mr Lee, **to whom I spoke** at the meeting, is interested in our proposal.
- ○ Fortunately we had a good map, **without which** we would have got lost.

In spoken English we often keep the preposition after the verb in the relative clause:

- ○ Katherine told me she works for a company called 'Latoma', **which** I'd never **heard of** before.

We do not use **whom** when the preposition is in this position:

- ○ Mr Lee, **who I spoke to** at the meeting, is interested in our proposal.
  (*not* Mr Lee, whom I spoke to …)

For prepositions in relative clauses, see also Unit 93C.

B   all of / most of etc. + whom/which

You can say:

- ○ Helen has three brothers, **all of whom** are married.
- ○ They asked me a lot of questions, **most of which** I couldn't answer.

In the same way you can say:

| many of whom | some of whom | neither of whom | etc. | (for people) |
| none of which | both of which | one of which | etc. | (for things) |

- ○ Martin tried on three jackets, **none of which** fitted him.
- ○ Two men, **neither of whom** I had seen before, came into the office.
- ○ They have three cars, **two of which** they rarely use.
- ○ Sue has a lot of friends, **many of whom** she was at school with.

You can also say:

the cause of which   **the name of which**   *etc.*

- ○ The house was damaged in a fire, **the cause of which** was never established.
- ○ We stayed at a beautiful hotel, **the name of which** I don't remember now.

C   which (*not* what)

Study this example:

Joe got the job . This surprised everybody.   *(2 sentences)*

Joe got the job , which surprised everybody.   *(1 sentence)*
——relative clause——

In this example, **which** = 'the fact that Joe got the job'. We use **which** (*not* what) in sentences like these:

- ○ Sarah couldn't meet us, **which** was a shame. (*not* what was a shame)
- ○ The weather was good, **which** we hadn't expected. (*not* what we hadn't expected)

For **what** and **that**, see Units 92D and 93D.

>> all of / most of etc. → Unit 88   both of etc. → Unit 89   Relative clauses 1–4 → Units 92–95

Exercises

96.1 Complete the sentences. Use a preposition + whom or which. Choose a preposition from:

| after | for | in | of | of | to | with | ~~without~~ |

1 Fortunately we had a good map, _without which_ we would have got lost.
2 The accident, _____ two people were injured, happened late last night.
3 I share an office with my boss, _____ I get on really well.
4 The wedding, _____ only family members were invited, was a lovely occasion.
5 Ben showed me his new car, _____ he's very proud.
6 Sarah showed us a picture of her son, _____ she's very proud.
7 Laura bought a very nice leather bag, _____ she paid twenty pounds.
8 We had lunch, _____ we went for a long walk.

96.2 Use the information in the first sentence to complete the second one. Use all of / most of etc.

1 All of Helen's brothers are married.
  Helen has three brothers, _all of whom are married_ .
2 Most of the information we were given was useless.
  We were given a lot of information, _____ .
3 None of the ten people who applied for the job was suitable.
  Ten people applied for the job, _____ .
4 My neighbours have two cars. They never use one of them.
  My neighbours have two cars, _____ .
5 James won a lot of money. He gave half of it to his parents.
  James won £100,000, _____ .
6 Both of Julia's sisters are lawyers.
  Julia has two sisters, _____ .
7 Jane replied to neither of the emails I sent her.
  I sent Jane two emails, _____ .
8 I went to a party – I knew only a few of the people there.
  There were a lot of people at the party, _____ .

Now use the ... of which ... .

9 You stayed in a hotel when you were on holiday but you don't remember the name.
  We stayed at a very nice hotel, _the name of which I don't remember_ .
10 We drove along the road. The sides of the road were lined with trees.
  We drove along the road, the _____ .
11 The aim of the company's new business plan is to save money.
  The company has a new business plan, _____ .

96.3 Complete the sentences. Choose from the box and use which.

This is good news.	This makes it hard to contact her.
~~This was a shame.~~	This means we can't go away tomorrow.
She apologised for this	This makes it difficult to sleep sometimes.
This was very kind of her.	This meant I had to wait two hours at the airport.

1 Laura couldn't come to the party, _which was a shame._
2 The street I live in is noisy at night, _____
3 Kate let me stay at her house, _____
4 Jane doesn't have a phone, _____
5 Alex passed his exams, _____
6 My flight was delayed, _____
7 Our car has broken down, _____
8 Amy was twenty minutes late, _____

-ing and -ed clauses (the woman **talking to Tom**, the boy **injured in the accident**)

A

A *clause* is a part of a sentence. Some clauses begin with -ing. For example:

Who is the woman **talking to Tom**?
└─ **-ing** *clause* ─┘

the woman talking to Tom

TOM

We use **-ing** clauses to say what somebody (or something) is (or was) doing at a particular time:
- ○ Who is the woman **talking to Tom**? (the woman **is talking** to Tom)
- ○ Police **investigating the crime** are looking for three men. (police **are investigating** the crime)
- ○ Who were those people **waiting outside**? (they **were waiting**)
- ○ I was woken up by a bell **ringing**. (a bell **was ringing**)

You can also use an **-ing** clause to say what happens all the time, not just at a particular time:
- ○ The road **connecting the two villages** is very narrow. (the road **connects** the two villages)
- ○ I have a large room **overlooking the garden**. (the room **overlooks** the garden)
- ○ Can you think of the name of a flower **beginning with T**? (the name **begins** with T)

B

Some clauses begin with -ed (**injured**, **painted** etc.). For example:

The boy **injured in the accident** was taken to hospital.
└────── **-ed** *clause* ──────┘

the boy injured in the accident

-**ed** clauses have a *passive* meaning:
- ○ The boy **injured in the accident** was taken to hospital.
  (he **was injured** in the accident)
- ○ George showed me some pictures **painted by his father**.
  (they **were painted** by his father)
- ○ The gun **used in the robbery** has been found.
  (the gun **was used** in the robbery)

Injured/painted/used are *past participles*. Most past participles end in **-ed**, but many are irregular (**stolen/made/built** etc.):
- ○ The police never found the money **stolen in the robbery**.
- ○ Most of the goods **made in this factory** are exported.

C

You can use **there is / there was** (etc.) + **-ing** and **-ed** clauses:
- ○ **There were** some children **swimming** in the river.
- ○ **Is there** anybody **waiting**?
- ○ **There was** a big red car **parked** outside the house.

We use **left** in this way, with the meaning 'not used, still there':
- ○ We've eaten nearly all the chocolates. **There are** only a few **left**.

>>   **see/hear** somebody **doing** something ➔ Unit 67   -ing clauses ➔ Unit 68   there (**is**) ➔ Unit 84
Irregular past participles (**made/stolen** etc.) ➔ Appendix 1

Exercises

97.1 Make one sentence from two. Complete the sentence using an **-ing** clause.

1 A bell was ringing. I was woken up by it.
I was woken up by ...*a bell ringing*... .

2 A taxi was taking us to the airport. It broke down.
The .... broke down.

3 There's a path at the end of this street. The path leads to the river.
At the end of the street there's ....

4 A factory has just opened in the town. It employs 500 people.
.... has just opened in the town.

5 A man was sitting next to me on the plane. He was asleep most of the time.
The .... was asleep most of the time.

6 The company sent me a brochure. It contained the information I needed.
The company sent me a ....

97.2 Complete the sentence with an **-ed** clause. Choose from:

damaged in the storm	made at the meeting	~~injured in the accident~~
involved in the project	stolen from the museum	surrounded by trees

1 The boy ...*injured in the accident*........ was taken to hospital.
2 The paintings .... haven't been found yet.
3 We've repaired the gate ....
4 Most of the suggestions .... were not practical.
5 Our friends live in a beautiful house ....
6 Everybody .... worked very well.

97.3 Complete the sentences. Use the following verbs in the correct form:

blow   call   cause   invite   live   offer   ~~paint~~   read   ~~ring~~   sit   study   work

1 I was woken up by a bell ...*ringing*..... .
2 George showed me some pictures ...*painted*........ by his father.
3 Some of the people .... to the party can't come.
4 Somebody .... Jack phoned while you were out.
5 Life must be very unpleasant for people .... near busy airports.
6 A few days after the interview, I received an email .... me the job.
7 The building was badly damaged in a fire .... by an electrical fault.
8 Did you see the picture of the trees .... down in the storm?
9 The waiting room was empty except for an old man .... in the corner
   .... a magazine.
10 Ian has a brother .... in a bank in London and a sister ....
    economics at university in Manchester.

97.4 Use the words in brackets to make sentences with **There is / There was** etc.

1 That house is empty. (nobody / live / in it) ...*There's nobody living in it.*...
2 The accident wasn't serious. (nobody / injure) ...*There was nobody injured.*........
3 I can hear footsteps. (somebody / come) There ....
4 I've spent all the money I had. (nothing / leave) There ....
5 The train was full. (a lot of people / travel)
   ....
6 We were the only guests at the hotel. (nobody else / stay there)
   ....
7 The piece of paper was blank. (nothing / write / on it)
   ....
8 The college offers English courses in the evening. (a course / begin / next Monday)
   ....

A Many adjectives end in -**ing** and -**ed**, for example: **boring** and **bored**.
Study this example situation:

bored

boring

Jane has been doing the same job for a very long time. Every day she does exactly the same thing again and again. She doesn't enjoy her job any more and would like to do something different.

Jane's job is **boring**.

Jane is **bored** with her job.

Somebody is **bored** or gets **bored** if something (or somebody else) is **boring**.
If something is **boring**, you get **bored** with it.
So:
○ Jane is **bored** because her job is **boring**.
○ Jane's job is **boring**, so Jane is **bored**. (*not* Jane is boring)

If a person is **boring**, this means that they make other people **bored**:
○ Paul always talks about the same things. He's really **boring**.

B Compare adjectives ending in -**ing** and -**ed**:

○ My job is
{
boring
interesting
tiring
satisfying
depressing (etc.)

○ I'm **bored** with my job.
○ I'm not **interested** in my job any more.
○ I get very **tired** doing my job.
○ I'm not **satisfied** with my job.
○ My job makes me **depressed**. (etc.)

In these examples, the -**ing** adjective tells you about the job

In these examples, the -**ed** adjective tells you how somebody feels (about the job).

Compare these examples:

interesting
○ Julia thinks politics is **interesting**.

○ Did you meet anyone **interesting** at the party?

surprising
○ It was **surprising** that he passed the exam.

disappointing
○ The movie was **disappointing**.
We expected it to be better.

shocking
○ The news was **shocking**.

interested
○ Julia is **interested** in politics.
(*not* interesting in politics)
○ Are you **interested** in buying a car?
I'm trying to sell mine.

surprised
○ Everybody was **surprised** that he passed the exam.

disappointed
○ We were **disappointed** with the movie.
We expected it to be better.

shocked
○ I was **shocked** when I heard the news.

Exercises

98.1 Complete the sentences for each situation. Use the word in brackets + **-ing** or **-ed**.

1 The movie wasn't as good as we had expected. (**disappoint**…)
   a The movie was ....*disappointing*..... .
   b We were ....*disappointed*..... with the movie.
2 Donna teaches young children. It's a very hard job, but she enjoys it. (**exhaust**…)
   a She enjoys her job, but it's often ....
   b At the end of a day's work, she is often ....
3 It's been raining all day. I hate this weather. (**depress**…)
   a This weather is ....
   b This weather makes me ....
   c It's silly to get .... because of the weather.
4 Clare is going to Mexico next month. She's never been there before. (**excit**…)
   a It will be an .... experience for her.
   b Going to new places is always ....
   c She is really .... about going to Mexico.

98.2 Choose the correct word.

1 I was ~~disappointing~~ / disappointed with the movie. I had expected it to be better.
   (disappointed *is correct*)
2 I'm not particularly interesting / interested in football.
3 The new project sounds exciting / excited. I'm looking forward to working on it.
4 It can be embarrassing / embarrassed when you have to ask people for money.
5 Do you easily get embarrassing / embarrassed?
6 I'd never expected to get the job. I was amazing / amazed when I was offered it.
7 She's learnt very fast. She's made amazing / amazed progress.
8 I didn't find the situation funny. I was not amusing / amused.
9 I'm interesting / interested in joining the club. How much does it cost?
10 It was a really terrifying / terrified experience. Everybody was very shocking / shocked.
11 Why do you always look so boring / bored? Is your life really so boring / bored?
12 He's one of the most boring / bored people I've ever met. He never stops talking and he
    never says anything interesting / interested.

98.3 Complete each sentence using a word from the box.

amusing/amused	annoying/annoyed	boring/bored
confusing/confused	disgusting/disgusted	exciting/excited
exhausting/exhausted	interesting/interested	~~surprising~~/surprised

1 You work very hard. It's not ....*surprising*.......... that you're always tired.
2 Some people get .... very easily. They always need something new.
3 The teacher's explanation was .... Nobody understood it.
4 The kitchen hadn't been cleaned for ages. It was really ....
5 I don't go to art galleries very often. I'm not very .... in art.
6 There's no need to get .... just because I'm a few minutes late.
7 The lecture was .... I fell asleep.
8 I've been working very hard all day and now I'm ....
9 I'm starting a new job next week. I'm very .... about it.
10 Steve is good at telling funny stories. He can be very ....
11 Helen is a very .... person. She knows a lot, she's travelled a lot and she's
    done lots of different things.

Adjectives: a **nice new** house, you look **tired**

A   Sometimes we use two or more adjectives together:
- My brother lives in a **nice new** house.
- In the kitchen there was a **beautiful large round wooden** table.

Adjectives like **new/large/round/wooden** are *fact* adjectives. They give us information about age, size, colour etc.

Adjectives like **nice/beautiful** are *opinion* adjectives. They tell us what the speaker thinks of something or somebody.
Opinion adjectives usually go before fact adjectives.

	opinion	*fact*	
a	**nice**	**long**	summer holiday
an	**interesting**	**young**	man
	delicious	**hot**	vegetable soup
a	**beautiful**	**large round wooden**	table

B   Sometimes we use two or more fact adjectives together. Usually (not always) we put fact adjectives in this order:

1 how big?	→	2 how old?	→	3 what colour?	→	4 where from?	→	5 what is it made of?	→	NOUN

a **tall young** man (1 → 2)   a **large wooden** table (1 → 5)
big blue eyes (1 → 3)   an **old Russian** song (2 → 4)
a **small black plastic** bag (1 → 3 → 5)   an **old white cotton** shirt (2 → 3 → 5)

Adjectives of size and length (**big/small/tall/short/long** etc.) usually go before adjectives of shape and width (**round/fat/thin/slim/wide** etc.):
a **large round** table   a **tall thin** girl   a **long narrow** street

When there are two or more colour adjectives, we use **and**:
a **black and white** dress   a **red**, **white and green** flag
This does not usually happen with other adjectives before a noun:
a **long black** dress   (*not* a long and black dress)

C   We use adjectives after **be/get/become/seem**:
- **Be careful**!
- I**'m tired** and I**'m getting hungry**.
- As the film went on, it **became** more and more **boring**.
- Your friend **seems** very **nice**.

We also use adjectives to say how somebody/something looks, feels, sounds, tastes or smells:
- You **look tired**. / I **feel tired**. / She **sounds tired**.
- The dinner **smells good**.
- This tea **tastes** a bit **strange**.

But to say *how* somebody *does something* you must use an *adverb* (see Units 100–101):
- Drive **carefully**!   (*not* Drive careful)
- Suzanne plays the piano very **well**.   (*not* plays … very good)

D   We say 'the **first two** days', 'the **next few** weeks', 'the **last ten** minutes' etc. :
- I didn't enjoy the **first two** days of the course.   (*not* the two first days)
- They'll be away for the **next few** weeks.   (*not* the few next weeks)

≫   Adverbs → **Units 100–101**   Comparative (**cheaper** etc.) → **Units 105–107**
Superlative (**cheapest** etc.) → **Unit 108**

Exercises

99.1 Put the adjectives in brackets in the correct position.

1. a beautiful table (wooden / round)   a beautiful round wooden table
2. an unusual ring (gold)
3. an old house (beautiful)
4. red gloves (leather)
5. an American film (old)
6. pink flowers (tiny)
7. a long face (thin)
8. big clouds (black)
9. a sunny day (lovely)
10. an ugly dress (yellow)
11. a wide avenue (long)
12. important ideas (new)
13. a new sweater (green / nice)
14. a metal box (black / small)
15. long hair (black / beautiful)
16. an old painting (interesting / French)
17. a large umbrella (red / yellow)
18. a big cat (black / white / fat)

99.2 Complete each sentence with a verb (in the correct form) and an adjective from the boxes.

feel	look	~~seem~~	awful	nervous	interesting
smell	sound	taste	nice	~~upset~~	wet

1. Helen ___seemed upset___ this morning. Do you know what was wrong?
2. I can't eat this. I've just tried it and it ....
3. It's normal to .... before an exam or an interview.
4. What beautiful flowers! They .... too.
5. You .... Have you been out in the rain?
6. James told me about his new job. It .... – much better than his old job.

99.3 Put in the correct word.

1. This tea tastes a bit ___strange___ . (strange / strangely)
2. I usually feel .... when the sun is shining. (happy / happily)
3. The children were playing .... in the garden. (happy / happily)
4. You look ....! Are you all right? (terrible / terribly)
5. There's no point in doing a job if you don't do it .... (proper / properly)
6. The soup tastes .... Can you give me the recipe? (good / well)
7. Please hurry up! You're always so .... (slow / slowly)
8. A customer in the restaurant was behaving .... (bad / badly)
9. The customer became .... when the manager asked him to leave. (violent / violently)

99.4 Write the following in another way using the first ... / the next ... / the last ... .

1. the first day and the second day of the course   the first two days of the course
2. next week and the week after   the next two weeks
3. yesterday and the day before yesterday
4. the first week and the second week of May
5. tomorrow and a few days after that
6. questions 1, 2 and 3 in the exam
7. next year and the year after
8. the last day of our holiday and the two days before that

→ **Additional exercise 31** (page 320)

Adjectives and adverbs 1 (**quick**/**quickly**)

A

You can say:
- ○ Our holiday was too short – the time passed very **quickly**.
- ○ Two people were **seriously** injured in the accident.

Quickly and **seriously** are *adverbs*. Many adverbs are *adjective* + **-ly**:

adjective	quick	serious	careful	bad	heavy	terrible
adverb	**quickly**	**seriously**	**carefully**	**badly**	**heavily**	**terribly**

For spelling, see Appendix 6.

Not all words ending in **-ly** are adverbs. Some *adjectives* end in **-ly** too, for example:
friendly   lively   elderly   lonely   lovely
- ○ It was a **lovely** day.

B

Adjective or adverb?

Adjectives (**quick**/**careful** etc.) tell us about a *noun* (somebody or something). We use adjectives before nouns:

- ○ Sam is a **careful driver**.
  (*not* a carefully driver)
- ○ We didn't go out because of the **heavy rain**.

Adverbs (**quickly**/**carefully** etc.) tell us about a *verb* (*how* somebody does something or *how* something happens):

- ○ Sam **drove carefully** along the narrow road. (*not* drove careful)
- ○ We didn't go out because it was **raining heavily**. (*not* raining heavy)

Compare:

- ○ She speaks **perfect English**.

  adjective + noun

- ○ She **speaks** English **perfectly**.

  verb + noun + adverb

C

We use adjectives after some verbs, especially **be**, and also **look**/**feel**/**sound** etc.
Compare:

- ○ Please **be quiet**.
- ○ My exam results **were** really **bad**.
- ○ Why do you always **look** so **serious**?
- ○ I **feel happy**.

- ○ Please **speak quietly**.
- ○ I **did** really **badly** in the exam.
- ○ Why do you never **take** me **seriously**?
- ○ The children were **playing happily**.

D

You can also use adverbs before *adjectives* and *other adverbs*. For example:

reasonably cheap   (*adverb + adjective*)
terribly sorry   (*adverb + adjective*)
incredibly quickly   (*adverb + adverb*)

- ○ It's a **reasonably cheap** restaurant and the food is **extremely good**.
- ○ I'm **terribly sorry**. I didn't mean to push you.
- ○ Maria learns languages **incredibly quickly**.
- ○ The exam was **surprisingly easy**.

You can also use an adverb before a *past participle* (**injured**/**organised**/**written** etc.):
- ○ Two people were **seriously injured** in the accident. (*not* serious injured)
- ○ The conference was **badly organised**.

>> Adjectives after **be**/**look**/**feel** etc. → **Unit 99C**   Adjectives and adverbs 2 → **Unit 101**

Exercises

100.1 Complete each sentence with an adverb. The first letters of the adverb are given.

1 We didn't go out because it was raining he **avily** .
2 I had no problem finding a place to live. I found a flat quite ea........................ .
3 We had to wait a long time, but we didn't complain. We waited pat........................ .
4 Nobody knew that Simon was coming to see us. He arrived unex........................ .
5 Mike keeps fit by playing tennis reg........................ .
6 I don't speak French very well, but I can understand per........................ if people speak
   sl........................ and cl........................ .

100.2 Put in the correct word.

1 Sam drove ....**carefully**........ along the narrow road. (careful / carefully)
2 I think you behaved very .... (selfish / selfishly)
3 The weather changed .... (sudden / suddenly)
4 There was a .... change in the weather. (sudden / suddenly)
5 Liz fell and hurt herself really .... (bad / badly)
6 I think I have flu. I feel .... (awful / awfully)
7 Tanya is .... upset about losing her job. (terrible / terribly)
8 I could sit in this chair all day. It's very .... (comfortable / comfortably)
9 I explained everything as .... as I could. (clear / clearly)
10 Be careful on that ladder. It doesn't look very .... (safe / safely)
11 Have a good trip and I hope you have a .... journey. (safe / safely)
12 I'm glad you had a good trip and got home .... (safe / safely)

100.3 Complete each sentence using a word from the box. Sometimes you need the adjective (careful etc.) and sometimes the adverb (carefully etc.).

careful(ly)	complete(ly)	dangerous(ly)	financial(ly)	fluent(ly)
frequent(ly)	nervous(ly)	perfect(ly)	permanent(ly)	special(ly)

1 Sam doesn't take risks when he's driving. He's always ....**careful**........ .
2 He's late sometimes, but it doesn't happen ....
3 Maria's English is very .... although she makes quite a lot of mistakes.
4 I cooked this meal .... for you, so I hope you like it.
5 Everything was very quiet. There was .... silence.
6 I tried on the shoes and they fitted me ....
7 I'd like to buy a car, but it's .... impossible for me at the moment.
8 I'm staying here only a few weeks. I won't be living here ....
9 Do you usually feel .... before exams?
10 Dan likes to take risks. He lives ....

100.4 Choose two words (one from each box) to complete each sentence.

absolutely	badly	completely	changed	cheap	damaged
happily	reasonably	seriously	enormous	ill	long
slightly	unnecessarily	unusually	married	planned	quiet

1 I thought the restaurant would be expensive, but it was ....**reasonably cheap**........ .
2 Will's mother is .... in hospital.
3 This house is so big! It's ....
4 It wasn't a serious accident. The car was only ....
5 Our children are normally very lively, but they're .... today.
6 When I returned home after 20 years, everything had ....
7 The movie was .... It could have been much shorter.
8 I'm surprised Amy and Joe have separated. I thought they were ....
9 A lot went wrong during our holiday because it was ....

→ **Additional exercise 31** (page 320)

Adjectives and adverbs 2 (well, fast, late, hard/hardly)

A good and well

Good is an *adjective*. The *adverb* is **well**:
- ○ Your English is **good**.　　*but*　You **speak** English **well**.
- ○ Sophie is a **good** pianist.　*but*　Sophie **plays** the piano **well**.

We use **well** (*not* good) with *past participles* (**known/educated** etc.). For example:
well-known　**well-educated**　**well-paid**　**well-behaved**
- ○ Sophie's father is a **well-known** writer.

Well is also an adjective meaning 'in good health':
- ○ 'How are you today?'　'I'm very **well**, thanks.'

B fast, hard and late

These words are both adjectives and adverbs:

adjective	*adverb*
○ Darren **is** a **fast runner**.	Darren can **run fast**.
○ It**'s hard** to find a job right now.	Kate **works hard**. (*not* works hardly)
○ Sorry I**'m late**.	I **got up late**.

lately = recently:
- ○ Have you seen Kate **lately**?

C hardly

hardly = very little, almost not:
- ○ Sarah wasn't very friendly at the party. She **hardly** spoke to me.
  (= she spoke to me very little)
- ○ We've only met once or twice. We **hardly** know each other.

Compare **hard** and **hardly**:
- ○ He tried **hard** to find a job, but he had no luck. (= he tried a lot, with a lot of effort)
- ○ I'm not surprised he didn't find a job. He **hardly** tried. (= he tried very little)

Hardly goes before the verb:
- ○ We **hardly know** each other. (*not* We know each other hardly)

I **can hardly** do something = it's very difficult for me, almost impossible:
- ○ Your writing is terrible. I **can hardly** read it. (= it is almost impossible to read it)
- ○ My leg was hurting. I **could hardly** walk.

D

You can use **hardly + any/anybody/anyone/anything/anywhere**:
- ○ A: How much money do we have?
  B: **Hardly any**. (= very little, almost none)
- ○ These two cameras are very similar. There's **hardly any** difference between them.
- ○ The exam results were bad. **Hardly anybody** in our class passed. (= very few students passed)
- ○ She was very quiet. She said **hardly anything**. *or* She **hardly** said **anything**.

> There's **hardly anything** in the fridge.

hardly ever = almost never:
- ○ I'm nearly always at home in the evenings. I **hardly ever** go out.

Hardly also means 'certainly not'. For example:
- ○ It's **hardly surprising** that you're tired. You haven't slept for three days.
  (= it's certainly not surprising)
- ○ The situation is serious, but it's **hardly a crisis**. (= it's certainly not a crisis)

Adjectives after verbs ('**You look tired**' etc.) → Unit 99C　　Adjectives and adverbs 1 → Unit 100

Exercises

101.1 **Put in good or well.**

1 I play tennis but I'm not very ...._good_.... .
2 Joe's exam results were very ....
3 Joe did .... in his exams.
4 I didn't sleep .... last night.
5 I like your hat. It looks .... on you.
6 Can you speak up? I can't hear you very ....
7 I've met her a few times, but I don't know her ....
8 Lucy speaks German .... She's .... at languages.

101.2 **Complete these sentences using well + the following words:**

~~behaved~~	informed	kept	known	paid	written

1 The children were very good. They were ...._well-behaved_.... .
2 I'm surprised you haven't heard of her. She is quite ....
3 Our neighbours' garden is neat and tidy. It is very ....
4 I enjoyed the book. It's a great story and it's very ....
5 Tanya knows about everything. She is very ....
6 Jane works very hard in her job, but she isn't very ....

101.3 **Which is right?**

1 I'm tired because I've been working hard / ~~hardly~~. (hard *is correct*)
2 I wasn't in a hurry, so I was walking slow / slowly.
3 I haven't been to the cinema late / lately.
4 Slow down! You're walking too fast / quick for me.
5 I tried hard / hardly to remember her name, but I couldn't.
6 This coat is practically unused. I've hard / hardly worn it.
7 Laura is a good tennis player. She hits the ball very hard / hardly.
8 It's really dark in here. I can hardly see / see hardly.
9 Ben is going to run a marathon. He's been training hard / hardly.

101.4 **Complete the sentences. Use hardly + the following verbs (in the correct form):**

change	hear	~~know~~	recognise	say	sleep	speak

1 Scott and Tracy have only met once before. They ...._hardly know_.... each other.
2 You're speaking very quietly. I can .... you.
3 I don't feel good this morning. I .... last night.
4 We were so shocked when we heard the news, we could ....
5 Kate was very quiet this evening. She .... anything.
6 Gary looks just like he looked 15 years ago. He has ....
7 David looked different without his beard. I .... him.

101.5 **Complete these sentences with hardly + any/anybody/anything/anywhere/ever.**

1 I'll have to go shopping. There's ...._hardly anything_.... to eat.
2 It was a very warm day and there was .... wind.
3 'Do you know much about computers?' 'No, ... ,'
4 The hotel was almost empty. There was .... staying there.
5 I listen to the radio a lot, but I .... watch TV.
6 It was very crowded in the room. There was .... to sit.
7 We used to be good friends, but we .... see each other now.
8 We invited lots of people to the party, but .... came.
9 It didn't take us long to drive there. There was .... traffic.
10 There isn't much to do in this town. There's .... to go.

→ Additional exercise 31 (page 320)

so and such

A Compare **so** and **such**:

We use **so** + *adjective/adverb*:
so stupid	**so quick**
so nice	**so quickly**

○ I didn't like the book. The story was **so stupid**.

○ Everything happened **so quickly**.

We use **such** + *noun*:
such a story   **such people**
We also use **such** + *adjective* + *noun*:
such a stupid **story**   **such** nice **people**

○ I didn't like the book. It was **such** a stupid **story**. (*not* a so stupid story)

○ I like Liz and Joe. They are **such nice people**. (*not* so nice people)

We say **such a** … (*not* a such):
such a big **dog**

B **So** and **such** make the meaning stronger:

○ I've had a busy day. I'm **so tired**. (= really tired)

○ It's difficult to understand him. He talks **so quietly**.

You can use **so** … **that**:
○ I was **so tired that** I fell asleep in the armchair.

We usually leave out **that**:
○ I was **so tired** I fell asleep.

○ We had a great trip. We had **such a good time**. (= a really good time)

○ You always think good things are going to happen. You're **such an optimist**.

You can use **such** … **that**:
○ It was **such nice weather that** we spent the whole day on the beach.

We usually leave out **that**:
○ It was **such nice weather** we spent …

C **So** and **such** also mean 'like this':

○ Somebody told me the house was built 100 years ago. I didn't realise it was **so old**. (= as old as it is)

○ I'm tired because I got up at six. I don't usually get up **so early**.

○ I expected the weather to be cooler. I'm surprised it is **so warm**.

○ I didn't realise it was **such an old house**.

○ You know it's not true. How can you say **such a thing**? (= a thing like this)

Note the expression **no such** … :
○ You won't find the word 'blid' in the dictionary. There's **no such word**. (= this word does not exist)

D Compare:

so long
○ I haven't seen her for **so long** I've forgotten what she looks like.

such a long time
○ I haven't seen her for **such a long time**. (*not* so long time)

so far
○ I didn't know it was **so far**.

such a long way
○ I didn't know it was **such a long way**.

so much, so many
○ I'm sorry I'm late – there was **so much** traffic.

such a lot (of)
○ I'm sorry I'm late – there was **such a lot** of traffic.

› not so … as → Unit 107A   such as → Unit 117A

Exercises

102.1 **Put in so, such or such a.**

1 It was a great holiday. We had ___such a___ good time.
2 Everything is _____ expensive these days, isn't it?
3 He always looks good. He wears _____ nice clothes.
4 I couldn't believe the news. It was _____ shock.
5 What a nice garden! These are _____ lovely flowers.
6 The party was great. It was _____ shame you couldn't come.
7 I was glad to see that he looked _____ well after his recent illness.
8 I have to go. I didn't realise it was _____ late.
9 Why does it always take you _____ long time to get ready?
10 Everything went wrong. We had _____ bad luck.

102.2 **Make one sentence from two. Choose from the box, and then complete the sentences using so or such.**

> The music was loud.   It was horrible weather.   I've got a lot to do.
> I had a big breakfast.   It was a beautiful day.   Her English is good.
> The bag was heavy.   I was surprised.   The hotel was a long way.

1 ___It was such a beautiful day___ , we decided to go to the beach.
2 _____ , she couldn't lift it.
3 _____ , I don't know where to begin.
4 _____ , I didn't know what to say.
5 _____ , it could be heard from miles away.
6 _____ , we spent the whole day indoors.
7 _____ , you would think it was her native language.
8 _____ , it took us ages to get there.
9 _____ , I didn't eat anything for the rest of the day.

102.3 **Put the words in the right order.**

1 I got up at six this morning. I ___don't usually get up so early___ .
   (get up / early / usually / so / don't)
2 Why _____ ? There's plenty of time.
   (a / such / hurry / you / in / are)
3 It took us an hour to get here. I'm _____ .
   (long / it / surprised / so / took)
4 He said he worked for a company called Elcron, but _____ .
   (such / there's / company / no)
5 I regret what I did. I don't know why _____ .
   (such / thing / I / did / a / stupid)
6 Why _____ ? Can't you drive faster?
   (driving / so / you / slowly / are)
7 Two months? How did you _____ ?
   (English / time / learn / short / a / such / in)
8 Why _____ ? You could have got a cheaper one.
   (expensive / you / an / phone / did / such / buy)

102.4 **Use your own ideas to complete these sentences.**

1 We enjoyed our holiday. We had such ___a good time___ .
2 I like Kate. She's so _____ .
3 I like Kate. She's such _____ .
4 It's good to see you again! I haven't seen you for so _____ .
5 I thought the airport was near the city. I didn't realise it was such _____
6 The streets were crowded. There were so _____

enough and too

I'm not **fit enough**.

A enough

Enough goes *after* adjectives and adverbs:
- ○ I can't run very far. I'm not **fit enough**. (*not* enough fit)
- ○ Let's go. We've waited **long enough**.

Enough normally goes *before* nouns:
- ○ We have **enough money**. We don't need any more.
- ○ There weren't **enough chairs**. Some of us had to sit on the floor.

We also use **enough** alone (without a noun or adjective):
- ○ We don't need more money. We have **enough**.

B too and enough

Compare **too** ... and **not** ... **enough**:
- ○ You never stop working. You work **too hard**.
  (= more than is necessary)
- ○ You're lazy. You **don't** work **hard enough**.
  (= less than is necessary)

Compare **too much/many** and **enough**:
- ○ There's **too much furniture** in this room. There's not **enough space**.
- ○ There were **too many people** and not **enough chairs**.

C enough/too + for ... and to ...

We say **enough/too ... for** somebody/something:
- ○ Does Joe have enough experience **for the job**?
- ○ This bag isn't big enough **for all my clothes**.
- ○ That shirt is too small **for you**. You need a larger size.

We say **enough/too ... to** do something. For example:
- ○ Does Joe have enough experience **to do** the job?
- ○ Let's get a taxi. It's too far **to walk** home from here.
- ○ She's not old enough **to have** a driving licence.

The next example has both **for** ... and **to** ... :
- ○ The bridge is just wide enough **for two cars to pass** one another.

D too hot to eat etc.

We say:

> The food was very hot. We couldn't eat **it**.
> *and*
> The food was so hot that we couldn't eat **it**.
> *but*
> The food was **too hot to eat**. (*not* to eat it)

The wallet doesn't fit in my pocket.

In the same way we say:
- ○ These boxes are **too heavy to carry**. (*not* to carry them)
- ○ The wallet was **too big to put in my pocket**. (*not* to put it)
- ○ This chair isn't **strong enough to stand on**. (*not* to stand on it)

›› to ... and for ... (purpose) ➜ **Unit 64**   Adjective + to ... (**difficult to understand** etc.) ➜ **Unit 65**

Exercises

103.1 Complete the sentences using **enough** + the following words:

| buses | ~~chairs~~ | cups | ~~hard~~ | room | tall | time | vegetables | warm | wide |

1 You're lazy. You don't work ___hard enough___ .
2 Some of us had to sit on the floor. There weren't ___enough chairs___ .
3 Public transport isn't good here. There aren't _____ .
4 I can't park the car here. The space isn't _____ .
5 I always have to rush. There's never _____ .
6 You need to change your diet. You don't eat _____ .
7 I'm not good at basketball. I'm not _____ .
8 The car is quite small. Do you think there's _____ for five of us?
9 Are you _____ ? Or shall I switch on the heating?
10 We can't all have coffee at the same time. We don't have _____ .

103.2 Complete the answers to the questions. Use **too** or **enough** + the word(s) in brackets.

1	Does Sophie have a driving licence?	(old)	No, she's not old enough to have a driving licence.
2	I need to talk to you about something.	(busy)	Well, I'm afraid I'm _____ _____ to you now.
3	Let's go to the cinema.	(late)	No, it's _____ to the cinema.
4	Why don't we sit outside?	(warm)	It's not _____ outside.
5	Would you like to be a politician?	(shy)	No, I'm _____ _____ a politician.
6	Would you like to be a teacher?	(patience)	No, I don't have _____ _____ a teacher.
7	Did you hear what he was saying?	(far away)	No, we were _____ _____ what he was saying.
8	Can he read a newspaper in English?	(English)	No, he doesn't know _____ _____ a newspaper.

103.3 Make one sentence from two. Complete the new sentence using **too** or **enough** + **to … .**

1 We couldn't carry the boxes. They were too heavy.
   ___The boxes were too heavy to carry.___
2 I can't drink this coffee. It's too hot.
   This coffee is _____
3 Nobody could move the piano. It was too heavy.
   The piano _____
4 Don't eat these apples. They're not ripe enough.
   These apples _____
5 I can't explain the situation. It is too complicated.
   The situation _____
6 We couldn't climb over the wall. It was too high.
   The wall _____
7 Three people can't sit on this sofa. It isn't big enough.
   This sofa _____
8 You can't see some things without a microscope. They are too small.
   Some _____

quite, pretty, rather and fairly

A   **Quite** and **pretty** are similar in meaning (= less than 'very', but more than 'a little'):
- ○ I'm surprised you haven't heard of her. She's **quite famous**. *or* She's **pretty famous**.
  (= less than 'very famous', but more than 'a little famous')
- ○ Anna lives **quite near** me, so we see each other **pretty often**.

Pretty is an informal word and is used mainly in spoken English.

Quite goes before **a/an**:
- ○ We live in **quite an old house**. (*not* a quite old house)

Compare:
- ○ Sarah has **quite a** good job.
- Sarah has **a pretty** good job.

You can also use **quite** (but not **pretty**) in the following ways:

quite a/an + *noun* (without an adjective):
- ○ I didn't expect to see them. It was **quite a surprise**. (= quite a big surprise)

quite a lot (of …):
- ○ There were **quite a lot of** guests at the wedding.

quite + verb, especially **like** and **enjoy**:
- ○ I **quite like** tennis, but it's not my favourite sport.

B   **Rather** is similar to **quite** and **pretty**. We often use **rather** for negative ideas (things we think are not good):
- ○ The weather isn't so good. It's **rather cloudy**.
- ○ Paul is **rather shy**. He doesn't talk very much.

Quite is also possible in these examples.

When we use **rather** for positive ideas (**good/nice** etc.), it means 'unusually' or 'surprisingly':
- ○ These oranges are **rather good**. Where did you get them?

C   **Fairly** is weaker than **quite/rather/pretty**. For example, if something is **fairly good**, it is not very good and it could be better:
- ○ My room is **fairly big**, but I'd prefer a bigger one.
- ○ We see each other **fairly often**, but not as often as we used to.

D   **Quite** also means 'completely'. For example:
- ○ 'Are you sure?' 'Yes, **quite sure**.' (= completely sure)

Quite means 'completely' with a number of adjectives, especially:

sure	right	true	clear	different	incredible	amazing
certain	wrong	safe	obvious	unnecessary	extraordinary	impossible

- ○ She was **quite different** from what I expected. (= completely different)
- ○ Everything they said was **quite true**. (= completely true)

We also use **quite** (= completely) with some verbs. For example:
- ○ I **quite agree** with you. (= I completely agree)

not quite = not completely:
- ○ **I don't quite understand** what you mean.
- ○ 'Are you ready yet?' '**Not quite**.' (= not completely)

Compare the two meanings of **quite**:
- ○ The story is **quite interesting**. (= less than 'very interesting')
- ○ The story is **quite true**. (= completely true)

Exercises

104.1 Complete the sentences using quite ... . Choose from:

| ~~famous~~ | hungry | late | noisy | often | old | surprised |

1 I'm surprised you haven't heard of her. She's __quite famous__ .
2 I'm _____ . Is there anything to eat?
3 We go to the cinema _____ – maybe once a month.
4 We live near a very busy road, so it's often _____ .
5 I didn't expect Lisa to contact me. I was _____ when she phoned.
6 I went to bed _____ last night, so I'm a bit tired this morning.
7 I don't know exactly when this house was built, but it's _____ .

104.2 Put the words in the right order to complete the sentences.

1 The weather was better than we had expected.
It was __quite a nice day__ (a / nice / quite / day).
2 Tom likes to sing.
He has _____ (voice / quite / good / a).
3 The bus stop wasn't near the hotel.
We had to walk _____ (quite / way / a / long).
4 It's not so warm today.
There's _____ (a / wind / cold / pretty).
5 The roads were busy.
There was _____ (lot / traffic / a / of / quite).
6 I'm tired.
I've had _____ (pretty / day / a / busy).
7 Sarah hasn't been working here long.
She _____ (fairly / started / recently).

104.3 Use your own ideas to complete these sentences. Use rather + adjective.

1 The weather isn't so good. It's __rather cloudy__ .
2 I enjoyed the film, but it was _____ .
3 Chris went away without telling anybody, which was _____ .
4 Lucy doesn't like having to wait. Sometimes she's _____ .
5 They have some lovely things in this shop, but it's _____ .

104.4 What does quite mean in these sentences? Tick (✓) the right meaning.

	more than 'a little', less than 'very' (Section A)	'completely' (Section D)
1 It's <u>quite cold</u>. You need a coat.	✓	
2 'Are you sure?' 'Yes, <u>quite sure</u>.'		✓
3 Anna's English is <u>quite good</u>.		
4 I couldn't believe it. It was <u>quite incredible</u>.		
5 My bedroom is <u>quite big</u>.		
6 I'm <u>quite tired</u>. I think I'll go to bed.		
7 I <u>quite agree</u> with you.		

104.5 Complete these sentences using quite ... . Choose from:

| different | impossible | right | safe | sure | ~~true~~ |

1 I didn't believe her at first, but in fact what she said was __quite true__ .
2 You won't fall. The ladder is _____ .
3 I'm afraid I can't do what you ask. It's _____ .
4 I completely agree with you. You are _____ .
5 You can't compare the two things. They are _____ .
6 I think I saw them go out, but I'm not _____ .

A Look at these examples:

How shall we travel? Shall we drive or go by train?

> Let's drive. It's **cheaper**.
> Don't go by train. It's **more expensive**.

Cheaper and **more expensive** are *comparative* forms.

After comparatives you can use **than** (see Unit 107):
- It's **cheaper** to drive **than** go by train.
- Going by train is **more expensive than** driving.

B The comparative form is **-er** or **more** … .

We use **-er** for short words (one syllable):

cheap → cheaper	fast → faster
large → larger	thin → thinner

We also use **-er** for two-syllable words that end in **-y** (**-y** → **-ier**):

lucky → luckier	early → earlier
easy → easier	pretty → prettier

We use **more** … for longer words (two syllables or more):

more serious	more expensive
more often	more comfortable

We also use **more** … for adverbs that end in **-ly**:

more slowly	more seriously
more easily	more quietly

For spelling, see Appendix 6.

Compare these examples:

- You're **older** than me.
- The exam was quite easy – **easier** than I expected.
- Can you walk a bit **faster**?
- I'd like to have a **bigger** car.
- Last night I went to bed **earlier** than usual.

- You're **more patient** than me.
- The exam was quite difficult – **more difficult** than I expected.
- Can you walk a bit **more slowly**?
- I'd like to have a **more reliable** car.
- I don't play tennis much these days. I used to play **more often**.

We use both **-er** *or* **more** … with some two-syllable adjectives, especially:

clever   **narrow**   **quiet**   **shallow**   **simple**
- It's too noisy here. Can we go somewhere **quieter**? *or* … somewhere **more quiet**?

C A few adjectives and adverbs have irregular comparative forms:

good/well → better
- The garden looks **better** since you tidied it up.
- I know him well – probably **better** than anybody else knows him.

bad/badly → worse
- 'How's your headache? Better?' 'No, it's **worse**.'
- He did very badly in the exam – **worse** than expected.

far → further (*or* **farther**)
- It's a long walk from here to the park – **further** than I thought. (*or* **farther** than)

Note that **further** (*but not* farther) also means 'more' or 'additional':
- Let me know if you hear any **further** news. (= any more news)

>> Comparative 2–3 → Units 106–107   Superlative (**cheapest** / **most expensive** etc.) → Unit 108

Exercises

105.1 Complete the sentences using a comparative form (older / more important etc.).

1 This restaurant is very expensive. Let's go somewhere _cheaper_ .
2 This coffee is very weak. I like it ....
3 The town was surprisingly big. I expected it to be ....
4 The hotel was surprisingly cheap. I expected it to be ....
5 The weather is too cold here. I'd like to live somewhere ....
6 Sometimes my job is a bit boring. I'd like to do something ....
7 It's a shame you live so far away. I wish you lived ....
8 It was quite easy to find a place to live. I thought it would be ....
9 Your work isn't very good. I'm sure you can do ....
10 Don't worry. The situation isn't so bad. It could be ....
11 You hardly ever call me. Why don't you call me .... ?
12 You're too near the camera. Can you move a bit .... away?

105.2 Complete the sentences. Use the comparative forms of the words in the box. Use **than** where necessary.

> big   ~~early~~   high   important   interested   peaceful   ~~reliable~~   serious   slowly   thin

1 I was feeling tired last night, so I went to bed _earlier than_ usual.
2 I'd like to have a _more reliable_ car. The one I have keeps breaking down.
3 Unfortunately the problem was .... we thought at first.
4 You look .... Have you lost weight?
5 We don't have enough space here. We need a .... apartment.
6 James doesn't study very hard. He's .... in having a good time.
7 Health and happiness are .... money.
8 I like living in the country. It's .... living in a town.
9 I'm sorry I don't understand. Can you speak .... , please?
10 In some parts of the country, prices are .... in others.

105.3 Complete the sentences. Choose from:

> **than**   **more**   **worse**   **quietly**   ~~**longer**~~   **better**   **careful**   **frequent**

1 Getting a visa was complicated. It took _longer_ than I expected.
2 Sorry about my mistake. I'll try and be more .... in future.
3 Your English has improved. It's .... than it was.
4 You can travel by bus or by train. The buses are more .... than the trains.
5 You can't always have things immediately. You have to be .... patient.
6 I'm a pessimist. I always think things are going to get ....
7 We were busier .... usual in the office today. It's not usually so busy.
8 You're talking very loudly. Can you speak more .... ?

105.4 Read the situations and complete the sentences. Use a comparative form (**-er** or **more ...**).

1 Yesterday the temperature was six degrees. Today it's only three degrees.
  It's _colder today than_ it was yesterday.
2 Dan and I went for a run. I ran ten kilometres. Dan stopped after eight kilometres.
  I ran .... Dan.
3 The journey takes four hours by car and five hours by train.
  The journey takes .... train .... car.
4 I expected my friends to arrive at about 4 o'clock. In fact they arrived at 2.30.
  My friends .... I expected.
5 There is always a lot of traffic here, but today the traffic is really bad.
  The traffic today .... usual.

Comparative 2 (**much better / any better** etc.)

A much / a lot etc. + comparative

Before comparatives you can use:

much   **a lot**   **far** (= a lot)   **a bit**   **a little**   **slightly** (= a little)

○ I felt ill earlier, but I feel **much better** now. (*or* **a lot better**)
○ Don't go by train. It's **a lot more expensive**. (*or* **much more expensive**)
○ Could you speak **a bit more slowly**? (*or* **a little more slowly**)
○ This bag is **slightly heavier** than the other one.
○ The problem is **far more serious** than we thought at first.

B any / no + comparative

You can use **any** and **no** + comparative (**any longer / no bigger** etc.):
○ I've waited long enough. I'm not waiting **any longer**. (= not even a little longer)
○ We expected their apartment to be very big, but it's **no bigger** than ours.
   or …it is**n't any bigger** than ours. (= not even a little bigger)
○ How do you feel now? Do you feel **any better**?
○ This hotel is better than the other one, and it's **no more expensive**.

C better and better, more and more etc.

We repeat comparatives (**better and better** etc.) to say that something changes continuously:
○ Your English is improving. It's getting **better and better**.
○ The city has grown fast in recent years. It's got **bigger and bigger**.
○ As I listened to his story, I became **more and more convinced** that he was lying.
○ **More and more tourists** are visiting this part of the country.

D the … the …

You can say **the sooner the better**, **the more the better** etc. :
○ A: What time shall we leave?
   B: **The sooner the better**. (= as soon as possible)
○ A: What sort of bag do you want? A big one?
   B: Yes, **the bigger the better**. (= as big as possible)
○ When you're travelling, **the less luggage** you have **the better**.

We also use **the … the …** to say that one thing depends on another thing:
○ **The sooner** we leave, **the earlier** we'll arrive. (= if we leave sooner, we'll arrive earlier)
○ **The younger** you are, **the easier** it is to learn.
○ **The more expensive** the hotel, **the better** the service.
○ **The more** I thought about the plan, **the less** I liked it.

E older and elder

The comparative of **old** is **older**:
○ David looks **older** than he really is. (*not* looks elder)

We use **elder** only when we talk about people in a family (**my elder sister**, **their elder son** etc.).
You can also use **older**:
○ **My elder sister** is a TV producer. (*or* My **older** sister …)

But we do not say that 'somebody is elder':
○ My sister is **older** than me. (*not* elder than me)

>> **any/no** → Unit 86   Comparative 1, 3 → **Units 105**, **107**   **eldest** → Unit 108C
even + comparative → Unit 112C

Exercises

106.1 Use the words in brackets to complete the sentences. Use much / a bit etc. + a comparative form. Use than where necessary.

1 The problem is <u>much more serious than</u> we thought at first. (much / serious)
2 This bag is too small. I need something .... (much / big)
3 I liked the museum. It was .... I expected. (a lot / interesting)
4 It was very hot yesterday. Today it's .... (a little / cool)
5 I'm afraid the problem is .... it seems. (far / complicated)
6 You're driving too fast. Can you drive .... ? (a bit / slowly)
7 I thought he was younger than me, but in fact he's .... (slightly / old)

106.2 Complete the sentences using any/no + comparative. Use than where necessary.

1 I've waited long enough. I'm not waiting <u>any longer</u> .
2 I'm sorry I'm a bit late, but I couldn't get here ....
3 This shop isn't expensive. The prices are .... anywhere else.
4 I need to stop for a rest. I can't walk ....
5 The traffic isn't especially bad today. It's .... usual.

106.3 Complete the sentences using ... and ... (see Section C).

1 It's getting <u>more and more difficult</u> to find a job. (difficult)
2 That hole in your sweater is getting .... (big)
3 I waited for my interview and became .... (nervous)
4 As the day went on, the weather got .... (bad)
5 Health care is becoming .... (expensive)
6 Since Anna went to Canada, her English has got .... (good)
7 These days I travel a lot. I'm spending .... away from home. (time)

106.4 Complete the sentences using the ... the ... .

1 You learn things more easily when you're young.
   The <u>younger you are</u> , the easier it is to learn.
2 It's hard to concentrate when you're tired.
   The more tired you are, the ....
3 We should decide what to do as soon as possible.
   The .... , the better.
4 I know more, but I understand less.
   The .... , the less I understand.
5 If you use more electricity, your bill will be higher.
   The more electricity you use, ...
6 Kate had to wait a long time and became more and more impatient.
   The .... , the more ....

106.5 Use the words on the right to complete the sentences.

1 I like to travel light. The <u>less</u> luggage, the better.
2 The problem is getting .... and more serious.
3 The more time I have, the .... it takes me to do things.
4 I'm walking as fast as I can. I can't walk .... faster.
5 The higher your income, ... more tax you have to pay.
6 I'm surprised Anna is only 25. I thought she was ....
7 Jane's .... sister is a nurse.
8 I was a little late. The journey took .... longer than I expected.
9 Applications for the job must be received .... later than 15 April.
10 Don't tell him anything. The .... he knows, the ....

any
better
elder
~~less~~
less
longer
more
no
older
slightly
the

213

Comparative 3 (**as … as / than**)

Study this example situation:

SARAH   *JOE*   *DAVID*

Sarah, Joe and David are all very rich.
Sarah has $20 million, Joe has $15 million
and David has $10 million. So:

Joe is rich.

He is **richer than** David.

But he **isn't as rich as** Sarah.
(= Sarah is **richer than** he is)

Some more examples of **not as** … (**as**):
- ○ Jack **isn't as old as** he looks. (= he looks **older than** he is)
- ○ The town centre **wasn't as crowded as** usual. (= it is usually **more crowded**)
- ○ Lisa **didn't** do **as well** in the exam **as** she had hoped. (= she had hoped to do **better**)
- ○ The weather is better today. It's **not as cold**. (= yesterday was **colder than** today)
- ○ **I don't** know **as many** people **as** you do. (= you know **more** people **than** me)
- ○ 'How much was it? Fifty dollars?'   'No, **not as much** as that.' (= **less than** fifty dollars)

You can also say **not so** … (**as**):
- ○ It's not warm, but it's **not so** cold **as** yesterday. (= it's not **as** cold **as** …)

Less than is similar to **not as** … **as**:
- ○ I spent **less** money **than** you. (= I **didn't** spend **as** much money **as** you)
- ○ The city centre was **less** crowded **than** usual. (= it **wasn't as** crowded **as** usual)
- ○ I play tennis **less than** I used to. (= I **don't** play **as** much **as** I used to)

We also use **as** … **as** (*but not* so … as) in positive sentences and in questions:
- ○ I'm sorry I'm late. I got here **as fast as** I could.
- ○ There's plenty of food. You can have **as much as** you want.
- ○ Can you send me the information **as soon as** possible, please?
- ○ Let's walk. It's just **as quick as** taking the bus.

also **twice as** … **as**, **three times as** … **as** etc. :
- ○ Petrol is **twice as expensive as** it was a few years ago.
- ○ Their house is about **three times as big as** ours.
   (*or* …**three times the size of** ours)

We say **the same as** (*not* the same like):
- ○ Laura's salary is **the same as** mine.   *or*   Laura gets **the same** salary **as** me.
- ○ David is **the same** age **as** James.
- ○ Sarah hasn't changed. She still looks **the same as** she did ten years ago.

than me / than I am etc.

You can say:
- ○ You're taller **than me**.   *or* You're taller **than I am**.
   (*not usually* You're taller than I)
- ○ He's not as clever **as her**.   *or* He's not as clever **as she is**.
- ○ They have more money **than us**. *or* They have more money **than we have**.
- ○ I can't run as fast **as him**.   *or* I can't run as fast **as he can**.

Comparative 1–2 → **Units 105–106**   as long as → **Unit 115B**   as and like → **Unit 117**

Exercises

107.1 **Complete the sentences using as ... as.**

1 I'm tall, but you are taller. I'm not ___as tall as you___ .
2 My salary is high, but yours is higher. My salary isn't _____ .
3 You know a bit about cars, but I know more.
You don't _____ .
4 We are busy today, but we were busier yesterday.
We aren't _____ .
5 I still feel bad, but I felt a lot worse earlier.
I don't _____ .
6 Our neighbours have lived here for quite a long time, but we've lived here longer.
Our neighbours haven't _____ .
7 I was a little nervous before the interview, but usually I'm a lot more nervous.
I wasn't _____ .

107.2 **Write a new sentence with the same meaning.**

1 Jack is younger than he looks. Jack isn't ___as old as he looks___ .
2 I didn't spend as much money as you. You ___spent more money than me___ .
3 The station was nearer than I thought. The station wasn't _____ .
4 The meal didn't cost as much as I expected. The meal cost _____ .
5 I watch TV less than I used to. I don't _____ .
6 Karen's hair isn't as long as it used to be. Karen used to _____ .
7 I know them better than you do. You don't _____ .
8 There are fewer students in this class than in the other one.
There aren't _____ .

107.3 **Complete the sentences using as ... as. Choose from:**

~~fast~~	hard	long	often	quietly	soon	well

1 I'm sorry I'm late. I got here ___as fast as___ I could.
2 It was a difficult question. I answered it _____ I could.
3 'How long can I stay with you?' 'You can stay _____ you like.'
4 I need the information quickly, so let me know _____ possible.
5 I like to keep fit, so I go swimming _____ I can.
6 I didn't want to wake anybody, so I came in _____ I could.
7 You always say how tiring your job is, but I work just _____ you.

107.4 **Write sentences using the same as.**

1 David and James are both 22 years old. David ___is the same age as___ James.
2 You and I both have dark brown hair. Your hair _____ mine.
3 I arrived at 10.25 and so did you. I arrived _____ you.
4 My birthday is 5 April. It's Tom's birthday too. My birthday _____ Tom's.

107.5 **Complete the sentences. Choose from:**

as	him	is	less	me	much	~~soon~~	than	twice

1 I'll let you know as ___soon___ as I have any more news.
2 My friends arrived earlier _____ I expected.
3 I live in the same street _____ Katherine. We're neighbours.
4 He doesn't know much. I know more than _____ .
5 This morning there was _____ traffic than usual.
6 I don't watch TV as _____ as I used to.
7 Your bag is quite light. Mine is _____ as heavy as yours.
8 We were born in the same year. I'm a little older than she _____ .
9 I was really surprised. Nobody was more surprised than _____ .

Superlative (**the longest / the most enjoyable** etc.)

A Look at these examples:

> What is **the longest** river in the world?
> What was **the most enjoyable** holiday you've ever had?

> **Longest** and **most enjoyable** are *superlative* forms.

The superlative form is **-est** or **most** .... In general, we use **-est** for short words and **most** ... for longer words.

long → long**est**	**hot** → hott**est**	**easy** → easi**est**	**hard** → hard**est**
but **most** famous	**most** boring	**most** enjoyable	**most** difficult

A few superlative forms are irregular:

> good → **best**   bad → **worst**   far → **furthest** *or* **farthest**

The rules are the same as those for the comparative – see Unit 105.
For spelling, see Appendix 6.

B We normally use **the** (or **my/your** etc.) with a superlative:
- ○ Yesterday was **the hottest** day of the year.
- ○ The Louvre in Paris is one of **the most famous** museums in the world.
- ○ She is really nice – one of **the nicest** people I know.
- ○ What's **the best** movie you've ever seen, and what's **the worst**?
- ○ How old is **your youngest** child?

Compare the superlative and the comparative:
- ○ This hotel is **the cheapest** in town. *(superlative)*
  It's **cheaper** than all the others in town. *(comparative)*
- ○ He's **the most patient** person I've ever met.
  He's much **more patient** than I am.

C **oldest** and **eldest**

The superlative of **old** is **oldest**:
- ○ That church is **the oldest** building in the town. *(not* the eldest)

We use **eldest** only when we talk about people in a family (you can also use **oldest**):
- ○ **Their eldest son** is 13 years old. *(or* Their **oldest** son)
- ○ Are you **the eldest** in your family? *(or* the **oldest**)

D After superlatives we normally use **in** with places:
- ○ What's the longest river **in the world**? *(not* of the world)
- ○ We had a nice room. It was one of the best **in the hotel**. *(not* of the hotel)

We also use **in** for organisations and groups of people (a class / a company etc.):
- ○ Who is the youngest student **in the class**? *(not* of the class)

For a period of time (**day**, **year** etc.), we normally use **of**:
- ○ Yesterday was the hottest day **of the year**.
- ○ What was the happiest day **of your life**?

E We often use the *present perfect* (I **have done**) after a superlative (see also Unit 8A):
- ○ What's **the most important** decision **you've** ever **made**?
- ○ That was **the best** holiday **I've had** for a long time.

   >>   Comparative (**cheaper / more expensive** etc.) → Units 105–107   elder → Unit 106E

Exercises

108.1 Complete the sentences. Use the superlative forms (-est or most …) of the words in the box.

bad   ~~cheap~~   good   honest   popular   short   tall

1 We didn't have much money, so we stayed at ____the cheapest____ hotel in the town.
2 This building is 250 metres high, but it's not _____ in the city.
3 It was an awful day. It was _____ day of my life.
4 What is _____ sport in your country?
5 I like the morning. For me it's _____ part of the day.
6 Sarah always tells the truth. She's one of _____ people I know.
7 A straight line is _____ distance between two points.

108.2 Complete the sentences. Use a superlative (-est or most …) or a comparative (-er or more …).

1 We stayed at ____the cheapest____ hotel in the town. (cheap)
2 Our hotel was ____cheaper____ than all the others in the town. (cheap)
3 I wasn't feeling well yesterday, but I feel a bit _____ today. (good)
4 What's _____ thing you've ever bought? (expensive)
5 I prefer this chair to the other one. It's _____. (comfortable)
6 Amy and Ben have three daughters. _____ is 14 years old. (old)
7 Who is the _____ person you know? (old)
8 What's _____ way to get to the station? (quick)
9 Which is _____ – the bus or the train? (quick)
10 I can remember when I was three years old. It's _____ memory. (early)
11 Everest is _____ mountain in the world. It is _____
   than any other mountain. (high)
12 A: This knife isn't very sharp. Do you have a _____ one?
   B: No, it's _____ one I have. (sharp)

108.3 Complete the sentences. Use a superlative (-est or most …) + a preposition (of or in).

1 It's a very good room. It's ____the best room in____ the hotel.
2 Brazil is a very large country. It's _____ South America.
3 It was a very happy day. It was _____ my life.
4 This is a very valuable painting. It's _____ the museum.
5 Spring is a very busy time for me. It's _____ the year.

In the following sentences use one of + a superlative + a preposition.

6 It's a very good room. It's ____one of the best rooms in____ the hotel.
7 He's a very rich man. He's one _____ the country.
8 She's a very good student. She's _____ the class.
9 It was a very bad experience. It was _____ my life.
10 It's a very famous university. It's _____ the world.

108.4 What do you say in these situations? Use a superlative + ever.

1 You've just been to the cinema. The movie was extremely boring. You tell your friend:
   (boring / movie / ever / see) That's ____the most boring movie I've ever seen____ .
2 Someone has just told you a joke which you think is very funny. You say:
   (funny / joke / ever / hear) That's _____ .
3 You're drinking coffee with a friend. It's really good coffee. You say:
   (good / coffee / ever / taste) This _____ .
4 You have just run ten kilometres. You've never run further than this. You say:
   (far / ever / run) That _____ .
5 You gave up your job. Now you think this was a very bad mistake. You say:
   (bad / mistake / ever / make) It _____ .
6 Your friend meets a lot of people, some of them famous. You ask your friend:
   (famous / person / ever / meet?) Who _____ ?

Word order 1: verb + object; place and time

A Verb + object

The *verb* and the *object* normally go together. We do not usually put other words between them:

	verb	object		
I	**like**	**my job**	very much.	(*not* I like very much)
Our guide	**spoke**	**English**	fluently.	(*not* spoke fluently English)
I didn't	**use**	**my phone**	yesterday.	
Do you	**eat**	**meat**	every day?	

Two more examples:
- ☐ I lost all my money and I also **lost my passport**.
  (*not* I lost also my passport)
- ☐ At the end of this street you'll **see a supermarket** on your left.
  (*not* see on your left a supermarket)

B Place

The *verb* and *place* (where?) normally go together:
   go home   **live in a city**   **walk to work** etc.

If the verb has an *object*, the order is:

	verb	object	place	
We	**took**	**the children**	**to the zoo**.	(*not* took to the zoo the children)
Don't	**put**	**anything**	**on the table**.	
Did you	**learn**	**English**	**at school**?	

C Time

Normally *time* (when? / how often? / how long?) goes after *place*:

	place	time
Ben walks	**to work**	**every morning**. (*not* every morning to work)
I'm going	**to Paris**	**on Monday**.
They've lived	**in the same house**	**for a long time**.
We need to be	**at the airport**	**by 8 o'clock**.
Sarah gave me a lift	**home**	**after the party**.
You really shouldn't go	**to bed**	**so late**.

Sometimes we put *time* at the beginning of the sentence:
- ☐ **On Monday** I'm going to Paris.
- ☐ **After the party** Sarah gave me a lift home.

Some time words (for example, **always**/**never**/**usually**) go with the verb in the middle of the sentence. See Unit 110.

Exercises

109.1 Is the word order OK or not? Correct the sentences where necessary.

1 Did you see your friends yesterday?   *OK*
2 Ben walks every morning to work.   *Ben walks to work every morning.*
3 Joe doesn't like very much football.
4 Dan won easily the race.
5 Tanya speaks German quite well.
6 Have you seen recently Chris?
7 I borrowed from a friend some money.
8 Please don't ask that question again.
9 I ate quickly my breakfast and went out.
10 Did you invite to the party a lot of people?
11 Sam watches all the time TV.
12 Does Kevin play football every weekend?

109.2 Complete the sentences. Put the parts in the correct order.

1 We (the children / to the zoo / took).   We *took the children to the zoo* .
2 I (a friend of mine / on my way home / met).   I ....
3 I (to put / on the envelope / a stamp / forgot).   I ....
4 We (a lot of fruit / bought / in the market).   We ....
5 They (opposite the park / a new hotel / built).   They ....
6 Did you (at school / today / a lot of things / learn)?
   Did you .... ?
7 We (some interesting books / found / in the library).
   We ....
8 Please (at the top / write / of the page / your name).
   Please ....

109.3 Complete the sentences. Put the parts in the correct order.

1 They (for a long time / have lived / in the same house).
   They *have lived in the same house for a long time* .
2 I (to the supermarket / every Friday / go).
   I ....
3 Why (home / did you come / so late)?
   Why .... ?
4 Sarah (her children / takes / every day / to school).
   Sarah ....
5 I haven't (been / recently / to the cinema).
   I haven't ....
6 I (her name / after a few minutes / remembered).
   I ....
7 We (around the town / all morning / walked).
   We ....
8 My brother (has been / since April / in Canada).
   My brother ....
9 I (on Saturday night / didn't see you / at the party).
   I ....
10 Lisa (her umbrella / last night / in a restaurant / left).
    Lisa ....
11 The moon (round the earth / every 27 days / goes).
    The moon ....
12 Anna (Italian / for the last three years / has been teaching / in London).
    Anna ....

Word order 2: adverbs with the verb

A   Some adverbs (for example, **always**, **also**, **probably**) go with the verb in the middle of a sentence:
- ○   Emily **always drives** to work.
- ○   We were feeling very tired and we **were also** hungry.
- ○   The meeting **will probably be cancelled**.

B   If the verb is one word (**drives**/**cooked** etc.), the adverb goes *before* the verb:

	adverb	verb	
Emily	**always**	**drives**	to work.
I	**almost**	**fell**	as I was going down the stairs.

- ○   I cleaned the house and **also cooked** the dinner. (*not* cooked also)
- ○   Laura **hardly ever watches** television and **rarely reads** newspapers.
- ○   'Shall I give you my address?'   'No, I **already have** it.'

Note that these adverbs (**always**/**usually**/**also** etc.) go before **have to** … :
- ○   Joe never phones me. I **always have to** phone him. (*not* I have always to phone)

But adverbs go *after* **am**/**is**/**are**/**was**/**were**:
- ○   We were feeling very tired and we **were also** hungry. (*not* also were)
- ○   You**'re always** late. You**'re never** on time.
- ○   The traffic **isn't usually** as bad as it was this morning.

C   If the verb is two or more words (for example, **can remember** / **will be cancelled**), the adverb usually goes *after the first verb* (**can**/**doesn't**/**will** etc.):

	verb 1	adverb	verb 2	
I	**can**	**never**	**remember**	her name.
Clare	**doesn't**	**usually**	**drive**	to work.
	Are you	**definitely**	**going**	away next week?
The meeting	**will**	**probably**	**be**	cancelled.

- ○   You**'ve always been** very kind to me.
- ○   Jack can't cook. He **can't even boil** an egg.
- ○   **Do** you **still work** for the same company?
- ○   The house **was only built** a year ago and it**'s already falling** down.

Note that **probably** goes before a negative (**isn't**/**won't** etc.). So we say:
- ○   I **probably won't see** you.   *or*
  I'll **probably not** see you. (*but not* I won't probably)

D   We also use **all** and **both** with the verb in the middle of a sentence:
- ○   We **all felt** ill after the meal. (*not* felt all ill)
- ○   My parents **are both** teachers.
- ○   Sarah and Jane **have both applied** for the job.
- ○   My friends **are all going** out tonight.

E   Sometimes we use **is**/**will**/**did** etc. instead of repeating part of a sentence (see Unit 51):
- ○   Tom says he isn't clever, but I think he **is**. (= he **is clever**)

When we do this, we put **always**/**never** etc. *before* the verb:
- ○   He always says he won't be late, but he **always is**. (= he **is always** late)
- ○   I've never done it and I **never will**. (= I **will never** do it)

>>   Word order 1 ➜ **Unit 109**

Exercises

Unit
110

110.1 Is the word order OK or not? Correct the sentences where necessary.

1 Helen <u>drives always</u> to work.   Helen always drives to work.
2 I cleaned the house and also cooked the dinner.   OK
3 I have usually a shower in the morning.
4 I'm usually hungry when I get home from work.
5 Steve gets hardly ever angry.
6 I called him and I sent also an email.
7 You don't listen! I have always to repeat things.
8 I never have worked in a factory.
9 I never have enough time. I'm always busy.
10 When I arrived, my friends already were there.

110.2 Rewrite the sentences to include the word in brackets.

1 Clare doesn't drive to work. (usually)   Clare doesn't usually drive to work.
2 Katherine is very generous. (always)
3 I don't have to work on Sundays. (usually)
4 Do you watch TV in the evenings? (always)
5 Martin is learning Spanish, and he is learning Japanese. (also)
   Martin is learning Spanish and he
6 a We were on holiday in Spain. (all)
   b We were staying at the same hotel. (all)
   c We had a great time. (all)
7 a The new hotel is expensive. (probably)
   b It costs a lot to stay there. (probably)
8 a I can help you. (probably)
   b I can't help you. (probably)

110.3 Complete the sentences. Use the words in brackets in the correct order.

1 What's her name again? I can never remember (remember / I / never / can) it.
2 Our cat .... (usually / sleeps) under the bed.
3 There are plenty of hotels here. .... (usually / it / easy / is)
   to find a place to stay.
4 Mark and Amy .... (both / were / born) in Manchester.
5 Lisa is a good pianist. .... (sing / she / also / can) very well.
6 How do you go to work? .... (usually / you / do / go) by bus?
7 I see them every day, but .... (never / I / have / spoken) to them.
8 We haven't moved. .... (we / still / are / living) in the same place.
9 This shop is always busy. .... (have / you / always / to wait)
   a long time to be served.
10 This could be the last time I see you. .... (meet / never / we / might)
   again.
11 Thanks for the invitation, but .... (probably / I / be / won't)
   able to come to the party.
12 I'm going out for an hour. .... (still / be / you / will) here when
   I get back?
13 Helen goes away a lot. .... (is / hardly ever / she) at home.
14 If we hadn't taken the same train, ...
   (never / met / we / would / have) each other.
15 The journey took a long time today. .... (doesn't / take / it / always)
   so long.
16 .... (all / were / we) tired, so .... (all / we / fell) asleep.
17 Tanya .... (says / always) that she'll phone me, but
   .... (does / she / never).

221

A

We use **still** to say that a situation or action is continuing. It hasn't changed or stopped:
- ○ It's ten o'clock and Joe is **still** in bed.
- ○ When I went to bed, Chris was **still** working.
- ○ Do you **still** want to go away or have you changed your mind?

Still also means 'in spite of this'. For example:
- ○ He has everything he needs, but he's **still** unhappy.

Still usually goes in the middle of the sentence with the verb. See Unit 110.

B

We use **not** … **any more** or **not** … **any longer** to say that a situation has changed.
Any more and **any longer** go at the end of a sentence:
- ○ Lucy **doesn't** work here **any more**. She left last month. *or*
  Lucy **doesn't** work here **any longer**.
- ○ We used to be good friends, but we **aren't any more**. *or* …we aren't **any longer**.

You can write **any more** (2 words) or **anymore** (1 word).

You can also use **no longer**. **No longer** goes in the middle of the sentence:
- ○ Lucy **no longer** works here.

We do not normally use **no more** in this way:
- ○ We are **no longer** friends. (*not* we are no more friends)

Compare **still** and **not** … **any more**:
- ○ Sally **still** works here, but Lucy **doesn't** work here **any more**.

C

We use **yet** mainly in negative sentences (**He isn't** here **yet**) and questions (**Is he** here **yet**?).
Yet (= until now) shows that the speaker expects something to happen.

Yet usually goes at the end of a sentence:
- ○ It's 10 o'clock and Joe **isn't** here **yet**.
- ○ **Have** you **decided** what to do **yet**?
- ○ 'Where are you going on holiday?'   'We **don't** know **yet**.'

We often use **yet** with the *present perfect* ('**Have** you **decided** … **yet**?'). See Unit 7C.

Compare **yet** and **still**:
- ○ Mike lost his job six months ago and **is still** unemployed.
  Mike lost his job six months ago and **hasn't found** another job **yet**.
- ○ **Is** it **still** raining?
  Has it **stopped** raining **yet**?

Still is also possible in *negative* sentences (before the negative):
- ○ She said she would be here an hour ago and she **still hasn't** come.

This is similar to 'she hasn't come **yet**'. But **still** … **not** shows a stronger feeling of surprise or impatience. Compare:
- ○ I sent him an invitation last week. He **hasn't** replied **yet**. (but I expect he will reply soon)
- ○ I sent him an invitation weeks ago and he **still hasn't** replied. (he should have replied before now)

D

We use **already** to say that something happened sooner than expected.
- ○ 'What time is Sue leaving?'   'She has **already** left.' (= sooner than you expected)
- ○ Shall I tell Joe what happened or does he **already** know?
- ○ I've just had lunch and I'm **already** hungry.

Already usually goes in the middle of a sentence (see Unit 110) or at the end:
- ○ She's **already** left. *or* She's left **already**.

>> Present perfect + **already/yet** ➔ Unit 7C   Word order ➔ **Unit 110**

Exercises

111.1 Compare what Paul said a few years ago with what he says now. Some things are the same as before and some things have changed. Write sentences with **still** and **any more**.

Paul a few years ago

I travel a lot.
I work in a shop.
I write poems.
I want to be a teacher.
I'm interested in politics.
I'm single.
I go fishing a lot.

Paul now

I travel a lot.
I work in a hospital.
I gave up writing poems.
I want to be a teacher.
I'm not interested in politics.
I'm single.
I haven't been fishing for years.

1 (travel)   _He still travels a lot._
2 (shop)   _He doesn't work in a shop_
             any more.
3 (poems) He _____
4 (teacher) _____

5 (politics) _____
             _____
6 (single) _____
7 (fishing) _____
8 (beard) _____

Now write three sentences about Paul using **no longer**.

9   _He no longer works in a shop._
10 _____

11 _____
12 _____

111.2 For each sentence (with **still**) write a sentence with a similar meaning using **not … yet**. Choose from these verbs:

| decide | find | finish | go | ~~stop~~ | take off | wake up |

1 It's still raining.   _It hasn't stopped raining yet._
2 Gary is still here.   He _____
3 They're still repairing the road.   They _____
4 The children are still asleep.   They _____
5 Kate is still looking for a job.   She _____
6 I'm still wondering what to do.   I _____
7 The plane is still waiting on the runway.   It _____

111.3 Put in **still**, **yet**, **already** or **any more**.

1 Mike lost his job a year ago and he is ____still____ unemployed.
2 Shall I tell Joe what happened or does he ___already___ know?
3 Do you _____ live in the same place or have you moved?
4 I'm hungry. Is dinner ready _____ ?
5 I was hungry earlier, but I don't feel hungry _____ .
6 Can we wait a few minutes? I don't want to go out _____ .
7 Amy used to work at the airport, but she doesn't work there _____ .
8 I used to live in Amsterdam. I _____ have a lot of friends there.
9 There's no need to introduce me to Joe. We've _____ met.
10 John is 80 years old, but he's _____ very fit and healthy.
11 Would you like something to eat, or have you _____ eaten?
12 'Where's Helen?' 'She's not here _____ . She'll be here soon.'
13 Mark said he'd be here at 8.30. It's 9 o'clock now and he _____ isn't here.
14 Do you want to join the club or are you _____ a member?
15 It happened a long time ago, but I _____ remember it very clearly.
16 I've put on weight. These trousers don't fit me _____ .

even

A

Study this example situation:

Tina loves watching TV.

She has a television in every room of the house, **even the bathroom**.

We use **even** to say that something is unusual or surprising. It is not usual to have a television in the bathroom.

Some more examples:

- These pictures are really awful. **Even I** take better pictures than these. (and I'm certainly not a good photographer)
- He always wears a coat, **even in hot weather**.
- The print was very small. I couldn't read it, **even with glasses**.
- Nobody would help her, **not even her best friend**. *or*
  Not even her best friend would help her.

B

You can use **even** with the verb in the middle of a sentence (see Unit 110):

- Laura has travelled all over the world. She's **even** been to the Antarctic.
- They are very rich. They **even** have their own private jet.

You can use **even** with a negative (**not even**, **can't even**, **don't even** etc.):

- I can't cook. I **can't even** boil an egg. (and boiling an egg is very easy)
- They weren't very friendly to us. They **didn't even** say hello.
- Jessica is very fit. She's been running quite fast and she's **not even** out of breath.

C

You can use **even** + *comparative* (**cheaper** / **more expensive** etc.):

- I got up very early, but Jack got up **even earlier**.
- I knew I didn't have much money, but I have **even less** than I thought.
- We were very surprised to get an email from her. We were **even more surprised** when she came to see us a few days later.

D

even though / even when / even if

We use **even though** / **even when** / **even if** + *subject* + *verb*:

- **Even though Tina can't** drive, she has a car.

  subject + verb

- He never shouts, **even when he's** angry.
- This river is dangerous. It's dangerous to swim in it, **even if you're** a strong swimmer.

We do not use **even** + *subject* + *verb*. We say:

- **Even though she can't** drive, she has a car. (*not* even she can't drive)
- I can't reach the shelf **even if I stand** on a chair. (*not* even I stand)

Compare **even if** and **even** (without **if**):

- It's dangerous to swim here **even if you're** a strong swimmer. (*not* even you are)
- The river is dangerous, **even for strong swimmers**.

Compare **even if** and **if**:

- We're going to the beach tomorrow. It doesn't matter what the weather is like. We're going **even if** the weather is bad.
- We want to go to the beach tomorrow, but we won't go **if** the weather is bad.

>> if and **when** → Unit 25D   **though** / **even though** → Unit 113E

Exercises

112.1 Amy, Kate and Lisa are three friends who went on holiday together. Use the information given about them to complete the sentences using **even** or **not even**.

AMY	KATE	LISA
is usually happy is usually on time likes to get up early is very interested in art	isn't very keen on art is usually miserable usually hates hotels doesn't use her camera much	is almost always late is a keen photographer loves staying in hotels isn't very good at getting up

1 They stayed at a hotel. Everybody liked it, _even Kate_ .
2 They arranged to meet. They all arrived on time, _____ .
3 They went to an art gallery. Nobody enjoyed it, _____ .
4 Yesterday they had to get up early. They all managed to do this, _____ .
5 They were together yesterday. They were all in a good mood, _____ .
6 None of them took any pictures, _____ .

112.2 Make sentences with **even**. Use the words in brackets.

1 Laura has been all over the world. (the Antarctic) _She has even been to the Antarctic._
2 We painted the whole room. (the floor) We _____
3 Rachel has met lots of famous people. (the prime minister)
   She _____
4 You could hear the noise from a long way away. (from the next street)
   You _____

Now make sentences with a negative + **even** (**didn't even**, **can't even** etc.).

5 They didn't say anything to us. (hello) _They didn't even say hello._
6 I can't remember anything about her. (her name)
   I _____
7 There isn't anything to do in this town. (a cinema)
   _____
8 He didn't tell anybody where he was going. (his wife)
   _____
9 I don't know anyone in our street. (my neighbours)
   _____

112.3 Complete the sentences using **even** + comparative.

1 It was very hot yesterday, but today it's _even hotter_ .
2 The church is 700 years old, but the house next to it is _____ .
3 That's a very good idea, but I've got an _____ one.
4 The first question was very difficult to answer. The second one was _____
5 I did very badly in the exam, but most of my friends did _____ .
6 Neither of us was hungry. I ate very little and my friend ate _____ .

112.4 Complete the sentences. Choose from: **if   even   even if   even though**

1 _Even though_ she can't drive, she has a car.
2 The bus leaves in five minutes, but we can still catch it _____ we run.
3 The bus leaves in two minutes. We won't catch it now _____ we run.
4 Mark's Spanish isn't very good, _____ after three years in Spain.
5 Mark's Spanish isn't very good, _____ he lived in Spain for three years.
6 _____ with the heating on, it was cold in the house.
7 I couldn't sleep _____ I was very tired.
8 I won't forgive them for what they did, _____ they apologise.
9 _____ I hadn't eaten anything for 24 hours, I wasn't hungry.

→ **Additional exercise 32** (page 321)

Unit 113

although though even though
in spite of despite

A Study this example situation:

Last year Paul and Sarah had a holiday by the sea.
It rained a lot, but they had a good time.

You can say:

Although it rained a lot, they had a good time.
(= It rained a lot, but they …)
or

In spite of
   Despite } **the rain**, they had a good time.

B After **although** we use a *subject + verb*:
- ○ **Although it rained** a lot, they had a good time.
- ○ I didn't apply for the job **although I had** the necessary qualifications.

Compare the meaning of **although** and **because**:
- ○ We went out **although** it was raining heavily.
- ○ We didn't go out **because** it was raining heavily.

C After **in spite of** or **despite**, we use a *noun*, a *pronoun* (**this/that/what** etc.) or **-ing**:
- ○ **In spite of the rain**, we had a good time.
- ○ She wasn't well, but **in spite of this** she continued working.
- ○ **In spite of what** I said yesterday, I still love you.
- ○ I didn't apply for the job **in spite of having** the necessary qualifications.

Despite is the same as **in spite of**. We say **in spite of**, but **despite** (*without* of):
- ○ She wasn't well, but **despite this** she continued working. (*not* despite of this)

You can say '**in spite of the fact** (that) …' and '**despite the fact** (that) …':
- ○ I didn't apply for the job { **in spite of the fact** (that) }
                                   { **despite the fact** (that) } I had the necessary qualifications.

Compare **in spite of** and **because of**:
- ○ We went out **in spite of the rain**. (*or* … **despite the rain**.)
- ○ We didn't go out **because of the rain**.

D Compare **although** and **in spite of / despite**:
- ○ **Although the traffic was** bad,
     In spite of the traffic, } we arrived on time. (*not* in spite of the traffic was bad)

- ○ I couldn't sleep { **although I was** very tired.
                       { **despite being** very tired. (*not* despite I was tired)

E **though** = **although**:
- ○ I didn't apply for the job **though** I had the necessary qualifications.

In spoken English we often use **though** at the end of a sentence:
- ○ The house isn't so nice. I like the garden **though**. (= but I like the garden)
- ○ I see them every day. I've never spoken to them **though**. (= but I've never spoken to them)

Even though (*but not* 'even' alone) is similar to **although**:
- ○ **Even though** I was really tired, I couldn't sleep. (*not* even I was really tired)

>> **even → Unit 112**

Exercises

113.1 Complete the sentences. Use **although** + a sentence from the box.

> I didn't speak the language well ~~she has a very important job~~
> I had never seen her before we don't like them very much
> it was quite cold the heating was on
> I'd met her twice before we've known each other a long time

1   _Although she has a very important job_ , she isn't well-paid.
2   _____, I recognised her from a photo.
3   Sarah wasn't wearing a coat _____ .
4   We decided to invite them to the party _____ .
5   _____, I managed to make myself understood.
6   _____, the room wasn't warm.
7   I didn't recognise her _____ .
8   We're not close friends _____ .

113.2 Complete the sentences with **although** / **in spite of** / **because** / **because of**.

1   _Although_ it rained a lot, we had a good time.
2   a   _____ all our careful plans, a lot of things went wrong.
    b   _____ we'd planned everything carefully, a lot of things went wrong.
3   a   I went home early _____ I was feeling unwell.
    b   I went to work the next day _____ I was still feeling unwell.
4   a   Chris only accepted the job _____ the salary, which was very high.
    b   Sam accepted the job _____ the salary, which was rather low.
5   a   _____ there was a lot of noise, I slept quite well.
    b   I couldn't get to sleep _____ the noise.

Use your own ideas to complete the following sentences:

6   a   He passed the exam although _____ .
    b   He passed the exam because _____ .
7   a   I didn't eat much although _____ .
    b   I didn't eat much in spite of _____ .

113.3 Make one sentence from two. Use the word(s) in brackets in your sentences.

1   I couldn't sleep. I was very tired. (despite)
    I couldn't sleep despite being very tired.
2   We played quite well. We lost the game. (in spite of)
    In spite _____
3   I'd hurt my foot. I managed to walk home. (although)
    _____
4   I enjoyed the film. The story was silly. (in spite of)
    _____
5   We live in the same building. We hardly ever see each other. (despite)
    _____
6   They came to the party. They hadn't been invited. (even though)
    _____

113.4 Use the words in brackets to make a sentence with **though** at the end.

1   The house isn't very nice. (like / garden)   _I like the garden though._
2   I enjoyed reading the book. (very long) _____
3   We didn't like the food. (ate) _____
4   Laura is very nice. (don't like / husband) I _____

→ **Additional exercise 32** (page 321)

in case

A

Study this example situation:

Your car should have a spare wheel **in case** you have a puncture.
(= because it is possible you will have a puncture)

in case something happens =
because it is possible it will happen

Some more examples of **in case**:
- ○ I'd better write down my password **in case I forget it**.
  (= because it is possible I will forget it)
- ○ Shall I draw a map for you **in case you have a problem** finding our house?
  (= because it is possible you will have problems finding it)
- ○ I'll remind them about the meeting **in case they've forgotten**.
  (= because it is possible they have forgotten)

We use **just in case** for a smaller possibility:
- ○ I don't think it will rain, but I'll take an umbrella **just in case**. (= **just in case** it rains)

We do not use **will** after **in case** (see also Unit 25):
- ○ I'll write down my password **in case** I **forget** it. (*not* in case I will forget)

B

In case and **if** are not the same. We use **in case** to say *why* somebody does (or doesn't do) something.
You do something *now* **in case** something happens *later*.

Compare:

in case	**if**
○ We'll buy some more food **in case** Tom comes. (= Maybe Tom will come. We'll buy some more food now, whether he comes or not. Then we'll *already* have the food *if* he comes.)	○ We'll buy some more food **if** Tom comes. (= Maybe Tom will come. If he comes, we'll buy some more food. If he doesn't come, we won't buy any more food.)
○ I'll give you my phone number **in case** you need to contact me.	○ You can call me on this number **if** you need to contact me.
○ You should insure your bike **in case** it is stolen.	○ You should inform the police **if** your bike is stolen.

C

You can use **in case** + *past* to say why somebody did something:
- ○ I gave him my phone number **in case he needed** to contact me.
  (= because it was possible that he would need to contact me)
- ○ I drew a map for Sarah **in case she had** a problem finding our house.
- ○ We rang the doorbell again **in case they hadn't heard** it the first time.

D

in case of = if there is … (especially on notices, instructions etc.):
- ○ **In case of fire**, please leave the building as quickly as possible. (= if there is a fire)
- ○ **In case of emergency**, call this number. (= if there is an emergency)

>> if → Units 25, 38–40

Exercises

114.1 Sophie is going for a long walk in the country. You're worried about her because:

> perhaps she'll be thirsty   she might need to call somebody   maybe she'll get lonely
> ~~it's possible she'll get lost~~   perhaps she'll get hungry   maybe it will rain

You advise her to take some things with her. Complete the sentences using in case.

1 Take a map   *in case you get lost*   .
2 You should take some chocolate   .
3 You'll need an anorak   .
4 Take plenty of water   .
5 Don't forget your phone   .
6 Shall I come with you   ?

114.2 What do you say in these situations? Use in case.

1 It's possible that Jane will need to contact you, so you give her your phone number.
   You say: I'll give you my phone number   *in case you need to contact me*   .

2 A friend of yours is going away for a long time. Maybe you won't see her again before she
   goes, so you decide to say goodbye now.
   You say: I'll say goodbye now   .

3 You are buying food in a supermarket with a friend. You think you have everything you need,
   but maybe you've forgotten something. Your friend has the list. You ask her to check it.
   You say: Can you   ?

4 You're shopping with a friend. She's just bought some jeans, but she didn't try them on.
   Maybe they won't fit her, so you advise her to keep the receipt.
   You say: Keep   .

114.3 Complete the sentences using in case.

1 It was possible that it would rain, so I took an umbrella.
   I took an umbrella   *in case it rained*   .
2 I thought that I might forget the name of the book. So I wrote it down.
   I wrote down the name of the book   .
3 I thought my parents might be worried about me. So I phoned them.
   I phoned my parents   .
4 I sent an email to Lisa, but she didn't reply. So I sent another email because maybe she didn't
   get the first one.
   I sent her another email   .
5 I met some people when I was on holiday in France. They said they might come to London
   one day. I live in London, so I gave them my phone number.
   I gave them my phone number   .

114.4 Put in in case or if.

1 I'll draw a map for you   *in case*   you have a problem finding our house.
2 You should tell the police   *if*   you have any information about the crime.
3 I hope you'll come to Australia sometime. _____ you come, you must visit us.
4 I made a copy of the document _____ something happens to the original.
5 This book belongs to Kate. Can you give it to her _____ you see her?
6 Write your name and phone number on your bag _____ you lose it.
7 Go to the lost property office _____ you lose your bag.
8 The burglar alarm will ring _____ somebody tries to break into the house.
9 You should lock your bike to something _____ somebody tries to steal it.
10 I was advised to get insurance _____ I needed medical treatment while I was abroad.

➜ Additional exercise 32 (page 321)

Unit 115   unless   as long as   provided

A   unless

Study this example situation:

The club is for members only.

You can't go in **unless you are a member**.

This means:
You can't go in *except if* you are a member.
You can go in *only if* you are a member.

unless = except if

Some more examples of **unless**:
- ○ I'll see you tomorrow **unless I have to work late**.
  (= except if I have to work late)
- ○ There are no buses to the beach. **Unless you have a car**, it's difficult to get there.
  (= except if you have a car)
- ○ A: Shall I tell Lisa what happened?
  B: **Not unless** she asks you. (= tell her only if she asks you)
- ○ Ben hates to complain. He wouldn't complain about something **unless it was really bad**.
  (= except if it was really bad)
- ○ We can take a taxi to the restaurant – **unless you'd prefer to walk**. (= except if you'd prefer to walk)

Instead of **unless** it is often possible to say **if** … **not**:
- ○ **Unless we leave now**, we'll be late. *or* **If we don't leave now**, we'll …

B   as long as / so long as and provided / providing

You can say **as long as** or **so long as** (= if, on condition that):
- ○ You can borrow my car { **as long as** / **so long as** } you promise not to drive too fast.
  (= You can borrow my car, but you must promise not to drive too fast. This is a condition.)

You can also say **provided** (**that**) or **providing** (**that**):
- ○ Travelling by car is convenient { **provided** (**that**) / **providing** (**that**) } you have somewhere to park.
  (= It's convenient but only if you have somewhere to park.)

- ○ { **Providing** (**that**) / **Provided** (**that**) } the room is clean, I don't mind which hotel we stay at.
  (= The room must be clean, but otherwise I don't mind.)

C   unless / as long as etc. for the future

When we are talking about the future, we do *not* use **will** after **unless** / **as long as** / **so long as** / **provided** / **providing**. We use a *present* tense (see Unit 25):
- ○ I'm not going out **unless** it **stops** raining. (*not* unless it will stop)
- ○ **Providing** the weather **is** good, we're going to have a picnic tomorrow.
  (*not* providing the weather will be good)

>> if → Units 25, 38–40

Exercises

115.1 Write a new sentence with the same meaning. Use unless in your sentence.

1 You must try a bit harder, or you won't pass the exam.
You won't pass the exam unless you try a bit harder.

2 Listen carefully, or you won't know what to do.
You won't know what to do ....

3 She must apologise to me, or I'll never speak to her again.
....

4 You have to speak very slowly, or he won't understand you.
....

5 Business must improve soon, or the company will have to close.
....

6 We need to do something soon, or the problem will get worse.
....

115.2 Write sentences with unless.

1 The club isn't open to everyone. You're allowed in only if you're a member.
You aren't allowed in the club unless you're a member.

2 I don't want to go to the party alone. I'm going only if you go too.
I'm not going ....

3 Don't worry about the dog. It will chase you only if you move suddenly.
The dog ....

4 Ben isn't very talkative. He'll speak to you only if you ask him something.
Ben ....

5 Today is a public holiday. The doctor will see you only if it's an emergency.
The doctor ....

115.3 Which is correct?

1 You can borrow my car ~~unless~~ / as long as you promise not to drive too fast.
(as long as _is correct_)

2 We're going to the beach tomorrow <u>unless / providing</u> the weather is bad.

3 We're going to the beach tomorrow <u>unless / providing</u> the weather is good.

4 I don't mind if you come home late <u>unless / as long as</u> you come in quietly.

5 I'm going now <u>unless / provided</u> you want me to stay.

6 I don't watch TV <u>unless / as long as</u> I have nothing else to do.

7 Children are allowed to use the swimming pool <u>unless / provided</u> they are with an adult.

8 <u>Unless / Provided</u> they are with an adult, children are not allowed to use the swimming pool.

9 We can sit here in the corner <u>unless / as long as</u> you'd rather sit by the window.

10 A: Our holiday cost a lot of money.
B: Did it? Well, that doesn't matter <u>unless / as long as</u> you enjoyed yourselves.

115.4 Use your own ideas to complete these sentences.

1 We'll be late unless _we take a taxi._

2 I like hot weather as long as ....

3 It takes 20 minutes to drive to the airport provided ....

4 I don't mind walking home as long as ....

5 I like to walk to work in the morning unless ....

6 We can meet tomorrow unless ....

7 I'll lend you the money providing ....

8 I'll tell you a secret as long as ....

9 You won't achieve anything unless ....

➜ **Additional exercise 32** (page 321)

as (as I walked … / as I was … etc.)

A   as = at the same time as

You can use **as** when two things happen together at the same time:
- We all waved goodbye to Liz **as she drove away**.
  (we **waved** and she **drove** away at the same time)
- **As I walked along the street**, I looked in the shop windows.
- Can you turn off the light **as you go out**, please?

Or you can say that something happened **as you were doing** something else (in the middle of doing something else):
- Kate slipped **as she was getting off the bus**.
- We met Paul **as we were leaving the hotel**.

For the *past continuous* (**was getting** / **were going** etc.), see Unit 6.

You can also use **just as** (= exactly at that moment):
- **Just as I sat down**, the doorbell rang.
- I had to leave **just as** the conversation was getting interesting.

We also use **as** when two things happen together in a longer period of time:
- **As the day went on**, the weather got worse.
- I began to enjoy the job more **as I got used to it**.

> the day went on
> the weather got worse

Compare **as** and **when**:

We use **as** only if two things happen at the same time.
- **As I drove home**, I listened to music.
  (= at the same time)

Use **when** (*not* as) if one thing happens after another.
- **When I got home**, I had something to eat.
  (*not* as I got home)

B   as = because

As also means 'because':
- **As I was hungry**, I decided to find somewhere to eat.
  (= because I was hungry)
- **As it's late and we're tired**, let's get a taxi home. (= because it's late …)
- We watched TV all evening **as we didn't have anything better to do**.
- **As I don't watch TV any more**, I gave my television to a friend of mine.

You can also use **since** in this way:
- **Since** it's late and we're tired, let's get a taxi home.

Compare **as** (= because) and **when**:

- David wasn't in the office **as he was on holiday**. (= because he was on holiday)

- David lost his passport **when he was on holiday**.
  (= during the time he was away)

- **As they lived near us**, we used to see them quite often.
  (= because they lived near us)

- **When they lived near us**, we used to see them quite often.
  (= at the time they lived near us)

>> as … as → Unit 107   like and as → Unit 117   as if → Unit 118

Exercises

116.1 In this exercise **as** means 'at the same time as'. Use **as** to join sentences from the boxes.

1 ~~We all waved goodbye to Liz~~
2 I listened
3 I burnt myself
4 The spectators cheered
5 A dog ran out in front of the car

we were driving along the road.
I was taking a hot dish out of the oven.
~~she drove away.~~
she told me her story.
the two teams came onto the field.

1   We all waved goodbye to Liz as she drove away.
2   ....
3   ....
4   ....
5   ....

116.2 In this exercise **as** means 'because'. Join sentences from the boxes beginning with **as**.

1 ~~I was hungry~~
2 today is a public holiday
3 I didn't want to disturb anybody
4 I can't go to the concert
5 it was a nice day

we went for a walk by the canal
I tried to be very quiet
~~I decided to find somewhere to eat~~
all government offices are shut
you can have my ticket

1   As I was hungry, I decided to find somewhere to eat.
2   ....
3   ....
4   ....
5   ....

116.3 What does **as** mean in these sentences?

	because	at the same time as
1 **As** they lived near us, we used to see them quite often.	✓	
2 Kate slipped **as** she was getting off the bus.		✓
3 **As** I was tired, I went to bed early.		
4 Unfortunately, **as** I was parking the car, I hit the car behind me.		
5 **As** we climbed the hill, we got more and more tired.		
6 We decided to go out to eat **as** we had no food at home.		
7 **As** we don't use the car very often, we've decided to sell it.		

116.4 In some of these sentences, **as** is not correct. Correct the sentences where necessary.

1 Julia got married <u>as she was 22</u>.   when she was 22
2 As the day went on, the weather got worse.   OK
3 He dropped the glass as he was taking it out of the cupboard.   ....
4 I lost my phone as I was in London.   ....
5 As I left school, I didn't know what to do.   ....
6 The train slowed down as it approached the station.   ....
7 I used to live near the sea as I was a child.   ....
8 We can walk to the hotel as it isn't far from here.   ....

116.5 Use your own ideas to complete these sentences.

1 Just as I sat down, the doorbell rang.
2 I saw you as ....
3 It started to rain just as ....
4 As she doesn't have a phone, ...
5 Just as I took the picture, ...

→ Additional exercise 32 (page 321)

A

Like = similar to, the same as:
- ○ What a beautiful house! It's **like a palace**. (*not* as a palace)
- ○ Be careful! The floor has been polished. It's **like walking on ice**. (*not* as walking)
- ○ It's raining again. I hate weather **like this**. (*not* as this)
- ○ 'What's that noise?' 'It sounds **like a baby crying**.' (*not* as a baby crying)

In these examples, **like** is a *preposition*. So it is followed by a *noun* (like **a palace**), a *pronoun* (like **this**) or **-ing** (like walk**ing**).

Sometimes **like** = for example. You can also use **such as**:
- ○ I enjoy water sports, **like** surfing, scuba diving and water-skiing. *or*
  I enjoy water sports, **such as** surfing …

B

As = in the same way as, in the same condition as.
We use **as** with *subject (S) + verb (V)*:
- ○ I didn't move anything. I left everything **as it was**.
- ○ You should have done it **as I showed** you.

	S + V	
as	it	was
as	I	showed

We also use **like** in this way (+ *subject + verb*):
- ○ I left everything **like it was**.

Compare **as** and **like**. You can say:
- ○ You should have done it **as I showed you**. *or* … **like I showed you**.
- *but* You should have done it **like this**. (*not* as this)

We say **as usual / as always**:
- ○ You're late **as usual**.
- ○ **As always**, Nick was the first to complain.

We say **the same as** … :
- ○ Your phone is **the same as** mine. (*not* the same like)

C

Sometimes **as** (+ *subject + verb*) has other meanings. For example, after **do**:
- ○ You can do **as you like**. (= do what you like)
- ○ They did **as they promised**. (= They did what they promised.)

We also say **as you know / as I said / as she expected / as I thought** etc. :
- ○ **As you know**, it's Emma's birthday next week. (= you know this already)
- ○ Andy failed his driving test, **as he expected**. (= he expected this before)

Like is not usual in these expressions, except with **say** (**like I said**):
- ○ **As I said** yesterday, I'm sure we can solve the problem. *or* **Like I said** yesterday …

D

As can also be a *preposition* (**as** + noun), but the meaning is different from **like**.
Compare:

- ○ **As a taxi driver**, I spend most of my working life in a car.
  (I am a taxi driver, it's my job.)

- ○ Everyone in the family wants me to drive them to places. I'm **like a taxi driver**.
  (I'm not a taxi driver, but I'm like one.)

As (*preposition*) = in the position of, in the form of etc. :
- ○ Many years ago I worked **as a photographer**. (I was a photographer)
- ○ Many words, for example 'work' and 'rain', can be used **as verbs or nouns**.
- ○ London is fine **as a place to visit**, but I wouldn't like to live there.
- ○ The news of the tragedy came **as a great shock**.

>> as … as → Unit 107   as (= at the same time as / because) → Unit 116   as if → Unit 118

Exercises

117.1 In some of these sentences, you need like (not as). Correct the sentences where necessary. Write '*OK*' if the sentence is correct.

1 It's raining again. I hate weather as this. — I hate weather like this.
2 You should have done it as I showed you. — OK
3 Do you think James looks as his father?
4 He gets on my nerves. I can't stand people as him.
5 Why didn't you do it as I told you to do it?
6 As her mother, Katherine has a very good voice.
7 You never listen. Talking to you is as talking to the wall.
8 I prefer the room as it was, before we decorated it.
9 I'll phone you tomorrow as usual, OK?
10 She's a very good swimmer. She swims as a fish.

117.2 Which goes with which?

1 I won't be able to come to the party.	a It was full, as I expected.	1 __c__
2 I like Tom's idea.	b As I've told you before, it's boring.	2
3 I'm fed up with my job.	c As you know, I'll be away.	3
4 You drive too fast.	d You can do as you like.	4
5 You don't have to take my advice.	e Let's do as he suggests.	5
6 I couldn't get a seat on the train.	f You should take more care, as I keep telling you.	6

117.3 Complete the sentences using like or as + the following:

a beginner	blocks of ice	a palace	a birthday present
a child	a theatre	winter	a tour guide

1 This house is beautiful. It's __like a palace__ .
2 My feet are really cold. They're .
3 I've been playing tennis for years, but I still play .
4 Marion once had a part-time job .
5 I wonder what that building is. It looks .
6 My brother gave me this watch a long time ago.
7 It's very cold for the middle of summer. It's .
8 He's 22 years old, but he sometimes behaves .

117.4 Put in like or as. Sometimes either word is possible.

1 We heard a noise __like__ a baby crying.
2 I wish I had a car _____ yours.
3 Hannah has been working _____ a waitress for the last two months.
4 We saw Kevin last night. He was very cheerful, _____ always.
5 You waste a lot of time doing things _____ sitting in cafes all day.
6 _____ you can imagine, we were very tired after such a long journey.
7 Tom showed me some photos of the city _____ it was thirty years ago.
8 My neighbour's house is full of interesting things. It's _____ a museum.
9 In some countries in Asia, _____ Japan, Indonesia and Thailand, traffic drives on the left.
10 The weather hasn't changed. It's the same _____ yesterday.
11 You're different from the other people I know. I don't know anyone else _____ you.
12 The news that they are getting married came _____ a complete surprise to me.
13 This tea is awful. It tastes _____ water.
14 Suddenly there was a terrible noise. It was _____ a bomb exploding.
15 Right now I'm working in a shop. It's not great, but it's OK _____ a temporary job.
16 Brian is a student, _____ most of his friends.

like   as if

A

We use **like** or **as if** to say how somebody/something looks, sounds or feels:

- ◯ That house **looks like** it's going to fall down. *or*
  That house **looks as if** it's going to fall down.
- ◯ Amy **sounded like** she had a cold, didn't she? *or*
  Amy **sounded as if** she had a cold, didn't she?
- ◯ I've just had a holiday, but I feel very tired.
  I don't **feel like** I've had a holiday. *or*
  I don't **feel as if** I've had a holiday.

That house **looks like** it's going to fall down.

You can also use **as though** in these examples:
- ◯ I don't **feel as though** I've had a holiday.

Compare:
- ◯ You **look tired**. (**look** + *adjective*)
- ◯ You **look like you haven't slept**. ⎫
  You **look as if you haven't slept**. ⎭ (**look like / as if** + *subject* + *verb*)

B

We say: **it looks like** … *or* **it looks as if** …
          it sounds like … *or* **it sounds as if** …

It sounds like they're having a party next door.

- ◯ Sarah is very late. **It looks like** she isn't coming.
  or **It looks as if** she isn't coming.
- ◯ **It looked like** it was going to rain, so we took
  an umbrella.
  or **It looked as if** it was going to rain …
- ◯ The noise is very loud next door.
  It sounds like they're having a party.
  or **It sounds as if** they're …

You can also use **as though**:
- ◯ **It sounds as though** they're having a party.

C

You can use **like / as if / as though** with other verbs to say how somebody does something:
- ◯ He ran **like he was running for his life**.
- ◯ After the interruption, the speaker went on talking **as if nothing had happened**.
- ◯ When I told them my plan, they looked at me **as though I was mad**.

D

After **as if**, we sometimes use the *past* when we are talking about the *present*.
For example:
- ◯ I don't like him. He talks **as if** he **knew** everything.

The meaning is not past. We use the past (as if he **knew**) because the idea is not real: he does *not* know everything. We use the past in the same way with **if** and **wish** (see Unit 39).
We do not normally use **like** in this way.

Some more examples:
- ◯ She's always asking me to do things for her – **as if I didn't** have enough to do already.
  (I *have* enough to do already)
- ◯ Joe's only 40. Why do you talk about him **as if he was** an old man? (he *isn't* an old man)

When you use the past in this way, you can use **were** instead of **was**:
- ◯ Why do you talk about him **as if he were** an old man?
- ◯ They treat me **as if I were** their own son. *or* … **as if I was** their own son.
  (I'm *not* their son)

≫ **if I was/were → Unit 39C**   **look/sound** etc. + adjective **→ Unit 99C**   **like** and **as → Unit 117**

Exercises

118.1 What do you say in these situations? Use the words in brackets to make your sentence.

1 You meet Bill. He has a black eye and blood on his face. (look / like / be / a fight)
   You say to him: _You look like you've been in a fight._
2 Claire comes into the room. She looks absolutely terrified. (look / as if / see / a ghost)
   You say to her: What's the matter? You ....
3 You have just run one kilometre, but you are exhausted. (feel / like / run / a marathon)
   You say: I ....
4 Joe is on holiday. He's talking to you on the phone and sounds happy.
   (sound / as if / have / a good time)
   You say to him: You ....

118.2 Make sentences beginning It looks like ... or It sounds like ... .

you should see a doctor	**there's been an accident**	**they're having an argument**
it's going to rain	~~**she isn't coming**~~	**they don't have any**

1 Sarah said she would be here an hour ago.
   You say: _It looks like she isn't coming._
2 The sky is full of black clouds.
   You say: It ....
3 You hear two people shouting at each other next door.
   You say: ....
4 You see an ambulance, some policemen and two damaged cars at the side of the road.
   You say: ....
5 You and a friend are in a supermarket. You're looking for bananas, but without success.
   You say: ....
6 Dave isn't feeling well. He tells you all about it.
   You say: ....

118.3 Complete the sentences with as if. Choose from the box, putting the verbs in the correct form.

she / enjoy / it	**I / be / crazy**	**he / not / eat / for a week**
~~**he / need / a good rest**~~	**she / hurt / her leg**	**he / mean / what he / say**
I / not / exist	**she / not / want / come**	

1 Mark looks very tired. He looks _as if he needs a good rest_ .
2 I don't think Paul was joking. He looked ....
3 What's the matter with Lisa? She's walking ....
4 Paul was extremely hungry and ate his dinner very quickly.
   He ate ....
5 I looked at Sarah during the movie. She had a bored expression on her face.
   She didn't look ....
6 I told my friends about my plan. They were amazed.
   They looked at me ....
7 I phoned Kate and invited her to the party, but she wasn't very enthusiastic.
   She sounded ....
8 I went into the office, but nobody spoke to me or looked at me.
   Everybody ignored me ....

118.4 These sentences are like the ones in Section D. Complete each sentence using as if.

1 Andy is a terrible driver. He drives _as if he were_ the only driver on the road.
2 I'm 20 years old, so please don't talk to me .... a child.
3 Steve has never met Nicola, but he talks about her .... his best friend.
4 We first met a long time ago, but I remember it .... yesterday.

during   for   while

during

during = at a time between the start and end of something:
- ○ I fell asleep **during the movie**. (= at a time between the start and end of the movie)
- ○ We met some really nice people **during our holiday**.
- ○ The ground is wet. It must have rained **during the night**.

With 'time words' (**the morning, the night, the summer** etc.), you can usually say **in** or **during**:
- ○ It rained **in the night**. *or* … **during the night**.
- ○ It's lovely here **during the summer**. *or* … **in the summer**.

I fell asleep **during the movie**.

for and **during**

We use **for** (+ a period of time) to say how long something goes on:
- ○ We watched TV **for two hours** last night.
- ○ Jess is going away **for a week** in September.
- ○ How are you? I haven't seen you **for ages**.
- ○ Are you going away **for the weekend**?

We do not use **during** to say *how long* something goes on. We do not say 'during two hours', 'during five years' etc. :
- ○ It rained **for** three days without stopping. (*not* during three days)

We use **during** to say *when* something happens (*not* how long). Compare **during** and **for**:
- ○ '**When** did you fall asleep?' '**During the movie**.'
- ○ '**How long** were you asleep?' '**For half an hour**.'

during and **while**

Compare:

We use **during** + *noun*:
- ○ I fell asleep **during the movie**.
  ⌞ noun ⌟

- ○ We met a lot of interesting people **during our holiday**.

- ○ Robert suddenly began to feel ill **during the exam**.

We use **while** + *subject* + *verb*:
- ○ I fell asleep **while I was watching** TV.
  ⌞ subject + verb ⌟

- ○ We met a lot of interesting people **while we were on holiday**.

- ○ Robert suddenly began to feel ill **while he was doing the exam**.

Some more examples of **while**:
- ○ We saw Clare **while we were waiting** for the bus.
- ○ **While you were** out, there was a phone call for you.
- ○ Alex read a book **while** Amy **watched** TV.

When we are talking about the future, we use the *present* after **while**. Do not use 'will' (see Unit 25):
- ○ I'm going to Moscow next week. I hope the weather will be good **while I'm** there. (*not* while I will be)
- ○ What are you going to do **while you're** waiting? (*not* while you'll be waiting)

ALEX   AMY

Alex read a book **while Amy watched** TV.

>> for and since → Unit 12A   while + -ing → Unit 68B

Exercises

119.1 **Put in for or during.**

1 It rained ......*for*...... three days without stopping.
2 I fell asleep .....*during*..... the movie.
3 I went to the theatre last night. I met Sue .... the interval.
4 I felt really ill last week. I could hardly eat anything .... three days.
5 The traffic was bad. We were stuck in a traffic jam .... two hours.
6 Production at the factory was seriously affected .... the strike.
7 Sarah was very angry with me. She didn't speak to me .... a week.
8 I don't have much free time .... the week, but I relax at weekends.
9 I need a break. I think I'll go away .... a few days.
10 The president gave a short speech. She spoke .... only ten minutes.
11 We were hungry when we arrived. We hadn't eaten anything .... the journey.
12 We were hungry when we arrived. We hadn't eaten anything .... eight hours.

119.2 **Put in during or while.**

1 We met a lot of interesting people .....*while*..... we were on holiday.
2 We met a lot of interesting people .....*during*..... our holiday.
3 I met Mike .... I was shopping.
4 .... I was on holiday, I didn't use my phone at all.
5 I learnt a lot .... the course. The teachers were very good.
6 There was a lot of noise .... the night. What was it?
7 I'd been away for many years. Many things had changed .... that time.
8 What did they say about me .... I was out of the room?
9 When I fly anywhere, I never eat anything .... the flight.
10 Please don't interrupt me .... I'm speaking.
11 .... the festival, it's almost impossible to find a hotel room here.
12 We were hungry when we arrived. We hadn't eaten anything .... we were travelling.

119.3 **Put in during, for or while.**

1 I used to live in Berlin. I lived there .... five years.
2 One of the runners fell .... the race but managed to get up and continue.
3 Nobody came to see me .... I was in hospital.
4 Try to avoid travelling .... the busy periods of the day.
5 I was very tired. I slept .... ten hours.
6 Can you hold my bag .... I try on this jacket?
7 I'm not sure when we'll arrive, but it will be sometime .... the afternoon.
8 I wasn't well last week. I hardly ate anything .... three days.
9 My phone rang .... we were having dinner.
10 Nobody knows how many people were killed .... the war.

119.4 **Use your own ideas to complete these sentences.**

1 I fell asleep while ...*I was watching TV.*...
2 I fell asleep during ...*the movie.*...
3 Can you wait for me while ....
4 Most of the students looked bored during ....
5 I was asked a lot of questions during ....
6 Don't open the car door while ....
7 The lights suddenly went out while ....
8 What are you going to do while ....
9 It started to rain during ....
10 It started to rain while ....

➔ Additional exercise 33 (page 321)

by and **until**   **by the time** ...

A

by ... = not later than:

- ○ I sent the documents today, so they should arrive **by Monday**.
  (= on or before Monday, not later than Monday)

- ○ We'd better hurry. We have to be home **by 5 o'clock**.
  (= at or before 5 o'clock, not later than 5 o'clock)

- ○ Where's Sarah? She should be here **by now**.
  (= now or before now – so she should already be here)

This milk has to be used
by 14 August.

B

We use **until** (or **till**) to say *how long* a situation continues:

- ○ A: Shall we go now?
  B: No, let's **wait until** it stops raining. *or* ...**till** it stops raining.

- ○ I was very tired this morning. { I **stayed in bed until** half past ten.
                                 I **didn't get up until** half past ten.

Compare **until** and **by**:

Something *continues* **until** a time in the future:	Something *happens* **by** a time in the future:
○ Joe **will be away until** Monday. (so he'll be back *on* Monday)	○ Joe **will be back by** Monday. (= not later than Monday)
○ I**'ll be working until** 11.30. (so I'll stop working *at* 11.30)	○ I**'ll have finished my work by** 11.30. (= I'll finish it not later than 11.30)

C

You can say '**by the time** something happens':

- ○ It's too late to go to the bank now. **By the time we get there**, it will be closed.
  (= it will close between now and the time we get there)

- ○ You'll need plenty of time at the airport. **By the time you check in and go through security**,
  it will be time for your flight.
  (= check-in and security will take a long time)

- ○ Hurry up! **By the time we get to the cinema**, the film will already have started.

You can say '**by the time** something happened' (for the past):

- ○ Karen's car broke down on the way to the party last night. **By the time she arrived**, most of the
  other guests had left.
  (= it took her a long time to get there and most of the guests left during this time)

- ○ I had a lot of work to do yesterday evening. I was very tired **by the time I finished**.
  (= it took me a long time to do the work, and I became more and more tired)

- ○ We went to the cinema last night. It took us a long time to find somewhere to park the car.
  By the time we got to the cinema, the film had already started.

You can say **by then** or **by that time**:

- ○ Karen finally got to the party at midnight, but **by then** most of the other guests had left.
  or ... but **by that time**, most of the other guests had left.

>>   **will be doing** and **will have done** → Unit 24   **by** (other uses) → Units 42B, 60B, 128

Exercises

120.1 Complete the sentences with **by**.

1 We have to be home not later than 5 o'clock.
   We have to be home ____by 5 o'clock____ .
2 I have to be at the airport not later than 8.30.
   I have to be at the airport _____ .
3 Let me know not later than Saturday whether you can come to the party.
   _____ whether you can come to the party.
4 Please make sure that you're here not later than 2 o'clock.
   Please make sure that _____ .
5 If we leave now, we should arrive not later than lunchtime.
   If we leave now, _____ .

120.2 Put in **by** or **until**.

1 Steve has gone away. He'll be away ____until____ Monday.
2 Sorry, but I must go. I have to be home _____ 5 o'clock.
3 According to the forecast, the bad weather will continue _____ the weekend.
4 I don't know whether to apply for the job or not. I have to decide _____ Friday.
5 I think I'll wait _____ Thursday before making a decision.
6 I'm still waiting for Tom to call me. He should have called me _____ now.
7 I need to pay this bill. It has to be paid _____ tomorrow.
8 Don't pay the bill today. Wait _____ tomorrow.
9 We haven't finished painting the house yet. We hope to finish _____ Tuesday.
10 'Will you still be in the office at 6.30?' 'No, I'll have gone home _____ then.'
11 I'm moving into my new flat next week. I'm staying with a friend _____ then.
12 I've got a lot of work to do. _____ the time I finish, it will be time to go to bed.
13 We have plenty of time. The film doesn't start _____ 8.30.
14 It is hoped that the new bridge will be completed _____ the end of the year.

120.3 Use your own ideas to complete these sentences. Use **by** or **until**.

1 David is away at the moment. He'll be away ____until Monday____ .
2 David is away at the moment. He'll be back ____by Monday____ .
3 I'm just going out. I won't be long. Wait here _____ .
4 I'm just going out. It's 4.30 now. I won't be long. I'll be back _____ .
5 If you want to apply for the job, your application must be received _____ .
6 My passport is valid _____ .
7 I missed the last bus and had to walk home. I didn't get home _____ .

120.4 Read the situations and complete the sentences using **By the time ...** .

1 I was invited to a party, but I got there much later than I intended.
   ____By the time I got to the party____ , most of the other guests had left.
2 I intended to catch a train, but it took me longer than expected to get to the station.
   _____ , my train had already left.
3 I wanted to go shopping after work. But I finished work much later than expected.
   _____ , it was too late to go shopping.
4 I saw two men who looked as if they were trying to steal a car. I called the police,
   but it was some time before they arrived.
   _____ , the two men had disappeared.
5 We climbed a mountain and it took us a long time to get to the top. There wasn't much
   time to enjoy the view.
   _____ , we had to come down again.

at/on/in (time)

A Compare **at**, **on** and **in**:
- ○ They arrived **at 5 o'clock**.
- ○ They arrived **on Friday**.
- ○ They arrived **in June**. / They arrived **in 2012**.

We use:

at for the time of day

at five o'clock	at 11.45	at midnight	at lunchtime	at sunset etc.

on for days and dates

on Friday / on Fridays	on 16 May 2012	on New Year's Day	on my birthday

in for longer periods (months/years/seasons etc.)

in June	in 2012	in the 1990s	in the 20th century	in the past	in winter

B We say:

at the moment / at the minute / at present / at this time (= now):
- ○ Can we talk later? I'm busy **at the moment**.

at the same time
- ○ Kate and I arrived **at the same time**.

at the weekends / at weekends (*or* **on the weekend** / **on weekends** in American English):
- ○ Will you be here **at the weekend**? (*or* … **on** the weekend)

at Christmas (*but* **on Christmas Day**)
- ○ Do you give each other presents **at Christmas**?

at night (= during nights in general), **in the night** (= during a particular night):
- ○ I don't like working **at night**. *but* I was woken up by a noise **in the night**.

C We say:

in the morning(s)	*but*	on Friday morning(s)
in the afternoon(s)		on Sunday afternoon(s)
in the evening(s)		on Monday evening(s) etc.

- ○ I'll see you **in the morning**.
- ○ Do you work **in the evenings**?

- ○ I'll see you **on Friday morning**.
- ○ Do you work **on Saturday evenings**?

D We do not use **at/on/in** before **last/next/this/every**:
- ○ I'll see you **next Friday**. (*not* on next Friday)
- ○ They got married **last June**.

We often leave out **on** before days. So you can say:
- ○ I'll see you **on Friday**. *or* I'll see you **Friday**.
- ○ I don't work **on Monday mornings**. *or* I don't work **Monday mornings**.

E We say that something will happen **in a few minutes / in six months** etc. :
- ○ The train will be leaving **in a few minutes**. (= a few minutes from now)
- ○ Andy has gone away. He'll be back **in a week**. (= a week from now)
- ○ They'll be here **in a moment**. (= a moment from now, very soon)

We also use **in** … to say how long it takes to do something:
- ○ I learnt to drive **in four weeks**. (= it took me four weeks to learn)

>> on/in time, at/in the end ➜ Unit 122   in/at/on (position) ➜ Units 123–125   in/at/on (other uses) ➜ Unit 127
American English ➜ Appendix 7

Exercises

121.1 **Put in at, on or in.**

1 Mozart was born in Salzburg ....in.... 1756.
2 I've been invited to a wedding .... 14 February.
3 Amy's birthday is .... May, but I don't know which date.
4 This park is popular and gets very busy .... weekends.
5 I haven't seen Kate for a few days. I last saw her .... Tuesday.
6 Jonathan is 63. He'll be retiring from his job .... two years.
7 I'm busy right now. I'll be with you .... a moment.
8 Sam isn't here .... the moment, but he'll be here this afternoon.
9 There are usually a lot of parties .... New Year's Eve.
10 I don't like the dark. I try to avoid going out .... night.
11 It rained very hard .... the night. Did you hear it?
12 My car is being repaired at the garage. It will be ready .... two hours.
13 The bus station was busy. A lot of buses were leaving .... the same time.
14 Helen and David always go out for dinner .... their wedding anniversary.
15 It was a short book and easy to read. I read it .... a day.
16 .... midday, the sun is at its highest point in the sky.
17 This building is very old. It was built .... the fifteenth century.
18 The office is closed .... Wednesday afternoons.
19 In the UK many people go home to see their families .... Christmas.
20 My flight arrives .... 5 o'clock .... the morning.
21 The course begins .... 7 January and ends sometime .... April.
22 I might not be at home .... Tuesday morning, but I'll be there .... the afternoon.

121.2 **Complete the sentences. Use at, on or in + the following:**

the evening	about 20 minutes	~~1756~~	the same time	the 1920s
the moment	21 July 1969	night	Saturdays	11 seconds

1 Mozart was born ....in 1756.. .
2 If the sky is clear, you can see the stars ....
3 After working hard during the day, I like to relax ....
4 Neil Armstrong was the first man to walk on the moon ....
5 It's difficult to listen if everyone is speaking ....
6 Jazz became popular in the United States ....
7 I'm just going out to the shop. I'll be back ....
8 I don't think we need an umbrella. It's not raining ....
9 Ben is a very fast runner. He can run 100 metres ....
10 Lisa works from Monday to Friday. Sometimes she also works ....

121.3 **Which is correct: a, b, or both of them?**

1 a I'll see you on Friday.   b I'll see you Friday.   _both_
2 a I'll see you on next Friday.   b I'll see you next Friday.   _b_
3 a Paul got married in April.   b Paul got married April.   ....
4 a I play tennis on Sunday mornings.   b I play tennis Sunday mornings.   ....
5 a We were ill at the same time.   b We were ill in the same time.   ....
6 a What are you doing at the weekend? b What are you doing on the weekend? ....
7 a Oliver was born at 10 May 1993. b Oliver was born on 10 May 1993. ....
8 a He left school last June.   b He left school in last June.   ....
9 a Will you be here on Tuesday?   b Will you be here Tuesday?   ....
10 a I don't like driving in night.   b I don't like driving at night.   ....

→ Additional exercise 33 (page 321)

on time and in time   at the end and in the end

on time and **in time**

on time = punctual, not late

If something happens **on time**, it happens at the time that was planned:

- ◯ The 11.45 train left **on time**. (= it left at 11.45)
- ◯ Please be **on time**. Don't be late.
- ◯ The conference was well-organised. Everything began and finished **on time**.

in time (for something / to do something) = soon enough

- ◯ Will you be home **in time for dinner**? (= soon enough for dinner)
- ◯ I sent Amy a birthday present. I hope it arrives **in time**.
  (= on or before her birthday)
- ◯ I'm in a hurry. I want to get home **in time to watch** the game on TV.
  (= soon enough to see the game)

The opposite of **in time** is **too late**:
- ◯ I got home **too late** to watch the game on TV.

You can say **just in time** (= almost too late):
- ◯ We got to the station **just in time** for our train.
- ◯ A child ran into the road in front of the car, but I managed to stop **just in time**.

at the end and **in the end**

at the end (of something) = at the time when something ends

For example:

at the end of the month	**at the end of January**	**at the end of the game**
at the end of the film	**at the end of the course**	**at the end of the concert**

- ◯ I'm going away **at the end of January** / **at the end of the month**.
- ◯ **At the end of the concert**, everyone applauded.
- ◯ The players shook hands **at the end of the game**.

We do not say '**in** the end of …'. For example, we do not say 'in the end of January'.

The opposite of **at the end** is **at the beginning**:
- ◯ I'm going away **at the beginning of January**. (*not* in the beginning)

in the end = finally

We use **in the end** when we say what the final result of a situation was:
- ◯ We had a lot of problems with our car. We sold it **in the end**. (= finally we sold it)
- ◯ He got more and more angry. **In the end** he just walked out of the room.
- ◯ Alan couldn't decide where to go for his holidays. He didn't go anywhere **in the end**.
  (*not* at the end)

The opposite of **in the end** is **at first**:
- ◯ **At first** we didn't get on very well, but **in the end** we became good friends.

Exercises

122.1 **Complete the sentences with on time or in time.**

1 The bus is usually ......*on time*...... , but it was late this morning.
2 The film was supposed to start at 8.30, but it didn't begin ....
3 The train service isn't very good. The trains are rarely ....
4 We nearly missed our train. We got to the station just ....
5 We want to start the meeting .... , so please don't be late.
6 I've just washed this shirt. I want to wear it this evening, so I hope it will be dry ....
7 I almost forgot that it was Joe's birthday. Fortunately I remembered ....
8 Why are you never ....? You always keep everybody waiting.
9 It is hoped that the new stadium will be ready .... for the tournament later this year.

122.2 **Read the situations and make sentences using just in time.**

1 A child ran into the road in front of your car. You saw the child at the last moment.
   (manage / stop) .....*I managed to stop just in time.*.....
2 You were walking home. Just after you got home, it started to rain very heavily.
   (get / home) I ....
3 Your friend was going to sit on the chair you had just painted. You said, 'Don't sit on that chair!', so
   he didn't. (stop / him) I ....
4 You and a friend went to the cinema. You were late, and you thought you would miss the beginning
   of the film. But the film began just as you sat down in the cinema.
   (get / cinema / beginning / film)
   We ....

122.3 **Complete the sentences using at the end + the following:**

the course	~~the game~~	the interview	the month	the race

1 The players shook hands ....*at the end of the game*.. .
2 I get paid ....
3 The students had a party ....
4 Two of the runners collapsed ....
5 I was surprised when I was offered the job ....

122.4 **Write sentences with in the end. Use the verb in brackets.**

1 We had a lot of problems with our car. (sell) ....*In the end we sold it.*.....
2 Anna got more and more fed up with her job.
   (resign) ....
3 I tried to learn Japanese, but I found it too difficult.
   (give up) ....
4 We couldn't decide whether to go to the party or not.
   (not / go) ....

122.5 **Put in at or in.**

1 I'm going away .....*at*..... the end of the month.
2 It took Gary a long time to find work. .... the end he got a job as a bus driver.
3 I couldn't decide what to buy Amy for her birthday. I didn't buy her anything .... the end.
4 I'm going away .... the end of this week.
5 We waited ages for a bus. .... the end we had to get a taxi.
6 .... the end of the lesson, all the students left the classroom.
7 We had a few problems at first, but .... the end everything was OK.
8 You were in a difficult position. What did you do .... the end?
9 The journey took a very long time, but we got there .... the end.
10 Are you going away .... the beginning of August or .... the end?

in/at/on (position) 1

in

in a room
in a building
in a box
etc.

in a garden
in a town
in the city centre
etc.

in a pool
in the sea
in a river
etc.

○ There's no-one **in the room** / **in the building** / **in the garden**.
○ What do you have **in your hand** / **in your mouth**?
○ When we were **in Italy**, we spent a few days **in Venice**.
○ I have a friend who lives **in a small village in the mountains**.
○ There were some people swimming **in the pool** / **in the sea** / **in the river**.

at

at the bus stop

at the door

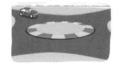

at the roundabout

at her desk

○ Who is that man standing **at the bus stop** / **at the door** / **at the window**?
○ Turn left **at the traffic lights** / **at the next junction** / **at the roundabout** / **at the church**.
○ We have to get off the bus **at the next stop**.
○ When you leave the hotel, please leave your key **at reception**. (= at the reception desk)

Compare **in** and **at**:
○ There were a lot of people **in the shop**. It was crowded.
   Go along this road, then turn left **at the shop**.
○ I'll meet you **in the hotel lobby**. (= in the building)
   I'll meet you **at the entrance to the hotel**. (= outside the building)

on

on the wall
on the door
on the ceiling
on the floor
on the table

on her nose

on a page

on an island

○ I sat **on the floor** / **on the ground** / **on the grass** / **on the beach** / **on a chair**.
○ There's a dirty mark **on the ceiling** / **on your nose** / **on your shirt**.
○ Did you see the notice **on the wall** / **on the door**?
○ You'll find details of TV programmes **on page seven** of the newspaper.
○ The hotel is **on a small island** in the middle of a lake.

Compare **in** and **on**:
○ There is some water **in the bottle**.
   There is a label **on the bottle**.

in the bottle
on the bottle

Compare **at** and **on**:
○ There is somebody **at the door**. Shall I go and see who it is?
   There is a notice **on the door**. It says 'Do not disturb'.

>> in/at/on (position) 2–3 ➜ Units 124–125

Exercises

123.1 Answer the questions about the pictures. Use **in**, **at** or **on** with the words below the pictures.

1 (bottle)	2 (arm)
3 (traffic lights)	4 (door)
5 (wall)	6 (Paris)
7 (gate)	8 (beach)

1 Where's the label? __On the bottle.__
2 Where's the fly? ....
3 Where's the car waiting? ....
4 Where's the notice? .... Where's the key? ....
5 Where are the shelves? ....
6 Where's the Eiffel Tower? ....
7 Where's the man standing? .... Where's the bird? ....
8 Where are the children playing? ....

123.2 Complete the sentences. Use **in**, **at** or **on** + the following:

the window	his hand	the mountains	that tree
my guitar	~~the river~~	the island	junction 14

1 There were some people swimming __in the river__ .
2 One of the strings .... is broken.
3 Leave the motorway .... and then turn left.
4 He was holding something .... , but I couldn't see what it was.
5 The leaves .... are a beautiful colour.
6 You can go skiing .... near here. There's plenty of snow.
7 There's nobody living .... It's uninhabited.
8 He spends most of the day sitting .... and looking outside.

123.3 Complete the sentences with **in**, **at** or **on**.

1 There was a long queue of people __at__ the bus stop.
2 Nicola was wearing a silver ring .... her little finger.
3 There was a security guard standing .... the entrance to the building.
4 I wasn't sure whether I had come to the right office. There was no name .... the door.
5 There are plenty of shops and restaurants .... the town centre.
6 You'll find the weather forecast .... the back page of the newspaper.
7 The headquarters of the company are .... California.
8 I wouldn't like an office job. I couldn't spend the whole day sitting .... a desk.
9 The man the police are looking for has a scar .... his right cheek.
10 If you come here by bus, get off .... the stop after the traffic lights.
11 Have you ever been camping? Have you ever slept .... a tent?
12 Emily was sitting .... the balcony reading a book.
13 My brother lives .... a small village .... the south-west of England.
14 I like that picture hanging .... the wall .... the kitchen.

➔ Additional exercise 34 (page 322)

A We say that somebody/something is:

in a line, **in a row**, **in a queue**	**in an office**, **in a department**
in a picture, **in a photo(graph)**	**in the sky**, **in the world**
in a newspaper, **in a magazine**, **in a book**	**in the country** (= not in a town)

○ When I go to the cinema, I like to sit **in the front row**.
○ Amy works **in the sales department**.
○ Who is the woman **in that picture**?
○ Do you live in a city or **in the country**?
○ It's a lovely day. There isn't a cloud **in the sky**.

They're standing **in a row**.

B We say that somebody/something is:

on the left, **on the right**   (or **on the left-hand side**, **on the right-hand side**)
○ Do you drive **on the left** or **on the right** in your country?

on the ground floor, **on the first floor**, **on the second floor** etc.
○ Our apartment is **on the second floor** of the building.

on a map, **on a menu**, **on a list**, **on a page**, **on a website**
○ Here's the shopping list. Don't buy anything that's not **on the list**.
○ You'll find the information you need **on our website**.

We say that a place is **on a river** / **on a road** / **on the coast**:
○ Vienna is **on the (river) Danube**.
○ The town where you live – is it **on the coast** or is it inland?

We say **on the way** (from one place to another):
○ We stopped at a shop **on the way** home.

C We say:
at the top (of . . .), **at the bottom** (of . . .), **at the end** (of . . .)
○ Write your name **at the top of the page**.
○ Jane lives **at the other end of the street**.

at the top (of the page)

at the bottom (of the page)

D We say:
in the front, **in the back** of a car
○ I was **in the back** (of the car) when we had the accident.

at the front, **at the back** of a building / theatre / group of people etc.
○ The garden is **at the back of the house**.
○ Let's sit **at the front** (of the cinema).
○ We were **at the back**, so we couldn't see very well.

on the front, **on the back** of an envelope / a piece of paper etc.
○ I wrote the date **on the back of the photo**.

at the back

at the front

E We say:
in the corner of a room
○ The TV is **in the corner** of the room.

at the corner or **on the corner** of a street
○ There is a small shop **at the corner** (of the street).
   or . . . **on the corner** (of the street).

in the corner   at or on the corner

>> **in the world** → Unit 108D   **in/at/on** (position) → **Units 123, 125**   American English → **Appendix 7**

Exercises

124.1 Answer the questions about the pictures. Use **in**, **at** or **on** with the words below the pictures.

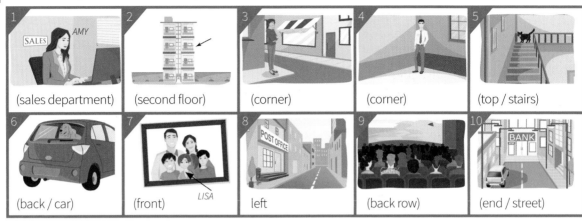

1 (sales department)	2 (second floor)	3 (corner)	4 (corner)	5 (top / stairs)
6 (back / car)	7 (front) *LISA*	8 left	9 (back row)	10 (end / street)

1 Where does Amy work? *In the sales department.*
2 Amy lives in this building. Where's her flat exactly?
3 Where is the woman standing?
4 Where is the man standing?
5 Where's the cat?
6 Where's the dog?
7 Lisa is in this group of people. Where is she?
8 Where's the post office?
9 Gary is at the cinema. Where is he sitting?
10 Where is the bank?

124.2 Complete the sentences. Use **in**, **at** or **on** + the following:

the west coast	the world	the back of the class	~~the sky~~
the front row	the right	the back of this card	the way to work

1 It's a lovely day. There isn't a cloud *in the sky* .
2 In most countries people drive
3 What is the tallest building   ?
4 I met a friend of mine   this morning.
5 San Francisco is   of the United States.
6 We went to the theatre last night. We had seats   .
7 I couldn't hear the teacher. She spoke quietly and I was sitting   .
8 I don't have your address. Could you write it   ?

124.3 Complete the sentences with **in**, **at** or **on**.

1 Write your name *at* the top of the page.
2 Is your sister _____ this photo? I don't recognise her.
3 They live in a small house _____ the bottom of the hill.
4 We normally use the front entrance to the building, but there's another one _____ the back.
5 We had to wait _____ a queue for an hour to check in at the airport.
6 There was a list of names, but my name wasn't _____ the list.
7 Is there anything interesting _____ today's newspaper?
8 I love to look up at the stars _____ the sky at night.
9 When I'm a passenger in a car, I prefer to sit _____ the front.
10 I live in a very small village. You probably won't find it _____ your map.
11 Joe works _____ the furniture department of a large store.
12 Paris is _____ the (river) Seine.
13 I don't like cities. I'd much prefer to live _____ the country.
14 My office is _____ the top floor. It's _____ your left as you come out of the lift.

→ Additional exercise 34 (page 322)

in/at/on (position) 3

A in hospital / at work etc.

We say that somebody is **in bed** / **in hospital** / **in prison**:
- ○ James isn't up yet. He's still **in bed**.
- ○ Anna's mother is **in hospital**.

We say that somebody is **at home** / **at work** / **at school** / **at university** / **at college**:
- ○ I'll be **at work** until 5.30.
- ○ My sister is **at university**. My brother is still **at school**.

We say **be at home** or **be home** (with or without **at**), but **do something at home** (with **at**):
- ○ I'll **be home** all evening. *or* I'll **be at home** all evening.
- ○ Shall we go to a restaurant or **eat at home**?

B at a party / at a concert etc.

We say that somebody is **at** an event (**at a party**, **at a conference** etc.):
- ○ Were there many people **at the party** / **at the meeting** / **at the wedding**?
- ○ I saw Steve **at a conference** / **at a concert** on Saturday.

C in and at for buildings

You can often use **in** or **at** with buildings. For example, you can eat **in a restaurant** or **at a restaurant**; you can buy food **in a supermarket** or **at a supermarket**.

We usually say **at** when we say where an event takes place (a concert, a party, a meeting etc.):
- ○ We went to a concert **at the National Concert Hall**.
- ○ The meeting took place **at the company's head office** in Frankfurt.
- ○ There was a robbery **at the supermarket**.

We say **at** somebody's house:
- ○ I was **at Helen's house** last night. *or* I was **at Helen's** last night.

In the same way we say **at the doctor's**, **at the hairdresser's** etc.

We use **in** when we are thinking about the building itself. Compare **at** and **in**:
- ○ I was **at Helen's** (house) last night.
  It's always cold **in Helen's house**. The heating doesn't work well. (*not* at Helen's house)
- ○ We had dinner **at the hotel**.
  All the rooms **in the hotel** have air conditioning. (*not* at the hotel)

We say **at the station** / **at the airport**:
- ○ There's no need to meet me **at the station**. I can get a taxi.

D in and at for towns etc.

We normally use **in** with cities, towns and villages:
- ○ The Louvre is a famous art museum **in Paris**. (*not* at Paris)
- ○ Sam's parents live **in a village** in the south of France. (*not* at a village)

We use **at** when we think of the place as a point or station on a journey:
- ○ Does this train stop **at Oxford**? (= at Oxford station)

E on a bus / in a car etc.

We usually say **on a bus** / **on a train** / **on a plane** / **on a ship** *but* **in a car** / **in a taxi**:
- ○ **The bus** was very full. There were too many people **on it**.
- ○ Laura arrived **in a taxi**.

We say **on a bike** (= bicycle) / **on a motorbike** / **on a horse**:
- ○ Jane passed me **on her bike**.

>> at school / in hospital etc. → Unit 74   in/at/on (position) → Units 123–124   to/at/in/into → Unit 126
by car / by bike etc. → Unit 128B

Exercises

125.1 Complete the sentences about the pictures. Use **in, at** or **on** with the words below the pictures.

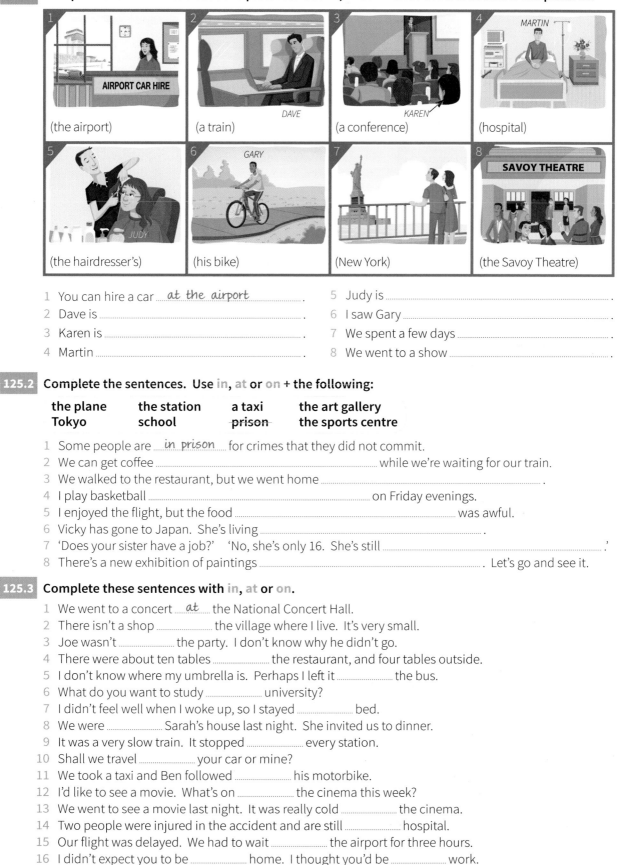

1		2	3	4 MARTIN
AIRPORT CAR HIRE		DAVE	KAREN	
(the airport)	(a train)	(a conference)	(hospital)
5	6 GARY	7	8 SAVOY THEATRE
JUDY			
(the hairdresser's)	(his bike)	(New York)	(the Savoy Theatre)

1 You can hire a car ....*at the airport*..... .
2 Dave is ....
3 Karen is ....
4 Martin ....

5 Judy is ....
6 I saw Gary ....
7 We spent a few days ....
8 We went to a show ....

125.2 Complete the sentences. Use **in, at** or **on** + the following:

the plane	the station	a taxi	the art gallery
Tokyo	school	~~prison~~	the sports centre

1 Some people are ....*in prison*..... for crimes that they did not commit.
2 We can get coffee .... while we're waiting for our train.
3 We walked to the restaurant, but we went home ....
4 I play basketball .... on Friday evenings.
5 I enjoyed the flight, but the food .... was awful.
6 Vicky has gone to Japan. She's living ....
7 'Does your sister have a job?' 'No, she's only 16. She's still ....?'
8 There's a new exhibition of paintings .... Let's go and see it.

125.3 Complete these sentences with **in, at** or **on**.

1 We went to a concert ....*at*.... the National Concert Hall.
2 There isn't a shop .... the village where I live. It's very small.
3 Joe wasn't .... the party. I don't know why he didn't go.
4 There were about ten tables .... the restaurant, and four tables outside.
5 I don't know where my umbrella is. Perhaps I left it .... the bus.
6 What do you want to study .... university?
7 I didn't feel well when I woke up, so I stayed .... bed.
8 We were .... Sarah's house last night. She invited us to dinner.
9 It was a very slow train. It stopped .... every station.
10 Shall we travel .... your car or mine?
11 We took a taxi and Ben followed .... his motorbike.
12 I'd like to see a movie. What's on .... the cinema this week?
13 We went to see a movie last night. It was really cold .... the cinema.
14 Two people were injured in the accident and are still .... hospital.
15 Our flight was delayed. We had to wait .... the airport for three hours.
16 I didn't expect you to be .... home. I thought you'd be .... work.

→ **Additional exercise 34** (page 322)

to, at, in and into

A

We say **go/come/travel** (etc.) **to** a place or event. For example:

go to China	**go to** work	**come to** my house	TO → ☐
go back to Italy	**go to** the bank	**drive to** the airport	
return to London	**go to** a party	**be taken to** hospital	

- ○ When are your friends **going back to Italy**? (*not* going back in Italy)
- ○ Three people were injured in the accident and **taken to hospital**.

In the same way we say **Welcome to** …, a **trip to** …, a **visit to** …, on **my way to** … etc. :
- ○ **Welcome to our country**! (*not* Welcome in)
- ○ We had to cancel **our trip to Paris**.

Compare **to** (for *movement*) and **in/at** (for *position*):
- ○ They are **going to** France.   *but*   They **live in** France.
- ○ Can you **come to** the party?   *but*   I'll **see you at** the party.

We say '(I've) **been to**' a place or an event:
- ○ I've **been to Italy** four times, but I've never **been to Rome**.
- ○ Amanda has never **been to a football match** in her life.

B

get and **arrive**

We say **get to** a place:
- ○ They **got to the hotel** at midnight.
- ○ What time did you **get to the party**?

We say **arrive in** … or **arrive at** … (*not* arrive to).
We say **arrive in** a town or country:
- ○ They **arrived in Madrid / in Spain** a week ago.

For other places (buildings etc.) or events, we say **arrive at**:
- ○ What time did you **arrive at the hotel / at the airport / at the party**?

C

home

We say: **go home**, **come home**, **get home**, **arrive home**, **on the way home** etc. (no preposition).
We do not say 'to home':
- ○ What time did you **get home**? (*not* get to home)
- ○ I met Lisa **on my way home**.

D

into

go into, **get into** … etc. = enter (a room / a building / a car etc.):
- ○ I opened the door, **went into the room** and sat down.
- ○ A bird **flew into the kitchen** through the window.   INTO →
- ○ Every month my salary **is paid** directly **into my bank account**.

With some verbs (especially **go/get/put**) we often use **in** (instead of **into**):
- ○ She **got in the car** and drove away.   *or*   She **got into** the car …
- ○ I read the letter and **put it** back **in the envelope**.

The opposite of **into** is **out of**:
- ○ She **got out of** the car and **went into** a shop.

For buses, trains and planes, we usually say **get on** and **get off**:
- ○ She **got on the bus** and I never saw her again.
- ○ You need to **get off** (the train) at the next station.

≫ **been to** → Units 7–8   **in/at/on** (position) → Units 123–125   **at home** → Unit 125A
into and **in** → Unit 138A

Exercises

Unit
126

126.1 Put in **to/at/in/into** where necessary. If no preposition is necessary, leave the space empty.

1 Three people were taken ......*to*...... hospital after the accident.
2 I'm tired. Let's go ......−...... home now. *(no preposition)*
3 We left our luggage .... the station and went to find something to eat.
4 Shall we take a taxi .... the station or shall we walk?
5 I have to go .... the bank today. What time does it open?
6 The Amazon flows .... the Atlantic Ocean.
7 I missed the bus, so I walked .... home.
8 Have you ever been .... Canada?
9 I lost my key, but I managed to climb .... the house through a window.
10 We got stuck in a traffic jam on our way .... the airport.
11 We had lunch .... the airport while we were waiting for our plane.
12 It took us four hours to get .... the top of the mountain.
13 Welcome .... the hotel. We hope you enjoy your stay here.
14 We drove along the main road and then turned .... a narrow side street.
15 Did you enjoy your visit .... the zoo?
16 I did some shopping on my way .... home.
17 Marcel is French. He has just returned .... France after two years .... Brazil.
18 Carl was born .... Chicago, but his family moved .... Boston when he was three.

126.2 Write sentences about places you have been to. Use **I've been to / I've never been to** + the words in brackets.

1 (never)   *I've never been to Egypt.*
2 (once)   ....
3 (never)   ....
4 (a few times)   ....
5 (many times)   ....

126.3 Put in **to/at/in** where necessary. If no preposition is necessary, leave the space empty.

1 What time does this train get ......*to*...... London?
2 They arrived .... Barcelona a few days ago.
3 What time did you get .... home last night?
4 What time do you usually arrive .... work in the morning?
5 When we got .... the cinema, there was a long queue outside.
6 We were delayed and arrived .... home very late.

126.4 Write sentences using **got** + **into / out of / on / off**.

1 You were walking home. A friend passed you in her car. She saw you, stopped and offered you a lift.
   She opened the door. What did you do?   *I got into the car.*
2 You were waiting at the bus stop. At last your bus came and stopped. The doors opened.
   What did you do then? I .... the bus.
3 You drove home in your car. You stopped outside your house and parked the car.
   What did you do then? ....
4 You were travelling by train to Manchester. When the train got to Manchester, what did you do?
   ....
5 You needed a taxi. After a few minutes a taxi stopped for you. You opened the door.
   What did you do then? ....
6 You were travelling by plane. At the end of your flight, your plane landed at the airport and stopped.
   The doors were opened, you took your bag and stood up.
   What did you do then? ....

→ **Additional exercise 34** (page 322)

253

A   in

in the rain / in the sun / in the shade / in the dark / in bad weather etc.
- ○ We sat **in the shade**. It was too hot to sit **in the sun**.
- ○ Don't go out **in the rain**. Wait until it stops.

in a language / **in** a currency etc.
- ○ How do you say 'thank you' **in Russian**?
- ○ How much is a hundred pounds **in dollars**?

(be/fall) **in love** (**with** somebody)
- ○ They're very happy together. They're **in love**.

in a (good/bad) **mood**
- ○ You seem to be **in a bad mood**. What's the matter?

in (my) **opinion**
- ○ **In my opinion** the movie wasn't very good.

in the shade

B   on

on TV / on television	○ I didn't see the news **on TV**.
on the radio	○ I heard the weather forecast **on the radio**.
on the phone	○ I've never met her, but I've spoken to her **on the phone**.
on fire	○ Look! That car is **on fire**.
on purpose (= intentionally)	○ I'm sorry. I didn't mean to hurt you. I didn't do it **on purpose**.
on the whole (= in general)	○ Sometimes I have problems at work, but **on the whole** I enjoy my job.

C   on holiday / on a trip etc.

(be/go) **on holiday / on vacation**	○ I'm going **on holiday** next week.
(be/go) **on a trip / on a tour / on a cruise** etc.	○ One day I'd like to go **on a world tour**.
(be/go to a place) **on business**	○ Emma's away **on business** at the moment.
(be/go) **on strike**	○ There are no trains today. The drivers are **on strike**.
(be/go) **on a diet**	○ I've put on weight. I'll have to go **on a diet**.

We also say 'go somewhere **for a** holiday':
- ○ Steve has gone to France **for a holiday**.

D   at the age of ... etc.

at the age of 16 / at 90 miles an hour / at 100 degrees etc. :
- ○ Tracy left school **at 16**. *or*
  Tracy left school **at the age of 16**.
- ○ The train was travelling **at 120 miles an hour**.
- ○ Water boils **at 100 degrees Celsius**.

> We are now flying **at a speed** of 800 kilometres an hour and **at an altitude** of 9,000 metres.

➤➤   **in/at/on** (time) ➜ **Unit 121**   **in/at/on** (position) ➜ **Units 123–125**

Exercises

127.1 Complete the sentences using **in** + the following:

the mood French	cold weather ~~the rain~~	love kilometres	my opinion the shade

1 Don't go out __in the rain__ . Wait until it stops.
2 Matt likes to keep warm, so he doesn't go out much _____ .
3 The movie was _____ with English subtitles.
4 They fell _____ almost immediately and were married in a few weeks.
5 I don't feel like going to a party tonight. I'm not _____ .
6 It's too hot here. I'm going to sit _____ under that tree.
7 Amanda thought the restaurant was OK, but _____ it wasn't very good.
8 Fifty miles? What's that _____ ?

127.2 Complete the sentences using **on** + the following:

business ~~the radio~~	a cruise purpose	a diet strike	fire TV	holiday a tour	her phone the whole

1 I heard the weather forecast __on the radio__ . It's going to get warmer.
2 Workers at the company have gone _____ for better pay and conditions.
3 Don't go _____ if you don't like being at sea.
4 There was panic when people realised that the building was _____ .
5 Soon after we arrived, we were taken _____ of the city.
6 Emma has lots of useful apps _____ .
7 I feel lazy this evening. Is there anything worth watching _____ ?
8 I'm sorry. It was an accident. I didn't do it _____ .
9 If you are _____ , there are certain things you're not allowed to eat.
10 We'll be _____ from Friday. We're going to the mountains.
11 Jane's job involves a lot of travelling. She often has to go away _____ .
12 Some of the exam questions were hard, but _____ it was OK.

127.3 Complete the sentences with **in**, **on** or **at**.

1 Water boils __at__ 100 degrees Celsius.
2 When I was 14, I went _____ a trip to France organised by my school.
3 Julia's grandmother died recently _____ the age of 90.
4 Can you turn the light on, please? I don't want to sit _____ the dark.
5 We didn't go _____ holiday last year. We stayed at home.
6 I hate driving _____ fog. You can't see anything.
7 Technology has developed _____ great speed.
8 David got married _____ 19, which is rather young to get married.
9 I listened to an interesting programme _____ the radio this morning.
10 I wouldn't like to go _____ a cruise. I think I'd get bored.
11 The earth travels round the sun _____ 107,000 kilometres an hour.
12 I shouldn't eat too much. I'm supposed to be _____ a diet.
13 A lot of houses were damaged _____ the storm last week.
14 I won't be here next week. I'll be _____ holiday.
15 I wouldn't like his job. He spends most of his time talking _____ the phone.
16 'Did you enjoy your holiday?' 'Not every minute, but _____ the whole, yes.'
17 _____ your opinion, what should I do?
18 Ben is a happy sort of person. He always seems to be _____ a good mood.
19 I don't think violent films should be shown _____ TV.
20 The museum guidebook is available _____ several languages.

➜ **Additional exercise 34** (page 322)

A You can say that something happens **by mistake / by accident / by chance**:
- ○ We hadn't arranged to meet. We met **by chance**.

But we say 'do something **on purpose**' (= you mean to do it):
- ○ I didn't do it **on purpose**. It was an accident.

Note that we say **by chance**, **by accident** etc. (*not* by the chance / by an accident).
In these expressions we use **by** + *noun* without **the** or **a**.

B We use **by** … to say how somebody travels. For example, you can travel:
  by car   by train   by plane   by boat   by ship   by bus   by bike etc.
- ○ Jess usually goes to work **by bus / by bike / by car**.

We do not use **by** if we say <u>my car</u> / <u>the train</u> / <u>a taxi</u> etc. We say:
  by car   *but*   **in my** car   (*not* by my car)
  by train   *but*   **on the** train   (*not* by the train)

We use **in** for cars and taxis:
- ○ They didn't come **in their car**. They came **in a taxi**.
We use **on** for bikes and public transport (buses, trains etc.):
- ○ We travelled **on the 6.45 train**, which arrived at 8.30.

Note that we usually say **on foot** (*not usually* by foot):
- ○ Did you come here **by car** or **on foot**?

We also use **by** to say how we do other things. For example, you can:
  send something **by post**   pay **by card / by cheque**   do something **by hand**
- ○ Can I pay **by credit card**?
But note that we say **pay cash** or **pay in cash** (*not usually* by cash).

C We say that 'something is done **by** …' *(passive)*:
- ○ Have you ever been bitten **by a dog**?
- ○ The programme was watched **by millions of people**.

Compare **by** and **with**:
- ○ The door must have been opened **with a key**. (*not* by a key)
  (= somebody used a key to open it)
- ○ The door must have been opened **by somebody** with a key.

We say: a play **by Shakespeare**, a painting **by Rembrandt**, a novel **by Tolstoy** etc.
- ○ Have you read any poems **by Shakespeare**?
- ○ '**Who** is this painting **by**? Picasso?' 'I have no idea.'

D **By** also means 'next to / beside':
- ○ The light switch is **by the door**.
- ○ Come and sit **by me**. (= next to me)

LIGHT SWITCH →

E You can also use **by** … to show the difference between two things:
- ○ Clare's salary has increased **by ten per cent**.
  (= it's now ten per cent more than before)
- ○ Carl won the race **by five metres**.
  (= he was five metres in front of the other runners)

← 5 METRES →

CARL

Passive + **by** → **Unit 42B**   **by** + **-ing** → **Unit 60B**   **by myself** → **Unit 83C**   **by** (time) → **Unit 120**

Exercises

128.1 Complete the sentences. Choose from the box.

1 We don't need cash. We can pay __by credit card__ .
2 Kate and James keep in touch with one another mainly ....
3 I didn't intend to take your umbrella. I took it ....
4 I think he arrived late .... He wanted to keep us waiting.
5 Some things are planned. Other things happen ....
6 Don't put my sweater in the washing machine. It has to be washed ....

by mistake
by hand
~~by credit card~~
by chance
by email
on purpose

128.2 Put in by, in or on.

1 Jess usually goes to work __by__ bus.
2 I saw Jane this morning. She was .... the bus.
3 How did you get here? Did you come .... train?
4 I couldn't find a seat .... the train. It was full.
5 How much will it cost to the airport .... taxi?
6 Did you come here .... Sarah's car or yours?
7 The injured man was taken to hospital .... ambulance.
8 How long does it take to cross the Atlantic .... ship?
9 He doesn't drive much. He goes everywhere .... bike or .... foot.

128.3 Complete these sentences about books, paintings etc. Choose from the box.

1 I was woken up in the night __by a strange noise__ .
2 These pictures were taken ....
3 I hate getting bitten ....
4 'Mona Lisa' is a famous painting ....
5 We lost the game because of a mistake ....
6 The plane was damaged .... , but landed safely.
7 This music is .... , but I can't remember what
   it's called.

by mosquitoes
by one of our players
by lightning
by Beethoven
~~by a strange noise~~
by Leonardo da Vinci
by a professional
   photographer

128.4 Put in by, in, on or with.

1 Have you ever been bitten __by__ a dog?
2 We managed to put the fire out .... a fire extinguisher.
3 Who's that man standing .... the window?
4 Do you travel much .... bus?
5 We travelled .... my friend's car because it is larger and more comfortable than mine.
6 It was only .... accident that I discovered the error.
7 These pictures were taken .... a very good camera.
8 My friends live in a beautiful house .... the sea.
9 There were only a few people .... the plane. It was almost empty.
10 The new railway line will reduce the journey time .... two hours (from five hours to three).
11 There was a small table .... the bed .... a lamp and a clock .... it.

128.5 Complete the sentences using by.

1 Carl won the race. He was five metres in front of the other runners.
   Carl __won by five metres.__
2 Ten years ago the population of the country was 50 million. Now it is 56 million.
   In the last ten years the population has ....
3 There was an election. Helen won. She got 25 votes and James got 23.
   Helen won ....
4 I went to Kate's office to see her, but she had left work five minutes before I arrived.
   I missed ....

Noun + preposition (**reason for**, **cause of** etc.)

A   *noun +* **for** …

a demand / **a need FOR** …
- ◯ The company went out of business. There was no **demand for** its product any more.
- ◯ There's no excuse for behaviour like that. There's no **need for** it.

a reason FOR …
- ◯ The train was late, but nobody knew the **reason for** the delay. (*not* reason of)

B   *noun +* **of** …

a cause OF …
- ◯ The **cause of** the explosion is unknown.

a picture / **a photo** / **a photograph** / **a map** / **a plan** / **a drawing** (etc.) **OF** …
- ◯ Rachel showed me some **pictures of** her family.
- ◯ I had a **map of** the town, so I was able to find my way around.

an advantage / **a disadvantage OF** …
- ◯ The **advantage of living alone** is that you can do what you like.

but

there is an advantage **IN** doing something *or* **TO** doing something:
- ◯ **There are** many advantages **in** living alone.   *or* … many advantages **to** living alone.

C   *noun +* **in** …

an increase / **a decrease** / **a rise** / **a fall IN** (prices etc.)
- ◯ There has been an **increase in** the number of road accidents recently.
- ◯ Last year was a bad one for the company. There was a big **fall in** sales.

D   *noun +* **to** …

damage TO …
- ◯ The accident was my fault, so I had to pay for the **damage to** the other car.

an invitation TO … (a party / a wedding etc.)
- ◯ Did you get an **invitation to** the wedding?

a solution TO a problem / a **key TO** a door / an **answer TO** a question / a **reply TO** a letter / a **reaction TO** something
- ◯ I hope we find a **solution to** the problem. (*not* a solution of the problem)
- ◯ I was surprised at her **reaction to** my suggestion.

an attitude TO … *or* an **attitude TOWARDS** …
- ◯ His **attitude to** his job is very negative.   *or*   His **attitude towards** his job …

E   *noun +* **with** … / **between** …

a relationship / a **connection** / **contact WITH** …
- ◯ Do you have a good **relationship with** your parents?
- ◯ The police want to question a man in **connection with** the robbery.

a relationship / a **connection** / **contact** / a **difference BETWEEN** two things or people
- ◯ The police believe that there is no **connection between** the two crimes.
- ◯ There are some **differences between** British and American English.

129.1 Complete the second sentence so that it has the same meaning as the first.

1 What caused the explosion?
   What was the cause ....*of the explosion*..?
2 We're trying to solve the problem.
   We're trying to find a solution ....
3 Sue gets on well with her brother.
   Sue has a good relationship ....
4 The cost of living has gone up a lot.
   There has been a big increase ....
5 I don't know how to answer your question.
   I can't think of an answer ....
6 I don't think that a new road is necessary.
   I don't think there is any need ....
7 I think that living in a big city has many advantages.
   I think that there are many advantages ....
8 Food prices fell last month.
   Last month there was a fall ....
9 Nobody wants shoes like these any more.
   There is no demand ....
10 In what way is your job different from mine?
   What is the difference ....?

129.2 Complete the sentences using these nouns + a preposition:

cause	connection	contact	damage	invitation
key	~~map~~	photos	reason	reply

1 On the classroom wall there were some pictures and a ......*map of*...... the world.
2 Thank you for the .... your birthday party.
3 Anna has little .... her family these days. She rarely sees them.
4 I can't open this door. Do you have a .... the other door?
5 The .... the fire at the hotel is still unknown.
6 Did you get a .... the email you sent?
7 The two companies are separate. There is no .... them.
8 Jane showed me some .... the city as it looked 100 years ago.
9 Emily has decided to give up her job. I don't know her .... doing this.
10 It wasn't a bad accident. The .... the car wasn't serious.

129.3 Complete the sentences with the correct preposition.

1 There are some differences ....*between*.... British and American English.
2 Money isn't the solution .... every problem.
3 There has been an increase .... the amount of traffic using this road.
4 The advantage .... having a car is that you don't have to rely on public transport.
5 There are many advantages .... being able to speak a foreign language.
6 Everything can be explained. There's a reason .... everything.
7 When Paul left home, his attitude .... many things seemed to change.
8 Ben and I used to be good friends, but I don't have much contact .... him now.
9 James did a very good drawing .... his father. It looks just like him.
10 What was Sarah's reaction .... the news?
11 Nicola took a picture .... me holding the baby.
12 The show is very popular and there has been a great demand .... tickets.
13 There has been a lot of debate about the causes .... climate change.
14 The fact that Jane was offered a job in the company has no connection .... the fact that she is a friend of the managing director.

➜ **Additional exercise 35** (page 322)

Adjective + preposition 1

A
nice of you, nice to me

nice / kind / good / generous / polite / honest / stupid / silly etc. **OF** somebody (to do something)
- ○ Thank you. It was very **nice of** you to help me.
- ○ It was **stupid of** me to go out without a coat in such cold weather.

(be) **nice / kind / good / generous / polite / rude / friendly / cruel** etc. **TO** somebody
- ○ They have always been very **nice to** me. (*not* with me)
- ○ Why were you so **unfriendly to** Lucy?

B
adjective + **about** / **with**

angry / annoyed / furious / upset { **ABOUT** something
{ **WITH** somebody **FOR** doing something
- ○ There's no point in getting **angry about** things that don't matter.
- ○ Are you **annoyed with** me **for** being late?
- ○ Lisa is **upset about** not being invited to the party.

excited / worried / nervous / happy etc. **ABOUT** something
- ○ Are you **nervous about** the exam?

pleased / satisfied / happy / delighted / disappointed WITH something you get or experience
- ○ They were **delighted with** the present I gave them.
- ○ Were you **happy with** your exam results?

C
adjective + **at** / **by** / **with** / **of**

surprised / shocked / amazed / astonished / upset AT / BY something
- ○ Everybody was **surprised at** the news. *or* ... **by** the news.
- ○ I hope you weren't **shocked by** what I said. *or* ... **at** what I said.

impressed WITH / BY somebody/something
- ○ I'm very **impressed with** (*or* **by**) her English. It's very good.

fed up / bored WITH something
- ○ I don't enjoy my job any more. I'm **fed up with** it. / I'm **bored with** it.

tired OF something
- ○ Come on, let's go! I'm **tired of** waiting.

D
sorry about / for

sorry ABOUT a situation or something that happened
- ○ I'm **sorry about** the mess. I'll clear it up later.
- ○ **Sorry about** last night. (= Sorry about something that happened last night)

sorry FOR / ABOUT something you did or caused
- ○ I'm **sorry for** shouting at you yesterday. (*or* **sorry about** shouting)
- ○ **Sorry for** the delay. (*or* **Sorry about** the delay)

You can also say 'I'm sorry I (did something)':
- ○ I'm **sorry I shouted** at you yesterday.

feel / be sorry FOR somebody in a bad situation
- ○ I **feel sorry for** Mark. He's had a lot of bad luck. (*not* I feel sorry about Mark)

➤➤ Preposition + -ing ➡ Unit 60   Adjective + **to** ... ➡ Unit 65   sorry to / sorry for ... ➡ Unit 66C
Adjective + preposition 2 ➡ **Unit 131**

Exercises

130.1 Complete the sentences using nice of ..., kind of ... etc.

1	Tom offered to drive me to the airport.	(nice) That was ____ nice of him.	
2	I needed money and Lisa gave me some.	(generous) That ____ her.	
3	They didn't invite us to their party.	(not very nice) That wasn't ____	
4	Can I help you with your luggage?	(very kind) That's ____	
5	Kevin never says 'thank you'.	(not very polite) That isn't ____	
6	They've had an argument and now they refuse to speak to each other.	(a bit childish) That's a bit ____	

130.2 Complete the sentences using an adjective + preposition. Choose from:

amazed   **angry**   **bored**   **careless**   **excited**   **impressed**   **kind**   ~~**nervous**~~

1 Are you ____ nervous about ____ the exam?
2 Thank you for all you've done. You've been very ____ me.
3 What have I done wrong? Why are you ____ me?
4 You must be very ____ your trip next week. It sounds really great.
5 I wasn't ____ the service in the restaurant. We had to wait ages.
6 Ben isn't very happy at college. He says he's ____ the course he's doing.
7 I'd never seen so many people before. I was ____ the crowds.
8 It was ____ you to leave the car unlocked while you were shopping.

130.3 Put in the correct preposition.

1 They were delighted ____ with ____ the present I gave them.
2 It was nice ____ you to come and see me when I was ill.
3 Why are you always so rude ____ people? Why can't you be more polite?
4 We always have the same food every day. I'm fed up ____ it.
5 We had a good holiday, but we were disappointed ____ the hotel.
6 I can't understand people who are cruel ____ animals.
7 I was surprised ____ the way he behaved. It was completely out of character.
8 I've been trying to learn Japanese, but I'm not very satisfied ____ my progress.
9 Tanya doesn't look very well. I'm worried ____ her.
10 I'm sorry ____ yesterday. I completely forgot we'd arranged to meet.
11 There's no point in feeling sorry ____ yourself. It won't help you.
12 Are you still upset ____ what I said to you yesterday?
13 Some people say Kate is unfriendly, but she's always been very nice ____ me.
14 I'm tired ____ doing the same thing every day. I need a change.
15 We interviewed ten people for the job, and we weren't impressed ____ any of them.
16 Vicky is annoyed ____ me because I didn't agree with her.
17 I'm sorry ____ the smell in this room. I've just finished painting it.
18 I was shocked ____ what I saw. I'd never seen anything like it before.
19 Jack is sorry ____ what he did. He won't do it again.
20 The hotel was incredibly expensive. I was amazed ____ the price of a room.
21 Paul made the wrong decision. It was honest ____ him to admit it.
22 You've been very generous ____ me. You've helped me a lot.
23 Our neighbours were very angry ____ the noise we made.
24 Our neighbours were furious ____ us ____ making so much noise.

→ Additional exercise 35 (page 322)

Adjective + preposition 2

A   adjective + **of**

afraid / scared / frightened / terrified OF …
- ○ 'Are you **afraid of** spiders?'   'Yes, I'm **terrified of** them.'

fond / proud / ashamed / jealous / envious OF …
- ○ Why is he so **jealous of** other people?

suspicious / critical / tolerant OF …
- ○ They didn't trust me. They were **suspicious of** my motives.

aware / conscious OF …
- ○ 'Did you know he was married?'   'No, I wasn't **aware of** that.'

capable / incapable OF …
- ○ I'm sure you are **capable of** doing the job well.

full / short OF …
- ○ Amy is a very active person. She's always **full of** energy.
- ○ I'm a bit **short of** money. Can you lend me some?

typical OF …
- ○ He's late again. It's **typical of** him to keep everybody waiting.

certain / sure OF or **ABOUT** …
- ○ I think she's arriving this evening, but I'm not **sure of** that. *or* … not **sure about** that.

B   adjective + **at / to / from / in / on / with / for**

good / bad / brilliant / better / hopeless etc. **AT** …
- ○ I'm not very **good at** repairing things. (*not* good in repairing things)

married / engaged TO …
- ○ Louise is **married to** an American. (*not* married with)
- *but*   Louise is married **with three children**. (= she is married and has three children)

similar TO …
- ○ Your handwriting is **similar to** mine.

different FROM   *or*   **different TO** …
- ○ The film was **different from** what I'd expected. *or* … **different to** what I'd expected.

interested IN …
- ○ Are you **interested in** art?

keen ON …
- ○ We stayed at home. Chris wasn't **keen on** going out.

dependent ON … (*but* **independent OF** …)
- ○ I don't want to be **dependent on** anybody.

crowded WITH (people etc.)
- ○ The streets were **crowded with** tourists. (*but* … **full of** tourists)

famous FOR …
- ○ The Italian city of Florence is **famous for** its art treasures.

responsible FOR …
- ○ Who was **responsible for** all that noise last night?

>> Preposition + -ing → **Unit 60**   afraid of/to … → **Unit 66A**   Adjective + preposition 1 → **Unit 130**
American English → **Appendix 7**

Exercises

131.1 Complete the sentences using an adjective + of. Choose from:

ashamed   aware   capable   envious   proud   scared   ~~short~~   typical

1 I'm a bit ..... *short of* ..... money. Can you lend me some?
2 My children have done very well. I'm .... them.
3 What I did was very bad. I'm .... myself.
4 She always behaves like that. It's .... her.
5 He wouldn't be able to run his own business. He's not .... it.
6 I don't like going up ladders. I'm .... heights.
7 Nobody told me she was ill. I wasn't .... it.
8 I wish I had what Sarah has. I'm .... her.

131.2 Write sentences about yourself. Are you good at these things or not? You can use:

good   pretty good   not very good   hopeless

1 (repairing things) .... *I'm not very good at repairing things.* ....
2 (telling jokes) ....
3 (maths) ....
4 (remembering names) ....
5 (making decisions) ....

131.3 Complete the sentences using an adjective + preposition. Choose from:

afraid   capable   different   interested   proud   responsible   similar   ~~sure~~

1 I think she's arriving this evening, but I'm not .... *sure of* .... that.
2 Your camera is .... mine, but it isn't exactly the same.
3 Don't worry. I'll look after you. There's nothing to be ....
4 I never watch the news on TV. I'm not .... the news.
5 The editor is the person who is .... what appears in a newspaper.
6 Sarah is a keen gardener and is very .... her garden.
7 I was surprised when I first met Tina. She was .... what I expected.
8 Ben could become world champion one day. He's .... it.

131.4 Complete the second sentence so that it means the same as the first.

1 There were lots of tourists in the streets.   The streets were crowded .... *with tourists* .... .
2 There was a lot of furniture in the room.   The room was full ....
3 I don't like sport very much.   I'm not very keen ....
4 We don't have enough time.   We're short ....
5 Helen does her job very well.   Helen is very good ....
6 Steven's wife is a doctor.   Steven is married ....
7 I don't trust Robert.   I'm suspicious ....
8 My problem is not the same as yours.   My problem is different ....

131.5 Put in the correct preposition.

1 Amy is always full .... *of* .... energy.
2 My home town is not a very interesting place. It's not famous .... anything.
3 Kate is very fond .... her younger brother.
4 You look bored. You don't seem interested .... what I'm saying.
5 'Our flight departs at 10.35.' 'Are you sure .... that?'
6 I wanted to go out for a meal, but nobody else was keen .... the idea.
7 These days everybody is aware .... the dangers of smoking.
8 The station platform was crowded .... people waiting for the train.
9 Mark has no money of his own. He's completely dependent .... his parents.
10 We're short .... staff in our office right now. We need more people to do the work.

→ Additional exercise 35 (page 322)

Verb + preposition 1 **to** and **at**

A   *verb +* **to**

talk / speak TO somebody (**talk/speak with** is also possible)
- ☐ Who were you **talking to**?

listen TO ...
- ☐ When I'm driving, I like to **listen to** the radio. (*not* listen the radio)

apologise TO somebody (for ...)
- ☐ They **apologised to me** for their mistake. (*not* apologised me)

explain something **TO** somebody
- ☐ Can you **explain** this word **to me**? (*not* explain me this word)
explain / describe (**to** somebody) what/how/why ...
- ☐ I **explained to them** why I was worried. (*not* I explained them)
- ☐ Let me **describe to you** what I saw. (*not* Let me describe you)

B   **phone** somebody, **ask** somebody etc. (*without* **to**)

phone / call / email / text somebody
- ☐ I **called the airline** to cancel my flight. (*not* called to the airline)
But we say '**write** (a letter) **to** somebody'.

answer somebody/something
- ☐ You didn't **answer my email**. (*not* answer to my email)
But we say **reply to** (an email / a letter etc.).

ask somebody (a question)
- ☐ If there's anything you want to know, you can **ask me**. (*not* ask to me)

thank somebody (**for** ...)
- ☐ He **thanked me** for helping him. (*not* He thanked to me)

C   *verb +* **at**

look / stare / glance AT ..., **have a look / take a look AT** ...
- ☐ Why are you **looking at** me like that?

laugh AT ...
- ☐ I look stupid with this haircut. Everybody will **laugh at** me.

aim / point (something) **AT** ..., **shoot / fire** (a gun) **AT** ...
- ☐ Don't **point** that knife **at** me. It's dangerous.
- ☐ We saw someone with a gun **shooting at** birds, but he didn't hit any.

D   Some verbs can be followed by **at** or **to**, with a difference in meaning. For example:

shout AT somebody (when you are angry or aggressive)
- ☐ He got very angry and started **shouting at** me.
shout TO somebody (so that they can hear you)
- ☐ He **shouted to** me from the other side of the street.

throw something **AT** somebody/something (to hit them)
- ☐ Somebody **threw** an egg **at** the politician.
throw something **TO** somebody (for somebody to catch)
- ☐ Lisa shouted 'Catch!' and **threw** the keys **to** me from the window.

» Verb + preposition 2–5 → Units 133–136   ask for → Unit 133B
apologise for / thank somebody for → Unit 135B   Other verbs + to → Unit 136D

Exercises

132.1 **Which is correct?**

1 a Can you explain this word to me? (a *is correct*)
  b ~~Can you explain me this word?~~

2 a I got angry with Mark. Afterwards, I apologised to him.
  b I got angry with Mark. Afterwards, I apologised him.

3 a Amy won't be able to help you. There's no point in asking to her.
  b Amy won't be able to help you. There's no point in asking her.

4 a I need somebody to explain me what I have to do.
  b I need somebody to explain to me what I have to do.

5 a They didn't understand the system, so I explained it to them.
  b They didn't understand the system, so I explained it them.

6 a I like to sit on the beach and listen to the sound of the sea.
  b I like to sit on the beach and listen the sound of the sea.

7 a I asked them to describe me exactly what happened.
  b I asked them to describe to me exactly what happened.

8 a We'd better phone the restaurant to reserve a table.
  b We'd better phone to the restaurant to reserve a table.

9 a It was a difficult question. I couldn't answer to it.
  b It was a difficult question. I couldn't answer it.

10 a I explained everybody the reasons for my decision.
   b I explained to everybody the reasons for my decision.

11 a I thanked everybody for all the help they had given me.
   b I thanked to everybody for all the help they had given me.

12 a My friend texted to me to let me know she was going to be late.
   b My friend texted me to let me know she was going to be late.

132.2 **Complete the sentences. Use these verbs + the correct preposition:**

~~explain~~	~~laugh~~	listen	look	point	reply	speak	throw	throw

1 I look stupid with this haircut. Everybody will ___*laugh at*___ me.
2 I don't understand this. Can you ___*explain*___ it ___*to*___ me?
3 We live in the same building, but we've never _____ one another.
4 Be careful with those scissors! Don't _____ them _____ me!
5 You shouldn't _____ directly _____ the sun. You'll damage your eyes.
6 Please _____ me! I've got something important to tell you.
7 Don't _____ stones _____ the birds!
8 If you don't want that sandwich, _____ it _____ the birds. They'll eat it.
9 I tried to contact Tina, but she didn't _____ my emails.

132.3 **Put in to or at.**

1 They apologised ___*to*___ me for what happened.
2 I glanced _____ my watch to see what time it was.
3 Please don't shout _____ me! Try to calm down.
4 I saw Lisa and shouted _____ her, but she didn't hear me.
5 Don't listen _____ what he says. He doesn't know what he's talking about.
6 What's so funny? What are you laughing _____ ?
7 Is it all right if I have a look _____ your magazine?
8 I'm lonely. I need somebody to talk _____ .
9 She was so angry she threw a book _____ the wall.
10 The woman sitting opposite me on the train kept staring _____ me.
11 Do you have a moment? I need to speak _____ you.

➜ Additional exercise 36 (page 323)

A   *verb* + **about**

talk / read / know ABOUT …
- ☐ We **talked about** a lot of things at the meeting.

have a discussion ABOUT something
- ☐ We had **a discussion about** what we should do.

But we say '**discuss** something' (no preposition):
- ☐ We **discussed** what we should do. (*not* discussed about)

do something/nothing **ABOUT** something = *do something/nothing to improve a situation*
- ☐ If you're worried about the problem, you should **do** something **about** it.

B   *verb* + **for**

ask (somebody) **FOR** …
- ☐ I sent an email to the company **asking** them **for** more information about the job.

But we say 'ask somebody **the way / the time**' etc. (no preposition):
- ☐ I **asked** somebody **the way to the station**.

apply (**TO** a company etc.) **FOR** a job etc.
- ☐ I think you could do this job. Why don't you **apply for** it?

wait FOR somebody, **wait FOR** something (to happen)
- ☐ Don't **wait for** me. I'll join you later.
- ☐ I'm not going out yet. I'm **waiting for** the rain to stop.

search (a person / a place / a bag etc.) **FOR** …
- ☐ I've **searched** the house **for** my keys, but I still can't find them.

leave (a place) **FOR** another place
- ☐ I haven't seen her since she **left** (home) **for** work. (*not* left to work)

C   **take care of**, **care for** and **care about**

take care OF … = *look after, keep safe, take responsibility for*
- ☐ Don't worry about me. I can **take care of** myself.
- ☐ I'll **take care of** the travel arrangements. You don't need to do anything.

care FOR somebody = *take care of them, keep them safe*
- ☐ Alan is 85 and lives alone. He needs somebody to **care for** him.

I don't **care FOR** something = *I don't like it*
- ☐ I don't **care for** hot weather. (= I don't like …)

care ABOUT … = *think that somebody/something is important*
- ☐ He's very selfish. He doesn't **care about** other people.

care what/where/how … etc. (*without* **about**)
- ☐ You can do what you like. I don't **care what** you do.

D   **look for** and **look after**

look FOR … = *search for, try to find*
- ☐ I've lost my keys. Can you help me to **look for** them?

look AFTER … = *take care of, keep safe or in good condition*
- ☐ Alan is 85 and lives alone. He needs somebody to **look after** him. (*not* look for)
- ☐ You can borrow this book, but please **look after** it.

Verbs + **about/of** (**think/hear** etc.) ➜ Unit 134   Other verbs + **for** ➜ Unit 135B

Exercises

133.1 Which is right?

1 We ~~searched everywhere Joe~~ / searched everywhere for Joe, but we couldn't find him.
   (searched everywhere for Joe *is correct*)
2 I sent her an email. Now I'm waiting for her to reply / waiting her to reply.
3 A security guard searched my bag / searched for my bag as I entered the building.
4 I paid the taxi driver and asked him a receipt / asked him for a receipt.
5 I wanted to get to the city centre, so I stopped a man to ask the way / to ask for the way.
6 We discussed about the problem / discussed the problem, but we didn't reach a decision.
7 There are many problems, but the government does nothing for them / nothing about them.
8 My flight is at 9.30. What time do I need to leave the hotel to the airport / for the airport?

133.2 Put in the correct preposition. If no preposition is necessary, leave the space empty.

1 I'm not going out yet. I'm waiting ....*for*.... the rain to stop.
2 I've applied .... three universities. I hope one of them accepts me.
3 If you don't want the job, there's no point in applying .... it.
4 I don't want to talk .... what happened last night. Let's forget it.
5 I don't want to discuss .... what happened last night. Let's forget it.
6 We had an interesting discussion .... the problem, but we didn't reach a decision.
7 My friends are in Italy. They're in Rome now and tomorrow they leave .... Milan.
8 The roof of the house is in bad condition. We need to do something .... it.

133.3 Put in the correct preposition after care. If no preposition is necessary, leave the space empty.

1 He's very selfish. He doesn't care ....*about*.... other people.
2 Who's going to take care .... you when you are old?
3 She doesn't care .... the exam. She doesn't care whether she passes or fails.
4 I don't like this coat very much. I don't care .... the colour.
5 Don't worry about the shopping. I'll take care .... that.
6 He gave up his job to care .... his elderly father.
7 I want to have a good holiday. I don't care .... the cost.
8 I want to have a good holiday. I don't care .... how much it costs.

133.4 Complete the sentences with look for or look after. Use the correct form of look (looks/ looked/looking).

1 I ....*looked for*.... my keys, but I couldn't find them anywhere.
2 Kate is .... a job. I hope she finds one soon.
3 Who .... you when you were ill?
4 The car park was full, so we had to .... somewhere else to park.
5 A child minder is somebody who .... other people's children.
6 I'm .... Lisa. I need to ask her something. Have you seen her?

133.5 Complete the sentences with these verbs (in the correct form) + a preposition:

| apply | ask | do | leave | look | ~~search~~ | talk | wait |

1 Police are ....*searching for*.... a man who escaped from prison.
2 Sarah wasn't ready. We had to .... her.
3 I think Amy likes her job, but she doesn't .... it much.
4 Don't .... me .... money. I don't have any.
5 Ben is unemployed. He has .... several jobs, but hasn't had any luck.
6 If something is wrong, why don't you .... something .... it?
7 Helen's car is very old, but she .... it. It's in excellent condition.
8 Diane is from Boston, but now she lives in Paris. She .... Boston .... Paris when she was 19.

➜ Additional exercise 36 (page 323)

A

hear ABOUT … = *be told about something*
- ○ Did you **hear about** the fire at the hotel?

hear OF … = *know that somebody/something exists*
- ○ A: Who is Tom Hart?
  B: I have no idea. I've never **heard of** him. (*not* heard from him)

hear FROM … = *be in contact with somebody*
- ○ A: Have you **heard from** Jane recently?
  B: Yes, she called me a few days ago.

B

think ABOUT something = consider it, concentrate your mind on it:
- ○ I've **thought about** what you said and I've decided to take your advice.
- ○ A: Will you lend me the money?
  B: I'll **think about** it. (*not* think of it)

think OF something = produce an idea:
- ○ It was my idea. I **thought of** it first. (*not* thought about it)
- ○ I felt embarrassed. I couldn't **think of** anything to say. (*not* think about anything)

We also use **think of** when we ask for or give an opinion:
- ○ A: What did you **think of** the movie?
  B: I didn't **think** much **of** it. (= I didn't like it much)

Sometimes the difference is very small and you can use **of** or **about**:
- ○ When I'm alone, I often **think of** you. *or* … **think about** you.

You can say **think of** *or* **think about** doing something (for possible future actions):
- ○ My sister is **thinking of** going to Canada. *or* … **thinking about** going …

C

dream ABOUT … (when you are asleep)
- ○ I **dreamt about** you last night.

dream OF/ABOUT being something / doing something = *imagine*
- ○ Do you **dream of** being rich and famous? *or* … **dream about** being rich …

I **wouldn't dream OF** doing something = *I would never do it*
- ○ 'Don't tell anyone what I said.' 'No, I **wouldn't dream of** it.'

D

complain (**TO** somebody) **ABOUT** … = *say that you are not satisfied*
- ○ We **complained to** the manager of the restaurant **about** the food.

complain OF a pain, an illness etc. = *say that you have a pain etc.*
- ○ We called the doctor because George was **complaining of** a pain in his stomach.

E

remind somebody **ABOUT** … = *tell somebody not to forget*
- ○ It's good you **reminded** me **about** the meeting. I'd completely forgotten about it.

remind somebody **OF** … = *cause somebody to remember*
- ○ This house **reminds** me **of** the one I lived in when I was a child.
- ○ Look at this photograph of Richard. Who does he **remind** you **of**?

>> **remind** somebody **to** … → Unit 55B

Exercises

134.1 Complete the sentences using hear or heard + a preposition (about/of/from).

1 I'm surprised you haven't ....*heard of*.... her. She's quite famous.
2 'Did you .... the accident last night?' 'No, what happened?'
3 Sarah used to call me quite often, but I haven't .... her for a long time now.
4 'Have you .... William Hudson?' 'No. Who is he?'
5 Thanks for your email. It was good to .... you.
6 'Do you want to .... our trip?' 'Not now. Tell me later.'
7 I live in a very small town. You've probably never .... it.

134.2 Complete the sentences using think about or think of. Sometimes both about and of are possible.
Use the correct form of think (think/thinking/thought).

1 I've ...*thought about*.... what you said and I've decided to take your advice.
2 I need time to make decisions. I like to .... things carefully.
3 You look serious. What are you .... ?
4 That's a good idea. Why didn't I .... that?
5 I don't really want to meet Tom tonight. I'll have to .... an excuse.
6 I'm .... buying a new car. What would you advise me to buy?
7 When I was offered the job, I didn't accept immediately. I went away and .... it
for a while. In the end I decided to take the job.
8 A: I've just finished reading the book you lent me.
  B: What did you .... it? Did you like it?
9 A: Will you be able to help me?
  B: I'm not sure. I'll .... it.
10 I don't .... much .... this coffee. It's like water.
11 Katherine is homesick. She's always .... her family back home.
12 A: Do you think I should apply to do the course?
  B: I can't .... any reason why not.

134.3 Put in the correct preposition.

1 Did you hear ....*about*.... the fire at the hotel yesterday?
2 I love living here. I wouldn't dream .... going anywhere else.
3 A: I had a strange dream last night.
  B: Did you? What did you dream .... ?
4 I love this music. It reminds me .... a warm day in spring.
5 A: We've got no money. What are we going to do?
  B: Don't worry. I'll think .... something.
6 Our neighbours complained .... us .... the noise we made.
7 Paul was complaining .... pains in his chest, so he went to the doctor.
8 He loves his job. He thinks .... it all the time, he dreams .... it, he talks .... it
and I'm fed up with hearing .... it.

134.4 Complete the sentences using these verbs (in the correct form) + a preposition:

complain	dream	hear	remind	remind	~~think~~	think

1 It was my idea. I ....*thought of*.... it first.
2 Ben is never satisfied. He's always .... something.
3 I can't make a decision yet. I need time to .... your proposal.
4 He's not a well-known singer. Not many people have .... him.
5 A: You wouldn't go away without telling me, would you?
  B: Of course not. I wouldn't .... it.
6 I would have forgotten my appointment if you hadn't .... me .... it.
7 Do you see that man over there? Does he .... you .... anybody you know?

➜ Additional exercise 36 (page 323)

A   *verb +* **of**

accuse / **suspect** somebody **OF** …
- ◯ Tina **accused** me **of** being selfish.
- ◯ Some students were **suspected of** cheating in the exam.

approve / **disapprove OF** …
- ◯ His parents don't **approve of** what he does, but they can't stop him.

die OF *or* **die FROM** an illness etc.
- ◯ 'What did he **die of**?'   'A heart attack.'

consist OF …
- ◯ We had an enormous meal. It **consisted of** seven courses.

B   *verb +* **for**

pay (somebody) **FOR** …
- ◯ We didn't have enough money to **pay for** the meal. (*not* pay the meal)
But we say '**pay** a bill / a fine / a fee / tax / rent / a sum of money' etc. (no preposition)
- ◯ We didn't have enough money to **pay the rent**.

thank / **forgive** somebody **FOR** …
- ◯ I'll never **forgive** them **for** what they did.

apologise (**TO** somebody) **FOR** …
- ◯ When I realised I was wrong, I **apologised** (**to** them) **for** my mistake.

blame somebody/something **FOR** …, somebody is **to blame FOR** …
- ◯ Everybody **blamed** me **for** the accident.
- ◯ Everybody said that I was **to blame for** the accident.
blame (a problem etc.) **ON** …
- ◯ It wasn't my fault. Don't **blame** it **on** me.

C   *verb +* **from**

suffer FROM an illness etc.
- ◯ There's been an increase in the number of people **suffering from** heart disease.

protect somebody/something **FROM** …
- ◯ Sun cream **protects** the skin **from** the sun.

D   *verb +* **on**

depend ON …, **rely ON** …
- ◯ I don't know what time we'll arrive. It **depends on** the traffic.
- ◯ You can **rely on** Anna. She always keeps her promises.
You can use **depend** + **when**/**where**/**how** etc. with or without **on**:
- ◯ 'Are you going to buy it?' 'It **depends how much** it is.' (*or* 'It depends **on** how much …')

live ON money/food
- ◯ Michael's salary is very low. It isn't enough to **live on**.

congratulate / **compliment** somebody **ON** …
- ◯ I **congratulated** her **on** doing so well in her exams.
- ◯ The meal was really good. I **complimented** Mark **on** his cooking skills.

135.1 **Put in the correct preposition. If no preposition is necessary, leave the space empty.**

1 Some students were suspected ....*of*.... cheating in the exam.
2 Are you going to apologise .... what you did?
3 The apartment consists .... three rooms, a kitchen and bathroom.
4 I was accused .... lying, but I was telling the truth.
5 We finished our meal, paid .... the bill, and left the restaurant.
6 The accident was my fault, so I had to pay .... the repairs.
7 Some people are dying .... hunger, while others eat too much.
8 I called Helen to thank her .... the present she sent me.
9 The government is popular. Most people approve .... its policies.
10 Do you blame the government .... our economic problems?
11 When something goes wrong, you always blame it .... other people.
12 Forgive me .... interrupting, but I'd like to ask you something.

135.2 **Complete the second sentence so that it means the same as the first.**

1 Sue said that I was selfish.
Sue accused me ....*of being selfish*.................... .
2 The misunderstanding was my fault, so I apologised.
I apologised ....
3 Jane won the tournament, so I congratulated her.
I congratulated ....
4 He has enemies, and he has a bodyguard to protect him.
He has a bodyguard to protect ....
5 Sandra eats only bread and eggs.
Sandra lives ....
6 You can't say that the bad weather is my fault.
You can't blame ....
7 The police thought my friend had stolen a car.
The police suspected ....

135.3 **Complete the sentences using these verbs (in the correct form) + a preposition:**

| accuse | apologise | ~~approve~~ | congratulate | depend | live | pay | suffer |

1 His parents don't ....*approve of*.... what he does, but they can't stop him.
2 When you went to the theatre with Paul, who .... the tickets?
3 It's not pleasant when you are .... something you didn't do.
4 We hope to go to the beach tomorrow, but it .... the weather.
5 Things are cheap there. You can .... very little money.
6 You were rude to Lisa. I think you should .... her.
7 Alex .... back pain. He spends too much time working at his desk.
8 I called Jack to .... him .... passing his driving test.

135.4 **Put in the correct preposition. If no preposition is necessary, leave the space empty.**

1 I'll never forgive them ....*for*.... what they did.
2 Vaccinations may protect you .... a number of diseases.
3 You know you can always rely .... me if you need any help.
4 Sophie will have to borrow money to pay .... her college fees.
5 She's often unwell. She suffers .... very bad headaches.
6 I don't know whether I'll go out tonight. It depends .... how I feel.
7 Anna doesn't have a job. She depends .... her parents for money.
8 My usual breakfast consists .... fruit, cereal and coffee.
9 I complimented her .... her English. It was really good.

→ Additional exercise 36 (page 323)

A   verb + in

believe IN ... = *believe that something exists, believe that it's good to do something*
- ☐ Do you **believe in** God? (= do you believe that God exists?)
- ☐ I **believe in** saying what I think. (= I believe it is right to say what I think)

but '**believe** something' (= believe that it is true), '**believe** somebody' (= believe what they say):
- ☐ The story can't be true. I don't **believe it**. (*not* believe in it)

specialise IN ...
- ☐ Helen is a lawyer. She **specialises in** company law.

succeed IN ...
- ☐ I hope you **succeed in** finding the job you want.

B   verb + into

break INTO ...
- ☐ Our house was **broken into** a few days ago, but nothing was stolen.

crash / drive / bump / run INTO ...
- ☐ He lost control of the car and **crashed into** a wall.

divide / cut / split something **INTO** two or more parts
- ☐ The book is **divided into** three parts.

translate a book etc. **FROM** one language **INTO** another
- ☐ She's a famous writer. Her books have been **translated into** many languages.

C   verb + with

collide WITH ...
- ☐ There was an accident this morning. A bus **collided with** a car.

fill something **WITH** ... (*but* **full of** – see Unit 131A)
- ☐ Take this saucepan and **fill** it **with** water.

provide / supply somebody **WITH** ...
- ☐ The school **provides** all its students **with** books.

D   verb + to

happen TO ...
- ☐ What **happened to** that gold watch you used to have? (= where is it now?)

invite somebody **TO** a party / a wedding etc.
- ☐ They only **invited** a few people **to** their wedding.

prefer one thing **TO** another
- ☐ I **prefer** tea **to** coffee.

E   verb + on

concentrate ON ...
- ☐ I tried to **concentrate on** my work, but I kept thinking about other things.

insist ON ...
- ☐ I wanted to go alone, but some friends of mine **insisted on** coming with me.

spend (money) **ON** ...
- ☐ How much do you **spend on** food each week?

Exercises

136.1 Complete the sentences using these verbs (in the correct form) + a preposition:

> believe   break   concentrate   divide   drive   fill   happen   ~~insist~~   invite   succeed

1 I wanted to go alone, but my friends ....*insisted on*.... coming with me.
2 I haven't seen Mike for ages. I wonder what has .... him.
3 It's a very large house. It's .... four apartments.
4 We've been .... the party, but unfortunately we can't go.
5 I don't .... ghosts. I think people imagine that they see them.
6 Steve gave me an empty bucket and told me to .... it .... water.
7 A burglar is someone who .... a house to steal things.
8 Don't try and do two things together. .... one thing at a time.
9 It wasn't easy, but in the end we .... finding a solution to the problem.
10 The car in front of me stopped suddenly. Unfortunately I couldn't stop in time and .... the back of it.

136.2 Complete the second sentence so that it means the same as the first.

1 There was a collision between a bus and a car.
   A bus collided ....*with a car*.. .
2 I don't mind big cities, but I prefer small towns.
   I prefer ....
3 I got all the information I needed from the company.
   The company provided me ....
4 This morning I bought a pair of shoes, which cost eighty pounds.
   This morning I spent ....
5 There are ten districts in the city.
   The city is divided ....

136.3 Put in the correct preposition. If the sentence is already complete, leave the space empty.

1 The school provides all its students ....*with*.... books.
2 A strange thing happened .... me a few days ago.
3 Mark decided to give up sport to concentrate .... his studies.
4 Money should be used well. I don't believe .... wasting it.
5 My present job isn't wonderful, but I prefer it .... what I did before.
6 I hope you succeed .... getting what you want.
7 Ben was injured playing football when he collided .... another player.
8 There was an awful noise as the car crashed .... a tree.
9 Patrick is a photographer. He specialises .... sports photography.
10 Joe doesn't spend much money .... clothes.
11 I was amazed when I heard the news. I couldn't believe .... it.
12 Somebody broke .... my car and stole my bag.
13 I was quite cold, but Tom insisted .... having the window open.
14 The teacher decided to split the class .... four groups.
15 I filled the tank, but unfortunately I filled it .... the wrong kind of fuel.
16 Some things are difficult to translate .... one language .... another.

136.4 Use your own ideas to complete these sentences. Use a preposition.

1 I wanted to go out alone, but my friend insisted ....*on coming with me*............................ .
2 I spend a lot of money ....
3 I saw an accident. A car crashed ....
4 Chris prefers basketball ....
5 The restaurant we went to specialises ....
6 Shakespeare's plays have been translated ....

➜ **Additional exercise 36** (page 323)

A   We often use verbs with:

in	on	up	away	by	about	over	round *or* around
out	off	down	back	through	along	forward	

So you can say **look out** / **get on** / **take off** / **run away** etc. These are *phrasal verbs*.

We often use **on/off/out** etc. with verbs of movement. For example:

get on	○	The bus was full. We couldn't **get on**.
drive off	○	A woman got into the car and **drove off**.
come back	○	Sarah is leaving tomorrow and **coming back** on Saturday.
turn round	○	When I touched him on the shoulder, he **turned round**.

B   Often the second word (**on/off/out** etc.) gives a special meaning to the verb. For example:

break down	○	Sorry I'm late. The car **broke down**. (= the engine stopped working)
find out	○	I never **found out** who sent me the flowers. (= I never discovered)
take off	○	It was my first flight. I was nervous as the plane **took off**. (= went into the air)
give up	○	I tried many times to contact her. In the end I **gave up**. (= stopped trying)
get on	○	How was the exam? How did you **get on**? (= How did you do?)
get by	○	My French isn't good, but it's enough to **get by**. (= enough to manage)

For more phrasal verbs, see Units 138–145.

C   Sometimes a phrasal verb is followed by a *preposition*. For example:

phrasal verb	*preposition*		
look up	**at**	○	We **looked up at** the plane as it flew above us.
run away	**from**	○	Why did you **run away from** me?
keep up	**with**	○	You're walking too fast. I can't **keep up with** you.
look forward	**to**	○	Are you **looking forward to** your trip?

D   Sometimes a phrasal verb has an *object*. For example:

○ I turned on **the light**. (**the light** is the *object*)

Usually there are two possible positions for the object. You can say:

○ I **turned on** the light.   *or*   I **turned** the light **on**.
       object   *object*

But if the object is a *pronoun* (**it/them/me/him** etc.), only one position is possible:

○ I turned **it** on. (*not* I turned on it)

In the same way, you can say:

○ I'm going to { **take off** my shoes.
                 { **take** my shoes **off**.

but   These shoes are uncomfortable. I'm going to **take them off**. (*not* take off them)

○ Don't { **wake up** the baby.
          { **wake** the baby **up**.

but   The baby is asleep. Don't **wake her up**. (*not* wake up her)

○ Don't { **throw away** this box.
          { **throw** this box **away**.

but   I want to keep this box, so don't **throw it away**. (*not* throw away it)

Phrasal verbs 2–9 ➜ **Units 138–145**   American English ➜ **Appendix 7**

Exercises

137.1 Complete each sentence using a verb from A (in the correct form) + a word from B.

A   be   get   fly   sit   B   away   by   on   round
    break   get   go   speak   ~~back~~ down   off   up
    ~~come~~ get   look   take   back   down   out   up

1 Sarah is leaving tomorrow and ......*coming back*...... on Saturday.
2 I've been standing a long time. I'm going to .... for a bit.
3 It's a very busy airport. There are planes landing and .... all the time.
4 A cat tried to catch the bird, but it .... just in time.
5 We were trapped in the building. We couldn't ....
6 I can't hear you very well. Can you .... a little?
7 Ben's salary is very low, but it's enough to ....
8 Everything is so expensive now. Prices have .... a lot.
9 I heard a noise behind me, so I .... to see what it was.
10 I'm going out now to do some shopping. I'll .... in about an hour.
11 Our car .... on the motorway and we had to call for help.
12 How is your new job? How are you .... ?

137.2 Complete each sentence using a word from A and a word from B.

A   away   in   ~~up~~   back   B   at   to   ~~with~~ about
    out   up   up   forward   at   to   with   through

1 You're walking too fast. I can't keep ......*up with*...... you.
2 My holidays are nearly over. Next week I'll be .... work.
3 We went .... the top floor of the building to admire the view.
4 The meeting tomorrow is going to be difficult. I'm not looking .... it.
5 There was a bank robbery last week. The robbers got .... £50,000.
6 I love to look .... the stars in the night sky.
7 I was sitting in the kitchen when a bird flew .... the open window.
8 How do you know about the plan? How did you find .... it?

137.3 Complete the sentences. Use these phrasal verbs + it/them/me:

get out   give back   switch on   take off   ~~throw away~~   wake up

1 I want to keep this box. Don't ......*throw it away*...... .
2 I'm going to bed now. Can you .... at 6.30?
3 I've got something in my eye and I can't ....
4 I don't like it when people borrow things and don't ....
5 I want to use the hair dryer. How do I .... ?
6 My shoes are dirty. I'd better .... before going into the house.

137.4 Complete the sentences. Use the word in brackets.

1 Don't throw ......*away this box*...... . I want to keep it. (away)
2 I don't want this newspaper. You can throw ......*it away*...... . (away)
3 These books are Lisa's. I have to give .... to her. (back)
4 We can turn .... Nobody is watching it. (off)
5 Shh! My mother is asleep. I don't want to wake .... (up)
6 It's cold today. You should put .... if you go out. (on)
7 It was only a small fire. I was able to put .... easily. (out)
8 It's a bit dark in this room. Shall I turn .... ? (on)
9 A: The hotel is more expensive than when we stayed here last year.
   B: Yes, they've put .... (up)
10 A: How did the vase get broken?
   B: I'm afraid I knocked .... while I was cleaning. (over)

→ **Additional exercises 37–41** (pages 323–25)   **275**

A
Compare **in** and **out**:

in = into a room, a building, a car etc.
- ○ How did the thieves **get in**?
- ○ Here's a key, so you can **let yourself in**.
- ○ Lisa walked up to the edge of the pool and **dived in**. (= into the water)
- ○ I've got a new apartment. I'm **moving in** on Friday.
- ○ As soon as I got to the airport, I **checked in**.

In the same way you can say **go in**, **come in**, **walk in**, **break in** etc.

Compare **in** and **into**:
- ○ I'm moving **in** on Friday.
- ○ I'm moving **into my new flat** on Friday

out = out of a room, a building, a car etc.
- ○ Stay in the car. Don't **get out**.
- ○ I had no key, so I was **locked out**.
- ○ She swam up and down the pool, and then **climbed out**.
- ○ Andy opened the window and **looked out**.
- ○ We paid the hotel bill and **checked out**.

In the same way you can say **go out**, **get out**, **move out**, **let** somebody **out** etc.

Compare **out** and **out of**:
- ○ She climbed **out**.
- ○ She climbed **out of the pool**.

B
Other verbs + **in**

drop in = *visit somebody at home without arranging to do this*
- ○ I **dropped in** to see Chris on my way home.

join in = *take part in something that is already going on*
- ○ They were playing cards, so I **joined in**.

plug in an electrical machine = *connect it to the electricity supply*
- ○ The fridge isn't working because you haven't **plugged** it **in**.

PLUG IN

take somebody **in** = *deceive somebody*
- ○ The man said he was a policeman and I believed him. I was completely **taken in**.

fill in or **fill out** a form, a questionnaire etc. = *write the necessary information on a form*
- ○ Please **fill in** the application form and send it to us by 28 February. *or*
  Please **fill out** the application form ...

C
Other verbs + **out**

eat out = *eat at a restaurant, not at home*
- ○ There wasn't anything to eat at home, so we decided to **eat out**.

drop out of college / university / a course / a race = *stop before you have completely finished*
- ○ Gary went to university but **dropped out** after a year.

get out of something that you arranged to do = *avoid doing it*
- ○ I promised I'd go to the wedding. I don't want to go, but I can't **get out** of it now.

leave something **out** = *omit it, not include it*
- ○ In the sentence 'She said that she was ill', you can **leave out** the word 'that'.

cross something **out** = *write a line through something*
- ○ Some of the names on the list had been **crossed out**.   ~~Sarah~~   *CROSS OUT*

» Phrasal verbs 1 (Introduction) → Unit 137   More verbs + **out** → Unit 139

Exercises

138.1 **Complete the sentences.**

1 Here's a key so that you can ......*let*...... yourself in.
2 Lisa doesn't like cooking, so she .... out a lot.
3 If you're in our part of town, you should .... in and say hello.
4 Could you .... in this questionnaire? It will only take five minutes.
5 Amy isn't living in this house any more. She .... out a few weeks ago.
6 After breakfast, we .... out of the hotel and got a taxi to the airport.
7 I wanted to charge my phone, but there was nowhere to .... the charger in.
8 Paul started doing a Spanish course, but he .... out after a few weeks.
9 Be careful! The water isn't very deep here, so don't .... in.

138.2 **Complete the sentences with in, into, out or out of.**

1 I've got a new flat. I'm moving ......*in*...... on Friday.
2 We arrived at the hotel and checked ....
3 When are you moving .... your new flat?
4 The car stopped and the driver got ....
5 Thieves broke .... the house and stole some jewellery.
6 How did the thieves break .... ? Through a window?
7 He opened his wallet and something fell ....
8 Kate was angry and walked .... the meeting.

138.3 **Complete the sentences using a verb + in or out (of).**

1 Lisa walked to the edge of the pool, ...*dived in*... and swam to the other end.
2 Not all the runners finished the race. Three of them ....
3 I went to see Joe and Sophie in their new house. They .... last week.
4 I've told you everything you need to know. I don't think I've .... anything.
5 Some people in the crowd started singing. Then a few more people ....
   and soon everybody was singing.
6 Don't be .... by him. If I were you, I wouldn't believe anything he says.
7 I .... to see Laura a few days ago. She was fine.

138.4 **Complete the sentences. Use the word in brackets in the correct form.**

1 A: The fridge isn't working.
   B: That's because you haven't ...*plugged it in*... . (plug)
2 A: What do I have to do with these forms?
   B: .... and send them to this address. (fill)
3 A: I've made a mistake on this form.
   B: That's OK. Just .... and correct it. (cross)
4 A: Have you been to the new club I told you about?
   B: No. We went there, but they wouldn't .... because we weren't
      members. (let)
5 A: Can we meet tomorrow at ten?
   B: Probably. I have another meeting, but I think I can .... (get)

138.5 **Complete the second sentence so that it means the same as the first. Use a verb from Sections B or C.**

1 Let's go to a restaurant tonight.   Let's ...*eat out*... tonight.
2 Why didn't you finish college?   Why did you .... ?
3 Please complete the application form.   Please .... form .
4 I can't avoid going to the party.   I can't .... to the party.
5 I thought the email was genuine, but it wasn't. I was completely .... the email .
6 You must come and see us sometime.   You must .... sometime.
7 Steve was upset because he wasn't chosen   Steve was upset because he ....
   for the team.   the team.

➔ **Additional exercises 37–41** (pages 323–25)

A

out = not burning, not shining

go out	○ Suddenly all the lights in the building **went out**.
put out a fire / a cigarette / a light	○ I **put** the fire **out** with a fire extinguisher.
turn out a light	○ I **turned** the lights **out** before leaving.
blow out a candle	○ We don't need the candle. You can **blow** it **out**.

B work out

work out = *do physical exercises*
○ Rachel **works out** at the gym three times a week.

work out = *develop, progress*
○ Good luck for the future. I hope everything **works out** well for you.
○ A: Why did James leave the company?
  B: Things didn't **work out**. (= things didn't work out well)

work out (for calculations):
○ The total bill for three people is £97.35. That **works out** at £32.45 each.
work (something) **out** = *calculate*
○ 345 × 76? I need a calculator. I can't **work** it **out** in my head.

work out or **figure out** = *understand, think about a problem and find an answer*
○ Investigators are trying to **work out** what caused the accident. *or*
  Investigators are trying to **figure out** what caused the accident.

C Other verbs + **out**

carry out an order / an experiment / a survey / an investigation / a plan etc.
○ Soldiers are expected to **carry out** orders.
○ An investigation into the accident will be **carried out**.

find out that/what/when (etc.) … , **find out about** … = *get information about*
○ The police never **found out** who committed the crime.
○ I just **found out** that it's Helen's birthday today.
○ I checked a few websites to **find out** about hotels in the town.

give/hand things **out** = *give to each person*
○ At the end of the lecture, the speaker **gave out** information sheets to the audience.

point something **out** (**to** somebody) = *draw attention to it*
○ As we drove through the city, the tour guide **pointed out** all the sights.
○ I didn't realise I'd made a mistake until somebody **pointed** it **out to** me.

run out (of something)
○ We **ran out of** petrol on the motorway. (= we used all our petrol)

sort something **out** = *find a solution to, put in order*
○ There are a few problems we need to **sort out**.
○ All these papers are mixed up. I'll have to **sort** them **out**.

turn out to be … / **turn out** good/nice etc. / **turn out** that …
○ Nobody believed Paul at first, but he **turned out** to be right. (= it became clear in the end that he was right)
○ The weather wasn't so good in the morning, but it **turned out** nice later.
○ I thought they knew each other, but it **turned out** that they'd never met.

try out a machine, a system, a new idea etc. = *test it to see if it is OK*
○ The company is **trying out** some new software at the moment.

Phrasal verbs 1 (Introduction) → Unit 137   More verbs + **out** → Unit 138

Exercises

139.1 Which words can go together? Choose from the list.

| a candle | a fire | a~~light~~ | a new product | an order | a problem |

1 turn out ....*a light*....................................
2 blow out ....
3 carry out ....
4 put out ....
5 try out ....
6 sort out ....

139.2 Complete the sentences using a verb + out.

1 The company is ....*trying out*.... a new computer system at the moment.
2 Steve is very fit. He does a lot of sport and .... regularly.
3 The road will be closed for two days while building work is ....
4 We didn't manage to discuss everything at the meeting. We .... of time.
5 You have to .... the problem yourself. I can't do it for you.
6 I need to .... what happened exactly. It's not clear at the moment.
7 The new drug will be .... on a small group of patients.
8 I thought the two books were the same until someone .... the difference.
9 They got married a few years ago, but it didn't .... and they separated.
10 There was a power cut and all the lights ....
11 We thought she was American at first, but she .... to be Swedish.
12 Sometimes it .... cheaper to eat in a restaurant than to cook at home.
13 How did you .... about the project? Did somebody tell you?
14 It took firefighters two hours to .... the fire.
15 I can't .... how the water is getting into the house.

139.3 For each picture, complete the sentence using a verb + out.

1 They've ....*run out of petrol*.... .
2 The man with the beard is .... leaflets.
3 *earlier* *now* The weather has ....
4 Sally and Kim are .... at the gym.
5 Joe has .... water.
6 Lisa is trying to .... how ....

139.4 Complete the sentences. Each time use a verb + out.

1 A: Was the fire serious?
   B: No, we were able to ....*put it out*.. .
2 A: This recipe looks interesting.
   B: Yes, let's ....
3 A: How much money do I owe you exactly?
   B: Just a moment. I'll have to ....
4 A: What happened about your problem with your bank?
   B: It's OK now. I went to see them and we ....
5 A: You've written the wrong date on this form.
   B: Oh, so I have. Thanks for ....

→ Additional exercises 37–41 (pages 323–25)

A on and off for lights, machines etc.

We say:
the light **is on** / **put** the light **on** / **leave** the light **on** etc.
turn the light **on/off**   or   **switch** the light **on/off**

- ○ Shall I **leave** the lights **on** or **turn** them **off**?
- ○ 'Is the heating **on**?'   'No, I **switched** it **off**.'

also
put (music, a song) **on**, **put** the kettle **on**:
- ○ Let's **put** some music **on**. What would you like to hear?
- ○ We need boiling water, so I'll **put** the kettle **on**.

B on and off for events etc.

go on = *happen*
- ○ What's all that noise? What's **going on**? (= what's happening)

call something **off** = *cancel it*
- ○ The concert in the park had to be **called off** because of the weather.

put something **off**, **put off** doing something = *delay it*
- ○ The election has been **put off** until January.
- ○ We can't **put off** making a decision. We have to decide now.

C on and off for clothes etc.

put on clothes, glasses, make-up, a seat belt etc.
- ○ My hands were cold, so I **put** my gloves **on**.
put on weight = *get heavier*
- ○ I've **put on** two kilos in the last month.

try on clothes (to see if they fit)
- ○ I **tried on** a jacket in the shop, but it didn't look right.

take off clothes, glasses etc.
- ○ It was warm, so I **took off** my coat.

D off = away from a person or place

be off (to a place)
- ○ Tomorrow I**'m off** to Paris. / I**'m off** on holiday.
   (= I'm going to Paris / I'm going on holiday)

walk off / **run off** / **drive off** / **ride off** / **go off** (similar to **walk away** / **run away** etc.)
- ○ Anna got on her bike and **rode off**.
- ○ Mark left home at the age of eighteen and **went off** to Canada.

set off = *start a journey*
- ○ We **set off** early to avoid the traffic. (= We left early)

take off = *leave the ground (for planes)*
- ○ After a long delay, the plane finally **took off**.

see somebody **off** = *go with them to the airport/station to say goodbye*
- ○ Helen was going away. We went to the station with her to **see her off**.

Exercises

140.1 Complete the sentences using **put on** + the following:

    some music   the heating   the kettle   ~~the light~~   the oven

1 It was getting dark, so I ....*put the light on*......... .
2 It was getting cold, so I ....
3 I wanted to bake a cake, so I ....
4 I wanted to make some tea, so I ....
5 I wanted to relax, so I ....

140.2 Complete the sentences. Use a verb + **on** or **off**.

1 It was hot in the cinema, so I ....*took off*.... my jacket.
2 What are all these people doing? What's .... ?
3 The weather was too bad for the plane to .... , so the flight was delayed.
4 Rachel got into her car and .... at high speed.
5 Tim is too thin. He needs to .... weight.
6 We spent the whole day walking. We .... at 8 am and walked for ten hours.
7 Don't .... until tomorrow what you can do today.
8 They've changed their minds about getting married. The wedding has been ....
9 Are you cold? Shall I get you a sweater to .... ?
10 I .... some jeans in the shop, but they were too tight.
11 When I go away, I prefer to be alone at the station or airport. I don't like it when people come to .... me ....
12 I need to make an appointment to see the dentist, but I keep .... it ....

140.3 Look at the pictures and complete the sentences.

1 Her hands were cold, so she ....*put her gloves on*.... .

2 The plane .... at 10.55.

3 Maria .... , but it was too big for her.

4 The match .... because of the weather.

5 Mark's parents went to the airport to ....

6 He took his sunglasses out of his pocket and ....

A   *verb* + **on** = continue doing something

go on = *continue*
- ☐   The party **went on** until 4 o'clock in the morning.

go on / **carry on** doing something = *continue doing it*
- ☐   We can't **go on** spending money like this. We'll have nothing left soon.
- ☐   I don't want to **carry on** working here. I'm going to look for another job.

go on with / **carry on with** something = *continue it*
- ☐   Don't let me disturb you. Please **carry on with** what you're doing.

keep on doing (*or* **keep** doing) something = *do it continuously or repeatedly*
- ☐   He **keeps on** criticising me. It's not fair! (*or* He **keeps** criticising me.)

drive on / **walk on** / **play on** = *continue driving/walking/playing etc.*
- ☐   Shall we stop at this petrol station or shall we **drive on** to the next one?

B   **get on**

get on = *progress*
- ☐   How are you **getting on** in your new job? (= How is it going?)

get on (**with** somebody) = *have a good relationship*
- ☐   Joanne and Karen don't **get on**. They're always arguing.
- ☐   Richard **gets on** well **with** his neighbours. They're all very friendly.

get on with something = *continue something you have to do, usually after an interruption*
- ☐   I must **get on with** my work. I have a lot to do.

C   *verb* + **off**

doze off / **drop off** / **nod off** = *fall asleep*
- ☐   I **dozed off** during the lecture. It was very boring.

finish something **off** = *do the last part of it*
- ☐   A: Have you finished painting the kitchen?
  - B: Nearly. I'll **finish** it **off** tomorrow.

go off = *make an alarm sound*
- ☐   Did you hear the alarm **go off**?

put somebody **off** (doing) something *so that they don't want it or want to do it any more*
- ☐   We wanted to go to the exhibition, but we were **put off** by the long queue.
  (= we didn't go because of the long queue)
- ☐   What **put** you **off** applying for the job? Was the salary too low?

rip somebody **off** / be **ripped off** = *cheat somebody / be cheated*
- ☐   Did you really pay £2,000 for that painting? I think you were **ripped off**.
  (= you paid too much)

show off = *try to impress people with your ability, your knowledge etc.*
- ☐   Look at that boy on the bike riding with no hands. He's just **showing off**.

tell somebody **off** = *speak angrily to somebody because they did something wrong*
- ☐   Clare's mother **told** her **off** for wearing dirty shoes in the house.

»   go on / carry on / keep on → **Unit 53B**   Phrasal verbs 1 (Introduction) → **Unit 137**
More verbs + **on/off** → **Unit 140**   American English → **Appendix 7**

Exercises

141.1 **What do these sentences mean?**

1 I carried on studying.
   a ~~I started studying.~~   b I continued studying.   c ~~I put off studying.~~   (b *is correct*)

2 I nodded off.
   a I agreed.   b I felt sick.   c I fell asleep.

3 We were ripped off.
   a We were attacked.   b We paid too much.   c Our clothes were torn.

4 I told them off.
   a I criticised them.   b I was satisfied with them.   c I told them to go away.

5 They don't get on.
   a They don't like each other much.   b They are lazy.   c They don't know each other.

6 He was showing off.
   a He was joking.   b He was trying to impress us.   c He wasn't telling the truth.

141.2 **Complete each sentence using a verb + on or off.**

1 We can't ......*go on*...... spending money like this. We'll have nothing left soon.
2 I'm not ready to go home yet. I have a few things to ....
3 'Shall I stop the car here?'   'No, ... a bit further.'
4 Dan paid too much for the car he bought. I think he was ....
5 Emma is enjoying her course at university. She's .... very well.
6 The fire alarm .... and everybody had to leave the building.
7 Ben was .... by his boss for being late for work repeatedly.
8 The meeting has only just finished. It .... longer than expected.
9 I really like working with my colleagues. We all .... really well together.
10 I .... making the same mistake. It's very frustrating.
11 I've just had a coffee break, and now I must .... with my work.
12 Peter likes people to know how clever he is. He's always ....
13 We decided not to go to the concert. We were .... by the cost of tickets.
14 Jack paused for a moment and then .... with his story.
15 I was so tired at work today. I nearly .... at my desk a couple of times.

141.3 **Complete the sentences. Use a verb (in the correct form) + on or off. Sometimes you will need other words as well. Choose from:**

carry	finish	~~get~~	get	go	keep	rip	tell

1 A: How .....*are you getting on*..... in your new job?
   B: Fine, thanks. It's going very well.

2 A: What's Tanya like?
   B: She's very nice and easy-going. She .... everybody.

3 A: Is Gary going to retire soon?
   B: No, he likes his job and wants to .... working.

4 A: Have you written the letter you had to write?
   B: I've started it. I'll .... tomorrow.

5 A: We took a taxi to the airport. It cost £40.
   B: £40! Normally it costs about £20. You ....

6 A: Why were you late for work this morning?
   B: I overslept. My alarm clock didn't ....

7 A: Some children at the next table in the restaurant were behaving very badly.
   B: Why didn't their parents .... ?

8 A: Is Kate good at making decisions?
   B: No, she isn't. .... changing her mind.

➜ Additional exercises 37–41 (pages 323–25)

A Compare **up** and **down**:

put something **up** (on a wall etc.)
- ☐ I **put** a picture **up** on the wall.

pick something **up**
- ☐ There was a letter on the floor. I **picked** it **up** and looked at it.

stand up
- ☐ Alan **stood up** and walked out.

turn something **up**
- ☐ I can't hear the TV. Can you **turn** it **up** a bit?

take something **down** (from a wall etc.)
- ☐ I didn't like the picture, so I **took** it **down**.

put something **down**
- ☐ I stopped writing and **put down** my pen.

sit down / bend down / lie down
- ☐ I **bent down** to tie my shoelace.

turn something **down**
- ☐ The oven is too hot. **Turn** it **down** to 150 degrees.

B **knock down, cut down** etc.

knock down a building / **blow** something **down** / **cut** something **down** etc.
- ☐ Some old houses were **knocked down** to make way for the new shopping centre.
- ☐ Why did you **cut down** the tree in your garden?

be **knocked down** (by a car etc.)
- ☐ A man was **knocked down** by a car and taken to hospital.

burn down = *be destroyed by fire*
- ☐ They were able to put out the fire before the house **burnt down**.

C **down** = getting less

slow down = *go more slowly*
- ☐ You're driving too fast. **Slow down**.

calm (somebody) **down** = *become calmer, make somebody calmer*
- ☐ **Calm down**. There's no point in getting angry.

cut down (**on** something) = *eat, drink or do something less often*
- ☐ I'm trying to **cut down on** coffee. I drink too much of it.

D Other verbs + **down**

break down = *stop working (for machines, cars, relationships etc.)*
- ☐ The car **broke down** and I had to phone for help.
- ☐ Their marriage **broke down** after only a few months.

close down / shut down = *stop doing business*
- ☐ There used to be a shop at the end of the street. It **closed down** a few years ago.

let somebody **down** = *disappoint them because you didn't do what they hoped*
- ☐ You can always rely on Paul. He'll never **let** you **down**.

turn somebody/something **down** = *refuse an application, an offer etc.*
- ☐ I applied for several jobs, but I was **turned down** for all of them.
- ☐ Rachel was offered the job, but she decided to **turn** it **down**.

write something **down** = *write something on paper because you may need the information later*
- ☐ I can't remember Ben's address. I **wrote** it **down**, but I can't find it.

>> Phrasal verbs 1 (Introduction) → **Unit 137**   More verbs + **up** → **Units 143–144**

Exercises

142.1 Complete the sentences. Use a verb + up or down.

before   now   *before   now*   BUS STOP   VOLUME   LISA

1 There used to be a tree next to the house, but we ___cut it down___ .
2 There used to be some shelves on the wall, but I ....
3 The ceiling was so low, he couldn't .... straight.
4 She couldn't hear the radio very well, so she ....
5 While they were waiting for the bus, they .... on the ground.
6 A few trees .... in the storm last week.
7 We've got some new curtains, but we haven't .... yet.
8 Lisa dropped her keys, so she .... and ....

142.2 Complete the sentences. Use a verb (in the correct form) + down. Choose from:

| calm | cut | let | ~~take~~ | turn | write |

1 I don't like this picture on the wall. I'm going to ___take it down___ .
2 The music was too loud, so I ....
3 David was very angry. I tried to ....
4 I promised I would help Anna. I don't want to ....
5 I've forgotten my password. I should have ....
6 Those trees are beautiful. Please don't ....

142.3 Complete the sentences. Use a verb + down.

1 I stopped writing and ___put down___ my pen.
2 I was really angry. It took me a long time to ....
3 The train .... as it approached the station.
4 Sarah applied to study medicine at university, but she ....
5 Our car is very reliable. It has never ....
6 I spend too much money. I'm going to .... on things I don't need.
7 I didn't play well. I felt that I had .... the other players in the team.
8 The shop .... because it was losing money.
9 It's a very ugly building. Many people would like it to ....
10 I can't understand why you .... the chance of working in another country
   for a year. It would have been a great experience for you.
11 I didn't see the accident. Someone told me that a boy .... as he was
   crossing the road.
12 Peter got married when he was 20, but unfortunately the marriage .... a
   few years later.

A

go up, **come up**, **walk up** (**to** …) = *approach*
- ☐ A man **came up to** me in the street and asked me for money.

catch up (**with** somebody), **catch** somebody **up** = *move faster than people in front of you so that you reach them*
- ☐ I'm not ready to go yet. You go on and I'll **catch up with** you / I'll **catch** you **up**.

keep up (**with** somebody) = *continue at the same speed or level*
- ☐ You're walking too fast. I can't **keep up** (**with** you).
- ☐ You're doing well. **Keep** it **up**!

B

set up an organisation, a company, a business, a system, a website etc. = *start it*
- ☐ The government has **set up** a committee to investigate the problem.

take up a hobby, a sport, an activity etc. = *start doing it*
- ☐ Laura **took up** photography a few years ago. She takes really good pictures.

fix up a meeting etc. = *arrange it*
- ☐ We've **fixed up** a meeting for next Monday.

C

grow up = *become an adult*
- ☐ Amy was born in Hong Kong but **grew up** in Australia.

bring up a child = *raise, look after a child*
- ☐ Her parents died when she was a child and she was **brought up** by her grandparents.

D

clean up, **clear up**, **tidy up** = *make something clean, tidy etc.*
- ☐ Look at this mess! Who's going to **tidy up**? (*or* … to **tidy** it **up**)

wash up = *wash the plates, dishes etc. after a meal*
- ☐ I hate **washing up**. (*or* I hate **doing the washing-up**.)

E

end up somewhere, **end up** doing something etc.
- ☐ There was a fight in the street and three men **ended up** in hospital.
  (= that's what happened to these men in the end)
- ☐ I couldn't find a hotel and **ended up** sleeping on a bench at the station.
  (= that's what happened to me in the end)

give up = *stop trying*, **give** something **up** = *stop doing it*
- ☐ Don't **give up**. Keep trying!
- ☐ Sue got bored with her job and decided to **give** it **up**. (= stop doing it)

make up something, be **made up of** something
- ☐ Children under 16 **make up** half the population of the city.
  (= half the population are children under 16)
- ☐ Air is **made up** mainly **of** nitrogen and oxygen. (= Air consists of …)

take up space or time = *use space or time*
- ☐ Most of the space in the room was **taken up** by a large table.

turn up, **show up** = *arrive, appear*
- ☐ We arranged to meet David last night, but he didn't **turn up**.

use something **up** = *use all of it so that nothing is left*
- ☐ I'm going to make soup. We have a lot of vegetables and I want to **use them up**.

>> Phrasal verbs 1 (Introduction) ➜ **Unit 137**   More verbs + **up** ➜ **Units 142, 144**

Exercises

143.1 Look at the pictures and complete the sentences. Use <u>three</u> words each time, including a verb from Section A.

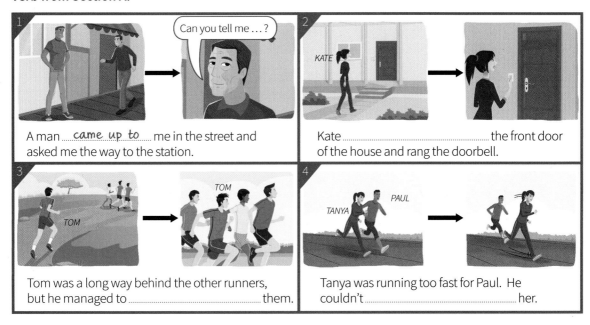

1   A man ...._came up to_.... me in the street and asked me the way to the station.

2   Kate .... the front door of the house and rang the doorbell.

3   Tom was a long way behind the other runners, but he managed to .... them.

4   Tanya was running too fast for Paul. He couldn't .... her.

143.2 Complete the sentences. Use a verb (in the correct form) + **up**. Choose from:

> ~~end~~   end   give   give   grow   make   take   take   turn   use   wash

1   I couldn't find a hotel and ...._ended up_.... sleeping on a bench at the station.
2   I'm feeling very tired now. I've .... all my energy.
3   After dinner I .... and put the dishes away.
4   People often ask children what they want to be when they ....
5   We arranged to meet Tom, but he didn't ....
6   Two years ago James .... his studies to be a professional footballer.
7   I don't do any sports right now, but I'm thinking of .... tennis.
8   You don't have enough determination. You .... too easily.
9   Karen travelled a lot for a few years and .... in Canada, where she still lives.
10 I do a lot of gardening. It .... most of my free time.
11 There are two universities in the city. Students .... 20 per cent of the population.

143.3 Complete the sentences. Use a verb + **up** (with any other necessary words). Choose from:

> bring   ~~catch~~   fix   ~~give~~   give   go   keep   keep   make   set   tidy

1   Sue got bored with her job and decided to ...._give it up_.... .
2   I'm not ready yet. You go on and I'll ...._catch up with_.... you.
3   The room is in a mess. I'd better ....
4   We expect to go away on holiday in July, but we haven't .... yet.
5   Steven is having problems at school. He can't .... the rest of the class.
6   I .... in the country, but I have always preferred cities.
7   Our team lost the game. We started well, but we couldn't ....
8   I saw Mike at the party, so I .... him and said hello.
9   Helen has her own website. A friend of hers helped her to ....
10 Ben was learning to play the guitar, but he found it hard and in the end he ....
11 When I was on holiday, I joined a tour group. The group .... two Americans, three Japanese, five Germans and myself.

➜ Additional exercises 37–41 (pages 323–25)

A

bring up a topic etc. = *introduce it in a conversation*
- ○ I don't want to hear any more about this. Please don't **bring** it **up** again.

come up = *be introduced in a conversation*
- ○ Some interesting things **came up** in our discussion yesterday.

come up with an idea, a suggestion etc. = *produce an idea*
- ○ Sarah is very creative. She's always **coming up with** new ideas.

make something **up** = *invent something that is not true*
- ○ What Kevin told you about himself wasn't true. He **made** it all **up**.

B

cheer up = *be happier*, **cheer** somebody **up** = *make somebody feel happier*
- ○ You look so sad! **Cheer up**!
- ○ Helen is depressed. What can we do to **cheer** her **up**?

save up for something / to do something = *save money to buy something*
- ○ Dan is **saving up** for a trip to New Zealand.

clear up = *become bright (for weather)*
- ○ It was raining when I got up, but it **cleared up** later.

C

blow up = *explode*, **blow** something **up** = *destroy it with a bomb etc.*
- ○ The engine caught fire and **blew up**.
- ○ The bridge was **blown up** during the war.

tear something **up** = *tear it into pieces*
- ○ I didn't read the letter. I just **tore** it **up** and threw it away.

beat somebody **up** = *hit someone repeatedly so that they are badly hurt*
- ○ A friend of mine was attacked and **beaten up**. He had to go to hospital.

D

break up, **split up** (**with** somebody) = *separate*
- ○ I'm surprised to hear that Kate and Paul have **split up**. They seemed very happy together.

do up a coat, a shoelace, buttons etc. = *fasten, tie etc.*
- ○ It's quite cold. **Do up** your coat before you go out.

do up a building, a room etc. = *repair and improve it*
- ○ The kitchen looks great now that it has been **done up**.

look something **up** in a dictionary/encyclopaedia etc.
- ○ If you don't know the meaning of a word, you can **look** it **up** (in a dictionary).

put up with something = *tolerate a difficult situation or person*
- ○ We live on a busy road, so we have to **put up with** a lot of noise from the traffic.

hold up a person, a plan etc. = *delay*
- ○ Don't wait for me. I don't want to **hold** you **up**.
- ○ Plans to build a new factory have been **held up** because of financial problems.

mix up people/things, **get** people/things **mixed up** = *you think one is the other*
- ○ The two brothers look very similar. People often **mix** them **up**.
  - *or* ... People often **get** them **mixed up**.

» Phrasal verbs 1 (Introduction) ➜ **Unit 137**   More verbs + **up** ➜ **Units 142–143**
American English ➜ **Appendix 7**

Exercises

144.1 **Which goes with which?**

1 He was angry and tore up	a a motorbike
2 Jane came up with	b a lot of bad weather
3 Paul is always making up	c your jacket
4 I think you should do up	d a good suggestion
5 I don't think you should bring up	e excuses
6 I'm saving up for	f ~~the letter~~
7 We had to put up with	g that subject

1 _f_
2 ....
3 ....
4 ....
5 ....
6 ....
7 ....

144.2 **Look at the pictures and complete the sentences. You will need two or three words each time.**

1 *this morning* / *now*
The weather was horrible this morning, but it's ..._cleared up_.... now.

2 Sorry I'm late.
LISA
Lisa was late because she was .... in the traffic.

3
They bought an old house and .... It's really nice now.

4 Come out for dinner with us!
JOE
Joe was really depressed. We took him out for a meal to ....

144.3 **Complete the sentences using a verb + up. Sometimes you will need other words as well.**

1 Some interesting things .....*came up*..... in our discussion yesterday.
2 The ship .... and sank. The cause of the explosion was never discovered.
3 James was attacked and .... by three men he'd never seen before.
4 Robert and Tina aren't together any more. They've ....
5 My hands were so cold, I found it hard to .... my shoelaces.
6 It's been raining all morning. Let's hope it .... this afternoon.
7 I turned up for the party on the wrong day. I got the dates ....

144.4 **Complete the sentences using a verb + up. You will need other words as well.**

1 Don't wait for me. I don't want to .....*hold you up*..... .
2 I don't know what this word means. I'll have to ....
3 I'm fed up with the way my boss treats me. I don't see why I should .... it.
4 I don't believe the story you're telling me. I think you're ....
5 The problem was complicated, but we managed to .... a solution.
6 Before you throw these documents away, you should ....
7 I'm trying to spend less money at the moment. I'm .... a holiday.
8 Tina doesn't like talking about the accident, so it's better not to ....
9 The words 'there' and 'their' sound the same, so it's easy to ....

→ Additional exercises 37–41 (pages 323–25)   289

Phrasal verbs 9 **away/back**

A
Compare **away** and **back**:

away = away from home
- ○ We're **going away** on holiday today.

away = away from a place, a person etc.
- ○ Sarah got into her car, started the engine and **drove away**.
- ○ I tried to take a picture of the bird, but it **flew away**.
- ○ I dropped the ticket, and it **blew away** in the wind.
- ○ The police searched the house and **took away** a computer.

In the same way you can say:
walk away, run away, look away etc.

back = back home
- ○ We'll **be back** in three weeks.

back = back to a place, a person etc.
- ○ A: I'm going out now.
  B: What time will you **be back**?
- ○ After eating at a restaurant, we **walked back** to our hotel.
- ○ I've still got Jane's keys. I forgot to **give** them **back** to her.
- ○ When you've finished with that book, can you **put** it **back** on the shelf?

In the same way you can say:
go back, come back, get back, take something **back** etc.

B
Other verbs + **away**

get away = escape, leave with difficulty
- ○ We tried to catch the thief, but she **got away**.

get away with something = do something wrong without being caught
- ○ I parked in a no-parking zone, but I **got away with** it. I didn't have to pay a fine.

keep away (**from** …) = don't go near
- ○ **Keep away from** the edge of the pool. You might fall in.

give something **away** = give it to somebody else because you don't want it any more
- ○ 'Did you sell your bike?' 'No, I **gave** it **away to a friend**.'

put something **away** = put it in the place where it is usually kept
- ○ When the children finished playing with their toys, they **put** them **away**.

throw something **away** = put it in the rubbish
- ○ I kept the letter, but I **threw away** the envelope.

C
Other verbs + **back**

wave back / **smile back** / **shout back** / **hit** somebody **back**
- ○ I waved to her, and she **waved back**.

call/phone/ring (somebody) **back** = return a phone call
- ○ I can't talk to you now. I'll **call** you **back** in ten minutes.

get back to somebody = reply to them by phone etc.
- ○ I sent him an email, but he never **got back to** me.

look back (**on** something) = think about what happened in the past
- ○ My first job was in a travel agency. I didn't like it much at the time but, **looking back on** it, I learnt a lot and it was a useful experience.

pay back money, **pay** somebody **back**
- ○ If you borrow money, you have to **pay** it **back**.
- ○ Thanks for lending me the money. I'll **pay** you **back** next week.

>> Phrasal verbs 1 (Introduction) → Unit 137

Exercises

145.1 **Look at the pictures and complete the sentences.**

1 She waved to him and he ...**waved back**... .

2 It was windy. I dropped a £20 note and it ....

3 She opened the letter, read it and ....in the envelope.

4 He tried to talk to her, but she just ....

5 Ellie threw the ball to Ben and he.................................... .
ELLIE   BEN

6 His shoes were worn out, so he.................................... .

145.2 **Complete the sentences. Use a verb +** away **or** back**.**

1 I was away all day yesterday. I ...**got back**... very late.

2 I haven't seen our neighbours for a while. I think they must ....

3 'I'm going out now.'   'OK. What time will you ....?'

4 I saw a man trying to break into a car. When he saw me, he ....

5 If you cheat in the exam, you might .... with it or you might get caught.

6 Be careful! That's an electric fence. Make sure you .... from it.

7 He wasn't very friendly. I smiled at him, but he didn't ....

145.3 **Complete the sentences. Use only one word each time.**

1 The woman got into her car, started the engine and ....**drove**.... away.

2 This box could be useful, so I won't .... it away.

3 Jane doesn't do anything at work. I don't know how she .... away with it.

4 I'm going out now. I'll .... back in about an hour.

5 You should think more about the future. Don't .... back all the time.

6 Gary is very generous. He won some money in the lottery and .... it all away.

7 I'll .... back to you as soon as I have the information you need.

8 I washed the dishes, dried them and .... them away.

145.4 **Complete the sentences. Use the verb in brackets +** away **or** back**.**

1 A: Do you still have my keys?
   B: No. Don't you remember? I ...**gave them back**... to you yesterday. (give)

2 A: Do you want this magazine?
   B: No, I've finished with it. You can .... (throw)

3 A: How are your new jeans? Do they fit you OK?
   B: No, they're too tight. I'm going to ....to the shop. (take)

4 A: Here's the money you asked me to lend you.
   B: Thanks. I'll ....as soon as I can. (pay)

5 A: What happened to all the books you used to have?
   B: I didn't want them any more, so I .... (give)

6 A: Did you phone Sarah?
   B: Yes, I left a message for her, but she hasn't .... (call)

→ **Additional exercises 37–41** (pages 323–25)

Appendix 1
Regular and irregular verbs

1.1 Regular verbs

If a verb is regular, the past simple and past participle end in **-ed**. For example:

infinitive	**clean**	**finish**	**use**	**paint**	**stop**	**carry**
past simple *past participle*	**cleaned**	**finished**	**used**	**painted**	**stopped**	**carried**

For spelling rules, see Appendix 6.

For the *past simple* (I **cleaned** / they **finished** / she **carried** etc.), see Unit 5.

We use the *past participle* to make the perfect tenses and all the passive forms.
Perfect tenses (**have/has/had** cleaned):
- ◯ I **have cleaned** the windows. (*present perfect* – see Units 7–8)
- ◯ They were still working. They **had**n't **finished**. (*past perfect* – see Unit 15)

Passive (**is** clean**ed** / **was** clean**ed** etc.):
- ◯ **He was carried** out of the room. (*past simple passive*) ⎫ see Units 42–44
- ◯ This gate has just **been painted**. (*present perfect passive*) ⎭

1.2 Irregular verbs

When the past simple and past participle do *not* end in **-ed** (for example, **I saw / I have seen**), the verb is *irregular*.

With some irregular verbs, all three forms (*infinitive*, *past simple* and *past participle*) are the same. For example, **hit**:
- ◯ Don't **hit** me. (*infinitive*)
- ◯ Somebody **hit** me as I came into the room. (*past simple*)
- ◯ I've never **hit** anybody in my life. (*past participle – present perfect*)
- ◯ George was **hit** on the head by a stone. (*past participle – passive*)

With other irregular verbs, the past simple is the same as the past participle (but different from the infinitive). For example, **tell → told**:
- ◯ Can you **tell** me what to do? (*infinitive*)
- ◯ She **told** me to come back the next day. (*past simple*)
- ◯ Have you **told** anybody about your new job? (*past participle – present perfect*)
- ◯ I was **told** to come back the next day. (*past participle – passive*)

With other irregular verbs, all three forms are different. For example, **wake → woke/woken**:
- ◯ I'll **wake** you up. (*infinitive*)
- ◯ I **woke** up in the middle of the night. (*past simple*)
- ◯ The baby has **woken** up. (*past participle – present perfect*)
- ◯ I was **woken** up by a loud noise. (*past participle – passive*)

1.3 The following verbs can be regular or irregular:

burn → burn**ed**	*or*	burn**t**	**smell** → smell**ed**	*or*	smel**t**
dream → dream**ed**	*or*	dream**t** [dremt]*	**spell** → spell**ed**	*or*	spel**t**
lean → lean**ed**	*or*	lean**t** [lent]*	**spill** → spill**ed**	*or*	spil**t**
learn → learn**ed**	*or*	learn**t**	**spoil** → spoil**ed**	*or*	spoil**t**

* pronunciation

So you can say:
- ◯ I **leant** out of the window. *or* I **leaned** out of the window.
- ◯ The dinner has been **spoiled**. *or* The dinner has been **spoilt**.

In British English the irregular form (**burnt/learnt** etc.) is more usual. For American English, see Appendix 7.

1.4   List of irregular verbs

infinitive	past simple	past participle
be	was/were	been
beat	beat	beaten
become	became	become
begin	began	begun
bend	bent	bent
bet	bet	bet
bite	bit	bitten
blow	blew	blown
break	broke	broken
bring	brought	brought
broadcast	broadcast	broadcast
build	built	built
burst	burst	burst
buy	bought	bought
catch	caught	caught
choose	chose	chosen
come	came	come
cost	cost	cost
creep	crept	crept
cut	cut	cut
deal	dealt	dealt
dig	dug	dug
do	did	done
draw	drew	drawn
drink	drank	drunk
drive	drove	driven
eat	ate	eaten
fall	fell	fallen
feed	fed	fed
feel	felt	felt
fight	fought	fought
find	found	found
flee	fled	fled
fly	flew	flown
forbid	forbade	forbidden
forget	forgot	forgotten
forgive	forgave	forgiven
freeze	froze	frozen
get	got	got/gotten
give	gave	given
go	went	gone
grow	grew	grown
hang	hung	hung
have	had	had
hear	heard	heard
hide	hid	hidden
hit	hit	hit
hold	held	held
hurt	hurt	hurt
keep	kept	kept
kneel	knelt	knelt
know	knew	known
lay	laid	laid
lead	led	led
leave	left	left
lend	lent	lent
let	let	let
lie	lay	lain

infinitive	past simple	past participle
light	lit	lit
lose	lost	lost
make	made	made
mean	meant	meant
meet	met	met
pay	paid	paid
put	put	put
read	read [red]*	read [red]*
ride	rode	ridden
ring	rang	rung
rise	rose	risen
run	ran	run
say	said	said
see	saw	seen
seek	sought	sought
sell	sold	sold
send	sent	sent
set	set	set
sew	sewed	sewn/sewed
shake	shook	shaken
shine	shone	shone
shoot	shot	shot
show	showed	shown/showed
shrink	shrank	shrunk
shut	shut	shut
sing	sang	sung
sink	sank	sunk
sit	sat	sat
sleep	slept	slept
slide	slid	slid
speak	spoke	spoken
spend	spent	spent
spit	spat	spat
split	split	split
spread	spread	spread
spring	sprang	sprung
stand	stood	stood
steal	stole	stolen
stick	stuck	stuck
sting	stung	stung
stink	stank	stunk
strike	struck	struck
swear	swore	sworn
sweep	swept	swept
swim	swam	swum
swing	swung	swung
take	took	taken
teach	taught	taught
tear	tore	torn
tell	told	told
think	thought	thought
throw	threw	thrown
understand	understood	understood
wake	woke	woken
wear	wore	worn
weep	wept	wept
win	won	won
write	wrote	written

* *pronunciation*

Appendix 2
Present and past tenses

	simple	*continuous*
present	**I do** *present simple* (→ Units 2–4) ○ Anna often **plays** tennis. ○ I **work** in a bank, but I **don't enjoy** it much. ○ **Do** you **like** parties? ○ It **doesn't rain** so much in summer.	**I am doing** *present continuous* (→ Units 1, 3–4) ○ 'Where's Anna?' 'She**'s playing** tennis.' ○ Please don't disturb me now. I**'m working**. ○ Hello! **Are** you **enjoying** the party? ○ It **isn't raining** at the moment.
present perfect	**I have done** *present perfect simple* (→ Units 7–8, 10–14) ○ Anna **has played** tennis many times. ○ I**'ve lost** my key. **Have** you **seen** it anywhere? ○ How long **have** you and Sam **known** each other? ○ A: Is it still raining? B: No, it **has stopped**. ○ The house is dirty. I **haven't cleaned** it for weeks.	**I have been doing** *present perfect continuous* (→ Units 9–11) ○ Anna is tired. She **has been playing** tennis. ○ You're out of breath. **Have** you **been running**? ○ How long **have** you **been learning** English? ○ It's still raining. It **has been raining** all day. ○ I **haven't been feeling** well recently. Perhaps I should go to the doctor.
past	**I did** *past simple* (→ Units 5–6, 13–14) ○ Anna **played** tennis yesterday afternoon. ○ I **lost** my key a few days ago. ○ There was a film on TV last night, but we **didn't watch** it. ○ What **did** you **do** when you finished work yesterday?	**I was doing** *past continuous* (→ Unit 6) ○ I saw Anna at the sports centre yesterday. She **was playing** tennis. ○ I dropped my key when I **was trying** to open the door. ○ The TV was on, but we **weren't watching** it. ○ What **were** you **doing** at this time yesterday?
past perfect	**I had done** *past perfect* (→ Unit 15) ○ It wasn't her first game of tennis. She **had played** many times before. ○ They couldn't get into the house because they **had lost** the key. ○ The house was dirty because I **hadn't cleaned** it for weeks.	**I had been doing** *past perfect continuous* (→ Unit 16) ○ Anna was tired yesterday evening because she **had been playing** tennis in the afternoon. ○ James decided to go to the doctor because he **hadn't been feeling** well.

For the passive, see Units 42–44.

Appendix 3
The future

3.1 *List of future forms:*

◯ I**'m leaving** tomorrow.	*present continuous*	(→ Unit 19A)
◯ My train **leaves** at 9.30.	*present simple*	(→ Unit 19B)
◯ I**'m going to leave** tomorrow.	**(be) going to**	(→ Units 20, 23)
◯ I**'ll leave** tomorrow.	**will**	(→ Units 21–23)
◯ I**'ll be leaving** tomorrow.	*future continuous*	(→ Unit 24)
◯ I**'ll have left** by this time tomorrow.	*future perfect*	(→ Unit 24)
◯ I hope to see you before I **leave** tomorrow.	*present simple*	(→ Unit 25)

3.2 *Future actions*

We use the present continuous (**I'm doing**) for arrangements:
- ◯ I**'m leaving** tomorrow. I've got my plane ticket. (already planned and arranged)
- ◯ 'When **are** they **getting** married?'   'On 24 July.'

We use the present simple (**I leave** / it **leaves** etc.) for timetables, programmes etc. :
- ◯ My train **leaves** at 11.30. (according to the timetable)
- ◯ What time **does** the film **begin**?

We use (**be**) **going to** … to say what somebody has already decided to do:
- ◯ I've decided not to stay here any longer. I**'m going to leave** tomorrow. (*or* I**'m leaving** tomorrow.)
- ◯ 'Your shoes are dirty.'   'Yes, I know. I**'m going to clean** them.'

We use **will** (**'ll**) when we decide or agree to do something at the time of speaking:
- ◯ A: I don't want you to stay here any longer.
  B: OK. I**'ll leave** tomorrow. (B decides this at the time of speaking)
- ◯ That bag looks heavy. I**'ll help** you with it.
- ◯ I **won't tell** anybody what happened. I promise. (**won't** = **will not**)

3.3 *Future happenings and situations*

Most often we use **will** to talk about future happenings ('something **will happen**') or situations ('something **will be**'):
- ◯ I don't think John is happy at work. I think he**'ll leave** soon.
- ◯ This time next year I**'ll be** in Japan. Where **will** you **be**?

We use (**be**) **going to** when the situation *now* shows what **is going to happen** *in the future*:
- ◯ Look at those black clouds. It**'s going to rain**. (you can see the clouds *now*)

3.4 *Future continuous and future perfect*

Will be (do)**ing** = will be in the middle of (doing something):
- ◯ This time next week I'll be on holiday. I**'ll be lying** on a beach or **swimming** in the sea.

We also use **will be -ing** for future actions (see Unit 24C):
- ◯ What time **will** you **be leaving** tomorrow?

We use **will have** (**done**) to say that something will already be complete before a time in the future:
- ◯ I won't be here this time tomorrow. I**'ll have** already **left**.

3.5 We use the *present* (*not* will) after **when/if/while/before** etc. (see Unit 25):
- ◯ I hope to see you **before I leave** tomorrow. (*not* before I will leave)
- ◯ **When** you **are** in London again, come and see us. (*not* When you will be)
- ◯ **If** we **don't hurry**, we'll be late.

Appendix 4
Modal verbs (**can/could/will/would** etc.)

This appendix is a summary of modal verbs. For more information, see Units 21–41.

4.1 Compare **can/could** etc. for actions:

can	○ I **can go** out tonight. (= there is nothing to stop me)
	○ I **can't go** out tonight.
could	○ I **could go** out tonight, but I'm not very keen.
	○ I **couldn't go** out last night. (= I wasn't able)
can *or* may	○ **Can** } I **go** out tonight? (= do you allow me?)
	○ **May** }
will/won't	○ I think I'**ll go** out tonight.
	○ I promise I **won't go** out.
would	○ I **would go** out tonight, but I have too much to do.
	○ I promised I **wouldn't go** out.
shall	○ **Shall I go** out tonight? (= do you think it is a good idea?)
should *or* ought to	○ I { **should** **ought to** } **go** out tonight. (= it would be a good thing to do)
must	○ I **must go** out tonight. (= it is necessary)
	○ I **mustn't go** out tonight. (= it is necessary that I do *not* go out)
needn't	○ I **needn't go** out tonight. (= it is not necessary)

Compare **could have** … / **would have** … etc. :

could	○ I **could have gone** out last night, but I decided to stay at home.
would	○ I **would have gone** out last night, but I had too much to do.
should *or* ought to	○ I { **should** **ought to** } **have gone** out last night. I'm sorry I didn't.
needn't	○ I **needn't have gone** out last night. (= I went out, but it was not necessary)

4.2 We use **will/would/may** etc. to say whether something is possible, impossible, probable, certain etc. Compare:

will	○ 'What time **will** she **be** here?' 'She'**ll be** here soon.'
would	○ She **would be** here now, but she's been delayed.
should *or* ought to	○ She { **should** **ought to** } **be** here soon. (= I expect she will be here soon)
may *or* might *or* could	○ She { **may** **might** **could** } **be** here now. I'm not sure. (= it's possible that she is here)
must	○ She **must be** here. I saw her come in.
can't	○ She **can't** possibly **be** here. I know for certain that she's away on holiday.

Compare **would have** … / **should have** … etc. :

will	○ She **will have arrived** by now. (= before now)
would	○ She **would have arrived** earlier, but she was delayed.
should *or* ought to	○ I wonder where she is. She { **should** **ought to** } **have arrived** by now.
may *or* might *or* could	○ She { **may** **might** **could** } **have arrived**. I'm not sure. (= it's possible that she has arrived)
must	○ She **must have arrived** by now. (= I'm sure – there is no other possibility)
can't	○ She **can't** possibly **have arrived** yet. It's much too early. (= it's impossible)

Appendix 5
Short forms (**I'm** / **you've** / **didn't** etc.)

5.1 In spoken English we usually say **I'm** / **you've** / **didn't** etc. *(short forms* or *contractions)* rather than **I am** / **you have** / **did not** etc. We also use these short forms in informal writing (for example, a letter or message to a friend).

When we write short forms, we use an *apostrophe* (') for the missing letter(s):

I'm = I <u>a</u>m   you've = you <u>have</u>   didn't = did n<u>o</u>t

5.2 List of short forms:

'm = am	I'm						
's = is *or* has		he's	she's	it's			
're = are					you're	we're	they're
've = have	I've				you've	we've	they've
'll = will	I'll	he'll	she'll		you'll	we'll	they'll
'd = would *or* had	I'd	he'd	she'd		you'd	we'd	they'd

's can be **is** or **has**:
- ○ She**'s** ill. (= She **is** ill.)
- ○ She**'s** gone away. (= She **has** gone)

but **let's** = let **us**:
- ○ Let**'s** go now. (= Let **us** go)

'd can be **would** or **had**:
- ○ I**'d** see a doctor if I were you. (= I **would** see)
- ○ I**'d** never seen her before. (= I **had** never seen)

We use some of these short forms (especially **'s**) after question words (**who/what** etc.) and after **that/there/here**:

who**'s**   what**'s**   where**'s**   how**'s**   that**'s**   there**'s**   here**'s**   who**'ll**   there**'ll**   who**'d**

- ○ **Who's** that woman over there? (= who **is**)
- ○ **What's** happened? (= what **has**)
- ○ Do you think **there'll** be many people at the party? (= there **will**)

We also use short forms (especially **'s**) after a noun:
- ○ **Katherine's** going out tonight. (= Katherine **is**)
- ○ **My best friend's** just got married. (= My best friend **has**)

You cannot use **'m** / **'s** / **'re** / **'ve** / **'ll** / **'d** at the end of a sentence (because the verb is stressed in this position):
- ○ 'Are you tired?' 'Yes, I **am**.' (*not* Yes, I'm.)
- ○ Do you know where she **is**? (*not* Do you know where she's?)

5.3 Negative short forms

isn't	(= is not)	don't	(= do not)	haven't	(= have not)
aren't	(= are not)	doesn't	(= does not)	hasn't	(= has not)
wasn't	(= was not)	didn't	(= did not)	hadn't	(= had not)
weren't	(= were not)				
can't	(= cannot)	couldn't	(= could not)	mustn't	(= must not)
won't	(= will not)	wouldn't	(= would not)	needn't	(= need not)
shan't	(= shall not)	shouldn't	(= should not)	daren't	(= dare not)

Negative short forms for **is** and **are** can be:

he **isn't** / she **isn't** / it **isn't**   *or*   he**'s not** / she**'s not** / it**'s not**
you **aren't** / we **aren't** / they **aren't**   *or*   you**'re not** / we**'re not** / they**'re not**

Appendix 6
Spelling

6.1 Nouns, verbs and adjectives can have the following endings:

noun + -**s**/-**es** (plural)	book**s**	idea**s**	match**es**
verb + -**s**/-**es** (after **he**/**she**/**it**)	work**s**	enjoy**s**	wash**es**
verb + -**ing**	work**ing**	enjoy**ing**	wash**ing**
verb + -**ed**	work**ed**	enjoy**ed**	wash**ed**
adjective + -**er** (comparative)	cheap**er**	quick**er**	bright**er**
adjective + -**est** (superlative)	cheap**est**	quick**est**	bright**est**
adjective + -**ly** (adverb)	cheap**ly**	quick**ly**	bright**ly**

When we use these endings, there are sometimes changes in spelling. These changes are listed below.

6.2 Nouns and verbs + -**s**/-**es**

The ending is -**es** when the word ends in -**s**/-**ss**/-**sh**/-**ch**/-**x**:

    bu**s**/bus**es**   mi**ss**/miss**es**   wa**sh**/wash**es**
    mat**ch**/match**es**   sear**ch**/search**es**   bo**x**/box**es**

Note also:

    potato/potato**es**   tomato/tomato**es**
    do/do**es**   go/go**es**

6.3 Words ending in -**y** (bab**y**, carr**y**, eas**y** etc.)

> If a word ends in a *consonant** + **y** (-**by**/-**ry**/-**sy**/-**vy** etc.)
>
> **y** changes to **ie** before the ending -**s**:
>   bab**y**/bab**ies**   stor**y**/stor**ies**   countr**y**/countr**ies**   secretar**y**/secretar**ies**
>   hurr**y**/hurr**ies**   stud**y**/stud**ies**   appl**y**/appl**ies**   try/tr**ies**
>
> **y** changes to **i** before the ending -**ed**:
>   hurr**y**/hurr**ied**   stud**y**/stud**ied**   appl**y**/appl**ied**   try/tr**ied**
>
> **y** changes to **i** before the endings -**er** and -**est**:
>   eas**y**/eas**ier**/eas**iest**   heav**y**/heav**ier**/heav**iest**   luck**y**/luck**ier**/luck**iest**
>
> **y** changes to **i** before the ending -**ly**:
>   eas**y**/eas**ily**   heav**y**/heav**ily**   temporar**y**/temporar**ily**

y does *not* change before -**ing**:

    hurry**ing**   study**ing**   apply**ing**   try**ing**

y does *not* change if the word ends in a *vowel** + **y** (-**ay**/-**ey**/-**oy**/-**uy**):

    pla**y**/pla**ys**/pla**yed**   monk**ey**/monk**eys**   enj**oy**/enj**oys**/enj**oyed**   b**uy**/b**uys**

An exception is: d**ay**/d**aily**
Note also: p**ay**/p**aid**   l**ay**/l**aid**   s**ay**/s**aid**

6.4 Verbs ending in -**ie** (d**ie**, l**ie**, t**ie**)

If a verb ends in -**ie**, **ie** changes to **y** before the ending -**ing**:

    d**ie**/d**ying**   l**ie**/l**ying**   t**ie**/t**ying**

---

* **a e i o u** are *vowel* letters.
The other letters (**b c d f g** etc.) are *consonant* letters.

6.5 Words ending in -**e** (hop**e**, danc**e**, wid**e** etc.)

Verbs

If a verb ends in -**e**, we leave out **e** before the ending -**ing**:

    hop**e**/hop**ing**   smil**e**/smil**ing**   danc**e**/danc**ing**   confus**e**/confus**ing**

Exceptions are **be**/**being** *and* verbs ending in -**ee**:

    s**ee**/s**eeing**   agr**ee**/agr**eeing**

If a verb ends in -**e**, we add -**d** for the past (of regular verbs):

    hop**e**/hop**ed**   smil**e**/smil**ed**   danc**e**/danc**ed**   confus**e**/confus**ed**

Adjectives and adverbs

If an adjective ends in -**e**, we add -**r** and -**st** for the comparative and superlative:

    wid**e**/wid**er**/wid**est**   lat**e**/lat**er**/lat**est**   larg**e**/larg**er**/larg**est**

If an adjective ends in -**e**, we *keep* **e** before -**ly** in the adverb:

    polit**e**/polit**ely**   extrem**e**/extrem**ely**   absolut**e**/absolut**ely**

If an adjective ends in -**le** (simp**le**, terrib**le** etc.), the adverb ending is -**ply**, -**bly** etc. :

    sim**ple**/sim**ply**   terri**ble**/terri**bly**   reasona**ble**/reasona**bly**

6.6 Doubling consonants (**stop**/**stopping**/**stopped**, **wet**/**wetter**/**wettest** etc.)

Sometimes a word ends in *vowel* + *consonant*. For example:

    st**op**   pl**an**   r**ub**   b**ig**   w**et**   th**in**   pref**er**   regr**et**

Before the endings -**ing**/-**ed**/-**er**/-**est**, we double the consonant at the end. So **p** → **pp**, **n** → **nn** etc. For example:

sto**p**	p → **pp**	sto**pp**ing	sto**pp**ed
pla**n**	n → **nn**	pla**nn**ing	pla**nn**ed
ru**b**	b → **bb**	ru**bb**ing	ru**bb**ed
bi**g**	g → **gg**	bi**gg**er	bi**gg**est
we**t**	t → **tt**	we**tt**er	we**tt**est
thi**n**	n → **nn**	thi**nn**er	thi**nn**est

If the word has more than one syllable (**prefer**, **begin** etc.), we double the consonant at the end *only if the final syllable is stressed*:

    preFER / prefe**rr**ing / prefe**rr**ed   perMIT / permi**tt**ing / permi**tt**ed

    reGRET / regre**tt**ing / regre**tt**ed   beGIN / begi**nn**ing

If the final syllable is not stressed, we do *not* double the final consonant:

    VISit / visi**t**ing / visi**t**ed   deVELop / develo**p**ing / develo**p**ed

    HAPpen / happe**n**ing / happe**n**ed   reMEMber / remembe**r**ing / remembe**r**ed

In British English, verbs ending in -**l** have -**ll**- before -**ing** and -**ed** whether the final syllable is stressed or not:

    trave**l** / trave**ll**ing / trave**ll**ed   cance**l** / cance**ll**ing / cance**ll**ed

For American spelling, see Appendix 7.

Note that

we do *not* double the final consonant if the word ends in *two* consonants (-**rt**, -**lp**, -**ng** etc.):

    sta**rt** / sta**rt**ing / sta**rt**ed   he**lp** / he**lp**ing / he**lp**ed   lo**ng** / lo**ng**er / lo**ng**est

we do *not* double the final consonant if there are *two* vowel letters before it (-**oil**, -**eed** etc.):

    b**oil** / b**oil**ing / b**oil**ed   n**eed** / n**eed**ing / n**eed**ed   expl**ain** / expl**ain**ing / expl**ain**ed

    ch**eap** / ch**eap**er / ch**eap**est   l**oud** / l**oud**er / l**oud**est   qu**iet** / qu**iet**er / qu**iet**est

we do *not* double **y** or **w** at the end of words. (At the end of words **y** and **w** are not consonants.)

    sta**y** / sta**y**ing / sta**y**ed   gro**w** / gro**w**ing   ne**w** / ne**w**er / ne**w**est

Appendix 7
American English

There are a few grammatical differences between British English and American English:

Unit	BRITISH	AMERICAN
7A–B and 13A	The *present perfect* is often used for new or recent happenings: ◯ I**'ve lost** my key. **Have** you **seen** it? ◯ Sally isn't here. She**'s gone** out. The *present perfect* is used with **just** and **already**: ◯ I'm not hungry. I**'ve just had** lunch. ◯ A: What time is Mark leaving? ◯ B: He**'s already left**.	The *past simple* is more common for new or recent happenings: ◯ I **lost** my key. **Did** you **see** it? ◯ Sally isn't here. **She went out**. The *past simple* is more common with **just** and **already**: ◯ I'm not hungry. I **just had** lunch. ◯ A: What time is Mark leaving? ◯ B: He **already left**.
17C	**have** a bath, **have** a shower **have** a break, **have** a holiday	**take** a bath, **take** a shower **take** a break, **take** a vacation
21D and 22D	**Will** or **shall** can be used with **I/we**: ◯ I **will/shall** be late this evening. **Shall I ... ?** and **shall we ... ?** are used to ask for advice etc. : ◯ Which way **shall we** go?	**Shall** is unusual: ◯ I **will** be late this evening. **Should I ... ?** and **should we ... ?** are used to ask for advice etc. : ◯ Which way **should we** go?
28	British speakers use **can't** to say they believe something is not probable: ◯ Sarah hasn't contacted me. She **can't have got** my message.	American speakers use **must not** in this situation: ◯ Sarah hasn't contacted me. She **must not have gotten** my message.
32	You can use **needn't** or **don't need to**: ◯ We **needn't** hurry. *or* We **don't need to** hurry.	**Needn't** is unusual. The usual form is **don't need to**: ◯ We **don't need to** hurry.
34A–B	**insist**, **demand** etc. + **should** ◯ I insisted that he **should apologise**. ◯ We demanded that something **should be** done about the problem.	**insist**, **demand** etc. + *subjunctive* (see Unit 34B) ◯ I insisted that he **apologize**.* ◯ We demanded that something **be done** about the problem.
51B	**Have you? / Isn't she?** etc. ◯ A: Lisa isn't very well today. ◯ B: **Isn't she?** What's wrong with her?	**You have? / She isn't?** etc. ◯ A: Lisa isn't very well today. ◯ B: **She isn't?** What's wrong with her?
59D	I**'d rather** you **did** something ◯ Are you going to tell Anna, or **would** you **rather** I **told** her?	I**'d rather** you **do** something ◯ Are you going to tell Anna, or **would** you **rather** I **tell** her?
70B	**Accommodation** is usually uncountable: ◯ There **is** plenty of excellent **accommodation** in the city.	**Accommodation** can be countable: ◯ There **are** plenty of excellent **accommodations** in the city.
74B	to/in **hospital** (without **the**) ◯ Joe had an accident and was taken to **hospital**.	to/in **the hospital** ◯ Joe had an accident and was taken to **the hospital**.

* Many verbs ending in **-ise** in British English (apolog**ise**/organ**ise**/special**ise** etc.) are spelt with **-ize** (apolog**ize**/organ**ize**/special**ize** etc.) in American English.

Unit	BRITISH	AMERICAN
79C	Nouns like **government/team/family** etc. can have a singular or plural verb: ☐ The team **is/are** playing well.	These nouns normally take a singular verb in American English: ☐ The team **is** playing well.
121B	**at the weekend / at weekends** ☐ Will you be here **at the weekend**?	**on the weekend / on weekends** ☐ Will you be here **on the weekend**?
124D	**at** the front / **at** the back (of a group etc.) ☐ (in a theatre) Let's sit **at the front**.	**in** the front / **in** the back (of a group etc.) ☐ (in a theater) Let's sit **in the front**.
131C	**different from** or **different to** ☐ The film was **different from/to** what I'd expected.	**different from** or **different than** ☐ The movie was **different from/than** what I'd expected.
137A	**round** or **around** ☐ He turned **round**. or He turned **around**.	**around** (not usually round) ☐ He turned **around**.
137C	**fill in** or **fill out** (a form etc.) ☐ Please **fill in** this form. or Please **fill out** this form.	**fill out** (a form) ☐ Please **fill out** this form.
141B	**get on** (with somebody) ☐ Richard **gets on** well with his neighbours.	**get along** (with somebody) ☐ Richard **gets along** well with his neighbors.
142B	**knock down** (a building) ☐ Some old houses were **knocked down** to make way for a new shopping centre.	**tear down** a building ☐ Some old houses were **torn down** to make way for a new shopping mall.
144D	**do up** a house etc. ☐ That old house looks great now that it has been **done up**.	**fix up** a house etc. ☐ That old house looks great now that it has been **fixed up**.

Appendix	BRITISH	AMERICAN
1.3	**Burn, spell** etc. can be regular or irregular (**burned** or **burnt**, **spelled** or **spelt** etc.). The past participle of **get** is **got**: ☐ Your English has **got** much better. (= has become much better) **Have got** is also an alternative to **have**: ☐ **I've got** a car. (= I **have** a car)	**Burn, spell** etc. are normally regular (**burned**, **spelled** etc.). The past participle of **get** is **gotten**: ☐ Your English has **gotten** much better. **Have got** = have (as in British English): ☐ **I've got** a car.
6.6	British spelling: travel → travelling / travelled cancel → cancelling / cancelled	American spelling: travel → traveling / traveled cancel → canceling / canceled

Additional exercises

These exercises are divided into the following sections:

Present and past

Units 1–6, Appendix 2

1   Put the verb into the correct form: present simple (**I do**), present continuous (**I am doing**), past simple (**I did**) or past continuous (**I was doing**).

1   We can go out now. ....It isn't raining.... (it / not / rain) any more.
2   Katherine ....was waiting.... (wait) for me when ....I arrived.... (I / arrive).
3   .... (I / get) hungry. Let's go and have something to eat.
4   What .... (you / do) in your spare time? Do you have any hobbies?
5   The weather was horrible when .... (we / arrive). It was cold and
     .... (it / rain) hard.
6   Louise usually .... (phone) me on Fridays, but
     .... (she / not / phone) last Friday.
7   A: When I last saw you, ... (you / think) of moving to a new flat.
     B: That's right, but in the end .... (I / decide) to stay where I was.
8   Why .... (you / look) at me like that? What's the matter?
9   It's usually dry here at this time of the year. .... (it / not / rain) much.
10   I waved to Ben, but he didn't see me. .... (he / not / look) in my
     direction.
11   Lisa was busy when .... (we / go) to see her yesterday. She had an
     exam today and .... (she / prepare) for it.
     .... (we / not / want) to disturb her, so ....
     (we / not / stay) very long.
12   When I first .... (tell) Tom what happened, ...
     (he / not / believe) me. .... (he / think) that ....
     (I / joke).

Present and past

2 **Which is correct?**

1 Everything is going well. We ~~didn't have~~ / haven't had any problems so far.
    (haven't had *is correct*)
2 Lisa <u>didn't go</u> / <u>hasn't gone</u> to work yesterday. She wasn't feeling well.
3 Look! That man over there <u>wears</u> / <u>is wearing</u> the same sweater as you.
4 I <u>went</u> / <u>have been</u> to New Zealand last year.
5 I <u>didn't hear</u> / <u>haven't heard</u> from Jess recently. I hope she's OK.
6 I wonder why James <u>is</u> / <u>is being</u> so nice to me today. He isn't usually like that.
7 Jane had a book open in front of her, but she <u>didn't read</u> / <u>wasn't reading</u> it.
8 I wasn't very busy. I <u>didn't have</u> / <u>wasn't having</u> much to do.
9 <u>It begins</u> / <u>It's beginning</u> to get dark. Shall I turn on the light?
10 After leaving school, Mark <u>worked</u> / <u>has worked</u> in a hotel for a while.
11 When Sue heard the news, she <u>wasn't</u> / <u>hasn't been</u> very pleased.
12 This is a nice hotel, isn't it? Is this the first time <u>you stay</u> / <u>you've stayed</u> here?
13 I need a new job. <u>I'm doing</u> / <u>I've been doing</u> the same job for too long.
14 'Anna has gone out.' 'Oh, has she? What time <u>did she go</u> / <u>has she gone</u>?'
15 'You look tired.' 'Yes, <u>I've played</u> / <u>I've been playing</u> basketball.'
16 Where <u>are you coming</u> / <u>do you come</u> from? Are you American?
17 I'd like to see Tina again. It's a long time <u>since I saw her</u> / <u>that I didn't see her</u>.
18 Robert and Maria have been married <u>since 20 years</u> / <u>for 20 years</u>.

3 **Complete each question using a suitable verb.**

1 A: I'm looking for Paul. ....*Have you seen*.... him?
    B: Yes, he was here a moment ago.

2 A: Why ....*did you go*.... to bed so early last night?
    B: I was feeling very tired.

3 A: Where .... ?
    B: Just to the shop at the end of the street. I'll only be ten minutes.

4 A: .... TV every day?
    B: No, only if there's something special on.

5 A: Your house is lovely. How long .... here?
    B: Nearly ten years.

6 A: How was your parents' holiday? .... a nice time?
    B: Yes, they really enjoyed it.

7 A: .... Sarah recently?
    B: Yes, we had lunch together a few days ago.

8 A: Can you describe the woman you saw? What .... ?
    B: A red sweater and black jeans.

9 A: I'm sorry to keep you waiting. .... long?
    B: No, only about ten minutes.

10 A: How long .... to get from here to the airport?
    B: Usually about 45 minutes. It depends on the traffic.

11 A: .... this song before?
    B: No, this is the first time. I like it.

12 A: .... to the United States?
    B: No, never, but I went to Canada a few years ago.

4 **Use your own ideas to complete B's sentences.**

1 A: What's Chicago like? Is it a good place to visit?
  B: I've no idea. __I've never been__ .... there.

2 A: How well do you know Ben?
  B: Very well. We .... since we were children.

3 A: Did you enjoy your holiday?
  B: Yes, it was really good. It's the best holiday ....

4 A: Is David still here?
  B: No, I'm afraid he isn't. .... about ten minutes ago.

5 A: I like your suit. I haven't seen it before.
  B: It's new. It's the first time ....

6 A: How did you cut your knee?
  B: I slipped and fell when .... tennis.

7 A: Do you ever go swimming?
  B: Not these days. I haven't .... a long time.

8 A: How often do you go to the cinema?
  B: Very rarely. It's nearly a year .... to the cinema.

9 A: I bought some new shoes. Do you like them?
  B: Yes, they're very nice. Where .... them?

Present and past   Units 1–17, 110, Appendix 2

5 **Put the verb into the correct form: past simple (I did), past continuous (I was doing), past perfect (I had done) or past perfect continuous (I had been doing).**

Yesterday afternoon Sarah ......__went__...... (go) to the station to meet Paul. When she
.... (get) there, Paul .... (already / wait)
for her. His train .... (arrive) early.

When I got home, Ben .... (lie) on the sofa. The TV was on,
but he .... (not / watch) it. He .... (fall)
asleep and .... (snore) loudly. I .... (turn) the
TV off and just then he .... (wake) up.

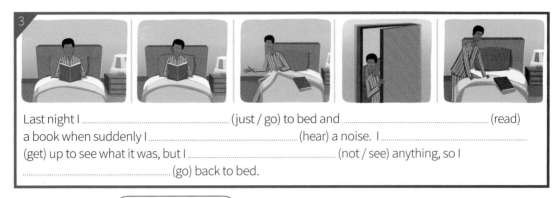

Last night I .... (just / go) to bed and .... (read)
a book when suddenly I .... (hear) a noise. I ....
(get) up to see what it was, but I .... (not / see) anything, so I
.... (go) back to bed.

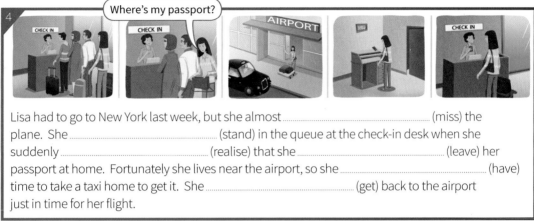

Lisa had to go to New York last week, but she almost .... (miss) the
plane. She .... (stand) in the queue at the check-in desk when she
suddenly .... (realise) that she .... (leave) her
passport at home. Fortunately she lives near the airport, so she .... (have)
time to take a taxi home to get it. She .... (get) back to the airport
just in time for her flight.

I .... (meet) Peter and Lucy yesterday as I ....
(walk) through the park. They .... (be) to the Sports Centre where they
.... (play) tennis. They .... (go) to a cafe and
.... (invite) me to join them, but I ....
(arrange) to meet another friend and .... (not / have) time.

6 Make sentences from the words in brackets. Put the verb into the correct form: present
perfect (I have done), present perfect continuous (I have been doing), past perfect (I had
done) or past perfect continuous (I had been doing).

1 Amanda is sitting on the ground. She's out of breath.
(she / run) *She has been running.*
2 Where's my bag? I left it under this chair.
(somebody / take / it) ....
3 We were all surprised when Jess and Nick got married last year.
(they / only / know / each other / a few weeks)
....
4 It's still raining. I wish it would stop.
(it / rain / all day) ....
5 Suddenly I woke up. I was confused and didn't know where I was.
(I / dream) ....

6 It was lunchtime, but I wasn't hungry. I didn't want to eat anything.
   (I / have / a big breakfast) ....
7 Every year Robert and Tina spend a few days at the same hotel by the sea.
   (they / go / there for years) ....
8 I've got a headache.
   (I / have / it / since I got up) ....
9 Next month Gary is going to run in a marathon.
   (he / train / very hard for it) ....

7 **Put the verb into the correct form.**

Sarah and Joe are old friends. They meet by chance at a train station.

SARAH: Hello, Joe. (1) .... (I / not / see)
       you for ages. How are you?
JOE: I'm fine. How about you?
       (2) .... (you / look) good.
SARAH: Thanks. You too.
       So, (3) .... (you / go) somewhere or
       (4) .... (you / meet) somebody?
JOE: (5) .... (I / go) to London for a business meeting.
SARAH: Oh. (6) .... (you / often / go) away on business?
JOE: Quite often, yes. And you? Where (7) .... (you / go)?
SARAH: Nowhere. (8) .... (I / meet) a friend. Unfortunately
       her train (9) .... (be) delayed –
       (10) .... (I / wait) here for nearly an hour.
JOE: How are your children?
SARAH: They're all fine, thanks. The youngest (11) .... (just / start)
       school.
JOE: How (12) .... (she / get) on?
       (13) .... (she / like) it?
SARAH: Yes, (14) .... (she / think) it's great.
JOE: (15) .... (you / work) at the moment? The last time I
       (16) .... (speak) to you, (17) ....
       (you / work) for an insurance company.
SARAH: That's right. Unfortunately the company (18) .... (go) out
       of business a couple of months after (19) .... (I / start)
       work there, so (20) .... (I / lose) my job.
JOE: And (21) .... (you / not / have) a job since then?
SARAH: Not a permanent job. (22) .... (I / have) a few temporary
       jobs. By the way, (23) .... (you / see) Matt recently?
JOE: Matt? He's in Canada.
SARAH: Really? How long (24) .... (he / be) in Canada?
JOE: About a year now. (25) .... (I / see) him a few days before
       (26) .... (he / go). (27) .... (he / be)
       unemployed for months, so (28) .... (he / decide) to try his
       luck somewhere else. (29) .... (he / really / look forward)
       to going.
SARAH: So, what (30) .... (he / do) there?
JOE: I have no idea. (31) .... (I / not / hear) from him since
       (32) .... (he / leave). Anyway, I have to go and catch my
       train. It was really good to see you again.
SARAH: You too. Bye! Have a good trip!
JOE: Thanks. Bye.

8 **Put the verb into the most suitable form.**

1 Who .... (invent) the bicycle?
2 'Do you still have a headache?' 'No, ... (it / go). I'm OK now.'
3 I was the last to leave the office last night. Everybody else .... (go)
   home when I .... (leave).
4 What .... (you / do) last weekend?
   (you / go) anywhere?
5 I like your car. How long .... (you / have) it?
6 It's a shame the trip was cancelled. I .... (look) forward to it.
7 Jane is an experienced teacher and loves her job. .... (she / teach)
   for 15 years.
8 Emily .... (buy) a new dress last week, but ....
   (she / not / wear) it yet.
9 A few days ago .... (I / meet) a man at a party whose face .... (be)
   very familiar. At first I couldn't think where .... (I / see)
   him before. Then suddenly .... (I / remember) who ....
   (he / be).
10 .... (you / hear) of Agatha Christie? .... (she / be)
   a writer who .... (die) in 1976. .... (she / write)
   more than 70 detective novels, but .... (I / not / read) any of them.
11 A: What .... (this word / mean)?
   B: I've no idea. .... (I / never / see) it before. Look it up in the
      dictionary.
12 A: .... (you / get) to the theatre in time for the play last night?
   B: No, we were late. By the time we got there, ...
      (it / already / start).
13 I went to Sarah's room and .... (knock) on the door, but there
   .... (be) no answer. Either .... (she / go) out
   or .... (she / not / want) to see anyone.
14 Dan asked me how to use the photocopier. .... (he / never / use)
   it before, so .... (he / not / know) what to do.
15 Lisa .... (go) for a swim after work yesterday. ....
   (she / need) some exercise because .... (she / sit) in an office all
   day in front of a computer.

Past continuous and *used to*   Units 6, 18

9 **Complete the sentences using the past continuous (was/were -ing) or used to … . Use the
verb in brackets.**

1 I haven't been to the cinema for ages now. We _used to go_ a lot. (go)
2 Ann didn't see me wave to her. She _was looking_ in the other direction. (look)
3 I .... a lot, but I don't use my car very much these days. (drive)
4 I asked the taxi driver to slow down. She .... too fast. (drive)
5 Rosemary and Jonathan met for the first time when they .... in the
   same bank. (work)
6 When I was a child, I .... a lot of bad dreams. (have)
7 I wonder what Joe is doing these days. He .... in Spain when I last
   heard from him. (live)
8 'Where were you yesterday afternoon?' 'I .... volleyball.' (play)
9 'Do you do any sports?' 'Not these days, but I .... volleyball.' (play)
10 George looked very smart at the party. He .... a very nice suit. (wear)

The future

10 What do you say to Joe in these situations? Use the words given in brackets. Use the present continuous (**I am doing**), **going to** or **will** (**I'll**).

1 You have made all your holiday arrangements. Your destination is Jamaica.
JOE: Have you decided where to go for your holiday yet?
YOU: ___I'm going to Jamaica.___ (I / go)

2 You have made an appointment with the dentist for Friday morning.
JOE: Shall we meet on Friday morning?
YOU: I can't on Friday. .... (I / go)

3 You and some friends are planning a holiday in Spain. You have decided to rent a car, but you haven't arranged this yet.
JOE: How do you plan to travel round Spain? By train?
YOU: No, ... (we / rent)

4 Joe reminds you that you have to call your sister. You completely forgot.
JOE: Did you call your sister?
YOU: No, I forgot. Thanks for reminding me. .... (I / call / now)

5 You have already arranged to have lunch with Sue tomorrow.
JOE: Are you free at lunchtime tomorrow?
YOU: No, ... (have lunch)

6 You are in a restaurant. You and Joe are looking at the menu. Maybe Joe has decided what to have. You ask him.
YOU: What ....? (you / have)
JOE: I don't know. I can't make up my mind.

7 Joe is reading, but it's getting dark. He's having trouble reading. You turn on the light.
JOE: It's getting dark and it's hard to read.
YOU: Yes, ... (I / turn on)

8 You and Joe are sitting in a room with the window open. It's getting cold. You decide to close the window. You stand up and walk towards it.
JOE: What are you doing?
YOU: .... (I / close)

11 Choose the best alternative.

1 '___Are you doing___ anything tomorrow evening?' 'No, why?'
A Do you do **B** Are you doing **C** Will you do (**B** *is the best alternative*)

2 'I can't open this bottle.' 'Give it to me. .... it.'
A I open **B** I'll open **C** I'm going to open

3 'Is Emily here yet?' 'Not yet. I'll let you know as soon as .... '
A she arrives **B** she's arriving **C** she'll arrive

4 'Are you free tomorrow afternoon?' 'No, ... '
A I work **B** I'm working **C** I'll work

5 'What time is the film tonight?' '............................... at 8.40.'
A It starts **B** It's going to start **C** It will start

6 'Are you going to the beach tomorrow?' 'Yes, if the weather .... good.'
A is going to be **B** will be **C** is

7 'What time .... tomorrow?' 'How about 8.30?'
A do we meet **B** are we meeting **C** shall we meet

8 'When ....?' 'Tomorrow.'
A does the festival finish **B** is the festival finished **C** is the festival finishing

12 Put the verb into the most suitable form. Sometimes there is more than one possibility.

1 *A has decided to learn a language.*

A: I've decided to try and learn a foreign language.

B: Have you? Which language (1) ..... *are you going to learn* ..... (you / learn)?

A: Spanish.

B: (2) .... (you / do) a course?

A: Yes, (3) .... (it / start) next week.

B: That's great. I'm sure (4) .... (you / enjoy) it.

A: I hope so. But I think (5) .... (it / be) difficult.

2 *A wants to know about B's holiday plans.*

A: I hear (1) .... (you / go) on holiday soon.

B: That's right. (2) .... (we / go) to Finland.

A: I hope (3) .... (you / have) a nice time.

B: Thanks. (4) .... (I / get) in touch with you when

(5) .... (I / get) back and maybe we can meet sometime.

3 *A invites B to a party.*

A: (1) .... (I / have) a party next Saturday. Can you come?

B: On Saturday? I'm not sure. Some friends of mine (2) .... (come) to

stay with me next week, but I think (3) .... (they / leave) by

Saturday. But if (4) .... (they / be) still here,

(5) .... (I / not / be) able to come to the party.

A: OK. Well, tell me as soon as (6) .... (you / know).

B: Right. (7) .... (I / call) you during the week.

4 *A and B are two secret agents arranging a meeting. They are talking on the phone.*

A: Well, what time (1) ....

(we / meet)?

B: Come to the cafe by the station at 4 o'clock.

(2) .... (I / wait) for you

when (3) .... (you / arrive).

(4) .... (I / sit) by the window

and (5) .... (I / wear) a bright green sweater.

A: OK. (6) .... (Agent 307 / come) too?

B: No, she can't be there.

A: Oh. (7) .... (I / bring) the documents?

B: Yes. (8) .... (I / explain) everything when

(9) .... (I / see) you. And don't be late.

A: OK. (10) .... (I / try) to be on time.

13 **Put the verb into the correct form. Choose from the following:**

present continuous (**I am doing**)   will ('**ll**) / **won't**
present simple (**I do**)   **will be doing**
going to (**I'm going to do**)   **shall**

1 I feel a bit hungry. I think .... (I / have) something to eat.
2 Why are you putting on your coat? .... (you / go) somewhere?
3 What time .... (I / phone) you tomorrow? About 10.30?
4 Look! That plane is flying towards the airport. .... (it / land).
5 We must do something soon, before .... (it / be) too late.
6 I'm sorry you've decided to leave the company. .... (I / miss) you
   when .... (you / go).
7 .... (I / give) you my phone number? If ....
   (I / give) you my number, ... (you / call) me?
8 Are you still watching that programme? What time .... (it / finish)?
9 .... (I / go) to a wedding next weekend. My cousin
   .... (get) married.
10 I'm not ready yet. .... (I / tell) you when ....
   (I / be) ready. I promise .... (I / not / be) very long.
11 .... (I / have) my hair cut tomorrow. I've just made an appointment.
12 She was very rude to me. I won't speak to her again until ....
   (she / apologise).
13 I wonder where .... (we / live) ten years from now.
14 What are you planning to do when .... (you / finish) your course
   at college?

---

14 **Use your own ideas to complete B's sentences.**

1 A: How did the accident happen?
   B: I __was going__ too fast and couldn't stop in time.
2 A: Is that a new coat?
   B: No, I .... it a long time.
3 A: Is that a new phone?
   B: Yes, I .... it a few weeks ago.
4 A: I can't talk to you right now. You can see I'm very busy.
   B: OK. I .... back in about half an hour.
5 A: This is a nice restaurant. Do you come here often?
   B: No, it's the first time I .... here.
6 A: Do you do any sport?
   B: No, I .... football, but I gave it up.
7 A: I'm sorry I'm late.
   B: That's OK. I .... long.
8 A: When you went to the US last year, was it your first visit?
   B: No, I .... there twice before.
9 A: Do you have any plans for the weekend?
   B: Yes, I .... to a party on Saturday night.
10 A: Do you know what Steve's doing these days?
   B: No, I .... him for ages.
11 A: Will you still be here by the time I get back?
   B: No, I .... by then.

15 Robert is travelling in North America. He sends an email to a friend in Winnipeg (Canada). Put the verb into the most suitable form.

Hi

(1) _I've just arrived_ (I / just / arrive) in Minneapolis. (2) _____ (I / travel) for more than a month now, and (3) _____ (I / begin) to think about coming home. Everything (4) _____ (I / see) so far (5) _____ (be) really interesting, and (6) _____ (I / meet) some really kind people.

(7) _____ (I / leave) Kansas City a week ago. (8) _____ (I / stay) there with Emily, the aunt of a friend from college. She was really helpful and hospitable and although (9) _____ (I / plan) to stay only a couple of days, (10) _____ (I / end up) staying more than a week. (11) _____ (I / enjoy) the journey from Kansas City to here. (12) _____ (I / take) the Greyhound bus and (13) _____ (meet) some really interesting people – everybody was really friendly.

So now I'm here, and (14) _____ (I / stay) here for a few days before (15) _____ (I / continue) up to Canada. I'm not sure exactly when (16) _____ (I / get) to Winnipeg – it depends what happens while (17) _____ (I / be) here. But (18) _____ (I / let) you know as soon as (19) _____ (I / know) myself.

(20) _____ (I / stay) with a family here – they're friends of some people I know at home. Tomorrow (21) _____ (we / visit) some people they know who (22) _____ (build) a house by a lake. It isn't finished yet, but (23) _____ (it / be) interesting to see what it's like. Anyway, that's all for now. (24) _____ (I / be) in touch again soon.

Robert

Modal verbs (*can*/*must*/*would* etc.)

Units 26–36, Appendix 4

16 Which alternatives are correct? Sometimes only one alternative is correct, and sometimes two of the alternatives are possible.

1 'What time will you be home tonight?' 'I'm not sure. I __A or B__ late.'
   A may be   **B** might be   **C** can be *(both A and B are correct)*

2 I can't find the theatre tickets. They _____ out of my pocket.
   A must have fallen   **B** should have fallen   **C** had to fall

3 Somebody ran in front of the car as I was driving. Luckily, I _____ just in time.
   A could stop   **B** could have stopped   **C** managed to stop

4 We have plenty of time. We .... yet.
   A mustn't go   **B** don't have to go   **C** don't need to go
5 I didn't go out yesterday. I .... with my friends, but I didn't feel like it.
   A could go   **B** could have gone   **C** must have gone
6 I looked everywhere for Helen, but I .... her.
   A couldn't find   **B** couldn't have found   **C** wasn't able to find
7 'What do you think of my theory?'   'You .... right, but I'm not sure.'
   A could be   **B** must be   **C** might be
8 Our flight was delayed. We .... for two hours.
   A must wait   **B** must have waited   **C** had to wait
9 I'm not sure whether I'll be free on Saturday. I ....
   A must have to work   **B** may have to work   **C** might have to work
10 At first they didn't believe me when I told them what had happened, but in the end
   I .... them that I was telling the truth.
   A was able to convince   **B** managed to convince   **C** could convince
11 I promised I'd call Amy this evening. I ....
   A mustn't forget   **B** needn't forget   **C** don't have to forget
12 Why did you leave without me? You .... for me.
   A must have waited   **B** had to wait   **C** should have waited
13 Lisa called me this morning. She suggested .... lunch together.
   A we have   **B** we should have   **C** to have
14 That jacket looks good on you. .... it more often.
   A You'd better wear   **B** You should wear   **C** You ought to wear
15 Do you think I should buy a car? What .... in my position?
   A will you do   **B** would you do   **C** should you do

17 **Complete the sentences using the words in brackets.**

1 Don't phone them now. (might / have)
   They ..._might be having_.. lunch.
2 I ate too much and now I feel sick. (shouldn't / eat)
   I .... so much.
3 I wonder why Tom didn't call me. (must / forget)
   He ....
4 Why did you go home so early? (needn't / go)
   You .... home so early.
5 You've signed the contract. (can't / change)
   It .... now.
6 I'm not sure where the children are. (may / watch)
   They .... TV.
7 I saw Laura standing outside the cinema. (must / wait)
   She .... for somebody.
8 He was in prison at the time that the crime was committed. (couldn't / do)
   He .... it.
9 Why are you so late? (should / be)
   You .... here an hour ago.
10 Why didn't you contact me? (could / phone)
   You .... me.
11 I'm surprised you weren't told that the road was dangerous. (should / warn)
   You .... about it.
12 We had a great day at the beach yesterday. (ought / come)
   You .... with us.

18 Complete B's sentences using can/could/might/must/should/would + the verb in brackets. In some sentences you need to use have: must have ... / should have ... etc. In some sentences you need the negative (can't/couldn't etc.).

1 A: I'm hungry.
  B: But you've just had lunch. You ___can't be___ hungry already. (be)
2 A: I haven't seen our neighbours for ages.
  B: No. They ___must have gone___ away. (go)
3 A: What's the weather like? Is it raining?
  B: Not at the moment, but it _____ later. (rain)
4 A: Where's Julia?
  B: I'm not sure. She _____ out. (go)
5 A: I didn't see you at Michael's party last week.
  B: No, I had to work that night, so I _____ . (go)
6 A: I think I saw Ben in town this morning.
  B: No, you _____ him this morning. He's away on holiday. (see)
7 A: What time will we get to Sue's house?
  B: Well, it takes about one and a half hours, so if we leave at 3 o'clock, we
     _____ there by 4.30. (get)
8 A: When was the last time you saw Max?
  B: Years ago. I _____ him if I saw him now. (recognise)
9 A: Did you hear the explosion?
  B: What explosion?
  A: There was a loud explosion about an hour ago. You _____ it. (hear)
10 A: We weren't sure which way to go. In the end we turned right.
   B: You went the wrong way. You _____ left. (turn)

---

if (conditional)

Units 25, 38–40

19 Put the verb into the correct form.

1 If ___you found___ a wallet in the street, what would you do with it? (you / find)
2 I'd better hurry. My friend will be annoyed if ___I'm not___ on time. (I / not / be)
3 I didn't realise that Gary was in hospital. If ___I'd known___ he was in hospital, I would have gone to visit him. (I / know)
4 If the doorbell _____ , don't answer it. (ring)
5 I can't decide what to do. What would you do if _____ me? (you / be)
6 A: What shall we do tomorrow?
  B: Well, if _____ a nice day, we can go to the beach. (it / be)
7 A: Let's go to the beach.
  B: No, it's not warm enough. If _____ warmer, I'd go. (it / be)
8 A: Did you go to the beach yesterday?
  B: No, it was too cold. If _____ warmer, we might have gone. (it / be)
9 If _____ enough money to go anywhere in the world, where would you go? (you / have)
10 I didn't have my phone with me, so I couldn't call you. I would have called you if
   _____ my phone. (I / have)
11 The accident was your fault. If you'd been driving more carefully,
   _____ . (it / not / happen).
12 A: Why do you watch the news every day?
   B: Well, if _____ it, I wouldn't know what was happening in the world. (I / not / watch)

20 Complete the sentences.

1 Lisa is tired all the time. She shouldn't go to bed so late.
If Lisa __didn't go__ to bed so late, she __wouldn't be__ tired all the time.
2 It's getting late. I don't think Sarah will call me now.
I'd be surprised if Sarah .... now.
3 I'm sorry I disturbed you. I didn't know you were busy.
If .... you were busy, I .... you.
4 There are a lot of accidents on this road. There is no speed limit.
There .... so many accidents if .... a speed limit.
5 You didn't tell me about the problem, so I didn't try to help you.
If .... the problem, ... you.
6 It started to rain, but fortunately I had an umbrella.
I .... very wet if .... an umbrella.
7 Mark failed his driving test. He was very nervous and that's why he failed.
If he .... so nervous, he .... the test.

21 Use your own ideas to complete the sentences.

1 I'd go out tonight if ....
2 I'd have gone out last night if ....
3 If you hadn't reminded me, ...
4 If I had more free time, ...
5 If you give me the camera, ...
6 Who would you phone if .... ?
7 We wouldn't have been late if ....
8 If I'd been able to get a ticket, ...
9 If I'd done better at the interview, ...
10 You wouldn't be hungry now if ....
11 Cities would be nicer places if ....
12 If there was no internet, ...

Passive

Units 42–45

22 Put the verb into the most suitable passive form.

1 There's somebody behind us. I think __we're being followed__ (we / follow).
2 A mystery is something that __can't be explained__ (can't / explain).
3 We didn't play football yesterday. The game .... (cancel).
4 The TV .... (repair). It's working again now.
5 The village church .... (restore) at the moment. The work is almost finished.
6 The tower is the oldest part of the church. .... (it / believe) to be over 600 years old.
7 If I didn't do my job properly, ... (I / would / fire).
8 A: I left a newspaper on the desk last night and it isn't there now.
B: .... (it / might / throw) away.
9 Joe learnt to swim when he was very young. .... (he / teach) by his mother.
10 After .... (arrest), I was taken to the police station.
11 '.. (you / ever / arrest)?'   'No, never.'
12 Two people .... (report) to .... (injure) in an accident at a factory in Birmingham early this morning.

23 **Put the verb into the correct form, active or passive.**

1 This house is quite old. It __was built__ (build) over 100 years ago.

2 My grandfather was a builder. He __built__ (build) this house many years ago.

3 'Is your car still for sale?' 'No, I .... (sell) it.'

4 A: Is the house at the end of the street still for sale?
   B: No, it .... (sell).

5 Sometimes mistakes .... (make). It's inevitable.

6 It's not a good idea to leave your car unlocked. It .... (might / steal).

7 My bag has disappeared. It .... (must / steal).

8 I can't find my umbrella. Somebody .... (must / take) it by mistake.

9 It's a serious problem. I don't know how it .... (can / solve).

10 We didn't leave early enough. We .... (should / leave) earlier.

11 Very often when I travel by plane, my flight .... (delay).

12 A new bridge .... (build) across the river. Work started last year
    and the bridge .... (expect) to open next year.

24 **Read these newspaper reports and put the verbs into the most suitable form.**

1
Castle Fire

Winton Castle (1) __was damaged__ (damage) in a fire last night. The fire, which (2) .... (discover) at about 9 o'clock, spread very quickly. Nobody (3) .... (injure), but two people had to (4) .... (rescue) from an upstairs room. A number of paintings (5) .... (believe / destroy). It (6) .... (not / know) how the fire started.

2
Shop Robbery

In Paxham yesterday a shop assistant (1) .... (force) to hand over £500 after (2) .... (threaten) by a man with a knife. The man escaped in a car which (3) .... (steal) earlier in the day. The car (4) .... (later / find) in a car park where it (5) .... (abandon) by the thief. A man (6) .... (arrest) in connection with the robbery and (7) .... (still / question) by the police.

3
Road Delays

Repair work started yesterday on the Paxham–Longworth road. The road (1) .... (resurface) and there will be long delays. Drivers (2) .... (ask) to use an alternative route if possible. The work (3) .... (expect) to last two weeks. Next Sunday the road (4) .... (close), and traffic (5) .... (divert).

4
Accident

A woman (1) .... (take) to hospital after her car collided with a lorry near Norstock yesterday. She (2) .... (allow) home later after treatment. The road (3) .... (block) for an hour after the accident, and traffic had to (4) .... (divert). A police inspector said afterwards: 'The woman was lucky. She could (5) .... (kill).'

315

Reported speech   Units 47–48, 50

25   **Complete the sentences using reported speech.**

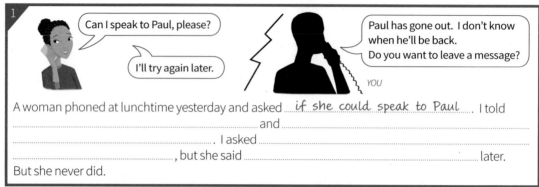

A woman phoned at lunchtime yesterday and asked ....*if she could speak to Paul*.... I told
.... and ....
.... I asked ....
...., but she said .... later.
But she never did.

I went to London recently, but my visit didn't begin well. I had reserved a hotel room, but
when I got to the hotel they told ....
.... When I asked ....,
they said ...., but ....
There was nothing I could do. I just had to look for somewhere else to stay.

After getting off the plane, we had to queue for an hour to get through immigration. Finally,
it was our turn. The immigration officer asked us ....
...., and we told ....
Then he wanted to know .... and
....
He seemed satisfied with our answers, checked our passports and wished us a pleasant stay.

A: What time is Sue arriving this afternoon?
B: About three. She said ....
....

A: Aren't you going to meet her?
B: No, she said not .... She said
   that ....

316

5

What's your job?

How much do you earn?

Mind your own business!

YOU

A few days ago a man phoned from a marketing company and started asking me questions. He wanted to know .... and asked .... I don't like people phoning and asking questions like that, so I told .... and ended the call.

6

NOW

I'll be at the restaurant at 7.30.

EARLIER

I know where the restaurant is.

Phone me if there's a problem.

LOUISE *SARAH*

PAUL *SARAH*

Sarah and Louise are in a restaurant waiting for Paul.

SARAH: I wonder where Paul is. He said ....
LOUISE: Maybe he got lost.
SARAH: I don't think so. He said ....
And I told ....

7

I'm not hungry.

I don't like bananas, so don't buy any.

JOE

JANE

Five minutes later

JOE: Is there anything to eat?
JANE: You just said ....
JOE: Well, I am now. I'd love a banana.
JANE: A banana? But you said ....
You told ....

-ing and to ...

Units 53–66

26   **Put the verbs into the correct form.**

1 How old were you when you learnt ....*to drive*....? (drive)
2 I don't mind ....*walking*.... home, but I'd rather ....*get*.... a taxi. (walk, get)
3 I can't make a decision. I keep .... my mind. (change)
4 He had made his decision and refused .... his mind. (change)
5 Why did you change your decision? What made you .... your mind? (change)
6 It was a really good holiday. I really enjoyed .... by the sea again. (be)

Additional exercises

7 Did I really tell you I was unhappy? I don't remember .... that. (say)
8 'Remember .... Tom tomorrow.' 'OK. I won't forget.' (call)
9 The water here is not very good. I'd avoid .... it if I were you. (drink)
10 I pretended .... interested in the conversation, but really it was very boring. (be)
11 I got up and looked out of the window .... what the weather was like. (see)
12 I don't have far to go. It's not worth .... a taxi. (take)
13 I have a friend who claims .... able to speak five languages. (be)
14 I like .... carefully about things before .... a decision. (think, make)
15 I had a flat in the centre of town but I didn't like .... there, so I decided .... (live, move)
16 Steve used .... a footballer. He had to stop .... because of an injury. (be, play)
17 After .... by the police, the man admitted .... the car but denied .... at 100 miles an hour. (stop, steal, drive)
18 A: How do you make this machine .... ? (work)
   B: I'm not sure. Try .... that button and see what happens. (press)

27 **Make sentences from the words in brackets.**

1 I can't find the tickets. (I / seem / lose / them)
  I seem to have lost them.

2 I don't have far to go. (it / not / worth / take / a taxi)
  It's not worth taking a taxi.

3 I'm feeling a bit tired. (I / not / fancy / go / out)

4 James isn't very reliable. (he / tend / forget / things)

5 I've got a lot of luggage. (you / mind / help / me?)

6 There's nobody at home. (everybody / seem / go out)

7 We don't like our apartment. (we / think / move)

8 The vase was very valuable. (I / afraid / touch / it)

9 I wanted to get to the station in plenty of time. (I / afraid / miss / my train)

10 I don't recommend the movie. (it / not / worth / see)

11 I'm very tired after that long walk. (I / not / used / walk / so far)

12 Sue is on holiday. She called me yesterday and sounded happy. (she / seem / enjoy / herself)

13 Dan took lots of pictures while he was on holiday. (he / insist / show / them to me)

14 I don't want to do the shopping. (I'd rather / somebody else / do / it)

318

28 **Complete the second sentence so that the meaning is similar to the first.**

1 I was surprised I passed the exam.
I didn't expect _to pass the exam_ .

2 Did you manage to solve the problem?
Did you succeed _in solving the problem_ ?

3 I don't read newspapers any more.
I've given up .

4 I'd prefer not to go out tonight.
I'd rather .

5 He finds it difficult to sleep at night.
He has trouble .

6 Shall I phone you this evening?
Do you want ?

7 Nobody saw me come in.
I came in without .

8 Some people said I was a cheat.
I was accused .

9 It will be good to see them again.
I'm looking forward .

10 What do you think I should do?
What do you advise me ?

11 It's a pity I couldn't go out with you last night.
I'd like .

12 I wish I'd taken your advice.
I regret .

---

a/an and *the*

Units 69–78

29 **Put in a/an or the where necessary. Leave the space empty if the sentence is already complete.**

1 I don't usually like staying at ___–___ hotels, but last summer we spent two weeks at ___a___ very nice hotel by ___the___ sea.

2 If you go to live in _____ foreign country, you should try and learn _____ language.

3 Helen is _____ economist. She lives in _____ United States and works for _____ investment company.

4 I love _____ sport, especially _____ tennis. I play two or three times _____ week if I can, but I'm not _____ very good player.

5 I won't be home for _____ dinner this evening. I'm meeting some friends after _____ work and we're going to _____ cinema.

6 When _____ unemployment is high, it's difficult for _____ people to find _____ work. It's _____ big problem.

7 There was _____ accident as I was going _____ home last night. Two people were taken to _____ hospital. I think _____ most accidents are caused by _____ people driving too fast.

8 A: What's _____ name of _____ hotel where you're staying?
B: _____ Ambassador. It's in _____ Queen Street in _____ city centre. It's near _____ station.

9 I have two brothers. _____ older one is training to be _____ pilot. _____ younger one is still at _____ school. When he leaves _____ school, he wants to go to _____ university to study _____ law.

Pronouns and determiners

Units 82–91

30 Which alternatives are correct? Sometimes only one alternative is correct, and sometimes two alternatives are possible.

1 I don't remember .....**A**..... about the accident. (A *is correct*)

   (**A**) anything   **B** something   **C** nothing

2 Chris and I have known .... for quite a long time.

   A us   **B** each other   **C** ourselves

3 'How often do the buses run?' '.. twenty minutes.'

   A All   **B** Each   **C** Every

4 I shouted for help, but .... came.

   A nobody   **B** no-one   **C** anybody

5 Last night we went out with some friends of ....

   A us   **B** our   **C** ours

6 It didn't take us a long time to get here. .... traffic.

   A It wasn't much   **B** There wasn't much   **C** It wasn't a lot

7 Can I have .... milk in my coffee, please?

   A a little   **B** any   **C** some

8 Sometimes I find it difficult to ....

   A concentrate   **B** concentrate me   **C** concentrate myself

9 There's .... on at the cinema that I want to see, so there's no point in going.

   A something   **B** anything   **C** nothing

10 I drink .... water every day.

   A much   **B** a lot of   **C** lots of

11 .... in the city centre are open on Sunday.

   A Most of shops   **B** Most of the shops   **C** The most of the shops

12 There were about twenty people in the photo. I didn't recognise .... of them.

   A any   **B** none   **C** either

13 I've been waiting .... for Sarah to phone.

   A all morning   **B** the whole morning   **C** all the morning

14 I can't afford to buy anything in this shop. .... so expensive.

   A All is   **B** Everything is   **C** All are

Adjectives and adverbs

Units 98–108

31 There are mistakes in some of these sentences. Correct the sentences where necessary. Write 'OK' if the sentence is already correct.

1 The building was <u>total destroyed</u> in the fire.   *totally destroyed*

2 I didn't like the book. It was such a stupid story.   OK

3 The city is very polluted. It's the more polluted place I've ever been to.

4 I was disappointing that I didn't get the job. I was well-qualified and the interview went well.

5 It's warm today, but there's quite a strong wind.

6 Joe works hardly, but he doesn't get paid very much.

7 The company's offices are in a modern large building.

8 Dan is a very fast runner. I wish I could run as fast as him. ....
9 I missed the three last days of the course because I was ill. ....
10 You don't look happy. What's the matter? ....
11 The weather has been unusual cold for the time of the year. ....
12 The water in the pool was too dirty to swim in it. ....
13 I got impatient because we had to wait so long time. ....
14 Is this box big enough or do you need a bigger one? ....
15 This morning I got up more early than usual. ....

Conjunctions
Units 25, 38, 112–118

32 Which is correct?

1 I'll try to be on time, but don't worry if / ~~when~~ I'm late. (if *is correct*)
2 Don't throw that bag away. If / When you don't want it, I'll have it.
3 Please report to reception if / when you arrive at the hotel.
4 We've arranged to go to the beach tomorrow, but we won't go if / when it's raining.
5 Tanya is in her final year at school. She still doesn't know what she's going to do if / when she leaves.
6 What would you do if / when you lost your keys?
7 I hope I'll be able to come to the party, but I'll let you know if / unless I can't.
8 I don't want to be disturbed, so don't phone me if / unless it's something important.
9 Please sign the contract if / unless you're happy with the conditions.
10 I like travelling by ship as long as / unless the sea is not rough.
11 You might not remember the name of the hotel, so write it down if / in case you forget it.
12 It's not cold now, but take your coat with you if / in case it gets cold later.
13 Take your coat with you and then you can put it on if / in case it gets cold later.
14 They always have the TV on, even if / if nobody is watching it.
15 Even / Although I left home early, I got to work late.
16 Despite / Although we've known each other a long time, we're not particularly close friends.
17 'When did you leave school?' 'As / When I was 17.'
18 I think Amy will be very pleased as / when she hears the news.

Prepositions (time)
Units 12, 119–122

33 Put in one of the following: at   on   in   during   for   since   by   until

1 Jack has gone away. He'll be back ...*in*... a week.
2 We're having a party .... Saturday. Can you come?
3 I've got an interview next week. It's .... Tuesday morning .... 9.30.
4 Sue isn't usually here .... weekends. She goes away.
5 The train service is very good. The trains are nearly always .... time.
6 It was a confusing situation. Many things were happening .... the same time.
7 I couldn't decide whether or not to buy the sweater. .... the end I decided not to.
8 The road is busy all the time, even .... night.
9 I met a lot of nice people .... my stay in New York.
10 I saw Helen .... Friday, but I haven't seen her .... then.
11 Robert has been doing the same job .... five years.
12 Lisa's birthday is .... the end of March. I'm not sure exactly which day it is.
13 We have friends staying with us .... the moment. They're staying .... Friday.
14 If you're interested in applying for the job, your application must be received .... Friday.
15 I'm just going out. I won't be long – I'll be back .... ten minutes.

Prepositions (position and other uses)   Units 123–128

34   Put in the missing preposition.

1   I'd love to be able to visit every country .... the world.
2   Jessica White is my favourite author. Have you read anything .... her?
3   There's a small shop .... the end of this road.
4   Tom is away at the moment. He's .... holiday.
5   We live .... the country, a long way from the nearest town.
6   I've got a stain .... my jacket. I'll have to have it cleaned.
7   We went .... a party .... Lisa's house on Saturday.
8   Boston is .... the east coast of the United States.
9   Look at the leaves .... that tree. They're a beautiful colour.
10 I've never been .... Japan, but I'd like to go very much.
11 Mozart died .... Vienna in 1791 .... the age of 35.
12 'Are you .... this photo?' 'Yes, that's me, ... the left.'
13 We went .... the theatre last night. We had seats .... the front row.
14 If you want to turn the light on, the switch is .... the wall .... the door.
15 It was late when we arrived .... the hotel.
16 I couldn't decide what to eat. There was nothing .... the menu that I liked.
17 We live .... a tower block. Our apartment is .... the fifteenth floor.
18 Some parts of the film were a bit stupid, but .... the whole I enjoyed it.
19 'When you paid the restaurant bill, did you pay cash?' 'No, I paid .... credit card.'
20 'How did you get here? Did you come .... the bus?' 'No, ... car.'
21 I watched a really interesting programme .... TV last night.
22 Helen works for a large company. She works .... the customer services department.
23 Anna spent two years working .... London before returning .... Italy.
24 How was your trip .... the beach? Did you have a good day?
25 On our first day in Paris, we went .... a trip round the city.

Noun/adjective + preposition   Units 129–131

35   Put in the missing preposition.

1   The plan has been changed, but nobody seems to know the reason .... this.
2   Don't ask me to decide. I'm not very good .... making decisions.
3   Some people say that Sue is unfriendly, but she's always very nice .... me.
4   What do you think is the best solution .... the problem?
5   Recently there has been a big increase .... the number of tourists visiting the city.
6   He lives a rather lonely life. He doesn't have much contact .... other people.
7   Paul is a keen photographer. He likes taking pictures .... people.
8   Michael got married .... a woman he met when he was studying at college.
9   He's very brave. He's not scared .... anything.
10 I'm surprised .... the traffic today. I didn't think it would be so busy.
11 Thank you for lending me the guidebook. It was full .... useful information.
12 I'm afraid I've had to change my plans, so I can't meet you tomorrow. I'm sorry .... that.

Verb + preposition
Units 132–136

36 **Complete each sentence with a preposition where necessary. If no preposition is necessary, leave the space empty.**

1 She works quite hard. You can't accuse her .... being lazy.
2 Who's going to look .... your children while you're at work?
3 The problem is becoming serious. We have to discuss .... it.
4 The problem is becoming serious. We have to do something .... it.
5 I prefer this chair .... the other one. It's more comfortable.
6 I need to call .... the office to tell them I won't be at work today.
7 The river divides the city .... two parts.
8 'What do you think .... your new boss?' 'She's all right, I suppose.'
9 Can somebody please explain .... me what I have to do?
10 I said hello to her, but she didn't answer .... me.
11 'Do you like staying at hotels?' 'It depends .... the hotel.'
12 'Have you ever been to Borla?' 'No, I've never heard .... it. Where is it?'
13 You remind me .... somebody I knew a long time ago. You look just like her.
14 This is wonderful news! I can't believe .... it.
15 George is not an idealist – he believes .... being practical.
16 What's funny? What are you laughing .... ?
17 What did you do with all the money you had? What did you spend it .... ?
18 If Alex asks .... you .... money, don't give him any.
19 I apologised .... Sarah .... keeping her waiting so long.
20 Lisa was very helpful. I thanked .... her .... everything she'd done.

Phrasal verbs
Units 137–145

37 **A says something and B replies. Which goes with which?**

A

1 I've made a mistake on this form.
2 I'm too warm with my coat on.
3 This jacket looks nice.
4 Your reference number is 318044BK.
5 This room is in a mess.
6 What's 45 euros in dollars?
7 How was the mistake discovered?
8 I'm not sure whether to accept their offer or not.
9 I need a place to stay when I'm in London.
10 It's a subject he doesn't like to talk about.
11 I don't know what this word means.

B

a Don't worry. I'll clear it up.
b That won't be a problem. I can fix it up.
c Kate pointed it out.
d That's OK. Cross it out and correct it.
e Yes, why don't you try it on?
f OK, I won't bring it up.
g Just a minute. I'll write it down.
h Why don't you take it off then?
i You can look it up.
j I think you should turn it down.
k Give me a moment. I'll work it out.

1 _d_
2 ....
3 ....
4 ....
5 ....
6 ....
7 ....
8 ....
9 ....
10 ....
11 ....

38 Only one alternative is correct. Which is it?

1 Nobody believed Paul at first but he ....*B*.... to be right. (B *is correct*)
   A came out   **B** turned out   **C** worked out   **D** carried out

2 Here's some good news. It will ....
   A turn you up   **B** put you up   **C** blow you up   **D** cheer you up

3 The children were behaving badly, so I ....
   A told them up   **B** told them off   **C** told them out   **D** told them over

4 The club committee is .... of the president, the secretary and seven other members.
   A set up   **B** made up   **C** set out   **D** made out

5 Why did you decide not to apply for the job? What .... ?
   A put you off   **B** put you out   **C** turned you off   **D** turned you away

6 I had no idea that he was lying to me. I was completely ....
   A taken in   **B** taken down   **C** taken off   **D** taken over

7 Helen started a course at college, but she .... after six months.
   A went out   **B** fell out   **C** turned out   **D** dropped out

8 You can't predict everything. Often things don't .... as you expect.
   A make out   **B** break out   **C** turn out   **D** get out

9 What's all this noise? What's .... ?
   A going off   **B** getting off   **C** going on   **D** getting on

10 It's a very busy airport. There are planes .... or landing every few minutes.
   A going up   **B** taking off   **C** getting up   **D** driving off

11 The road was blocked by a bus that had ....
   A broken down   **B** dropped out   **C** driven off   **D** held up

12 How are you .... in your new job? Are you enjoying it?
   A keeping on   **B** going on   **C** carrying on   **D** getting on

39 Complete the sentences. Use two words each time.

1 Keep ....*away from*.... the edge of the pool. You might fall in.
2 I didn't notice that the two pictures were different until Amy pointed it .... me.
3 I asked Max if he had any suggestions about what we should do, but he didn't come .... anything.
4 I'm glad Sarah is coming to the party. I'm really looking .... seeing her again.
5 Things are changing all the time. It's difficult to keep .... all these changes.
6 I don't want to run .... food for the party. Are you sure we have enough?
7 We had a short break and then carried .... our work.
8 I've had enough of being treated like this. I'm not going to put .... it any more.
9 I didn't enjoy the trip very much at the time, but when I look .... it now, I realise it was a good experience and I'm glad I went on it.
10 The wedding was supposed to be a secret, so how did you find .... it? Who told you?
11 There is a very nice atmosphere in the office where I work. Everybody gets .... everybody else.

40 **Complete each sentence using a phrasal verb that has a similar meaning to the words in brackets.**

1 The concert in the park had to be ..... *called off* ..... because of the weather. (cancelled)
2 The story Kate told wasn't true. She ..... *made it up* ..... . (invented it)
3 Paul finally .... an hour late. (arrived)
4 Here's an application form. Can you .... and sign it, please? (complete it)
5 Some houses will have to be .... to make way for the new road. (demolished)
6 Be positive! You must never ....! (stop trying)
7 I was very tired and .... in front of the TV. (fell asleep)
8 After eight years together, they've decided to .... (separate)
9 The noise is terrible. I can't .... any longer. (tolerate it)
10 We don't have a lot of money, but we have enough to .... (manage)
11 I'm sorry I'm late. The meeting .... longer than I expected. (continued)
12 We need to make a decision today at the latest. We can't .... any longer. (delay it)

41 **Complete the sentences. Use one word each time.**

1 You're driving too fast. Please ..... *slow* ..... down.
2 It was only a small fire and I managed to .... it out with a bucket of water.
3 The house is empty right now, but I think the new tenants are .... in next week.
4 I've .... on weight. My clothes don't fit any more.
5 Their house is really nice now. They've .... it up really well.
6 I was talking to the woman next to me on the plane, and it .... out that she works for the same company as my brother.
7 I don't know what happened yet, but I'm going to .... out.
8 There's no need to get angry. .... down!
9 If you're going on a long walk, plan your route carefully before you .... off.
10 Sarah has just phoned to say that she'll be late. She's been .... up.
11 You've written my name wrong. It's Martin, not Marin – you .... out the T.
12 Three days at £45 a day – that .... out at £135.
13 We had a really interesting discussion, but Jane didn't .... in. She just listened.
14 Jonathan is pretty fit. He .... out in the gym every day.
15 Come and see us more often. You can .... in any time you like.
16 We are still discussing the contract. There are still a couple of things to .... out.
17 My alarm clock .... off in the middle of the night and .... me up.

Study guide

This guide is to help you decide which units you need to study. The sentences in the guide are grouped together (*Present and past*, *Articles and nouns* etc.) in the same way as the units in the *Contents* (pages iii–vi).

Each sentence can be completed using one or more of the alternatives (A, B, C etc.). There are between two and five alternatives each time. IN SOME SENTENCES MORE THAN ONE ALTERNATIVE IS POSSIBLE.

If you don't know or if you are not sure which alternatives are correct, then you probably need to study the unit(s) in the list on the right. You will also find the correct sentence in this unit. (If two or three units are listed, you will find the correct sentence in the first one.)

There is a key to this study guide on page 372.

IF YOU ARE NOT SURE WHICH IS RIGHT	STUDY UNIT

Present and past

1.1 At first I didn't like my job, but .... to enjoy it now.
A I'm starting   **B** I start
1, 3

1.2 I don't understand this sentence. What ....?
A does mean this word   **B** does this word mean   **C** means this word
2, 49

1.3 Robert .... away two or three times a year.
A is going usually   **B** is usually going   **C** usually goes   **D** goes usually
2, 3, 110

1.4 How .... now? Better than before?
A you are feeling   **B** do you feel   **C** are you feeling
4

1.5 It was a boring weekend. .... anything.
A I didn't   **B** I don't do   **C** I didn't do
5

1.6 Matt .... while we were having dinner.
A phoned   **B** was phoning   **C** has phoned
6, 14

Present perfect and past

2.1 James is on holiday. He .... to Italy.
A is gone   **B** has gone   **C** has been
7

2.2 Everything is going well. There .... any problems so far.
A weren't   **B** have been   **C** haven't been
8

2.3 Sarah has lost her passport again. This is the second time this ....
A has happened   **B** happens   **C** happened   **D** is happening
8

2.4 Why are you out of breath? ....?
A Are you running   **B** Have you run   **C** Have you been running
9

2.5 Where's the book I gave you? What .... with it?
A have you done   **B** have you been doing   **C** are you doing
10

2.6 'How long .... Jane?' 'A long time. Since we were at school.'
A do you know   **B** have you known   **C** have you been knowing
11, 10

2.7 Sally has been working here ....
A for six months   **B** since six months   **C** six months ago   **D** six months
12

IF YOU ARE NOT SURE WHICH IS RIGHT

2.8   It's two years .... Joe.   **12**
       A that I don't see   **B** that I haven't seen   **C** since I didn't see
       D since I last saw

2.9   It .... raining for a while, but now it's raining again.   **13**
       A stopped   **B** has stopped   **C** was stopped

2.10   My mother .... in Italy.   **13**
       A grew up   **B** has grown up   **C** had grown up

2.11   .... a lot of sweets when you were a child?   **14**
       A Have you eaten   **B** Had you eaten   **C** Did you eat

2.12   Jack .... in New York for ten years. Now he lives in Los Angeles.   **14, 11**
       A lived   **B** has lived   **C** has been living

2.13   The people sitting next to me on the plane were nervous. .... before.   **15**
       A They haven't flown   **B** They didn't fly   **C** They hadn't flown
       D They'd never flown   **E** They weren't flying

2.14   Katherine was lying on the sofa. She was tired because .... very hard.   **16**
       A she was working   **B** she's been working   **C** she'd been working

2.15   .... a car when you were living in Paris?   **17, 14**
       A Had you   **B** Were you having   **C** Have you had   **D** Did you have

2.16   I .... tennis a lot, but I don't play very much now.   **18**
       A was playing   **B** was used to play   **C** used to play

Future

3.1   I'm tired. .... to bed now. Goodnight.   **19**
       A I go   **B** I'm going

3.2   .... tomorrow, so we can go out somewhere.   **19, 21**
       A I'm not working   **B** I don't work   **C** I won't work

3.3   That bag looks heavy. .... you with it.   **21**
       A I'm helping   **B** I help   **C** I'll help

3.4   I think the weather .... nice later.   **23, 22**
       A will be   **B** is   **C** is going to be   **D** shall be

3.5   'Anna is in hospital.' 'Yes, I know. .... her this evening.'   **23, 20**
       A I visit   **B** I'm going to visit   **C** I'll visit

3.6   We're late. The film .... by the time we get to the cinema.   **24**
       A will already start   **B** will be already started   **C** will already have started

3.7   Don't worry .... late tonight.   **25**
       A if I'm   **B** when I'm   **C** when I'll be   **D** if I'll be

IF YOU ARE NOT SURE WHICH IS RIGHT	STUDY UNIT

Modals

4.1 The fire spread quickly, but everybody .... from the building. — **26**
   A was able to escape   **B** managed to escape   **C** could escape

4.2 I'm so tired I .... for a week. — **27**
   A can sleep   **B** could sleep   **C** could have slept

4.3 The story .... be true, but I don't think it is. — **27, 29**
   A might   **B** can   **C** could   **D** may

4.4 Why did you stay at a hotel? You .... with me. — **27**
   A can stay   **B** could stay   **C** could have stayed

4.5 I lost one of my gloves. I .... it somewhere. — **28**
   A must drop   **B** must have dropped   **C** must be dropping
   D must have been dropping

4.6 'Why wasn't Amy at the meeting yesterday?'   'She .... about it.' — **29**
   A might not know   **B** may not know   **C** might not have known
   D may not have known

4.7 What .... to get a new driving licence? — **31**
   A have I to do   **B** do I have to do   **C** I must do   **D** I have to

4.8 We have plenty of time. We .... hurry. — **32**
   A don't need to   **B** mustn't   **C** needn't

4.9 You missed a great party last night. You .... Why didn't you? — **33**
   A must have come   **B** should have come   **C** ought to have come
   D had to come

4.10 Jane won the lottery. I suggested .... a car with the money she won. — **34**
   A that she buy   **B** that she should buy   **C** her to buy
   D that she bought

4.11 You're always at home. You .... out more often. — **35**
   A should go   **B** had better go   **C** had better to go

4.12 It's late. It's time .... home. — **35**
   A we go   **B** we must go   **C** we should go   **D** we went   **E** to go

4.13 .... a little longer, but I really have to go now. — **36**
   A I'd stay   **B** I'll stay   **C** I can stay   **D** I'd have stayed

if and wish

5.1 I'm not tired enough to go to bed. If I .... to bed now, I wouldn't sleep. — **38, 39**
   A go   **B** went   **C** had gone   **D** would go

5.2 If I were rich, ... a lot. — **39**
   A I'll travel   **B** I can travel   **C** I would travel   **D** I travelled

5.3 I wish I .... have to work tomorrow, but unfortunately I do. — **39, 41**
   A don't   **B** didn't   **C** wouldn't   **D** won't

IF YOU ARE NOT SURE WHICH IS RIGHT	STUDY UNIT

5.4 The view was wonderful. I would have taken some pictures if .... a camera with me.   **40**
  A I had   **B** I would have   **C** I would have had   **D** I'd had

5.5 The weather is horrible. I wish it .... raining.   **41**
  A would stop   **B** stopped   **C** stops   **D** will stop

Passive

6.1 We .... by a loud noise during the night.   **42**
  A woke up   **B** are woken up   **C** were woken up   **D** were waking up

6.2 A new supermarket is going to .... next year.   **43**
  A build   **B** be built   **C** be building   **D** building

6.3 There's somebody walking behind us. I think **43**
  A we are following   **B** we are being following   **C** we are followed
  D we are being followed

6.4 'Where ....?' 'In Chicago.'   **44**
  A were you born   **B** are you born   **C** have you been born
  D did you born

6.5 There was a fight, but nobody **44**
  A was hurt   **B** got hurt   **C** hurt

6.6 Jane .... to phone me last night, but she didn't.   **45**
  A supposed   **B** is supposed   **C** was supposed

6.7 Where ....? Which hairdresser did you go to?   **46**
  A did you cut your hair   **B** have you cut your hair
  C did you have cut your hair   **D** did you have your hair cut

Reported speech

7.1 Paul left the room suddenly. He said he .... to go.   **48, 47**
  A had   **B** has   **C** have

7.2 (*You meet Joe in the street.*)   **48, 47**
  Joe, this is a surprise. Rachel said you .... in hospital.
  A are   **B** were   **C** was

7.3 Anna .... and left.   **48**
  A said goodbye to me   **B** said me goodbye   **C** told me goodbye

Questions and auxiliary verbs

8.1 'What time ....?' 'At 8.30.'   **49**
  A starts the film   **B** does start the film   **C** does the film start

8.2 'Do you know where ....?' 'No, he didn't say.'   **50**
  A Tom has gone   **B** has Tom gone   **C** has gone Tom

8.3 The police officer stopped us and asked us where **50**
  A were we going   **B** are we going   **C** we are going   **D** we were going

IF YOU ARE NOT SURE WHICH IS RIGHT

8.4 'Do you think it will rain?'   '_____.'
     A I hope not   **B** I don't hope   **C** I don't hope so

51

8.5 'You don't know where Karen is, _____?' 'Sorry, I have no idea.'
     A don't you   **B** do you   **C** is she   **D** are you

52

-ing and to ...

9.1 You can't stop people _____ what they want.
     A doing   **B** do   **C** to do   **D** from doing

53, 62

9.2 I'd better go now. I promised _____ late.
     A not being   **B** not to be   **C** to not be   **D** I wouldn't be

54, 36

9.3 Do you want _____ with you or do you want to go alone?
     A me coming   **B** me to come   **C** that I come   **D** that I will come

55

9.4 I know I locked the door. I clearly remember _____ it.
     A locking   **B** to lock   **C** to have locked

56

9.5 She tried to be serious, but she couldn't help _____ .
     A laughing   **B** to laugh   **C** that she laughed   **D** laugh

57

9.6 Paul lives in Berlin now. He likes _____ there.
     A living   **B** to live

58

9.7 It's not my favourite job, but I like _____ the kitchen as often as possible.
     A cleaning   **B** clean   **C** to clean   **D** that I clean

58

9.8 I'm tired. I'd rather _____ out this evening, if you don't mind.
     A not going   **B** not to go   **C** don't go   **D** not go

59

9.9 I'd rather _____ anyone what I said.
     A you don't tell   **B** not you tell   **C** you didn't tell   **D** you wouldn't tell

59

9.10 Are you looking forward _____ on holiday?
     A going   **B** to go   **C** to going   **D** that you go

60, 62

9.11 When Lisa first came to Britain, she wasn't used _____ on the left.
     A driving   **B** to driving   **C** to drive   **D** drive

61

9.12 I'm thinking _____ a house. Do you think that's a good idea?
     A to buy   **B** of to buy   **C** of buying   **D** about buying

62, 66

9.13 I had no trouble _____ a place to stay. In fact it was surprisingly easy.
     A find   **B** found   **C** to find   **D** finding

63

9.14 I called the restaurant _____ a table.
     A for reserve   **B** to reserve   **C** for reserving   **D** for to reserve

64

9.15 James doesn't speak clearly. _____ .
     A It is hard to understand him   **B** He is hard to understand
     C He is hard to understand him

65

IF YOU ARE NOT SURE WHICH IS RIGHT — STUDY UNIT

9.16 The path was icy, so we walked very carefully. We were afraid .... — 66
A of falling B from falling C to fall D to falling

9.17 I didn't hear you .... in. You must have been very quiet. — 67
A come B to come C came

9.18 .... a hotel, we looked for somewhere to eat. — 68
A Finding B After finding C Having found D We found

Articles and nouns

10.1 It wasn't your fault. It was .... — 69
A accident B an accident C some accident

10.2 Where are you going to put all your .... ? — 70
A furniture B furnitures

10.3 'Where are you going?' 'I'm going to buy ....' — 70
A a bread B some bread C a loaf of bread

10.4 Sandra is .... She works at a large hospital. — 71, 72
A nurse B a nurse C the nurse

10.5 Helen works six days .... week. — 72
A in B for C a D the

10.6 There are millions of stars in .... — 73
A space B a space C the space

10.7 Every day .... starts at 9 and finishes at 3. — 74
A school B a school C the school

10.8 .... changed a lot in the last thirty years. — 75
A Life has B The life has C The lives have

10.9 When .... invented? — 76
A was camera B were cameras C were the cameras D was the camera

10.10 Have you been to .... ? — 77
A Canada or United States B the Canada or the United States
C Canada or the United States D the Canada or United States

10.11 On our first day in Moscow, we visited .... — 78
A Kremlin B a Kremlin C the Kremlin

10.12 I have some news for you. .... — 79, 70
A It's good news B They are good news C It's a good news

10.13 It took us quite a long time to get here. It was .... journey. — 80
A three hour B a three-hours C a three-hour

10.14 This isn't my book. It's .... — 81
A my sister B my sister's C from my sister D of my sister
E of my sister's

IF YOU ARE NOT SURE WHICH IS RIGHT

	STUDY UNIT

Pronouns and determiners

11.1 What time shall we .... tomorrow?
    A meet   **B** meet us   **C** meet ourselves
82

11.2 I'm going to a wedding on Saturday. .... is getting married.
    A A friend of me   **B** A friend of mine   **C** One my friends
83

11.3 They live on a busy road. .... a lot of noise from the traffic.
    A It must be   **B** It must have   **C** There must have   **D** There must be
84

11.4 He's lazy. He never does .... work.
    A some   **B** any   **C** no
85

11.5 'What would you like to eat?' 'I don't mind. .... – whatever you have.'
    A Something   **B** Anything   **C** Nothing
85

11.6 The course didn't go well. .... of the students were happy.
    A All   **B** No-one   **C** None   **D** Nobody
86

11.7 We went shopping and spent .... money.
    A a lot of   **B** much   **C** lots of   **D** many
87

11.8 I was ill yesterday. I spent .... in bed.
    A the most of day   **B** most of day   **C** the most of the day   **D** most of the day
88

11.9 I asked two people how to get to the station, but .... of them knew.
    A none   **B** either   **C** both   **D** neither
89

11.10 Our holiday was a disaster. .... went wrong.
    A Everything   **B** All   **C** All things   **D** All of things
90

11.11 The bus service is excellent. There's a bus .... ten minutes.
    A each   **B** every   **C** all
90, 91

11.12 There were four books on the table. .... a different colour.
    A Each of books was   **B** Each of the books was   **C** Each book was
91

Relative clauses

12.1 I don't like stories .... have unhappy endings.
    A that   **B** they   **C** which   **D** who
92

12.2 I didn't believe them at first, but in fact everything .... was true.
    A they said   **B** that they said   **C** what they said
93

12.3 We helped some people ....
    A their car had broken down   **B** which car had broken down
    C whose car had broken down   **D** that their car had broken down
94

12.4 Anna told me about her new job, ... a lot.
    A that she's enjoying   **B** which she's enjoying   **C** she's enjoying
    D she's enjoying it
95

12.5 Sarah couldn't meet us, ... was a shame.
    A that   **B** it   **C** what   **D** which
96

12.6 George showed me some pictures .... by his father.
    A painting   **B** painted   **C** that were painted   **D** they were painted
97, 92

IF YOU ARE NOT SURE WHICH IS RIGHT

Adjectives and adverbs

13.1 Jane doesn't enjoy her job any more. She's .... because every day she does exactly the same thing.
A boring   **B** bored

98

13.2 Lisa was carrying a .... bag.
A black small plastic   **B** small and black plastic   **C** small black plastic
D plastic small black

99

13.3 Maria's English is excellent. She speaks ....
A perfectly English   **B** English perfectly   **C** perfect English
D English perfect

100

13.4 He .... to find a job, but he had no luck.
A tried hard   **B** tried hardly   **C** hardly tried

101

13.5 I haven't seen her for .... , I've forgotten what she looks like.
A so long   **B** so long time   **C** a such long time   **D** such a long time

102

13.6 Don't stand on that chair. It isn't ....
A enough strong to stand on   **B** strong enough to stand on it
C strong enough to stand on   **D** strong enough for stand on

103

13.7 Sarah is doing OK at the moment. She has ....
A a quite good job   **B** quite a good job   **C** a pretty good job

104

13.8 The exam was quite easy – .... I expected.
A more easy that   **B** more easy than   **C** easier than   **D** easier as

105

13.9 The more expensive the hotel, ...
A the service will be better   **B** will be better the service
C the better the service   **D** better the service will be

106

13.10 Patrick is a fast runner. I can't run as fast as ....
A he   **B** him   **C** he can

107

13.11 What's .... you've ever made?
A most important decision   **B** the more important decision
C the decision more important   **D** the most important decision

108

13.12 Ben likes walking. ....
A Every morning he walks to work   **B** He walks to work every morning
C He walks every morning to work   **D** He every morning walks to work

109

13.13 Joe never phones me. ....
A Always I have to phone him   **B** I always have to phone him
C I have always to phone him   **D** I have to phone always him

110

13.14 Lucy .... She left last month.
A still doesn't work here   **B** doesn't still work here   **C** no more works here
D doesn't work here any more   **E** no longer works here

111

13.15 .... she can't drive, she has a car.
A Even   **B** Even when   **C** Even if   **D** Even though

112, 113

IF YOU ARE NOT SURE WHICH IS RIGHT	STUDY UNIT

Conjunctions and prepositions

14.1 I couldn't sleep .... very tired.

    A although I was   **B** despite I was   **C** despite of being   **D** in spite of being   **113**

14.2 You should insure your bike .... stolen.

    A in case it will be   **B** if it will be   **C** in case it is   **D** if it is   **114**

14.3 The club is for members only. You .... you're a member.

    A can't go in if   **B** can go in only if   **C** can't go in unless   **115**

    D can go in unless

14.4 Yesterday we watched TV all evening .... we didn't have anything better to do.   **116**

    A when   **B** as   **C** while   **D** since

14.5 'What's that noise?' 'It sounds .... a baby crying.'   **117, 118**

    A as   **B** like   **C** as if   **D** as though

14.6 They are very kind to me. They treat me .... their own son.   **118**

    A like I'm   **B** as if I'm   **C** as if I was   **D** as if I were

14.7 I'm going to be in Moscow next week. I hope the weather will be good **119**

    A while I'll be there   **B** while I'm there   **C** during my visit

    D during I'm there

14.8 Joe is away at the moment. I don't know exactly when he's coming back, but I'm sure he'll be back .... Monday.   **120**

    A by   **B** until

Prepositions

15.1 Bye! I'll see you **121**

    A at Friday morning   **B** on Friday morning   **C** in Friday morning

    D Friday morning

15.2 I'm going away .... the end of January.   **122**

    A at   **B** on   **C** in

15.3 When we were in Italy, we spent a few days .... Venice.   **123, 125**

    A at   **B** to   **C** in

15.4 Our apartment is .... the second floor of the building.   **124**

    A at   **B** on   **C** in   **D** to

15.5 I saw Steve .... a conference on Saturday.   **125**

    A at   **B** on   **C** in   **D** to

15.6 What time did you .... the hotel?   **126**

    A arrive to   **B** arrive at   **C** arrive in   **D** get to   **E** get in

15.7 I'm going .... holiday next week. I'll be away for two weeks.   **127**

    A at   **B** on   **C** in   **D** for

15.8 We travelled .... 6.45 train, which arrived at 8.30.   **128**

    A in the   **B** on the   **C** by the   **D** by

15.9 'Who is this painting .... ? Picasso?' 'I have no idea.'   **128**

    A of   **B** from   **C** by

IF YOU ARE NOT SURE WHICH IS RIGHT

15.10   The accident was my fault, so I had to pay for the damage.............................. the other car.
       A of   **B** for   **C** to   **D** on   **E** at
    129

15.11   I like them very much. They have always been very nice.............................. me.
       A of   **B** for   **C** to   **D** with
    130

15.12   I'm not very good.............................. repairing things.
       A at   **B** for   **C** in   **D** about
    131

15.13   I don't understand this sentence. Can you.............................. ?
       A explain to me this word   **B** explain me this word
       C explain this word to me
    132

15.14   If you're worried about the problem, you should do something.............................. it.
       A for   **B** about   **C** against   **D** with
    133

15.15   'Who is Tom Hart?' 'I have no idea. I've never heard.............................. him.'
       A about   **B** from   **C** after   **D** of
    134

15.16   I don't know what time we'll arrive. It depends.............................. the traffic.
       A of   **B** for   **C** from   **D** on
    135

15.17   I prefer tea.............................. coffee.
       A to   **B** than   **C** against   **D** over
    136, 59

Phrasal verbs

16.1   These shoes are uncomfortable. I'm going to.............................. .
       A take off   **B** take them off   **C** take off them
    137

16.2   They were playing cards, so I.............................. .
       A joined in   **B** came in   **C** got in   **D** broke in
    138

16.3   Nobody believed Paul at first, but he.............................. to be right.
       A worked out   **B** came out   **C** found out   **D** turned out
    139

16.4   We can't.............................. making a decision. We have to decide now.
       A put away   **B** put over   **C** put off   **D** put out
    140

16.5   'Have you finished painting the kitchen?' 'Nearly. I'll.............................. tomorrow.'
       A finish it up   **B** finish it over   **C** finish it off
    141

16.6   You can always rely on Paul. He'll never.............................. .
       A put you up   **B** let you down   **C** take you over   **D** see you off
    142

16.7   Children under 16.............................. half the population of the city.
       A make up   **B** put up   **C** take up   **D** bring up
    143

16.8   I'm surprised to hear that Kate and Paul have.............................. . They seemed very happy together.
       A broken up   **B** ended up   **C** finished up   **D** split up
    144

16.9   I parked in a no-parking zone, but I.............................. it.
       A came up with   **B** got away with   **C** made off with   **D** got on with
    145

Key to Exercises

In some of the exercises you have to use your own ideas to write sentences. Example answers are given in the Key. If possible, check your answers with somebody who speaks English well.

UNIT 1

1.1
2 He's tying / He is tying
3 They're crossing / They are crossing
4 He's scratching / He is scratching
5 She's hiding / She is hiding
6 They're waving / They are waving

1.2
2	e	6	h
3	g	7	b
4	a	8	c
5	d		

1.3
2 Why are you crying?
3 Is she working today?
4 What are you doing these days?
5 What is she studying? / What's she studying?
6 What are they doing?
7 Are you enjoying it?
8 Why are you walking so fast?

1.4
3 I'm not listening / I am not listening
4 She's having / She is having
5 He's learning / He is learning
6 they aren't speaking / they're not speaking / they are not speaking
7 it's getting / it is getting
8 isn't working / 's not working / is not working
9 I'm looking / I am looking
10 It's working / It is working
11 They're building / They are building
12 He's not enjoying / He is not enjoying
13 The weather's changing / The weather is changing
14 He's starting / He is starting

UNIT 2

2.1
2 go
3 causes
4 closes
5 live
6 take
7 connects

2.2
2 do the banks close
3 don't use
4 does Maria come
5 do you do
6 does this word mean
7 doesn't do
8 takes ... does it take

2.3
3 rises
4 make
5 don't eat
6 doesn't believe
7 translates
8 don't tell
9 flows

2.4
2 Does your sister play tennis?
3 How often do you go to the cinema?
4 What does your brother do?
5 Do you speak Spanish?
6 Where do your grandparents live?

2.5
2 I promise
3 I insist
4 I apologise
5 I recommend
6 I agree

UNIT 3

3.1
3 is trying
4 phones
5 OK
6 are they talking
7 OK
8 OK
9 It's getting / It is getting
10 I'm coming / I am coming
11 He always starts
12 OK

3.2
2 a Are you listening
  b Do you listen
3 a flows
  b is flowing / 's flowing
4 a I don't do
  b do you usually do
5 a She's staying / She is staying
  b She always stays

3.3
2 She speaks
3 Everybody's waiting / Everybody is waiting
4 do you pronounce
5 isn't working / is not working / 's not working
6 is improving
7 lives
8 I'm starting / I am starting
9 They're visiting / They are visiting
10 does your father do
11 it doesn't take
12 I'm learning / I am learning ... is teaching / 's teaching

3.4
2 It's always breaking down.
3 I'm always making the same mistake. / ... that mistake.
4 You're always leaving your phone at home.

UNIT 4

4.1
2 believes
3 I don't remember / I do not remember or I can't remember
4 I'm using / I am using
5 I need
6 consists
7 does he want
8 is he looking
9 Do you recognise
10 I'm thinking / I am thinking
11 do you think
12 he seems

4.2
2 I'm thinking.
3 Who does this umbrella belong to?
4 This smells good.
5 Is anybody sitting there?
6 These gloves don't fit me.

4.3
3 OK (I feel is also correct)
4 does it taste
5 OK
6 do you see
7 OK

4.4
2 's / is
3 's being / is being
4 're / are
5 are you being
6 Are you

UNIT 5

5.1
2 had
3 She walked to work
4 It took her (about) half an hour
5 She started work
6 She didn't have (any) lunch. / ... eat (any) lunch.
7 She finished work
8 She was tired when she got home.
9 She cooked / She made
10 She didn't go
11 She went to bed
12 She slept

5.2

2 taught
3 sold
4 fell ... hurt
5 threw ... caught
6 spent ... bought ... cost

5.3

2 did you travel / did you go
3 did it take (you) / was your trip / were you there
4 did you stay
5 Was the weather
6 Did you go to / Did you see / Did you visit

5.4

3 didn't disturb
4 left
5 were
6 didn't sleep
7 didn't cost
8 flew
9 didn't have
10 wasn't

UNIT 6

6.1

2 wasn't listening
3 were sitting
4 was working
5 weren't looking
6 was snowing
7 were you going
8 was looking

6.2

2 e   5 c
3 a   6 d
4 g   7 b

6.3

1 didn't see ... was looking
2 was cycling ... stepped ... was going ... managed ... didn't hit

6.4

2 were you doing
3 Did you go
4 were you driving ... happened
5 took ... wasn't looking
6 didn't know ... did
7 saw ... was trying
8 was walking ... heard ... was following ... started
9 wanted ... changed
10 dropped ... was doing ... didn't break

UNIT 7

7.1

2 Her English has improved.
3 My bag has disappeared.
4 Lisa has broken her leg.
5 The bus fare has gone up.
6 Dan has grown a beard.
7 It's stopped raining. / It has stopped raining.
8 My sweater has shrunk. / My sweater's shrunk.

7.2

2 been   4 gone
3 gone   5 been

7.3

2 Have you seen it
3 I've forgotten / I have forgotten
4 he hasn't replied
5 has it finished
6 The weather has changed
7 You haven't signed
8 have they gone
9 He hasn't decided yet
10 I've just seen her / I have just seen her
11 He's already gone / He has already gone
12 Has your course started yet
   *You can also use the past simple (**Did** you **see**, he **didn't reply** etc.) in this exercise.*

7.4

2 he's just gone out / he has just gone out *or* he just went out
3 I haven't finished yet. *or* I didn't finish yet.
4 I've already done it. / I have already done it. *or* I already did it. / I did it already.
5 Have you found a place to live yet? *or* Did you find a place ...?
6 I haven't decided yet. *or* I didn't decide yet.
7 she's just come back / she has just come back *or* she just came back

UNIT 8

8.1

2 Have you ever been to California?
3 Have you ever run a marathon?
4 Have you ever spoken to a famous person?
5 What's the most beautiful place you've ever visited? / ... you have ever visited?

8.2

3 haven't eaten
4 I haven't played (it)
5 I've had / I have had
6 I haven't read
7 I've never been / I haven't been
8 it's happened / it has happened *or* that's happened / that has happened
9 I've never tried / I haven't tried *or* I've never eaten / I haven't eaten
10 's been / has been
11 I've never seen / I haven't seen

8.3

Example answers:

2 I haven't travelled by bus this week.
3 I haven't been to the cinema recently.
4 I haven't read a book for ages.
5 I haven't lost anything today.

8.4

2 It's the first time they've seen a giraffe. / ... they have seen ...
3 She's / She has never ridden a horse before.
4 This is the second time they've been to Japan. / ... they have been to Japan.
5 It's not the first time she's / she has / Emily has stayed at this hotel.
6 He's / He has / Ben has never played tennis before. *or* He/Ben hasn't played tennis before.

UNIT 9

9.1

2 's been watching TV / has been watching TV *or* ... watching television
3 've been playing tennis / have been playing tennis
4 's been running / has been running

9.2

2 Have you been waiting long?
3 What have you been doing?
4 How long have you been working here?
5 How long have you been doing that?

9.3

2 've been waiting / have been waiting
3 've been learning Japanese / have been learning Japanese
4 She's been working there / She has been working there
5 They've been going there / They have been going there *or* ... going to Italy

9.4

2 I've been looking / I have been looking
3 are you looking
4 She's been teaching / She has been teaching
5 I've been thinking / I have been thinking
6 he's working / he is working
7 She's been working / She has been working
8 you're driving / you are driving
9 has been travelling

UNIT 10

10.1

2 She's been travelling / She has been travelling …
   She's visited / She has visited …
3 He's won / He has won …
   He's been playing tennis / He has been playing …
4 They've been making / They have been making …
   They've made / They have made …

10.2

2 Have you been waiting long?
3 Have you caught any fish?
4 How many people have you invited?
5 How long have you been teaching?
6 How many books have you written?
   How long have you been writing books?
7 How long have you been saving (money)?
   How much money have you saved?

10.3

2 Somebody's broken / Somebody has broken
3 Have you been working
4 Have you ever worked
5 has she gone
6 I've had / I have had
7 I've been watching / I have been watching
8 He's appeared / He has appeared
9 I haven't been waiting
10 you've been crying / you have been crying
11 it's stopped / it has stopped
12 They've been playing / They have been playing
13 I've lost / I have lost … Have you seen
14 I've been reading / I have been reading … I haven't finished
15 I've read / I have read

UNIT 11

11.1

2 have you lived
3 It's raining
4 has been
5 Have you been waiting
6 We're living
7 I haven't known
8 She's
9 have you had
10 I've been feeling

11.2

2 How long have you known Katherine?
3 How long has your sister been in Australia?
4 How long have you been teaching English? / How long have you taught English?
5 How long have you had that jacket?
6 How long has Joe been working at the airport? / How long has Joe worked at the airport?
7 Have you always lived in Chicago?

11.3

3 's been / has been
4 's / is
5 haven't played
6 've been waiting / have been waiting
7 've known / have known
8 hasn't been
9 lives *or* 's living / is living
10 's lived / has lived *or* 's been living / has been living
11 's been watching / has been watching
12 haven't watched
13 've had / have had
14 haven't been
15 've always wanted / have always wanted

UNIT 12

12.1

2 for (*also correct without* for)
3 for (*also correct without* for)
4 since
5 for
6 since
7 since
8 for

12.2

2 How long have you had this car?
3 How long have you been waiting?
4 When did your course start?
5 When did Anna arrive in London?
6 How long have you known each other?

12.3

3 He has been ill/unwell since Sunday.
4 She got married a year ago.
5 I've had a headache since I woke up.
6 The meeting started/began at 9 o'clock.
7 I've been working in a hotel for six months. / I've been working there …
8 Kate started learning Japanese a long time ago.

12.4

2 No, I haven't seen Lisa/her for about a month.
3 No, I haven't been swimming for a long time.
4 No, I haven't ridden a bike for ages.
6 No, it's about a month since I (last) saw Lisa/her. *or*
   No, it's been about a month since …
7 No, it's a long time since I (last) went swimming. *or*
   No, it's been a long time since …
8 No, it's ages since I (last) rode a bike. *or* No, it's been ages since …

UNIT 13

13.1

2 has gone   5 had
3 forgot   6 has broken
4 went

13.2

3 did William Shakespeare write
4 *OK*
5 Who invented
6 *OK*
7 We washed
8 Where were you born?
9 *OK*
10 Albert Einstein was the scientist who developed

13.3

3 I've forgotten / I have forgotten
4 arrested
5 it's improved / it has improved
6 Have you finished
7 I applied
8 It was
9 There's been / There has been
10 did you find … It was
11 He's / He has broken … *or* He broke … did that happen … He fell

UNIT 14

14.1

3 *OK*
4 I bought
5 Where were you
6 Maria left school
7 *OK*
8 *OK*
9 *OK*
10 When was this bridge built?

14.2

2 The weather has been cold recently.
3 It was cold last week.
4 I didn't eat any fruit yesterday.
5 I haven't eaten any fruit today.
6 Emily has earned a lot of money this year.
7 She didn't earn so much last year.
8 Have you had a holiday recently?

14.3

3 I didn't sleep
4 There was … there were
5 worked … he gave
6 She's lived / She has lived
7 died … I never met
8 I've never met / I have never met
9 I haven't seen
10 Did you go … was
11 It's been / It has been … it was
12 have you lived / have you been living … did you live … did you live

14.4

Example answers:
2 I haven't bought anything today.
3 I didn't watch TV yesterday.
4 I went out with some friends yesterday evening.
5 I haven't been to the cinema recently.
6 I've read a lot of books recently.

UNIT 15

15.1

3 It had changed a lot.
4 I hadn't heard it before.
5 She'd arranged to do something else. / She had arranged …
6 The film had already started.
7 We hadn't been there before.
8 I hadn't seen him for five years.
9 They'd just had lunch. / They had just had …
10 He'd never played before. / He had never played …

15.2

2 there was …
She'd gone / She had gone
3 He'd just come back from / He had just come back from … He looked
4 got a phone call
He was
He'd sent her / He had sent her … she'd never replied (to them) / she had never replied (to them)

15.3

2 I went
3 had gone
4 he'd already travelled / he had already travelled
5 broke
6 we saw … had broken … we stopped

UNIT 16

16.1

2 They'd been playing football. / They had been playing …
3 I'd been looking forward to it. / I had been looking forward …
4 She'd been having a bad dream. / She had been having …
5 He'd been watching a film. / He had been watching …
6 They'd been waiting a long time. / They had been waiting …

16.2

2 I'd been waiting / I had been waiting … I realised (that) I was (in …)
3 went … had been working   *or*   had worked
4 had been playing … started
5 *Example answer:*
I'd been walking for about ten minutes when a car suddenly stopped just behind me.

16.3

2 We'd been travelling
3 He was looking
4 She'd been running
5 He was walking
6 I'd had it
7 I'd been going
8 I've been training
9 (When I finally arrived,) she was waiting … she'd been waiting (such a long time)
10 a he was already working
b had already been working
c He's been working

UNIT 17

17.1

2 h
3 c
4 g
5 b
6 a
7 e
8 f

17.2

3 don't have / haven't got (haven't *is less usual*)
4 didn't have
5 doesn't have / hasn't got (hasn't *is less usual*)
6 do you have / have you got (have you *is less usual*)
7 didn't have
8 Does he have / Has he got (Has he *is less usual*)
9 did you have
10 don't have / haven't got
11 had … didn't

17.3

3 I didn't have / hadn't got my phone
4 I have a cold   *or*   I've got a cold
5 *OK*
6 I didn't have any energy
7 *OK (or* It hasn't got many shops.)
8 Did you have (Had you *is unusual*)
9 *OK*
10 he had a beard
11 *OK (or* We've got plenty of time.)
12 do you have a shower

17.4

2 has a break
3 had a party
4 have a look
5 's having / is having a nice time
6 had a chat
7 Did you have trouble
8 had a baby
9 was having a shower
10 haven't had a holiday / haven't had a break

UNIT 18

18.1

2 used to have/ride
3 used to live
4 used to be
5 used to eat/like/love
6 used to take
7 used to be
8 used to work

18.2

2 used
3 used to be
4 did
5 used to
6 use
7 to
8 be able
9 didn't

18.3

2–6
• She used to be very lazy, but she works very hard these days.
• She didn't use to like cheese, but she eats lots of cheese now.   *or*   She used not to like cheese, but …
• She used to play the piano, but she hasn't played the piano for a long time. / … played it for a long time.
• She didn't use to drink tea, but she likes it now.   *or*   She used not to drink tea, but …
• She used to have a dog, but it died two years ago.

18.4

Example answers:

3 I used to be a vegetarian, but now I eat meat sometimes.
4 I used to watch TV a lot, but I don't watch it much now.
5 I used to hate getting up early, but now it's no problem.
7 I didn't use to drink coffee, but I drink it every day now.
8 I didn't use to like hot weather, but now I love it.

UNIT 19

19.1

2 How long are you going for?
3 When are you leaving?
4 Are you going alone?
5 Are you travelling by car?
6 Where are you staying?

19.2

2 We're having
3 I'm not working
4 I'm leaving
5 are you going
6 Laura isn't coming / Laura's not coming
7 I'm going
8 He's working / He is working

19.3

Example answers:

2 I'm working tomorrow morning.
3 I'm not doing anything tomorrow evening.
4 I'm going swimming next Sunday.
5 I'm going to a party this evening.

19.4

2 Are you going
3 he's moving / he is moving
4 I'm going / I am going … does it start
5 we're meeting / we are meeting
6 Are you doing
7 does this term end … starts
8 We're going / We are going … Who's getting / Who is getting
9 Are you watching
10 leaves … arrives
11 It finishes
12 I'm not using / I am not using

UNIT 20

20.1

2 What are you going to wear?
3 Where are you going to put it?
4 Who are you going to invite?
5 How are you going to cook it?

20.2

2 I'm going to try
3 I'm going to say
4 I'm going to wash
5 I'm not going to accept
6 I'm going to learn
7 I'm going to run
8 I'm going to complain
9 I'm not going to tell

20.3

2 He's going to be late.
3 The boat is going to sink.
4 They're going to run out of petrol.
5 It's going to cost a lot (of money) to repair the car.

20.4

2 was going to buy
3 were going to play
4 was going to phone
5 was going to be
6 was going to give up
7 were you going to say

UNIT 21

21.1

2 I'll turn / I'll switch / I'll put
3 I'll check
4 I'll do
5 I'll show
6 I'll have
7 I'll stay / I'll wait
8 I'll try

21.2

2 I think I'll go to bed.
3 I think I'll go for a walk.
4 I don't think I'll have (any) lunch.
5 I don't think I'll go swimming today.

21.3

3 I'll meet
4 I'll stay
5 I'm having
6 I won't forget
7 we're going
8 Are you doing
9 Will you do
10 Do you go
11 won't tell
12 I'll do

21.4

2 Where shall we go (on holiday)?
3 Shall I buy it?
4 Shall we get a taxi (or) (shall we) walk?
5 What shall I give/buy/get Helen (for her birthday)?
6 What time shall we meet?

UNIT 22

22.1

2 won't	5 'll / will	
3 'll / will	6 won't	
4 won't		

22.2

2 It will look
3 you'll like / you will like
4 You'll enjoy / You will enjoy
5 You'll get / You will get
6 people will live
7 we'll meet / we will meet
8 she'll come / she will come
9 she'll mind
10 it will be

22.3

2 Do you think it will rain?
3 When do you think it will end?
4 How much do you think it will cost?
5 Do you think they'll get married? / … they will get married?
6 What time do you think you'll be back? / … you will be back?
7 What do you think will happen?

22.4

Example answers:

2 I'll be in bed.
3 I'll be at work.
4 I'll probably be at home.
5 I don't know where I'll be.

22.5

2 I'll never forget it.
3 You'll laugh
4 I'm going
5 will win
6 is coming
7 It won't hurt
8 What will happen
9 we're going

UNIT 23

23.1

2 I'll lend
3 I'm going to wash
4 I'll show
5 are you going to paint
6 I'm going to buy
7 I'll have
8 I'm not going to finish
9 (What) is he going to study / (What)'s he going to study
10 I'll call
11 he's going to have … he's going to do

23.2

2 I'll see
3 I'm going to sell
4 you'll find (you're going to find *is also possible*)
5 a I'm going to throw
5 b I'll have it.
6 a I'll take
6 b Amy is going to take (*or* Amy is taking)

23.3

2 d	6 a	
3 h	7 e	
4 g	8 b	
5 c		

UNIT 24

24.1
2 b *is true*
3 a *and* c *are true*
4 b *and* d *are true*
5 c *and* d *are true*
6 c *is true*

24.2
2 be going
3 won't be playing
4 will be starting
5 be watching
6 will you be doing
7 won't be going
8 will be landing

24.3
2 we'll be playing / we will be playing
3 She'll be waiting / She will be waiting
4 it will have finished (*or* it will be finished)
5 you'll still be living / you will still be living
6 she'll have travelled / she will have travelled
7 I'll be staying / I will be staying
8 he'll have spent / he will have spent
9 I won't be doing / I will not be doing

UNIT 25

25.1
2 we'll let
3 starts
4 it changes
5 I'll make
6 I'm 40
7 I'll wait
8 he grows up
9 you're
10 is
11 will be
12 you've had

25.2
2 she goes
3 you know
4 I'll wait / I will wait … you're / you are
5 Will you still be … I get
6 there are … I'll let / I will let
7 You won't recognise / You will not recognise … you see
8 you need … I'm / I am

25.3
2 it gets dark
3 you decide *or* you've decided / you have decided
4 you're in Hong Kong / you go to Hong Kong
5 build the new road *or* 've built the new road / have built the new road
6 she apologises *or* she's apologised / she has apologised

25.4
2 if
3 If
4 when
5 If
6 When
7 if
8 if

UNIT 26

26.1
3 can
4 be able to
5 been able to
6 can (*or* will be able to)
7 be able to
8 can
9 be able to

26.2
Example answers:
2 I used to be able to run fast.
3 I'd like to be able to play the piano.
4 I've never been able to get up early.

26.3
2 could run
3 can wait
4 couldn't sleep
5 can't hear
6 couldn't believe

26.4
2 was able to finish it
3 were able to solve it
4 was able to get away

26.5
4 couldn't
5 managed to
6 could
7 managed to
8 could
9 couldn't
10 managed to

UNIT 27

27.1
2 e
3 b
4 f
5 a
6 d

27.2
2 could
3 can
4 could
5 can
6 can
7 could
8 can
9 could
10 could

27.3
2 could have come
3 could be
4 could have been
5 could have
6 could come
7 have moved
8 gone

27.4
3 couldn't wear
4 couldn't have managed
5 couldn't have been
6 couldn't afford (*or* couldn't manage)
7 couldn't have studied
8 couldn't stand

UNIT 28

28.1
2 must
3 can't
4 must
5 must
6 can't
7 must
8 can't
9 must
10 can't
11 must

28.2
3 know
4 have left
5 be
6 have been
7 be looking
8 have heard
9 have been
10 be joking
11 get / be getting *or* have

28.3
3 It must have been very expensive.
4 They must have gone away.
5 I must have left it in the restaurant last night.
6 It can't have been easy for her.
7 He must have been waiting for somebody.
8 She can't have understood what I said. *or* She couldn't have understood what I said.
9 I must have forgotten to lock it.
10 They must have been having a party.
11 The driver can't have seen the red light. *or* The driver couldn't have seen …
12 He can't have worn them much.

UNIT 29

29.1
2 might know
3 might be Brazilian
4 may not be possible
5 may be Tom's
6 might be driving
7 might have one
8 may not be feeling well

29.2
2 have been
3 have arrived
4 be waiting
5 have told
6 have gone
7 be watching
8 have
9 have left
10 have heard
11 have forgotten

29.3
2 might not have wanted
3 couldn't have been
4 couldn't have tried
5 might not have been American

UNIT 30

30.1
2 I'm going to get
3 He might come
4 I might hang
5 She's going
6 I might go away

30.2
2 might wake
3 might spill
4 might need
5 might hear
6 might slip

30.3
2 might have to leave
3 might be able to meet
4 might have to pay
5 might have to wait
6 might be able to fix

30.4
2 I might not recognise him.
3 We might not be able to get tickets for the game.
4 I might not have time to do the shopping.
5 I might not be able to go to the wedding.

30.5
2 I might as well buy a new one.
3 I might as well paint the bathroom too.
4 We might as well watch it.

UNIT 31

31.1
3 I have to go / I'll have to go
4 do you have to go / will you have to go
5 he has to get up
6 We had to run
7 does she have to work
8 I had to do
9 do you have to be
10 We had to close
11 did you have to pay

31.2
3 have to make
4 don't have to decide
5 had to ask
6 don't have to pay
7 didn't have to go
8 has to make
9 had to stand
10 will have to drive / 'll have to drive / is going to have to drive

31.3
3 OK (I **have to** remember *is also correct*)
4 I **had to** walk home.
5 OK (You **have to** come *is also correct*)
6 He **has to** study
7 We **have to** go
8 She **has had to** wear glasses since … *For the present perfect (**has had**) with **since**, see Units 11–12.*

31.4
3 don't have to
4 mustn't
5 don't have to
6 doesn't have to
7 don't have to
8 mustn't
9 mustn't
10 don't have to

UNIT 32

32.1
2 d   5 g
3 b   6 a
4 e   7 c

32.2
2 must
3 mustn't
4 don't need to
5 mustn't
6 needn't
7 mustn't
8 don't need to
9 needn't … must

32.3
2 needn't come
3 needn't walk
4 needn't keep
5 needn't worry

32.4
2 You needn't have walked home. You could have taken a taxi.
3 They needn't have stayed at a hotel. They could have stayed with us.
4 She needn't have phoned me at 3 am. She could have waited until the morning.
5 You needn't have shouted at me. You could have been more patient.

32.5
3 You **needn't shout**. / You **don't need to** shout. / You **don't have to** shout.
4 I **didn't need to go** out. / I **didn't have to go** out.
5 *OK*
6 You **needn't** lock the door. / You **don't need to** lock the door. / You **don't have to** lock the door.
7 I **didn't need to say** anything. / I **didn't have to say** anything.
8 *OK*

UNIT 33

33.1
2 You should look for another job.
3 He shouldn't stay up so late.
4 You should take a picture.
5 She shouldn't worry so much.
6 He should put some pictures on the walls.

33.2
2 should be here soon
3 should be working OK
4 shouldn't take long
5 should receive
6 should be much warmer
7 shouldn't cost more
8 should solve

33.3
3 should do
4 should have done
5 should have won
6 should come
7 should have turned
8 should have done

33.4
2 We should have reserved a table.
3 I should have written down her address. / I should have written her address down. *or* I should have written it down.
4 The shop should be open (now / by now). / The shop should have opened by now. *or* It should …
5 I shouldn't have been looking at my phone. *or*
I should have looked / been looking where I was going.
6 She shouldn't be doing 50. / She shouldn't be driving so fast. / She should be driving more slowly.
7 I shouldn't have gone to work (yesterday).
8 Team A should win (the match).
9 The driver in front shouldn't have stopped without warning. / … shouldn't have stopped so suddenly.

UNIT 34

34.1

2 I should stay / I stay / I stayed a little longer
3 they should visit / they visit / they visited the museum after lunch
4 we should pay / we pay / we paid the rent by Friday
5 we should go / we go / we went to the cinema

34.2

2 *OK*
   ('suggested that we should meet' *is also correct*)
3 What do you suggest I do / I should do
4 *OK*
   ('suggest I buy' *is also correct*)
5 I suggest you read / you should read …
6 *OK*
   ('suggested that Anna should learn', 'suggested that Anna learns' *and* 'suggested that Anna learnt/learned' *are also correct*)

34.3

2 should say
3 should worry
4 should leave
5 should ask
6 should vote
7 should be done

34.4

2 If it should rain
3 If there should be any problems
4 If anyone should ask
6 Should it rain
7 Should there be any problems
8 Should anyone ask

34.5

2 I should keep
3 I should call
4 I should get

UNIT 35

35.1

2 We'd better reserve a table.
3 You'd better put a plaster on it.
4 You'd better not go to work this morning.
5 I'd/We'd better check what time the film starts.
6 I'd better not disturb her right now.

35.2

2 *OK*
3 You **should** come more often.
4 *OK*
5 *OK*
6 everybody **should** learn a foreign language
7 *OK*

35.3

2 had
3 not
4 should
5 to
6 I'd
7 were
8 better
9 hadn't
10 do
11 did
12 was

35.4

2 It's time I had a holiday.
3 It's time the children were in bed. / … went to bed.
4 It's time I started cooking (the) dinner.
5 It's time she/Kate stopped complaining about everything.
6 It's time (some) changes were made

UNIT 36

36.1

Example answers:
2 I wouldn't like to be a teacher.
3 I'd love to learn to fly a plane.
4 It would be nice to have a big garden.
5 I'd like to go to Mexico.

36.2

2 'd enjoy / would enjoy
3 'd have enjoyed / would have enjoyed
4 would you do
5 'd have stopped / would have stopped
6 would have been
7 'd be / would be
8 would have

36.3

2 e   5 a
3 b   6 d
4 f

36.4

2 He promised he'd call. / … he would call.
3 You promised you wouldn't tell her. *or* … wouldn't tell anyone/anybody.
4 They promised they'd wait (for us). / … they would wait.

36.5

2 wouldn't tell
3 wouldn't speak
4 wouldn't let

36.6

2 would shake
3 would share
4 would always forget
5 would stay
6 would always smile

UNIT 37

37.1

2 g
3 d
4 b
5 a
6 h
7 f
8 c

37.2

2 Would you like
3 I'd like
4 Would you like to come
5 Can I take
6 I'd like to
7 Would you like to try
8 Do you mind

37.3

2 Can/Could I/we have the bill, please? *or* … get the bill?
3 Can/Could you check these forms (for me)? *or* Do you think you could check …?
4 Can/Could you turn the music down, please? / … turn it down? *or* Do you think you could turn …?
5 Is it OK if I close the window? *or* Is it all right if …? *or* Can I close …? *or* Do you mind if I close …?
6 Would you like to sit down? *or* Would you like a seat? *or* Can I offer you a seat?
7 Can/Could you tell me how to get to the station? *or* … the way to the station? *or* … where the station is?
8 Can/Could I try on these trousers? *or* Can/Could I try these (trousers) on? *or* I'd like to try on these trousers. *or* Is it OK if I try …
9 Can/Could I get your autograph? / … have your autograph? *or* Do you think I could get/have your autograph?

UNIT 38

38.1

2 dropped
3 lost
4 happened
5 went
6 did
7 was

38.2

2 b
3 a
4 b
5 b
6 a
7 b

38.3

2 I bought
3 would you invite
4 he asked
5 I'd be / I would be
6 somebody gave … I'd have / I would have
7 Would you be … you met
8 would you do … you were … it stopped

38.4

2 If we stayed at a hotel, it would cost too much.
3 If I told you what happened, you wouldn't believe me. or … believe it.
4 If she left her job, it would be hard to find another one.
5 If he applied for the job, he wouldn't get it.

UNIT 39

39.1

3 I'd help / I would help
4 It would taste
5 we lived
6 we'd live / we would live
7 I was / I were
8 it wasn't / it weren't
9 I wouldn't wait … I'd go / I would go
10 you didn't go … you wouldn't be
11 there weren't … there wouldn't be
12 would you do if you didn't have

39.2

2 I'd / I would buy them if they weren't so expensive.
3 We'd / We would go on holiday if we could afford it.
4 We could have lunch outside if it weren't/wasn't raining.
5 If I wanted his advice, I'd / I would ask for it.

39.3

2 I wish I had more free time.
3 I wish Helen were/was here.
4 I wish it weren't/wasn't (so) cold.
5 I wish I didn't live in a big city.
6 I wish I could find my phone.
7 I wish I was/were feeling well/better.
8 I wish I didn't have to get up early tomorrow.
9 I wish I knew more about science.

39.4

Example answers:

1 I wish I was at home.
2 I wish I had a big garden.
3 I wish I could tell jokes.
4 I wish I was taller.

UNIT 40

40.1

2 If she'd missed / she had missed (the train), she'd have missed / she would have missed (her flight too).
3 I'd have forgotten / I would have forgotten (if) you hadn't reminded
4 I'd had / I had had (your email address) I'd have sent / I would have sent (you an email)
5 they'd have enjoyed / they would have enjoyed (it more if the weather) had been (better)
6 It would have been (quicker if) we'd walked / we had walked
7 you'd told / you had told (me) I'd have tried / I would have tried
8 I were / I was
9 I'd been / I had been

40.2

2 If the road hadn't been icy, the accident wouldn't have happened.
3 If I'd known / If I had known (that you had to get up early), I'd have woken / I would have woken you up.
4 If I hadn't lost my phone (or If I'd had my phone), I'd have called you. or … I would have called you. or … I could have called you.
5 If Karen hadn't been wearing a seat belt, she'd have been injured / she would have been injured (in the crash). or … she might have been injured or … she could have been injured
6 If you'd had / If you had had (some) breakfast, you wouldn't be hungry now.
7 If I'd had / If I had had enough money, I'd have got / I would have got a taxi. (or … taken a taxi)
8 If Dan had done well/better at school, he could/would have gone to university.

40.3

2 I wish I'd learned / I wish I had learned to play a musical instrument (when I was younger). or I wish I could play … / I wish I was able to play …
3 I wish I hadn't painted it red. or … the gate red. or I wish I had painted it a different colour.
4 I wish we'd gone / I wish we had gone by train. or
   I wish we hadn't gone by car.
5 I wish we'd had / I wish we had had more time (to do all the things we wanted to do).
6 I wish I hadn't moved (to my new flat). or I wish I'd stayed where I was. / … stayed in my old flat.

UNIT 41

41.1

2 hope
3 wish
4 wished
5 hope
6 wish
7 hope

41.2

2 wasn't/weren't
3 'd told / had told
4 had / could have
5 could
6 hadn't bought
7 didn't have
8 have gone

41.3

2 I wish she would come. or … would hurry up.
3 I wish somebody would give me a job.
4 I wish the/that dog would stop barking.
5 I wish you wouldn't drive so fast.
6 I wish you wouldn't leave the door open (all the time).
7 I wish people wouldn't drop litter in the street.

41.4

3 I knew
4 we hadn't gone
5 the bus would come
6 I could come
7 it was/were
8 I'd taken / I had taken
9 you'd listen / you would listen
10 you wouldn't complain or you didn't complain
11 it wasn't/weren't
12 the weather would change
13 I had / I could have
14 we could have stayed

UNIT 42

42.1

2 is made
3 was damaged
4 are shown
5 were invited
6 's/is found
7 were overtaken
8 are held
9 was injured
10 is surrounded
11 was sent
12 is owned

42.2

2 When was television invented?
3 How are mountains formed?
4 When was DNA discovered?
5 What is silver used for?

42.3

2 a covers
   b is covered
3 a was stolen
   b disappeared
4 a died
   b were brought up
5 a sank
   b was rescued
6 a was fired
   b resigned
7 a doesn't bother
   b 'm/am not bothered
8 a was knocked
   b fell
9 a are they called
   b do you call

42.4

2 All flights were cancelled because of fog.
3 I was accused of stealing money.
4 How is this word used?
5 All taxes are included in the price.
6 We were warned not to go out alone.
7 This office isn't / is not used any more.
8 Five hundred people were invited to the wedding.

UNIT 43

43.1

3 be made
4 be kept
5 have been repaired
6 be carried
7 have been arrested
8 be delayed
9 have been caused
10 be knocked
11 be known
12 have been forgotten

43.2

3 It's been stolen! / It has been stolen!
4 Somebody has taken it. *or*
   … taken my umbrella.
5 He hasn't been seen since then.
6 I haven't seen her for ages.
7 Have you ever been stung by a bee?
8 It's / It is being repaired at the moment.
9 It hasn't / It has not been found yet.
10 The furniture had been moved.

43.3

2 A new road is being built
3 Two new hotels have been built
4 some new houses were being built
5 The date of the meeting has been changed.
6 I didn't know that our conversation was being recorded.
7 Is anything being done about the problem?
8 They hadn't / had not been cleaned for ages.

UNIT 44

44.1

2 was given
3 wasn't told / was not told
4 's paid / is paid
5 been shown
6 was asked
7 weren't given / were not given
8 to be offered

44.2

2 being invited
3 being given
4 being knocked down
5 being bitten
6 being treated
7 being stuck

44.3

2 got stung
3 get used
4 got stolen
5 get paid
6 get broken
7 get asked
8 got stopped

44.4

3 were
4 given
5 lost
6 being
7 get
8 doesn't
9 was
10 weren't

UNIT 45

45.1

2 Many people are reported to be homeless after the floods.
3 The thieves are thought to have got in through a window in the roof.
4 The driver (of the car) is alleged to have been driving at 110 miles an hour. *or* … to have driven at …
5 The building is reported to have been badly damaged by the fire.
6 The company is said to be losing a lot of money.
7 The company is believed to have lost a lot of money last year.
8 The company is expected to make a loss this year.

45.2

2 they're / they are supposed to be
3 it's / it is supposed to have been
4 they're / they are supposed to have won
5 the view is supposed to be
6 she's / she is supposed to be living

45.3

2 You're / You are supposed to be my friend.
3 I'm / I am supposed to be on a diet.
4 It was supposed to be a joke.
5 Or maybe it's / it is supposed to be a flower.
6 You're / You are supposed to be working.
7 It's supposed to be open every day.

45.4

2 're / are supposed to start
3 was supposed to phone
4 aren't / 're not / are not supposed to put
5 was supposed to depart
6 isn't / 's not / is not supposed to lift

UNIT 46

46.1

1 b
2 a
3 a
4 b

46.2

2 Sarah has her car serviced once a year.
3 Have you had your eyes tested recently?
4 I don't like having my hair cut.
5 It cost fifteen pounds to have my suit cleaned.
6 You need to get this document translated as soon as possible.

46.3

2 I had it cut.
3 We had them cleaned.
4 He had it built.
5 I had them delivered.
6 She had them repaired.

46.4

2 f
3 a
4 e
5 c
6 b

46.5

2 We had our bags searched.
3 I've had my salary increased. *or* I had my salary increased.
4 He's had his application refused. *or* He had his application refused.

UNIT 47

47.1

2 (that) it was too far
3 (that) she didn't want to go
4 (that) he would let me know next week.
5 (that) he hadn't seen her for a while
6 (that) I could borrow hers.
7 (that) she wasn't enjoying it very much
8 (that) he sold it a few months ago
   or he'd sold it … / he had sold it …
9 (that) she didn't know
10 (that) there were twenty students in her class

47.2

Example answers:

2 wasn't coming / was going somewhere else / couldn't come
3 they didn't like each other / they didn't get on with each other / they couldn't stand each other
4 he didn't know anyone
5 she would be away / she was going away
6 you were staying at home
7 you couldn't speak / you didn't speak any other languages
8 he'd seen you / he saw you last weekend

UNIT 48

48.1

2 But you said you didn't like fish.
3 But you said you couldn't drive.
4 But you said she had a very well-paid job.
5 But you said you didn't have any brothers or sisters.
6 But you said you'd / you had never been to the United States.
7 But you said you were working tomorrow evening.
8 But you said she was a friend of yours.

48.2

2 Tell
3 Say
4 said
5 told
6 said
7 told
8 said
9 tell … said
10 tell … say

48.3

2 her to slow down
3 her not to worry
4 asked Tom to give me a hand   *or* … to help me
5 asked/told me to open my bag
6 told him to mind his own business
7 asked her to marry him
8 told her not to wait (for me) if I was late

UNIT 49

49.1

2 Were you born there?
3 Are you married?
4 How long have you been married?
5 What do you do?
6 What does your wife do?
7 Do you have (any) children?   *or* Have you got (any) children?
8 How old are they?

49.2

3 Who paid the bill? / Who paid it?
4 What are you worried about?
5 What happened?
6 What did she/Diane say?
7 Who does it / this book belong to?
8 Who lives in that house? / Who lives there?
9 What did you fall over?
10 What fell off the shelf?
11 What does it / this word mean?
12 Who was she/Sarah with?
13 What are you looking for?
14 Who does she/Emma remind you of?

49.3

2 How is cheese made?
3 Why isn't Sue working today?
4 What time are your friends arriving?
5 Why was the meeting cancelled?
6 When was paper invented?
7 Where were your parents born?
8 Why didn't you come to the party?
9 How did the accident happen?
10 Why aren't you happy?
11 How many languages can you speak?

49.4

2 Don't you like him?
3 Isn't it good?
4 Don't you have any?   *or*   Haven't you got any?

UNIT 50

50.1

2 c
3 a
4 b
5 b
6 c
7 b
8 a

50.2

2 How far is it to the airport?
3 I wonder how old Tom is.
4 How long have they been married?
5 Do you know how long they have been married?
6 Could you tell me where the station is?
7 I don't know whether anyone was injured in the accident.
8 Do you know what time you will arrive tomorrow?

50.3

2 She asked me how long I'd been in London.   *or* … how long I had been …
3 They asked me if/whether I'd been to London before.   *or* … I had been …
4 She asked me if/whether I liked London.
5 He asked me where I was staying.
6 She asked me how long I was going to stay.
7 She asked me if/whether I thought London was expensive.   *or* … is expensive.
8 They asked me why I'd come to London.   *or* … why I had come …   *or* … why I came …

UNIT 51

51.1

2 doesn't
3 was
4 has
5 will
6 should
7 won't
8 do
9 didn't
10 might
11 am … isn't   *or*   'm not … is   *or* can't … can   *or*   can't … is
12 would … could … can't

51.2

3 Do you? I don't.
4 Didn't you? I did.
5 Aren't you? I am.
6 Did you? I didn't.

51.3

Example answers:

3 So did I.   *or* Did you? What did you watch?
4 Neither will I.   *or* Won't you? Where will you be?
5 So do I.   *or* Do you? What sort of books do you like?
6 So would I.   *or* Would you? Where would you like to live?
7 Neither can I.   *or* Can't you? Why not?
8 So am I.   *or* Are you? Are you doing something nice?

51.4

2 I hope so.   6 I'm afraid so.
3 I hope not.   7 I think so.
4 I don't think so.   8 I'm afraid not.
5 I suppose so.

UNIT 52

52.1

3 don't you
4 were you
5 does she
6 isn't he
7 did it
8 can't you
9 will they
10 aren't there
11 shall we
12 is it
13 aren't I
14 would you
15 hasn't she
16 should I
17 had he
18 will you

52.2

2 It's (very) expensive, isn't it?
3 The course was great, wasn't it?
4 You've had your hair cut, haven't you? *or*
   You had your hair cut, didn't you?
5 She has a good voice, doesn't she?
   or She has a good voice, hasn't she?
   or She's got / She has got a good voice, hasn't she?
6 It doesn't look right, does it?
7 This bridge isn't very safe, is it? *or*
   … doesn't look very safe, does it?

52.3

2 Joe, you couldn't help me (with this table), could you?
3 Lisa, you don't know where Sarah is, do you? *or*
   … you haven't seen Sarah, have you?
4 Helen, you don't have a tennis racket, do you? *or*
   … you haven't got a tennis racket, have you?
5 Anna, you couldn't take me to the station, could you? *or*
   … you couldn't give me a lift to the station, could you?
6 Robert, you haven't seen my keys, have you?

UNIT 53

53.1

2 playing tennis
3 going for a walk
4 causing the accident
5 waiting a few minutes
6 not telling the truth *or*
   (She admitted) lying.

53.2

2 making
3 listening
4 applying
5 reading
6 living
7 travelling
8 forgetting
9 paying
10 trying
11 losing
12 interrupting

53.3

2 I don't mind you driving it.
3 Can you imagine anybody being so stupid?
4 We can't stop it raining.
5 I don't want to keep you waiting.

53.4

Example answers:

2 going out
3 sitting on the floor
4 having a picnic
5 laughing
6 breaking down

UNIT 54

54.1

2 to help him
3 to carry her bag (for her)
4 to meet at 8 o'clock
5 to tell him her name / to give him her name
6 not to tell anyone *or* (She promised) she wouldn't tell anyone.

54.2

2 to get
3 to live
4 to play
5 to tell
6 say *or* to say

54.3

2 to look
3 to move
4 waiting
5 to finish
6 barking
7 to be
8 having
9 missing
10 to say

54.4

2 Tom appears to be worried about something.
3 You seem to know a lot of people.
4 My English seems to be getting better.
5 That car appears to have broken down.
6 Rachel seems to be enjoying her job.
7 They claim to have solved the problem.

54.5

2 what to do
3 how to ride
4 whether to go
5 where to put
6 how to use

UNIT 55

55.1

2 or do you want me to lend you some
3 or would you like me to shut it
4 or would you like me to show you
5 or do you want me to repeat it
6 or do you want me to wait

55.2

2 to stay with them
3 to call Joe.
4 him to be careful
5 her to give him a hand

55.3

2 I didn't expect it to rain.
3 Let him do what he wants.
4 Tom's glasses make him look older.
5 I want you to know the truth.
6 Sarah persuaded me to apply for the job.
7 My lawyer advised me not to say anything to the police.
8 I was warned not to believe everything he says.
9 Having a car enables you to get around more easily.

55.4

2 to do
3 cry
4 to study
5 finish
6 do
7 to do
8 drive
9 change
10 to work

UNIT 56

56.1

2 driving
3 to go
4 going
5 to win
6 asking
7 asking
8 to answer
9 causing
10 to do
11 being
12 to climb
13 to tell
14 talking … to see

56.2

2 He doesn't remember crying
3 He remembers falling into the river.
4 He doesn't remember saying he wanted to be a doctor. *or* He doesn't remember wanting to be a doctor.
5 He doesn't remember being bitten by a dog.
6 He remembers his sister being born (when he was four).

56.3

1 b meeting
  c leaving/putting
  d to say
  e lending
  f to call/phone
2 a doing
  b to say
  c wearing / having / taking / putting on
  d leaving / giving up
3 a to become
  b working
  c reading
  d going up / rising / increasing

UNIT 57

57.1

2 to reach
3 knocking
4 to put
5 to concentrate
6 asking
7 calling
8 to remember
9 restarting

57.2

2 It needs cutting.
3 They need cleaning.
4 They need tightening.
5 It needs emptying.

57.3

2 washing
3 looking
4 to think
5 cutting
6 to go
7 to iron
8 ironing

57.4

2 look *or* to look
3 overhearing
4 smiling
5 make *or* to make
6 organise *or* to organise
7 thinking
8 get *or* to get

UNIT 58

58.1

Example answers:
2 I don't mind playing cards.
3 I don't like being alone. *or* … to be alone.
4 I enjoy going to museums.
5 I love cooking. *or* I love to cook.
6 I hate getting up early.

58.2

2 She likes teaching biology.
3 He likes taking pictures. *or* He likes to take pictures.
4 I didn't like working there.
5 She likes studying medicine.
6 He doesn't like being famous.
7 She doesn't like taking risks. *or* She doesn't like to take risks.
8 I like to know things in advance.

58.3

2 to sit
3 turning
4 doing *or* to do
5 to get
6 being
7 to come / to go
8 living / being
9 to talk
10 to have / to know / to get / to hear / to be told
11 to wait
12 losing *or* to lose

58.4

2 I would like / I'd like to have seen the programme.
3 I would hate / I'd hate to have lost my watch.
4 I would love / I'd love to have met your parents.
5 I wouldn't like to have been alone.
6 I would prefer / I'd prefer to have travelled by train.

UNIT 59

59.1

Example answers:
2 I prefer basketball to football.
3 I prefer going to the cinema to watching movies at home.
4 I prefer being very busy to having nothing to do.
6 I prefer to go to the cinema rather than watch movies at home. *or* I prefer going to the cinema rather than watching movies at home.
7 I prefer to be very busy rather than have nothing to do. *or* I prefer being very busy to having nothing to do.

59.2

3 prefer
4 eat / stay
5 I'd rather (wait) / I'd prefer to (wait)
6 to go
7 (I'd) rather (think) / (I'd) prefer to (think)
8 I'd prefer
9 go
11 I'd rather listen to some music than watch TV.
12 I'd prefer to eat/stay at home rather than go to a restaurant.
13 I'd rather go for a swim than play tennis. *or* … than have a game of tennis.
14 I'd prefer to think about it for a while rather than decide now.

59.3

2 (would you rather) I paid it
3 would you rather I did it
4 would you rather I phoned her

59.4

2 came
3 watch
4 than
5 didn't
6 was
7 to watch
8 didn't
9 did
10 rather than

UNIT 60

60.1

2 applying for the job
3 remembering names
4 winning the lottery
5 being late
6 eating at home
7 having to queue *or* (without) queuing
8 being 90 years old

60.2

2 by standing
3 by pressing
4 by borrowing
5 by driving
6 by putting

60.3

2 paying/settling
3 going
4 making
5 being/travelling/sitting
6 going
7 asking/telling/consulting/informing
8 doing/having
9 turning/going
10 taking
11 bending
12 buying

60.4

2 I'm looking forward to seeing her (again).
3 I'm not looking forward to going to the dentist (tomorrow).
4 She's looking forward to leaving school (next summer).
5 They're looking forward to moving (to their new apartment).

UNIT 61

61.1

2 used to going
3 used to working / used to being
4 used to walking
5 used to living

61.2

1 It took her a few months to **get used to** it. ...
   She**'s used to working** nights. / She **is used to working** nights.
2 When Jack started working in this job, he **wasn't used to** driving two hours to work every morning, but after some time he **got used to** it.
   ... He**'s used to driving** two hours every morning. / He **is used to driving** ...

61.3

2 No, I'm used to sleeping on the floor.
3 I'm used to working long hours.
4 I'm not used to the crowds (of people).

61.4

2 They soon got used to her. / ... to the/their new teacher.
3 She had to get used to living in a much smaller house.
4 She can't get used to the weather.
5 He had to get used to having less money.

61.5

2 drink
3 eating
4 having
5 have/own
6 go
7 be
8 being

UNIT 62

62.1

2 doing
3 coming/going
4 doing/trying
5 buying/having
6 solving
7 buying/having/owning
8 seeing

62.2

2 of stealing
3 from taking off
4 of getting
5 on telling
6 to eating
7 for being
8 from walking (or ... stop people walking)
9 for inviting
10 of using
11 of (not) trying

62.3

2 on taking Ann to the station
3 on getting married
4 Sue for coming to see her
5 (to me) for being late
6 me of not caring about other people

UNIT 63

63.1

2	h	6	a
3	d	7	e
4	g	8	c
5	b		

63.2

2 There's no point in working if you don't need money.
3 There's no point in trying to study if you feel tired. *or*
   There's no point in studying if ...
4 There's no point in hurrying if you have plenty of time.

63.3

2 remembering people's names
3 finding a job / getting a job
4 getting a ticket for the game
5 understanding one another

63.4

2 going / travelling / getting
3 getting
4 watching
5 going / climbing / walking
6 getting / being
7 practising
8 working
9 applying
10 trying

63.5

2 went swimming
3 go skiing
4 goes riding
5 's/has gone shopping *or* went shopping

UNIT 64

64.1

2 I opened the box to see what was in it.
3 I moved to a new apartment to be nearer my friends.
4 I couldn't find a knife to chop the onions. *or*
   ... a knife to chop the onions with.
5 I called the police to report the accident.
6 I called the hotel to find out if they had any rooms free.
7 I employed an assistant to help me with my work.

64.2

2 to do
3 to walk
4 to drink
5 to put / to carry
6 to discuss / to consider / to talk about
7 to go / to travel
8 to talk / to speak
9 to wear / to put on
10 to celebrate
11 to help / to assist
12 to be

64.3

2 to
3 for
4 to
5 for
6 for
7 to
8 for ... to

64.4

2 so that I wouldn't get/be cold.
3 so that he could contact me. / ... would be able to contact me.
4 so that nobody else would hear us. / so that nobody else could hear us. / ... would be able to hear us.
5 so that we can start the meeting on time. / so that we'll be able to start ...
6 so that we wouldn't forget anything.
7 so that the car behind me could overtake. / ... would be able to overtake.

UNIT 65

65.1

2 The window was difficult to open.
3 Some words are impossible to translate.
4 A car is expensive to maintain.
5 This meat isn't safe to eat.
6 My house is easy to get to from here.

65.2

2 It's an easy mistake to make.
3 It's a great place to live.
4 It was a strange thing to say.

Key to Exercises

65.3

2	glad	6	amazed
3	to hear	7	to make
4	of you	8	not
5	to help	9	silly

65.4

2 Paul was the last (person) to arrive.
3 Emily was the only student to pass (the exam). / … the only one to pass (the exam).
4 I was the second customer/person to complain.
5 Neil Armstrong was the first person/ man to walk on the moon.

65.5

2 You're / You are bound to be tired
3 He's / He is sure to forget
4 It's / It is not likely to rain   *or*
   It isn't likely to rain
5 There's / There is sure to be

UNIT 66

66.1

3 I'm afraid of losing it.
4 I was afraid to tell her.
5 We were afraid of missing our train.
6 We were afraid to look.
7 I was afraid of dropping it.
8 Don't be afraid to ask.
9 I was afraid of running out of petrol.

66.2

2 interested in starting
3 interested to know / interested to hear
4 interested in studying
5 interested to hear / interested to know (interested in hearing/knowing *is also possible here*)
6 interested in looking

66.3

2 sorry to hear
3 sorry for saying / sorry I said
4 sorry to see
5 sorry for making / sorry I made

66.4

1 b to leave
   c from leaving
2 a to solve
   b to solve
   c in solving
3 a of going / about going
   b to go (*or* on going)
   c to go
   d to going
4 a to buy
   b on buying
   c to buy
   d of buying

UNIT 67

67.1

1 b give
2 a stopped
   b stop
3 a open
   b opened
4 a say
   b said (says *is also possible*)
5 a fell
   b fall

67.2

2 We saw Clare eating/sitting in a restaurant.
3 We saw David and Helen playing tennis.
4 We could smell something burning.
5 We could hear Bill playing his/the guitar.
6 We saw Linda jogging/running.

67.3

3	say	8	explode
4	happen	9	crawling
5	crying	10	riding
6	put	11	slam
7	tell	12	lying

UNIT 68

68.1

2 Amy was sitting in an armchair reading a book.
3 Nicola opened the door carefully trying not to make a noise.
4 Sarah went out saying she would be back in an hour.
5 Lisa worked in Rome for two years teaching English.
6 Anna walked around the town looking at the sights and taking pictures.

68.2

2 I got very wet walking in the rain.
3 Laura had an accident driving to work.
4 My friend slipped and fell getting off a bus.
5 Emily hurt her back trying to lift a heavy box.
6 Two people were overcome by smoke trying to put out the fire.

68.3

Example answers:

2 Having bought our tickets / Having got our tickets
3 Having discussed the problem / Having talked about the problem / Having thought about the problem
4 Having said he was hungry
5 Having lost his job / Having given up his job / Having been fired from his job
6 Having spent most of his life / Having lived (for) most of his life

68.4

2 Thinking they might be hungry, …
3 Being a vegetarian, …
4 Not having a phone, …
5 Having travelled a lot, …
6 Not being able to speak the local language, …
7 Having spent nearly all our money, …

UNIT 69

69.1

3 We went to **a** very nice restaurant …
4 *OK*
5 I use **a** toothbrush …
6 … if there's **a** bank near here?
7 … for **an** insurance company.
8 *OK*
9 … we stayed in **a** big hotel.
10 If you have **a** problem …
11 … It's **an** interesting idea.
12 *OK*
13 … It's **a** good game.
14 *OK*
15 … wearing **a** beautiful necklace.
16 … have **an** airport?

69.2

3	a key	8	a question
4	a coat	9	a moment
5	ice	10	blood
6	a biscuit	11	a decision
7	electricity	12	an interview

69.3

2	days	8	air
3	meat	9	patience
4	a queue	10	an umbrella
5	jokes	11	languages
6	friends	12	space
7	people		

UNIT 70

70.1

1 b there's a lot of noise
2 a Light
   b a light
3 a time
   b a great time
4 a a glass of water
   b broken glass
5 a a very nice room
   b room

70.2

2 bad luck
3 journey
4 complete chaos
5 doesn't
6 some lovely scenery
7 very hard work
8 paper
9 heavy traffic
10 Your hair is … it

70.3

2	furniture	7	advice
3	chair**s**	8	experience
4	hair	9	experience**s**
5	progress	10	damage
6	permission		

70.4

2 I'd like some information about places to visit (in the town).
3 Can you give me some advice about which courses to do? / ... courses I can do?
4 I've (just) got some good news. / I've (just) had some good news. / I (just) got some good news.
5 It's a beautiful view (from here), isn't it?
6 What horrible/awful weather!

UNIT 71

71.1

3 They're vegetables.
4 It's a flower.
5 They're planets.
6 It's a game.
7 They're tools.
8 They're rivers.
9 It's an insect.
10 They're languages.

71.2

2 He's a waiter.
3 She's a journalist.
4 He's a surgeon.
5 He's a chef.
6 He's a plumber.
7 She's a tour guide.
8 She's an interpreter.

71.3

2 a careful driver
3 some books
4 books
5 sore feet
6 a sore throat
7 a lovely present
8 some students
9 without an umbrella
10 Some people

71.4

4 a
5 Some
6 an
7 – (You're always asking questions!)
8 a
9 – (Do you like staying in hotels?)
10 Some
11 – (Those are nice shoes.)
12 You need **a** visa to visit **some** countries
13 Kate is **a** teacher. Her parents were teachers too.
14 He's **a** liar. He's always telling lies.

UNIT 72

72.1

1 ... and **a** magazine. **The** book is in my bag, but I can't remember where I put **the** magazine.
2 I saw **an** accident this morning. **A** car crashed into **a** tree. **The** driver of **the** car wasn't hurt, but **the** car was badly damaged.
3 ... **a** blue one and **a** grey one. **The** blue one belongs to my neighbours. I don't know who **the** owner of **the** grey one is.
4 My friends live in **an** old house in **a** small village. There is **a** beautiful garden behind **the** house. I would like to have **a** garden like that.

72.2

1	a	a		4	a	the
	b	the			b	a
	c	the			c	an
2	a	a		5	a	the
	b	a			b	a
	c	the			c	a
3	a	the				
	b	the				
	c	a				

72.3

2 **the** dentist
3 **the** door
4 **a** problem
5 **the** station
6 **the** post office
7 **a** very good player
8 **an** airport
9 **The** nearest airport
10 **the** floor
11 **the** book
12 **a** job in **a** bank
13 **a** small apartment in **the** city centre
14 **a** shop at **the** end of **the** street

72.4

Example answers:

2 About once a month.
3 Once or twice a year.
4 About seven hours a night.
5 Two or three times a week.
6 About two hours a day.
7 50 kilometres an hour.

UNIT 73

73.1

1 **a** lift
2 **a** nice holiday ... **the** best holiday
3 **the** nearest shop ... **the** end of this street
4 **a** lovely day ... **a** cloud in **the** sky
5 **the** most expensive hotel ... **a** cheaper hotel
6 to travel **in space** ... go to **the** moon
7 think of **the** movie ... I thought **the** ending ...
8 Is it **a** star? No, it's **a** planet. It's **the** largest planet in **the** solar system.

73.2

2 TV
3 the radio
4 The television
5 dinner
6 the same name
7 for breakfast
8 vitamin C
9 the internet
10 the ground ... the sky
11 The next train ... platform 3

73.3

2 ... doing **the** same thing
3 **Room 25** is on **the** second floor.
4 It was **a** very hot day. It was **the** hottest day of **the** year.
5 We had **lunch** in **a** nice restaurant by **the** sea.
6 What's on at **the** cinema ...
7 I had **a** big breakfast ...
8 You'll find **the** information you need at **the** top of **page 15**.

73.4

2 **the** sea
3 question 3
4 **the** cinema
5 **the** question
6 breakfast
7 Gate 24
8 **the** gate

UNIT 74

74.1

2 school
3 the school
4 school
5 ... get to and from school
6 the school
7 school
8 ... walk to school. The school isn't ...

74.2

1 b university
   c university
   d the university
2 a hospital
   b the hospital
   c the hospital
   d hospital
3 a prison
   b the prison
   c prison
4 a church
   b church
   c the church

74.3

2 to work
3 bed
4 at home
5 the bed
6 after work
7 in bed
8 home
9 work
10 like home

74.4

2 to school
3 at home *or* stayed home
   (*without* at)
4 to work
5 at university
6 in bed
7 to hospital
8 in prison

UNIT 75

75.1

Example answers:
2–5 I like cats.
   I don't like zoos.
   I don't mind snow.
   I'm not interested in boxing.

75.2

1 b the apples
2 a the people
   b people
3 a names
   b the names
4 a The First World War
   b war
5 a hard work
   b the work

75.3

3 spiders
4 meat
5 the questions
6 the people
7 Biology
8 lies
9 The hotels
10 The water
11 the grass
12 patience

75.4

1 stories
2 the words
3 the rooms
4 public transport
5 All the books
6 Life
7 The weather
8 water
9 films ('films with unhappy endings'
   in general)

UNIT 76

76.1

1 b the cheetah
   c the kangaroo (and the rabbit)
2 a the swan
   b the penguin
   c the owl
3 a the wheel
   b the laser
   c the telescope
4 a the rupee
   b the (Canadian) dollar
   c the …

76.2

2	a	7	a
3	the	8	The
4	a	9	the
5	the	10	a
6	the		

76.3

2 the sick
3 the unemployed
4 the injured
5 the elderly
6 the rich

76.4

2 a German
   Germans / German people
3 a Frenchman/Frenchwoman
   the French / French people
4 a Russian
   Russians / Russian people
5 a Japanese
   the Japanese / Japanese people
6 a Brazilian
   Brazilians / Brazilian people
7 an Englishman/Englishwoman
   the English / English people
8 …

UNIT 77

77.1

2 The doctor
3 Doctor Thomas
4 Professor Brown
5 the President
6 President Kennedy
7 Inspector Roberts
8 the Wilsons
9 the United States
10 France

77.2

3 *OK*
4 … and **the** United States
5 … than **the** north
6 *OK*
7 *OK*
8 … in **the** Swiss Alps
9 **The** UK …
10 **The** Seychelles … in **the** Indian Ocean
11 *OK*
12 **The** River Volga flows into **the**
   Caspian Sea.

77.3

2 (in) South America
3 **the** Nile
4 Sweden
5 **the** United States
6 **the** Rockies
7 **the** Mediterranean
8 Australia
9 **the** Pacific
10 **the** Indian Ocean
11 **the** Thames
12 **the** Danube
13 Thailand
14 **the** Panama Canal
15 **the** Amazon

UNIT 78

78.1

2 Turner's in Carter Road
3 **the** Crown (Hotel) in Park Road
4 St Peter's in Market Street
5 **the** City Museum in George Street
6 Blackstone's in Forest Avenue
7 Mario's in George Street
8 Victoria Park at the end of Market
   Street

78.2

2 **The** Eiffel Tower
3 Buckingham Palace
4 **The** White House
5 **The** Kremlin
6 Broadway
7 **The** Acropolis
8 Gatwick Airport

78.3

2 St Paul's Cathedral
3 Central Park
4 **the** Great Wall
5 Dublin Airport
6 **The** Classic
7 Liverpool University
8 **the** National Museum
9 Harrison's
10 Cathay Pacific
11 **The** Morning News
12 **the** Leaning Tower
13 Cambridge University Press
14 **the** College of Art
15 **The** Imperial Hotel is in Baker Street.
16 **The** Statue of Liberty is at the
   entrance to New York Harbor.

UNIT 79

79.1

2	don't	6	pair
3	doesn't	7	are
4	some	8	a
5	them	9	it

79.2

2	means	6	news
3	series	7	species
4	species	8	means
5	series		

79.3

2 don't
3 want
4 was
5 are
6 is *or* are
7 Do
8 do *or* does
9 enjoy
10 is *or* are

79.4

2 **is** too hot
3 **isn't** enough money
4 **isn't** long enough
5 **is** a lot to carry

79.5

3 … wearing black jeans.
4 … very nice **people**.
5 *OK*
6 There was **a police officer / a policeman / a policewoman** …
7 **These** scissors **aren't** …
8 *OK* (The company **has** *is also correct*)
9 … is **a** very rare species.
10 Twelve hours **is** …

UNIT 80

80.1

3 train ticket
4 ticket machine
5 hotel staff
6 exam results
7 race horse
8 horse race
9 running shoes
10 shoe shop
11 shop window
12 window cleaner
13 a construction company scandal
14 car factory workers
15 road improvement scheme
16 New York department store

80.2

2 seat belt
3 credit card
4 weather forecast
5 washing machine
6 wedding ring
7 room number
8 birthday party
9 truck driver

80.3

2 school football team
3 film production company
4 life insurance policy
5 tourist information office

80.4

2 two-hour
3 two hours
4 twenty-pound
5 ten-pound
6 15-minute
7 60 minutes
8 twelve-storey
9 five days
10 Five-star
11 six years old
12 six-year-old

UNIT 81

81.1

3 your friend's umbrella
4 *OK*
5 James's daughter
6 Helen and Andy's son
7 *OK*
8 *OK*
9 Your children's friends
10 *OK*
11 Our neighbours' garden
12 David's hair
13 *OK*
14 my best friend's party
15 *OK*
16 Ben's parents' car
17 *OK*
18 *OK* (the government's policy *is also OK*)

81.2

2 father's
3 apples
4 Children's
5 Switzerland's
6 parents'
7 photos
8 someone else's
9 Shakespeare's

81.3

2 Last week's storm caused a lot of damage.
3 The town's only cinema has closed down.
4 Britain's weather is very changeable.
5 The region's main industry is tourism.

81.4

2 twenty minutes' walk
3 two weeks' holiday / fourteen days' holiday / a fortnight's holiday
4 an/one hour's sleep

UNIT 82

82.1

2 hurt himself
3 blame herself
4 put yourself
5 enjoyed themselves
6 burn yourself
7 express myself

82.2

2 me
3 myself
4 us
5 yourself
6 you
7 ourselves
8 them
9 themselves

82.3

3 feel
4 dried myself
5 concentrate
6 defend yourself
7 meeting
8 relax

82.4

2 themselves
3 each other
4 each other
5 themselves
6 each other
7 ourselves
8 each other
9 introduced **ourselves** to **each other**

82.5

2 I made it myself
3 Laura told me herself / Laura herself told me
4 know themselves
5 cuts it himself
6 do it yourself?

UNIT 83

83.1

2 We met a **relative of yours**.
3 Jason borrowed **a book of mine**.
4 I met Lisa and **some friends of hers**.
5 We had dinner with **a neighbour of ours**.
6 I went on holiday with **two friends of mine**.
7 I met **a friend of Amy's** at the party.
8 It's always been **an ambition of mine** to travel round the world.

83.2

2 his own opinions
3 her own business
4 our own words
5 its own private beach

Key to Exercises

83.3
2 your own fault
3 her own ideas
4 your own problems
5 his own decisions

83.4
2 make her own (clothes)
3 clean your own (shoes)
4 bake our own (bread)
5 write their own (songs)

83.5
2 myself
3 our own
4 themselves
5 himself
6 their own
7 yourself
8 her own

83.6
2 Sam and Chris are colleagues of **mine**.
3 I was scared. I didn't want to go out **on** my own.
4 In my last job I had **my** own office.
5 He must be lonely. He's always **by** himself.
6 My parents have gone away with some friends of **theirs**.
7 Are there any countries that produce all **their** own food?

UNIT 84

84.1
3 There's / There is
4 there wasn't
5 Is it
6 Is there
7 there was
8 It isn't / It's not
9 There wasn't
10 It's / It is … there isn't
11 It was
12 Is there … there's / there is
13 It's / It is … There's / There is
14 there was … It was

84.2
2 There's / There is a lot of salt in the soup. *or* … too much salt …
3 There was nothing in the box.
4 There were about 50 people at the meeting.
5 There's / There is a lot of violence in the film.
6 *(example answers)*
There is a lot to do in this town. /
… plenty to do in this town. /
… a lot happening in this town. *or*
There are a lot of places to go in this town.

84.3
2 There may be
3 There won't be
4 There's / There is going to be
5 There used to be
6 there should be
7 there wouldn't be

84.4
3 **there** will be an opportunity
4 **There** must have been a reason.
5 *OK*
6 *OK*
7 **There** used to be a lot of tourists
8 **There**'s no signal.
9 *OK*
10 **There**'s sure to be a car park somewhere.
11 *OK*
12 **there** would be somebody … but **there** wasn't anybody.

UNIT 85

85.1
2 some
3 any
4 some
5 any … some
6 any
7 some
8 any
9 some
10 any
11 some … any

85.2
2 somebody/someone
3 anybody/anyone
4 anything
5 something
6 anything *or* anybody/anyone
7 anybody/anyone
8 somewhere
9 anybody/anyone
10 something
11 Anybody/Anyone
12 somebody/someone … anybody/anyone
13 anywhere
14 anything
15 something
16 something … anybody/anyone
17 somebody/someone … anybody/anyone
18 anybody/anyone anything

85.3
2 Any day
3 Anything
4 anybody/anyone
5 Any job *or* Anything
6 anywhere
7 Anybody/Anyone

UNIT 86

86.1
3 no
4 any
5 None
6 no
7 none
8 any
9 no
10 any
11 none
12 no
13 any
14 no

86.2
2 Nobody/No-one.
3 None.
4 Nowhere.
5 None.
6 Nothing.
8 I'm not waiting for anybody/anyone.
9 I didn't buy any (bread).
10 I'm not going anywhere.
11 I haven't read any (books).
12 It doesn't cost anything.

86.3
2 nobody/no-one
3 Nowhere
4 anything.
5 Nobody/No-one
6 anywhere
7 Nothing
8 **Nothing**. I couldn't find **anything** I wanted.
9 **Nobody/No-one** said **anything**.

86.4
2 nobody
3 anyone
4 Anybody
5 Nothing
6 Anything
7 anything
8 any
9 No-one … anyone

UNIT 87

87.1
3 *OK*
4 It cost **a lot** to …
5 *OK*
6 You have **a lot of** luggage.
7 *OK*
8 … know **many** people *or* … know **a lot of** people
9 *OK*
10 He travels **a lot**.

87.2
2 He has (got) plenty of money.
3 There's plenty of room.
4 … she still has plenty to learn.
5 There is plenty to see.
6 There are plenty of hotels.

87.3

2 little
3 many
4 few
5 little
6 many
7 little
8 much
9 few

87.4

2 a few dollars
3 little traffic
4 a few years ago
5 a little time
6 only a few words
7 Few people

87.5

2 a little
3 a few
4 few
5 little
6 a little
7 little
8 a few
9 a few
10 a little

UNIT 88

88.1

3 —
4 of
5 —
6 —
7 of
8 of
9 — (**of** is also correct)
10 —
11 —
12 of

88.2

3 of my spare time
4 accidents
5 of the buildings
6 of her friends
7 of the population
8 birds
9 of the players
10 of her opinions
11 European countries
12 (of) my dinner

88.3

Example answers:
2 the time
3 my friends
4 (of) the questions
5 the pictures / the photos / the photographs
6 (of) the money

88.4

2 All of them
3 none of us
4 some of it
5 none of them
6 Some of them
7 all of it
8 none of it

UNIT 89

89.1

2 Neither
3 both
4 Either
5 Neither
6 both

89.2

2 either
3 both
4 Neither of
5 **neither** driver … **both / both the / both of the** cars
6 both / both of

89.3

2 either of them
3 both of them
4 Neither of us
5 neither of them

89.4

3 The movie was both boring and long.
4 Neither Joe nor Sam has a car. *or* … has got a car.
5 Emily speaks both German and Russian.
6 Ben neither watches TV nor reads newspapers.
7 That man's name is either Richard or Robert.
8 I have neither the time nor the money to go on holiday.
9 We can leave either today or tomorrow.

89.5

2 either   5 any
3 any   6 either
4 none   7 neither

UNIT 90

90.1

3 Everybody/Everyone
4 Everything
5 all
6 everybody/everyone
7 everything
8 All
9 everybody/everyone
10 All
11 everything
12 Everybody/Everyone
13 All
14 everything

90.2

2 The whole team played well.
3 He ate the whole box (of chocolates).
4 They searched the whole house.
5 The whole family plays tennis. *or* … play tennis.
6 Sarah/She worked the whole day.
7 It rained the whole week.
8 Sarah worked all day.
9 It rained all week.

90.3

2 every four hours
3 every four years
4 every five minutes
5 every six months

90.4

2 every day
3 all day
4 The whole building
5 Every time
6 all the time
7 all my luggage

UNIT 91

91.1

3 Each
4 Every
5 Each
6 every
7 each
8 every

91.2

3 Every
4 Each
5 every
6 every
7 each of
8 every
9 each
10 Every
11 each of
12 each

91.3

2 Sonia and I had ten pounds each. *or* Sonia and I each had ten pounds.
3 Those postcards cost a pound each / … one pound each. *or* Those postcards are a pound each / … one pound each
4 We paid 200 dollars each. *or* We each paid 200 dollars.

91.4

2 everyone
3 every one *(2 words)*
4 Everyone
5 every one *(2 words)*

UNIT 92

92.1

2 A customer is someone who buys something from a shop.
3 A burglar is someone who breaks into a house to steal things.
4 A coward is someone who is not brave.
5 A tenant is someone who pays rent to live somewhere.
6 A shoplifter is someone who steals from a shop.
7 A liar is someone who doesn't tell the truth.
8 A pessimist is someone who expects the worst to happen.

92.2

2 The waiter who/that served us was impolite and impatient.
3 The building that/which was destroyed in the fire has now been rebuilt.
4 The people who/that were arrested have now been released.
5 The bus that/which goes to the airport runs every half hour.

92.3

2 who/that runs away from home
3 that/which were hanging on the wall
4 that/which cannot be explained
5 who/that has stayed there
6 that/which happened in the past
7 who/that developed the theory of relativity
8 that/which can support life

92.4

3 the nearest shop **that**/**which** sells
4 some things about me **that**/**which** were
5 The driver **who**/**that** caused
6 *OK* (the person **who** took *is also correct*)
7 a world **that**/**which** is changing
8 *OK*
9 the horse **that**/**which** won

UNIT 93

93.1

3 *OK* (the people **who**/**that** we met *is also correct*)
4 The people **who**/**that** work in the office
5 *OK* (the people **who**/**that** I work with *is also correct*)
6 *OK* (the money **that**/**which** I gave you *is also correct*)
7 the money **that**/**which** was on the table
8 *OK* (the worst film **that**/**which** you've ever seen *is also correct*)
9 the best thing **that**/**which** has ever happened to you

93.2

2 you're wearing *or*
   that/which you're wearing
3 you're going to see *or*
   that/which you're going to see
4 I/we wanted to visit *or*
   that/which I/we wanted to visit
5 I/we invited to the party *or*
   who/whom/that we invited …
6 you had to do *or*
   that/which you had to do
7 I/we rented *or* that/which I/we rented

93.3

2 the wedding we were invited to
3 the hotel you told me about
4 the job I applied for
5 the concert you went to
6 somebody you can rely on
7 the people you were with

93.4

3 – (that *is also correct*)
4 what
5 that
6 what
7 – (that *is also correct*)
8 what
9 – (that *is also correct*)

UNIT 94

94.1

2 whose wife is an English teacher
3 who owns a restaurant
4 whose ambition is to climb Everest
5 who have just got married
6 whose parents used to work in a circus

94.2

2 *more formal* I went to see a lawyer **whom** a friend of mine (had) recommended.
   less formal I went to see a lawyer a friend of mine (had) recommended.
3 *more formal* The person **to whom** I spoke wasn't very helpful.
   less formal The person I spoke **to** wasn't very helpful.
4 *more formal* The woman **with whom** Tom was in love wasn't in love with him.
   less formal The woman Tom was in love **with** wasn't in love with him.

94.3

2 where
3 who
4 whose
5 where
6 whose
7 whom
8 where

94.4

Example answers:

2 The reason I left my job was that the salary was too low.
3 I'll never forget the time I got stuck in a lift.
4 2009 was the year Amanda got married.
5 The reason they don't have a car is that neither of them can drive.
6 The last time I saw Sam was about six months ago.
7 Do you remember the day we first met?

UNIT 95

95.1

3 We drove to the airport, which was not far from the city.
4 Kate's husband, who I've never met, is an airline pilot. *or* … whom I've never met …
5 Lisa, whose job involves a lot of travelling, is away from home a lot.
6 Paul and Emily have a daughter, Alice, who has just started school.
7 The new stadium, which will be finished next month, will hold 90,000 spectators.
8 My brother lives in Alaska, which is the largest state in the US.
9 Our teacher, whose name I have forgotten, was very kind.
10 We enjoyed our visit to the museum, where we saw a lot of interesting things.

95.2

2 The strike at the factory, which began ten days ago, has now ended.
3 I've found the book I was looking for this morning. *or* … the book that/which I was looking for …
4 My car, which I've had for 15 years, has never broken down.
5 Few of the people who/that applied for the job had the necessary qualifications.
6 Amy showed me a picture of her son, who is a police officer.

95.3

2 My office**, which** is on the second floor**,** is very small.
3 *OK*
   (The office I'm using … *and* The office **which** I'm using … *are also correct*)
4 Sarah's father**, who** used to be in the army**,** now works for a TV company.
5 *OK* (The doctor **who** examined me … *is also correct*)
6 The sun**, which** is one of millions of stars in the universe**,** provides us with heat and light.

UNIT 96

96.1
2 in which
3 with whom
4 to which
5 of which
6 of whom
7 for which
8 after which

96.2
2 most of which was useless
3 none of whom was suitable
4 one of which they never use
5 half of which he gave to his parents
6 both of whom are lawyers
7 neither of which she replied to
8 only a few of whom I knew
10 sides of which were lined with trees
11 the aim of which is to save money

96.3
2 which makes it difficult to sleep sometimes.
3 which was very kind of her.
4 which makes it hard to contact her.
5 which is good news.
6 which meant I had to wait two hours at the airport.
7 which means we can't go away tomorrow.
8 which she apologised for or for which she apologised

UNIT 97

97.1
2 The taxi taking us to the airport
3 a path leading to the river
4 A factory employing 500 people
5 man sitting next to me on the plane
6 brochure containing the information I needed

97.2
2 stolen from the museum
3 damaged in the storm
4 made at the meeting
5 surrounded by trees
6 involved in the project

97.3
3 invited
4 called
5 living
6 offering
7 caused
8 blown
9 sitting … reading
10 working … studying

97.4
3 There's somebody coming.
4 There's nothing left.
5 There were a lot of people travelling.
6 There was nobody else staying there.
7 There was nothing written on it.
8 There's a course beginning next Monday.

UNIT 98

98.1
2 a exhausting
  b exhausted
3 a depressing
  b depressed
  c depressed
4 a exciting
  b exciting
  c excited

98.2
2 interested
3 exciting
4 embarrassing
5 embarrassed
6 amazed
7 amazing
8 amused
9 interested
10 terrifying … shocked
11 (look so) bored … (really so) boring
12 boring … interesting

98.3
2 bored
3 confusing
4 disgusting
5 interested
6 annoyed
7 boring
8 exhausted
9 excited
10 amusing
11 interesting

UNIT 99

99.1
2 an unusual gold ring
3 a beautiful old house
4 red leather gloves
5 an old American film
6 tiny pink flowers
7 a long thin face
8 big black clouds
9 a lovely sunny day
10 an ugly yellow dress
11 a long wide avenue
12 important new ideas
13 a nice new green sweater
14 a small black metal box
15 beautiful long black hair
16 an interesting old French painting
17 a large red and yellow umbrella
18 a big fat black and white cat

99.2
2 tastes/tasted awful
3 feel nervous
4 smell nice
5 look wet
6 sounds/sounded interesting

99.3
2 happy
3 happily
4 terrible
5 properly
6 good
7 slow
8 badly
9 violent

99.4
3 the last two days
4 the first two weeks of May
5 the next few days
6 the first three questions (in the exam)
7 the next two years
8 the last three days of our holiday

UNIT 100

100.1
2 easily
3 patiently
4 unexpectedly
5 regularly
6 perfectly … slowly … clearly

100.2
2 selfishly
3 suddenly
4 sudden
5 badly
6 awful
7 terribly
8 comfortable
9 clearly
10 safe
11 safe
12 safely

100.3
2 frequently
3 fluent
4 specially
5 complete
6 perfectly
7 financially or completely
8 permanently
9 nervous
10 dangerously

100.4
2 seriously ill
3 absolutely enormous
4 slightly damaged
5 unusually quiet
6 completely changed
7 unnecessarily long
8 happily married
9 badly planned

UNIT 101

101.1
2 good
3 well
4 well
5 good
6 well
7 well
8 well … good

101.2
2 well-known
3 well-kept
4 well-written
5 well-informed
6 well-paid

101.3
2 slowly
3 lately
4 fast
5 hard
6 hardly
7 hard
8 hardly see
9 hard

101.4
2 hardly hear
3 hardly slept
4 hardly speak
5 hardly said
6 hardly changed
7 hardly recognised

101.5
2 hardly any
3 hardly anything
4 hardly anybody/anyone
5 hardly ever
6 hardly anywhere
7 hardly or hardly ever
8 hardly anybody/anyone
9 hardly any
10 hardly anywhere

UNIT 102

102.1
2 so
3 such
4 such a
5 such
6 such a
7 so
8 so
9 such a
10 such

102.2
2 The bag was **so** heavy
3 I've got **such** a lot to do
4 I was **so** surprised
5 The music was **so** loud
6 It was **such** horrible weather
7 Her English is **so** good
8 The hotel was **such** a long way
9 I had **such** a big breakfast

102.3
2 Why are you in such a hurry?
3 I'm surprised it took so long.
4 … but there's no such company.
5 … why I did such a stupid thing.
6 Why are you driving so slowly?
7 How did you learn English in such a short time?
8 Why did you buy such an expensive phone?

102.4
Example answers:
2 She's so **friendly**.
3 She's such **a nice person**.
4 I haven't seen you for so **long**.
5 I didn't realise it was such **a long way**.
6 There were so **many people**.

UNIT 103

103.1
3 enough buses
4 wide enough
5 enough time
6 enough vegetables
7 tall enough
8 enough room
9 warm enough
10 enough cups

103.2
2 too busy to talk
3 too late to go
4 warm enough to sit
5 too shy to be
6 enough patience to be
7 too far away to hear
8 enough English to read

103.3
2 This coffee is too hot to drink.
3 The piano was too heavy to move.
4 These apples aren't / are not ripe enough to eat.
5 The situation is too complicated to explain.
6 The wall was too high to climb over.
7 This sofa isn't / is not big enough for three people (to sit on).
8 Some things are too small to see without a microscope. or … to be seen without a microscope.

UNIT 104

104.1
2 quite hungry
3 quite often
4 quite noisy
5 quite surprised
6 quite late
7 quite old

104.2
2 quite a good voice
3 quite a long way
4 a pretty cold wind
5 quite a lot of traffic
6 a pretty busy day
7 started fairly recently

104.3
Example answers:
2 rather long
3 rather strange
4 rather impatient
5 rather expensive

104.4
3 more than a little …
4 completely
5 more than a little …
6 more than a little …
7 completely

104.5
2 quite safe
3 quite impossible
4 quite right
5 quite different
6 quite sure

UNIT 105

105.1
2 stronger
3 smaller
4 more expensive
5 warmer / hotter
6 more interesting / more exciting
7 nearer / closer
8 harder / more difficult / more complicated
9 better
10 worse
11 more often
12 further / farther

105.2
3 more serious than
4 thinner
5 bigger
6 more interested
7 more important than
8 more peaceful than
9 more slowly
10 higher than

105.3
2 careful
3 better
4 frequent
5 more
6 worse
7 than
8 quietly

105.4
2 I ran further/farther than Dan.
3 The journey takes longer by train than by car.
4 My friends arrived earlier than I expected.
5 The traffic today is worse than usual.

UNIT 106

106.1
2 much bigger
3 a lot more interesting than
4 a little cooler
5 far more complicated than
6 a bit more slowly
7 slightly older

106.2
2 any sooner / any earlier
3 no higher than / no more expensive than / no worse than
4 any further/farther
5 no worse than

106.3
2 bigger and bigger
3 more and more nervous
4 worse and worse
5 more and more expensive
6 better and better
7 more and more time

106.4
2 The more tired you are, the harder it is to concentrate.
3 The sooner we decide (what to do), the better.
4 The more I know, the less I understand.
5 The more electricity you use, the higher your bill will be.
6 The more / The longer she had to wait, the more impatient she became.

106.5
2 more
3 longer
4 any
5 the
6 older
7 elder *or* older
8 slightly
9 no
10 (The) less (he knows, the) better

UNIT 107

107.1
2 My salary isn't as high as yours.
3 You don't know as much about cars as me. *or* …as I do. *or* …as I know.
4 We aren't as busy today as we were yesterday. *or* …as busy today as yesterday.
5 I don't feel as bad as I did earlier. *or* …as I felt earlier.
6 Our neighbours haven't lived here as long as us. *or* …as long as we have.
7 I wasn't as nervous (before the interview) as I usually am. *or* …as usual.

107.2
3 The station wasn't as far as I thought.
4 The meal cost less than I expected.
5 I don't watch TV as much as I used to. *or* …as often as I used to.
6 Karen used to have longer hair.
7 You don't know them as well as me. *or* …as I do.
8 There aren't as many students in this class as in the other one.

107.3
2 as well as
3 as long as
4 as soon as
5 as often as
6 as quietly as
7 as hard as

107.4
2 Your hair is the same colour as mine.
3 I arrived (at) the same time as you.
4 My birthday is (on) the same day as Tom's. *or* My birthday is the same as Tom's.

107.5
2 than
3 as
4 him
5 less
6 much
7 twice
8 is
9 me

UNIT 108

108.1
2 the tallest
3 the worst
4 the most popular
5 the best
6 the most honest
7 the shortest

108.2
3 better
4 the most expensive
5 more comfortable
6 The eldest *or* The oldest
7 oldest
8 the quickest
9 quicker
10 my earliest
11 … **the highest** mountain in the world … It is **higher** than …
12 Do you have a **sharper** one? No, it's **the sharpest** one I have.

108.3
2 It's the largest country in South America.
3 It was the happiest day of my life.
4 It's the most valuable painting in the museum.
5 It's the busiest time of the year.
7 He's one of the richest men in the country.
8 She's one of the best students in the class.
9 It was one of the worst experiences of my life.
10 It's one of the most famous universities in the world.

108.4
2 That's the funniest joke I've ever heard.
3 This is the best coffee I've ever tasted.
4 That's the furthest/farthest I've ever run.
5 It's the worst mistake I've ever made. *or* It was the worst …
6 Who's the most famous person you've ever met?

UNIT 109

109.1
3 Joe doesn't like football very much.
4 Dan won the race easily.
5 *OK*
6 Have you seen Chris recently?
7 I borrowed some money from a friend.
8 *OK*
9 I ate my breakfast quickly and went out. *or* I quickly ate my breakfast and …
10 Did you invite a lot of people to the party?
11 Sam watches TV all the time.
12 *OK*

109.2
2 I met a friend of mine on my way home.
3 I forgot to put a stamp on the envelope.
4 We bought a lot of fruit in the market.
5 They built a new hotel opposite the park.
6 Did you learn a lot of things at school today?
7 We found some interesting books in the library.
8 Please write your name at the top of the page.

109.3
2 I go to the supermarket every Friday.
3 Why did you come home so late?
4 Sarah takes her children to school every day.
5 I haven't been to the cinema recently.
6 I remembered her name after a few minutes.
7 We walked around the town all morning.
8 My brother has been in Canada since April.
9 I didn't see you at the party on Saturday night.
10 Lisa left her umbrella in a restaurant last night.
11 The moon goes round the earth every 27 days.
12 Anna has been teaching Italian in London for the last three years.

UNIT 110

110.1
3 I usually have …
4 *OK*
5 Steve hardly ever gets angry.
6 … and I also sent an email.
7 I always have to repeat …
8 I've never worked / I have never worked …
9 *OK*
10 … my friends were already there. *or* … my friends were there already.

110.2
2 Katherine is always very generous.
3 I don't usually have to work on Sundays.
4 Do you always watch TV in the evenings?
5 … he is also learning Japanese.
6 a We were all on holiday in Spain.
   b We were all staying at the same hotel.
   c We all had a great time.
7 a The new hotel is probably expensive.
   b It probably costs a lot to stay there.
8 a I can probably help you.
   b I probably can't help you.

110.3
2 usually sleeps
3 It's / It is usually easy to … *or* Usually it's / it is easy to …
4 were both born
5 She can also sing
6 Do you usually go …
7 I have / I've never spoken
8 We're / We are still living …
9 You always have to wait …
10 We might never meet
11 I probably won't be
12 Will you still be
13 She's / She is hardly ever
14 We would / We'd never have met
15 It doesn't always take
16 We were all … we all fell
17 always says … she never does

UNIT 111

111.1
3 He doesn't write poems any more.
4 He still wants to be a teacher.
5 He isn't / He's not interested in politics any more.
6 He's still single.
7 He doesn't go fishing any more.
8 He doesn't have a beard any more. *or* He hasn't got …
10–12
   He no longer writes poems.
   He is / He's no longer interested in politics.
   He no longer goes fishing.
   He no longer has a beard. / He's no longer got a beard.

111.2
2 He hasn't gone yet.
3 They haven't finished (it) yet. / … finished repairing the road yet.
4 They haven't woken up yet.
5 She hasn't found one yet. / … found a job yet.
6 I haven't decided (what to do) yet.
7 It hasn't taken off yet.

111.3
3 still
4 yet
5 any more
6 yet
7 any more
8 still
9 already
10 still
11 already
12 yet
13 still
14 already
15 still
16 any more

UNIT 112

112.1
2 even Lisa
3 not even Amy
4 even Lisa
5 even Kate
6 not even Lisa

112.2
2 We even painted the floor.
3 She's even met the prime minister.
4 You could even hear it from the next street. / You could even hear the noise from … *or* You could hear it / the noise even from the next street.
5
6 I can't even remember her name.
7 There isn't even a cinema.
8 He didn't even tell his wife (where he was going).
9 I don't even know my neighbours.

112.3
2 even older
3 even better
4 even more difficult
5 even worse
6 even less

112.4
2 if
3 even if
4 even
5 even though
6 Even
7 even though
8 even if
9 Even though

UNIT 113

113.1
2 Although I had never seen her before
3 although it was quite cold
4 although we don't like them very much
5 Although I didn't speak the language well
6 Although the heating was on
7 although I'd met her twice before
8 although we've known each other a long time

113.2
2 a In spite of (*or* Despite)
   b Although
3 a because
   b although
4 a because of
   b in spite of (*or* despite)
5 a Although
   b because of
Example answers:
6 a he hadn't studied very hard
   b he had studied very hard
7 a I was hungry
   b being hungry / my hunger / the fact (that) I was hungry

113.3
2 In spite of playing quite well, we lost the game. *or* In spite of the fact (that) we played quite well …
3 Although I'd hurt my foot, I managed to walk home. *or* I managed to walk home although I'd …
4 I enjoyed the film in spite of the silly story. / … in spite of the story being silly. / … in spite of the fact (that) the story was silly. *or* In spite of …, I enjoyed the film.
5 Despite living in the same building, we hardly ever see each other. *or* Despite the fact (that) we live in … *or* We hardly ever see each other despite …
6 They came to the party even though they hadn't been invited. *or* Even though they hadn't been invited, they came to the party.

113.4
2 It's very long though.
3 We ate it though.
4 I don't like her husband though.

UNIT 114

114.1
2 in case you get hungry / … you are hungry
3 in case it rains
4 in case you get thirsty / … you are thirsty
5 in case you need to call somebody
6 in case you get lonely / … you are lonely

114.2

2 I'll say goodbye now in case I don't see you again (before you go).
3 Can you check the list in case we've forgotten something? / … in case we forgot something?
4 Keep the receipt in case they don't fit you (and you have to take them back to the shop).

114.3

2 in case I forgot it.
3 in case they were worried (about me).
4 in case she didn't get the first one. / in case she hadn't got …
5 in case they came/come to London (one day).

114.4

3 If
4 in case
5 if
6 in case
7 if
8 if
9 in case
10 in case

UNIT 115

115.1

2 You won't know what to do unless you listen carefully.
3 I'll never speak to her again unless she apologises (to me). *or* Unless she apologises (to me), I'll …
4 He won't understand you unless you speak very slowly. *or* Unless you speak very slowly, he …
5 The company will have to close unless business improves soon. *or* Unless business improves soon, the company …
6 The problem will get worse unless we do something soon. *or* Unless we do something soon, the problem …

115.2

2 I'm not going (to the party) unless you go too. / … unless you're going too.
3 The dog won't chase you unless you move suddenly.
4 Ben won't speak to you unless you ask him something.
5 The doctor won't see you unless it's an emergency. / … unless it's an emergency.

115.3

2 unless
3 providing
4 as long as
5 unless
6 unless
7 provided
8 Unless
9 unless
10 as long as

115.4

Example answers:

2 it's not too hot.
3 there isn't too much traffic.
4 it isn't raining.
5 I'm in a hurry.
6 you have something else to do.
7 you pay it back next week.
8 you don't tell anyone else.
9 you take risks.

UNIT 116

116.1

2 I listened as she told me her story.
3 I burnt myself as I was taking a hot dish out of the oven.
4 The spectators cheered as the two teams came onto the field.
5 A dog ran out in front of the car as we were driving along the road.

116.2

2 As today is a public holiday, all government offices are shut.
3 As I didn't want to disturb anybody, I tried to be very quiet.
4 As I can't go to the concert, you can have my ticket.
5 As it was a nice day, we went for a walk by the canal.

116.3

3 because
4 at the same time as
5 at the same time as
6 because
7 because

116.4

3 OK
4 when I was in London
5 When I left school
6 OK
7 when I was a child
8 OK

116.5

Example answers:

2 I saw you as you were getting into your car.
3 It started to rain just as we started playing tennis.
4 As she doesn't have a phone, it's quite difficult to contact her.
5 Just as I took the picture, somebody walked in front of my phone.

UNIT 117

117.1

3 … like his father
4 … people like him
5 OK
6 Like her mother …
7 … like talking to the wall
8 OK
9 OK
10 like a fish

117.2

2 e
3 b
4 f
5 d
6 a

117.3

2 like blocks of ice
3 like a beginner
4 as a tour guide
5 like a theatre
6 as a birthday present
7 like winter
8 like a child

117.4

2 like
3 as
4 as
5 like
6 As
7 as
8 like
9 like *or* such as
10 as
11 like
12 as
13 like
14 like
15 as
16 like

UNIT 118

118.1

2 You look as if you've seen a ghost. / … as if you saw a ghost.
3 I feel like I've (just) run a marathon. / … like I (just) ran a marathon.
4 You sound as if you're having a good time.

118.2

2 It looks like it's going to rain.
3 It sounds like they're having an argument.
4 It looks like there's been an accident.
5 It looks like they don't have any.
6 It sounds like you should see a doctor.

118.3

2 as if he meant what he said
3 as if she's hurt her leg / as if she hurt her leg
4 as if he hadn't eaten for a week
5 as if she was enjoying it
6 as if I was crazy / as if I were crazy
7 as if she didn't want to come
8 as if I didn't exist

118.4

2 as if I was/were
3 as if she was/were
4 as if it was/were

UNIT 119

119.1

3 during
4 for
5 for
6 during
7 for
8 during (or in)
9 for
10 for
11 during
12 for

119.2

3 while   8 while
4 While   9 during
5 during   10 while
6 during (or in) 11 During
7 during (or in) 12 while

119.3

1 for
2 during
3 while
4 during (or in)
5 for
6 while
7 during (or in)
8 for
9 while
10 during

119.4

Example answers:
3 Can you wait for me while I make a quick phone call?
4 Most of the students looked bored during the lesson.
5 I was asked a lot of questions during the interview.
6 Don't open the car door while the car is moving.
7 The lights suddenly went out while we were watching TV.
8 What are you going to do while you're on holiday?
9 It started to rain during the game.
10 It started to rain while we were walking home.

UNIT 120

120.1

2 by 8.30
3 Let me know by Saturday
4 you're here by 2 o'clock.
5 we should arrive by lunchtime.

120.2

2 by
3 until
4 by
5 until
6 by
7 by
8 until
9 by
10 by
11 until
12 By
13 until
14 by

120.3

Example answers:
3 until I come back
4 by 5 o'clock
5 by 3 April
6 until 2028
7 until midnight

120.4

2 By the time I got to the station
3 By the time I finished (work)
4 By the time the police arrived
5 By the time we got to the top (of the mountain)

UNIT 121

121.1

2 on
3 in
4 at (or **on** *in American English*)
5 on (or I last saw her Tuesday.)
6 in
7 in
8 at
9 on (or There are usually a lot of parties New Year's Eve.)
10 at
11 in
12 in
13 at
14 on
15 in
16 At
17 in
18 on
19 at
20 **at** 5 o'clock **in** the morning
21 **on** 7 January … **in** April
22 **on** Tuesday morning … **in** the afternoon *or* at home Tuesday morning … **in** the afternoon

121.2

2 at night
3 in the evening
4 on 21 July 1969
5 at the same time
6 in the 1920s
7 in about 20 minutes
8 at the moment
9 in 11 seconds
10 on Saturdays *or* … works Saturdays

121.3

3 a
4 *both*
5 a
6 *both*
7 b
8 a
9 *both*
10 b

UNIT 122

122.1

2 on time
3 on time
4 in time
5 on time
6 in time
7 in time
8 on time
9 in time

122.2

2 I got home just in time.
3 I stopped him just in time.
4 We got to the cinema just in time for the beginning of the film. / … just in time to see the beginning of the film.

122.3

2 at the end of the month
3 at the end of the course
4 at the end of the race
5 at the end of the interview

122.4

2 In the end she resigned (from her job). *or* She resigned (from her job) in the end.
3 In the end I gave up (trying to learn Japanese / learning Japanese). *or* I gave up (learning Japanese) in the end.
4 In the end we decided not to go (to the party). *or* In the end we didn't go (to the party). *or* We decided not to go (to the party) in the end. *or* We didn't go (to the party) in the end.

122.5

2	In	7	in
3	in	8	in
4	at	9	in
5	In	10	at … at
6	At		

UNIT 123

123.1

2 On his arm. *or* On the man's arm.
3 At the traffic lights.
4 On the door. (notice)
   In the door. (key)
5 On the wall.
6 In Paris.
7 At the gate. (man)
   On the gate. (bird)
8 On the beach.

123.2

2 on my guitar
3 at junction 14
4 in his hand
5 on that tree
6 in the mountains
7 on the island
8 at the window

123.3

2 on
3 at
4 on
5 in
6 on
7 in
8 at
9 on
10 at
11 in
12 on
13 **in** a small village **in** the south-west
14 **on** the wall **in** the kitchen

UNIT 124

124.1

2 On the second floor.
3 On the corner. *or* At the corner.
4 In the corner.
5 At the top of the stairs.
6 In the back of the car.
7 At the front.
8 On the left.
9 In the back row.
10 At the end of the street.

124.2

2 on the right
3 in the world
4 on the way to work
5 on the west coast
6 in the front row
7 at the back of the class
8 on the back of this card

124.3

2	in		
3	at		
4	at		
5	in		
6	on		
7	in		
8	in		
9	in		
10	on		
11	in		
12	on		
13	in		
14	on … on		

UNIT 125

125.1

2 on a train
3 at a conference
4 is in hospital / in the hospital
5 at the hairdresser's
6 on his bike
7 in New York
8 at the Savoy Theatre

125.2

2 at the station
3 in a taxi
4 at the sports centre
5 on the plane
6 in Tokyo
7 at school
8 at the art gallery

125.3

2	in	10	in
3	at	11	on
4	in	12	at
5	on	13	in
6	at	14	in
7	in	15	at
8	at	16	at … at
9	at		

UNIT 126

126.1

3 at
4 to
5 to
6 into
7 – *(no preposition)*
8 to
9 into
10 to
11 at
12 to
13 to
14 into
15 to
16 – *(no preposition)*
17 to (France) … in (Brazil)
18 in (Chicago) … to (Boston)

126.2

2 I've been to … once.
3 I've never been to …
4 I've been to … a few times.
5 I've been to … many times.

126.3

2 in
3 – *(no preposition)*
4 at
5 to
6 – *(no preposition)*

126.4

2 I got on
3 I got out (of the/my car).
4 I got off (the train).
5 I got into the taxi. *or*
   I got in the taxi. *or*
   I got in.
6 I got off (the plane).

UNIT 127

127.1

2 in cold weather
3 in French
4 in love
5 in the mood
6 in the shade
7 in my opinion
8 in kilometres

127.2

2 on strike
3 on a cruise
4 on fire
5 on a tour
6 on her phone
7 on TV
8 on purpose
9 on a diet
10 on holiday
11 on business
12 on the whole

127.3

2 on
3 at
4 in
5 on
6 in
7 at
8 at
9 on
10 on
11 at
12 on
13 in
14 on
15 on
16 on
17 In
18 in
19 on
20 in

UNIT 128

128.1
2 by email
3 by mistake
4 on purpose
5 by chance
6 by hand

128.2
2 on
3 by
4 on
5 by
6 in
7 by
8 by
9 **by** bike (*or* **on his** bike) … **on** foot

128.3
2 by a professional photographer
3 by mosquitoes
4 by Leonardo da Vinci
5 by one of our players
6 by lightning
7 by Beethoven

128.4
2 with
3 by
4 by
5 in
6 by
7 with
8 by
9 on
10 by
11 **by** the bed **with** a lamp and a clock **on** it

128.5
2 In the last ten years the population has gone up / increased / grown / risen by 6 million.
3 Helen won (the election) by two votes.
4 I missed her/Kate by five minutes.

UNIT 129

129.1
2 to the problem
3 with her brother
4 in the cost of living
5 to your question
6 for a new road
7 in/to living in a big city
8 in food prices
9 for shoes like these any more
10 between your job and mine

129.2
2 invitation to
3 contact with
4 key to (key for *is also possible*)
5 cause of
6 reply to
7 connection between
8 photos of
9 reason for
10 damage to

129.3
2 to
3 in
4 of
5 in *or* to
6 for
7 to *or* towards
8 with
9 of
10 to
11 of
12 for
13 of
14 with

UNIT 130

130.1
2 That was generous of her.
3 That wasn't very nice of them.
4 That's very kind of you.
5 That isn't very polite of him.
6 That's a bit childish of them.

130.2
2 kind to
3 angry with
4 excited about
5 impressed by / impressed with
6 bored with (bored by *is also possible*)
7 amazed at / amazed by
8 careless of

130.3
2 of
3 to
4 with
5 with (by *or* in *are also possible*)
6 to
7 at/by
8 with
9 about
10 about
11 for
12 about/by/at
13 to
14 of
15 by/with
16 with
17 about
18 at/by
19 for/about
20 at/by
21 of
22 to
23 about
24 furious **with** us **for** making

UNIT 131

131.1
2 proud of
3 ashamed of
4 typical of
5 capable of
6 scared of
7 aware of
8 envious of

131.2
Example answers:
2 I'm hopeless at telling jokes.
3 I'm not very good at maths.
4 I'm pretty good at remembering names.
5 I'm good at making decisions.

131.3
2 similar to
3 afraid of
4 interested in
5 responsible for
6 proud of
7 different from / different to (different than *is also correct*)
8 capable of

131.4
2 of furniture
3 on sport
4 of time
5 at her job
6 to a doctor
7 of him / of Robert
8 from yours / from your problem *or* to yours / to your problem (different than *is also correct*)

131.5
2 for
3 of
4 in
5 of
6 on
7 of
8 with
9 on
10 of

UNIT 132

132.1
2 a
3 b
4 b
5 a
6 a
7 b
8 a
9 b
10 b
11 a
12 b

132.2

3 spoken to
4 point (them) at
5 look (directly) at
6 listen to
7 throw (stones) at
8 throw (it) to
9 reply to

132.3

2 at
3 at
4 to
5 to
6 at
7 at
8 to
9 at
10 at
11 to

UNIT 133

133.1

2 waiting for her to reply
3 searched my bag
4 asked him for a receipt
5 to ask the way
6 discussed the problem
7 nothing about them
8 for the airport

133.2

2 to
3 for
4 about
5 – (*no preposition*)
6 about
7 for
8 about

133.3

2 of
3 about
4 for
5 of
6 for
7 about
8 – (*no preposition*)

133.4

2 looking for
3 looked after
4 look for
5 looks after
6 looking for

133.5

2 wait for
3 talk about
4 ask (me) for
5 applied for
6 do (something) about
7 looks after   *or*   has looked after
8 left (Boston) for

UNIT 134

134.1

2 hear about
3 heard from
4 heard of
5 hear from
6 hear about
7 heard of

134.2

2 think about
3 thinking about
4 think of
5 think of
6 thinking of   *or*   thinking about
7 thought about
8 think of
9 think about
10 think (much) of
11 thinking about   *or*   thinking of
12 think of

134.3

2 of
3 about
4 of
5 of
6 to (us) about
7 of
8 about … about … about … about

134.4

2 complaining about
3 think about
4 heard of
5 dream of
6 reminded (me) about
7 remind (you) of

UNIT 135

135.1

2 for
3 of
4 of
5 – (*no preposition*)
6 for
7 of/from
8 for
9 of
10 for
11 on
12 for

135.2

2 for the misunderstanding
3 her on winning the tournament
4 him from his enemies
5 on bread and eggs
6 me for the (bad) weather   *or*
   the (bad) weather on me
7 my friend of stealing a car   *or*
   (that) my friend had stolen a car

135.3

2 paid for
3 accused of
4 depends on
5 live on
6 apologise to
7 suffers from
8 congratulate (him) on

135.4

2 from
3 on
4 – (*no preposition*)
5 from
6 depends how (*no preposition*)   *or*
   depends **on** how
7 on
8 of
9 on

UNIT 136

136.1

2 happened to
3 divided into
4 invited to
5 believe in
6 fill (it) with
7 breaks into
8 Concentrate on
9 succeeded in
10 drove into

136.2

2 I prefer small towns to big cities.
3 The company provided me with all
   the information I needed.
4 This morning I spent eighty pounds
   on a pair of shoes.
5 The city is divided into ten districts.

136.3

2 to
3 on
4 in
5 to
6 in
7 with
8 into
9 in
10 on
11 – (*no preposition*)
12 into
13 on
14 into
15 with
16 from (one language) into (another)

136.4

Example answers:

2 on petrol
3 into a wall
4 to volleyball
5 in seafood
6 into many languages

UNIT 137

137.1
2 sit down
3 taking off
4 flew away / flew off
5 get out
6 speak up
7 get by
8 gone up
9 looked round
10 be back
11 broke down
12 getting on

137.2
2 back at
3 up to
4 forward to
5 away with
6 up at
7 in through
8 out about

137.3
2 wake me up
3 get it out
4 give them back
5 switch it on
6 take them off

137.4
3 I have to give **them back** to her.
4 We can turn **the TV/television off**. *or* We can turn **off the TV/television**.
5 I don't want to wake **her up**.
6 (*example answer*) You should put **your coat on** *or* You should put **on your coat**.
7 I was able to put **it out**
8 Shall I turn **the light(s) on**? *or* Shall I turn **on the light(s)**?
9 (*example answer*) they've put **the price(s) up** *or* they've put **up the price(s)**
10 I knocked **it over**

UNIT 138

138.1
2 eats
3 drop
4 fill
5 moved
6 checked
7 plug
8 dropped
9 dive

138.2
2 in		6 in	
3 into		7 out	
4 out		8 out of	
5 into			

138.3
2 dropped out
3 moved in
4 left out
5 joined in
6 taken in
7 dropped in

138.4
2 Fill them in *or* Fill them out
3 cross it out
4 let us in
5 get out of it

138.5
2 drop out of college
3 fill in / fill out the application form
4 get out of going to the party
5 taken in by the email
6 drop in (and see us) sometime
7 was left out of the team *or* had been left out …

UNIT 139

139.1
2 a candle
3 an order
4 a fire
5 a new product
6 a problem

139.2
2 works out
3 carried out
4 ran out
5 sort out
6 find out / work out / figure out
7 tried out
8 pointed out
9 work out
10 went out
11 turned out
12 works out / turns out
13 find out
14 put out
15 figure out / work out

139.3
2 giving/handing out
3 turned out nice/fine/sunny
4 working out
5 run out of
6 work out how to use the camera *or* figure out how to …

139.4
2 try it out
3 work it out
4 sorted it out / worked it out
5 pointing it out

UNIT 140

140.1
2 put the heating on
3 put the oven on
4 put the kettle on
5 put some music on

140.2
2 going on
3 take off
4 drove off / went off
5 put on
6 set off
7 put off
8 called off
9 put on
10 tried on
11 see (me) off
12 putting (it) off

140.3
2 took off
3 tried on a/the hat *or* tried a/the hat on
4 was called off
5 see him off
6 put them on

UNIT 141

141.1
2 c
3 b
4 a
5 a
6 b

141.2
2 finish off
3 drive on / carry on / go on
4 ripped off
5 getting on
6 went off
7 told off
8 went on
9 get on
10 keep on / keep
11 get on / carry on
12 showing off
13 put off
14 went on / carried on
15 dozed off / dropped off / nodded off

141.3
2 gets on with
3 carry on / go on / keep / keep on
4 finish it off
5 were ripped off
6 go off
7 tell them off
8 She keeps on / She keeps

UNIT 142

142.1

2 took them down
3 stand up
4 turned it up
5 put their bags down
6 were blown down
7 put them up
8 bent down (and) picked them up

142.2

2 turned it down
3 calm him down
4 let her down
5 written it down
6 cut them down

142.3

2 calm down
3 slowed down
4 was turned down
5 broken down
6 cut down
7 let down
8 closed down / has closed down
9 be knocked down
10 turned down
11 was knocked down
12 broke down

UNIT 143

143.1

2 went up to / walked up to
3 catch up with
4 keep up with

143.2

2 used up
3 washed up
4 grow up
5 turn up / show up
6 gave up
7 taking up
8 give up
9 ended up
10 takes up
11 make up

143.3

3 tidy it up / tidy up
4 fixed it up
5 keep up with
6 was brought up
7 keep it up
8 went up to
9 set it up
10 gave it up / gave up
11 was made up of

UNIT 144

144.1

2 d
3 e
4 c
5 g
6 a
7 b

144.2

2 held up
3 did it up
4 cheer him up

144.3

2 blew up
3 beaten up
4 broken up / split up
5 do up
6 clears up / will clear up
7 mixed up

144.4

2 look it up
3 put up with
4 making it up
5 come up with
6 tear them up
7 saving up for
8 bring it up
9 mix them up / get them mixed up

UNIT 145

145.1

2 blew away
3 put it back
4 walked away
5 threw it back (to her)
6 threw them away

145.2

2 be away / have gone away
3 be back
4 ran away
5 get away
6 keep away / keep back
7 smile back

145.3

2 throw
3 gets
4 be
5 look
6 gave
7 get
8 put

145.4

2 throw it away
3 take them back
4 pay you back / pay it back
5 gave them away
6 called back / called me back

Key to Additional exercises *(see page 302)*

1

3 I'm getting / I am getting
4 do you do
5 we arrived … it was raining
6 phones … she didn't phone
7 you were thinking … I decided
8 are you looking
9 It doesn't rain
10 He wasn't looking
11 we went … she was preparing … We didn't want … we didn't stay
12 told … he didn't believe … He thought … I was joking

2

2 didn't go
3 is wearing
4 went
5 haven't heard
6 is being
7 wasn't reading
8 didn't have
9 It's beginning
10 worked
11 wasn't
12 you've stayed
13 I've been doing
14 did she go
15 I've been playing
16 do you come
17 since I saw her
18 for 20 years

3

3 are you going
4 Do you watch
5 have you lived / have you been living / have you been
6 Did they have
7 Have you seen
8 was she wearing
9 Have you been waiting / Have you been here
10 does it take
11 Have you heard
12 Have you been / Have you ever been

4

2 've known each other / have known each other *or* 've been friends / have been friends
3 I've ever had / I've ever been on / I've had for ages *(etc.)*
4 He went / He went home / He went out / He left
5 I've worn it
6 I was playing
7 been swimming for

8 since I've been / since I went / since I last went
9 did you buy / did you get

5

1 got … was already waiting … had arrived
2 was lying … wasn't watching … 'd fallen / had fallen … was snoring … turned … woke
3 'd just gone / had just gone … was reading … heard … got … didn't see … went
4 missed … was standing … realised … 'd left / had left … had … got
5 met … was walking … 'd been / had been … 'd been playing / had been playing … were going … invited … 'd arranged / had arranged … didn't have

6

2 Somebody has taken it.
3 They'd only known / They had only known each other (for) a few weeks.
4 It's been raining / It has been raining all day. *or* It's rained / It has rained all day.
5 I'd been dreaming. / I had been dreaming.
6 I'd had / I had had a big breakfast.
7 They've been going / They have been going there for years.
8 I've had it / I have had it since I got up.
9 He's been training / He has been training very hard for it.

7

1 I haven't seen
2 You look / You're looking
3 are you going
4 are you meeting
5 I'm going
6 Do you often go
7 are you going
8 I'm meeting
9 has been (delayed) / is (delayed)
10 I've been waiting
11 has just started / just started
12 is she getting
13 Does she like
14 she thinks
15 Are you working
16 spoke
17 you were working
18 went
19 I started / I'd started
20 I lost

21 you haven't had
22 I've had
23 have you seen
24 has he been
25 I saw
26 he went
27 He'd been
28 he decided / he'd decided
29 He was really looking forward
30 is he doing
31 I haven't heard
32 he left

8

1 invented
2 it's gone / it has gone
3 had gone … left
4 did you do … Did you go
5 have you had
6 was looking *or* 'd been looking / had been looking
7 She's been teaching / She has been teaching
8 bought … she hasn't worn *or* she didn't wear
9 I met … was … I'd seen / I had seen … I remembered … he was
10 Have you heard … She was … died … She wrote … I haven't read
11 does this word mean … I've never seen
12 Did you get … it had already started
13 knocked … was … she'd gone / she had gone … she didn't want
14 He'd never used / He had never used … he didn't know
15 went … She needed *or* She'd needed / She had needed … she'd been sitting / she had been sitting

9

3 used to drive
4 was driving
5 were working
6 used to have
7 was living
8 was playing
9 used to play
10 was wearing

10

2 I'm going to the dentist.
3 No, we're going to rent a car.
4 I'll call her now.
5 I'm having lunch with Sue.
6 What are you going to have? / What are you having?
7 I'll turn on the light.
8 I'm going to close the window.

11

2 B
3 A
4 B
5 A
6 C
7 C
8 A

12

1 (2) Are you going to do / Are you doing
   (3) it starts
   (4) you'll enjoy / you're going to enjoy
   (5) it will be / it's going to be
2 (1) you're going
   (2) We're going
   (3) you have
   (4) I'll get
   (5) I get
3 (1) I'm having / I'm going to have
   (2) are coming
   (3) they'll have left
   (4) they're
   (5) I won't be / I will not be
   (6) you know
   (7) I'll call
4 (1) shall we meet
   (2) I'll be waiting
   (3) you arrive
   (4) I'll be sitting
   (5) I'll be wearing
   (6) Is Agent 307 coming / Is Agent 307 going to come / Will Agent 307 be coming
   (7) Shall I bring
   (8) I'll explain / I'm going to explain
   (9) I see
   (10) I'll try

13

1 I'll have
2 Are you going
3 shall I phone
4 It's going to land
5 it's / it is
6 I'll miss / I'm going to miss … you go / you've gone
7 Shall I give … I give … will you call
8 does it finish
9 I'm going … is getting
10 I'll tell … I'm … I won't be
11 I'm going to have / I'm having
12 she apologises
13 we'll be living / we'll live
14 you finish / you've finished

14

2 I've had / I have had
3 I bought or I got

4 I'll come / I will come or I'll be / I will be
5 I've been / I have been or I've eaten / I have eaten
6 I used to play
7 I haven't been waiting or I haven't been here
8 I'd been / I had been or I was
9 I'm going / I am going
10 I haven't seen or I haven't heard from
11 I'll have gone / I will have gone or I'll have left / I will have left

15

2 I've been travelling
3 I'm beginning
4 I've seen
5 has been
6 I've met
7 I left
8 I stayed or I was staying
9 I'd planned or I was planning
10 I ended up
11 I enjoyed
12 I took
13 met
14 I'm staying or I'm going to stay or I'll be staying or I'll stay
15 I continue
16 I'll get
17 I'm
18 I'll let
19 I know
20 I'm staying
21 we're going to visit or we're visiting
22 are building or have been building
23 it will be
24 I'll be

16

2 A
3 C
4 B or C
5 B
6 A or C
7 A or C
8 C
9 B or C
10 A or B
11 A
12 C
13 A or B
14 B or C
15 B

17

2 shouldn't have eaten
3 must have forgotten
4 needn't have gone
5 can't be changed
6 may be watching
7 must have been waiting

8 couldn't have done
9 should have been
10 could have phoned
11 should have been warned
12 ought to have come

18

3 could rain / might rain
4 might have gone / could have gone
5 couldn't go
6 couldn't have seen / can't have seen
7 should get
8 wouldn't recognise / might not recognise
9 must have heard
10 should have turned

19

4 rings
5 you were
6 it's / it is
7 it was or it were
8 it had been
9 you had
10 I'd had / I had had
11 it wouldn't have happened
12 I didn't watch

20

2 called (me)
3 (If) I'd known / I had known …
   (I) wouldn't have disturbed (you).
4 (There) wouldn't be (so many accidents if) there was … or
   … (if) there were …
5 (If) you'd told me about (the problem), I would have tried to help / I'd have tried to help (you). or
   … I would have helped / I'd have helped
6 (I) would have got/gotten (very wet if) I hadn't had …
7 (If he) hadn't been / hadn't got / hadn't gotten … (he) wouldn't have failed / would have passed / 'd have passed …

21

Example answers:
1 I wasn't feeling so tired
2 I hadn't had so much to do
3 I would have forgotten Amy's birthday
4 I'd probably waste it
5 I'll take a picture of you
6 you were in trouble
7 you hadn't taken so long to get ready
8 I would have gone to the concert
9 I might have got the job
10 you'd eaten lunch
11 there was less traffic
12 it would be harder to get information

22

3 was cancelled
4 has been repaired
5 is being restored
6 It's believed / It is believed
7 I'd be fired / I would be fired
8 It might have been thrown
9 He was taught
10 being arrested / having been
   arrested   *or*   I was arrested
11 Have you ever been arrested
12 are reported … have been injured

23

3 've sold / have sold   *or*   sold
4 's been sold / has been sold   *or*
   was sold
5 are made
6 might be stolen
7 must have been stolen
8 must have taken
9 can be solved
10 should have left
11 is delayed
12 is being built … is expected

24

1 **Castle Fire**
2 was discovered
3 was injured
4 be rescued
5 are believed to have been destroyed
6 is not known
2 **Shop Robbery**
1 was forced
2 being threatened
3 had been stolen
4 was later found
5 had been abandoned
6 has been arrested / was
   arrested
7 is still being questioned
3 **Road Delays**
1 is being resurfaced
2 are asked / are being asked /
   have been asked
3 is expected
4 will be closed / is going to be closed
5 will be diverted / is going to be diverted
4 **Accident**
1 was taken
2 was allowed
3 was blocked
4 be diverted
5 have been killed

25

1 I told **her (that) Paul had gone out**
   and **I didn't know when he'd be
   back**.
   I asked (**her**) **if/whether she
   wanted to leave a message**, but
   she said (**that**) **she'd try again** later.

2 I had reserved a hotel room, but
   when I got to the hotel they told
   **me (that) they had no record of a
   reservation in my name**.
   When I asked (**them**) **if/whether
   they had any rooms free anyway**,
   they said (**that**) **they were sorry**,
   but **the hotel was full**.
3 The immigration officer asked us
   why we were visiting the country,
   and we told **him (that) we were on
   holiday**.
   Then he wanted to know **how long
   we intended to stay** and **where we
   would be staying during our visit**.
4 She said (**that**) **she'd phone us
   from the airport when she arrived**.
   or   She said (**that**) **she'll phone us
   from the airport when she arrives**.
   No, she said not **to come to the
   airport**. She said that **she'd take
   the bus**.   *or*   She said that **she'll
   take the bus**.
5 He wanted to know **what my job
   was** and asked (**me**) **how much I
   earned**.   *or*   He wanted to know
   what my job is and asked (**me**)
   how much I earn.
   … so I told **him to mind his own
   business** and ended the call.
6 He said (**that**) **he'd be at the
   restaurant at 7.30**.
   He said (**that**) **he knew where the
   restaurant was**. And I told **him to
   phone me if there was a problem**.
7 You just said (**that**) **you weren't
   hungry**.
   But you said (**that**) **you didn't like
   bananas**. You told **me not to buy
   any**.

26

3 changing
4 to change
5 change
6 being
7 saying
8 to call
9 drinking
10 to be
11 to see
12 taking
13 to be
14 to think … making
15 living … to move
16 to be … playing
17 being stopped … stealing … driving
18 work … pressing

27

3 I don't fancy going out.
4 He tends to forget things.
5 Would you mind helping me? /
   Do you mind helping me?

6 Everybody seems to have gone out.
7 We're / We are thinking of moving.
8 I was afraid to touch it.
9 I was afraid of missing my train.
10 It's / It is not worth seeing.
11 I'm not used to walking so far.
12 She seems to be enjoying
   herself.   *or*   She seemed …
13 He insisted on showing them to me.
14 I'd rather somebody else did it.

28

3 I've given up reading newspapers.
4 I'd rather not go out tonight. / …
   stay at home tonight.
5 He has trouble sleeping at night.
6 Do you want me to phone
   you this evening?
7 I came in without anybody/anyone
   seeing me. / … without being seen.
8 I was accused of being a cheat. /
   … of cheating.
9 I'm looking forward to seeing
   them again.
10 What do you advise me to do?
11 I'd like to have gone out with
   you last night.
12 I regret not taking your advice. /
   … that I didn't take your advice.

29

2 **a** foreign country … **the** language
3 **an** economist … in **the** United
   States … for **an** investment company
4 I love sport, especially tennis … two
   or three times **a** week … not **a** very
   good player
5 for dinner … after work … to **the**
   cinema
6 When unemployment is … for
   people to find work … **a** big problem
7 **an** accident … going home …
   taken to hospital / taken to **the**
   hospital … I think most accidents …
   by people driving
8 **the** name of **the** hotel … **The**
   Ambassador … in Queen Street in
   the city centre … near **the** station
9 **The** older one … **a** pilot … **The**
   younger one … at school … he
   leaves school …
   go to university … study law

30

2 B
3 C
4 A *or* B
5 C
6 B
7 A *or* C
8 A
9 C
10 B *or* C
11 B

12 A
13 A *or* B
14 B

31

3 It's the **most** polluted place …
4 I was **disappointed** that …
5 *OK*
6 Joe works **hard**, but …
7 … in a **large modern** building.
8 *OK* (as fast as he can *is also correct*)
9 I missed the **last three** days …
10 *OK*
11 The weather has been **unusually** cold …
12 The water in the pool was too dirty to swim in.
13 … to wait **such a** long time.
    or to wait so long.
14 *OK*
15 … I got up **earlier** than usual.

32

2 If
3 when
4 if
5 when
6 if
7 if
8 unless
9 if
10 as long as
11 in case
12 in case
13 if
14 even if
15 Although
16 Although
17 When
18 when

33

2 on
3 **on** Tuesday morning **at** 9.30
4 at / on
5 on
6 at
7 In
8 at
9 during
10 **on** Friday … **since** then
11 for
12 at
13 **at** the moment … **until** Friday
14 by
15 in

34

1 in
2 by
3 at
4 on
5 in
6 on

7 **to** a party **at** Lisa's house
8 on
9 on
10 to
11 **in** Vienna … **at** the age of 35
12 **in** this photo … **on** the left
13 **to** the theatre … **in** the front row
14 **on** the wall **by** the door / **next to** the door / **beside** the door
15 at
16 on
17 **in** a tower block … **on** the fifteenth floor
18 on
19 by
20 **on** the bus … **by** car
21 on
22 in
23 **in** London … **to** Italy
24 to
25 on

35

1 for
2 at
3 to
4 to
5 in
6 with
7 of
8 to
9 of
10 at/by
11 of
12 about

36

1 of
2 after
3 – *(no preposition)*
4 about
5 to
6 – *(no preposition)*
7 into
8 of (about *is also possible*)
9 to
10 – *(no preposition)*
11 on
12 of
13 of
14 – *(no preposition)*
15 in
16 at (about *is also possible*)
17 on
18 If Alex **asks you for** money
19 I **apologised to Sarah for** keeping …
20 I **thanked her for** everything …

37

2 h
3 e
4 g
5 a

6 k
7 c
8 j
9 b
10 f
11 i

38

2 D
3 B
4 B
5 A
6 A
7 D
8 C
9 C
10 B
11 A
12 D

39

2 out to
3 up with
4 forward to
5 up with
6 out of
7 on with
8 up with
9 back on
10 out about
11 on with

40

3 turned up / showed up
4 fill it in / fill it out
5 knocked down / pulled down / torn down
6 give up
7 dozed off / dropped off / nodded off
8 split up / break up
9 put up with it
10 get by
11 went on
12 put it off

41

2 put
3 moving
4 put
5 done
6 turned / turns
7 find
8 Calm
9 set
10 held
11 left / 've left / have left *or* missed / 've missed / have missed
12 works
13 join
14 works
15 drop / call
16 sort / work
17 **went** off … **woke** me up

Key to Study guide

Present and past

1.1	A
1.2	B
1.3	C
1.4	B, C
1.5	C
1.6	A

Present perfect and past

2.1	B
2.2	C
2.3	A
2.4	C
2.5	A
2.6	B
2.7	A, D
2.8	D
2.9	A
2.10	A
2.11	C
2.12	A
2.13	C, D
2.14	C
2.15	D
2.16	C

Future

3.1	B
3.2	A
3.3	C
3.4	A, C
3.5	B
3.6	C
3.7	A

Modals

4.1	A, B
4.2	B
4.3	A, C, D
4.4	C
4.5	B
4.6	C, D
4.7	B
4.8	A, C
4.9	B, C
4.10	A, B, D
4.11	A
4.12	D, E
4.13	A

if and wish

5.1	B
5.2	C
5.3	B
5.4	D
5.5	A

Passive

6.1	C
6.2	B
6.3	D
6.4	A
6.5	A, B
6.6	C
6.7	D

Reported speech

7.1	A
7.2	B
7.3	A

Questions and auxiliary verbs

8.1	C
8.2	A
8.3	D
8.4	A
8.5	B

-ing and to …

9.1	A, D
9.2	B, D
9.3	B
9.4	A
9.5	A
9.6	A
9.7	C
9.8	D
9.9	C
9.10	C
9.11	B
9.12	C, D
9.13	D
9.14	B
9.15	A, B
9.16	A
9.17	A
9.18	B, C

Articles and nouns

10.1	B
10.2	A
10.3	B, C
10.4	B
10.5	C
10.6	A
10.7	A
10.8	A
10.9	D
10.10	C
10.11	C
10.12	A
10.13	C
10.14	B

Pronouns and determiners

11.1	A
11.2	B
11.3	D
11.4	B
11.5	B
11.6	C
11.7	A, C
11.8	D
11.9	D
11.10	A
11.11	B
11.12	B, C

Relative clauses

12.1	A, C
12.2	A, B
12.3	C
12.4	B
12.5	D
12.6	B, C

Adjectives and adverbs

13.1	B
13.2	C
13.3	B, C
13.4	A
13.5	A, D
13.6	C
13.7	B, C
13.8	C
13.9	C
13.10	B, C
13.11	D
13.12	A, B
13.13	B
13.14	D, E
13.15	D

Conjunctions and prepositions

14.1	A, D
14.2	C
14.3	B, C
14.4	B, D
14.5	B
14.6	C, D
14.7	B, C
14.8	A

Prepositions

15.1	B, D
15.2	A
15.3	C
15.4	B
15.5	A
15.6	B, D
15.7	B
15.8	B
15.9	C
15.10	C
15.11	C
15.12	A
15.13	C
15.14	B
15.15	D
15.16	D
15.17	A

Phrasal verbs

16.1	B
16.2	A
16.3	D
16.4	C
16.5	C
16.6	B
16.7	A
16.8	A, D
16.9	B

Index

Index

Trusted by millions, RIGHT FOR YOU.

CHOOSE IN USE

For over 30 years, in Use has helped millions of learners around the world improve their grammar, vocabulary and pronunciation.

With clear explanations and essential practice exercises, in Use is perfect for self-study or to supplement the classroom.

cambridge.org/chooseinuse